WORK HOLIDAYS

Published annually by the Central Bureau for
Educational Visits & Exchanges, Seymour Mews
House, Seymour Mews, London W1H 9PE,
England

THE INFORMATION IN THIS EDITION OF WORKING
HOLIDAYS IS VALID ONLY FOR THE DURATION OF
1991

—1991—

Thirty ninth edition

Copyright Central Bureau for Educational Visits &
Exchanges 1990

ISBN 0 900087 86 2

Distributed worldwide by the Central Bureau for
Educational Visits & Exchanges, Seymour Mews House,
Seymour Mews, London W1H 9PE

Telephone 071-486 51 01
Telex 21368 CBEVEX G
Dialcom 87:WQQ383
Fax 071-935 5741

Distributed in the UK by the Central Bureau and
Intrepid Travel Publications, 44 Top Dartford Road,
Hextable, Kent BR8 7SQ

Available in mainland Europe from

GIJK, Am Gasschen 24, Postfach 20 05 62, 5300 Bonn 2,
Federal Republic of Germany *Telephone* (49 228) 32 10 71

Eurovac, 55 rue Nationale, 37000 Tours, France
Telephone 47 20 20 57

IZV, Edificio España, Grupo 4o, Planta 11, Of 4, 28013
Madrid, Spain *Telephone* (91) 542 10 89

Available in North America from

Institute of International Education, 809 United Nations
Plaza, New York, NY10017, United States of America
Telephone (212) 984 5412

Working Holidays 1991 was compiled and edited by the
Print, Marketing & IT Unit, Central Bureau for
Educational Visits & Exchanges, London

Typographic imaging and print production by the
Print, Marketing & IT Unit, Central Bureau for
Educational Visits & Exchanges, London

Printed & bound by BPCC Hazell Books Ltd, Aylesbury

CONTENTS

A-Z

Practical advice and information to provide you with all you need to know to help you make your working holiday go smoothly.

WORK PROFILES

Details on the categories of work available, enabling you to decide where, when and how your skills and enthusiasms may be best employed.

JOBS INDEX

All the details on over 500 employers and 85,000 opportunities, paid and voluntary, from au pair work to workcamps, from Australia to Zaire, and in periods of from 3-365 days long.

INDEX

Full index on all the employers and sources of
information and advice detailed throughout this guide.

REPORT FORM

When you have been on your working holiday please
complete and return this form. Up-to-date reports
enable us to improve the accuracy and standard of the
information given in **Working Holidays.**

APPLYING FOR A JOB

Read carefully all the information given before
applying. Check in particular:

* the necessary skills/experience required

* the full period of employment expected

* any restrictions of age, sex or nationality

* application deadlines

* any other points, particularly details of
insurance cover provided, and other costs
such as travel and accommodation.

When applying be sure to include:

* name, address, date of birth, marital status,
nationality, sex

* education, qualifications, relevant
experience

* period of availability

* details of languages spoken

* a large stamped, self-addressed envelope
plus, if overseas, 2 International Reply
Coupons

* a passport-size photo, particularly if you are
to have contact with the public

* any registration or membership fees

USING THIS GUIDE

The job opportunities in **Working Holidays 1991** are given alphabetically by country, and arranged under various categories (see the **Work Profiles** section for further details). At the beginning of each country section you will find a list of useful addresses including embassies, consulates, tourist offices and youth and student travel centres - all vital sources of further information and advice as you plan your working holiday. Tourist offices and embassies are generally unable to help in finding employment but they may be able to provide useful lists, for example of hotels that may employ temporary staff, or other information sheets. The **Information** section under each country details entry and work permit regulations, possibilities for low-cost travel and accommodation, relevant publications and information centres. The available jobs are listed under each employer, including a description of the work, any skills or qualifications required, general conditions, wages, and application procedures.

Certain organisations provide facilities for, or will consider applications from those with handicaps. Those services and job opportunities that are open to those with restricted ability are indicated by:

B   Blind
D   Deaf and hearing impaired
PH Physically handicapped

Most prices and salaries have been given in £ Sterling, though in some cases costs have been quoted in the currency of the host country. When this guide was compiled the exchange rates were (all rates = £1 Sterling):

Australia 2.35 $
Austria 20.3 Sch
Belgium 59.6 F
Canada 2.13 $
Denmark 11.09 Kr
Finland 6.90 M
France 9.72 F
FR Germany 2.89 M
Greece 281.00 Drc
Ireland 1.09 £
Israel 3.00 Sh
Italy 2130.0 Lire
Japan 278.00 Yen
Malta 0.57 £
Netherlands 3.27 Fl
New Zealand 3.00 $
Norway 11.27 Kr
Portugal 256.00 Esc
Spain 177.25 Pts
Sweden 10.82 Kr
Switzerland 2.44 F
Turkey 4700.00 Lira
United States 1.86 $
Yugoslavia 46160 Dnr

A-Z

The main section of this guide, the **Jobs Index**, not only provides full details on the thousands of paid and voluntary opportunities to work around the world, but also gives sources of information that can help in planning your working holiday and provide advice on accommodation, travel and on getting to know the area and country in which you will be working. This A-Z of practical advice and information provides virtually everything else you need to know to make your working holiday a success.

A

ADVERTISING This guide lists thousands of job opportunities and details the categories of work available and where they are advertised, such as youth information centres, newspapers and magazines. Details of British representatives that can place advertisements in the *Situations Wanted* sections of foreign publications can be found in the **Job advertising** section under the respective countries. The following media directories can be consulted in reference libraries.

Benn's Media Directories are comprehensive sources of information for anyone wishing to consult or advertise in foreign or British media. *The International Volume* provides details of major newspapers and magazines, embassies and chambers of commerce in over 197 countries. *The UK Volume* provides a comprehensive guide to over 450 major UK publishers of newspapers and magazines, and listings of periodicals, directories and media organisations. Published by Benn Business Information Services Ltd, PO Box 20, Sovereign Way, Tonbridge, Kent TN9 1RQ Tel Tonbridge 362666.

Willings Press Guide provides information on over 21,000 publications worldwide, listing newspapers, periodicals and annuals in the UK, and details of major overseas newspapers and periodicals in over 116 countries. Published by Reed Information Services Ltd, Windsor Court, East Grinstead House, East Grinstead, West Sussex RH19 1XA Tel East Grinstead 326972.

B

BAGGAGE What to include or exclude from your suitcase or rucksack can make or break your working holiday. The basic list of what to take may already be drawn up for you by virtue of the job you are going to. If you are having to taking your own tent, sleeping bag, equipment and work clothes, then you are unlikely to have little room for much else. Even where accommodation is provided, your own sleeping bag may provide a touch of home comfort while working, and allow you some flexibility in accommodation if you are going to travel around afterwards. If you propose to do a fair amount of travelling, think carefully about the method of carrying your load, possibly investing in a good frame rucksack. Travel light, consider whether one pair of jeans or shoes, for example, would suffice, rather than two. Some companies will provide work clothes, from basic overalls to complete uniforms, allowing you the space to pack more casual and social clothes. However, if you are providing your own work clothes, consider how much free time you will have either during or after the working period, and whether you really will need a change of clothes for those occasions. Try to get as much background information as you can on the area or country you are visiting, investigate the climate and weather patterns so that you will be taking the right sort of clothes, particularly if you will be involved in much outdoor work.

C

CUSTOMS It is vital that if you are going to work in another country you are fully aware of the Customs regulations governing all the countries you will be visiting. Full details of UK Customs regulations are given in *Planning To Go Green?* obtainable from HM Customs & Excise or from Customs at ports and airports in the UK. There are prohibitions and restrictions on the importation of certain goods including controlled drugs, firearms, ammunition, explosives, flick knives and certain other offensive weapons, horror comics, indecent or obscene books, magazines, video tapes, meat, poultry, plants, vegetables, fruit, certain radio transmitters and cordless telephones, animals and birds, articles derived from endangered species, goods bearing a false or misleading indication of origin, and certain counterfeit goods. Further details from HM Customs & Excise, CDE5, Room 201, Dorset House, Stamford Street, London SE1 9PS Tel 071-928 0533.

D

DRUGS If you are taking prescribed drugs it is advisable to carry a doctor's letter giving details of the medical condition and the medication, avoiding the possibility of confusion. It will also be useful to find out the generic rather the brand name of the medicine, so that if need arises further supplies can be obtained abroad. If you are given any tablets or medicine when overseas, it may not be legal to bring them back into your own country; if in doubt, declare the drugs at Customs when you return. Some community service projects and workcamps involve working with ex-drug abusers, and participants will be asked to refrain from the use of tobacco, alcohol and other drugs whilst working on these projects. Those who feel that they will be unable to cope with this should not apply; conversely, those who have drug-related problems themselves should also think very carefully about participating in such work. The social and legal conditions relating to the use of controlled drugs in the country you are visiting should be understood, particularly in relation to importation and usage.

E

EMBASSIES Addresses and telephone numbers of embassies are given under each country throughout this guide. It should be noted that they cannot help in finding work, cannot provide money (except in certain specific emergencies), telex or telephone facilities, interpretation or legal advice services, or pay bills, whether legal, medical, hotel, travel or any other debts, though in an emergency may help in repatriation.

British citizens should note that there are consular offices at British Embassies in foreign capitals and at Consulates in some provincial

cities. Consuls maintain a list of English-speaking doctors and will advise or help in cases of serious difficulty or distress. As a last resort a consul can arrange for a direct return to the UK by the cheapest possible passage, providing the person concerned agrees to have his passport withdrawn and gives written confirmation that he will pay the travel expenses involved. If the consul's urgent help is needed you should telephone or telegraph. The telegraphic address of all British Embassies is *Prodrome* and of all British Consulates *Britain*, followed in each case by the name of the appropriate town.

F

FOOD One of the joys of any holiday abroad is sampling the local food. On a working holiday this is no exception, though depending on the job being undertaken, for example working in a holiday centre, regular access to authentic local cuisine may be somewhat difficult. Local tourist offices are good sources of information on shopping for local produce and in identifying good, cheap ethnic restaurants. In many instances the working holiday will involve cooking for yourself. Given that you may be involved in heavy manual labour you should ensure that you are eating well, and consider resolving any conflict you may have if the best you have achieved in home cooking depends on the freezer contents. On some workcamps catering is undertaken on a rota basis; if the thought of self-catering may bring on doubts, how confident are you at catering for up to thirty other starving workers? Before you inflict your culinary skills on yourself let alone others, you may care to buy a basic but practical cookery guide. The Coordinating Committee for International Voluntary Service, UNESCO, 1 rue Miollis, 750915 Paris, France publish *Cookbook for Workcamps* which contains a variety of nutritious recipes and tips on cooking cheaply for large numbers.

G

GUIDES Under the **Information** heading for each country **Working Holidays 1991** details a number of down-to-earth guides to areas and countries in which you will find yourself working and travelling. A good travellers guidebook and map can make all the difference between a missed opportunity and a memorable experience. Forward planning and advance reading can give you a flavour of the country and some idea of sights worth seeing.

Your local library should give you the opportunity to compare the available guides before buying your own copies. Tourist offices are a good initial source of free maps and guides. A good map of the area can help you make the most of your free time; locally available maps, for example those issued free at petrol stations can be invaluable.

H

HEALTH In the UK the Department of Health issues a leaflet *T1 The Traveller's Guide to Health* with vital information for those travelling overseas. It includes details of compulsory and recommended vaccinations, other measures that can be taken to protect one's health, information on yellow fever, cholera, infectious hepatitis, typhoid, tetanus, polio, malaria, rabies and AIDS, and action to take in an emergency. There is also advice on types of food and on water supplies which may be a source of infection. Available from post offices, by telephoning 0800 555 777 or from Health Publications Unit, No 2 Site, Heywood Stores, Manchester Road, Heywood OL10 2PZ.

I

INSURANCE All workers should ensure that they have full insurance cover against risk of accident, illness and possible disability. Most large insurance companies offer comprehensive policies at reasonable cost, and workcamp organisations are sometimes able to arrange full cover for participants in their programmes. However, the insurance cover provided automatically by many employers is often solely against third party risks and accidents. You are therefore strongly advised to obtain precise details on this point and, if necessary, to take out individual policies.

There are health care arrangements between all the EC countries (Belgium, Britain, Denmark,

France, Federal Republic of Germany, Greece, Ireland, Italy, Luxembourg, Netherlands, Portugal and Spain).

British citizens resident in the UK will receive free or reduced cost emergency treatment in other EC countries only on production of form *E111*. Leaflet *T1, The Travellers Guide to Health*, explains who is covered by the arrangements and how to apply for form *E111*. It lists all the countries where free or reduced cost emergency medical treatment is available, including details of what treatment is free or at reduced cost in EC countries, and gives the procedures which must be followed to get treatment in countries where form *E111* is not needed (usually Denmark, Ireland and Portugal). Form *E111* is issued with information on how to get emergency medical treatment in other EC countries. Form *E111* or leaflet *T1* must be taken abroad and, if emergency treatment is needed, the correct procedures must be followed.

There are also reciprocal health care arrangements between Britain and Australia, Austria, Bulgaria, Channel Islands, Czechoslovakia, Finland, German Democratic Republic, Gibraltar, Hong Kong, Hungary, Iceland, Isle of Man, Malta, New Zealand, Norway, Poland, Romania, Sweden, USSR, Yugoslavia and British Dependent Territories of Anguilla, British Virgin Islands, Falkland Islands, Montserrat, St Helena, and Turks and Caicos Islands. However, private medical insurance may still be needed to supplement the cover provided under the arrangements detailed in leaflet *T1*. Free or subsidised medical treatment in countries other than those listed in the leaflet is not available, and it is therefore strongly advisable to take out adequate private medical insurance.

If you are going away for more than 3 months you should hand your NHS medical card to the immigration officer at the point of departure, or send it to the local Family Practitioner Committee (England and Wales), Area Health Board (Scotland) or Central Services Agency (Northern Ireland), with a note of your date of departure. If you have lost or mislaid the card you should write to the same address (see local telephone directory), giving date of departure, last permanent address in this country, name and address of your doctor, and NHS medical numbers. If you are going to Australia, British Dependent Territories, Bulgaria, Hong Kong, Iceland, Poland or Romania you may need the NHS medical card to get free treatment, so should not hand it in. See leaflet *T1* for details.

KNOWLEDGE

The International Student Insurance Service policy provides, at competitive rates, a wide range of benefits covering death, disablement, medical and other personal expenses, loss of luggage, personal liability and cancellation, loss of deposits or curtailment. The use of farm or industrial machinery is, however, excluded. ISIS policies include worldwide travel for up to 2 years. An advantage of this policy is that medical expenses can be settled on the spot in many countries by student organisations cooperating with ISIS; the medical limit for these expenses relates to each claim and therefore the cover is, in effect, limitless. A 24 hour assistance service is provided to handle all medical emergencies. Details in the UK from local Endsleigh Insurance centres.

J

JABS In addition to the compulsory vaccinations required for foreign travel, anyone about to undertake any sort of manual work is strongly advised to have an anti-tetanus injection. A certificate of vaccination against certain diseases is an entry requirement for some countries, and it is wise to consult embassies on this point, since requirements are continually subject to review. You should be aware of the length of cover of any injections given, and you may also need a course of medication. You should check with your own doctor as to the benefit of obtaining booster inoculations against, for example, polio, even if you are remaining within Europe. British Airways Travel Clinics Tel 071-831 5333, offer the latest health news, advice and a comprehensive range of immunisations. Whilst abroad it is unwise to have your skin pierced by injection such as acupuncture, tattooing or ear piercing, unless you can be sure that the equipment is sterile. A major cause of the spread of viruses, including AIDS, is the use of infected needles and equipment. In some countries blood for transfusions is not screened for the presence of the AIDS virus, but

there may be arrangements for obtaining screened blood. The local doctor treating you or the nearest consulate or embassy may be able to offer advice.

K

KNOWLEDGE This edition of **Working Holidays** builds on over forty years of our knowledge in gathering together information on opportunities to experience life through a period of work in another environment. Every employer listed in this guide has been selected as offering a genuine working holiday; that is, you may be on holiday, but you will be expected to do a real job of work. Those employers who we feel cannot offer an authentic experience are not included; neither are those who can offer only one or two vacancies. However, we need your help in monitoring that the jobs on offer live up to their promise. To this end we include a report form at the end of this guide; when you have been on your working holiday we would value your comments. Completed report forms enable us to continually improve on the information and advice we offer.

L

LANGUAGE Fluency in another language will increase the range of work opportunities open to you; in addition it will make your time in another country that much more enjoyable. Local education authorities offer a range of evening classes to develop foreign language skills. The vocabulary and confidence gained will stand you in good stead when you find yourself abroad, even if, unless tuition is undertaken well in advance, you are unlikely to be totally fluent in the new language. *Study Holidays* £6.70 including UK postage, is a comprehensive guide to over 600 organisations offering European language courses in 25 countries, from 1 week to 12 months. Detailed practical information on language resources and sources of grants is also given. Published by the Central Bureau, Seymour Mews, London W1H 9PE. While you are abroad, even the best phrase books will have limited use; if you are keen to develop your vocabulary a pocket dictionary will prove better value.

M

MONEY It's important that you work out how much money you'll need. The exact amount will depend on a variety of factors, including the location, the country itself, the total length of time you will be away, including what proportion of this period will be spent travelling rather than working, and the type of work you are undertaking. You will need some money to live on until your first pay day; this may need only be pocket money if food and accommodation are being found for you. On the other hand, you may have to pay for your board, lodging and other needs, and you may be paid monthly, not weekly.

If you're undertaking voluntary work in a remote location, with food and accommodation provided, pocket money may be enough to cover your needs, and you may even find difficulty in finding somewhere to spend that!

A good guide as to how much to take is to make sure you've got enough to pay for at least two night's accommodation and food, a long-distance telephone call, and return travel, if not already accounted for. If you do run out of funds it is possible to arrange for money to be transferred to a bank abroad, provided of course that you have the necessary funds available back home. Large amounts of money may be best taken as travellers' cheques; when obtaining these from a bank or travel agency you'll generally need to give a few days notice, and produce your passport. Shop around beforehand to compare commission rates charged. Read carefully any instructions given, particularly with regard to signing cheques and keeping note of the numbers. Some travellers' cheques can be replaced while you're still abroad; others will be honoured by the issuing bank on your return.
If you have a bank current account you will probably be able to obtain a supply of Eurocheques and a cheque card. These can be cashed abroad at banks where the Eurocheque sign is displayed, and in many cases are accepted by shops and restaurants. You'll need to carry some foreign currency; you can get this at major travel agents and banks. Again, shop around for the best exchange and commission rates.

N

NATIONALITY The information given in this guide, particularly with reference to entry, work and health regulations, applies to British citizens and, as applicable, European Community (EC) citizens. Where possible full details on work opportunities and on employment regulations for other nationalities have been given, but applicants should check out job availability, entry and work permit regulations with employers and the consular sections of the appropriate embassies. In the main, voluntary work opportunities are open to all nationalities, with a letter of invitation acting as an entry permit; paid jobs usually require work permits, which depending on the country may be issued only for the job in question, and may not be available to certain nationalities.

O

OPPORTUNITIES The thousands of opportunities to undertake paid and voluntary work, from as short as one weekend up to 52 weeks, are all detailed under the **Jobs Index** section of this guide. The next section, **Work Profiles** details the categories of work on offer, and if you are in any doubt as to what type of work and in which country will be best suited to your needs, the work profiles will help you to decide where your skills and enthusiasms may best be employed. It will also answer some of the basic questions like where and when does the grape harvest take place, what is involved in being an au pair, exactly what is a kibbutz, where can I literally dig up the past, and how can I practically contribute to the conservation of this planet?

P

PASSPORTS If you intend to work abroad and are not in possession of a valid passport, application for one should be made at least three months in advance. In most countries you will need to hold a full passport in order to undertake work, even though you can travel on a visitor's passport or identity card. If a passport is lost or stolen while abroad the local

NATIONALITY

OPPORTUNITIES

PASSPORTS

police should be notified immediately; if necessary your nearest embassy or consulate will issue a substitute.

Within western Europe, excluding the German Democratic Republic, East Berlin and Cyprus, and certain other countries, British citizens can travel on a British Visitor's Passport, but those travelling for purposes of work should obtain a standard passport. Application forms and BVPs, valid for 12 months, are obtainable from any main UK post office, Monday-Saturday; they are not obtainable from passport offices other than the Passport Office, Belfast, and are only available to British citizens, British Dependent Territories citizens, and British Overseas citizens for holiday purposes of up to three months. Full UK passports, valid for 10 years, can be obtained from the regional offices listed below.

Passport Office, Clive House, 70-78 Petty France, London SW1H 9HD Tel 071-279 3434

Passport Office, 5th Floor, India Buildings, Water Street, Liverpool L2 0QZ Tel 051-237 3010

Passport Office, Olympia House, Upper Dock Street, Newport, Gwent NPT 1XA Tel Newport 244500

Passport Office, Aragon Court, Northminster Road, Peterborough, Cambridgeshire PE1 1QG Tel Peterborough 895555

Passport Office, 3 Northgate, 96 Milton Street, Cowcaddens, Glasgow G4 0BT Tel 041-332 0271

Passport Office, Hampton House, 47-53 High Street, Belfast BT1 2QS Tel Belfast 232371

Essential information for holders of UK passports who intend to travel overseas contains notes on illness or injury while abroad, insurance, vaccinations, NHS medical cards, consular assistance overseas, British Customs and other useful advice, and is available from all passport offices.

Nationals of other countries will need to consult their own passport-issuing authorities as to the issuing and validity of passports, and should read carefully details given under the **Information** and other headings for each

QUALIFICATIONS

REDUCTIONS

country in this guide, so they are aware of the restrictions governing certain nationalities and their freedom to take certain jobs, particularly where the work is paid.

Q

QUALIFICATIONS Although this guide has a large number of opportunities for those with no particular qualifications other than enthusiasm and a willingness to be fully involved with the job in hand, before applying for any job check that you fully meet any credentials required. These need not be formal requirements either: for example, it's no use opting for farmwork if you suffer from hay fever; it's no use settling for a volunteer post if you must cover all your expenses; and it's no use choosing a workcamp if you don't like working hard and mixing with an international group. On the formal side, the more you can offer as regards language skills, teaching or training certificates, formal education or previous experience, then the wider the range of options you will have, and consequently the better the chance of being selected. It is always worthwhile listing relevant qualifications and experience when applying for any job; the competition for many of these jobs is strong, and employers can afford to be very selective.

R

REDUCTIONS Youth and student cards offer a range of reductions on travel, accommodation, restaurants, shopping and entry to cultural sites, and if you are eligible it is worth getting one of the available cards. The International Student Identity Card scheme is operated by the International Student Travel Confederation, a group of major official student travel bodies worldwide. ISIC provides internationally accepted proof of student status and consequently ensures that students may enjoy many special facilities, including fare reductions, cheap accommodation, reduced rate or free entry to museums, art galleries and historic sites. Obtainable from official student travel offices, the card is available to all full-time students, along with the International Student Travel Guide detailing the discounts and facilities available worldwide. Valid for up to 16 months (1 September-31 December of the following year). Details in the UK from ISIC Administration, NUS Services Ltd, Bleaklow House, Howard Town Mills, Mill Street, Glossop SK13 8PT Tel Glossop 868003.

The Federation of International Youth Travel Organisations (FIYTO) aims to promote educational, cultural and social travel among young people. The FIYTO Youth International Exchange Card is a recognised card offering concessions to young travellers including transport, accommodation, restaurants, excursions, cultural events and reduced rates or free entry to many museums, art galleries, theatres and cinemas. Available to all those under 26, together with a booklet giving details of the concessions. Available in the UK from Campus Travel, 52 Grosvenor Gardens, London SW1W 0AG Tel 071-730 3402.

S

SOCIAL SECURITY If a person undertakes paid employment abroad in a country having reciprocal social security arrangements, advice as to their position should be sought from their own social security authority.

The UK has reciprocal agreements with Australia, Austria, Bermuda, Canada, Cyprus, Finland, Iceland, Isle of Man, Israel, Jamaica, Jersey and Guernsey, Malta, Mauritius, New Zealand, Norway, Philippines, Sweden, Switzerland, Turkey, United States and Yugoslavia.

Leaflet SA29, available from the Overseas Branch of the Department of Social Security, see below, gives details of the social security rights available to UK nationals working in the EC and how and where to claim them. In addition separate booklets are available describing the social security arrangements (including health services) in certain EC countries. Leaflet NI38 Social Security Abroad is a guide to National Insurance contributions and social security benefits in non-EC and non-reciprocal agreement countries.

For further information contact the Department of Social Security, Overseas Branch, Newcastle upon Tyne NE98 1YX Tel 091-225 3002.

T

TRAINING The Job Book 1990 £13.95, lists jobs and training schemes offered by over 1,000 UK employers. Editorial guidance identifies the job and training opportunities on offer, indexes help pinpoint the employers who match individual needs and employer profiles give a more in-depth view on each organisation. Available from CRAC Publications, Hobsons Publishing Group, Bateman Street, Cambridge CB2 1LZ Tel Cambridge 354551.

Community Service Volunteers, 237 Pentonville Road, London N1 9NJ Tel 071-278 6601 is the UK national volunteer agency which aims to involve people in community service and to encourage social change. It invites all 16-35 year olds to join the National Volunteer Network and work with people in need: homeless people in the inner city, children in care, people with disabilities, elderly people, children with handicaps. Volunteers work away from home, alongside professionals, for 4+ months, receiving board, lodging, travel costs and pocket money.

There is also a programme for overseas volunteers aged 18-35, with good English and able to meet British visa requirements. Overseas volunteers work on the same projects as UK volunteers, and receive board, lodging, pocket money and travel costs within Britain. Cost £395 for 4-12 months, or £190 for 10-16 week summer programme. PH

The Youth Training Scheme (YTS) run by the Training Agency aims to provide training to equip young British people for working life. It gives most 16 year old school leavers 2 years of training, and most 17 year olds 1 year, with special arrangements for disabled young people and some other groups.
It offers off-the-job training and planned work experience, with the opportunity to gain a recognised vocational qualification or a credit towards one. Two year trainees receive an allowance of £29.50 per week increasing to £35 in the second year. Those joining with a 1 year entitlement receive £29.50 per week for the first 13 weeks, £35 per week for the latter 39 weeks. For further information contact your local careers office or Jobcentre. PH

Vacation Traineeships for Students 1991 £6.95, is a guide to short-term opportunities available to students, sixth formers and school leavers interested in obtaining work experience or training during the vacation period. Includes jobs in accountancy, business and management, computers and electronics, the Civil Service, education, publishing, construction and engineering, medicine, law, insurance and banking. Published by Vacation Work, 9 Park End Street, Oxford OX1 1HJ Tel Oxford 241978.

U

UNEMPLOYMENT BENEFIT If you are an EC citizen and unemployed and want to look for work in another EC country, except Portugal or Spain, you may be able to get unemployment benefit there for up to 3 months. Claimants must have registered at an unemployment benefit office or a careers office in their own country, normally for at least 4 weeks, and must be getting benefit when they leave. They must immediately register for work and also for benefit in all the countries they go to but may encounter problems if they cannot speak the languages of the countries they visit. Unemployed British citizens should ask for leaflet *UBL22*, or contact the Department of Employment, St Vincent House, 30 Orange Street, London WC2H 7HT Tel 071-839 5600.

Those who qualify for benefit, and are staying temporarily at workcamps away from their home areas in Great Britain, Northern Ireland or the Isle of Man run by charities or local authorities and providing a service to the community, may receive unemployment benefit for one period of up to 14 days in a calendar year provided they continue to be available for work during this period. They will not be required to attend the unemployment office during the workcamp. On return, their claims will be considered to see whether they continued to satisfy the conditions for the payment of unemployment benefit. It is essential, however, that they give the office details of the workcamp in advance. Unemployed people may earn up to £2 per day when working for voluntary groups, charities or the community, without having to forfeit their unemployment benefit, providing that they also remain available for work.

V

VISAS For entry to some countries a visa or visitor's pass is required, and in many a work and/or residence permit will be required. Requirements and regulations are noted in this guide under the **Information** headings for each country. Entry and work regulation requirements vary considerably, particularly outside the EC, and it is advisable to apply early to the relevant embassy or consulate as it may take some time to obtain the necessary documentation.

W

WORKING FULL TIME This guide does not attempt to cover regular paid employment abroad; those interested in finding such employment should apply through normal channels and advertisements. From time to time employment offices receive details of overseas vacancies, mainly in the EC. The majority of vacancies are for skilled persons aged 18+ with a good working knowledge of the language of the country chosen; applicants must be prepared to work abroad for 6 months or more. In Britain contact the Training Agency, Employment Service Division, through your local Jobcentre or employment office, for further information.

Professionally qualified people wishing to work in their particular field should send a SAE/IRC to the Federation of Recruitment and Employment Services Ltd, 36/38 Mortimer Street, London W1N 7RB for a list of member agencies dealing in overseas recruitment. Knowledge of a foreign language is usually preferred.

The Directory of Jobs and Careers Abroad £7.95, is a guide to permanent career opportunities worldwide, and outlines methods of finding work. It includes information on jobs in computer services, oil, mining and engineering, medicine and nursing, journalism, banking and accountancy, transport and tourism, and also gives information on work permits, visas, taxes and social security. Published by Vacation Work, 9 Park End Street, Oxford OX1 1HJ Tel Oxford 241978.

The leaflet *Working Abroad* gives broad guidelines relevant to working abroad, with useful information for UK nationals on how to apply for an overseas job and what they should ask before accepting it. Published by the Department of Employment and available from Jobcentres and employment offices.

X

XENOPHOBIA If you suffer from this condition, then a working holiday in another country, experiencing a different life and culture, and speaking another language, could prove to be just the cure. Even in your own country, taking part in an international workcamp could provide relief from some of the more extreme symptoms of xenophobia. However, if the condition has persisted for some time, then a working holiday, where international teamwork, shared experiences, opportunities to make and develop new friendships, and the challenges of new situations in far away environments are just some of the highlights, is probably not for you!

Y

YEAR BETWEEN A number of options are open to school leavers who choose to widen their experience by taking a year off before going on to higher education or settling into a permanent job. Like a working holiday, it is a valuable opportunity to develop personal skills, become more self reliant and to achieve an understanding of your own strengths and weaknesses.

The Central Bureau for Educational Visits & Exchanges administers the Junior Language Assistants Scheme which enables school leavers with an interest in improving their knowledge of the language of the target country to spend two or three terms helping in the teaching of English in a school in France, the Federal Republic of Germany or Spain; *see pages 103, 122 and 259 for further information.*

GAP Activity Projects Ltd, 44 Queen's Road, Reading, Berkshire, RG1 4BB Tel Reading 594914 offers work opportunities overseas for school leavers aged 18-19 with a year before

going on to further education. The aim is to broaden horizons by providing opportunities to live and work for 4-12 months in another country. Projects include working in hospitals, acting as teachers' aides in schools, farmwork, domestic work, conservation and general office work in Australia, Canada, Chile, China, Indonesia, France, the Falkland Islands, the Federal Republic of Germany, India, Israel, Mexico, Nepal, New Zealand, Pakistan and the USSR. Board, lodging and pocket money provided, but applicants pay their own return fare and insurance. *UK nationals only; apply early in September of final school year.*

The Project Trust, Breacachadh Castle, Isle of Coll, Argyll PA78 6TB Tel Coll 444 is an educational trust sending British school leavers overseas for a year between school and university or employment. Volunteers are placed in projects which are of real use to their host communities; these include teaching English, arts and sciences; working as teachers' aides or helping at Outward Bound schools; looking after deprived or handicapped children; medical work and health care; and working on sheep or cattle stations. Placements are arranged in Australia, Brazil, China, Egypt, Honduras, Hong Kong, Indonesia, Jamaica, Jordan, Namibia, Nigeria, South Africa/Transkei, Sri Lanka, and Zimbabwe. Volunteers live in the same type of accommodation as local workers, with an appropriate subsistence wage. Cost £2,100. Successful candidates are given guidance on fundraising. Volunteers must be aged 17¼-19½ years at the time of going overseas. Compulsory 1 week training course. *Apply early; applications close January.*

Year Off, Year On £2.95 is a guide to temporary jobs, voluntary service, vacation jobs, study courses, scholarships, travel and expeditions, available from Careers Research and Advisory Centre (CRAC) Publications, Hobsons Ltd, Bateman Street, Cambridge CB2 1LZ Tel Cambridge 354551.

Jobs in the Gap Year £2 is a booklet for those intending to work during their year between. It details opportunities for voluntary work, teaching, office work, engineering and science, attachment to the armed forces, and the leisure industry. Intended mainly for public school students, but useful for all. Published by the Independent Schools Careers Organisation, 129-189 Princess Way, Camberley, Surrey GU15 3SP Tel Camberley 21188.

Volunteer Work £4.20 including UK postage is the authoritative guide to medium and long-term voluntary work and service. Thirty four of the 100 volunteer-sending agencies listed run projects tailored to the needs of those taking a year between. Information on each agency covers its background and objectives, countries of operation, projects, experience and personal qualities required of the volunteer, and details of orientation and debriefing. Practical information includes details on preparation and training, understanding development, advisory bodies, insurance, travel, social security and health requirements, and advice for returned volunteers. Published by the Central Bureau for Educational Visits & Exchanges.

Z

Z As in algebra, so in a working holiday, Z is the third unknown quantity. Having decided on a job and the country in which you want to work, the third variable is **you** yourself. No matter that this guide lists thousands of opportunities all over the world, and provides a wealth of advice and information, at the end of the day you will have needed to use your own initiative, determination and imagination in order to have obtained the job you wanted. Those with faint hearts will never get that opportunity to work their way round the world, undertaking for example, courier work on the Cote d'Azur in France, working in the orchard groves of a moshavim in Israel, picking pears in the Murray Valley in Australia, teaching sports at an American summer camp, and doing conservation work in Iceland. On the other hand, those without a wanderlust will find a host of opportunities nearer home. To all, the best of luck.

When writing to any organisation it is essential to mention Working Holidays 1991 and enclose a large stamped, self-addressed envelope, or if overseas, a large addressed envelope and at least two International Reply Coupons.

WORK PROFILES

The following profiles on the categories of work detailed in this guide may enable applicants to decide where their skills and enthusiasms may best be employed. More detailed information will be found under the respective categories for individual countries, and with particular employers, but these profiles outline the wide range of jobs on offer throughout **WORKING HOLIDAYS 1991**, and highlight the main opportunities available, with general details on age limits, requirements and periods of work.

ARCHAEOLOGY

Sitting in the bottom of a trench for hours on end, carefully brushing away decades of deposits is not everyone's idea of pleasure, but involvement in a project that may discover important finds of Palaeolithic, Bronze Age or Roman habitation has particular rewards. The range of archaeological projects available to participants is immense. Typical opportunities include studying the life of Magdalenian reindeer hunters through the excavation of Upper Palaeolithic sites in France; working on Roman, Anglo-Saxon and medieval city sites in Britain; excavations of a castle and village with Crusader, Mamluk and Ottoman remains in Israel; site surveys and excavations of a Copper Age site with Beaker culture evidence on Majorca; and revealing warehouses, chandlers' and tanners' premises on a 200 year old waterfront in the United States. Although complete beginners are welcome on many excavation sites, applicants for archaeological work are often expected to have a formal interest in history or the classics, or to be studying archaeology at college or university level. It is also important to realise that on most excavations overseas, the site directors prefer to recruit those with experience; this may be best first acquired on sites in your own country. Archaeological work can be hard and may continue in almost all weathers, and participants should be prepared accordingly. Any relevant skills should be made clear when applying; those with graphic, topographic or photographic skills are often particularly welcome. If you have an archaeological interest but no directly related skills or experience you may nevertheless be able to contribute in other ways, for example in administration or catering. Beginners will usually receive board and lodging in return for their labours, and occasionally a small amount of pocket money. Wages and/or travelling expenses may be offered to more experienced volunteers. Basic accommodation is normally provided, but volunteers may have to take their own tents and cooking equipment. The minimum age for participants is usually 13; those under 13 may be welcome provided they are accompanied by a participating adult. Families may also participate on many projects. Work may be available almost all year round, but owing to the nature of the work, projects are most often undertaken in the summer season. Anyone involved in excavation work is strongly advised to have a prior anti-tetanus injection.

AU PAIR/CHILDCARE

Working as an au pair can be an economic way to spend some time learning the language and experiencing the way of life in another country. It can be an invaluable way to widen your experience, particularly in the year between school and college/university or starting a career, for example, or in taking a break between job moves. Although au pair positions in most countries are now usually open to both sexes, many families traditionally specify females and as agencies recruit accordingly, male applicants will find opportunities more limited. One exception is the au pair programmes in Canada and the United States, see below and in the respective sections. The majority of positions are for 6+ months, although a limited number of short-term posts are available in the summer months.

The regulations of respective governments give an au pair the status of that of a member of a family, not that of a domestic. In return for board, lodging and pocket money au pairs are expected to help with light household duties including simple cooking and the care of any children, for a maximum of 30 hours per week. This should allow sufficient time to meet friends, go sightseeing and to take a part-time course in the language. Unfortunately, there is no guarantee that these conditions will be met as the arrangements depend almost totally on

AU PAIR/CHILDCARE

goodwill and cooperation between the host family and the au pair, and au pairs should be aware of these potential problems before accepting a post. However, if an au pair post is found through one of the reputable agencies listed in this guide, most of the problems can be avoided as both family and au pair should be fully briefed.

Au pair positions outside the UK are open to those aged 17-27/30; stays are usually for a minimum of six months. There may be a limited number of short-term summer stays of 2/3 months, depending on the country. The work involves general household chores such as ironing, bedmaking, dusting, vacuuming, sewing, washing up, preparing simple meals and taking the children to and from school, plus general childcare duties.
A typical working day is of 5/6 hours, with 3/4 evenings babysitting in a 6 day week. The remainder of the evening, 1 full day and 3 afternoons per week are usually free. In addition to board and lodging approx £25 per week pocket money is provided. There is usually an agency service charge of up to £50, and applicants are responsible for their travel and insurance costs, although most agencies can provide information and advice. In some cases, normally after a stay of 12 months or more, the host family will pay a single or return fare.

The au pair programmes in Canada and the United States are open equally to males as well as females, with the emphasis as much on community involvement as on childcare. To be eligible you must be a citizen of a western European country with at least a fair degree of fluency in English. Character references and a medical certificate are required, and you will also need to have some childcare experience and, particularly as some of the communities are rural, be able to drive. 5-9 hour day, 5½ day week with 1 weekend free each month. The day is made up of up to6 hours of active duties including feeding and playing with the children, and 3 hours of passive supervision including babysitting. Ages 18-25. The positions last 12 months. The return flight plus approx $80-$100 per week pocket money, board and accommodation, $250-$300 for a course of study, 2 weeks holiday, and opportunities to travel are provided.

Au pair posts in Britain are open to unmarried girls aged 17-27, without dependants, and who wish to learn English while living as a member of an English-speaking family. Only nationals of western European countries, including Cyprus, Malta, Turkey and Yugoslavia are eligible. As a general rule au pairs in Britain can expect to work up to 5 hours per day with one fixed day per week free. They should have their own room and receive approximately £28+ per week pocket money. EC nationals wishing to stay for longer than 6 months must obtain a residence permit.

Under current regulations UK au pair agencies must be licensed by the Department of Employment, and can charge up to a maximum of £46 for finding an au pair position provided that they use an agent abroad as an intermediary. This fee is payable only after the applicant has been offered and accepted a position.

It is the responsibility of the agency to ensure that the correct arrangements are made for entry into the chosen country; however it is wise for applicants to check these requirements themselves with the relevant consulates, and details are given in this guide under the respective headings. Applicants should ascertain who is responsible for making travel arrangements and paying the fares; usually agencies will give advice on travel, but applicants make their own arrangements and pay the costs. It is essential to have sufficient funds to pay the fare home in case of emergency. Before leaving au pairs should make sure they have a valid passport, a visa/ work permit as necessary, and a letter of invitation from the host family, setting out details of the arrangements that have been made, including details of pocket money and any contributions that may be payable to national insurance or other schemes in the destination country. Au pair posts should not be confused with regular domestic employment, posts as nannies or mother's helps, or posts advertised as demi-pair or au pair plus, which are covered by quite different employment and entry regulations. Applicants for nannies and mother's help posts will generally need to have NNEB or other nursery qualifications in addition to some experience, and will work longer hours for a higher salary.

Whereas au pair posts have the learning of a foreign language and the experience of life in another country as their basis, which means that au pairs cannot be placed in their home countries or countries where their own language is the native tongue, these restrictions do not apply to other childcare and domestic posts. For those with an interest in working with children but who are unavailable for the minimum periods of service of au pair and other childcare posts, or who do not possess the relevant qualifications or experience, a variety of less formal opportunities exist, particularly in the areas of community work, courier work and working as leaders or monitors; see below and under the respective headings for each country throughout this guide.

The Au Pair and Nanny's Guide to Working Abroad £5.95, is a comprehensive guide for those considering au pair, nanny or domestic work. Published by Vacation Work, 9 Park End Street, Oxford OX1 1HJ Tel Oxford 241978.

COMMUNITY WORK

Short-term voluntary work in community service can be of great social and educational value, and there are many opportunities in Britain and abroad to actively participate in improving community life. However, applicants should be aware that any period of community work involves commitment. The ideas and attitudes of voluntary service which used to be expressed as *helping those less fortunate than ourselves* or as *giving benefit to people in need* are inappropriate and patronising in society today. Working to overcome the extremes of wealth and poverty, bad housing, illiteracy, high unemployment and discrimination against an immigrant population are worthwhile challenges. The work can be undertaken in a variety of forms; for example construction, carpentry, painting and decorating work in community centres and homes can be of equal value to helping directly in the care of the homeless, rootless, inadequate, disadvantaged or disabled members of society.

Typical projects include helping to run playschemes for able-bodied or handicapped children; working in day centres/night shelters for ex-drug addicts, alcoholics or the homeless; nursing and entertaining the elderly or physically handicapped; working with immigrant communities; and taking children from deprived inner city areas on holidays in the countryside. Examples include helping with fundraising, teaching first aid and on preparation for disasters, in New Delhi; working in a 12th century monastery in Finland, an ecumenical centre for Christians of differing traditions and nationalities; supervising activities at an adventure centre for needy children in Lille, France; helping in Parish deanery and diocesan missions in the Federal Republic of Germany; working in night shelters, reception and community houses for the homeless, the isolated and unemployable, in London; working with residents on manual projects and organising activities at training centres for those with mental disabilities, in Torino, Italy; helping run youth camps, projects and family weeks for children and families under stress and from troubled areas, in Northern Ireland; helping children at a holiday centre in Switzerland, aiming to fight isolation and creating opportunities for new friendships; and working with Sioux Indians on small, remote reservations in South Dakota, developing recreational and educational activities for children.

For those contemplating study or a career in areas of social or community service, or for those currently studying or working in these areas, a period of community work can be a particularly rewarding experience. Applicants for community work schemes may need a good command of the host language, although many workcamp projects exist for those with enthusiasm but few formal skills or experience; see below under **Workcamps**. The minimum age is 18, although younger applicants may be accepted on the basis of interests, experience and individual maturity.

Many of the community work projects can be particularly physically and emotionally draining, and potential applicants should read carefully all the literature provided on the project and consider their own strengths and weaknesses before formally applying. The ability to take initiatives within the framework of the project team, to cope with crises, to exert discipline without being authoritarian, and to maintain a sense of humour and perspective, is essential.

CONSERVATION

The Earth is 4,600 million years old; in the last century we have come very close to upsetting the ecological balance that has developed since the planet's creation, coming ever closer to destroying the supportable environment altogether. Earth's inhabitants have raided the planet for fuels, used the land, sea and air as rubbish tips, and caused the extinction of over 500 species of animals. For those who would like to make some contribution towards the health and management of planet Earth, no matter how small, a variety of conservation work projects in Britain and around the world offer the opportunity to turn concerns into practical use. Volunteers can contribute to the conservation of the natural environment, from the coasts of Britain to the rain cloud forests of Costa Rica, and in the protection and restoration of neglected buildings of historic or environmental interest.

Work can be undertaken on a wide range of tasks, including drystone walling, railway/canal and other industrial heritage restoration, restoring churches, castles or agricultural buildings; cleaning rivers and ponds, protecting rare plants, trees and animals, stabilising sand dunes; working in national parks, reserves and mountain pastures; renovating abandoned hamlets and maintaining footpaths, forest trails and bridleways.

Typical opportunities include creating a wetlands education site in the Northern Territories of Australia; leading environmental conservation camps focusing on species protection, waste recycling and action against sea pollution, in Belgium; environmental protection work on the Faroe Islands; sand dune stabilisation and urban conservation in France's Northern Regional Park; restoration work on the British canal network; the restoration of an 11th century convent in Tuscany; biological and geological studies in natural caves in Portalegre, Portugal; trail routing and maintenance in a rare tropical white oak cloud forest in Costa Rica; work on an environmental education centre, organic farm and ecological park in Valencia, Spain; and assisting with the relocation of black bears in the Great Smokey Mountains, United States.

Some projects include training on particular aspects of conservation and preservation work. All tasks involve work which could not otherwise be achieved without volunteer assistance. The minimum age is usually 13, although families with younger children will often be welcome. Those with relevant skills are particularly welcome. The projects are normally undertaken during the summer months, though opportunities exist at other times, and sometimes all year round. Basic accommodation is provided in church or village halls, schools, farm buildings or hostels, depending on the situation. Self-catering facilities are usually provided, though volunteers may have to contribute towards the cost of food and pay their own travel costs. Work can be strenuous; all volunteers should be fit and are strongly advised to have an anti-tetanus injection before joining any project.

COURIERS/REPS

The holiday market, particularly the package holiday sector, is a vast business, and provides a great number of seasonal work opportunities. Around 14 million Britons annually take a package holiday overseas, 5 million of them in Spain. However, for a variety of reasons there has been a recent drop of up to 80% in these numbers, with a further drop predicted for coming years. These statistics, coupled with an anticipated increase in holiday costs may well mean a corresponding reduction in the number of opportunities for seasonal employment, particularly overseas.

Many holiday companies employ couriers to escort groups on holiday, between holiday areas, or from Britain to destinations overseas, in both the winter and summer seasons, December-April and May-August/October. Couriers are also required on an increasing number of European campsites, acting as resident representatives, setting up and cleaning tents and mobile homes, responding to problems and emergencies, maintaining equipment, and arranging both children's and adult's entertainment programmes. Other representatives are needed at hotels and centres in resorts worldwide, providing client information and looking after welfare and other needs. Applicants need to be 18/21+, mature, reliable, with a good knowledge of

anguages. The ability to
dent, efficient, sensible,
iable is essential.
either courier work or
ic in similar situations
... many holiday operators will
prefer to employ a courier or representative for
the whole of the season, and consequently will
give preference to those applicants available
for long periods. Salaries and accommodation
will vary according to qualifications,
experience, resorts and seasons worked. There
will usually be enough free time to make use of
the hotel's or centre's facilities.

DOMESTIC WORK

Hotels and holiday centres take on extra
kitchen assistants, waiters, waitresses, bar
staff, cleaners, chambermaids and other
domestic staff during the holiday seasons.
However the comments made above under
Couriers/reps with regard to the future volume
of work generated by the package holiday
industry should be noted. Domestic work can
be very hard with long, unsociable hours. The
ability to work as part of a team is essential.
Knowledge of the local language may be
needed, particularly where contact with the
public is made, and those with some relevant
skills or experience will find successful
application easier. Salaries, living conditions,
tips or bonuses vary according to placement.
Often the facilities open to clients will be
available for use during free time. The
minimum age will be 17/18, and those with
experience or relevant qualifications are
particularly sought, although there are posts
such as kitchen assistants and porters where
previous experience is not necessary.
Preference will usually be given to those able
to work the whole of either the winter or
summer season, usually December-April/May
and April-October, respectively. The
Federation of Recruitment and Employment
Services, 36/38 Mortimer Street, London W1N
7RB, is the UK trade association for the private
recruitment service and produces a list of
members who recruit domestic, catering and
hotel staff in Britain and overseas, available on
receipt of SAE/IRCs. In Britain Jobcentres and
employment offices often have details of
summer jobs in the hotel/catering industries.

FARMWORK/GRAPE PICKING

A variety of work is available on international
farmcamps, on agricultural establishments,
including organic and bee farms, and in
vineyards in a number of European countries
and as far afield as Australia and Canada.
Participants must be fit and ready to undertake
whatever picking or other agricultural work
they are required to do. The work is often very
hard and patience is required; hours can be
long and it is sometimes necessary to work
weekends. As most picking jobs are paid at
piece-work rates, it is important to remember
that inclement weather can affect ripening, the
amount of crops to be picked and thus the
wages; if no work is available due to bad
weather or for any other reason, no wages will
be paid. The wage is normally enough to cover
food, accommodation and other charges and
leave a small net gain, varying according to the
efficiency of the picker the weather, and the
quality and quantity of the harvest. Living
conditions are often simple, with self-catering
accommodation in dormitory huts or tents. On
farmcamps participants may have to provide
their own tents and cooking equipment, and a
registration fee will be payable. Some
international farmcamps provide facilities for
sports and other leisure activities and may
arrange excursions to places of interest.

Summer farmwork in Britain includes general
farm labouring as well as vegetable harvesting
and soft fruit picking, often on international
farmcamps. The work is mainly in Scotland,
East Anglia, the South, the West Country and
Kent, where it includes the traditional English
working holiday of hop picking. Other crops to
be picked include cherries, raspberries,
strawberries, blackcurrants, loganberries,
blackberries, plums, gooseberries, apples,
pears, potatoes, courgettes and beans. A range
of ancillary work such as strawing, weeding,
irrigation, fruit inspection, packing, indoor
processing, tractor driving or working in the
oast houses may also be available.
The work can be on individual, often family-
run farms, on smallholdings or with
cooperatives, or on international farmcamps.
The general number of hours worked are 40-45

FARMWORK/GRAPE PICKING

per week and for 5-6 days. The length of the working season varies, depending on the crop being harvested, the weather and the location of the farm. The harvesting of soft fruit is normally undertaken between mid June and August, although in some areas picking may start as early as May. The picking of hops, apples and other crops runs from late August to October.

Work is also available on community and alternative farming projects. It can include assisting in the breeding of rare domestic animals; working with underprivileged children on farmsteads during their summer holidays; helping organic farmers and smallholders replace the use of herbicides, chemical fertilisers and heavy machinery by manpower; helping on city farms and community garden projects; and working with the handicapped, disabled and disadvantaged on rehabilitation projects on the basis of a common interest in plants and animals.

Hop picking has traditionally been undertaken as a working holiday by many of the families of London's East End and their counterparts in the Black Country, once England's industrial heart. Although this tradition is still carried on today, the majority of the several hundred pickers working annually in the hop gardens of Hampshire, Kent, Sussex and Worcestershire are overseas students, local workers and Travellers. Hops are climbing bines, their bitter cones used in the flavouring of beer. At one time there were over 1,000 hop farms in southern England, supplying cones to brewers all over the world. However, since mainland Europe and the United States began plantations to provide for most of their own needs, and since drinking fashion turned to lighter beers and lagers, the number of English hop producers has dwindled to around 250. Consequently the number of seasonal workers taken on is now substantially less than it once was. Generally a flat rate of pay, up to £25 per day, is paid rather than piece-work rates.

On farmcamps the emphasis is as much on living and working in an international community, with sports and social activities, as on earning money. The wages paid may only be sufficient to cover food and accommodation costs and to provide a little pocket money. The social and sports facilities provided can include swimming pools, tennis courts, games fields, games and television rooms, video, bars, discos and dances. The majority of workers will be in the 17-30 age range, and families are often welcome. On some camps English language tuition may be available for overseas workers during free time. For those from outside Britain working on farmcamps, work permits are not required, but those from countries outside the European Community subject to immigration control will require a letter of invitation. This letter, issued by the farmcamp organisers, allows entry into Britain but does not entitle the visitor to take paid work of any other kind during the visit.

Most soft fruit picking is a slow and painstaking job, and workers will often be required to pick to a very high standard. All agricultural work is physically demanding and can involve long hours in all weathers. The living conditions offered are often simple, with self-catering accommodation in farm cottages, caravans, dormitory huts or tents. In some instances participants may have to take their sleeping bags, if not their own tents and camping equipment. Insurance cover is usually provided against accidents or illness, but personal insurance cover will normally be necessary. Community and alternative farmwork projects are generally of a voluntary nature, and some financial contribution towards board and accommodation may be required. The work can include hedging, ditching, pond and scrub clearance, haymaking, fruit and vegetable cropping, dairy work, bee keeping, stone walling, sheep shearing, animal rearing, building renovation, peat cutting, scything and compost making.

Grape picking under the sun in the south of France, tasting the product, living at the vineyard, taking *déjeuner sur l'herbe* with the grower and his family may conjure a colourful and idyllic scene. It certainly can be with proper planning, a genuine job awaiting you, and the true picture of what grape picking involves clearly defined. If not, then the reality can be very different. The hours of work are long, you need to be fit as the work is hard, the accommodation may be basic and often, during bad weather, only those hours actually worked will be paid. The decreasing need for manual labour owing to mechanisation together with the regular army of seasonal workers being swelled by the numbers of unemployed has also led to increased competition for jobs. Despite this, and providing you have a realistic assessment of just what a grape picking holiday involves, the grape harvest can provide an enjoyable summer job, as you toil away alongside the locals and workers from all over the world.

The main opportunities available, with brief details on age limits, requirements and periods of work are given below. The dates of the harvest should be regarded as approximate; they may vary by two weeks either way. Changes in the weather may also mean that you are given as little as 48 hours notice before work is due to commence. The quality and quantity of the harvests can vary enormously. 1986 was a good harvest, swelling the European wine lake to 6070 million litres; 1987 was not indifferent in quality but was far from generous in quantity. The effects of a good year can make for lower production in subsequent years. In any case, wine consumption in the main wine producing areas is falling. Also, since the dollar weakened, the United States has lost some of its taste for European wines, and Australian and New Zealand wines have become increasingly popular. The USSR which has traditionally absorbed some of the European wine surplus is now increasing its own production capacity and has planted 25% more vines over the last decade.

There are also fewer acres of vines, many farmers taking advantage of EC subsidies to turn their land into more lucrative forms of agriculture. In France the total vineyard area has decreased from 3 million acres to 2.4 million in the last ten years. Nevertheless France, Italy and Portugal have an 80 litres per head, per year, wine consumption rate, compared to Britain's 10 litres per head. The net result, at least as far as summer workers are concerned, is that in France the quality areas such as Burgundy, Beaune and Bordeaux are where grape picking will prove to be most fruitful.

For those looking further afield for farmwork, in addition to opportunities on kibbutzim and moshavim, see below for further details, the fruitgrowing regions of the Goulbourn/ Murray Valley in Australia, offer fruitpicking jobs from late January to April each year. These regions are situated approximately 300 miles south west of Sydney, and 100 miles due north of Melbourne; they are one of the most productive fruit growing regions of Australia, producing an annual crop of around 200,000 tonnes of fruit. The season starts in January with the harvesting of Bartletts pears, used mainly for canning. Other pear varieties and peaches extend the season through March and into April, finishing with apple harvesting. Piece-work rates apply, and although accommodation is offered on many orchards, those with rucksack and tent will find the climate conducive.

KIBBUTZIM/ MOSHAVIM

Hundreds of kibbutzim and moshavim all over Israel offer the opportunity to experience the challenge of living and working in a small, independent community. This in itself is potentially rewarding, as is living in a country whose society and culture are so different from one's own. The first kibbutz was established in 1909 by a group of individuals who wanted to form a community where there was no exploitation and no drive to accumulate individual wealth. The desire to establish a just society is the basis principle guiding kibbutz life, together with a commitment to undertake tasks important to the development of Israel and the Jewish people. There are now 250 kibbutzim throughout Israel providing a way of life for nearly 100,000, in which all means of production are owned by the community as a whole. The workforce consists of all members and any volunteers, who receive no wages but give their labour according to ability and in return receive in accordance with their needs.

Kibbutzim are democratic societies and all members have a voice in determining how the kibbutz is run. A general assembly meets weekly and a number of committees discuss and resolve specialist problems. Kibbutzim welcome volunteers who are prepared to live and work within the community and abide by the kibbutz way of life. Volunteers share all communal facilities with kibbutz members, and should be capable of adapting to a totally new society. The majority of work for volunteers is in the communal dining room, the laundry and possibly in children's houses. On most kibbutzim children live in houses apart from their parents, spending only part of the afternoons and evenings with them. This allows for mothers to become active in the life of the kibbutz, and ensures an equality of education where the community as a whole is responsible for the care and education of the children. Some of the work during summer months includes citrus, melon and soft fruit harvesting, and volunteers may also be involved in haymaking, gardening or working in the fish ponds, cow sheds or chicken houses. Part of the time is also likely to be spent in non-specialist, light industrial work. Volunteers work approximately an 8 hour day, 6 day week with Saturdays free. Work outdoors often starts at 05.00 and finishes at 14.00, the hottest part of the afternoons being free. Volunteers live together in wood cabins, 2-4 to a room, with food provided in the communal dining room.

Moshavim are collective settlements of from 10-100 individual smallholders. Each family works and develops its own area of land or farm while sharing the capital costs of equipment, marketing and necessary services. There are almost 1,000 moshavim where volunteers can live and work as members of Israeli families, mainly in the Jordan valley, the Arava and the western Negev. Most of the work is on the land, particularly in flower growing, market gardening and specialist fruit farming.

Kibbutzim or moshavim volunteers should be aged between 18 and 32, in good physical and mental health, and will need references, a medical certificate and a special entry visa. Pregnant women or families with young children will not be accepted. Prospective volunteers should bear in mind that the work is often physically arduous, that conditions can be uncomfortable, and the hours long. The effect of living in relatively close confinement with a group of fellow volunteers is also something that should not be underestimated. Working holidays on kibbutzim and moshavim can last from 5 weeks up to one year.

LEADERS & GUIDES

A wide range of opportunities exist for those with organising and leadership skills. This includes leading a range of adventure holidays and expeditions, both by truck or foot, in countries in Africa, Asia and South America; organising welfare and entertainment activities for groups of young people and adults on activity holidays throughout Europe; organising and running sports and activities at adventure holiday centres in a number of countries including France and Britain; running an adventure centre on the Isle of Mull, cooking and leading canoeing and hillwalking outings; and looking after children on holiday in Spanish coastal resorts, arranging entertainments, competitions and parties. Depending to some extent on the individual job, applicants will need at least some of the following qualities : to be energetic, reliable and mature, self-motivated, resourceful, adaptable, with good stamina, tolerance, flexibility, initiative and a sense of humour. Previous travel experience and a knowledge of foreign languages will be an advantage. The minimum age is normally 21, and the period of work from 8 weeks-6 months. It is often necessary to attend a short training course, and previous experience of working with children is a definite advantage.

MONITORS, TEACHERS & INSTRUCTORS

For those with some teaching or instructing skills and qualifications there are a number of posts in a wide range of countries. Most of the opportunities will require formal qualifications, although a number will be open to those with at least relevant experience.

Monitors and teachers are required to teach English at language camps in Austria, Hungary, Poland and Turkey. Applicants should be native English speakers and have experience of working with or teaching children; organisational ability in sports, music and crafts is an advantage. Various posts also exist for qualified EFL teachers, particularly working in summer schools in Britain.

Camp counsellors are needed on North American summer camps, and on similarly run day and residential camps in some European countries. General counsellors are responsible for the care and supervision of a group of 8-10 children aged 6-16. The work involves playing and living with the children 24 hours a day, and duties include supervising the camp, helping to maintain a high level of morale, supervising rest hours and conducting activities. Specialist counsellors are responsible for instructing the children in specific activities such as sports, watersports, sciences, arts and crafts, pioneering and performing arts. Applicants are normally aged 18-35, and must be flexible, cooperative and adaptable, like and actively get on with children, and be prepared to work with young people intensively in an outdoor environment.

Teaching posts also include those suitable for students taking a year between school and higher education or a career. These include work in independent schools in Australia, January-August, helping with sports, games, arts and science activities; and helping to teach English and taking conservation classes in schools in France, Germany and Spain, January-June.

A variety of instructor posts are open, including those for ski instructors, usually with BASI or ASSI qualifications, working the winter season, December-April. Qualified sports, watersports and other activity instructors are also required in a number of countries, usually in the summer seasons, April or May-August or September. All instructors must have the ability to teach to a good basic level and impart their knowledge in an imaginative, interesting way, particularly as many of the posts involve work with children. On many holiday centres the emphasis is on informality and enjoyment; safety, fun and participation is often the main aim, rather than on pure sports teaching. To this end the ability to manage and organise, and to work within a team, is as important as technical ability.

PEACE CAMPS

Forty five million people worldwide lost their lives in the Second World War. If this statistic was not troubling enough in itself, over two thirds of those killed were civilians, innocent bystanders killed not on the field of war, but in cities and concentration camps. In order that we may not simply forget the horrors of the Second World War or previous or subsequent conflicts, a number of organisations run peace camps in several countries, particularly in Europe. Their aim is through the understanding of events and history to prevent the repetition of the savageries of war. The work on peace camps often involves the maintenance of Second World War concentration camps as monuments, warning symbols and as a means of raising awareness of history. The camps also support peace information and activity centres, promote international discussion of the nuclear threat, alternative security policies and non-violence, and bring together peace movements in different countries. Volunteers should be aware that they may be confronted with very disturbing situations and they should give a lot of thought to the subject of war and peace, before participating. Equally, volunteers should be aware that they have the potential to make an important contribution to promoting tolerance and justice. Discussion forums and educational and cultural activities form an integral part of all peace camp activities. Ages 18+. Applicants should be interested in peace work, and have some knowledge of the political background of the host country.

WORKCAMPS

International workcamps are a form of short-term voluntary service, providing an opportunity for people of different racial, cultural and religious backgrounds to live and work together on a common project providing a constructive service to the community. By bringing together a variety of skills, talents and experiences from different nations, volunteers not only provide a service to others but also receive an opportunity for personal growth and greater awareness of their responsibility to the society in which they live

WORKCAMPS

and work. Workcamp participants have an opportunity to learn about the history, culture and social conditions of the host country and to partake in the life of the local community. Workcamps run for periods of 2-4 weeks, April-October; some are also run at Christmas, Easter and at other times throughout the year. Young people participating in workcamps need to be mature enough not to require adult supervision and should be prepared to take responsibility for the successful running of the projects, group recreation activities and discussions. The minimum age is around 17, with the exception of a number of youth projects, usually with a minimum age of 13.

The type of work undertaken varies considerably depending on both the area and the country in which the camp is being held. The work can include building, gardening and decorating, providing roads and water supplies to rural villages or constructing adventure playgrounds, and is within the capacity of normally fit volunteers. Virtually all workcamp organisers will consider volunteers with disabilities providing the nature of the work allows their active participation. Any manual work undertaken is usually for 7-8 hours a day, 5 or 6 days a week. Workcamps can also involve community or conservation projects with work other than that of a manual nature. A few camps have shorter working hours and an organised study programme concerned with social problems or dealing with wider international issues.

Accommodation is provided in a variety of building such as schools, community centres or hostels, and may sometimes be under canvas. Living conditions and sanitation vary considerably and can be very basic; in some cases running water may not be readily available. Food is generally provided, although it is often on a self-catering basis, with volunteers preparing and cooking their own meals, sometimes on a rota basis. In many camps food will be vegetarian. Most workcamps consist of 10-30 volunteers from several countries. English is in common use as the working language, especially in Europe; the other principal working language is French. A knowledge of the host country's language is sometimes essential, especially for community work. Workcamp applicants will generally pay a registration fee and arrange and pay for their own travel and possibly insurance. Volunteers may occasionally be expected to make a contribution towards the cost of their board and lodging, and should take pocket money to cover basic needs. Although many organisations provide insurance cover for their volunteers, this is often solely against third party risks and accidents. Volunteers are strongly advised to obtain precise details on this and, where necessary, take out individual policies against illness, disablement and loss or damage to personal belongings. In addition to the compulsory vaccinations required for foreign travel, anyone joining a manual workcamp programme is strongly advised to have an anti-tetanus injection.

Workcamp leaders are volunteers, usually in their early 20s, selected for general suitability and experience, and briefly trained. They have no special privileges on the camp, arc expected to work as much as everyone else and can only be distinguished from their fellow volunteers by their extra responsibilities; most workcamps have two co-leaders of equal status. Domestic affairs are the responsibility of the group; the key function of the leaders is to enable the volunteers to form a cohesive group within which each volunteer feels expected and able to contribute fully to the work and life of the camp. An important function of the leaders is to act as the link between people professionally concerned with social need and volunteers whose willingness to help may not be matched, at least initially, with enough understanding of the problems involved and how to meet them. Besides basic training regarding the functions of leadership, workcamp organisations run special courses to prepare leaders for particular types of projects, such as children's playgroup leadership or the care of the mentally handicapped. Anyone interested in attending workcamp leadership training courses in Britain should contact one of the major UK workcamp organisations, details below.

Workcamp Organisers lists nearly 280 national and international voluntary service organisations sponsoring workcamps in approx 90 countries. It includes the duration of the camps, months in which they take place, type of work, financial conditions and other details. Published every 3 years in cooperation with the Youth Division of UNESCO by the Coordinating Committee for International Voluntary Service, UNESCO, 1 rue Miollis, 75015 Paris, France. Cost FF12 or 14 IRCs.

When applying to join a workcamp in your own country it is essential to include a large stamped self-addressed envelope when you write to the organisers. If you would like to join a workcamp overseas, you should apply through the recruiting organisation in your own country, and not direct. The UK and overseas organisations that cooperate in the recruitment of volunteers on international workcamps are either given at the end of each entry or are detailed below. If no cooperating organisation is listed, or you need to write direct to an overseas workcamp organiser for any other reason, it is essential that you enclose a large self-addressed envelope and at least two International Reply Coupons (IRCs), available from post offices.

The three main UK organisations either running workcamps in Britain or recruiting volunteers for international workcamps overseas, together with their cooperating partner organisations worldwide are as follows:

CMP Christian Movement for Peace, Bethnal Green United Reformed Church, Pott Street, London E2 0EF Tel 071-729 1877.
Registration fee £15 (UK camps) or £24 (overseas)

IVS International Voluntary Service, 162 Upper Walk, Leicester LE1 7QA Tel Leicester 549430.
Registration fee £20 (UK camps) or £40 (overseas). Membership fee £25 (students £15, unwaged £10).

UNA United Nations Association, International Youth Service,Welsh Centre for International Affairs, Temple of Peace, Cathays Park, Cardiff CF1 3AP Tel Cardiff 223088.
Registration fee £25 (UK camps) or from £35 (overseas).

AUSTRIA
SCI, Schottengasse 3a 1/4/59, 1010 Wien **IVS**

BANGLADESH
SCI, GPO Box 3254, Dhaka 2 **IVS**

BELGIUM
MJP, boulevard de l'Empereur 15, 1000 Bruxelles **CMP**

VIA, Venusstraat 28, 2000 Antwerpen **IVS**

SCI, rue Van Elewyck 35, 1050 Bruxelles **IVS**

BENIN
CCAB, BP 1109, Carre 964, Cotonou 1 **IVS**

BOTSWANA
BWA, PO Box 1185, Mochudi **IVS**

BULGARIA
Argo-M, Boulevard Stamboliski 2A, Sofia 1000 **IVS UNA**

CAMEROON
UCJG, BP 89, Foyer de Jeunesse Protestant, Douala **IVS UNA**

CANADA
CMP, 427 Bloor Street West, Toronto, Ontario M5S 1X7 **CMP**

CBIE, 85 Albert Street, 14th Floor, Ottawa, Ontario K1P 6A4 **IVS UNA**

CZECHOSLOVAKIA
CKM, Zitna Ulice 12, 121 05 Praha 1 **CMP IVS UNA**

DENMARK
MS, Borgergade 10-14, 1300 Kobenhavn K **CMP IVS UNA**

FINLAND
KVT, Rauhanasema, Veturitori, 00520 Helsinki 52 **CMP IVS**

FRANCE
MCP, 38 rue du Faubourg St Denis, 75010 Paris **CMP**

SCI, 129 rue du Faubourg Poissonnière, 75009 Paris **IVS**

Jeunesse et Reconstruction, 10 rue de Trévise, 75009 Paris **UNA**

Concordia, 27 rue du Pont-Neuf, BP 238, 75024 Paris Cedex 01 **UNA**

Etudes et Chantiers International, 33 rue Campagne Premiere, 75014 Paris **UNA**

FEDERAL REPUBLIC OF GERMANY
CFD, 6000 Frankfurt-Bornheim 60,
Rendelerstrasse 9-11 CMP

SCI, 5300 Bonn 1, Blücherstrasse 14 IVS

NDF, 6000 Frankfurt-am-Main 1, Auf der
Kornerwiese 5 UNA

IJGD, 5300 Bonn 1, Kaiserstrasse 43 UNA

ADJ, 3550 Marburg/Lahn, Bahnhofstrasse 26
UNA

GERMAN DEMOCRATIC REPUBLIC
FDJ, Unter den Linden 36-38, 1086 Berlin IVS

GHANA
VOLU, PO Box 1540, Accra IVS UNA

GREECE
SCI, 59 Kefallimias Street, 11251 Athens IVS

HUNGARY
KISZ, PO Box 72, 1138 Budapest IVS UNA

INDIA
SCI, K5 Green Park, New Delhi 110016 IVS

IRELAND
VSI, 37 North Great George Street, Dublin 1
IVS

Comhchairdeas, 7 Lower Ormond Quay,
Dublin 1 UNA

ITALY
MCP, via Rattazi 24, 00185 Roma CMP UNA

SCI, via dei Laterani 28, 00184 Roma IVS

IVORY COAST
AICV, 04 BP 714, Abidjan IVS

JAPAN
SCI, 5-5-32-206, Mukodai, Tanashi-shi, Tokyo
168 IVS

LESOTHO
LWA, PO Box 6, Maseru 100 IVS UNA

MALAYSIA
SCI, c/o 29 Jalan Gajah, 11200 Tanjung Bungah,
Penang IVS

MAURITIUS
SVI, c/o Amicale, Arcades Rambour, Route
Royale, Rose Hill IVS

MOROCCO
CSM, BP 456, Rabat RP CMP UNA

NEPAL
SCI, 11/141 Kalmachi Tole, Kathmandu IVS

NETHERLANDS
ICVD, Pesthuislaan 25, 1054 RH Amsterdam
CMP

VIA, Pesthuislaan 25, 1054 RH Amsterdam IVS

SIV, Willemstraat 7, 3511 RJ Utrecht IVS UNA

NIGERIA
VWAN, PO Box 2189, Lagos IVS UNA

NORTHERN IRELAND
IVS, 122 Great Victoria Street, Belfast BT2 7BG
IVS

NORWAY
ID, Rozenkrantzgate 18, 0160 Oslo 1 IVS

POLAND
Almatur, ul Kopernika 23, 00-359 Warsaw
CMP

OHP, ul Kosynierow 22, 04-641 Warsaw IVS
CMP UNA

PORTUGAL
Cristaos Para a Paz, Rua Citade de Poitiers No
44-1, Monte Formosa, 3000 Coimbra CMP

Instituto da Juventude, Avenida Duque d'Avila
137, 1100 Lisboa IVS UNA

Turicoop, Rua Pascoal de Melo 15-1 Dt, 1100
Lisboa UNA

SIERRA LEONE
SALVAS, PMB 655, Freetown IVS

VWASL, PO Box 1205, Freetown IVS UNA

SLOVENIA
RK-ZSMS, Dalmatinova 4, Dom Sindikatov,
Llubljana IVS UNA

SPAIN
Instituto de la Juventud, Jose Ortega y Gasset 71, 28006 Madrid **CMP UNA**

SCI-SCCT, Rambla Catalunya 5, pral 2a, 08007 Barcelona **IVS**

SRI LANKA
SCI, No 7, Vihare Lane, Suduhumpola, Kandy **IVS**

SWAZILAND
SWA, PO Box A, 129 Swazi Plaza, Mbabane **IVS**

SWEDEN
IAL, Barnangsgatan 23, 11641 Stockholm **IVS**

SWITZERLAND
CFD, Falkenhoheweg 8, 3001 Bern **CMP**

SCI, Waldhoheweg 33a, Postfach 246, 3000 Bern 25 **IVS**

TANZANIA
CCM/YL, PO Box 19985, Dar es Salaam **IVS**

TOGO
ASTOVOCT, BP 97, Kpalime **IVS**

TUNISIA
Association Tunisienne d'Action Volontaire, Maison du RCD, boulevard du 9 avril 1938, La Kasbah, 1002 Tunis **UNA**

TURKEY
Genctur, PO Box 1263, Sirkeci, Istanbul **CMP IVS UNA**

UNITED STATES
CIEE, 205 East 42nd Street, New York, NY 10017 **UNA**

Volunteers for Peace, Tiffany Road, Belmont, Vermont 05730 **CMP IVS UNA**

SCI, Innisfree Village, Route 2, Box 506, Crozet, Virginia 22932 **IVS**

YUGOSLAVIA
RK-ZSMSS, Dalmatinova 4, Dom Sindikatov, 61000 Llubljana **IVS UNA**

WORKCAMPS

APPLYING FOR A JOB

Read carefully all the information given before applying. Check in particular:

* the necessary skills/experience required

* the full period of employment expected

* any restrictions of age, sex or nationality

* application deadlines

* any other points, particularly details of insurance cover provided, and other costs such as travel and accommodation.

When applying be sure to include:

* name, address, date of birth, marital status, nationality, sex

* education, qualifications, relevant experience

* period of availability

* details of languages spoken

* a large stamped, self-addressed envelope plus, if overseas, 2 International Reply Coupons

* a passport-size photo, particularly if you are to have contact with the public

* any registration or membership fees

NOTES

Working Holidays 1991 is published by the Central Bureau for Educational Visits & Exchanges, the UK national office responsible for the provision of information and advice on all forms of educational visits and exchanges; the development and administration of a wide range of curriculum-related pre-service and in-service exchange programmes; the linking of educational establishments and local education authorities with counterparts abroad; and the organisation of meetings and conferences related to professional international experience. Its information and advisory services extend throughout the educational field. In addition, over 20,000 individual enquiries are answered each year. Publications cater for the needs of people of all ages seeking information on the various opportunities available for educational contacts and travel abroad.

The Central Bureau was established in 1948 by the British government and is funded by the Department of Education and Science, the Scottish Education Department, and the Department of Education for Northern Ireland.

Chairman of the Board: JA Carter

Director: AH Male

Deputy Director: WE Musk

Seymour Mews House, Seymour Mews, London W1H 9PE
Telephone 071-486 5101
Telex 21368 CBEVEX G
Dialcom 87:WQQ 383
Fax 071-935 5741

3 Bruntsfield Crescent, Edinburgh EH10 4HD
Telephone 031-447 8024
Dialcom 87:WCP 034
Fax 031-452 8569

16 Malone Road, Belfast BT9 5BN
Telephone 0232-664418/9
Fax 0232-661275

AFRICA

See also Morocco, Tunisia and Worldwide

Cameroon Embassy
84 Holland Park, London W11 3SB
Tel 071-727 0771

Ghana High Commission
13 Belgrave Square, London SW1X 8PR
Tel 071-235 4142

Ivory Coast Embassy
2 Upper Belgrave Street, London SW1X 8BJ
Tel 071-235 6991

Kenya High Commission
45 Portland Place, London W1N 4AS
Tel 071-636 2371

Lesotho High Commission
10 Collingham Road, London SW5 0NR
Tel 071-373 8581

Mauritius High Commission
32/33 Elvaston Place, London SW7 5NW
Tel 071-581 0294

Nigeria High Commission
Nigeria House, 9 Northumberland Avenue,
London WC2N 5BX Tel 071-839 1244

Senegal Embassy
11 Phillimore Gardens, London W8 7QG
Tel 071-937 0925

Sierra Leone High Commission
33 Portland Place, London W1N 3AG
Tel 071-636 6483

Swaziland High Commission
58 Pont Street, London SW1X 0AE
Tel 071-581 4976

Tanzania High Commission
43 Hertford Street, London W1Y 8DB
Tel 071-499 8951

Togo Embassy
30 Sloane Street, London SW1X 9NE
Tel 071-235 0147

Zaire Embassy
26 Chesham Place, London SW1X 8HG
Tel 071-235 6137

Zimbabwe High Commission
Zimbabwe House, 429 Strand, London WC2R
0SA Tel 071-836 7755

INFORMATION

Entry regulations Details of work permits and entry requirements can be obtained in Britain from the embassies/high commissions above.

Travel North-South Travel, Moulsham Mill, Parkway, Chelmsford CM2 7PX Tel Chelmsford 492882 arranges competitively priced, reliably planned flights to all parts of Africa. Profits are paid into a trust fund for the assignment of aid to projects in the poorest areas of the South.

STA Travel, 74 Old Brompton Road, London SW7 3LQ Tel 071-937 9962 operates flexible, low-cost flights with open jaw facility - enter one country, leave by another - to destinations throughout Africa. Internal flights, accommodation and tours also available, plus advice from STA's Africa Desk at 117 Euston Road, London NW1 Tel 071-465 0486.

Africa on a Shoestring £9.95 is a useful handbook for travellers making their own way through Africa. A country by country guide with details on climate and geography, plus practical information on where to stay and what to visit. Also *Travellers Guides* to Central Africa, East Africa, the Middle East, North Africa, and West Africa, each £6.95, as well as *Backpackers Africa* £6.95. All available from Trailfinders, 194 Kensington High Street, London W8 7RG Tel 071-938 3939.

AFRICA

The Rough Guide to Kenya £6.95 is a practical handbook with details on travelling, hiking, village life and wildlife; plus information on how to get around the country and on cheap places to stay. Published by Harrap Columbus, Chelsea House, 26 Market Square, Bromley, Kent BR1 1NA.

CONSERVATION

CONSERVATION

EARTHWATCH EUROPE Belsyre Court, 57 Woodstock Road, Oxford, Oxfordshire OX2 6HU Tel Oxford 311600
Aims to support field research in a wide range of disciplines including archaeology, ornithology, animal behaviour, nature conservation and ecology. Support is given to researchers as a grant and in the form of volunteer assistance.
Recent projects have included studying the biological and cultural responses of traditional cultures to food shortages in the Cameroons; studying the problem of a drop in the water level of Lake Navaisha, one of Kenya's largest freshwater lakes; recording damage caused by fire and elephants in one of Zimbabwe's crowded wildlife parks; and assisting at an archaeological excavation investigating traces left by early man in Zaire.
Ages 16-80. No special skills are required although each expedition may, because of its nature, demand some talent or quality of fitness. Volunteers should be generally fit, able to cope with new situations, able to mix and work with people of different ages and backgrounds, and a sense of humour will help. 2-3 weeks, all year. Members share the costs of the expedition, from £500, which includes meals, transport and all necessary field equipment, but not travel, although assistance may be given in arranging it. Membership fee £22 includes magazines and newsletters providing all the information on joining an expedition.

FARMWORK

When writing to any organisation it is essential to mention Working Holidays 1991 and enclose a large stamped, self-addressed envelope, or if overseas, a large addressed envelope and at least two International Reply Coupons.

FARMWORK

GORMORGOR AGRICULTURAL DEVELOPMENT ORGANISATION c/o Njala University College, Private Mail Bag, Freetown, Sierra Leone
Volunteers are needed throughout the year to help upgrade subsistence farming on cash-crop enterprises in Kenema-Vaogboi and surrounding villages, Dasse Chiefdom Moyamba district, Sierra Leone. Volunteers help with, and supervise, projects such as the production of rice, maize, bananas, pineapples and a variety of vegetables.
Ages 15+. Experience usually necessary. Volunteers should have commonsense, be independent, willing to live in an isolated village, be physically and mentally fit and socially and culturally adaptable. They should also be flexible and prepared to participate in other activities such as town planning, accounting, report writing, health education courses, handicrafts, primary and adult education, and cultural activities on days when there are no supervisory duties. The working week will vary according to the season and to the projects in operation. Half board accommodation in village staff house provided, and native entertainments arranged on some evenings. Volunteers arrange and pay their own travel and insurance, and contribute towards food. Orientation course arranged upon arrival. English-speaking volunteers preferred. Applications should be typed and include a cv, passport photo and a 50p postal order. *For further information contact William Pratesi, 102 Savernake Road, London NW3.*

LEADERS & GUIDES

EXODUS EXPEDITIONS 9 Weir Road, London SW12 0LT Tel 081-675 7996
Operates a large range of expeditions including those by truck to Africa plus foot treks and shorter adventure holidays to Kenya, Morocco and Tanzania. Expedition leaders are needed to lead and drive expeditions; each expedition lasts 4-6 months, but leaders can expect to be

out of the country for up to 12 months at a time. The work involves driving, servicing and when necessary repairing the vehicle; controlling and accounting for expedition expenditure; dealing with border formalities and other official procedures; helping clients with any problems that may arise and informing them on points of interest in the countries visited.

Ages 25-30. Applicants must be single and unattached, and able to commit themselves for at least 2 years. For this reason, and because of the amount of travelling and flexibility involved, applicants should have no personal or financial commitments. Driving experience of large vehicles plus HGV/PSV licence and a good basic knowledge of mechanics required. Applicants must be resourceful, adaptable and have leadership qualities and a good sense of humour. Previous travel experience and a knowledge of foreign languages an advantage.

Basic training will be given to suitable candidates who do not have all the necessary qualifications; trainees will spend 2 months in the company's Wiltshire workshop and will then go on an expedition with an experienced leader before leading on their own. Salary £50 per week with food and accommodation provided on site when training and £20 salary and £28 expenses per week plus food and accommodation on the first expedition. Salary £80-£115 per week for a full expedition leader plus food and accommodation.

WORKCAMPS

AFRICA VOLUNTARY SERVICE OF SIERRA LEONE Private Mail Bag 717, Freetown, Sierra Leone
Aims to take part in development projects and to enhance international peace, understanding and cooperation. Volunteers are needed for agricultural, medical or renovation work in rural areas. Previous experience not always necessary. Ages 15+. Good spoken English essential. 35 hour week, end July-end August. Food and accommodation provided; some excursions and discussions organised. Volunteers pay own insurance and travel.

CHRISTIAN STUDENTS' COUNCIL OF KENYA Ufungamano House, State House, Mamlaka Road, PO Box 54579, Nairobi, Kenya
Promotes cooperation and Christian unity in study, service and commitment among Christian students, and organises workcamps, exchanges, afforestation, refugee awareness and women's programmes, seminars and conferences. Organises rural and urban projects providing an opportunity to participate directly in the work of the churches and social welfare agencies in an attempt to meet the needs and relieve the suffering of local people in desperate situations. Agriculturists, architects, poultry farmers, carpenters and those with experience in building are especially needed. Knowledge of English necessary. April, August and December. 8 hour day. Visits arranged to self-sufficiency farms and tree nursery. Accommodation provided, but volunteers pay for travel and insurance.

INTERNATIONAL VOLUNTARY SERVICE Development Education & Exchange Programme (DEEP), 109 Pilgrim Street, Newcastle upon Tyne NE1 6QF Tel 091-261 1649
IVS is the British branch of Service Civil International which promotes international reconciliation and peace through work and study projects. Opportunities are available to take part in the Development Education & Exchange Programme, coordinated by SCI and partner organisations in Africa, which encourages people to become active in working for change. The exchange programme enables people to learn about another culture and society while living and working together on the basis of equality and comradeship, participating in local community development projects.

Volunteers may apply for projects in West African countries including Cape Verde, Ghana, Togo, Sierra Leone and Senegal (June-September); in the Southern African frontline states of Lesotho and Swaziland (December/January and June-August); and in Mauritius (June-August). Typical projects involve helping in the construction of a school or community centre, building or repairing a road, agricultural and ecological work, constructing latrines and community work. The programme

AFRICA

involves compulsory orientation and information weekends before departure plus evaluation weekends and follow-up development education activities on return. Participants are required to raise at least £50 for African participants to Britain. Applicants must have workcamp experience or substantial involvement in voluntary youth or community work in Britain, and should support the aims and ideals of IVS/SCI. Ages 18+. Approx 4-10 weeks. A fee of up to £50 is charged towards the cost of food, accommodation and local transport. Participants pay their own travel costs. Advice on travel and health care, reading and resource lists, briefing material, fundraising ideas and follow-up activities available at orientation weekends. Membership fee £25 (students £15, unemployed £10). Registration fee £45. *Apply by October for exchange the following year.* D PH

DEEP is currently focusing on promoting development education activities within the youth and community sector, and particularly encourages applications from both young people and youth and community workers. DEEP also provides opportunities to participate in a variety of practical and educational weekends, and workcamps in Britain on development themes such as aid, racism, women, the media, Third World struggles and solidarity work, one of the main aims being to show how these development issues are linked to individual lives and similar issues in Britain.

GENERAL

KENYA VOLUNTARY DEVELOPMENT ASSOCIATION The Director, PO Box 48902, Nairobi, Kenya
Offers young people from Africa and overseas the opportunity to serve the country's rural or needy areas during their free time or holidays. Volunteers work alongside members of the local community helping with rural development projects such as irrigation schemes, tree planting, food growing, tilling, goat and hen rearing; and the construction of schools and clinics, helping with roofing and foundation digging. Discussions, games and other entertainments arranged, often involving the community. Working languages are English and Swahili. Emergency projects are also organised in times of catastrophe or disaster. Ages 18+. Volunteers are expected to

participate in all activities and to adapt fully to the local way of life. 6 hour day, 6 day week. Each workcamp lasts 2-3 weeks, April, July, August and December. Food and accommodation in local schools provided. Volunteers arrange and pay their own travel. Registration fee $160 for 1 camp or $210 for 2 camps; $2 postage costs.

NIGERIA VOLUNTARY SERVICE ASSOCIATION (NIVOSA) General Secretary, GPO Box 11837, Ibadan, Nigeria
Brings together Nigerian and other nationals interested in promoting voluntary service, and organises international workcamps and promotes understanding and cooperation among communities. Projects include workcamps in the states of the Federation (Lagos, Oyo, Ogun and Ondo) involving the construction of hospitals, post offices, markets and schools. Tasks include site clearance, making and laying blocks, plastering, carpentry and digging, all with the help of community artisans. Volunteers live and work in villages, cooking in groups. Ages 18+. 6 hour day, 2 weeks, July-September. Volunteers pay own insurance and travel. Excursions, lectures and debates. Workcamps are usually preceded by 2/3 day leadership courses which include an orientation programme for new volunteers. Participation fee $5.

GENERAL

THE AFRICAN-AMERICAN INSTITUTE 833 United Nations Plaza, New York, NY 10017, United States
Can provide information on opportunities in Africa for employment in technical assistance positions, teaching posts and volunteer work experience.

When writing to any organisation it is essential to mention Working Holidays 1991 and enclose a large stamped, self-addressed envelope, or if overseas, a large addressed envelope and at least two International Reply Coupons.

ASIA

Bangladesh High Commission
28 Queens Gate, London SW7 5JA
Tel 071-584 0081

Embassy of the People's Republic of China
49-51 Portland Place, London W1N 3AH
Tel 071-636 5726

The High Commission of India
India House, Aldwych, London WC2B 4NA
Tel 071-836 8484

Indonesian Embassy
38 Grosvenor Square, London W1X 9AD
Tel 071-499 7661

Korean Embassy
4 Palace Gate, London W8 5NF
Tel 071-581 0247

Royal Nepalese Embassy
12a Kensington Palace Gardens, London W8
4QU Tel 071-229 1594

Pakistan High Commission
35 Lowndes Square, London SW1X 9JN
Tel 071-235 2044

Sri Lanka High Commission
13 Hyde Park Gardens, London W2 2LU
Tel 071-262 1841

INFORMATION

Entry regulations Details of work permits and entry requirements can be obtained in Great Britain from the embassies/high commissions above.

Travel SD Enterprises Ltd, 21 York House, Empire Way, Wembley, Middlesex HA9 0PA Tel 081-903 3411 issues the Indrail Pass which allows unlimited travel on all trains throughout India, with no charge for night sleepers or reservations. Available for periods of 1, 7, 15, 21, 30, 60 or 90 days. Cost from $10.

Indian Airlines operate a youth fare scheme entitling those aged 12-30 to a discount of 25% off the normal fare, all year. Also Discover India scheme entitling the holder to unlimited air travel within India. 21 days, all year. Cost $400. Further information from the Government of India Tourist Office, 7 Cork Street, London W1X 2AB Tel 071-437 3677.

North-South Travel, Moulsham Mill, Parkway, Chelmsford CM2 7PX Tel Chelmsford 492882 arranges competitively priced, reliably planned flights to all parts of Asia. Profits are paid into a trust fund for the assignment of aid to projects in the poorest areas of the South.

STA Travel, 74 Old Brompton Road, London SW7 3LQ Tel 071-937 9962 operates flexible, low-cost flights with open jaw facility - enter one country, leave by another - to destinations throughout Asia. Internal flights, accommodation and tours also available. Also offer an Asian Overland Travel Pass, £278, which covers overland air-conditioned bus or train transport between Bangkok and Singapore, plus the ferry to Penang and 6 nights' accommodation in selected hotels en route. Valid 3 months.

Trailfinders Travel Centre, 42-50 Earls Court Road, London W8 6EJ Tel 071-938 3366 and Trailfinders, 194 Kensington High Street, London W8 7RG Tel 071-938 3939 operate low-cost flights between London and destinations throughout Asia. Also arrange a Bangkok-Bali Rover, which provides the opportunity to travel east via Thailand, Malaysia, Singapore and Indonesia by road, rail and air. 20 days, departures all year. Cost £345, flight extra. Also have a travellers' library and information centre, and an immunisation centre for overseas travel vaccinations.

Travellers Survival Kit to the East £6.95, is a practical guide to travelling between Turkey and Indonesia, following the overland route from Europe that remains accessible. Advice on preparations, transport and route planning, hitch hiking, frontier regulations, medical

ASIA

facilities, plus useful addresses. Published by Vacation Work, 9 Park End Street, Oxford OX1 1HJ Tel Oxford 241978.

All Asia Guide £9.95, gives comprehensive information on a country by country basis, on history, overland/air entry, health regulations, language, climate, transport, accommodation, tours, events, useful addresses plus street maps. *North East Asia on a Shoestring* £4.95, *South East Asia on a Shoestring* £6.95, *West Asia on a Shoestring* £5.95, are useful handbooks for anyone wanting to travel from Hong Kong to Australia and anywhere in between. Information given includes cheap accommodation, getting about, street and country maps, student reductions, visas, history, geography and things to see. *Bangladesh - A Travel Survival Kit* £4.95, *India - A Travel Survival Kit* £11.95, *Indonesia - A Travel Survival Kit* £9.95, *Korea and Taiwan - A Travel Survival Kit* £4.95, *Sri Lanka - A Travel Survival Kit* £4.95 and *Pakistan - A Travel Survival Kit* £4.95 are comprehensive guides with information on where to stay, what to eat, the best places to visit and how to travel around. All available from Trailfinders, see above.

COMMUNITY WORK

Bangladesh Today - A Profile contains essential information on the geography, climate, culture and wildlife of Bangladesh plus details of entry and exit regulations, currency, events, festivals, places to visit, accommodation, transport and other facilities. Available from the Bangladesh High Commission, Press Division, 28 Queen's Gate, London SW7 5JA Tel 071-584 0081.

Travel Information provides information on accommodation, currency, climate, customs, health/entry regulations, inland travel and languages. Available from the Government of India Tourist Office, see above.

Pakistan Tourist Guide is a small booklet containing details of the history, people and language, plus information on travel, where to stay, sport and recreation, visa/health regulations and places of interest. Available from the Pakistan Development Corporation, 52-54 High Holborn, London WC1V 6RB Tel 071-242 3131.

Sri Lanka Official Tourist Handbook is a comprehensive booklet containing information for visitors, including entry and visa formalities, places of interest, travel, medical services, national parks, plus background information and useful addresses. Available from the Sri Lanka Tourist Board, see below.

Accommodation The Sri Lanka Tourist Board, London House, 53/54 Haymarket, London SW1Y 4RP Tel 071-925 0177 issues the *Sri Lanka Accommodation Guide* containing information on a wide range of accommodation and restaurants.

The Government of India Tourist Office, 7 Cork Street, London W1X 2AB Tel 071-437 3677 issues a booklet *Accommodation* containing information on hostels set up and run by the Department of Tourism in 25 states/Union territories.

COMMUNITY WORK

JOINT ASSISTANCE CENTRE H-65, South Extension 1, New Delhi 110049, India
A voluntary action group for disaster assistance needs volunteers to help on workcamps with environmental, agricultural, construction, health and sanitation work, fundraising, teaching first aid, and on preparation work for disasters. Also opportunities to help in the office, editing the journal and working on the wordprocessor or in a small improvised library. 2 weeks-6 months, all year. Short visits/stays on projects all over India, with opportunities to meet and work with local people, and to learn yoga, nature cures and Hindi. Disaster management programmes and exhibitions arranged in November, workcamp/disaster conferences arranged throughout the year.

Ages 18+. All nationalities welcome, no experience necessary. Cost from £60 per month covers accommodation with self-catering facilities. Conditions are primitive and the summer is very hot. No travel, insurance or pocket money provided. Registration fee £10. *Enclose 3 IRCs.*

THE LEPROSY MISSION Personnel Director, 80 Windmill Road, Brentford, Middlesex TW8 0QH Tel 081-569 7292
A medical missionary society whose main object is to minister in the name of Christ to the physical, mental and spiritual needs of leprosy sufferers, to assist in their rehabilitation and to work towards the eradication of leprosy. Volunteers should have a Christian commitment in one of the Protestant denominations, be elective medical students in their fourth and final year of studies with suitable training and experience and who have completed at least 1 full clinical year, and be considering work in the Third World after qualifying. 8 weeks, all year. Part assistance towards travel expenses and free board and lodging at the centre provided.

LEADERS & GUIDES

EXODUS EXPEDITIONS 9 Weir Road, London SW12 0LT Tel 081-675 7996
Operates a large range of expeditions including those by truck to Asia plus foot treks and shorter adventure holidays to Nepal, Pakistan, India, Indonesia and China. Expedition leaders are needed to lead and drive expeditions; each expedition lasts 4-6 months, but leaders can expect to be out of the country for up to 12 months at a time. The work involves driving, servicing and when necessary repairing the vehicle; controlling and accounting for expedition expenditure; dealing with border formalities and other official procedures; helping clients with any problems that may arise and informing them on points of interest in the countries visited. Ages 25-30. Applicants must be single and unattached, and able to commit themselves for at least 2 years. For this reason, and because of the amount of travelling and flexibility involved, applicants should have no personal or financial commitments. Driving experience of large vehicles plus HGV/PSV licence and a good basic knowledge of mechanics required. Applicants must be resourceful, adaptable and have leadership qualities and a good sense of humour. Previous travel experience and a knowledge of foreign languages an advantage. Basic training will be given to suitable candidates who do not have all the necessary qualifications; trainees will spend 2 months in the company's Wiltshire workshop and will then go on an expedition with an experienced leader before leading on their own. Salary £50 per week with food and accommodation provided on site when training and £20 salary and £28 expenses per week plus food and accommodation on the first expedition. Salary £80-£115 per week for a full expedition leader plus food and accommodation.

MONITORS & TEACHERS

GAP ACTIVITY PROJECTS LTD 44 Queen's Road, Reading, Berkshire RG1 4BB Tel Reading 594914
A small number of attachments are available for volunteers to act as assistants to the English teaching staff in universities and senior teaching establishments. The placements are away from the main tourist areas of Java and Bali, on comparatively infrequently visited islands. Applicants should be school leavers aged 18-19, with up to a year before going on to further education, and will be required to undertake a one week TEFL course before departure. Placements begin in January for a period of approx 6 months. Cost £300, plus airfare, insurance and TEFL course.

Also small number of work attachments available at schools in three provinces in the People's Republic of China. The work is to conduct conversation classes in English with both staff and students (12-17 year olds), as well as participating, as a member of staff, in a wide range of school activities. Genuine interest in China and its culture desirable. Applicants should be school leavers aged 18-19, with up to a year before going on to further education, and will be required to undertake a one week TEFL course before departure. Placements begin September or February. Board, lodging and a small amount of pocket money provided. Cost £300 plus airfare, insurance and TEFL course.
Apply early September of last school year; applications close March. UK nationals only.

WORKCAMPS

INTERNATIONAL VOLUNTARY SERVICE Development Education & Exchange Programme (DEEP), 109 Pilgrim Street, Newcastle upon Tyne NE1 6QF Tel 091-261 1649
IVS is the British branch of Service Civil International which promotes international reconciliation and peace through work and study projects. Opportunities are available to take part in the Development Education & Exchange Programme, which encourages people to become active in working for change. The programme enables people to learn about another culture and society while living and working together on the basis of equality and comradeship. Volunteers may apply for manual work on community development projects in Bangladesh (July-August and November-January), India (July-August and November-December), Sri Lanka (July-August), Nepal (October-November), Malaysia and Thailand. Typical projects involve helping in the construction of a school or community centre, building or repairing a road, planting trees to reduce soil erosion or preparing a vegetable garden. The programme involves compulsory orientation and information weekends before departure plus evaluation weekends and development education activities on return. Participants are required to raise at least £50 for Asian participants to Britain. Applicants must have workcamp experience or substantial involvement in voluntary youth or community work in Britain, and should support the ideals of IVS/SCI. Ages 21+. Approx 6-10 weeks. A charge towards the cost of food, accommodation and local transport may be made. Participants pay their own travel costs. Advice on travel and health care, reading and resource lists, briefing material, fundraising ideas and follow-up activities available. Membership fee £25 (students £15, unemployed £10). Registration fee £45. *Apply by October for the following year.*

DEEP is currently focusing on promoting development education activities within the youth and community sector, and particularly encourages applications from young people and youth and community workers. DEEP also provides opportunities to participate in a variety of practical and educational weekends, and workcamps in Britain on development themes, one of the main aims being to show how these development issues are linked to individual lives and similar issues in Britain.

UNESCO YOUTH CENTRE Korean National Commission for UNESCO, PO Box Central 64, Seoul, Korea 100
Organises an international youth camp with the aim of furthering international understanding and cooperation through working and living together in Korea. Discussions, lectures and workshops are held on international problems such as development and cultural identity. Recreational activities, including involvement with local villagers, are organised. Volunteers learn about the history and culture of Korea through a 3 day study tour. Of the 100 volunteers working on the camp, half will be from Korea, and the official languages are English and Korean. Volunteers live in 5 camps of various nationalities. 10 days, July. Food, accommodation, transport within Korea and medical expenses provided. Participation fee $90. *Apply by 20 June.*

GENERAL

GAP ACTIVITY PROJECTS LTD 44 Queen's Road, Reading, Berkshire RG1 4BB Tel Reading 594914
Offers a number of attachments in India, Nepal and Pakistan, ranging from service in community homes to teaching in schools. Social work applicants must show a readiness to work amongst the disadvantaged in almost any capacity; a contribution towards board and lodging may be required. Work in schools may involve teaching English, science, music, drama and sport; accommodation, food and pocket money usually provided, but contributions may be required. Applicants should be school leavers aged 18-19, with up to a year before going on to further education. Those wishing to teach take a one week TEFL course before departure. Usually 6 months beginning September or January; Nepal 3 months, at various times of the year. Cost £235 India and Pakistan, £150 Nepal, plus airfare, insurance and TEFL course, if applicable. *Apply early September of last school year; applications close March. UK nationals only.*

AUSTRALIA

Australia High Commission
Australia House, The Strand, London WC2B 4LA Tel 071-379 4334

British High Commission
Commonwealth Avenue, Yarralumta ACT 2600

Tourist office
Australian Tourist Commission, Gemini House, 10-18 Putney Hill, Putney, London SW15 6AA Tel 081-780 1424

Youth hostels
Australian YHA, 60 Mary Street, Surrey Hills NSW 2010

Youth & student information
Australian Union of Students, 97 Drummond Street, Carlton, Victoria 3053

INFORMATION

Entry regulations A visa is required for a working holiday, and will be granted subject to certain conditions. The prime purpose of the visit must be a temporary stay for a holiday of specific duration and the applicant must have a return ticket, or sufficient funds to pay for this, plus sufficient funds to cover maintenance for a substantial part of the holiday period; employment must be incidental to the holiday and only to supplement holiday funds; employment in Australia must not be pre-arranged except on a private basis and on the applicant's own initiative; there should be reasonable prospects of obtaining temporary employment; full-time employment of more than 3 months with the same employer should not be undertaken; departure should be at the expiration of the authorised period of temporary entry; and applicants must meet normal health and character standards. If all these conditions are met the initial period of stay normally authorised is for 6 months, maximum 12 months. A period of up to 8 weeks should be allowed to obtain a working holiday visa and travel tickets should not be purchased before a visa is obtained.
Applicants should be single people or married couples without children who are aged between 18 and 25 inclusive (exceptionally ages up to 30 will be considered) and holders of valid Irish, Canadian or Dutch passports, or if normally resident in Britain, holders of British passports endorsed with the words *British Citizen*. Visa applications should be made to the nearest Migration Office. There

are offices in Britain at Australia House, see above, the Australian Consulate, Chatsworth House, Lever Street, Manchester M1 2DL and at the Australian Consulate, Hobart House, 80 Hanover Street, Edinburgh EH2 2DL.
The objective of the working holiday scheme is essentially to provide young people with opportunities for cultural exchange, the work undertaken being part-time or of a casual nature. Personal qualities such as initiative, self-reliance, adaptability, resourcefulness and open-mindedness are the important attributes, enabling the participant to profit from the experience and to provide Australians with an insight into cultural differences.

Travel Travellers are recommended to obtain relevant inoculations for their own personal protection during their journey to Australia depending on the route they take and the countries in which they stay.

Campus Travel, 52 Grosvenor Gardens, London SW1W 0AG Tel 071-730 3402 offers competitive fares to destinations in Australia with open jaw facility which allows travel out to one destination and return from another. Special student fares available to ISIC cardholders.

North-South Travel, Moulsham Mill, Parkway, Chelmsford CM2 7PX Tel Chelmsford 492882 arranges competitively priced, reliably planned flights to all parts of Australia. Profits are paid into a trust fund for the assignment of aid to projects in the poorest areas of the South.

AUSTRALIA

STA Travel, 74 Old Brompton Road, London SW7 3LQ Tel 071-937 9962 operates flexible, low-cost flights with open jaw facility - enter one country, leave by another - to destinations throughout Australia. Internal flights, accommodation and tours also available.

See Australia Fares provide a 25% discount on domestic jet routes. Details from Australian Airlines, 7 Swallow Street, London W1R 8DU Tel 071-434 3864.

Greyhound International Travel Inc, 14-16 Cockspur Street, London SW1Y 5BL Tel 071-839 5591 issues the Greyhound Australia Bus-Pass, which offers unlimited bus travel on Australia's largest express route, with discounts on accommodation, sightseeing and car rental. Valid for 7, 10, 15, 21, 30, 60, 90 or 120 days; cost AU$217-AU$1400.

Austrailpass entitles the holder to unlimited travel on Railways of Australia. 14-90 days, cost from AU$415. Details from Compass, 9 Grosvenor Gardens, London SW1W 0BH Tel 071-828 4111.

CONSERVATION

Traveller's Guide is a comprehensive booklet which includes all the facts to plan a trip: travel to and around the country, where to stay, general information on seasons, climate, time zones, currency, health services, customs, entry/visa requirements and useful addresses. Available free from the Australian Tourist Commission, see above.

Australia - A Travel Survival Kit £9.95, is an essential handbook for travellers in Australia, with comprehensive information on where to stay, what to eat, the best places to visit and how to travel around. Available from Trailfinders, 194 Kensington High Street, London W8 7RG Tel 071-938 3939.

How to Live and Work in Australia £7.95 explains how to become a temporary or permanent Australian resident, gives information on tax, housing, health, further addresses and contacts. Available from Jobsearch Publications, Broads Lane, Mylor, Falmouth, Cornwall TR11 5UL.

Travellers Survival Kit Australia & New Zealand £6.95, is a complete handbook for those going down under, giving information on travelling

as cheaply as possible, local culture, pubs and restaurants, beaches and reefs, flora and fauna, etc. Published by Vacation Work, 9 Park End Street, Oxford OX1 1HJ Tel Oxford 241978.

CONSERVATION

AUSTRALIAN TRUST FOR CONSERVATION VOLUNTEERS, National Director, PO Box 423, Ballarat 3350, Victoria
Involves volunteers in the management and care of the environment through practical conservation projects. Volunteers are needed to restore degraded areas affected by salinity or soil erosion which may be on farms, along rivers, at old mining sites or in urban areas. Recent projects have included working with fisheries' researchers in Kakadu National Park and the Jabiru mining site in Northern Territory; creating a wetlands education site after mining at Capel in Western Australia; planting trees to counteract the effects of salinity in affected pastoral areas; constructing part of the Hume and Hovell walking track in New South Wales; and collecting seed for revegetation programmes in the Murray-Darling river catchment area.

Ages 17+. Experience and qualifications relating to the environment welcome, but not essential. Applicants should be fit, willing to work and mix with people from many nations in teams of 8-10. A sound knowledge of English essential. Food, accommodation and travel whilst working provided; volunteers must take a sleeping bag. Cost AU$460 for 6 weeks.

EARTHWATCH EUROPE Belsyre Court, 57 Woodstock Road, Oxford, Oxfordshire OX2 6HU Tel Oxford 311600
Aims to support field research in a wide range of disciplines including archaeology, ornithology, animal behaviour, nature conservation and ecology. Support is given to researchers as a grant and in the form of volunteer assistance. Recent projects have included researching the effects of introduced honeybees on plants and honeyeaters in Kangaroo Island, South Australia; studying the social life of the kangaroo in New South Wales; and observing the behaviour of honey ants in Alice Springs. Ages 16-80. No special skills are required although each expedition may,

because of its nature, demand some talent or quality of fitness. Volunteers should be generally fit, able to cope with new situations, able to mix and work with people of different ages and backgrounds, and a sense of humour would help. 2-3 weeks, all year. Members share the costs of the expedition, from £500, which includes meals, transport and all necessary field equipment, but does not include the cost of travel, although assistance may be given in arranging it. Membership fee £22 includes magazines and newsletters providing all the information on joining an expedition.

INVOLVEMENT VOLUNTEERS PO Box 218, Port Melbourne, Victoria 3207
Aims to assist volunteers to participate in community based projects related to conservation and the environment. Can also introduce volunteers to paid work placements to fit in with their volunteer programme. Work includes urban or rural revegetation, planting, fruit picking, marine archaeology, the restoration of gardens and museums, bird observatory operations and assisting with sport for the disadvantaged. Work available all year round. Volunteers must have at least a working knowledge of English, and arrange their own work permits, visas, travel and insurance. Cost AU$300 includes planning, advice, meeting on arrival and accommodation. **B D PH**

CHILDCARE

ANGLIA AGENCY 15 Eastern Avenue, Southend-on-Sea, Essex Tel Southend 613888
Positions for mother's helps and nannies arranged throughout the year. Salary, board and lodging provided. Ages 18+. Travel costs paid by the applicant. Service charge £40.

FARMWORK

GAP ACTIVITY PROJECTS LTD 44 Queen's Road, Reading, Berkshire RG1 4BB Tel Reading 594914
Opportunities available for males, working on sheep, cattle and wheat farms or properties in the outback. 4-6 months starting January-April. Applicants must be school leavers aged 18-19 who have up to a year before going to

university or starting a career. They should also enjoy the outdoor life, be able to drive a tractor or ride a horse, be practical and capable of working hard. Board, lodging and approx AU$50 pocket money per week provided. Cost £325 plus airfare.

INTERNATIONAL AGRICULTURAL EXCHANGE ASSOCIATION YFC Centre, National Agricultural Centre, Kenilworth, Warwickshire CV8 2LG Tel Coventry 696578
Operates opportunities for agricultural students and young people to acquire practical work experience in the rural sector, to strengthen and improve their knowledge and understanding of the way of life in other countries. Participants are given an opportunity to study practical methods on approved training farms, and work as trainees, gaining further experience in their chosen field.

Types of farm include cattle and sheep; mixed (cattle, sheep and field crops); dairy; dairy and crops; sheep and crops; plus a limited number of pig, sheep and cattle farms and horticultural enterprises. Participants undertake paid work on the farm, approx 45 hours per week, and live as members of the host family. Full board and lodging, insurance cover and a minimum net weekly wage of £50-£60 provided. All programmes include 3/4 weeks unpaid holiday. 3/5 day orientation courses held at the beginning of each programme at agricultural colleges and universities throughout Australia. Educational sightseeing trips (2-4 days) in Singapore and Hawaii are arranged en route for all programmes. Ages 19-28. Applicants should be single, and have good practical experience in the chosen training category, plus a valid driving licence. 7 or 8 months (departing September), 9 months (departing April), 8 months (departing July), 14 months - 7 in Australia plus 7 in Canada/US (departing September) or 15 months - 7 months in Australia and 8 months in New Zealand (departing July). Cost from £1,250. £200 deposit payable. Costs cover airfare, work permit, administration fee and orientation courses. *Apply at least 4 months in advance; UK nationals holding full British passport only.*

Australian applicants requiring an exchange should apply to IAEA, 50 Oxford Street, Paddington, NSW 2021.

AUSTRALIA

TEACHERS & INSTRUCTORS

WORKCAMPS

NORTHERN VICTORIA FRUITGROWERS' ASSOCIATION PO Box 394, Shepparton, Victoria 3630

VICTORIAN PEACH AND APRICOT GROWERS' ASSOCIATION PO Box 39, Cobram, Victoria 3644

Fruit picking jobs are available under the Working Holidaymakers scheme. The Associations represent the 500 orchards in the Goulburn/Murray Valley, Victoria. The season commences in late January with the harvesting of Bartlett pears, used mainly for canning, and continues into March and April when crops include other pear varieties, peaches, and apples. Piece-work rates. Accommodation offered on many orchards; participants may camp in the orchards if they bring their own equipment. For latest details on location and availability of work, contact either of the Associations on arrival in Australia.

Addresses for personal callers: Northern Victoria Fruitgrowers' Association Ltd, 21 Nixon Street, Shepparton, Victoria Tel (058) 21 5844/Victorian Peach and Apricot Growers' Association, 21 Station Street, Cobram, Victoria Tel (058) 72 1729

WILLING WORKERS ON ORGANIC FARMS (WWOOF) Mt Murrindal Coop, Buchan, Victoria 3885
A non-profitmaking organisation which aims to provide a practical learning situation as well as to help farmers and smallholders who need manpower to replace the use of herbicides, chemical fertilisers and heavy machinery. Provides volunteers with first hand experience of organic farming and gardening, and a chance to spend some time in the country. Has approx 140 host farms all over Australia especially in the eastern and south eastern coastal areas. The work includes all types of farm work, field work, animal care and building. Placements of up to 6 months can be arranged for agricultural students. Ages 17+. 6 hour day. Full board and lodging provided in the farmhouse or outbuildings; volunteers should take a sleeping bag. No wages paid, and helpers must pay their own travel. Insurance and anti-tetanus vaccination recommended. Membership fee £10. PH

TEACHERS & INSTRUCTORS

GAP ACTIVITY PROJECTS LTD 44 Queen's Road, Reading, Berkshire RG1 4BB Tel Reading 594914
Work is available in independent day and boarding schools acting as teachers' aides. Duties include helping with activities such as sports, games, music, drama, weekend hikes, supervisory duties, laboratory assistant work and helping in the school office and with private tuition. Some placements also available in Bush Camps, where experience in Outward Bound or similar activities is essential.

Applicants should be school leavers aged 18/19 who have up to a year before going on to further education. Most placements start in September or January. Board, lodging and approx AU$50 pocket money per week provided. Cost £325 plus airfare and insurance. *Apply early in September of last school year; applications close in March. UK nationals only.*

WORKCAMPS

CHRISTIAN WORK CAMPS c/o Australian Council of Churches, Box C199, Clarence Street Post Office, Sydney 2000
An ecumenical group where volunteers work on projects that meet personal or community needs. Volunteers are needed to work on building projects in New South Wales, Central Australia and sometimes the Northern Territory and Queensland. Recent projects have included constructing, extending or renovating houses for Aboriginal families and communities, pre-school centres, campsites for handicapped children and the building of houses, craft rooms and other facilities.

Ages 18+. Special building skills are not necessary since there is a core of experienced workers to pass on their skills. The work is demanding, requiring the discipline and long hours of teamwork, but is rewarding. 60 hour week, 3-4 weeks immediately after Christmas, and sometimes 1-2 weeks, June/July. Accommodation provided in school/church halls; volunteers should take a sleeping bag. Cost approx AU$160 for 3 weeks includes food, insurance and use of tools. Volunteers pay their own travel costs.

GENERAL

BRITISH UNIVERSITIES NORTH AMERICA CLUB (BUNAC) 16 Bowling Green Lane, London EC1R 0BD Tel 071-251 3472

A non-profit, non-political educational student club venture which aims to encourage interest and understanding between students in Britain and Australia. Administers a Work Australia programme for those who wish to work and travel in Australia. Jobs do not have to be organised in advance, but those wishing to will be offered advice on how to do so. Orientation programmes on arrival give advice on finding and choosing a job, obtaining a visa, income tax, accommodation, travel, food and budgeting. The programme includes return flight, two night's accommodation followed by orientation in Australia, and the help of Student Services Australia. Ages 17-25. Cost £1,060 (1990), includes flight and registration. In order to obtain a visa, applicants must have evidence of funds, (up to £2,000 for a 12 month stay), and proof of round-trip transportation. *UK, Irish, Canadian and Dutch nationals only.*

CAREERS RESEARCH AND ADVISORY CENTRE (CRAC), Sheraton House, Castle Park, Cambridge CB3 0AX Tel Cambridge 460277

Opportunities are available to work, travel and live in Australia for up to 3 months. Applications are welcomed from British undergraduates for the Britain Australasia Vocational Exchange scheme. The aim is to widen the experience and understanding of industrial, commercial and business life, providing work experience to undergraduates to help them relate and apply their academic studies to career opportunities. 12 weeks, July-September. Work is for a period of 8 weeks in paid jobs relating wherever possible to university studies, and then approx 4 weeks holiday. Jobs have included work in a wide variety of fields: retail distribution, mining and metallurgy, farming, laboratories, engineering, geology, planning, marketing, personnel, accountancy, astronomy, banking, computing,

nursing and research. Those studying engineering, economics, commerce, computing or applied science stand a higher chance of being placed. Preference given to students in the penultimate year of a first degree course. Average weekly wage AU$350. Flight, visa, work permit and insurance organised. Participants pay their own airfare, but they should earn sufficient to cover board, lodging and living expenses. Insurance fee £60. Registration fee £8. *Application forms available November.*

When writing to any organisation it is essential to mention Working Holidays 1991 and enclose a large stamped, self-addressed envelope, or if overseas, a large addressed envelope and at least two International Reply Coupons.

NOTES

AUSTRIA

Austrian Embassy
18 Belgrave Mews West, London SW1X 8HU
Tel 071-235 3731

British Embassy
1030 Vienna, Jauresgasse 12

Tourist office
Austrian National Tourist Office, 30 St George
Street, London W1R 9FA Tel 071-629 0461

Youth hostels
Osterreichischer Jugendherbergsverband,
Gonzagagasse 22, 1010 Vienna

Youth & student information
Austrian Foreign Students' Service,
Rooseveltplatz 13, 1090 Vienna

Austrian Institute, 28 Rutland Gate, London
SW7 1PQ Tel 071-584 8653

Buro für Studentenreisen, Schreyvogelgasse 3,
1010 Vienna

OKISTA (Austrian Committee for International
Educational Exchange), Turkenstrasse 4, 1090
Vienna

Jugendinformationzentrum,
Kalvarienbergstrasse 2, 4560 Kirchdorf

Info-Center, Dambockgasse 1, 1060 Vienna

INFORMATION

Entry regulations Work permits are required
for all kinds of employment including au pair
positions. When a job has been found the
prospective employer must obtain a permit;
employees are not allowed to apply for a work
permit themselves. The number of work
permits issued to foreign nationals is limited
and a permit will only be granted if there is no
Austrian national to fill the post; this applies
particularly to clerical and secretarial work.
Permits will not be granted to foreign passport
holders while on a visit to Austria. Students
who find holiday work through one of the
official student exchange agencies can obtain
an equivalent certificate from them. The work
permit or equivalent should be submitted to
the Consular Section of the Austrian Embassy,
together with a valid passport, who will then
issue the necessary visa. Holders of British
passports do not require a visa for a work
period of less than 6 months.

Social security All employed persons except au
pairs must contribute to the health and social
security scheme, which covers most medical
expenses.

Employment offices The Austrian Embassy,
see above, can supply a list of provincial
employment offices. When applying to one of
the offices the following details should be
supplied in a letter typed in German: name,
address, date of birth, education, profession,
type of present employment, knowledge of
foreign languages, length of intended stay, and
type of job required. Applications for au pair
positions, however, cannot be accepted.

Addresses of some provincial employment
offices are:

Landesarbeitsamt für das Burgenland,
Permayerstrasse 10, 7001 Eisentstadt

Landesarbeitsamt für Karnten, Kumpfgasse 25,
9010 Klagenfurt

Landesarbeitsamt für Niederosterreich,
Hohenstauffengasse 2, 1013 Vienna

Landesarbeitsamt für Oberosterreich,
Grüberstrasse 63, 4010 Linz

AUSTRIA

Landesarbeitsamt für Salzburg,
Schiesstattstrasse 4, 5021 Salzburg

Landesarbeitsamt für Steiermark,
Babenbergerstrasse 33, 8021 Graz

Landesarbeitsamt für Tirol, Schopfstrasse 5,
6010 Innsbruck

Landesarbeitsamt für Vorarlberg, Rheinstrasse
32, 6901 Bregenz

Landesarbeitsamt für Wien, Weihburggasse 30,
1011 Vienna

For further information see *Working in Austria*
available from the Austrian Embassy.
Applications for work can also be made under
the International Clearing of Vacancies scheme;
for further details contact the Training Agency.

Job advertising Publicitas, 525/527 Fulham
Road, London SW6 1HF Tel 071-385 7723 can
accept job advertisements for a number of
Austrian newspapers.

Travel Reduced rate rail travel for ages up to
26 or full-time students is available from the
Anglo-Austrian Society, 46 Queen Anne's Gate,
London SW1H 9AU Tel 071-222 0366.

Austria Ticket allows unlimited travel for 9/16
days on railway and postal bus networks, and
a reduction on certain steamship services, and
is available from YHA Travel, 14 Southampton
Street, London WC2E 7HY Tel 071-836 8541.

Campus Travel, 52 Grosvenor Gardens, London
SW1W 0AG Tel 071-730 3402 offer Eurotrain
under 26 reduced fares to destinations in
Austria, and student/youth fares by air and
weekly charter flights to Vienna and Salzburg.

Accommodation Youth hostel accommodation
in Vienna and hotel accommodation in Vienna,
Innsbruck, Graz and Salzburg is available
through the Anglo-Austrian Society, see above.
For accommodation in hotels, pensions and
student hostels in Vienna, contact Büro für
Studentenreisen, Schreyvogelgasse 3, 1010
Vienna. OKISTA (Austrian Committee for
International Educational Exchange)
Turkenstrasse 4, 1090 Vienna can provide all
kinds of accommodation throughout Austria.

AU PAIR/CHILDCARE

AU PAIR/ CHILDCARE

Work permits for au pair positions are
obtained by the host family from the local
employment office and must be issued before
the au pair arrives in Austria. The application
should be accompanied by an agreement
signed by the au pair, the host family and the
au pair agency. Au pairs must be girls at least
18 years old, and can expect to receive board,
lodging and a minimum AS700 per week in
exchange for looking after the children and
helping in the house with light housework and
simple cooking. Au pairs do not pay income tax
and no contributions to the health and social
security scheme can be made, so it is essential
to join a private health insurance scheme.
Evidence of this must be produced by the host
family when applying for the work permit. Au
pairs must give an undertaking to return home
at the end of their stay, and prove that they
have sufficient funds for the journey.

**ARBEITSGEMEINSCHAFT AUSLANDS-
SOZIALDIENST Katholisches Jugendwerk
Osterreichs, Johannesgasse 16/1, 1010 Vienna**
Au pair positions in Vienna and other areas.
5-6 hour day with 2/3 evenings babysitting per
week. One full day a week and some
afternoons free. Full board and lodging
provided. Pocket money minimum AS700 per
week. Ages 18-28. Some experience in child
care or housework useful. 6+ months, all year.
Applicants pay their own fares and insurance.
Offers regular programmes of sightseeing,
theatre visits and opportunities to meet other
au pairs. Preferably apply for September or
January, when language classes begin.
Registration fee AS600. Limited number of
summer positions with families outside
Vienna, 8+ weeks, July and August; language
classes not available.

**HELPING HANDS AU PAIR & DOMESTIC
AGENCY 10 Hertford Road, Newbury Park,
Ilford, Essex IG12 7HQ Tel 081-597 3138**
Au pair and mother's help positions available
throughout the year. Au pairs work approx 30
hours plus 3 evenings babysitting each week

and earn approx £25 per week. Mother's helps work longer hours for a higher salary. Board and lodging provided. 6+ months. Ages 18-27. Applicants should be willing, helpful and adaptable. Insurance and travel costs paid by the applicant but assistance with arrangements provided. Introduction fee £40 on acceptance of a family. *UK nationals only*

INTERLINGUA CENTRE Torquay Road, Foxrock, Dublin 18, Ireland Tel Dublin 893876
Can place au pairs in Austrian families. 6+ months. 30 hour week with one full day and some evenings off. Time to attend language classes 2-3 mornings or afternoons per week. Experience desirable but not essential. Ages 18+. £25-£40 pocket money per week, full board, lodging and insurance provided. Travel paid by applicants. Placement fee £55.

INTERNATIONAL CATHOLIC SOCIETY FOR GIRLS (ACISJF) St Patrick's International Youth Centre, 24 Great Chapel Street, London W1V 3AF Tel 071-734 2156
Au pair posts are arranged for 9+ months. Ages 18+. The Society assists girls/young women who are travelling and living away from home. Information and counselling service.

MONDIAL AGENCY 32 Links Road, West Wickham, Kent BR4 0QW Tel 071-777 0510
Can place au pairs with families throughout the year in Vienna or the provinces. Au pairs work a 5-6 hour day with 2/3 afternoons free for language classes, and are expected to spend some evenings babysitting by arrangement with the family. Board and lodging provided. Pocket money approx £25-£30 per week. Ages 18-27. 6+ months. Applicants pay their own fares and insurance. Service charge £40.

OKISTA (Austrian Committee for International Educational Exchange) Au Pair Department, Berggasse 4, 1090 Vienna
Can help find au pair positions with Austrian families in Vienna, main cities and country areas. 5-6 hour day plus 2-3 evenings baby-sitting by arrangement. 1 day off per week plus time to attend language classes. Ages 18-28. Board, lodging and approx AS700 pocket money per week provided. 2-3 months summer, without language classes; 6-12 months, starting January or September. Registration fee AS400. Applicants pay own travel and insurance.

UNIVERSAL CARE Chester House, 9 Windsor End, Beaconsfield, Buckinghamshire HP9 2JJ Tel Beaconsfield 678811
Can place au pairs in families in Vienna, main cities and country areas. 6+ months, all year. 5/6 hour day, with occasional babysitting and 1 day off per week. Free time given for language classes. Ages 17-27. Knowledge of German necessary. Board and lodging provided. Salary approx £25 per week. Travel paid by applicants; families will sometimes help with return fare. Service charge £46.

COURIERS/REPS

BLADON LINES Personnel Department, 56-58 Putney High Street, London SW15 1SF Tel 081-785 2200
Opportunities for representatives to work in the ski resorts of St Anton, Kitzbühel, and Obergurgl. Work involves welcoming and looking after guests, providing information, helping with coach transfers, managing chalet staff and ensuring everything is running smoothly. Ages 24+. Relevant experience an advantage, and good spoken German, French or Italian essential. Hours very variable; applicants must be prepared to work hard but will get time to ski. Season lasts December-May. Board, lodging, return travel and insurance provided. Salary £50-£100 per week, depending on the size of the resort. Free ski pass, ski hire and company ski jacket. Training week held in London before departure. There are also a few places in each resort for ski guides who act as assistant reps and whose work involves showing guests around the slopes, helping with coach transfers and organising *après ski*. Age 22+ with good spoken German. Applicants should have good leadership qualities and be proficient skiers (minimum 20 weeks experience). Salary approx £50 per week. A week's training held in Val d'Isère before the season starts. *EC passport holders only*. PH depending on ability.

CANVAS HOLIDAYS LTD Bull Plain, Hertford SG14 1DY Tel Hertford 553535
Provides accommodation for holiday families in ready-erected fully equipped tents and cabins on campsites. Resident couriers are required. The work involves a daily routine of tent cleaning as customers arrive and depart,

providing information and advice on the local attractions and essential services, helping to sort out problems that might arise and organising activities for the children and get-togethers for the families. 7 day week with no fixed hours; the workload varies from day to day. At the beginning and end of the season there is a period of physical work when tents are put up and prepared or taken down and stored for the winter. Other tasks include administration, book keeping and stock control. Working knowledge of German essential.

Ages 18-25. Applicants should be those with a year between school and further education, undergraduates or graduates. They need to be enthusiastic, practical, reliable, self-motivated, able to turn their hand to new and varied tasks, and with a sense of humour. 10-14 weeks, early April-mid July or July-late September. Return travel (dependent on successful completion of contract), accommodation in frame tents and moped or bicycle for use on site provided. Salary approx £76 per week. *Applications accepted anytime; interviews commence early November for the following season. UK nationals only.*

EUROCAMP Courier Department, Edmundson House, Tatton Street, Knutsford, Cheshire WA16 6BG Tel Knutsford 50052
Organises self-drive holidays providing fully equipped tents and caravans on a campsite near Innsbruck. Resident couriers required. The work involves cleaning tents and equipment prior to the arrival of new customers; checking, replacing and making repairs on equipment; replenishing gas supplies; keeping the store tent in order; keeping basic accounts and reporting on a weekly basis to England. Couriers are also expected to meet new arrivals and assist holidaymakers with any problems that may arise; organise activities and parties; provide information on local tourist attractions and maintain an information noticeboard. At the beginning and end of the season couriers are expected to help in erecting and dismantling tents. There are no set working hours or free days, as these depend on unpredictable factors.
Ages 18-28, although older applicants will be considered. Applicants should be familiar with working and travelling abroad, preferably with

camping experience. They should also be adaptable, reliable, independent, efficient, hard working, sensible, sociable, tactful, patient and have a working knowledge of German. Applications from couples welcome.

Applicants are expected to work one half of the season, early/mid April-mid July or mid July-late September/early October - exact dates depend on the campsite. Work is also available for the whole season. Salary £80 per week. Accommodation in frame tent with cooking facilities, insurance, return fare and moped on site provided. *Early application advisable; interviews start September.*

QUEST TRAVEL Olivier House, 18 Marine Parade, Brighton, East Sussex BN2 1TL Tel Brighton 677777
Provides ski and summer tours for groups, mainly school parties, individuals and youth and adult organisations. Resort representatives are required for the summer and winter seasons, December-April and May-July/August, in St Michael, Lofer, Igls, Gotzens and other resorts. Duties include meeting groups at airports or hotels, room allocation, liaising with group leaders, organising entertainments, arranging ski passes and lessons, and promoting good local relations. Ages 21+. Applicants should be enthusiastic, have a flair for organising, enjoy hard, stimulating work, and speak fluent German. Representatives will be on call 24 hours per day. Salary £75-£110 per week. Full board and lodging in shared accommodation, medical insurance and return travel provided. Training course at beginning of season. B D PH limited opportunities.

SKIBOUND Blenheim House, 120 Church Street, Brighton, East Sussex BN1 1WH
Specialises in winter sports tours for schools and adults and in activity tours and excursions in spring/summer. Area managers, hotel/chalet managers and representatives are required for the winter and summer/spring seasons, December-April and May-August, in the Austrian Alps. Posts involve a considerable amount of client contact, and applicants must be presentable and keen to work hard. Ages 18+. Good knowledge of German required for representatives and preferably for managers; previous experience necessary. 48 hour week. Insurance, travel from port/airport and full

board accommodation provided. Wages dependent on position. *EC nationals only.*

SUPERTRAVEL Alpine Operations Department, 22 Hans Place, London SW1X 0EP Tel 071-589 5161

Arranges skiing holidays in the alpine resorts of Lech and St Anton. Opportunities for resort representatives, responsible for looking after guests and supervising staff. Work involves travelling to the airport each weekend to welcome guests; organising their ski passes, ski hire and ski school; informing them of local events; overseeing the work of chalet girls and ensuring that chalets are kept in perfect running order.

Applicants should be used to working on their own initiative, often under pressure. Stamina, a sense of humour and fluent German essential. Applicants must be available for the whole season, early December-end April. Approx 40+ hours per week. Board, lodging, ski pass, ski and boot hire and return travel provided; also insurance in return for approx £35 contribution. Salary £55-£85 per week, paid in local currency. Two day briefing held in London before departure, plus individual session to learn about the resort. *British passport holders only.*

DOMESTIC

BLADON LINES Personnel Department, 56-58 Putney High Street, London SW15 1SF Tel 081-785 2200

Opportunities for cooks and cleaners to work in the ski resorts of St Anton, Kitzbühel and Obergurgl. Also opportunities for chalet girls, cleaning chalets, making beds, caring for guests, shopping and preparing meals. Ages 20+. Experience and/or qualifications in catering or domestic work essential. Also positions for hostesses to work in larger chalets where no cooking experience is required. Hours very variable; applicants must be prepared to work hard but will get time to ski. Season lasts December-May. Salary approx £40 per week. Board, lodging, return travel, insurance, ski pass, ski hire and company ski jacket provided. One day briefing in London held before departure. *EC passport holders only.* PH depending on ability.

SKIBOUND Blenheim House, 120 Church Street, Brighton, East Sussex BN1 1WH

Specialises in winter sports tours for schools and adults and in activity tours and excursions in spring/summer. Staff are required for all grades of hotel work in the winter and summer/spring seasons, December-April and May-August, in the Austrian Alps. Posts involve client contact, and applicants must be presentable and keen to work hard. Ages 18+. Previous experience useful; catering experience required for some posts. 48 hour week. Insurance, travel from port/airport and full board accommodation provided. Wages dependent on position. *EC nationals only.*

SNOW WORLD (SUN LIVING LTD) Personnel Manager, Adventure House, 34-36 South Street, Lancing, West Sussex BN15 8AG Tel Lancing 750310

Opportunities exist for chalet maids in ski resorts. Work involves preparing meals, keeping chalets tidy and looking after guests. Ages 18-30. Relevant experience in catering essential plus Cordon Bleu or equivalent qualification. 8-10 hour day, 6 day week as a general rule, but hours vary depending on the needs of clients. Applicants should be prepared to work for the whole season December-April. Extra staff may also be required at peak times such as Christmas. Board, lodging and travel provided. Salary from £45 per week. Training given at the resort during the week before clients arrive.

SUPERTRAVEL Alpine Operations Department, 22 Hans Place, London SW1X 0EP Tel 071-589 5161

Arranges skiing holidays in the alpine resorts of Lech and St Anton. Opportunities for chalet girls responsible for looking after guests and keeping chalet clean and tidy. Ages 21-30. Work involves cooking, cleaning, acting as hostess, sitting down to dinner with guests, advising them on skiing areas and keeping them up to date with events in the resort. Chalet girls must work to a budget and account for expenditure. Applicants must have cooking experience and preferably qualifications, be capable of running a chalet of approx 8 guests and have an outgoing and helpful personality. Applicants must be available for the whole season, early December-end April. Approx 40+ hours per week. Board, lodging, ski pass, ski and boot hire and return travel provided; also insurance in return for approx £35 contribution. Salary £45 per week, paid in local currency. Briefings held in London before departure. *British passport holders only.*

FARMWORK

INTERNATIONAL FARM EXPERIENCE PROGRAMME YFC Centre, National Agricultural Centre, Kenilworth, Warwickshire CV8 2LG Tel Coventry 696584
Provides assistance to young farmers and nurserymen by finding places in farms/nurseries abroad, enabling them to broaden their knowledge of agricultural methods. Opportunities for practical horticultural and agricultural work usually on mixed farms. Applicants live and work with a farmer and his family and the work is matched as far as possible with the applicant's requirements. The work is physically hard. 8-10 hour day, 6 day week; every other weekend free. 3-12 months. Positions mostly available in spring and summer; some au pair positions for girls. Wages approx £30 plus board and lodging. Ages 18-26. Applicants must have at least 2 years' practical experience, 1 year of which may be at an agricultural college, and intend to make a career in agriculture/horticulture. Valid driving licence necessary. Applicants pay own fare. Registration fee £62. *British applicants only.*

Austrian applicants should apply to Präsidentenkonferenz der Landwirtschafts-kammern Osterreichs, I Lowelstrasse Nr 12, Postfach 124, 1014 Vienna.

MONITORS & INSTRUCTORS

SKI EUROPE Northumberland House, 2 King Street, Twickenham, Middlesex TW1 3RZ Tel 081-891 4400
Operates holidays for groups and school parties. Part-time ski instructors are required for winter sports centres in the Tyrol and Salzburgland. BASI or full ASSI qualifications essential. Knowledge of foreign languages useful but not essential, but fluent English a prerequisite. 6 hours teaching per day, 1-4 week periods over the New Year, February and April. Wages approx £75 per week, according to qualifications. Full board hotel accommodation and ski pass plus travel from London/resort. Access to the same facilities as the clients. *Interviews held May-November.*

SKIBOUND Blenheim House, 120 Church Street, Brighton, East Sussex BN1 1WH
Specialises in winter sports tours for schools and adults and in activity tours and excursions in spring/summer. Ski instructors are required for the winter season, December-April, in the Austrian Alps. Posts involve a considerable amount of client contact, and applicants must be presentable and keen to work hard. Ages 18+. BASI qualifications essential; previous experience necessary. 48 hour week. Insurance, travel from port/airport and full board accommodation provided. Wages dependent on location. *EC nationals only.*

SNOW WORLD (SUN LIVING LTD) Personnel Manager, Adventure House, 34-36 South Street, Lancing, West Sussex BN15 8AG Tel Lancing 750310
Opportunities exist for ski instructors. 8-10 hour day, 6 day week, although hours vary depending on needs of clients. Ages 18-30. Applicants must have BASI grade 3 or equivalent qualifications and should be prepared to work for the whole season, December-April. Extra staff may also be required at peak times such as Christmas. Also opportunities for ski technicians. Board, lodging and travel provided. Salary from £80 per week. Training given at the resort in the week before clients arrive.

YOUNG AUSTRIA Alpenstrasse 108a, 5020 Salzburg
Opportunities available for monitors and EFL teachers at English language camps for Austrian and German children. The camps are based at holiday centre chalets in the Salzburg region, and are organised for children aged 10-19 who are studying English at school. The aim is to improve their knowledge of the English language and the British way of life. Monitors and teachers are responsible for the daily welfare of a group of approx 15-20 children, for the organisation of indoor and outdoor

activities, including sports, music and crafts, excursions and for helping the children with English conversation. Teachers are responsible for the daily tuition (3½ hours) of English but also have to act as monitors. The language of the camps is English and a knowledge of German is not compulsory. Ages 21-40. Applicants should be native English speakers and have experience in working with or teaching children. Qualified teachers will be given priority for teaching posts. Applicant's ability and organisational skills in sports, music and crafts will be taken into consideration. 3 or 6 weeks, end June-beginning September. Board, accommodation, insurance and sports clothes provided. Pay AS4200, monitors or AS5200, teachers, per 3 week session, plus lump sum of AS200 for travel expenses. Compulsory interviews and briefing held in London in June. Organised with the support of the Central Bureau. *UK residents preferred; apply by end February.*

WORKCAMPS

INTERNATIONAL VOLUNTARY SERVICE 162 Upper New Walk, Leicester LE1 7QA Tel Leicester 549430

IVS is the British branch of Service Civil International which promotes international reconciliation through work projects. Volunteers are needed to live and work in international teams on workcamps. Recent projects have included working with a Croatian group to promote their culture, developing their centre and preparing their annual local festival in the Burgenland; making paths and vegetable gardens accessible to the disabled in Vienna; preserving and reviving plant species and converting a loft in the Waldviertel; working with children at a women's refuge in Vienna; and renovating farm buildings for use as a youth centre in the Weinviertel. Camps are linked to study themes. Workcamp languages are English and German. Ages 18+. Applicants should have previous workcamp experience, and be prepared to work hard and contribute to team life. 35-40 hour week, 2-4 weeks, June-September. Food, accommodation and insurance provided, but not travel. Volunteers prepare and cook their own meals. Membership fee £25 (students £15, unwaged £10). Registration fee £40. B D PH

Organised by Service Civil International, Schottengasse 3a/1/4/59, 1010 Vienna.

UK applications to IVS; overseas applications: see workcamp information on page 27.

OSTERREICHISCHER BAUORDEN PO Box 186, Hornesgasse 3, 1031 Vienna

An international volunteers' association with the aims of fighting misery and distress, and making a contribution towards a better understanding between nations. Volunteers are needed to work in international teams on behalf of the socially, mentally, economically and physically underprivileged. Projects have included construction, cleaning and renovation work at youth/social centres, churches, hostels, homes for the aged, kindergartens, schools, community centres and refugee resettlements; housing for socially deprived families and road/canal building for communities without means. Ages 18+. Applicants should have previous workcamp experience. 40 hour week, 3-4 weeks, July and August. Food, prepared by the volunteers, tent, family, school or centre accommodation, insurance and travel in Austria provided, but volunteers should take sleeping bags. Participation fee DM110. *Apply 2 months in advance.*

GENERAL

CANVAS HOLIDAYS LTD Bull Plain, Hertford SG14 1DY Tel Hertford 553535

Provides ready-erected fully equipped tents for family holidays. Require applicants to form flying squads, teams of 2/3 people who help set up and equip 200-250 6 berth frame tents in an area containing approx 12 campsites. Similar work is also available taking down tents and cleaning and storing equipment. Ages 18-25. Knowledge of German not required, but is an advantage as flying squad members sometimes have the opportunity to continue as couriers. Applicants must be sociable in order to work in a small community, fit and able to work hard for long hours under pressure, work without supervision and cope with living out of a rucksack. April-mid June, possibly longer to set up the tents, and September to dismantle them. Valid international driving licence an advantage. Salary approx £76 per week. Tented

AUSTRIA

accommodation and self-catering facilities provided. Outward travel paid by the company; return travel dependent on the completion of contract dates. *UK nationals only.*

GENERAL

EUROYOUTH LTD 301 Westborough Road, Westcliff-on-Sea, Essex SS0 9PT Tel Southend-on-Sea 341434
Holiday stays arranged where guests are offered board and lodging in return for an agreed number of hours English conversation with hosts or their children. Time is also available for guests to practise German if desired. Mainly ages 15-25, but there are sometimes opportunities for ages 13-16 and for older applicants. The scheme is open to anyone born and educated in the UK, interested in visiting Austria and living with a local family. 2-3 weeks, June-August. Travel and insurance paid by the applicant. Registration fee approx £80. Apply at least 12 weeks prior to scheduled departure date.

When applying to any organisation it is esential to mention Working Holidays 1991 and enclose a large stamped, self-addressed envelope, or if overseas, a large addressed envelope and at least two International Reply Coupons.

BELGIUM

Belgian Embassy
103 Eaton Square, London SW1W 9AB
Tel 071-235 5422

British Embassy
Britannia House, rue Joseph II 28, 1040 Brussels

Tourist office
Belgian National Tourist Office, Premier
House, 2 Gayton Road, Harrow, Middlesex
HA1 2XU Tel 081-861 3300

Youth hostels
Centrale Wallonne des Auberges de la
Jeunesse, rue Van Oost 52, 1030 Brussels

Vlaamse Jeugdherbergcentrale, Van
Stralenstraat 40, 2008 Antwerp

Youth & student information
InforJeunes, rue Marché aux Herbes 27, 1000
Brussels

Caravanes de Jeunesse Belge, rue Mercelis 6,
1050 Brussels

Accueil Jeunes, rue Declercq 76, 1150 Brussels

Centre J, rue des Dominicains 11, 4000 Liège

Nationaal Informatiecentrum voor jongeren,
Prinsstraat 15, 2000 Antwerp

INFORMATION

Entry regulations UK citizens intending to work in Belgium should have a full passport. EC nationals may stay in Belgium for up to 3 months in order to seek employment; once a job has been found, the applicant must register at the nearest town hall and apply for a residence permit. The number of opportunities available to foreign students is, however, extremely limited. The Belgian Embassy can supply a list of job centres for temporary work (T-Service) and also some specifically for students (Job Service).

Job advertising Advertisements for job vacancies, situations wanted, services offered and domestic help are included in the weekly news magazine for English-speaking residents in Belgium, *The Bulletin*, avenue Molière 329, 1060 Brussels.

Publicitas Ltd, 525/527 Fulham Road, London SW6 1HF Tel 071-385 7723 can place job advertisements in 12 Belgian newspapers and 17 magazines.

Travel Belgian National Railways, 10 Greycoat Place, London SW1P 1SP Tel 071-233 0360 operates a scheme where a bike can be hired at one of 61 Belgian stations and returned to any

one of 148. Advisable to reserve bikes in advance; cost from £2.25 per day.

Abonnement Réseau allows unlimited rail travel throughout the Belgian network. Valid 16 consecutive days, all year, cost BF3050. B-Tourrail Ticket allows unlimited travel for 5 days; cost for ages under 26, BF1400 and BF1700 for those over 26. Benelux Tourrail allows unlimited travel throughout the Belgium, Luxembourg and Netherlands rail networks; valid for 5 days during a period of 17 consecutive days. Cost for ages under 26, BF2490 and BF1790 for those over 26. All available from YHA Travel, 14 Southampton Street, London WC2E 7HY Tel 071-836 8541 and from stations in Belgium.

Campus Travel, 52 Grosvenor Gardens, London SW1W 0AG Tel 071-730 3402 offer Eurotrain under 26 rail fares to all main destinations in Belgium, plus youth and student airfares.

Information centres ACOTRA rue de la Madeleine 51, 1000 Brussels arranges youth and student travel and is able to give advice and make reservations for accommodation. Also books tours and excursions, cultural and activity holidays, and issues youth/student reduction and youth hostel cards. The ACOTRA Welcome Desk at Brussels airport provides information and reservations for accommodation and travel, including BIGE train tickets for those under 26.

Brussels Welcome Open Door, rue de Tabora 6, 1000 Brussels is a Catholic information service for visitors, residents, workers and students, providing advice on education, language classes, social services, legal aid and religion. Free interpreting and translation service. Open Monday-Saturday, 10.00-18.00.

Centre National Infor Jeunes, avenue Jean Volders 10, 1060 Brussels Tel 02 537 64 63, is the head office of the national youth information service that has 13 centres throughout Belgium open to the public. Information is available on legal rights, study, leisure, holidays, in fact anything that particularly affects young people. Publishes *Belgium, Use It*, BF70 including postage, a booklet in English, French and Dutch translations intended for young visitors to Belgium.

Accommodation *Camping*, a leaflet listing, by province, all camping sites and their facilities is available from the Belgian National Tourist Office, see above.

Le CHAB, Hotel de Jeunes, rue Traversière 8, 1030 Brussels is an inexpensive international accommodation centre, with 1-8 bedded rooms or dormitories. Cost from BF240 for bed and breakfast plus BF70 linen charge. Cycle hire, walking tours, and information on cultural activities.

Cheap accommodation for young people is available at Maison Internationale, chaussée de Wavre 205, 1040 Brussels, based in a former monastery. Cost from BF350 per night includes shower and breakfast. Also youth camping site situated in a large park, BF220 per night including breakfast.

Rijksuniversiteit Gent, Mrs K Van Den Broeck, Department of Guest Accommodation, Home A Vermeylen, Stalhof 6, 9000 Gent has cheap accommodation in single rooms in 2 halls of residence, 15 July-15 September. Bed and breakfast BF450 per night. Facilities include

restaurant, swimming pool and sports grounds.

AU PAIR/ CHILDCARE

ANGLIA AGENCY 15 Eastern Avenue, Southend-on-Sea, Essex Tel Southend 613888
Au pair, mother's helps and nanny positions arranged throughout the year. Long and short-term placements available, including summer period. Hours and salaries vary; au pairs work 30 hours per week plus babysitting, with 1 free day and £25+ pocket money per week. Board and lodging provided. Ages 17+. Travel costs paid by the applicant. Service charge £40.

AVALON AGENCY Thursley House, 53 Station Road, Shalford, Guildford, Surrey GU4 8HA Tel Guildford 63640
Can place au pairs. 25-36 hour week, 6-12 months. Ages 18-30. Basic knowledge of the language needed. Board, lodging and pocket money of BF4500 per month provided. Also opportunities for mother's helps and nannies, working longer hours. Salary depends on experience and on the family. Travel paid by the applicant, insurance provided. Service charge £40 on acceptance of placement.

HELPING HANDS AU PAIR & DOMESTIC AGENCY 10 Hertford Road, Newbury Park, Ilford, Essex IG2 7HQ Tel 081-597 3138
Au pair and mother's help positions available throughout the year. Au pairs work approx 30 hours plus 3 evenings babysitting each week and earn approx £25 per week. Mother's helps work longer hours for a higher salary. Board and lodging provided. Minimum stay 6 months. Ages 18-27. Applicants should be willing, helpful and adaptable. Insurance and travel costs paid by the applicant but assistance with the arrangements provided. Introduction fee £40 on acceptance of a family. *UK nationals only.*

INTERLINGUA CENTRE Torquay Road, Foxrock, Dublin 18, Ireland Tel Dublin 893876
Can place au pairs in Belgian families. 30 hour week with one full day and some evenings off.

Time to attend classes 2-3 mornings or afternoons per week. 6+ months. Experience desirable but not essential. Ages 18+. £25-£40 pocket money per week, full board, lodging and insurance provided. Travel paid by applicants. Placement fee £55.

INTERNATIONAL CATHOLIC SOCIETY FOR GIRLS (ACISJF) St Patrick's International Youth Centre, 24 Great Chapel Street, London W1V 3AF Tel 071-734 2156
Au pair posts arranged for 9+ months. Ages 18+. The Society assists girls/young women who are travelling and living away from home. Counselling and information service.

STUDENTS ABROAD AGENCY Elm House, 21b The Avenue, Hatch End, Middlesex HA5 4EN Tel 081-428 5823
Can place au pairs and mother's helps. Long-term positions available all year as well as a limited number of summer placements for a minimum of 2/3 months. Au pairs normally work a 5/6 hour day with 3-4 hours allowed for language classes, but curriculum changes and applicants must be flexible during temporary summer season when no schooling available. Usually 1 full day and 2/3 evenings free per week. Salary approx £25-£30 per week. Mother's helps work longer hours for a higher salary. Board and lodging provided. Ages 17-27. Basic knowledge of French required. Applicants should like, and have the ability to cope with, children, babies, light housework and simple cooking. Applicants pay their own fares, but advice given on travel and insurance. Service charge £40. *Apply early for temporary summer positions.*

UNIVERSAL CARE Chester House, 9 Windsor End, Beaconsfield, Buckinghamshire HP9 2JJ Tel Beaconsfield 678811
Can place au pairs and mother's helps, 6+ months, all year. Posts are limited during the summer. Au pairs work a 5/6 hour day, with occasional babysitting and 1 day off per week; regular free time for language classes. Ages 17-27. Mother's helps work an 8 hour day, without free time for classes. Ages 18-30. Basic French essential. Board and lodging provided, salaries vary, but are normally £25 per week, higher for mother's helps. Travel paid by applicant. Service charge £46. *Apply 2 months before work period desired.*

COMMUNITY WORK

ATD QUART MONDE Avenue Victor Jacobs 12, 1040 Brussels Tel 6479900
Strives to protect and guarantee the fundamental rights of the poorest and most disadvantaged and excluded families, which constitute the Fourth World. These rights include the right to family life, to education and training, and to representation. Volunteers are required to undertake varied manual and construction work on two centres in Brussels, under the direction of permanent, trained volunteers. Work includes masonry, carpentry, painting, roof and floor tiling. Ages 18+. No experience necessary but applicants should be interested in better understanding the causes and effects of persistent poverty, willing to work hard with others as a team. Approx 30 hour week. 2/3 weeks, July. Dormitory accommodation and insurance, but not travel, provided. Volunteers take it in turns to cook. Participants should take a sleeping bag and all-weather working clothes. Cost BF800.

ENTRAIDE ET AMITIE ASBL rue du Boulet 9, 1000 Brussels
Volunteers are needed throughout the year to help out in clinics and nursing homes in Brussels and Wallonia, with the emphasis on giving more personal attention to individual patients than can usually be provided by medical staff alone. Duties include making beds, serving meals, welcoming patients and their visitors, and generally helping the patients in their day-to-day lives. Ages 17+. 2-24 hour week. No experience necessary but volunteers should be in good health with a good knowledge of French. Participants must arrange their own board and lodging, but insurance is provided.

INTERNATIONAL VOLUNTARY SERVICE 162 Upper Walk, Leicester LE1 7QA Tel Leicester 549430
IVS is the British branch of Service Civil International which promotes international reconciliation through work projects. Volunteers are needed to work in international teams on various workcamps. Recent projects

have included renovating houses for the underprivileged in Liège and Brussels; running holiday activities for children in Ker'Yol; working at a crisis centre in Gent; adapting a house in Kapellen for mentally handicapped people; and cooking cheap meals for the poor in Naumur.

Ages 18+. Applicants should have previous workcamp experience and be highly motivated and prepared to work hard and contribute to team life. Knowledge of French needed on some camps. 35-40 hour week, 2-4 weeks, June-September. Food, accommodation and insurance provided, but not travel. Membership fee £25 (students £15, unwaged £10). Registration fee £40. PH

Organised by Vrijwillige Internationale Aktie (VIA), Venusstraat 28, 2000 Antwerp and SCI, rue Van Elewyck 35, 1050 Brussels.

Applications from outside the UK: please see workcamp information on page 27.

CONSERVATION

INTERNATIONAL VOLUNTARY SERVICE 162 Upper New Walk, Leicester, LE1 7QA Tel Leicester 549430
IVS is the British branch of Service Civil International which promotes international reconciliation through work projects. Volunteers are needed for conservation work on camps organised by two SCI branches in Belgium. Recent projects organised by Service Civil International have included making compost in Londerzeel; and helping with daily tasks on a cooperative farm in Namur. Projects organised by Vrijwillige Internationale Aktie have included building work for an alternative energy centre in Proven; and mowing and footpath-making to improve a green belt area for plants and wildlife in an Antwerp suburb. Good knowledge of French/Dutch needed for some camps.
Ages 18+. Applicants should have previous workcamp, voluntary work or community service experience and should be prepared to work hard and contribute to team life. 35-40 hour week, 2-4 weeks, June-September. Food, accommodation and insurance provided, but not travel. Membership fee £25 (student £15, unwaged £10). Registration fee £40. PH

Organised by Service Civil International, rue Van Elewyck 35, 1050 Brussels, and Vrijwillige Internationale Aktie (VIA), Venusstraat 28, 2000 Antwerp.

Applications from outside the UK: please see workcamp information on page 27.

NATUUR 2000 Flemish Youth Federation for the Study of Nature & for Environmental Conservation, Bervoetstraat 33, 2000 Antwerp
Organises conservation activities such as management of nature reserves and smaller landscape elements, species protection, waste recycling, action against sea pollution and solidarity action on acid rain, tropical rain forests, pesticides and Arctic/Antarctic problems. Arrange nature study and conservation camps in Dutch-speaking areas of Belgium. Volunteers, preferably with experience in field biology are required to help lead the study camps. Ages 15+. Knowledge of Dutch, French or English needed. July and August. Food, accommodation, insurance and travel from Antwerp to site provided. Visas/work permits arranged if necessary. Cost from BF1000, depending on type of camp, duration and location. Help is also needed in the office, 40 hour week, all year. Experience preferred.

COURIERS/REPS

EUROCAMP Courier Department, Edmundson House, Tatton Street, Knutsford, Cheshire WA16 6BG Tel Knutsford 50052
Resident couriers required to work on various campsites. Work involves cleaning tents and equipment prior to the arrival of new customers, checking, replacing and making repairs on equipment, replenishing gas supplies, keeping the store tent in order, keeping basic accounts and reporting on a weekly basis to England. Couriers are also expected to meet new arrivals and assist holidaymakers with any problems that may arise; organise activities and parties; provide information on local tourist attractions and maintain an information noticeboard. At the beginning and end of the season couriers are expected to help erect and dismantle tents. There are no set working hours or free days, as these depend on unpredictable factors. Ages

18-28; older applicants considered. Applications from couples welcome. Applicants should be familiar with working and travelling abroad, preferably with camping experience. They should also be adaptable, reliable, independent, efficient, hard working, sensible, sociable, tactful, patient and have a working knowledge of the language. Applicants are expected to work one half of the season, early/mid April-mid July or mid July-late September/early October; exact dates depend on the campsite. Work also available for the whole season. Accommodation in frame tent with cooking facilities, moped for use on site, insurance and return fare provided. Salary approx £80 per week. *Early application advisable; interviews start September.*

TEACHERS

BELGIAN EMBASSY 103 Eaton Square, London SW1W 9AB Tel 071-235 5422
Publish *Posts for Foreign Teachers in Belgium*, a list giving the addresses of international English-speaking schools that may be able to offer teaching posts.

WORKCAMPS

BOUWORDE VZW Tiensesteenweg 145, 3200 Leuven
A Catholic organisation which expresses solidarity with people in distress through creating better living environments. Volunteers undertake construction work under the guidance of experienced leaders. Recent projects have included rebuilding a residence for poor families; constructing a recreation ground for children with cerebral palsy; building youth hostels for invalid youngsters; and remodelling a home for the aged. Ages 18+. No experience required but a keen attitude necessary. 8 hour day, 5 day week. 3-4 weeks, July-September. Full board, lodging and insurance provided. Travel paid by applicants. Registration fee BF1500.

CHRISTIAN MOVEMENT FOR PEACE Bethnal Green United Reformed Church, Pott Street, London E2 0EF Tel 071-729 1877
An international movement open to all who share a common concern for lasting peace and

justice in the world. Volunteers are needed to work in international teams on summer projects aimed at offering a service in an area of need and promoting self-help within the community, promoting international understanding and the discussion of social problems, and offering young people the chance to live as a group and take these experiences into the context of daily life. Recent projects have included demolition, renovation and gardening work for a religious community which acts as a place of retreat for young people with problems; helping in a centre for the physically handicapped; and working with Spanish and Arabic immigrant families. Ages 18-30. Knowledge of French required on some camps. 6 hour day, 30-36 hour week. 2-4 weeks, July, August and October. Food, school, centre or tent accommodation and insurance provided; participants pay their own travel costs. Registration fee £24.

Organised by Mouvement des Jeunes pour la Paix, boulevard de l'Empereur 15, 1000 Brussels.

Applications from outside the UK: please see workcamp information on page 27.

INTERNATIONAL VOLUNTARY SERVICE 162 Upper New Walk, Leicester, LE1 7QA Tel Leicester 549430
IVS is the British branch of Service Civil International which promotes international reconciliation through work projects. Volunteers are needed to work in international teams on various workcamps. Recent projects have included building a playground at a holiday centre for Fourth World families, and for an alternative school at Oudenaarde; improving an Oxfam shop that sells Third World products; and constructing a greenhouse at a centre for mentally handicapped people. Ages 18+. Applicants should have previous workcamp experience and be highly motivated and prepared to work hard and contribute to team life. Knowledge of French/Dutch needed on some camps. 35-40 hour week, 2-4 weeks, June-September. Food, accommodation and insurance provided, but not travel. Membership fee £25 (student £15, unwaged £10). Registration fee £40. PH

Organised by Vrijwillige Internationale Aktie

BELGIUM

(VIA), Venusstraat 28, 2000 Antwerp.

Applications from outside the UK: please see workcamp information on page 27.

GENERAL

EUROYOUTH LTD 301 Westborough Road, Westcliff-on-Sea, Essex SSO 9PT
Tel Southend-on-Sea 341434
Holiday stays arranged where guests are offered board and lodging in return for an agreed number of hours English conversation with hosts or their children. Time is also available for guests to practise the native language if desired. Mainly ages 15-25, but there are sometimes opportunities for ages 13-16 and for older applicants. 2-3 weeks, June-August. Travel and insurance arranged by the applicant. Registration fee approx £60. Number of places limited. *Apply at least 12 weeks prior to scheduled departure date. UK nationals only.*

GENERAL

When applying to any organisation it is essential to mention Working Holidays 1991 and enclose a large stamped, self-addressed envelope, or if overseas, a large addressed envelope and at least two International Reply Coupons.

BULGARIA

Bulgarian Embassy
186-188 Queen's Gate, London SW7 5HL
Tel 071-584 9400

British Embassy
Boulevard Marshal Tolbukhin 65-67, Sofia 1000

Tourist office
Bulgarian National Tourist Office, 18 Princes

Street, London W1R 7RE Tel 071-499 6988

Youth hostels
Union Bulgare de Tourisme, Boulevard Marshal
Tolbukhin 18, Sofia

Youth & student information
Orbita Chain for Youth Tourism, Boulevard
Alexander Stamboliski 45a, Sofia

INFORMATION

Entry regulations Details of entry
requirements can be obtained from the Visa
Section of the Bulgarian Embassy. Workcamp
organisations will inform volunteers how to
obtain the necessary visa/permit and hold
orientation days for volunteers going to East
Europe, giving information on all aspects of the
work covered together with some political
background and practical information.

Travel Campus Travel, 52 Grosvenor Gardens,
London SW1 0AG Tel 071-730 3402 offer
Eurotrain under 26 fares and youth and student
airfares to Bulgaria.

Accommodation Orbita Chain for Youth
Tourism, see above, offer accommodation at
student hostels in Sofia, Varna, Veliko
Turnovo, and in the Rhodope Mountains
during July and August. Also maintain
international youth centres for recreation and
study.

The Rough Guide to Eastern Europe £7.95 is a
practical handbook covering Bulgaria,
Hungary and Romania, packed with useful and
unusual information. Published by Harrap
Columbus, Chelsea House, 26 Market Square,
Bromley, Kent BR1 1NA.

WORKCAMPS

**INTERNATIONAL VOLUNTARY SERVICE
162 Upper New Walk, Leicester, LE1 7QA
Tel Leicester 549430**

**UNITED NATIONS ASSOCIATION
International Youth Service, Welsh Centre for
International Affairs, Temple of Peace,
Cathays Park, Cardiff CF1 3AP Tel Cardiff
223088**

Apply to either of the above to participate on a
workcamp with more than 100 volunteers from
over 35 countries. Recent projects have
included archaeological excavations in Plovdiv;
renovating a children's theatre in Ravda; and
environmental work around the lakes of the
Rila Plateau. Also discussions on voluntary
youth service for peace, detente and

disarmament, East/West friendship, plus
solidarity and cultural/sports events. Ages
18-30. Previous workcamp experience and an
interest in East/West relations essential.
Knowledge of Russian or German useful. 8
hour day, 5 day week. 3 weeks, August. Board,
lodging, working clothes and travel within
Bulgaria provided. 5 day educational tour of
cultural and historical sites arranged after the
workcamp, for which a small fee may be
charged. Compulsory orientation for IVS
participants. *Limited places; apply by end May.*

Organised by Argo-M, Boulevard Stamboliski
2A, 1000 Sofia C.

*Applications from outside the UK: please see
workcamp information on page 27.*

NOTES

CANADA

Canadian High Commission
Canada House, Trafalgar Square, London
SW1Y 5BJ Tel 071-409 2071

Immigration Division: MacDonald House,
38 Grosvenor Street, London W1X 0AA
Tel 071-409 2071

British High Commission
80 Elgin Street, Ottawa, Ontario K1P 5K7

Tourist office
Tourism Canada, Canada House, Trafalgar
Square, London SW1Y 5BJ Tel 071-930 8540

Youth hostels
Canadian Hostelling Association, National
Office, 333 River Road, 3rd Floor, Vanier,
Ottawa, Ontario K1L 8H9

Youth & student information
Association of Student Councils (Canada),
171 College Street, Toronto, Ontario M5T 1P7

Canadian Bureau for International Education,
85 Albert Street, 14th floor, Ottawa, Ontario
K1P 6A4

Tourbec , 1178 Avenue Cartier, Quebec City,
Quebec G1R 2S7

INFORMATION

Entry regulations Employment Authorisation
is required for all types of employment, and
application should be made to the Canadian
Immigration Division Office. Authorisation
cannot be issued until the prospective
employer has obtained certification from a
Canadian employment centre to say that no
qualified Canadian citizen or landed
immigrant is available to fill the job in
question. An Authorisation only becomes valid
when stamped at the port of entry.
Employment opportunities for visitors are
therefore extremely restricted.
However, a limited number of foreign students
are admitted to Canada each year under an
international student summer employment
programme. Under this programme,
authorisation is granted to students who have
been offered employment in Canada, without
the vacancy first having been advertised to
Canadian nationals. Applicants must obtain an
offer of employment by their own means and
having done so, produce written proof of the
offer, showing position, salary, and working
conditions. Authorisation is issued only for the
job specified in the application, and is normally
valid for a maximum of 20 weeks. UK
applicants must produce written proof that
they are British citizens, and bona fide full-
time students of British or Irish universities or

similar institutions (including students who
have been accepted for admission in the current
year), and that they will be returning after the
vacation period to continue their course of
study. Those whose job involves handling food
or where hygiene is important, will be required
to undergo a medical examination, at a cost of
£50, before authorisation is issued. A number
of organisations in the UK operate Exchange
Visitor Programmes which help students to
find employment in Canada. As the number of
places is limited, applications should be made
as early as possible. An additional student
programme is now available whereby an offer
of pre-arranged employment is not required,
but evidence of funds needs to be produced
along with a medical certificate and evidence of
student status.
Those travelling to Canada and planning to
remain there for an extended period may be
required to prove at the time of entry that they
have sufficient means to maintain themselves
and have evidence of onward reservations.
Those under 18 not accompanied by an adult
should have a letter from a parent/guardian
giving them permission to travel to Canada.
Those wishing to work or study in Canada
should contact the High Commission for
further information before seeking admission.
Information sheets *Do You Want to Work*

Temporarily in Canada? and *Do You Want to Visit Canada?* can be obtained from the Immigration Division of the Canadian High Commission.

Travel North-South Travel, Moulsham Mill, Parkway, Chelmsford CM2 7PX Tel Chelmsford 492882 arranges competitively priced, reliably planned flights to all parts of Canada. Profits are paid into a trust fund for the assignment of aid to projects in the poorest areas of the South.

STA Travel, 74 Old Brompton Road, London SW7 3LQ Tel 071-937 9971 operates flexible, low-cost flights to destinations throughout Canada.

The Canrailpass provides unlimited travel at a fixed cost over the entire rail network or over any of 3 designated territories. Cost from Can$499, 45 days nationwide. Available from Compass Travel, 9 Grosvenor Gardens, London SW1W 0BH Tel 071-828 4111.

Canada Travel Information provides helpful practical hints covering health, climate, travel and accommodation. Available from Tourism Canada, see above.

The Moneywise Guide to North America £9.95 including postage, provides essential information for anyone travelling on a budget in Canada, the US and Mexico, with useful information on getting around, where to stay, what to eat and places to visit. Published by BUNAC, 16 Bowling Green Lane, London EC1R 0BD Tel 071-251 3472.

Travellers Survival Kit USA and Canada £6.95, is a down-to-earth, entertaining guide for travellers to North America. Describes how to cope with the inhabitants, officialdom and way of life in the Canada and the US. Published by Vacation Work Publications, 9 Park End Street, Oxford OX1 1HJ.

Information centres The Canadian Bureau for International Education, 85 Albert Street, 14th floor, Ottawa, Ontario K1P 6A4 provides information and publications on international work, study and exchange, and a reception service for incoming students at Canadian international airports in August and September.

Accommodation No-frills accommodation available in a hostel in the heart of Old Quebec. Cost Can$14-Can$15 includes bedding. 2-8 bedded rooms, washing facilities, tv lounge and baggage check-in. Cafeteria on premises. No age limit; no membership needed. Apply to Centre International de Séjour de Quebec, 19 rue Ste-Ursule, Quebec G1R 4E1.

The Ys Way, 356 West 34th Street, New York, NY10001, United States operate the Ys Way to Visit North America, a programme offering inexpensive accommodation in single/double rooms at YMCAs in major cities in Canada and the US. Cost from US$24 per night includes use of sports facilities. Apply to STA Travel, 74 Old Brompton Road, London SW7 3LQ Tel 071-937 9971.

CHILDCARE/ DOMESTIC

ANGLIA AGENCY 15 Eastern Avenue, Southend-on-Sea, Essex Tel Southend 613888 Positions for mother's helps and nannies arranged throughout the year. Salary, board and lodging provided. 6+ months. Ages 18+. Travel costs paid by the applicant. Service charge £40.

AVALON AGENCY Thursley House, 53 Station Road, Shalford, Guildford, Surrey GU4 8HA Tel Guildford 63640 Positions available for mother's helps, nannies and housekeepers. Mother's helps undertake general light housework, care of children, laundry and ironing, assisting in the kitchen and babysitting. Nannies take care of children, particularly very young ones, children's meals and clothes, with some babysitting and light housework. Housekeepers take care of children, do cooking, laundry and ironing, babysitting and generally run the household, often with some domestic assistance. Salary usually over Can$350 per month with full board, but varies according to family and area; west Canada pays approx Can$100 per month more than the east. Ages 18+. Applicants should be single females, preferably with NNEB, minimum 1 year experience, and a valid driving licence; non-smokers preferred.

Contract is for 11½ months. Accommodation in private room; 1½ days per week free. Travel paid by the applicant, but return fare may be paid. Medical insurance essential, approx Can$30-Can$40 per month.

EXPERIMENT IN INTERNATIONAL LIVING Au Pair/Study Canada, Otesaga, Upper Wyche, Malvern, Worcestershire WR14 4EN Tel Malvern 562577

A non-profitmaking organisation which aims to promote international understanding as a means of achieving world peace. Operates a government authorised programme to place au pairs with families throughout Canada. Maximum 25 hour week. Ages 18-24. Applicants should be non-smokers, hold a current driving licence, have good childcare/ babysitting experience and a genuine love of children. 12 months; placements available monthly, except December. Pre-departure orientation and session on arrival for host families and au pairs, with detailed training and advice on adaptation and getting the most out of the stay. Local coordinators arrange monthly meetings, providing support and guidance. Can$80 per week pocket money, accommodation, insurance, work permits, visas and Can$250 for course of study at local school or college provided. Two week paid holiday and opportunity to travel. £350 good faith bond, returnable at end of year; administration and orientation fee £150. *British nationals only.* B D PH

JOLAINE AGENCY 18 Escot Way, Barnet, Hertfordshire EN5 3AN Tel 081-449 1334

Mother's help posts arranged throughout the year. 8 hour day with 1½ days free per week, plus some evenings and other time by arrangement. Applicants must have at least 6 months live-in experience with a family with children. Positions for nannies, cooks and housekeepers also available. Full board and accommodation provided. Ages 18+. Minimum stay 1 year. Travel paid by applicant. Introduction fee £40.

NANNIES UNLIMITED INC PO Box 5864, Station A, Calgary, Alberta T2H 1X4

Can place nannies and domestics in Calgary, Edmonton, Toronto, Regina, Vancouver and the North West Territories. Applicants must have one year's previous experience in childcare, or

training, and a working knowledge of English. 47 hour week. Ages 18+. Salary from Can$540 per month and accommodation with family in own room provided. Travel and insurance sometimes paid. Assistance given with obtaining a visa.

STUDENTS ABROAD AGENCY Elm House, 21b The Avenue, Hatch End, Middlesex HA5 4EN Tel 081-428 5823

Can place mother's helps and sometimes housekeepers and nannies, for a minimum of 1 year. Ages 18+. Applicants should be experienced and/or NNEB qualified with good references and like, and have the ability to cope with, children, babies, light housework and simple cooking. Board and lodging provided. Salary, dependent on experience and qualifications, approx Can$560 per month after deductions. Applicants pay their own fare, but advice given on travel and insurance. Minimum of 3 months for work permit formalities, so early application advisable. Service charge £40.

CONSERVATION

CANADIAN PARKS SERVICE National Volunteer Coordinator, Room 200, 10 Wellington, Ottawa, Ontario K1A 0H3 Tel 819 994 5127

The federal agency responsible for protected examples of Canada's natural and cultural heritage. Aims to encourage public understanding, appreciation and enjoyment of this heritage in ways which will leave it unimpaired for future generations. Workers are needed in national parks, historic sites and canals across Canada. Paid positions exist in natural resource management, cultural resource management, interpretation, visitor services and maintenance. Voluntary positions also exist in the above categories and in assisting and enhancing new programmes. Volunteers may serve as assistants interpreting or animating the history of a park, hosting in a campground, collecting data on flora and fauna in a park, maintaining or building trails, designing posters, photographing historic artefacts or wildlife, or keeping library files. Experience essential for applicants from outside Canada; degrees desirable for some positions. Working languages English and

French; bilingual applicants particularly welcome. Fluency in Japanese or German also an advantage. 2-40 hour week, depending on project. No age restrictions. Direct expenses reimbursed and general liability insurance provided. Volunteers pay accommodation, food and travel costs. *Apply before January for summer and autumn positions; before July for winter and spring.* PH limited opportunities.

EARTHWATCH EUROPE Belsyre Court, 57 Woodstock Road, Oxford Tel Oxford 311600 Aims to support field research in a wide range of disciplines including archaeology, ornithology, animal behaviour, nature conservation and ecology. The support is given to researchers as a grant and in the form of volunteer assistance. Recent projects have included identifying and recording plants on Vancouver Island to see how the species diversity varies from that on the mainland; assisting with the study of migratory patterns of striped bass and other fish to discover the potential effects of a planned hydroelectric dam in the Bay of Fundy, Nova Scotia; and collecting ancient pollen from peat samples in Hudson Bay in order to study the correlation between climatic changes and the level of atmospheric carbon dioxide. Ages 16-80. No special skills are required although each expedition may, because of its nature, demand some talent or quality of fitness. Volunteers should be generally fit, able to cope with new situations, able to mix and work with people of different ages and backgrounds, and a sense of humour will help. 2-3 weeks, all year. Members share the costs of the expedition, from £500, which includes meals, transport and all necessary field equipment, but does not include the cost of travel, although assistance may be given in arranging it. Membership fee £22 includes magazines and newsletters providing all the information on joining an expedition.

FARMWORK

INTERNATIONAL AGRICULTURAL EXCHANGE ASSOCIATION YFC Centre, National Agricultural Centre, Kenilworth, Warwickshire CV8 2LG Tel Coventry 696578 Operates opportunities for agricultural students and young people to acquire practical work experience in the rural sector, and to strengthen and improve their knowledge and understanding of the way of life in other countries. Participants are given an opportunity to study practical methods on approved training farms, and work as trainees, gaining further experience in their chosen field. Types of farm include mixed (grain production and livestock); grain; dairy and crop; plus a limited number of bee farms and horticultural enterprises. Participants undertake paid work on the farm, approx 45 hours per week, and live as members of the host family. Full board and lodging, insurance cover and a net minimum weekly wage of £50-£60 provided. All programmes include 3/4 weeks unpaid holiday. 3-5 day orientation courses are held at the beginning of each programme at agricultural colleges and universities throughout Canada. Educational sightseeing trips (4 days-3 weeks) within Canada and in Australia, Thailand, Singapore, Fiji, Hawaii and the US are arranged for participants en route for the 13/14 month programme. Ages 19-28. Applicants should be single, and have good practical experience in the chosen training category, plus a valid driving licence. 7 months (departing April), 13 months - 6½ in Australia/New Zealand plus 6½ in Canada (departing October) or 14 months in Australia/Canada (departing September). Cost £1250 (7 months), £3550 (13/14 months). £200 deposit payable. Costs cover airfare, work permit, administration fee and orientation courses. *Apply at least 4 months in advance. British nationals only.*

Canadian applicants requiring an exchange should apply to IAEA, 206 1501-17 Avenue SW, Calgary, Alberta T2T 0E2.

INTERNATIONAL FARM EXPERIENCE PROGRAMME YFC Centre, National Agricultural Centre, Kenilworth, Warwickshire CV8 2LG Tel Coventry 696584 Provides assistance to young farmers and nurserymen by finding places in farms/nurseries abroad enabling them to broaden their knowledge of agricultural methods. Opportunities for practical farming, mostly dairying, in Ontario. Ages 18-26. Valid driving licence necessary. The work is hard; 10 hour day, 6 day week, every other weekend free. 6-12 months; places are found throughout the year. Wages Can$1100 monthly. Board and lodging provided, usually on the farm with the family. Applicants pay own fares and medical insurance. Registration fee £167. *UK nationals only.*

WILLING WORKERS ON ORGANIC FARMS (WWOOF) RR 2, Carlson Road, Nelson, British Columbia V1L 5P5

A non-profitmaking organisation which aims to help farmers and smallholders who need manpower to replace the use of herbicides, chemical fertilizers and heavy machinery. Provides unskilled voluntary workers with first hand experience of organic farming and gardening on approx 50 host farms throughout Canada, on homesteads on the East Coast (Nova Scotia and New Brunswick), in Ontario and the West Coast in British Columbia. The work can include weeding, milking cows, apple picking, cleaning out the stalls. Members receive a bi-monthly newsletter which details places needing help. Ages 16+. Hours vary from one farm to another. Work available all year but especially in early spring and late autumn. Full board and lodging in own room, cabin or tent provided, but volunteers should take a sleeping bag. Opportunity on some farms to learn skills. Insurance and anti-tetanus vaccination recommended. Membership fee £6.

UK applicants can apply to WWOOF, 19 Bradford Road, Lewes, Sussex BN7 1RB.

MONITORS & TEACHERS

BRITISH UNIVERSITIES NORTH AMERICA CLUB (BUNAC) 16 Bowling Green Lane, London EC1R 0BD Tel 071-251 3472

Opportunities for young people to work as counsellors on summer camps throughout Canada. The camps are permanent sites by lakes in woodland areas, and cater for 40-600 children at a time. Camps can be privately owned, or organised by the YMCA/Girl Scouts/Salvation Army, or they can be institutional camps for the physically, socially or mentally handicapped. Camp counselling involves living, working and playing with

groups of 3-8 children aged 6-16. General counsellors are responsible for the full-time supervision of their group and ensure that the children follow the routine set for them. They should be able to provide counsel and friendship and must therefore have fairly general experience and aptitude in the handling of children. Specialist counsellors must have a sporting/craft interest, qualifications or skills plus ability and enthusiasm to organise or teach specific activities. These include sports, watersports, music, arts and crafts, science, pioneering, entertainments and dance. Counsellors with secretarial skills are needed for office work. Ages 19½ (by 1 July)-35. Applicants can be any nationality, but must be resident in the UK, single, hard working as hours are long, with a genuine love of children and relevant experience. They should be able to show firm, fair leadership and be flexible, cooperative, energetic, conscientious, cheerful, patient, positive, able to adapt to new situations, and to function enthusiastically in a structured setting. 8/9+ weeks, with 1 day off most weeks, mid June-end August, followed by 1-6 weeks free for travel after the camp. Return flight, overnight hostel accommodation, transfer to camp, orientation and training plus board and lodging at the camp provided. Counsellors live with the children in log cabins or tents. Registration fee £48. Insurance fee approx £72. Salary approx US$360 (US$410 for those aged 21+). Suitable for students, teachers, nurses, social workers and those with other relevant qualifications. Interviews are held in major towns and cities throughout the UK, mid November-early May. Compulsory orientation programme held at Easter. Membership fee £3. *Early application advisable.*

Irish applicants should apply to USIT, Aston Quay, O'Connell Bridge, Dublin 2, Ireland Tel Dublin 778117.

GAP ACTIVITY PROJECTS LTD 44 Queen's Road, Reading, Berkshire RG1 4BB Tel Reading 594914

Opportunities available in schools across Canada as general assistants or teachers' aides; there are also a small number of places in business and outdoor education establishments. Successful applicants are expected to play an active role in the running of the school, particularly in sporting and cultural activities, with some supervisory duties in the evenings and at weekends. Most placements are currently in British Columbia. Applicants should be school leavers aged 18-19 who have up to a year before going on the further education. Most placements start September or early January. Board, lodging and pocket money provided. Cost £250 plus airfare and insurance costs. *Apply early September of last school year; applications close March. UK nationals only.*

PEACE CAMPS

CHRISTIAN MOVEMENT FOR PEACE
Bethnal Green United Reformed Church, Pott Street, London E2 2EF Tel 071-729 7985
An international movement open to all who share a common concern for lasting peace and justice in the world. Volunteers are required to work in international teams on summer projects aimed at offering a service in an area of need and promoting self-help within the community; promoting international understanding and the discussion of social problems; and offering young people the chance to live as a group and take these experiences into the context of daily life. Recent projects have included work as camp counsellors, activity leaders, kitchen helpers, housekeepers and maintenance workers at a cooperative centre for peace, justice and social issues, on Grindstone Island, Big Rideau Lake, Ontario. Ages 19+. Good knowledge of English essential. 6 hour day, 30-36 hour week. 3 weeks, July-September. Food, accommodation and insurance usually provided, although volunteers may have to contribute approx US$35 towards food on some camps. Participants pay their own travel costs. Registration fee approx £24.

Applications from outside the UK: please see workcamp information on page 27.

Applications from outside the UK: please see workcamp information on page 27.

When applying to any organisation it is essential to mention Working Holidays 1991 and enclose a large stamped, self-addressed envelope, or if overseas, a large addressed envelope and at least two International Reply Coupons

WORKCAMPS

FRONTIERS FOUNDATION INC Operation
Beaver, 2615 Danforth Avenue, Suite 203, Toronto, Ontario M4C 1L6
Volunteers are needed to work on practical community projects in cooperation with the native and non-native people in Northern Canada. Projects help to provide and improve adequate housing, training, and recreational facilities to developing regions. Recent projects have included constructing a fish storage cottage at Peerless Lake and a greenhouse at Wabasca in Alberta; building log houses at Fort Good Hope in the Northwest Territories; constructing frame houses at Big Trout Lake and a log ceremonial building for pow-wows at Rat Portage in Ontario; and landscaping at Moricetown in British Columbia. Volunteers with construction skills or previous voluntary service experience preferred for many projects. Ages 18-81. All year round or 2 months, July-August, including time for orientation and follow-up sessions. Salary not provided, though volunteers may be paid a modest living allowance after 2 months, depending on the length of extension. Accommodation, living and local travel expenses provided. Travel paid by volunteers. Long-term projects of up to 18 months also available.

INTERNATIONAL VOLUNTARY SERVICE
162 Upper New Walk, Leicester LE1 7QA Tel Leicester 549430

UNITED NATIONS ASSOCIATION
International Youth Service, Welsh Centre for International Affairs, Temple of Peace, Cathays Park, Cardiff CF1 3AP Tel Cardiff 223088

Apply to either of the above to work on manual, social and work/study camps. Recent projects have included excavating prehistoric Indian archaeological sites at Kenora in the Winnipeg river basin; preparing for international conferences on disarmament and conservation in Ottawa; building a garden for the blind and helping at a summer camp for mentally handicapped children in British Columbia; building an ocean adventure park for disabled children at Victoria; and helping handicapped visitors with activities at a holiday centre on Lake Joseph. Topics for discussion included the care of the handicapped in Canada. Ages 18+. 2-4 weeks, May-September. Opportunities for hiking, swimming, biking and canoeing. Food, accommodation in tents or cabins, and insurance provided, but not travel. **B D**

Organised by the Canadian Bureau for International Education, 85 Albert Street, 14th floor, Ottawa, Ontario K1P 6A4.

Applications from outside the UK: please see workcamp information on page 27.

GENERAL

BRITISH UNIVERSITIES NORTH AMERICA CLUB (BUNAC) 16 Bowling Green Lane, London EC1R 0BD Tel 071-251 3472
Aims to encourage interest and understanding between students in Britain and North America, a non-profit, non-political educational student club which has enabled many thousands of students to enjoy self-financing working vacations in North America. As well as arranging employment on children's summer camps through the BUNACAMP programme, BUNAC can also assist with an unlimited variety of jobs through their Work Canada programme organised in cooperation with the Canadian Federation of Students. The job does not have to be organised in advance, and participants are able to change jobs once in Canada, if necessary. Those who wish to organise jobs before arrival in Canada will be offered advice on how to do so, and may use BUNAC's own job directory. There are also places outside the summer season, for secondary students in their year between. The summer programme involves a compulsory orientation in Britain, return transatlantic flight, one night's accommodation followed by an orientation in Canada, work authorisation papers, a guidebook, and the services of BUNAC and CFS in North America. In order to obtain a visa, applicants must have evidence of student status, an orientation course certificate and proof of round-trip transportation. They must also provide evidence that they can support themselves whilst in Canada in either of the following three ways: definite evidence of a job, plus

proof that they are taking at least Can$500 with them; definite evidence of sponsorship, plus proof that they are taking at least Can$500 with them; or proof that they are taking at least Can$1000 with them and can thus support themselves with their own funds until they get a job. Ages 18-29. Applicants must be full British passport holders and must be returning at the end of the programme to continue their studies. 8/9+ weeks-6 months. Registration fee £49, return flight (1990) £345-£470, and insurance fee £72. A medical in Britain is necessary, to be conducted by a doctor designated by the Canadian High Commission; cost approx £65. Membership fee £3. *Apply from October/November; closing date mid-April. Job directory available from January.*

When writing to any organisation it is essential to mention Working Holidays 1991 and enclose a large stamped, self-addressed envelope, or if overseas, a large addressed envelope and at least two International Reply Coupons.

NOTES

CZECHOSLOVAKIA

Czechoslovak Embassy
25 Kensington Palace Gardens, London W8
4QY Tel 071-229 1255
Visa section: 28 Kensington Palace Gardens,
London W8 4QY Tel 071-727 3966

British Embassy
Thunovská 14, 11800 Prague 1

Tourist office
Cedok, 17-18 Old Bond Street, London W1X
3DA Tel 071-629 6058

Youth & student information
Czechoslovak Youth and Students Travel
Bureau (CKM), Zitna ulice 12, 12105 Prague 2

INFORMATION

Entry regulations Workcamp organisations will inform volunteers how to obtain the necessary visa/permit and hold orientation days giving information on all aspects of the work covered together with some political background and practical information. Visitors whose stay has not been prepaid will be asked to exchange the equivalent of DM30 per day of visit upon arrival at the Czechoslovak border.

Travel Campus Travel, 52 Grosvenor Gardens, London SW1W 0AG Tel 071-730 3402 offer Eurotrain under 26 fares and youth and student airfares to destinations in Czechoslovakia.

STA Travel, 86 Old Brompton Road, London SW7 3LQ Tel 071-937 9921 operates flexible, low-cost flights to Prague.

WORKCAMPS

CHRISTIAN MOVEMENT FOR PEACE Bethnal Green United Reformed Church, Pott Street, London E2 0EF Tel 071-729 1877

CONCORDIA (Youth Service Volunteers) Ltd, Recruitment Secretary, 8 Brunswick Place, Hove, Sussex BN3 1ET Tel Brighton 772086

INTERNATIONAL VOLUNTARY SERVICE 162 Upper New Walk, Leicester LE1 7QA Tel Leicester 549430

UNITED NATIONS ASSOCIATION International Youth Service, Welsh Centre for International Affairs, Temple of Peace, Cathays Park, Cardiff CF1 3AP Tel Cardiff 223088

Apply to one of the above to participate on a choice of approx 30 workcamps concerned with conservation, construction and agricultural work. Recent projects have included environmental protection work in forests and mountains, historic gardens and castles;

helping at the zoo; archaeological work; agricultural work on cooperative farms; and building and repair work at youth hostels, sports centres, camps, monasteries, old people's homes and cooperatives. Also work/study/peace camps. Lectures and discussions held on related topics. Excursions, lectures and discussions linked to projects, meetings with youth groups and visits to local families arranged. Ages 19-35. Previous workcamp experience or similar voluntary work experience essential. 40 hour, 5 day week. 2-3 weeks, July-September. Full board and simple lodging provided, but not pocket money. Tetanus injection required. Volunteers pay their own travel. Compulsory orientation meeting for participants applying through IVS. Working language usually English. *Limited places; apply before end May.* B D

Organised by Czechoslovak International Workcamps, CKM, Zitna ulice 12, 12105 Prague

Applications from outside the UK: please see workcamp information on page 27.

DENMARK

Royal Danish Embassy
55 Sloane Street, London SW1X 9SR
Tel 071-333 0200

British Embassy
Kastelsvej 38/40, 2100 Copenhagen Ø

Tourist office
Danish Tourist Board, Sceptre House, 169/173
Regent Street, London W1R 8PY Tel 071-734 2637

Youth hostels
Landsforeningen Danmarks Vandrerhjem,
Vesterbrogade 39, 1620 Copenhagen V

Youth & student information
Danmarks Internationale Studenterkomite,
Skindergade 36, 1159 Copenhagen K

Informationskontoret/Huset, Vester Alle 15,
8000 Arhus C

INFORMATION

Entry regulations A UK citizen intending to work in Denmark should have a full passport. EC nationals may stay for up to 3 months in order to seek employment. If employment is obtained within this period, the residence permit will be granted automatically. To qualify for a residence permit the job must fulfil certain conditions such as working hours, salary and membership of an employment fund. Once a job has been found it is necessary to obtain a personal registration number and social security certificate within 5 days by taking personal identification and a statement from the employer to the nearest Folkeregisteret. This entitles the employee to use the national health service.
There are no Danish offices operating exclusively as labour exchanges for foreigners; it is practically impossible to get a job without some knowledge of Danish, unless the work is in a restaurant or hotel where English is usually required. Permission to stay for more than 3 months must be obtained from the Department for Supervision of Aliens; for EC citizens this is a formality if they have a job.

Job advertising Frank L Crane (London) Ltd, International Press Representatives, 5/15 Cromer Street, Grays Inn Road, London WC1H 8LS Tel 071-837 3330 can place job advertisements in *Politiken*, *Jyllands-Posten* and *Ekstrabladet*, all leading Danish newspapers.

Travel The Nordic Tourist Ticket entitles the holder to unlimited travel on trains in

Denmark, Finland, Norway and Sweden, and is also valid on some inter-Scandinavian ferries. Valid for 21 days, cost £101 for ages under 26, and £135 for ages over 26. Available from Norwegian State Railways, 21-24 Cockspur Street, London SW1Y 5DA Tel 071-930 6666.

Campus Travel, 52 Grosvenor Gardens, London SW1W 0AG Tel 071-730 3402 offer Eurotrain under 26 fares and youth and student airfares to destinations in Denmark.

Map and General Travel Information leaflet provides information on travel, customs and entry formalities, residence and employment, the health service and other practical information.
Greenland brochure provides brief information on routes to Greenland, domestic transport, accommodation, mountain hiking, boat hire, dog sledges, excursions, entry formalities, health services and other useful facts for visitors.
The Faroe Islands booklet provides information including details on accommodation, food and drink, transport and activities, plus facts on the Faroes and practical information. All available from the Danish Tourist Board, see above.

The Rough Guide to Scandinavia £7.95 is a practical handbook which includes concise, up-to-date information on getting around Denmark and the Faroe Islands. Published by Harrap Columbus, Chelsea House, 26 Market Square, Bromley, Kent BR1 1NA.

DENMARK

AU PAIR/CHILDCARE

Information centres The Use-It Youth Information Centre Copenhagen, Radhusstraede 13, 1466 Copenhagen K issue an information pack including *Working in Denmark*, a leaflet outlining seeking and finding employment. Also produce *Playtime*, a newspaper intended as an alternative guide to Copenhagen for low-budget visitors, with advice on travel, food and accommodation, cultural attractions, practical information and a list of alternative organisations. Also provide poste restante and travel help/hitch hiking link services, plus free locker facilities.

Dick Phillips, Whitehall House, Nenthead, Alston, Cumbria CA9 3PS Tel Alston 381440 can provide information and various publications on the Faroe Islands covering historical background, physical environment and Faroese life, and stocks a selection of maps.

Guide for Young Visitors to Denmark is a booklet published by Denmark's Information Centre for International Study and Exchange (ICU), and deals not only with documents and procedures, travel, mail, money, accommodation, social services, leisure, language and people but also with study and work in Denmark. Available from the Central Bureau, Seymour Mews House, Seymour Mews, London W1H 9PE, price £3.20.

Accommodation The Danish Tourist Board, see above, publish *Camping*, a list of 500 officially approved camping sites. Free brochure also available on youth hostels in Denmark and the Faroe Islands.

Bellahoj Camping, Hvidkildevej, 2400 Copenhagen NV is a campsite 5 km from Copenhagen, open 1 June-1 September, cost DKr29 per night. A camping pass is required on all campsites in Copenhagen, obtainable from campsite wardens, price DKr21 and valid all year.

The Use-It Youth Information Centre Copenhagen, see above, publish *Where to Sleep, Eat and Relax* a leaflet listing accommodation in Copenhagen, including youth hostels, sleep-ins, cheap hotels, camping sites and pensions. Also *Housing in Copenhagen* giving information on private rooms for rent, flats, bedsits, student halls and communes.

Copenhagen Sleep-In, Per Henrik Lings Alle 6, 2100 Copenhagen Ø, is a hostel with 452 beds in 4-bedded rooms. Free hot showers. Open 19 June-28 August. Cost DKr60 per night, bed and breakfast; take your own sleeping bag.

A hostel within walking distance from Central Station is Vesterbro Ungdomsgard, Absalonsgade 8, 1658 Copenhagen V, with 160 beds; cost DKr90 per night, bed and breakfast. Open 5 May-end August.

AU PAIR/ CHILDCARE

ANGLIA AGENCY 15 Eastern Avenue, Southend-on-Sea, Essex Tel Southend 613888 Au pair, mother's helps and nanny positions arranged throughout the year. Long and short-term placements available, including summer vacation period. Hours and salaries vary; au pairs work 30 hours per week plus babysitting, with 1 free day per week, and receive £25+ per week pocket money. Board and lodging provided. Ages 17+. Travel costs paid by the applicant. Service charge £40.

AVALON AGENCY Thursley House, 53 Station Road, Shalford, Guildford, Surrey GU4 8HA Tel Guildford 63640 Positions available for au pairs, mother's helps and nannies. Mother's helps undertake general light housework, care of children, laundry and ironing, assisting in the kitchen and babysitting. Nannies take care of children, particularly very young ones, children's meals and clothes, with some babysitting and light housework. Board and lodging provided, with opportunity to attend language classes. 25-30 hour week, 4-12 months. Ages 18-30. Basic knowledge of Danish needed. Pocket money £28-£35 per week. Travel paid by applicant; insurance provided. Service charge £40 if placement accepted.

INTERLINGUA CENTRE Torquay Road, Foxrock, Dublin 18, Ireland Tel Dublin 893876 Can place au pairs in Danish families. 30 hour week with one full day and some evenings off. Time to attend language classes 2-3 mornings or afternoons per week. 6+ months. Ages 18+. Experience desirable but not essential. £25-£40 pocket money per week, full board, lodging and insurance provided. Travel paid by applicants. Placement fee £55.

UNIVERSAL CARE Chester House, 9 Windsor End, Beaconsfield, Buckinghamshire HP9 2JJ Tel Beaconsfield 678811
Can place au pairs/mother's helps in Danish families. 6-12 months. Girls normally work a 40 hour week, with weekends and most evenings free. Evening classes available in most cities. Opportunities for winter sports, sailing and a good social life. Ages 17-27. Knowledge of Danish and previous experience in a family useful. Board and lodging provided. Salaries vary, but are normally £25 per week, higher for those with experience. Travel paid by the applicant. Service charge £46. Apply 2 months before work period desired.

CONSERVATION

CHRISTIAN MOVEMENT FOR PEACE Bethnal Green United Reformed Church, Pott Street, London E2 0EF Tel 071-729 1877

INTERNATIONAL VOLUNTARY SERVICE 162 Upper New Walk, Leicester LE1 7QA Tel Leicester 549430

UNITED NATIONS ASSOCIATION International Youth Service, Welsh Centre for International Affairs, Temple of Peace, Cathays Park, Cardiff CF1 3AP Tel Cardiff 223088

Apply to one of the above for conservation work on international workcamps. Recent projects have included excavating an Iron Age village in Jutland; organic farming at a self-sufficient community near Frederikssund; restoring agricultural equipment for an open air museum in Glamsbjerg; constructing a biological garden for pupils at a school in Hadsten; environmental protection on the island of Bornholm and on the Faroe Islands; and constructing ornithology observation posts at Copenhagen. Also study camps on the environment. Ages 18+. 30-40 hour week. 2-3 weeks, June/August. Board and lodging in community houses, Scout huts, farms, youth

centres or schools and insurance provided. Mentally or physically handicapped volunteers welcome on most camps; places also available for families. **B D PH**

Organised by Mellemfolkeligt Samvirke (Danish Association for International Cooperation) Borgergade 10-14, 1300 Copenhagen K.

Applications from outside the UK: please see workcamp information on page 27.

FARMWORK

INTERNATIONAL FARM EXPERIENCE PROGRAMME YFC Centre, National Agricultural Centre, Kenilworth, Warwickshire CV8 2LG Tel Coventry 696584
Provides assistance to young farmers and nurserymen by finding places in farms/nurseries abroad enabling them to broaden their knowledge of agricultural methods. Opportunities for practical agricultural work, usually on mixed farms throughout Denmark. Applicants live and work with a farmer and his family and the work is matched as far as possible with the applicant's requirements. Physically hard work, 3-12 months. Positions available throughout the year, with the exception of the winter months. Wages approx £30; board and lodging provided. Applicants pay own fares. Also opportunities to take part in practical training schemes involving living and working on a farm for 3 months, starting June. 4 month practical training scheme also exists, preceded by a 5 week French/German language course in France, starting February or June. Wages £30 on farm, pocket money on the course; board and lodging provided. Some travel costs paid. Ages 18-26. Applicants must have at least 2 years practical experience, 1 year of which may be at agricultural college, and intend to make a career in agriculture. Valid driving licence necessary. Registration fee £62. *Apply at least 3 months in advance; British applicants only.*

ORBAEKGARD FRUGTPLANTAGE Odensevej 28, 5853 Orbaek Tel 65 33 12 57
Fruit pickers are needed to pick strawberries, 3-4 weeks, June/July. 06.00-13.00, Monday-Saturday. Piece-work rates paid. Ages 19+.

DENMARK

Pickers should take their own food and camping equipment; insurance and travel not provided. *EC nationals only.*

VI HJAELPER HINANDEN Inga Nielsen, Asenvej 35, 9881 Bindslev Tel 98 938607
A non-profitmaking organisation which aims to help farmers and smallholders who need manpower to replace the use of herbicides, chemical fertilisers and heavy machinery. Provides unskilled voluntary workers with first hand experience of organic farming and gardening, and a chance to spend some time in the country. Places exist on organic farms, smallholdings and gardens throughout Denmark. Members receive a bi-monthly newsletter which details places needing help on specific projects, and also lists job opportunities in the organic movement. Ages 16+. 25 hours per week. Full board and lodging provided in the farmhouse or outbuildings; volunteers should take a sleeping bag. No wages paid, and helpers must pay their own travel costs. Insurance and anti-tetanus vaccination recommended. Membership £6.

WORKCAMPS

CHRISTIAN MOVEMENT FOR PEACE Bethnal Green United Reformed Church, Pott Street, London E2 0EF Tel 071-729 1877

INTERNATIONAL VOLUNTARY SERVICE 162 Upper New Walk, Leicester LE1 7QA Tel Leicester 549430

UNITED NATIONS ASSOCIATION International Youth Service, Welsh Centre for International Affairs, Temple of Peace, Cathays Park, Cardiff CF1 3AP Tel Cardiff 223088

Apply to one of the above for social service and manual work on international workcamps. Provides the possibility to come into contact with the social problems found in every society and to help volunteers become more actively involved in the creation of a more just society. Recent projects have included preparing a big music festival in Skandeborg; producing a video on culture, tourism and trade; restoring and converting a disused tile works into a working museum in Jutland; and constructing

farmhouses from the Viking era in Odeuse. Also work/study and Nicaragua solidarity camps. Projects on the Faroe Islands included building an adventure playground and cleaning up beaches. Projects in Greenland have included helping the local people to build houses and plant indigenous vegetation. Ages 18+. 30-40 hour week. 2-3 weeks, July-September. Board and lodging in schools, youth centres, community houses, Scout huts or inns and insurance provided. Mentally or physically handicapped volunteers welcome on most camps, but camps on the Faroes and Greenland cannot take wheelchairs; places also available for families. **B D PH**

Organised by Mellemfolkeligt Samvirke (Danish Association for International Cooperation) Borgergade 10-14, 1300 Copenhagen K.

Applications from outside the UK: please see workcamp information on page 27.

U-LANDSFORENINGEN SVALERNE Osterbrogade 49, 2100 Copenhagen Ø
Volunteers are needed to join a 3 week Danish summer workcamp organised by the Swallows, an independent Third World organisation linked to Emmaus, which raises proceeds by recycling used items. The work involves collecting, sorting and selling paper, books, clothes, furniture and household items. Proceeds are directed to grassroots programmes in Bangladesh and India. Volunteers should be committed to sharing community life and solidarity. Ages 15+. Children welcome if accompanied by an adult. 8 hour day, 6 day week. Minimum 1 week, July. Board, accommodation and accident insurance provided, but volunteers pay their own travel costs and should take a sleeping bag and work clothes. **PH**

When writing to any organisation it is essential to mention Working Holidays 1991 and enclose a large stamped, self-addressed envelope, or if overseas, a large addressed envelope and at least two International Reply Coupons.

FINLAND

Finnish Embassy
38 Chesham Place, London SW1X 8HW
Tel 071-235 9531

British Embassy
Uudenmaankatu 16-20, 00120 Helsinki 12

Tourist office
Finnish Tourist Board, 66/68 Haymarket,
London SW1Y 4RF Tel 071-839 4048

Youth hostels
Suomen Retkeilymajajarjesto ry, Yrjonkatu 38B,
00100 Helsinki 10

Youth & student information
Travela-FSTS, Mannerheimintie 5C, 00100
Helsinki 10

Hotel Booking, Central Station, Asema-Aukio
3, Helsinki

INFORMATION

Entry regulations A work permit and a permit of residence are required for all kinds of employment, except for nationals of Denmark, Iceland, Norway and Sweden. Applications for a permit may not be made until an offer of work has been received and the prospective employer has provided a certificate giving details of salary, type and duration of work, plus personal information and a letter of recommendation. Once this has been received, a Labour Permit Application form, available from the Finnish Embassy, should be completed and returned, together with the certificate. These will be sent to the Office of Alien Affairs of the Finnish Ministry of the Interior in Helsinki who will consult the Ministry of Labour and reject or accept the application accordingly; this takes about 4 weeks. The applicants will then be notified of the decision by the Embassy. A work permit is only valid for the specific job for which it has been issued. It is usually granted for 3 months, after which it may or may not be extended. It is strongly emphasised that anyone intending to work in Finland should not enter the country before the necessary formalities have been completed. Foreign nationals may not apply for a permit whilst on holiday in Finland.

Job advertising Frank L Crane (London) Ltd, International Press Representatives, 5/15 Cromer Street, Grays Inn Road, London WC1H 8LS Tel 071-837 3330 are agents for *Helsingin Sanomat*, the leading newspaper in Finland, for which they can accept job advertisements.

Travel The Finnrailpass entitles the holder to unlimited travel on Finnish State Railways, cost from £56, 8 days. Available from Finlandia Travel, 223 Regent Street, London W1R 7DB Tel 071-409 7334.

The Nordic Tourist Ticket entitles the holder to unlimited travel on trains in Finland, Denmark, Norway and Sweden, and is also valid on some inter-Scandinavian ferries. Valid for 21 days, cost £101 for ages under 26 and £135 for ages over 26. Available from Norwegian State Railways, 21-24 Cockspur Street, London SW1Y 5DA Tel 071-930 6666.

Campus Travel, 52 Grosvenor Gardens, London SW1W 0AG Tel 071-730 3402 offer Eurotrain under 26 fares and youth and student airfares to destinations in Finland.

Finland Facts and Map covers travel to and within Finland, accommodation, customs and other useful information. Available from the Finnish Tourist Board, see above.

The Rough Guide to Scandinavia £7.95 is a practical handbook which includes concise, up-to-date information on getting around Finland. Published by Harrap Columbus, Chelsea House, 26 Market Square, Bromley, Kent BR1 1NA

Accommodation The Finnish Tourist Board, see above, publish *Camping and Youth Hostels* listing campsites and youth hostels with their

FINLAND

facilities and a map, and also *Hotels* which includes a section on hostels.

COMMUNITY WORK

COMMUNITY WORK

MONASTERY OF VALAMO
79850 Uusi - Valamo
Volunteers are invited on ecumenical and international workcamps at this ancient Eastern Orthodox religious community, whose history dates back to the 12th century. A popular pilgrimage site, it also serves as a meeting place for Christians of differing traditions and nationalities. Work involves helping in the monastery kitchen and garden, collecting brushwood, mushrooms and berries in the forest, and other common domestic tasks which community living involves. Camp languages are English and German. There is ample time for relaxation, traditional recreations such as sauna, and daily worship. Opportunities for talks and discussions on relevant topics, and excursions. Ages 18+. 34 hour week. 2 weeks, July and August; also opportunities throughout the year. Full board and hostel accommodation provided, but no pocket money or travel. Insurance provided for long-term workers. In free time volunteers may participate in courses or lectures at the Valamo Lay Academy. *All nationalities welcome.*

CONSERVATION

CONSERVATION

INTERNATIONAL VOLUNTARY SERVICE
162 Upper New Walk, Leicester LE1 7QA
Tel Leicester 549430
IVS is the British branch of Service Civil International which promotes international reconciliation through conservation workcamps. Recent projects have included helping village farmers collect hay and winter foodstuffs for reindeer feed at Rovaniemi; refitting an old Finnish schooner at Pori on the Eastern coast of the Gulf of Finland; organic gardening, harvesting and beekeeping in Juva; and renovation and repair work at a college researching into alternative lifestyles, in Harviala. Ages 18+. 35-40 hour week. 2-4

weeks, June-September. Board, lodging and insurance provided. Volunteers must be prepared to work hard and contribute to team life. Mentally or physically handicapped volunteers welcome on most camps; places also available for families. Membership fee £25 (students £15, unwaged £10). Registration fee £40. **B D PH**

Organised by Kansainvälinen Vapaaehtoinen Tyoleirijärjestory (KVT), Rauhanasema, Veturitori, 00520 Helsinki 52.

Applications from outside the UK: please see
workcamp information on page 27.

DOMESTIC

FINNISH FAMILY PROGRAMME Ministry of Labour, Fabianinkatu 32, PO Box 30, 00100 Helsinki 10
Offers native speakers of English, French or German an opportunity to get acquainted with the Finnish way of life, living as a member of a family. An essential part of the programme is for applicants to teach their mother tongue to the family. Applicants are treated as family members and not as employees. Host families include both farming and urban or suburban families who may move into the country for the summer. As well as language tuition, applicants are also expected to help with household chores and/or childcare. On farms the work also involves helping with haymaking, milking, gardening and fruit picking. Approx 25 hour, 5 day week. Board and lodging provided plus pocket money. Ages 18-23. 1-12 months, mostly June-August. *Applications for summer positions should be in Ministry of Labour by 31 March; for other positions at least 3 months in advance.*

UK applications to the Central Bureau, Vocational and Technical Education Department, Seymour Mews House, Seymour Mews, London W1H 9PE Tel 071-486 5101.

When writing to any organisation it is essential to mention Working Holidays 1991 and enclose a large stamped, self-addressed envelope, or if overseas, a large addressed envelope and at least two International Reply Coupons.

FARMWORK

INTERNATIONAL FARM EXPERIENCE PROGRAMME YFC Centre, National Agricultural Centre, Kenilworth, Warwickshire CV8 2LG Tel Coventry 696584
Provides assistance to young farmers and nurserymen by finding places in farms/ nurseries abroad, enabling them to broaden their knowledge of agricultural methods. Opportunities for practical horticultural or agricultural work, usually on mixed farms. Applicants live and work with a farmer and his family and the work is matched as far as possible with the applicant's requirements. 8 hour day, 5 day week. 2-12 months. Positions are mostly available in spring and summer. Wages approx £55 per week; board and lodging provided. Ages 18-30. Some practical experience required. Applicants pay own fare and insurance. Registration fee £62. *Apply at least 3 months in advance; British applicants only.*

Finnish applicants requiring an exchange should apply to International Trainee Exchanges, Ministry of Labour, Fabianinkatu 32, PO Box 30, 00101 Helsinki 10.

WORKCAMPS

INTERNATIONAL VOLUNTARY SERVICE 162 Upper New Walk, Leicester LE1 7QA Tel Leicester 549430
IVS is the British branch of Service Civil International which promotes international reconciliation through work projects. Volunteers are needed to work in international teams on workcamps organised by KVT, the Finnish branch of SCI. Aims to make people realise their responsibility and to work for constructive changes in the unjust areas of society. Projects are of a combined manual and social nature, with the aim of supporting communities either in remote depressed areas of Finland or those practising alternative methods of treating handicapped or underprivileged people.
Recent projects have included rigging sails and repairing a Third World exporter's trading ship at Turku; renovating an old reindeer farm in Lapland for conversion into a centre for young people; farming and gardening work at a home for the disabled and able-bodied in Jyväskylä; converting an old farmhouse in Aijala into a home for disabled persons; building small pottery and blacksmith workshops in Kaustinen, an alternative centre for arts and crafts; and repairing tools, bikes and farm machinery to send to Tanzania. Most of the camps have a study element, which involves the discussion of questions and folk traditions relevant to the community and work for peace. The main language of the camps is English. Ages 18+. Applicants should have previous workcamp experience, and should be prepared to work hard and contribute to team life. 35-40 hour week. 2-4 weeks, June-September. Food, accommodation in schools, barns, tents or log cabins and work accident insurance provided. Participants pay their own travel costs. Membership fee £25 (students £15, unwaged £10). Registration fee £40. B D PH

Organised by Kansainvälinen Vapaaehtoinen Toleirijärjestory (KVT), Rauhanasema, Veturitori, 00520 Helsinki 52.

Applications from outside the UK: please see workcamp information on page 27.

NOTES

FRANCE

French Embassy
58 Knightsbridge, London SW1X 7JT
Tel 071-235 8080
Consular Section: 21 Cromwell Road, London
SW7 2EW Tel 071-581 5292

British Embassy
35 rue de Faubourg St Honoré, 75008 Paris
Cedex 08

Tourist office
French Government Tourist Office, 178
Piccadilly, London W1V 0AL Tel 071-491 7622

Youth hostels
Fédération Unie des Auberges de Jeunesse,
6 rue Mesnil, 75016 Paris

Ligue Française pour les Auberges de la
Jeunesse, 38 boulevard Raspail, 75007 Paris

Youth & student information
Accueil des Jeunes en France, 12 rue des Barres,
75004 Paris *(for correspondence)* or 16 rue du
Pont Philippe/119 rue Saint-Martin, 75004
Paris *(for personal callers)*

Centre d'Information et de Documentation
Jeunesse (CIDJ), 101 quai Branly, 75740 Paris
Cedex 15

Organisation pour le Tourisme Universitaire,
137 boulevard St Michel, 75005 Paris

INFORMATION

Entry regulations UK citizens intending to
work in France should have full passports. EC
nationals may stay for up to 3 months to find a
job; once a job has been found, a residence
permit, *carte de séjour de ressortissant d'un état
membre de la CEE,* must be applied for.
Application forms are available from the
Prefecture de Police in Paris, or from the local
police station or town hall elsewhere. The
permit is valid for the period of employment if
this is less than 12 months. Those under 18
should have written parental consent and are
not allowed to work in bars. Details of
particular regulations applying to au pair
posts and seasonal agricultural work are given
under the relevant headings. Non-EC nationals
are not allowed to take up any form of
employment in France unless they have been
granted a permit before arrival. Several
agreements exist between France and some
African and South East Asian countries, Poland
and Lebanon, and nationals of these countries
are allowed to work in specific cases. Those
studying in France can work after their first
year. EC nationals living in Britain who intend
to work in France for more than 6 months can
apply for a job through a local Jobcentre or
employment office of the Training Agency, who

will forward all relevant applications to the
French employment service, Agence Nationale
pour l'Emploi (ANPE). Alternatively, they can
register at a local branch of the ANPE on
arrival in France. CIDJ, see below, publishes a
list, *ANPEs à Paris et en Région Parisienne.*
Addresses of ANPEs in the principal
agricultural and wine producing areas are
given under the **Farmwork/grape picking**
heading, below. The French Embassy issues a
leaflet *Employment in France of British nationals
and nationals of other EC countries,* available
from the Visa Section, PO Box 57, 6A Cromwell
Place, London SW7 2EW. A list of ANPEs and
notes about au pair posts and grape picking are
available from the Social Service at the
Consular Section of the French Embassy, see
above.

Job advertising The French Publishing Group,
21-23 Elizabeth Street, London SW1W 9RW Tel
071-730 3477 can place advertisements in most
French newspapers and magazines.

Travel Rent-a-bike scheme available at 280
stations, bookable in advance; FF300 deposit,
cost FF37 per day, decreasing as the number of
rental days increases. Two youth cards

FRANCE

available to ages 12-25, and sold in France only, are: Carre Jeune, offering 4 single or 2 return journeys at up to 50%; valid for 1 year; Carte Jeune, offering up to 50% reduction, June-September. Holiday Return (Séjour) Ticket concession of 25% if the journey covers more than 1000km, and if the holder includes a Sunday (or fraction of a Sunday) in the stay. Valid 2 months. France Vacances Pass gives unlimited travel on 4 days during a period of 15 or on any 9 days during a period of 1 month, all year, plus, among other concessions, a £14 cross-Channel fare by Hoverspeed. Cost £75/£127. Details of all from SNCF French Railways Ltd, French Railways House, 179 Piccadilly, London W1V 0BA. *Write for an information pack.*

Campus Travel, 52 Grosvenor Gardens, London SW1W 0AG Tel 071-730 3402 offer flexible youth and student charter flights to Lyon, Nice, Paris, Toulouse and other destinations, from £19 single, Paris. Also Eurotrain under 26 fares, including Eurotrain Tour de France Explorer, giving 9/15 days travel in a period of 1 month.

INFORMATION

Information centres Accueil des Jeunes en France, 12 rue des Barres, 75004 Paris is a general information and advisory service for young travellers. Can provide vouchers for low-cost restaurants and arrange cheap accommodation, see below, and also supply cheap rail and coach tickets.

Centre d'Information et de Documentation Jeunesse (CIDJ), 101 quai Branly, 75740 Paris Cedex 15 provides a comprehensive information service for young people, with branches throughout France. Practical help can be provided in finding work. Information is also available on accommodation, social, cultural, artistic, scientific and sports facilities, activities and holidays plus practical information on staying, travelling and studying in France and facilities for the disabled. Services include free legal aid and consumer protection. The centre also acts as the local branch of the ANPE and career advice/social security office. Publish a wide range of booklets and information sheets including *Recherche d'un Emploi Temporaire ou Occasionel; Séjour et Emploi des Etudiants Etrangers en France; Entrée, Séjour et Emploi des Etrangers en France; Réductions de Transports pour les Jeunes* and *Restaurants Bon Marché à Paris.* PH

Publications *Emplois d'Eté en France 1991* lists thousands of vacancies including waiting and bar staff, au pairs, sports instructors, receptionists, work in factories, shops, language schools and offices and on farms and children's summer camps. Also includes special information for foreign students, with details of authorisation to work in France. Published by Vac-job, 4 rue d'Alesia, 75014 Paris. Distributed in the UK by Vacation Work, 9 Park End Street, Oxford OX1 1HJ Tel Oxford 241978, price £6.95.

Hello France! is a booklet intended for young foreigners visiting France. It covers what to do before you leave, travel, money, food, postal services, accommodation, tourism and leisure; and also provides information on study and work in France. Published by the Centre d'Information et de Documentation Jeunesse (CIDJ), see above, and available from the Central Bureau, Seymour Mews House, Seymour Mews, London W1H 9PE, price £3.20 including UK postage.

1000 Pistes de Jobs FF89 including postage, is a comprehensive guide giving 1000 ideas and different ways of finding a holiday job, with practical advice and useful addresses. Although the book is primarily a guide for young French people, it is an invaluable source of reference for anyone wanting to work in France, providing they speak fluent French. Available from L'Etudiant, 27 rue du Chemin Vert, 75011 Paris.

Rough Guide to France £6.95 and *Rough Guide to Paris* £4.95 are practical handbooks providing first-hand information on travel, budget accommodation and things to see; everything the visitor needs to know about France and the French capital. Published by Harrap Columbus, Chelsea House, 26 Market Square, Bromley, Kent BR1 1NA.

Accommodation Accueil des Jeunes en France, 12 rue des Barres, 75004 Paris is a central booking office for youth accommodation with access to 11,000 beds in the summer. Has 4 offices which guarantee to find any young traveller decent, cheap accommodation in Paris, with immediate reservation. Cost approx FF80 per night. Contact AJF Beaubourg, 119 rue St-Martin, 75004 Paris; AJF Hotel de Ville,

16 rue du Pont Louis-Philippe, 75004 Paris; AJF Quartier Latin, 139 boulevard Saint-Michel, 75005 Paris; and AJF Gare du Nord, 75010 Paris.

Bureau des Voyages de la Jeunesse, 20 rue JJ Rousseau, 75001 Paris has 4 youth accommodation centres in Paris at Les Halles, Opera, Latin Quarter and Louvre. Cost FF80 bed and breakfast, FF130 half board, FF180 full board, per night, 1-8 bedded rooms.

Centre d'Information et de Documentation Jeunesse (CIDJ), 101 quai Branly, 75740 Paris Cedex 15 publish information sheets providing addresses of reasonable accommodation in youth centres, university halls and pensions, mainly in the Paris region: *Centres d'Hébergement Temporaires Paris et Région Parisienne; Hotels Bon Marché et Pensions de Famille à Paris; Logement des Jeunes Travailleurs;* and *Le Logement de L'Etudiant.*

Centre International de Séjour de Paris, 6 avenue Maurice-Ravel, 75012 Paris offers accommodation at two residential centres. Facilities include sports hall, workshops, swimming pools, library and restaurants. Cost from FF50 per night includes dormitory accommodation. Reservations should be made at least 3 months in advance.

Accommodation available for young workers at a modern residential centre where facilities include restaurant, bar, library, art, theatre and music studios/workshops and language courses. Maximum 2 weeks, all year. Cost from FF100 per night, bed only, or FF141 per night half board in 4-6 bedded rooms. Also centres at Evry and Nanterre. Reservations should be made 30 days in advance to Foyer International d'Accueil de Paris, 30 rue Cabanis, 75014 Paris. PH

Union des Centres de Rencontres Internationales de France (UCRIF), 4 rue JJ Rousseau, 75001 Paris publish a list of 63 youth accommodation centres and hostels, each providing a comprehensive tourist service in a friendly atmosphere. Facilities include swimming, riding, sports grounds, cycling, skating, skiing, sailing and language courses. PH

ARCHAEOLOGY

ASSOCIATION POUR LE DEVELOPPEMENT DE L'ARCHEOLOGIE URBAINE A CHARTRES 12 rue du Cardinal Pie, 28000 Chartres

Volunteers are needed for urban rescue excavation work on sites in Chartres. The project is a long term research programme on the archaeological and historical development of Chartres, covering its economic, cultural and social evolution from Roman to medieval times. Sites include Gallo-Roman buildings and constructions including amphitheatre, roads, houses, metal and pottery workshops, plus sites dating from the High Middle Ages. Talks/slides will be given on a variety of related subjects. July-September.

Volunteers should be prepared for hard, physical work in all weathers. Punctuality is expected. Volunteers also work in the laboratory, washing, classifying, repairing and drawing finds. Ages 18+ (occasionally 16+ with parental consent). Previous experience desirable and if possible applicants should enclose an archaeological cv. 8 hour day, 5 day week, with weekends free. 3+ weeks, preferably 4+, May-October. Food, accommodation and insurance provided, but no wages or fares paid. Volunteers should take their own sleeping bag. Registration fee FF100. *Apply 4 weeks in advance.*

CENTRE DE RECHERCHES ARCHEOLOGIQUES F Audouze, Centre National de la Recherche Scientifique, 1 place Aristide Briand, 92190 Meudon

Experienced volunteers are required for the excavation of the Upper Palaeolithic site of Verberie on the river Oise, 80 km north of Paris. The aim of the excavation is to study the everyday life of Magdalenian reindeer hunters. Work involves the digging of a living floor covered with flint tools and chips, bones and stones, plus mapping and restoring artefacts. Some knowledge of French preferred. Ages 18+. 8 hour day, 6 day week. 1 July-31 August. Food, camping accommodation and insurance provided. No fares or wages paid. Occasional visits to places of interest in the Oise area may be arranged. *Apply by end May.*

FRANCE

ARCHAEOLOGY

CERCLE ARCHEOLOGIQUE DE BRAY/ SEINE Claude & Daniel Mordant, rue du Tour de l'Eglise, Dannemoine, 89700 Tonnerre
Volunteers are required for the excavation of a late Bronze Age settlement at Grisy and Neolithic causewayed enclosures at Balloy. The aim is a study of the paleo environment in the Upper Seine Valley. Work involves excavating and cleaning pottery and bones, with lectures and visits to other sites. Volunteers should preferably have a knowledge of the periods involved. 8 hour day, 6 day week. 2-4 weeks June-September. Food and camping accommodation provided but participants should take their own tents and sleeping bags. No fares or wages offered. Registration fee FF30 includes insurance. *Apply by May/August.*

CHANTIERS D'ETUDES MEDIEVALES Centre d'Archéologie Mediévale de Strasbourg, 4 rue du Tonnelet Rouge, 67000 Strasbourg
Organise international workcamps devoted to the study, restoration and maintenance of monuments or sites dating back to the Middle Ages. Restoration and excavation work is being carried out on two 12th-14th century fortified castles in Ottrott, and restoration work on old houses in Strasbourg and the Ardèche town of Viviers. Beginners welcome. Teams of specialists in history, architecture, ceramics and archaeology accompany the participants on both restoration and excavation projects. Excavation techniques are taught and there are opportunities to study finds and draw conclusions.
Ages 16+. Those under 18 require parental consent. Applicants are accepted from all countries, and should be fit and willing to adapt to a community lifestyle. 36 hour, 6 day week. 12/15 days, July-September. Cost FF350/FF545 includes food and very basic accommodation in schools, houses, barracks, tents or hostels with self-catering facilities, plus insurance. Participants should take sleeping bags and work clothes. *Apply by May; applications may take several weeks to process.*

DEPARTMENT OF PREHISTORY & ARCHAEOLOGY Dr J Collis, The University, Sheffield, South Yorkshire S10 2TN
Volunteers are required, excavating, processing finds and surveying at the Iron Age-Roman sites near Mirefleurs, Clermont-Ferrand, in conjunction with the Service des Fouilles Historiques de l'Auvergne. A long-term project studying the impact of urbanisation on a rural settlement, 2nd century BC and 2nd century AD. Experience not necessary. 9 weeks, July-September. Campsite accommodation with communal cooking on a rota basis at nearby house. Cost approx FF30-FF40 per day. No wages or fares paid. *Apply by 31 March.*

GROUPE ARCHEOLOGIQUE DU MEMONTOIS M Louis Roussel, Directeur des Fouilles, 52 rue des Forges, 21000 Dijon
Volunteers are needed for excavation work at Malain on the Cote d'Or. The site consists of the Gallic and Roman town including roads, temples, squares, caves, houses and fields as well as a medieval castle and prehistoric earthworks. The object is to study the development of the town from its origins and explore its later development.
The camp is based on a collective life style, and volunteers share in supervising digs, discussions on finds, taking charge of exhibitions and preparing meals. Work involves documenting, classifying, washing, collecting, drawing and photographing finds, with lectures and excursions. 7 hour day, 5½ day week. 4 weeks, July-August. Camping accommodation provided; food at a cost of FF50 per week. Volunteers should preferably be experienced, and can take their own camping equipment. No wages or fares paid. *Apply by May.* PH

INSTITUT D'HISTOIRE Annie Renoux, Université de Mans, Route de Laval, 72017 Le Mans Cedex
Volunteers are required for excavation work at the site of the Château Comtal at Chavot, Epernay, Champagne. Recent work has concentrated on the 10th-13th century castle of the Count of Champagne and involves excavating, cleaning, marking and recording finds. Lectures on excavation techniques. Ages 18+. 8 hour day, 5½ day week. 15+ days, July and August. Experience not necessary. Lunch and accommodation in stone building provided, but no fares or wages paid. Volunteers should take a sleeping bag. Qualified volunteers staying more than 3 weeks may be offered full expenses. *Early application advisable.*

FRANCE

LABORATOIRE D'ANTHROPOLOGIE PREHISTORIQUE Université de Rennes I, Campus de Beaulieu, 35042 Rennes Cedex
Volunteers are required for excavations on prehistoric and protohistoric remains in Brittany. Ages 18+. 3-4 weeks, summer. Food and campsite accommodation provided but volunteers must take their own camping equipment. No fares or wages paid. *Apply in April for further details.*

MINISTERE DE LA CULTURE Circonscription des Antiquités Historiques et Préhistoriques de Bretagne, 6 rue du Chapitre, 35044 Rennes Cedex
Volunteers are needed to work on archaeological sites all over Brittany, ranging from Palaeolithic to medieval periods. Recent projects have included work on megalithic monuments and sites in Locmariaquer, St Laurent sur Ouse and Monteneuf; the excavation of a Gallic/Gallo-Roman site prior to the building of a new road near Rennes; work on Iron Age and Dark Ages sites at Locronan and Quimper; and uncovering the ancient area of shops near the site of the forum in the Gallo-Roman capital at Corseul.

Volunteers should be prepared for hard physical work. Experience useful but not essential; basic French necessary. Ages 18+. Approx 40 hour week. 1+ weeks, April-September. Board and lodging provided, varying from campsites to university halls of residence depending on the location. Cost FF50 per week plus travel to site. Participants should take a sleeping bag. Insurance provided. Anti-tetanus vaccination required. Excursions sometimes arranged. *Detailed list of sites available in March.*

MUSEE DES ANTIQUITES NATIONALES Henri Delporte, Conservateur en Chef, PO Box 30, 78103 Saint-Germain-en-Laye
Volunteers are required for the excavation of an upper Palaeolithic limestone cave site at Brassempouy in the Landes region. Tasks involve establishing precise date of female statuettes found. 15 days, July and August. Volunteers should be students of archaeology, preferably with some experience. Food and accommodation under canvas provided, but no fares or wages paid. *Apply in May/June.*

MUSEE DES SCIENCES NATURELLES ET D'ARCHEOLOGIE Service Archéologique du Musée de la Chartreuse, Pierre Demolon, Conservateur de Musée, 191 rue St-Albin, 59500 Douai
Beginners and experienced volunteers are required to help with urban rescue excavation in a quarter of Douai. The object is to trace the origins and development of the town from the 11th-16th century, concentrating on the medieval houses. Preference will be given to those sufficiently experienced to take over sections of the excavation. 7½ hour day. 2+ weeks, July-September. Knowledge of French useful. Ages 18+. Food and accommodation provided. No fares paid, but wages may be offered to specialists. Participants should take their own sleeping bag. Anti-tetanus vaccination compulsory. Registration fee FF100 covers insurance. *Apply by 15 June.*

MUSEUM NATIONAL D'HISTOIRE NATURELLE Laboratoire de Préhistoire, Institut de Paléontologie Humaine, Professeur Henry de Lumley, 1 rue René Panhard, 75013 Paris
Volunteers are required to work on various sites and grottoes in south east and south west France. Projects include investigating Acheulian and Tayacian industries, fauna, pre-Neanderthal human remains and dwelling structures at the Grotte du Lazaret in Nice and at Tautavel near Perpignan; studying and recording protohistoric rock engravings at a research centre in the Vallee des Merveilles in Tende; excavation at the Palaeolithic site of La Baume Bonne, Alpes de Haute Provence and at Les Eyzies, Dordogne. Opportunities to study finds. Specialists and amateurs welcome. Minimum stay 15 days in March/April or 1 month, June-August. Board provided at local campsites, but participants should take their own tents and equipment. No fares or wages paid.

MUSEUM D'HISTOIRE NATURELLE Jean Pierre Watte, Archéologue Municipal, Place du Vieux-Marché, 76600 Le Havre
Volunteers are required for excavation of a rare open-air Neolithic settlement site in Pays de Caux. The site is rich in stone artefacts and pottery. Work involves excavating, drawing, washing and documenting finds. Ages 16+. Minimum 15 days for beginners, July-August.

ARCHAEOLOGY

FRANCE

ARCHAEOLOGY

Apart from training on the dig, courses with slides, films and prehistoric tools are given every evening. Food and campsite provided; participants should take their own camping equipment. Anti-tetanus vaccination compulsory. No fares or wages paid.

REMPART (Union des Associations pour la Réhabilitation et l'Entretien des Monuments et du Patrimoine Artistique) 1 rue des Guillemites, 75004 Paris

Aims to improve the way of life through a better understanding of and a greater respect for the archaeological, architectural and natural heritage and environment, through the restoration of endangered buildings and monuments. It consists of a grouping of more than 140 local, departmental or regional associations, providing a wide variety of projects. Volunteers are needed for archaeological work on sites in Auvergne, Centre, Ile de France, Languedoc-Roussillon, Lorraine, Midi-Pyrénées, Normandie, Poitou-Charentes, Provence-Alpes-Cote d'Azur and Corsica. Sites include medieval towns and villages, châteaux, fortresses, abbeys and churches, prehistoric and Gallo-Roman towns, early Christian sites, amphitheatres and villas, and post-medieval fortresses and castles. Work involves excavation, cleaning and restoration. Participants are usually accompanied by experienced archaeologists and are involved in carrying out surveys, drawing plans, technical photography and learning archaeological methods and site history. Opportunities for swimming, tennis, riding, cycling, rambling, exploring the region, crafts and taking part in local festivities.

Ages 16/18+. There is no upper age limit, anyone feeling young is welcome. Some knowledge of French needed. 30-35 hour week. 2-4 weeks, Easter and June-September; a few camps are open throughout the year. Cost FF20-FF45 per day includes food and accommodation in huts, old buildings and tents, with self-catering facilities; a few camps are free. Volunteers help with camp duties, pay their own fares, and should take a sleeping bag. Applicants can choose which project they would like to work on in the workcamp programme and contact addresses are given. Registration fee FF200 includes insurance. Also arrange archaeology courses. *Enclose 3 IRCs.*

SERVICE D'ARCHEOLOGIE DU CONSEIL GENERAL DE VAUCLUSE Michel-Edouard Bellet, Archéologue Départemental, Hotel du Département, PO Box 318, 84021 Avignon Cedex

Aims to protect, research and document archaeological sites throughout Vaucluse. Volunteers are needed to participate in excavations on various sites. Recent excavations have included the prehistoric sites of Bonnieux and Courthezon, and the Gallo-Roman towns of Orange, Cavaillon and Vaison-la-Romaine. Volunteers should be prepared for hard physical work. Some experience is desirable; fluent French essential. 40 hour week, Easter and summer. Ages 18+. Accommodation, food and insurance provided; visits to other sites sometimes arranged.

SERVICE DE L'URBANISME - ARCHEOLOGIE, Gilles Blieck, Archéologue Municipal, Hotel de Ville, BP 667, 59033 Lille Cedex

Volunteers are needed to help excavate an important medieval and post-medieval site in the historic centre of Lille. 40 hour week; 1+ weeks, 1 July-31 August. Ages 17+. Experience preferred but not essential. Some knowledge of French preferred. Food, accommodation and insurance provided, but no wages or travel expenses. Excursions arranged each week to other excavations, museums or historic Flemish towns.

UNITE DE RECHERCHE ARCHEOLOGIQUE No 12, Centre National de la Recherche Scientifique, Dr Claude Constantin, 3 rue Michelet, 75006 Paris

Volunteers are needed for excavation work in the Vallée de l'Aisne. The project, organised in conjunction with the Université de Paris, involves the rescue of sites threatened by urban expansion, gravel extraction and motorway or canal construction, and the study of changes in settlement, subsistence and material culture within the valley over a 5,000 year period. Recent work has been undertaken on a number of Neolithic and early Iron Age settlement sites. Ages 18+. Archaeology students or experienced excavators preferred. 2+ weeks, late June-early September. Good food, dormitory accommodation in farm buildings or camping space and hot showers provided, but no fares or wages paid. *Apply by 15 June.*

AU PAIR/ CHILDCARE

Certain conditions apply to anyone working as an au pair in France, regardless of the organisation through which they apply. Both sexes can apply, and must be between 18 and 30. Work is for a minimum of 3 months and a maximum of 12 months, with the possibility of an extension to 18 months. As a rule, applicants should reach an agreement with the host family before leaving for France. It is then up to the host family or the organisation which arranged the placing to obtain, from the Direction Départementale du Travail et de l'Emploi (in Paris: Service de la Main-d'Oeuvre Etrangère, 80 rue de la Croix-Nivert, 75732 Paris Cedex 15), the form *Accord de placement au pair d'un stagiaire aide-familial*. This has to be signed by the family and returned together with a certificate of registration at a school in France specialising in teaching foreign students, proof of academic studies, and a current medical certificate. If the Direction Départementale are satisfied with the information supplied, they will stamp the *Accord de placement* and a copy will be sent to the applicant.

On arrival in France, an au pair from an EC country must obtain a *carte de séjour* from the local Commissariat de Police; an au pair from a non-EC country must obtain a *carte de séjour* and *autorisation provisoire de travail* from the Direction Départementale, on production of the *Accord de placement*. The host family must register the au pair with the national insurance scheme and pay quarterly contributions which cover the au pair for accidents at work, sickness and maternity. Au pairs can expect to live as a member of the family and to have sufficient free time for recreation and to attend language classes. Work involves light housework tasks including simple cooking, hand washing, cleaning, washing up, shopping, helping to prepare simple meals and care of the children for up to 5 hours a day, plus 2 nights' babysitting per week. At least 1 day per week free and this must include at least 1 Sunday per month. Pocket money FF1113.75-FF1336.50 per month.

An information sheet, *Au Pair Posts in France*, giving details of conditions and formalities governing au pair posts is available from the Visa Section of the French Embassy. *Séjour Au Pair en France (Stagiaire Aide-Familial)* is an information sheet including details of regulations and formalities for those applying to be au pairs, a list of organisations placing au pairs, plus addresses of Préfectures de Police in Paris. Also *Garde d'Enfants Temporaire et Baby-Sitting (Paris et Région Parisienne)*. Both published by the Centre d'Information et de Documentation Jeunesse (CIDJ), 101 quai Branly, 75740 Paris Cedex 15.

ANGLIA AGENCY 15 Eastern Avenue, Southend-on-Sea, Essex Tel Southend 613888
Au pair, mother's help and nanny positions arranged throughout the year. Long and short-term placements available, including summer vacation period. Hours and salaries vary; au pairs work 30 hours plus babysitting with 1 free day per week, and receive £25+ per week pocket money. Board and lodging provided. Ages 17+. Travel costs paid by the applicant. Service charge £40.

AVALON AGENCY Thursley House, 53 Station Road, Shalford, Guildford, Surrey GU4 8HA Tel Guildford 63640
Can place au pairs. Food, lodging and pocket money provided, with opportunities to attend language classes. 25-30 hour week. Most positions are for 6-12 months; limited vacancies for 2 months in summer. Ages 18-30. Basic knowledge of French needed. Pocket money per month, FF750 (2 month positions), FF900 (6+ months). Insurance provided. Positions also available for mother's helps and nannies. Service charge £40, if placement is accepted.

HOME FROM HOME 10 Tackley Place, Oxford, Oxfordshire OX2 6RR Tel Oxford 512628
Au pair positions available throughout France, all year. 6 day, 30 hour week. Ages 18+. Reasonable level of French essential. Pocket money £25 per week. Applicants pay own travel and insurance. Service charge £40.

HELPING HANDS AU PAIR & DOMESTIC AGENCY 10 Hertford Road, Newbury Park, Ilford, Essex IG2 7HQ Tel 081-597 3138
Au pair and mother's help positions available throughout the year. Au pairs work approx 30 hours plus 3 evenings babysitting each week

FRANCE

AU PAIR/CHILDCARE

and earn approx £25 per week. Mother's helps work longer hours for a higher salary. Board and lodging provided. 6+ months. Ages 18-27. Applicants should be willing, helpful and adaptable. Insurance and travel costs paid by the applicant but assistance with arrangements provided. Introduction fee £40 on acceptance of a family. *UK nationals only.*

INTERLINGUA CENTRE Torquay Road, Foxrock, Dublin 18, Ireland Tel Dublin 893876
Can place au pairs in French families. 30 hour week with one full day and some evenings off. Time to attend language classes 2-3 mornings or afternoons per week. 6+ months. Ages 18+. Experience desirable but not essential. £25-£40 pocket money per week, full board, lodging and insurance provided. Travel paid by applicants. Placement fee £50.

INTER-SEJOURS 179 rue de Courcelles, 75017 Paris Tel 47 63 06 81
Can place au pairs with families in Paris and the provinces. 5 hour day, with 2/3 evenings babysitting per week. One day free per week, with time for language classes and cultural activities. Ages 18-26. Minimum 6 months, preferably beginning September or January. Some posts arranged for 2-3 months, summer. Board, lodging and insurance provided. FF1500 pocket money per month. Travel not provided, but families sometimes help towards the cost if the au pair has spent the year with them. Registration fee FF580.

INTERNATIONAL CATHOLIC SOCIETY FOR GIRLS (ACISJF) St Patrick's International Youth Centre, 24 Great Chapel Street, London W1V 3AF Tel 071-734 2156
Au pair posts arranged for 3 months in summer or 9+ months, all year. Ages 18+. The Society assists girls/young women who are travelling and living away from home. Counselling and information service.

JOLAINE AGENCY 18 Escot Way, Barnet, Hertfordshire EN5 3AN Tel 081-449 1334
Au pair and mother's help posts arranged throughout the year. Au pairs work a 5 hour day and 3/4 evenings babysitting per week. Afternoons plus 1 full day free. Mother's helps work an 8 hour day with 1½ days free per week, plus some evenings and other time by arrangement. Ages 18+. 6+ months. Pocket

money per week from £25, au pairs, and £40, mother's helps. Travel paid by applicant. Introduction fee £35.

MONDIAL AGENCY 32 Links Road, West Wickham, Kent BR4 0QW Tel 081-777 0510
Can place au pairs with families in Paris or Nice throughout the year. Au pairs work a 5-6 hour day with 2/3 afternoons free for language classes, and are expected to spend some evenings babysitting by arrangement with the family. Board and lodging provided. Pocket money approx £25 per week. Ages 18-27. 6+ months. Applicants pay their own fares and insurance. Service charge £40.

SEJOURS INTERNATIONAUX LINGUISTIQUES ET CULTURELS 32 Rempart de l'Est, 16022 Angoulême Cedex Tel 45 95 83 56
Can place au pairs all over France. Stays are usually 6+ months all year or 2+ months summer. 5 hour day, 6 day week, plus 3/4 evenings per week babysitting. Pocket money approx FF300 per week. Board and lodging provided. Travel costs paid by the applicant. *Apply by March for summer placements, by end June for placements starting September.*

STUDENTS ABROAD AGENCY Elm House, 21b The Avenue, Hatch End, Middlesex HA5 4EN Tel 081-428 5823
Can place au pairs and sometimes mother's helps with families in Paris, Nice and other areas. Long-term positions available throughout the year; limited number of short-term (3+ months) summer placements. Au pairs are normally expected to work a 5/6 hour day with 3-4 hours per day for language classes. Usually 1 full day and 2/3 evenings free per week, but curriculum changes and applicants must be flexible during temporary summer season when no schooling available and families often go on holiday. Basic salary approx FF1200 per month. Mother's helps work longer hours for a higher salary. Board and lodging provided. Ages 18-27. Basic knowledge of French preferred. Applicants should like, and have the ability to cope with, children, babies, light housework and simple cooking. Applicants pay their own fare, but advice given on travel and insurance. Service charge £40. *Apply early for temporary summer positions.*

UNIVERSAL CARE Chester House, 9
Windsor End, Beaconsfield, Buckinghamshire
HP9 2JJ Tel Beaconsfield 678811
Can place au pairs and mother's helps in most
areas of France. Stays are usually 6+ months,
all year; summer positions available in the
south, 3+ months. Au pairs work a 5/6 hour
day, with 3-4 free evenings and 1 day off per
week. Regular free time for language classes.
Ages 17-27. Mother's helps work a 7/8 hour
day, with 2 full days off and 3-4 free evenings.
Ages 18-35. Most families require a minimum
knowledge of French. Board and lodging provided. Salary from FF1300 for au pairs and
FF1500 for mothers' helps, per month. Travel
paid by the applicant, although families will
sometimes help with return fare. Service charge
£46. Apply 2 months before work period desired.

COMMUNITY WORK

LES AMIS DE PAX CHRISTI 18 rue Cousté,
94230 Cachan
An international Catholic movement for peace,
organising centres for international encounter
during the summer which attempt to encourage
dialogue between different nations, races and
relations, to give a living witness that peace is
possible.
Volunteers are needed to work in Avignon,
Lourdes, Trebeurden and Vezelay. The hostels
are usually set up in school buildings, and
provide meals and accommodation. The aim is
for the volunteers to form a lively international
community. Work involves reception duties,
cleaning, cooking, shopping, laundry, publicity
and the setting up and dismantling of beds.
Volunteers also invite the visitors to join them
in reflection, dialogue and prayer. The work is
hard but often rewarding. Duties and free time
are allocated on a rota basis as far as possible
so that everyone shares menial as well as more
enjoyable aspects of the work.

Ages 18-30. Volunteers must have a real
commitment to peace. 3 weeks, July-early
September. Food, dormitory accommodation
and insurance provided. Volunteers pay their
own travel costs.

ASSOCIATION DES PARALYSES DE
FRANCE Service-Vacances, 17 boulevard
Auguste-Blanqui, 75013 Paris
A non-profitmaking organisation recruiting
volunteers to help physically handicapped
adults on holiday all over France. Participants
give aid and share their time with the
handicapped as appropriate, so there are no
fixed hours of work. July and August. Ages
18+. No experience necessary. Full board,
youth centre accommodation and insurance
provided, plus travel expenses from the French
border. Social activities and excursions
arranged are available to the volunteers.

INTERNATIONAL VOLUNTARY SERVICE
162 Upper New Walk, Leicester LE1 7QA
Tel Leicester 549430
IVS is the British branch of Service Civil
International which promotes international
reconciliation through workcamps. Volunteers
are needed to work on community projects.
Recent projects have included helping at a
medical and social centre for people with
physical disabilities at Montoire near Blois;
taking part in outdoor activities and daily
chores on activity holidays for disabled people
in the village of Ariege in the Pyrénées; helping
with the plastering and decorating of elderly
people's homes in Lille; and helping organise a
cycle tour to the North Sea coast for a group of
children. Ages 18+. Applicants should be
prepared to work hard and contribute to team
life. 35-40 hour week. 2-4 weeks, May-
September. Membership fee £25 (students £15,
unwaged £10). Registration fee £40. B D PH

Organised by Service Civil International, 129
rue du Faubourg Poissonnière, 75009 Paris

Applications from outside the UK: please see
workcamp information on page 27.

CONSERVATION

LES ALPES DE LUMIERE Prieuré de Salagon,
Mane, 04300 Forcalquier
Arranges conservation workcamps. Recent
projects have included restoring a Roman
chapel; renovating a cloistered and cobbled
courtyard in a Roman priory; constructing a
footpath; and creating a play area for children.
Ages 18+. 15+ days, July-September, approx 30

hour week with afternoons free for leisure activities. Concerts/shows and countryside excursions arranged. Volunteers should take a sleeping bag, working clothes, rucksack and walking shoes. Food, camping accommodation and insurance provided. Volunteers pay own travel and FF300-FF500 registration fee depending on length of stay.

ASSOCIATION LE MAT, Le Viel Audon, Balazuc, 07120 Ruoms

Volunteers needed to help in restoring a village in the Ardèche, developing its resources to create new jobs. Ten years of workcamps have resulted in the creation of a farm and a youth hostel, and educational courses are also held. Work involves masonry, carpentry, cooking and baking bread. Sports and social activities also organised. Ages 17-25. 6 hour day. Easter, July and August. Basic accommodation and communal meals provided. FF45 per day covers board. Volunteers pay own travel costs. Registration fee FF80 includes insurance.

ASSOCIATION OCCITANE POUR LA DEFENSE DE LA FORET (ASSODEF) Hotel de Ville, Chemin des Loutabas, 13860 Peyrolles

Volunteers required for summer workcamps. Recent projects have included helping to build a forest information centre based on solar energy, setting up observation posts and information boards, footpath maintenance, coppicing, and working to prevent forest fire. Ages 18+. No special skills or techniques required. 1/3 weeks, July-early September. Approx 30 hour week, with afternoons free for arranged leisure activities. Accommodation, food and insurance provided. Volunteers pay own travel . FF450 registration fee.

ASSOCIATION POUR LA PARTICIPATION A L'ACTION REGIONALE (APARE) 103 rue des Infirmières, 84000 Avignon

Offers participants the opportunity to discover Provence through projects aimed at protecting the region's environment and heritage. Recent projects have included restoring a Roman chapel in Vaucluse; cleaning up the rivers Recluse and Pesquier; helping to preserve cultivated terraces north of Avignon; and repairing a Roman bridge in Var. Ages 18+. 2-4 weeks, June-November. Approx 30 hour week, with afternoons and weekends free to discover the region on foot, by bike or canoe. Also opportunities to attend local festivals, theatre plays and poetry workshops. Volunteers should take a sleeping bag, working clothes, rucksack and walking shoes. Accommodation, food and insurance provided. Volunteers pay own travel. FF500 registration fee.

BRITISH TRUST FOR CONSERVATION VOLUNTEERS Room 1WH, 36 St Marys Street, Wallingford, Oxfordshire OX10 0EU

Britain's leading organisation for the promotion of practical conservation work for protecting the environment. Since 1983 volunteers have carried out board walk projects, dune stabilisation and footpath maintenance in the regional park of Nord Pas du Calais, working alongside local people. Ages 18-70. Cost £50 per week includes food and camping or dormitory accommodation. Shared cooking duties. Membership fee £10.

CHRISTIAN MOVEMENT FOR PEACE Bethnal Green United Reformed Church, Pott Street, London E2 0EF Tel 071-729 1877

An international movement open to all who share a common concern for lasting peace and justice in the world. Volunteers are required to work in international teams on summer projects aimed at offering a service in an area of need and promoting self-help within the community; promoting international understanding and the discussion of social problems; and offering young people the chance to live as a group and take these experiences into the context of daily life. Volunteers are needed to help in small rural communities, preserving their heritage by carrying out restoration and salvage work on old buildings and the environment. Recent projects have included restoring the ruins of a monument and organising a sound and light show to display the tower during a village festival; clearing and repairing footpaths, and restoring an old village in the Drome region; renovating medieval castles, churches, chapels and traditional country houses; clearing moats; renovating an old train and railway in the Gironde; clearing canals in the Cévennes, and repairing the banks of the river Hérault; studying the medicinal and nutritional virtues of forgotten plants, and creating a nature reserve. Sports, social activities and village festivities are organised. Ages 15-17 and 18+.

6 hour day, 30-36 hour week. 2-3 weeks, July-August. Food, accommodation in tents or barns and insurance provided, but participants pay their own travel costs, and sometimes contribute towards food expenses. Registration fee £24.

Organised by Mouvement Chrétien pour la Paix, 38 rue du Faubourg St Denis, 75010 Paris.

Applications from outside the UK: please see workcamp information on page 27.

CLUB DU VIEUX MANOIR 10 rue de la Cossonnerie, 75001 Paris
A national movement which brings together young people willing to devote time to the restoration and upkeep of historic and endangered monuments and sites and to the protection of the natural environment. Recent projects have included restoration work on an abbey at Sarlat in the Dordogne; restoring old buildings, including an 17th century chapel, 18th century fortresses, a 16th century church, and village sundials at Briançon in the Hautes-Alpes; restoring a tileworks at St Plantaire in Indre; restoration of the Cadraus Solaires in Paris; and restoring a 16th century wooden coaching inn at Casteljaloux in Lot-et-Garonne. Three permanent sites at Guise, Argy and Pontpoint serve as centres for introduction to the environment, architectural heritage and for specialised research and instruction on materials, techniques and tools. Some sites also run special programmes/festivals. All volunteers receive manual and technical tuition in archaeology, building techniques, restoration of buildings, architecture, history and handicrafts.
Ages 14/15+, depending on site chosen. Minimum age for specialised instruction is 16. 15+ days, Easter, July-September, Christmas and during the year. Simple self-catering accommodation provided in tents (summer) or under shelter (winter), sometimes without running water. Participants share in the day to day organisation of the camp, and discipline is strict. Cost FF55 per day includes board and lodging. Participants should take a sleeping bag. Volunteers aged 17+ staying for an extended period, other than during the summer, receive free board and lodging after a trial period of 15 days. Registration fee FF60 covers membership and insurance.

ENFANTS ET AMIS DE BEAUCHASTEL Christian Coulet, 33 rue de France, 69100 Villeurbanne
Volunteers are needed to help in the restoration of an abandoned medieval village in the Ardèche, developing its resources to create new jobs. Work involves masonry, carpentry, roof and floor tiling, paving and cooking. Ages 18+ No experience necessary, but knowledge of French useful. Approx 30 hour week, 1-15 August. Accommodation in village schoolhouse and meals provided; sports and social activities organised. Volunteers pay own travel costs. Cost FF350, 2 weeks, includes insurance. Anti-tetanus vaccination advisable.

KLAUS & JEAN ERHARDT Bardou, 34390 Olargues Tel 67 97 72 43
The village of Bardou is a living museum of medieval farming life and a retreat for artists and writers. Volunteers are required to help in the restoration of 16th century stone houses and on farm maintenance and care of a flock of 200 prize-winning Bizet sheep. Ages 20+. No experience necessary. 16 hour week. May-June and September-November. French useful but not essential. Accommodation in the village and social activities provided. Volunteers pay own food, insurance and travel costs.

ETUDES ET CHANTIERS INTERNATIONAL 33 rue Campagne Premiere, 75014 Paris
Founded to encourage and promote the participation of young people and adults in the redevelopment of rural communities, the conservation of the environment and the rehabilitation of old town areas. Workcamps are organised in many areas of France for groups of 15-20 volunteers. The work includes clearing silt and debris from rivers and streams, stabilising banks and clearing vegetation; clearing and maintaining footpaths, and constructing new ones to give access to rural sites; restoring old buildings and converting them into meeting or sports centres; rebuilding villages or buildings which have been abandoned or fallen into disrepair; and creating environmental education centres in existing green spaces or laying out playgrounds in towns. Technical help and advice given by local craftsmen. Sports and social activities include concerts, exhibitions, evenings with villagers, discovery of the region, crafts, sailing and windsurfing.

FRANCE

CONSERVATION

FRANCE

Ages 13-17 (25 hour week) and 17+ (35 hour week). Also family camps, 15-25 days, July-October and at Christmas and Easter. Food and lodging in gites, tents or schools provided. Cost FF60 per day for ages 13-17, free for ages 17+. Volunteers prepare food, help with chores and pay their own travel costs. Registration fee FF350. Long-term work also available.

Alternatively UK applicants may apply to United Nations Association, International Youth Service, Welsh Centre for International Affairs, Temple of Peace, Cathays Park, Cardiff CF1 3AP Tel Cardiff 223088.

CONSERVATION

INTERNATIONAL VOLUNTARY SERVICE 162 Upper New Walk, Leicester LE1 7QA Tel Leicester 549430
IVS is the British branch of Service Civil International which promotes international reconciliation through work projects. Volunteers are needed to work on conservation workcamps. Recent projects have included helping local farmers with the harvest, and protecting natural sites and rivers in Midi-Pyrénées; cleaning the Tarun river along three villages in Bretagne; draining a marshy area, tending a woodland and reinforcing drystone walls at an environmental centre in Escalusse; and repairing footpaths, cutting brushwood, pruning trees and building footbridges in the hills and mountains of Ariège. Ages 18+. Applicants should be fit, prepared to work hard and contribute to team life. Good knowledge of French required for some projects. 2/3 weeks, June-August. Food, accommodation and insurance provided, but not travel. Membership fee £25 (students £15, unwaged £10). Registration fee £40. B D PH

Organised by Service Civil International, 129 rue du Faubourg Poissonnière, 75009 Paris

Applications from outside the UK: please see workcamp information on page 27.

JEUNESSE ET RECONSTRUCTION 10 rue de Trévise, 75009 Paris
Aims to provide short-term practical aid towards the redevelopment of small rural communities, the understanding of the environment and to encourage local inhabitants to continue with the work. Recent projects have included clearing brushwood and

cleaning riverbanks, repaving village streets, restoring ancient ramparts, castles and churches in Drome; restoring a Roman road and medieval tower in Hautes-Alpes; restoring a 14th century château, a watermill and a bread oven in Haute-Loire; and thatching a summer house, cleaning and renovating a stone bridge, replanting grass on ski slopes and clearing rivers in Puy-de-Dome. Tasks involve masonry, woodwork, carpentry, painting, electrical work, roofing and other manual work. Discussions are held in the evenings and at weekends, centring on environmental problems. Camps are run on a democratic basis; volunteers decide how to go about the project, when to work, rest, shop and cook. Ages 17-35. Parental consent needed for those under 18. Applicants should preferably have previous workcamp experience. 7 hour day, 5 day week. 2/3+ weeks, April-November. Basic accommodation provided in schools, dormitories, tents, mills or barns. Volunteers should take a sleeping bag. Food, prepared by the volunteers, and insurance provided. Volunteers pay their own travel costs. Registration fee FF340.

Alternatively UK applicants may apply to Concordia (Youth Service Volunteers) Ltd, Recruitment Secretary, 8 Brunswick Place, Hove, Sussex BN3 1ET Tel Brighton 772086 or United Nations Association, International Youth Service, Welsh Centre for International Affairs, Temple of Peace, Cathays Park, Cardiff CF1 3AP Tel Cardiff 223088.

PIERRES SECHES DU VAUCLUSE La Cornette, 84800 Plan de Saumane
Arranges workcamps mainly based on drystone-walling techniques. Recent projects have included restoring a 17th century wall built across the plateau of Vaucluse during the time of the last Plague. Ages 18+. 1+ weeks, May-August. Approx 30 hour week with afternoons free for leisure activities. Country walks, swimming and canoeing arranged. Food and camping accommodation provided. Volunteers pay own travel, FF150 registration fee, plus FF100 per week for insurance.

PRO PEYRESQ Secrétariat, c/o Windberg 290, 1810 Wemmel, Belgium
Peyresq is an isolated mountain village in the Alpes de Haute Provence, 100km from Nice.

The village, once almost abandoned, has been mostly rebuilt and has become a cultural centre for young people. Cultural, artistic activities and courses include photography, dance, hang gliding, entomology, astronomy, botany and ecology. Also mountain walking, watersports, *pétanque* and ball games. Ages 18+. Participants must be prepared to take part in daily life and domestic tasks, and must respect rules of village community life. All nationalities accepted. 3+ days, July-August. Full board dormitory accommodation. Participants should take a sleeping bag and any useful tools are welcomed. Anti-tetanus injection required. There are no shops in the village. Registration fee FB200. Address after 19 June: Pro Peyresq, Peyresq, 04170 Saint-André-les-Alpes. *Apply at least 15 days in advance.*

REMPART (Union des Associations pour la Réhabilitation et l'Entretien des Monuments et du Patrimoine Artistique) 1 rue des Guillemites, 75004 Paris
Aims to improve the way of life through a better understanding of and a greater respect for the archaeological, architectural and natural heritage and environment, through the restoration of endangered buildings and monuments. It consists of a grouping of more than 140 autonomous associations, providing a wide variety of work projects involving the restoration of medieval towns, cities, châteaux, fortresses, religious buildings, farms, ancient villages, roads, forges, walls, wind/watermills, Gallo-Roman amphitheatres and baths, churches and post-medieval fortresses, houses, villages and castles, old industrial sites plus contemporary murals, ramparts, churches, underground passages, paths, ski runs and steam engines. Work includes masonry, woodwork, carpentry, roofing, interior decorating, restoration and clearance work, plus carrying out surveys, technical photography and filing. Opportunities for sports, exploring the region, crafts, music cinema and taking part in local festivities. Ages 16/18+. There is no upper age limit, anyone feeling young is welcome, and some camps accept families. Previous experience not necessary. Some knowledge of French needed. 30-35 hour week. 2-4 weeks, Easter and June-September; a few camps are open throughout the year. Cost FF20-FF45 per day (average

FF30) for food and accommodation in huts, old buildings or tents, with self-catering facilities; a few camps are free. Volunteers help with camp duties, pay their own fares, and should take a sleeping bag. Applicants can choose which project they would like to work on from the workcamp programme and contact addresses are given. Registration fee FF200 includes insurance. Also arranges courses in restoration techniques, artistic activities and environmental studies. *Enclose 3 IRCs.* B D PH

LA SABRANENQUE CENTRE INTERNATIONAL 30290 Saint Victor la Coste
A small, non-profitmaking organisation that has been working since 1969 to preserve, restore and reconstruct abandoned rural sites, and bring them back to life. Aims to give volunteers the chance to discover the pleasure of working directly on genuine rural restoration projects while being part of a cooperative team. After completing the reconstruction of the medieval village of Saint Victor la Coste, 25km north of Avignon, La Sabranenque now works on several sites in nearby villages. Volunteers work in small teams, learning traditional construction techniques on-the-job from experienced leaders. Work can include masonry, stone-cutting, floor or roof tiling, interior restoration, drystone walling, path paving and planting trees. 1 day per session spent visiting the region, which is rich in ancient monuments. Ages 18+. No experience necessary. 2+ weeks, 1 June-30 August. Cost FF65 per day includes full board accommodation in restored houses. Registration fee FF120.

SOLIDARITES JEUNESSES 38 rue du Faubourg St Denis, 75010 Paris
Originally took over, saved and restored old mills in the Creuse region, with the help of volunteers, which now form the basis of international workcamps. Projects include the continuing restoration of old mills and other old buildings for conversion into international meeting centres along the Creuse rivers, plus a feudal fortress in the Pyrénées-Atlantique and the protection of their environment including cleaning rivers and banks, gardening, upkeep of footpaths, nature trails and open spaces, plus flora and fauna. Camps involve working mornings with cultural activities in the

FRANCE

afternoons, including workshops and courses covering pottery, photography, carpentry, painting, ecology, wood carving, weaving and ironwork. Also courses in French and Esperanto. Opportunities exist for discovering the region and sports. Ages 13+. 2 weeks, Easter, Christmas and June-September. Cost FF90 per day includes board, insurance and tent, dormitory or pension accommodation. Membership fee FF100. Participants should take a sleeping bag and work clothes. Courses last approx 2 weeks, July and August; cost FF1800 includes board, lodging, tuition and materials. B D PH (no wheelchairs).

CONSERVATION

UNITED NATIONS ASSOCIATION
International Youth Service, Welsh Centre for International Affairs, Temple of Peace, Cathays Park, Cardiff CF1 3AP Tel Cardiff 223088
Volunteers are needed on approx 60 international workcamps which aim to help in the development of small communities in mountainous and isolated rural areas, including Auvergne, Bourgogne, Champagne, Midi-Pyrénées, Picardy and Alpes and give participants the chance to get to know the natural, economic and social environment. Typical conservation projects include restoring houses, chapels, churches, châteaux and forts, fountains, wells and wash-houses in villages and abandoned hamlets; clearing and signposting footpaths and hiking tracks; creating gardens and green spaces, bird hides and observatories; repairing traditional bread ovens, sheepfolds and mountain huts; restoring paintings and frescoes; and environmental protection in the Parc Naturel de la Vanoise. Volunteers are taught traditional building techniques by local craftsmen. Sports, crafts, and other cultural/social activities arranged. Ages 17-25. Good knowledge of French needed for some camps. Applicants should preferably have previous workcamp experience. 35 hour week. 3 weeks, June-November and 2 weeks, Easter and Christmas. Also camps for ages 15-17. 25 hour week. Projects include cleaning rivers, laying out paths for walkers, working in the forest and restoration work on endangered monuments. Full board, accommodation in schools, huts or community buildings and insurance provided. Volunteers pay their own travel costs. Registration fee FF550, FF800 for ages 15-17. B D PH

Walking/cycling holidays are organised to introduce the type of projects undertaken on workcamps and to discover the natural environment. Participants should be able to carry a rucksack and walk/cycle for 3-6 hours a day. Also arrange leader training seminars.

Organised by Concordia, 27 rue du Pont-Neuf, PO Box 238, 75024 Paris Cedex 01.

Applications from outside the UK: please see workcamp information on page 27.

COURIERS/REPS

BLADON LINES Personnel Department, 56-58 Putney High Street, London SW15 1SF Tel 081-785 2200
Opportunities for representatives to work in the ski resorts of Avoriaz, Méribel les Allues, Chatel, Flaine, Les Deux Alpes, Serre Chevalier, Risoul, Vars, Courchevel, Tignes and Val d'Isère. Work involves welcoming and looking after guests, providing information, helping with coach transfers and ensuring everything is running smoothly. Ages 24+. Relevant experience an advantage; good spoken French essential. Hours very variable; applicants must be prepared to work hard but will get time to ski. December-May. Salary £50-£100 per week, depending on the size of the resort. Board, lodging, return travel, insurance, ski pass, ski hire and company ski jacket provided. Training week held in London before departure.

CANVAS HOLIDAYS LTD Bull Plain, Hertford SG14 1DY Tel Hertford 553535
Resident couriers are required to work on over 100 campsites for a holiday company providing accommodation for families in ready-erected fully equipped tents and cabins. The work involves a daily routine of cleaning as customers arrive and depart, providing information and advice on the local attractions and essential services and helping to sort out any problems that might arise. 7 day week with no fixed hours; the workload varies from day to day. At the beginning and end of the season there is a period of physical work when tents are put up and prepared or taken down and stored for the winter. Other tasks include administration, book-keeping and stock control. On certain sites children's couriers are

also needed, responsible for a number of children during various periods of the day or evening. Children's couriers are expected to organise a variety of games, activities and competitions within the limitations of the site, and be flexible to cope with weather, varying numbers and limited preparation time. Applicants should have previous experience with children, through nursing, teacher training or group playschemes, and be able to use their initiative to develop ideas for activities. Ages 18-25. Applicants are normally those with a year between school and further education, undergraduates or graduates. They need to be enthusiastic, practical, reliable, self-motivated, able to turn their hand to new and varied tasks, and with a sense of humour. 10-14 weeks, early April-mid July or July-late September. Return travel, dependent on successful completion of contract, moped or bicycle for use on site and accommodation in frame tents provided. Salary approx £76 per week. *Applications accepted any time; interviews commence November for the following season.*

CAREFREE CAMPING LTD Operations Manager, 126 Hempstead Road, Kings Langley, Hertfordshire WD4 8AL Tel Watford 261316
Operates self-drive family holidays providing fully furnished and equipped tents and mobile homes. Vacancies exist for operations team members plus a limited number of children's couriers and campsite couriers. Operations teams consist of 3-5 members and a supervisor travelling around France, responsible for setting up or closing down campsites. 3-4 days are spent at each site and the work involves long car journeys and heavy lifting. Applicants must be fit and capable of working long hours, maybe in poor weather. They will be expected to show initiative and ability to work without supervision. 3-4 weeks, May or September, depending on factors such as weather. Children's couriers are required to look after children and organise a variety of games, races, competitions and treasure hunts. Applicants should have sound organisational ability and a mature, outgoing personality. French language ability essential for courier posts, useful for other positions. End May-beginning September. Work as campsite couriers entails preparing tents or mobile homes, welcoming clients, occasionally

organising social activities, and dealing with any problems which may arise. Mid May-mid July or mid July-mid September. Ages 19+. Salary approx £80 per week. Accommodation in tents with cooking facilities and insurance provided. Travel expenses paid, provided that company transport is used when available.

CLUB CANTABRICA HOLIDAYS LTD Overseas Department, Holiday House, 146-148 London Road, St Albans, Hertfordshire AL1 1PQ Tel St Albans 33141
Organises camping holidays, providing fully equipped tents, caravans and mobile homes. Vacancies exist for couriers and maintenance staff to work the whole summer season, mid May-early October, in Cavalier, Port Grimaud, Cavalaire and Canet. 6 day week. Ages 21+. Salary from £40 per week, plus bonus at end of season. Experience an advantage. Self-catering accommodation in tents or caravans, travel costs from Watford and insurance provided.

EUROCAMP Courier Department, Edmundson House, Tatton Street, Knutsford, Cheshire WA16 6BG Tel Knutsford 50052
Resident couriers are required on a number of campsites. The work involves cleaning tents and equipment prior to the arrival of new customers; checking, replacing and making repairs on equipment; replenishing gas supplies; keeping the store tent in order; keeping basic accounts and reporting on a weekly basis to England. Couriers are also expected to meet new arrivals and assist holidaymakers with any problems that may arise; organise activities and parties; provide information on local tourist attractions and maintain an information noticeboard. At the beginning and end of the season couriers are expected to help in erecting and dismantling tents. There are no set working hours or free days, as these depend on unpredictable factors. Ages 18-28, although older applicants will be considered. Applicants should be familiar with working and travelling abroad, preferably with camping experience. They should be reliable, adaptable, independent, efficient, sensible, hardworking, tactful, patient, sociable, with a working knowledge of French. Applications from couples welcome. Applicants are expected to work one half of the season, early/mid April-mid July or mid July-late September/early October - exact date depends on the

FRANCE

COURIERS/REPS

campsite. Work is also available for the whole season. Accommodation in frame tent with cooking facilities, insurance, return fare and moped on site provided. Salary approx £72.50 per week. Positions as senior couriers also available; salary £97 per week. *Early application advisable - interviews start November.*

FREEDOM OF FRANCE Personnel Department, Alton Court, Penyard Lane, Ross-on-Wye, Herefordshire HR9 5NR Tel Ross-on-Wye 767833
Provides luxury self-drive, self-catering holidays at campsites throughout France. Couriers are required to work from Brittany through to the Bordeaux coast and down to the Mediterranean. The work involves ensuring that tents are clean and tidy, meeting and greeting families on arrival, and lending a sympathetic ear to clients' requirements. Duties also include running entertainment programmes for children, who will be divided into different age groups. April-September. Ages 21+ Good command of French essential. Salary £75-£80 per week, self-catering tent accommodation, full liability and medical insurance and travel from UK port provided.

FRENCH LIFE MOTORING HOLIDAYS Overseas Personnel Manager, 26 Church Road, Horsforth, Leeds LS18 5LG Tel Leeds 390077
Organises self-drive holidays with fully equipped tents and caravans on campsites, and requires site representatives. Work involves welcoming clients and looking after them during their holiday, cleaning and maintaining tents and caravans, organising excursions, caring for and entertaining children, providing a babysitting service, and running evening entertainment activities such as barbecues, wine and cheese and fancy dress parties. On call 24 hours a day, usually 6 days a week. Ages 21+. Applicants should have experience of dealing with people, and be used to hard physical work. They should be dynamic, reliable, hard working, conscientious and loyal with the ability to work as part of a team, plus the staying power to last the whole season. Working knowledge of French essential. April-October, with some positions for students only in June/July. Accommodation in shared frame tents with own bedroom area, self-catering cooking facilities and return travel provided.

Salary approx £80 per week. All staff are required to take part in a training programme in April. *British or French nationals only. Early application advisable - recruitment starts December, interviews commence mid-January.*

HEAD WATER HOLIDAYS 146 London Road, Northwich, Cheshire CW9 5HH Tel Northwich 49599
Operates activity holidays involving cycling, walking and Canadian canoeing in Creuse, Jura, Lot and Vercors. Requires canoeing representatives with BCU Certificates, and cycling representatives with some experience of bicycle maintenance. The work includes briefing clients at the start of the holiday, helping with any queries or problems and canoe or bicycle familiarisation. Hours vary according to clients' needs. Mid May-beginning October. Ages 20+. Driving licence and fluent French desirable. Salary approx £105 per week plus expenses, self-catering accommodation in village houses, travel and insurance provided. Two training weekends before season starts.

KEYCAMP HOLIDAYS Courier Recruitment Department, 92-96 Lind Road, Sutton, Surrey SM1 4PL Tel 081-643 7510
Organises self-drive family holidays in tents and mobile homes on over 50 campsites in France. Campsite couriers are required to clean tents/mobile homes, welcome clients, run programme of social events, give local information, sort out problems, run children's clubs and maintain equipment. Applicants are required to work the whole season, March-October, or a half season, April-mid July or early July-end September. 48 hour week. Ages 18+. Knowledge of French desirable. Salary £78+ per week. Accommodation in 6 berth tents, compulsory insurance premium and return travel from London provided. *Apply September-March; telephone applications preferred.*

NAT HOLIDAYS, Overseas Personnel Manager, ILG Coach & Camping, Devonshire House, Elmfield Road, Bromley, Kent Tel 081-466 6660
Vacancies exist for representatives in hotels, apartments, and on campsites. Work involves welcoming, visiting and generally looking after clients, accompanying excursions, organising and taking part in evening entertainment. Staff are required to take an active part in their

resort entertainment programme. Ages 23+ (hotels/apartments), 21+ (campsites). April-October, with some positions for students only, June/July. Applicants must have the desire and ability to get on with people and to handle extreme pressure, and should be dynamic, conscientious, loyal, reliable, hard working, prepared to work as part of a team, and have enough staying power to last the season. Knowledge of French an advantage. Salary approx £57 per week. Accommodation and return travel provided. All staff are required to take part in a 2 week training programme in April. *Early application advisable; recruitment starts October, interviews commence mid December*

NSS RIVIERA HOLIDAYS 199 Marlborough Avenue, Hull, North Humberside HU5 3LG Tel Hull 42240
Owns 26 chalets and mobile homes at a holiday village near Fréjus, between St Tropez and Cannes. Facilities include swimming pools, tennis courts, bars, disco, shops, washeteria, take-away and restaurant. Couples or two friends required to act as representatives, June-September. Ages 26-40. Applicants must be caring, reliable, responsible and capable of working without supervision. Good general DIY skills, command of English, French and some German, sense of humour and own car essential. Non-smokers preferred. References required. Wages up to £90 per week, plus accommodation, gas, electricity, use of site amenities and help with ferry costs. Non-UK nationals with exceptionally good command of English considered. *Apply in writing only.*

PGL YOUNG ADVENTURE LTD Personnel Department, Alton Court, Penyard Lane, Ross-on-Wye, Herefordshire HR9 5NR Tel Ross-on-Wye 764211
Organises outdoor adventure holidays for young people and adults in the Ardèche and on the Mediterranean. Activities include canoeing, sailing, windsurfing and caving. Couriers/group leaders are required, accompanying children aged 12-17, starting and finishing in London. The position involves complete responsibility for the group whilst travelling and at the centre, dealing with pocket money, illness and general coordination, and helping with the evening programme. Ages 21+/25+. Applicants should have a strong sense of responsibility, total commitment, enjoy the

company of young people, be self-motivated, tolerant, flexible, positive, mature, with a good sense of humour, stamina, energy, enthusiasm, and a fairly extrovert personality. Good spoken French essential; experience in working with groups of young people, preferably abroad, in informal or formal settings, and ability to cope with demands on one's time needed. May-September. Couriers accompany groups on 8 day trips, and usually take 2/3 trips during the season. Return travel from London, full board, accommodation in frame tents and health insurance provided. Sports, social facilities available, plus participation in programmed activities. Pocket money FF300 per week, plus appropriate travelling expenses. *Apply ideally December-April.*

QUEST TRAVEL Olivier House, 18 Marine Parade, Brighton East Sussex BN2 1TL Tel Brighton 677777
Provides ski and summer tours for groups, mainly school parties, individuals and youth and adult organisations. Requires resort representatives for the winter and summer seasons, December-April and May-July/August, in La Clusaz, Tignes, Chatel, Crest Voland, Pra Loup and other resorts. Duties include meeting groups at airports or hotels, room allocation, liaising with group leaders, organising entertainments and promoting good local relations. Applicants should enjoy hard, stimulating work, be enthusiastic, have a flair for organising and be prepared to be on call 24 hours a day. Ages 21+. Fluent French essential. Salary £75-£110 per week, full board, lodging in shared accommodation, medical insurance and return travel provided. Training course at beginning of season. B D PH limited.

SNOWTIME LTD 96 Belsize Lane, Hampstead, London NW3 5BE Tel 071-433 3336
Organises luxury winter skiing holidays in Méribel. Representatives required to ensure standards are maintained and clients enjoy their holiday. Duties involve liaison with local companies, agents and suppliers; good command of French required. Applicants should be efficient, capable, friendly and outgoing, preferably with previous experience. Ages 24+. 30-50 hour week. December-May. Salary from £50 per week, plus return travel and insurance. *British nationals only.*

FRANCE

COURIERS/REPS

FRANCE

SOLAIRE INTERNATIONAL HOLIDAYS 1158 Stratford Road, Hall Green, Birmingham B28 8AF Tel 021-778 5061

Organises camping and mobile home holidays in Normandy, Paris, Brittany, the Loire and Vendee, Dordogne, South West France and on the Mediterranean. Staff are required to prepare the tents and mobile homes at the beginning of the season in May and then close down at the end of the season in October. During the season staff act as couriers, ensuring the smooth running of the camps, and undertake some maintenance work. No fixed hours. Ages 18+. No previous experience necessary. Foreign language fluency preferable but not essential. Wages £40-£60 per week. Accommodation in tents or mobile homes, insurance and travel provided.

DOMESTIC

SUPERTRAVEL Alpine Operations Department, 22 Hans Place, London SW1X 0EP Tel 071-589 5161

Arranges skiing holidays in the French alpine resorts of Méribel, Courchevel, Val d'Isère, Tignes, Avoriaz, La Plagne and Les Deux Alpes. Opportunities for resort representatives, responsible for looking after guests and supervising staff. Ages 24-34. Work involves travelling to the airport each weekend to welcome guests; organising their ski passes, ski hire and ski school; informing them of local events; overseeing the work of chalet girls and ensuring that chalets are kept in perfect running order. There are also opportunities for managers in the jumbo chalets (24-60 beds) who are responsible for the smooth running of their chalet and should be experienced in hotel work. Applicants must be available for the whole season, early December-end April. Approx 40+ hours per week. Board, lodging, ski pass, ski and boot hire and return travel provided; also insurance in return for approx £35 contribution. Salary £55-£85 per week, paid in local currency. Two day briefing held in London before departure, plus individual session to learn about the resort. *British passport holders only.*

When writing to any organisation it is essential to mention Working Holidays 1991 and enclose a large stamped, self-addressed envelope, or if overseas, a large addressed envelope and at least two International Reply Coupons.

DOMESTIC

ALPOTELS AGENCY PO Box 388, London SW1X 8LX

At the request of French hotels, carries out aptitude tests for work as waitresses and chambermaids or night-porters and dishwashers. Ages 18+. Good knowledge of French needed. All jobs involve long hours and hard work as part of a professional team of French workers. 8 hour day with 1/1½ days free per week. December-April or June-September. Pay approx £100 per week; board, lodging and insurance provided. Interview fee £1 plus subscription to JITA Club. *Closing dates for interviews 30 September (winter), 30 April (summer). EC nationals only.*

BLADON LINES Personnel Department, 56-58 Putney High Street, London SW15 1SF Tel 081-785 2200

Opportunities for cooks and cleaners to work in the French ski resorts of Méribel les Allues, Courchevel, Les Deux Alpes, Serre Chevalier, Risoul, Vars, Tignes and Val d'Isère. Also opportunities for chalet girls, whose work involves cleaning chalets, making beds, caring for guests, shopping and preparing meals. Limited amount of domestic work also available in Corsica, May-October. Ages 20+. Experience and/or qualifications in catering or domestic work essential. However, there are also a few positions for hostesses to work in the larger chalets where no cooking experience is required. Hours are very variable; applicants must be prepared to work hard but will get time to ski. Season lasts December-May. Salary approx £40 per week. Board, lodging, return travel, insurance, ski pass, ski hire and company ski jacket provided. One day briefing in London held before departure. *EC nationals only.* PH depending on ability.

PGL YOUNG ADVENTURE LTD Personnel Department, Alton Court, Penyard Lane, Ross-on-Wye, Herefordshire HR9 5NR Tel Ross-on-Wye 764211

Organises outdoor adventure holidays for young people and adults in the Ardèche and on the Mediterranean. Activities include canoeing, sailing, windsurfing, water skiing and caving. Kitchen assistants, housemaids, caterers/cooks and bar, shop staff and organisers are required.

FRANCE

DOMESTIC

Ages 20+; preference given to ages 21+. Applicants should have relevant experience and be energetic and enthusiastic, reliable and mature, adaptable, friendly and efficient, with a sense of humour. May-September. Jobs are usually for approx 8 week periods but are sometimes for the whole season. Staff are also recruited for very short periods over the spring bank holiday. Return travel from Dover, full board, accommodation in frame tents and health insurance provided. Sports and social facilities available, plus participation in programmed activities. 1 day free per week. Pocket money per week approx FF270 (housemaids, kitchen assistants and bar/shop staff, bar/shop organisers), or from FF800 (head cooks). *Applicants available in May and early July have a greater chance of selection. Applications should ideally be made December-April.*

QUEST TRAVEL Olivier House, 18 Marine Parade, Brighton, East Sussex BN2 1TL
Tel Brighton 677777
Provides ski and summer tours for groups, mainly school parties, individuals and youth and adult organisations. Requires staff for catering and domestic teams during the winter and summer seasons, December-April and May-July/August, in Notre Dame, Chatel, Crest, La Clusaz, Voland, Pra Loup and other resorts. Chefs/assistant chefs manage a small kitchen team, work to a strict budget, manage stock control and food ordering. Kitchen assistants help chefs with food preparation, washing up and general kitchen work. Domestic staff are responsible for maintaining a high standard of cleanliness. Bar staff are also required for hotel work. 54 hour week. Ages 18+. Knowledge of French and experience required according to post. Salary £50-£80 per week, full board, lodging in shared accommodation, medical insurance and return travel provided. Training course at beginning of season. B D PH limited opportunities.

SKI WHIZZ/SMALL WORLD Hillgate House, 13 Hillgate Street, London W8 7SP
Tel 071-221 9868
Arranges chalet holidays in the Alps. Chalet girls/boys are required to work in ski resorts in the Alps and the Dolomites. Work involves keeping chalets clean and tidy, making beds, cooking meals and acting as host. Ages 20+.

Cordon bleu cookery qualifications and/or sound experience of catering essential. Applicants should also have a basic knowledge of accounts/budgeting, some knowledge of French or German, an outgoing, friendly personality with the ability to put people at ease. They also need enough stamina and sense of humour to last through the average 1,200 beds made and 3,500 meals cooked during the season. Also positions for chalet helpers, for which not so much cooking experience is required. Hours variable; applicants must be prepared to work hard. 6 days per week, December-May. Wages up to £50 per week. Board, lodging, return travel, insurance, seasonal ski pass and ski hire provided.

SNOW WORLD (SUN LIVING LTD)
Personnel Manager, Adventure House, 34-36 South Street, Lancing, West Sussex BN15 8AG
Tel Lancing 751942
Opportunities exist for chalet maids to work in ski resorts. Work involves keeping chalets tidy, looking after guests and in certain cases preparing meals. Ages 18-30. Relevant domestic and/or catering experience essential. 8-10 hour day, 6 day week as a general rule, but hours vary depending on the needs of clients. Applicants should be prepared to work for the whole season, December-April. Extra staff may also be required at peak times such as Christmas. Board, lodging and travel provided. Salary from £45 per week. Training is given at the resort during the week before the clients arrive.

SNOWTIME LTD 96 Belsize Lane, Hampstead, London NW3 5BE
Tel 071-433 3336
Organises luxury winter skiing holidays in Méribel. Chalet girls required to run chalets, either single-handedly or in pairs. Duties include cooking to a high standard, shopping, budgeting, housekeeping and acting as hostess. Applicants should be experienced cooks, preferably holding a recognised cooking diploma. They should have a friendly, easygoing personality, and the ability to mix well with clients. Hotel girls also required to work in 2 chalet hotels. Work involves cleaning, housekeeping and waitressing, with a few bar vacancies also available. Cooking skills not essential, but experience in catering industry an advantage. Ages 18+. Knowledge

FRANCE

of French useful. 30-50 hours per week. Girls work for the whole season, December-May. Salary from £35 per week, plus return travel and insurance. *British nationals only.*

SUPERTRAVEL Alpine Operations Department, 22 Hans Place, London SW1X 0EP Tel 071-589 5161
Arranges skiing holidays in the French alpine resorts of Méribel, Courchevel, Val d'Isère, Tignes, Avoriaz, La Plagne and Les Deux Alpes. Opportunities for chalet girls responsible for looking after guests and keeping chalet clean and tidy. Ages 21-30. Work involves cooking, cleaning, acting as hostess, sitting down to dinner with guests, advising them on skiing areas and keeping them up to date with events in the resort. Chalet girls must work to a budget and account for expenditure. Applicants must have cooking experience and preferably qualifications, be capable of running a chalet of approx 8 guests and have an outgoing and helpful personality. In jumbo chalets (24-60 beds) there are opportunities for chalet girl helpers whose duties are similar to the chalet girls, but do not involve cooking and also for chalet boy helpers who look after the heavier duties such as the cleaning of general areas, washing up, snow clearing, maintenance and sometimes bar work. Ages 21+. Applicants must be available for the whole season, early December-end April. Approx 40+ hours per week. Board, lodging, ski pass, ski and boot hire and return travel provided; also insurance in return for approx £35 contribution. Salary £45 per week, paid in local currency. Briefings held in London before departure. *British nationals only.*

DOMESTIC

TOPS HOLIDAYS (SUN LIVING LTD) Personnel Manager, Adventure House, 34-36 South Street, Lancing, West Sussex BN15 8AG Tel Lancing 751942
Organises a range of specialised activity and outdoor education programmes for groups of schoolchildren aged 12-17 at campsites in the Ardèche and Les Tamaris in the south, and at a hotel in Hardelot in the north and at a centre in the Pyrénées. Each centre has its own team of staff who ensure that high standards of safety, instruction and enjoyment are maintained. Staff are required for catering and domestic teams: chefs/assistant chefs managing a small kitchen team, working to a strict budget, managing stock control and food ordering, as well as catering for up to 500 guests; kitchen assistants helping chefs with food preparation and general kitchen work; domestic staff responsible for maintaining a high standard of hygiene and cleanliness, and also assisting in the centre's activities. Staff often assist in all areas of the centre's operation and will need to be flexible. All posts involve direct contact with children and their activities, so applicants must be prepared to become completely involved.
Ages 18+; preference given to ages 20+. Experience required varies according to post: chefs and assistant chefs should come from a home cooking or small restaurant background. The jobs demand a high level of commitment both physically and mentally; applicants should enjoy being with children all day and have a genuine interest in their welfare. Fitness, stamina, enthusiasm and the ability to live and work as part of a team are also essential. 40+ hour week, 1 day free per week. 1+ months, May-September. Most staff work the full season; extra staff are also taken on for shorter periods during peak times at Easter and during July and August. Opportunities for staff to move from centre to centre. Travel costs from Dover, full board apartment or tent accommodation and insurance provided. Pay from £25 per week paid in local currency, and varying according to experience and responsibilities. Training is provided to ensure staff are confident and able to carry out their responsibilities. Social and recreational activities such as parties, barbecues and outings arranged for staff. *British nationals only.* B D PH limited opportunities.

FARMWORK/ GRAPE PICKING

Seasonal agricultural work is available May-October, for periods of approx 2/3 weeks. However, those looking for this type of work will be competing against a large number of students as well as seasonal workers. This, added to the number of unemployed looking for work and to the decreasing need for manual labour due to mechanisation, makes it more

FRANCE

and more difficult to find employment. Seasonal agricultural workers receive the national minimum wage, *le SMIC*, approx FF30 per hour. Food and accommodation are not always provided and workers should take their own camping and cooking equipment.

The grape harvest takes place between approx 20 September and 30 October in Beaujolais, Aquitaine, the Loire Valley, Central France, Burgundy, Midi-Pyrénées and Champagne. Three types of work are available - picking the grapes, collecting the baskets, or emptying baskets for which 20% more is paid. Work is generally for 8 hours a day and may include Sundays. Wages are usually slightly higher than *SMIC* rates; board and lodging provided by the farmer and deducted from gross earnings. Workers generally pay their own travel costs. All agricultural work is physically demanding and can involve working long hours in all-weather conditions; accommodation may be very basic.

Applicants are strongly advised to take enough money to cover the cost of their stay in France and their return fare should they be unable to find work. Applications for employment can be made to local national employment agencies (ANPEs) in the relevant areas. Applications should be written in French and sent several months before work is due to start. Applicants should state the type of work they are willing to undertake and the period for which they will be available. However, due to the heavy demand for this type of work, many ANPEs may be reluctant to enter into correspondence. If no reply is received applicants can call in person a few days before work is due to start, but the chances of finding employment are limited. Addresses of the ANPEs in the chief agricultural and wine growing regions are listed at the end of this section. All applicants should have a working knowledge of French and a full passport. A birth certificate may be required by some employers in order for affiliation to the national insurance scheme.

Advertisements for seasonal workers appear in the agricultural press, mainly during August and September. Principal papers are: *La France Agricole* (weekly) and *Motorisation et Technique Agricole* (monthly), 8 Cité Paradis, 75493 Paris Cedex 10.

The season for temporary agricultural work runs from May to October. With adjustments depending on the weather, the following periods represent the best opportunities for employment:

Mid May-end June
Cherry and strawberry picking in the Rhone River Valley, Central France and Périgord

June-August
Haymaking all over France

Mid July-mid August
Harvesting corn in Auvergne and the southwest

August-September
Tobacco harvesting in the southwest and east, males only

Mid September-end October
Grape picking throughout the regions

FARMWORK/GRAPE PICKING

CENTRE DE DOCUMENTATION ET D'INFORMATION RURALE 92 rue du Dessous des Berges, 75013 Paris
Acts as an official clearing house for seasonal agricultural employment, working in conjunction with local ANPEs. Receives notification of several thousand jobs, mainly maize-topping and grape picking. Applications should be made no earlier than 2 months before the proposed period of work. Successful applicants will be notified 8 days before work is due to start. Ages 16+. Compulsory membership FF20. *Applicants from EC countries only; fluent French essential.*

CENTRE D'INFORMATION ET DE DOCUMENTATION JEUNESSE (CIDJ) 101 quai Branly, 75740 Paris Cedex 15
Acts as the local ANPE branch and receives notification of vacancies for seasonal farmworkers; applicants must call in person.

CLAUDE SIREJOL Le Castagné-St Etienne, 46170 Castelnau-St Paul de Loubressac, Montrutier
A small number of volunteers interested in agriculture, and in particular organic farming, are needed to help with general farmwork throughout the year. Tasks include looking

FRANCE

FARMWORK/GRAPE PICKING

after livestock, crops and vegetables. No experience necessary. Applicants under 18 must have parental consent. Full board and lodging in farmhouse or campsite and a small payment at the end of the work provided. Volunteers pay their own travel and insurance costs.

FERME APICOLE DE SABLE Joseph Barale, 47400 Grateloup Tel 53 88 80 23
Volunteers interested in beekeeping are required on this bee farm of 500 hives. The farm produces honey, pollen, queen bees and beeswax, and ensures pollenisation of surrounding orchards. Volunteers take part in all aspects of work necessary for the smooth running of the farm. Slide shows held on various aspects of beekeeping, and excursions organised at weekends to places of apicultural or general interest. Non-smokers aged 18+, who enjoy outdoor life and have no allergies to bees. Experience desirable, but not essential; knowledge of French required. Approx 50 hours per week, March-October. Midday meal, farm/camping accommodation and insurance provided, plus a small payment at end of work period. **PH** depending on ability. *UK nationals only.*

INTERNATIONAL FARM EXPERIENCE PROGRAMME YFC Centre, National Agricultural Centre, Kenilworth, Warwickshire CV8 2LG Tel Coventry 696584
Provides assistance to young farmers and nurserymen by finding places in farms/nurseries abroad enabling them to broaden their knowledge of agricultural methods. Opportunities for applicants to live and work with a farmer and his family, the work being matched as far as possible with the applicant's requirements. 4 month practical training scheme preceded by a 6 week French language course in Lille or Strasbourg, starting in February or June. Wages £30 per week on farm and pocket money on the course; board and lodging provided plus some travel costs paid.

Ages 18-26. Applicants must have a minimum of 2 years practical experience, of which at least 1 year may be at agricultural college, and intend to make a career in agriculture or horticulture. Valid driving licence necessary. Registration fee £62. *EC nationals only; apply at least 3 months in advance.*

French applicants should apply to Centre Nationale des Jeunes Agriculteurs, 14 rue la Boetie, 75382 Paris.

JEUNESSE ET RECONSTRUCTION 10 rue de Trévise, 75009 Paris
Offers a large number of places on grape picking camps during the wine harvest in Beaujolais, Champagne, Chablis, and Cote d'Or. Ages 16-30; applicants under 18 must have parental consent. All participants must supply a medical certificate. Up to 9 hour day, 7 day week. Applicants should be free to work anytime, for at least 8-10 days, and good harvests last 15-20 days, September and October. As little as 48 hours' notice may be given before work is due to start, so it is essential that applicants are prepared to leave for France at any time. Food and basic accommodation usually provided on the farm but participants should take a sleeping bag. Wages FF200-FF250 per day, from which board, lodging and national insurance are deducted. Participants arrange and pay their own travel. Registration fee FF280. *Enclose IRCs to the value of FF10.*

NATURE ET PROGRES Service des Stages, Service de Remplacement, Michel Champy, chez Mr Roger Fransoret, Alancourt Mancy, 51200 Epernay
Offers a placement service on organic farms for those interested in gaining practical experience in methods of organic farming. Placements last a minimum of 3 months, with a maximum trial period of 3 weeks. Knowledge of French desirable. Board and lodging provided; pay varies and is at the discretion of the individual farmer. A few short-term places available during grape and fruit harvests. Priority is given to those expressing a genuine interest in pursuing a course of study or career in organic farming. *Write for application form, enclosing 5 IRCs.*

VACATION WORK INTERNATIONAL 9 Park End Street, Oxford, Oxfordshire OX1 1HJ Tel Oxford 241978
Wine harvest work, grape picking or basket carrying in Languedoc-Roussillon available, 15-20 days, September-October. Applicants should be flexible and available for the full harvest. Wages approx FF227-FF278 per day plus free wine, less a social security deduction

of 15%. Higher rates paid for porters and at weekends. Basic accommodation provided in barns or dormitories; participants should take a sleeping bag. Accommodation and self-catering facilities provided free. 8/9 hour day. Ages 16+. Applicants should be EC nationals, fit and prepared to work a 7 day week. Cost from £139 and FF100 registration fee, includes outward travel by train. Insurance extra. *Apply by 15 August.*

ANPEs IN THE WINE PRODUCING AREAS

Aquitaine Tour 2000, terrasse Front-du-Médoc, 33076 Bordeaux Cedex

Bourgogne 7 rue des Corroyeurs, 21033 Dijon Cedex

6 rue Claude Debussy, 71000 Macon

Centre 3 passage des Albanais, 45000 Orléans

Cité Administrative, Champ Girault, PO Box 2510, 37025 Tours Cedex

Champagne-Ardennes 40 rue de Talleyrand, 51057 Reims Cedex

Languedoc-Roussillon 44 avenue de Grande-Bretagne, 66000 Perpignan

Midi-Pyrénées 16 allée de Bellefontaine, 31081 Toulouse Cedex

16 rue Lavedan, 81004 Albi Cedex

Pays de la Loire 3 rue Celestin Frenet, 44000 Nantes Cedex

Square Lafayette, 49000 Angers

Poitou-Charentes 14 boulevard Chasseigne, Poitiers Cedex

Provence-Cote d'Azur 65 avenue Cantini, 13298 Marseille Cedex

Rhone-Alpes 87 rue de Seze, 69451 Lyon Cedex

ANPEs IN OTHER AGRICULTURAL AREAS

Alsace 8 rue de l'Auge, 68021 Colmar Cedex

18 rue Auguste-Lamey, 67005 Strasbourg

Aquitaine Residence A Fallières, rue Diderot, 47015 Agen Cedex

2 rue Henri-Farbos, 40000 Mont-de-Marsan

45 rue Emile Guichene, 64016 Pau Cedex

17 rue Louis Blanc, 24016 Périgueux Cedex

Auvergne 70 rue Blatin, 63000 Clermont-Ferrand

Languedoc-Roussillon 76 allée d'Iena, 11002 Carcassonne

25 boulevard Renouvier, 34000 Montpellier

80 avenue Jean-Jaurès, 30040 Nimes Cedex

Rhone-Alpes 98/100 rue Boileau, 69455 Lyon Cedex 3

14 rue du Jeu de Paume, 26001 Valence Cedex

LEADERS & GUIDES

There are around 23,000 holiday centres, *centres de vacances*, all over France recruiting camp counsellors or monitors to supervise young people using the facilities during the summer holidays. Applicants must speak good French and will need to acquire a *Brevet d'aptitude aux fonctions d'animateur* (BAFA) certificate by undertaking a week's study of theory, a 50 hour specialisation course, and a week of practical application in a *centre*. The two training courses will cost approx FF2000, although in some cases the potential employer will offer reimbursement, but payment will be made for the practical training work. The training associations usually also act as placement agencies. As a certified monitor the pay is approx FF4000 per month plus board and accommodation. Work is also available during other school holidays, and on Wednesdays during term time in *centres de*

FRANCE

loisirs. The following six organisations offer preparation courses for the BAFA:

ASSOCIATION NATIONALE SCIENCES ET TECHNIQUES JEUNESSE (ANSTJ) 17 avenue Gambetta, 91130 Ris-Orangis Tel 1 69 06 82 20

CENTRE D'ENTRAINMENT AUX METHODES D'EDUCATION ACTIVE (CEMEA) 76 boulevard de la Villette, 75019 Paris Tel 1 42 06 38 10

COMITE PROTESTANT DES CENTRES DE VACANCES (CPCV) 47 rue de Clichy, 75009 Paris Tel 1 42 80 06 99

STAJ 27 rue du Château d'Eau, 75010 Paris Tel 1 42 08 56 63

UNION FRANCAISE DES CENTRES DE VACANCES (UFCV) 19 rue Dareau, 75014 Paris Tel 1 45 35 25 26

UNION NATIONALE DES CENTRES SPORTIFS ET DE PLEIN AIR (UCPA) 62 rue de la Glacière, 75640 Paris Cedex 13 Tel 1 43 36 05 20

LEADERS & GUIDES

CLUB CANTABRICA HOLIDAYS LTD Overseas Department, Holiday House, 146-148 London Road, St Albans, Hertfordshire AL1 1PQ Tel St Albans 33141 Organises camping holidays, providing fully equipped tents, caravans and mobile homes. Kiddies representatives are required for the summer season, mid May-early October, in Cavalaire, Port Grimaud, Canet and Perpignan. 6 day week. Wages from £40 per week, plus bonus at end of season. Ages 21+. Nursery or NNEB qualifications required; experience an advantage. Self-catering accommodation in tents or caravans, travel costs from Watford and insurance provided.

PGL YOUNG ADVENTURE LTD Personnel Department, Alton Court, Penyard Lane, Ross-on-Wye, Herefordshire HR9 5NR Tel Ross-on-Wye 764211 Organises outdoor adventure holidays for young people and adults in the Ardèche and on the Mediterranean. Activities include canoeing, sailing, windsurfing, water skiing and caving. Group and activity organisers are

required. Group organisers are responsible for group welfare and for contributing to the entertainments programme when not participating in the main sports activities. Group organisers greet the group of approx 45 on its arrival and are responsible for them until their departure 3/4 days later. Entertainment organisers are responsible for the organisation and running of all evening activities and entertainments including disco, games, talent contests and competitive events for ages 12-18. Applicants should be energetic and enthusiastic, reliable and mature, self-motivated, with leadership qualities, stamina, tolerance, flexibility, initiative and a sense of humour. Experience in working with children and handling young people at leisure preferable.

Ages 21+. May-September. Jobs are usually for 8 week periods. Staff are also recruited for very short periods over the spring bank holiday. Return travel from Dover, full board, accommodation in frame tents and health insurance provided. Sports and social facilities available, plus participation in programmed activities. 1 day free per week. Pocket money FF320 per week. *Applications should ideally be made between December and April.*

TOPS HOLIDAYS (SUN LIVING LTD) Personnel Manager, Adventure House, 34-36 South Street, Lancing, West Sussex BN15 8AG Tel Lancing 751942 Organises a range of specialised activity and outdoor education programmes for groups of school children aged 12-17 at campsites in the Ardèche and Les Tamaris in the south, at a hotel in Hardelot in the north and at a centre in the Pyrénées. Each centre has its own team of staff to ensure that high standards of safety, instruction and enjoyment are maintained. Group leaders are required to work at these centres. Work involves looking after the general welfare of a group of up to 50 children and making sure they get the most from their holiday. Leaders are also responsible for ensuring their group arrives at activities, meals and events on time, sorting out problems and organising entertainments.

Ages 20+. Experience of working with children, and of at least one of the activities organised an advantage. The jobs demand a high level of commitment both physically and mentally; applicants should enjoy being with children all day, have a genuine interest in their welfare, be patient, sympathetic and diplomatic. Fitness, stamina, energy, enthusiasm and the ability to live and work as part of a team are also essential. 40+ hour week, 1 day free per week. 1+ months, May-September. Most staff work the full season; extra staff are also taken on for shorter periods during peak times at Easter and during July and August. There are opportunities for staff to move from centre to centre. Travel costs from Dover, full board apartment or tent accommodation and insurance provided. Pay from £35 per week, paid in local currency. Training provided to ensure staff are confident and able to carry out their responsibilities. Social and recreational activities such as parties, barbecues and outings arranged for staff. Senior positions also available. *British nationals only.* B D PH limited opportunities.

TEACHERS & INSTRUCTORS

CENTRAL BUREAU Assistants Department, Seymour Mews House, Seymour Mews, London W1H 9PE Tel 071-486 5101
Opportunities exist for *Assistants à Temps Partiel* (ATPs) to work in French state secondary schools, working under the supervision of the English teaching staff and assisting them in the classroom. ATPs may also take small groups of pupils to improve their command of spoken English and give them an insight into British life, customs and institutions, and are expected to participate fully in the life of the school.
Ages 18-20. Applicants must have A level French. Lodging provided and possibility of subsidised meals. Monthly allowance approx FF2000, payable in arrears. 8 hours teaching and 3 hours recreational activities per week. 2 terms, January-June. Short introductory course held in Paris before taking up duty, for which group travel and accommodation are arranged. Onward travel is the responsibility of the applicant. It should be possible to attend classes in local schools on subjects of particular interest. The number of posts is limited and

competition strong. Registration fee £5. *Application forms available from end March; apply by first week of June.*

CENTRE DE VOILE DE LANDEDA BP4, Aber Wrac'h, 29214 Landeda
Vacancies exist for qualified instructors to teach sailing and windsurfing at the centre situated in a small fishing village. Knowledge of French essential. Ages 19+. June-September. 40 hour week. Board, lodging and insurance provided. Salary FF550 per week. Excursions arranged to surrounding areas.

CENTRE REGIONAL DE NAUTISME DE GRANVILLE boulevard des Amiraux, Port de Herel, BP140, 50401 Granville Cedex
Staff are needed to teach and supervise sailing at all levels at the residential sailing school/ youth centre, equipped with dinghies, sailboards, catamarans, sea kayaks and cruisers. Ages 19+. July and August. 30-36 hour week. Board and lodging provided. Salary FF140 per day. Applicants must have good spoken French and a diploma awarded by the national sailing federation of their country of origin. Travel paid by the applicant.

FREEDOM OF FRANCE Personnel Department, 2-5 Market Place, Ross-on-Wye, Herefordshire HR9 5LD Tel Ross-on-Wye 767833
Provides luxury self-drive, self-catering holidays at campsites throughout France. Activity instructors in canoeing, sailing and windsurfing are required to work at 12 sites from Brittany through to the Bordeaux coast, and on the Mediterranean. Children of guests who will be divided into different age groups. Good command of French useful. Applicants should ideally have considerable experience, hold a RYA or BCU Certificate and have previously worked as an instructor. April-September, hours variable. Ages 21+. Salary £70-£75 per week, self-catering accommodation in large tents, full liability and medical insurance, and travel from UK port provided.

FRENCH EMBASSY Cultural Service, 23 Cromwell Road, London SW7 2EW
Publishes an information sheet *Teaching Posts in France* giving details of how to obtain posts as *lecteurs* and assistants in state and private schools.

FRANCE

TEACHERS & INSTRUCTORS

PGL YOUNG ADVENTURE LTD Personnel Department, Alton Court, Penyard Lane, Ross-on-Wye, Herefordshire HR9 5NR Tel Ross-on-Wye 764211
Organises outdoor adventure holidays for young people and adults in the Ardèche and on the Mediterranean. Activities include canoeing, sailing, windsurfing, water skiing and caving. Experienced or qualified Canadian canoeists, sailors, windsurfers and cavers are required as instructors and river leaders at the centres. River leaders, senior sailors, senior water skiers and their teams assist with the care and welfare and evening entertainment of a group, including total responsibility for their safety and enjoyment, as well as for canoeing/sailing instruction.

Ages 21+, occasionally 18+ with relevant qualifications or experience. Applicants should ideally have considerable experience, first aid and lifesaving experience, hold a RYA or BCU Certificate, and have previously worked as an instructor. A good basic level of skill is important as well as the ability to impart it to others with enthusiasm and interest. Applicants should also be able to adhere to strict safety standards, have the foresight to deal with emergencies, and recognise the limitations of each learner. The emphasis is on informality and enjoyment; the ability to manage and organise a team of staff is essential. Applicants should be fit, energetic and enthusiastic, reliable and mature, with leadership qualities, initiative and a sense of humour; experience of working with young people preferable. May-September; jobs are usually for 8 week periods but are sometimes for the whole season. Staff are also recruited for very short periods over the spring bank holiday. Return travel from Dover, full board, accommodation in frame tents and health insurance provided. Sports and social facilities available, plus participation in programmed activities. Pocket money per week FF320 (canoeists, sailors, windsurfers and cavers), FF370 (river leaders), and FF650 (senior watersports instructors in sailing, windsurfing and senior canoeists). *Applicants available in May and early July have a greater chance of selection. Applications should ideally be made between December and April.*

QUEST TRAVEL Olivier House, 18 Marine Parade, Brighton, East Sussex BN2 1TL Tel Brighton 677777
Provides ski and summer tours for groups, mainly school parties, individuals and youth and adult organisations. Requires ski instructors for the winter season, December-April, in Notre Dame, Chatel, Crest Voland, Pra Loup and other resorts. Applicants must hold a BASI Certificate, and should preferably have experience in teaching both children and adults. 48 hour week. Ages 21+. Salary £75-£130 per week, full board, lodging in shared accommodation, medical insurance and return travel provided. Training course at beginning of season. B D PH limited opportunities.

SKI EUROPE Northumberland House, 2 King Street, Twickenham, Middlesex TW1 3RZ Tel 081-891 4400
Operates holidays for groups and school parties. Part-time ski instructors are required for winter sports in Savoie, Vanoise and Hautes-Alpes. Work involves 6 hours teaching per day. BASI or full ASSI qualifications essential, together with a high level of teaching skill. A knowledge of foreign languages useful but not essential, but fluent English is a prerequisite. 1-2 week periods over Christmas, New Year, in February and April. Instructors receive full board hotel accommodation and ski pass plus travel expenses London/resort, and have access to the same facilities as the clients. Wages approx £75 per week, depending on qualifications. *Interviews take place May-November.*

SNOW WORLD (SUN LIVING LTD) Personnel Manager, Adventure House, 34-36 South Street, Lancing, West Sussex BN15 8AG Tel Lancing 751942
Opportunities exist for ski instructors. Ages 18-30. Applicants must have BASI grade 3 or equivalent qualifications. 8-10 hour day, 6 day week, although hours vary depending on needs of clients. Applicants should be prepared to work for the whole season, December-April. Extra staff may also be required at peak times such as Christmas. Also opportunities for ski technicians. Board, lodging and travel provided. Salary from £80 per week. Training is given at the resort in the week before clients arrive.

TOPS HOLIDAYS (SUN LIVING LTD)
Personnel Manager, Adventure House, 34-36 South Street, Lancing, West Sussex BN15 8AG
Tel Lancing 751942
Organises a range of specialised activity and outdoor education programmes for groups of school children aged 12-17 at campsites in the Ardèche and Les Tamaris in the south, at a hotel in Hardelot in the north and at a centre in the Pyrénées. Each centre has its own team of staff who ensure that high standards of safety, instruction and enjoyment are maintained. Activity instructors are required to teach horse riding, trail riding, sailing, windsurfing, canoeing, climbing, abseiling, archery, rifle shooting and motorsports. Instructors must have the ability to teach their sport to a good basic level and impart the knowledge to a variety of ages in an imaginative, interesting way. The emphasis is on safety, fun and participation rather than achievement. Ages 18+, preference given to ages 20+. Qualifications from the relevant sporting body are a definite advantage, but applicants with just teaching experience will be considered.

Instructors with experience in or an aptitude for BMX bikes, orienteering, assault course, photography, hill walking, camping, raft building, swimming and trials bikes are also needed. In these activities prior technical skills are less significant than personality and teaching ability; training is given and most staff learn to cope with and enjoy 2 or 3 new activities. In addition there are a number of senior instructor positions, such as River Leader and Head Activity Instructor, for which applicants with extensive experience and maturity will be considered. All jobs demand a high level of commitment both physically and mentally; applicants should enjoy being with children all day and have a genuine interest in their welfare. Fitness, stamina, energy, enthusiasm and the ability to live and work as part of a team are also essential. 40+ hour week, 1 day free per week. 1+ months, May-September. Most staff work the full season; extra staff are also taken on for shorter periods during peak times at Easter and during July and August. There are opportunities for staff to move from centre to centre. Travel costs from Dover, full board apartment or tent accommodation and insurance provided. Pay from £35 per week

paid in local currency, and varying according to experience and responsibilities. Training provided to ensure staff are confident and able to carry out their responsibilities. Social and recreational activities such as parties, barbecues and outings arranged for staff. *British nationals only.* B D PH limited opportunities.

WORKCAMPS

CENTRE DE LA FORMATION DE LA JEUNESSE DU QUART MOND, 29 rue du Stade, Champeaux, 77720 Mormant
Part of the Movement ATD Fourth World which aims to protect the fundamental rights of the poorest and most disadvantaged and excluded families, which constitute the Fourth World. These rights include the right to family life, to education and training, and to representation. Workcamps are organised at the youth centre, involving construction, carpentry, electrical installation, painting, gardening, office work and cooking. Evenings are reserved for discussions and the exchange of ideas about the fight against poverty, as well as the sharing of knowledge between young people of different social backgrounds. Ages 16-25. Volunteers should be concerned by persistent poverty and social exclusion. French speakers only. 6 hours of manual work daily. 5/6 days, April, August/September and November. Full board and accommodation provided. Volunteers pay their own travel and insurance. Volunteers should take a sleeping bag. Cost FF200.

CENTRE D'INFORMATION ET DE DOCUMENTATION JEUNESSE (CIDJ)
101 Quai Branly, 75740 Paris Cedex 15
Publishes an information sheet *Chantiers de Travail Volontaire* which gives details on workcamps with a list of addresses, type of work and dates.

CHANTIERS DE JEUNES PROVENCE-COTE D'AZUR (CJPCA) 3 rue Esprit Violet, 06400 Cannes
Arranges workcamps for young people during the summer. Recent projects have included converting buildings to create outdoor pursuits centres or meeting places for young people

FRANCE

WORKCAMPS

including the restoration of a 17th century fort on the Ile Sainte-Marguerite. Ages 14-18. 2 weeks, July and August. Nature walks and watersports arranged. Food, accommodation and insurance provided. Volunteers pay own travel and FF570-910 depending on workcamp. Membership fee FF100 per person, FF120 per family. Volunteers must have written parental consent and a medical certificate.

CHRISTIAN MOVEMENT FOR PEACE
Bethnal Green United Reformed Church, Pott Street, London E2 0EF Tel 071-729 1877
An international movement open to all who share a common concern for lasting peace and justice in the world. Volunteers are needed to work in international teams on summer projects aimed at offering a service in an area of need and promoting self-help within the community, promoting international understanding and the discussion of social problems, and offering young people the chance to live as a group and take these experiences into the context of daily life. Recent projects have included constructing a centre for meetings and group activities; building a new workshop in an educational centre; converting an old school into a rest centre in the Haute-Alpes; creating a natural ice rink; restoring a 12th century chapel for use as a museum on provincial history and traditions; converting a 16th century chapel into a hiker's shelter; and putting on a play in a renovated monastery. Sports and social activities organised. International seminars also arranged. Ages 15-17 and 18+. 6 hour day, 30-36 hour week. 2-3 weeks, July-September. Food, accommodation and insurance provided, but participants pay their own travel costs and sometimes contribute towards food expenses. Registration fee £24. **B D PH**

Organised by Mouvement Chrétien pour la Paix, 38 rue du Faubourg St Denis, 75010 Paris.

Applications from outside the UK: please see workcamp information on page 27.

INTERNATIONAL MOVEMENT ATD
FOURTH WORLD 107 avenue du Général Leclerc, 95480 Pierrelaye
Strives to protect the fundamental rights of the poorest and most disadvantaged and excluded families, which constitute the Fourth World. These rights include the right to family life, to education and training, and to representation. Volunteers are needed, helping to build the international centre at Méry sur Oise where training sessions take place. Work involves construction, carpentry, electrical installation, painting, plumbing, gardening, office work and cooking. Study preceding camp and during evenings arranged. Ages 18+. Volunteers should be concerned by persistent poverty and social exclusion. All nationalities accepted. Knowledge of French helpful but not essential. 7 hour day. 2 weeks, June-September. Full board, accommodation in tents and bungalows, and basic insurance provided. Volunteers should take a sleeping bag and work clothes. Cost FF400, 15 days. Travel paid by volunteers; 20% reduction on French rail network.

INTERNATIONAL VOLUNTARY SERVICE
162 Upper New Walk, Leicester LE1 7QA Tel Leicester 549430
IVS is the British branch of Service Civil International which promotes international reconciliation through work projects. Volunteers are needed on workcamps. Recent projects have included fitting out a horse and buggy holiday centre in northern Isère; painting and masonry work at a young people's meeting place in the Ariège mountains; travelling around Paris on a peace truck to provide information on peace education; and decorating and gardening at a holiday centre for underprivileged children in Rhone-Alpes. Projects are linked to study themes. A good knowledge of French is needed on some camps. Walking holidays in the mountains also arranged, which provide fundraising and a workcamp atmosphere for those unable to attend.
Ages 18+. Applicants should be prepared to work hard and contribute to team life. 35-40 hour week. 2-4 weeks, May-September; a few places at Christmas, Easter and in the autumn. Food, accommodation and insurance provided, but not travel. Membership fee £25 (students £15, unwaged £10). Registration fee £40. **B D PH**

Organised by Service Civil International, 129 rue du Faubourg Poissonnière, 75009 Paris.

UK applications to IVS; overseas applications: see workcamp information on page 27.

NEIGE ET MERVEILLES, La Minière de Valluria, 06430 Saint Dalmas de Tende
Arranges sports, leisure and cultural activities, and youth meetings; workcamps are organised in the mountain hamlet where the centre is based. Recent projects have included rebuilding a mountain shelter surrounded by Bronze Age rock carvings; constructing a road; chopping and gathering wood; and conservation work on the site of a nearby fort. Ages 16+. 20/35 hour week. 2 weeks, April-September. Mountain walks and excursions arranged. Volunteers should take a sleeping bag, warm, waterproof clothing and good walking shoes. Food, accommodation and insurance provided. Volunteers pay own travel and FF360 fee to cover costs.

UNITED NATIONS ASSOCIATION International Youth Service, Welsh Centre for International Affairs, Temple of Peace, Cathays Park, Cardiff CF1 3AP Tel Cardiff 223088
Volunteers are needed to work on a choice of approx 60 international workcamps which aim to help in the development of small communities in mountainous and isolated rural areas and give participants a chance to get to know their natural, political, economic and social environment. Typical projects involve constructing community centres for use by villagers, children or handicapped people, and renovating or converting existing agricultural buildings, abbeys and schools. Work includes masonry, carpentry, flooring, painting, roofing, tiling, woodwork, plumbing, electrical and insulation work. Also equipping mountain huts with water and electricity, building rest gites, demolition and repair or maintenance work. Volunteers are taught traditional building techniques by local craftsmen. The camps provide an opportunity to discover a region, its traditions and inhabitants, and to become involved in the life of a village community. Sports, crafts, dance, music, theatre, and other cultural activities arranged. Ages 17-25. Good knowledge of French needed for some camps. Applicants should preferably have previous workcamp experience. 35 hour week. 3 weeks, June-November and 2 weeks, Easter and Christmas. Also camps for ages 15-17; 25 hours per week. Projects include constructing a sports field and renovating holiday, youth and watersports centres. Full

board, accommodation in schools, huts or community buildings and insurance provided. Volunteers pay their own travel. Registration fee FF550; FF800 for ages 15-17. **B D PH**

Organised by Concordia, 27 rue du Pont-Neuf, PO Box 238, 75024 Paris Cedex 01.

Applications from outside the UK: please see workcamp information on page 27.

GENERAL

CANVAS HOLIDAYS LTD Bull Plain, Hertford, SG14 1DY Tel Hertford 553535
Provides ready-erected fully equipped tents for holiday families. Requires applicants to form a flying squad, a team of 2/3 people who help set up and equip 200-250 6 berth frame tents in an area containing approx 12 campsites. Similar work is also available dismantling tents and cleaning and storing equipment. A knowledge of French is not required but is an advantage as flying squad members sometimes have the opportunity to continue as couriers. Applicants must be sociable in order to work in a small community, fit, and able to work hard for long hours under pressure and without supervision, and to cope with living out of a rucksack. Ages 18-25. End April-mid June, possibly longer, to set up the tents, and September, to dismantle them. Valid driving licence an advantage. Salary approx £76 per week plus tented accommodation and self-catering facilities. Outward travel paid; return travel dependent on the completion of contract dates.

CAREFREE CAMPING LTD Operations Manager, 126 Hempstead Road, Kings Langley, Hertfordshire WD4 8AL Tel Watford 261316
Operates self-drive family holidays providing fully furnished and equipped tents and mobile homes. Vacancies exist for drivers and assistant drivers to deliver equipment to and from campsites immediately before and after the summer season. Applicants must have driving experience, preferably overseas and/or using vans. Good command of French desirable. Mid April-mid May or during September. Ages 19+. Salary approx £80 per week. Accommodation on sites, transport and insurance provided.

FRANCE

GENERAL

FRANCE

CENTRE D'INFORMATION ET DE DOCUMENTATION JEUNESSE (CIDJ) 101 quai Branly, 75740 Paris Cedex 15

Issues an information sheet listing branches throughout France which act as local branches of the ANPE. Temporary jobs for young EC nationals, usually in offices or working with children, are put on the noticeboards.

EUROYOUTH LTD 301 Westborough Road, Westcliff-on-Sea, Essex SS0 9PT Tel Southend-on-Sea 341434

Holiday guest stays are arranged whereby guests are offered board and lodging in return for an agreed number of hours' English conversation with hosts or their children. Time is also available for guests to practise French if desired. Mainly ages 15-25, but there are sometimes opportunities for older applicants. The scheme is open to anyone who was born and educated in the UK, interested in visiting France and living with a local family for a short time. 2-3 weeks, June-August. Insurance and travel arranged by the applicant, but tickets at reduced rates on request. Registration fee approx £80. *Apply at least 12 weeks prior to scheduled departure date. Limited places.*

GENERAL

FLOT'HOME UK/BARGE FRANCE 25 Kingswood Creek, Wraysbury, Staines Middlesex

Operates floating holidays on French canals, using cabin cruisers and hotel barges. Vacancies exist for barge crews and boat yard assistants in Burgundy, Alsace-Lorraine and the Midi area of southern France. Crews consist of 4 members, including an experienced bargemaster, and positions range from deckhand to mechanic. Ages 21+. 6+ months, throughout the year; peak season April-October. Crews work long hours, 50-80 per week, and must be fit. Previous experience of similar work preferred. Some knowledge of French or German essential. Salary £70-£125 per week, depending on experience, on-board accommodation and travel expenses provided. Applicants pay own insurance and food costs.

FREE TIME 9 bis boulevard de Italiens, 75002 Paris Tel 42 96 95 87
MACDONALDS 11 boulevard Saint Denis, 75002 Paris Tel 42 21 34 17

Fast food franchises in major cities take on extra staff on a part-time contractual basis,

particularly during holiday periods. Ages 18-25. Food, uniform and *le SMIC*, the national minimum wage provided. Applicants should either contact the managers of individual branches directly, or write to the main offices in Paris, addresses above.

GAP ACTIVITY PROJECTS LTD 44 Queen's Road, Reading, Berkshire, RG1 4BB Tel Reading 594914

A limited number of placements are available with banks, accountants, stockbrokers and law offices in Paris, Lille and Lyon for school leavers aged 18-19, with up to a year before going on to further education. 3-6 months departing September or January. Cost £260 plus travel costs. Accommodation and pocket money provided. *Apply in September of last school year; applications close in March.*

NAT HOLIDAYS, Overseas Personnel Officer, ILG Travel Ltd, Holiday House, Domestic Road, Leeds LS12 6HR Tel Leeds 434690

Vacancies exist for suitably qualified and experienced child minders, office staff, cashiers, bar staff, night security staff, electricians, plumbers and carpenters to work on campsites. Ages 21+/24+. April-October, with some positions available for students only in June/July. Applicants for all positions should be reliable, hard working, prepared to work as part of a team, and have enough staying power to last the season. Knowledge of French an advantage. All staff are required to take an active part in their resort entertainment programme, helping to organise events such as parties, barbecues, and games evenings. Salary from £57-£75 per week, depending on position. Accommodation in single or shared tents with self-catering cooking facilities and return travel provided. Compulsory 2 week training programme in April. *Early application advisable - recruitment starts December, interviews commence mid-January.*

NSS RIVIERA HOLIDAYS, 199 Marlborough Avenue, Hull, North Humberside HU5 3LG Tel Hull 42240

Owns 26 chalets and mobile homes at a holiday village near Fréjus, between St Tropez and Cannes. Facilities include 2 swimming pools, tennis courts, bars, disco, shops, washeteria, take-away and restaurant. Couples or two

FRANCE

friends with own car required as helpers for 4 weeks between Easter and Whitsun, or for 4 weeks in October to prepare or repair accommodation. Ages 24-60. Applicants should have good painting/decorating/DIY skills, or be electricians, joiners, builders, plumbers or gardeners. 3 days work per week. Accommodation, gas, electricity and use of site amenities provided. Caretakers also required to check holiday homes and keep gardens in good order. October-Easter. Fully equipped self-contained accommodation offered at £10 per week in return for work; some paid work available if required, 3 days per week. Ages 24+. Particularly suitable for writers or others seeking solitude. Own car essential. Non-smokers preferred; references necessary for all posts. *Apply in writing only.*

QUEST TRAVEL Olivier House, 18 Marine Parade, Brighton, East Sussex BN2 1TL Tel Brighton 677777
Provides ski and summer tours for groups, mainly school parties, individuals and youth and adult organisations. Requires hotel managers during the winter and summer seasons, December-April and May-July/August, in Notre Dame, Chatel, Crest Voland, Pra Loup and other resorts. Managers are responsible for stock control, management of personnel, PR work, ordering of stock, banking, insurance, fire precautions, rooming and general administration. 54 hour week, on call 24 hours per day. Ages 18+. Knowledge of French and experience essential. Salary £90-£100 per week, full board, lodging in shared accommodation, medical insurance and return travel provided. Training course at beginning of season. B D PH limited opportunities.

PGL YOUNG ADVENTURE LTD Personnel Department, Alton Court, Penyard Lane, Ross-on-Wye, Herefordshire HR9 5NR Tel Ross-on-Wye 764211
Organises outdoor adventure holidays for young people and adults in the Ardèche and on the Mediterranean. Activities include canoeing, sailing, windsurfing, water skiing and caving. Staff required at the centres include: nurses, mainly responsible for the treatment of minor ailments, maintaining the medicine stock and also helping in administration and welfare;

driver, site and stores assistants, responsible for transporting guests and staff, collecting and delivering food and equipment, ensuring the tidiness and cleanliness of the site and issuing and keeping a close check on all the equipment; general maintenance assistants, work involves painting, labouring, carpentry, gardening, driving and errands; lift operators, responsible for operating the goods lift, unloading and delivering goods; fibreglassers/canoe leaders, repairing and maintaining fibreglass canoes and accompanying canoe pick-up trips; tent repairers, responsible for tent and sleeping bag repairs; HGV and PSV drivers, responsible for delivering and collecting canoes; administrative assistants required for office work, public relations, costings, ordering, petty cash, wages, stock and giving information to the centres. Ages 20+, preference given to ages 21+. Applicants should be responsible, self-motivated, flexible, positive, energetic and enthusiastic, reliable and mature, with a sense of humour; supplies and services staff also need to be very fit. Staff working with the guests should preferably have experience of working with children. May-September; jobs are usually for 8 week periods but are sometimes for the whole season. Staff are also recruited for very short periods over the spring bank holiday. Fibreglassers, tent repairers, HGV drivers and general maintenance staff work March-October. Return travel from Dover, full board, accommodation in frame tents and health insurance provided. Sports and social facilities available, plus participation in programmed activities. 1 day free per week. Pocket money FF280-FF600 per week according to qualifications and position. *Applicants available in May and early July have a greater chance of selection. Applications should ideally be made December-April.*

GENERAL

SKI WHIZZ/SMALL WORLD Hillgate House, Hillgate Street, London W8 7SP Tel 071-221 9868
Arranges chalet holidays in the French Alps. Snow men required to work in ski resorts in the Alps and the Dolomites. Work is very varied and can involve acting as van driver, log chopper, wine merchant, impromptu cook and snow shoveller. Snow men also act as ski guides and will need to gain a good knowledge of skiing facilities in the area and become

FRANCE

familiar with the resort's *pistes* and lifts. Ages 22+. Applicants must be good skiers with a clean driving licence and a knowledge of mechanics. Experience of dealing with the general public, flexibility and basic knowledge of French or German also essential. Hours variable; applicants must be prepared to work hard. 6 days per week, December-May. Wages £50 per week. Board, lodging, ski pass and hire, return travel and medical insurance provided.

SNOWTIME LTD 96 Belsize Lane, Hampstead, London NW3 5BE Tel 071-433 3336
Organises luxury winter skiing holidays in Méribel. Requires practical, mechanically minded men to act as drivers and handymen. As duties involve liaison with local companies, agents and suppliers, a good command of French is required. Applicants should be efficient, capable, friendly and outgoing, preferably with experience of this type of work. Ages 25+. 30-50 hour week, depending on position. Staff work the whole season, December-May. Pay from £35 per week, return travel and insurance provided. *British nationals only.*

GENERAL

SOCIETE D'APPROVISIONNEMENT PLAGISTE boulevard d'Archimède, Zone Industrielle, 66200 Elne
Require people to sell ice creams, doughnuts and drinks on the beaches around Perpignan. Ages 18+. No experience necessary. 5 hour day, afternoons only. 7 days per week, July and August. Wages 25% of sales, approx £20-£30 per day. Accommodation available on campsites at approx £3 per night. Applicants should take their own tent, camping equipment and sleeping bag. Travel and insurance paid by applicant.

SUN LIVING LTD French Experience Programme, 34-36 South Street, Lancing, West Sussex BN15 8AG Tel Lancing 750310
Offers the opportunity for applicants to improve their French language skills and fluency by working in French-managed hotels, from the Alps to the Cote d'Azur. Staff are totally immersed in a French-speaking environment, becoming part of the local community. Waiters/waitresses, housemaids and kitchen assistants are required, and are expected to adjust to the host style of working

as part of a conscientious team providing a high standard of service. The work can be very hard and applicants must have the stamina to combine long hours with a frenetic social calendar. December-April and May-September. Ages 18+. Applicants must have a working knowledge of spoken French; previous experience of hotel or catering work an advanatage. Salary £40 per week, full board, accommodation and return travel provided, plus ski pass for winter season staff.

SUSI MADRON'S CYCLING FOR SOFTIES Lloyds House, 22 Lloyd Street, Manchester M2 5WA Tel 061-834 6800
Organises a variety of cycling holidays in the regions of Mayenne and Sarthe, Loire, Venise Verte, Cognac and Charente, Beaujolais and Jura, Rhone, Provence and Camargue, and the Dordogne and Garonne. Vacancies exist for holiday assistants. The work includes welcoming guests, maintaining cycles to a high standard, helping in emergencies and providing on-the-spot information about the region. 2-3 months, May-September. Ages 19/20+. Applicants should be self-confident and adaptable, able to liaise with diverse groups from guests to hoteliers. Fluent English and French essential. Hours variable with one day off per week. Salary £65 per week, bonus, self-catering flat or house accommodation, travel and insurance provided. Generally 2 assistants work together; full training given before work commences, and high support system in place.

TOPS HOLIDAYS (SUN LIVING LTD) Personnel Manager, Adventure House, 34-36 South Street, Lancing, West Sussex BN15 8AG Tel Lancing 751942
Organises a range of specialised activity and outdoor education programmes for groups of school children aged 12-17 at campsites in the Ardèche and Les Tamaris in the south, at a hotel in Hardelot in the North and a centre in the Pyrénées. Each centre has its own team of staff who ensure that high standards of safety, instruction and enjoyment are maintained.

Staff are required for the following positions: administration assistants, helping to run the centres and operate holiday programmes, preferably with experience of paperwork or accounts; qualified nurses, RGN, SRN or equivalent, providing medical care and supervising general welfare of staff and guests; support staff who have close contact with guests, requiring a basic level of skill in catering and mechanics, for example; maintenance staff who are expected to do minor repairs to equipment, tents, vehicles and outboard engines, and help with rubbish clearance, gardening, tent erection and driving jobs, with experience in trailer towing, minibus driving, vehicle maintenance useful, and willingness and aptitude to learn essential; centre managers, responsible for running the centres and directing a large team of young, inexperienced staff, with wide ranging experience, proven ability, total commitment, good administrative and organisational skills and a willingness to work hard for the whole operational period. Staff often assist with all areas of the centre's operation and will need to be flexible. All posts involve direct contact with children and their activities, so staff must be prepared to become completely involved.

Ages 18+, preference given to ages 20+. The jobs demand a high level of commitment, both physically and mentally; applicants should enjoy being with children all day and have a genuine interest in their welfare. Fitness, stamina, enthusiasm and the ability to live and work as part of a team are also essential. Knowledge of French useful for all posts, and essential for administrative posts. 40+ hour week, 1 day free per week. 1+ months, May-September. Most staff work the full season; extra staff are also taken on for shorter periods during peak times at Easter and during July and August. Opportunities for staff to move from centre to centre. Travel costs from Dover, full board, dormitory, apartment or tent accommodation and insurance provided. Pay approx £30-£50 per week depending on experience and responsibilities; centre managers' pay negotiable. Training provided to ensure staff are confident and able to carry out their responsibilities. Social and recreational activities such as parties, barbecues and outings arranged for staff. *British nationals only.* **B D PH** limited opportunities.

APPLYING FOR A JOB

Read carefully all the information given before applying. Check in particular:

* the necessary skills/experience required

* the full period of employment expected

* any restrictions of age, sex or nationality

* application deadlines

* any other points, particularly details of insurance cover provided, and other costs such as travel and accommodation.

When applying be sure to include:

* name, address, date of birth, marital status, nationality, sex

* education, qualifications, relevant experience

* period of availability

* details of languages spoken

* a large stamped, self-addressed envelope plus, if overseas, 2 International Reply Coupons

* a passport-size photo, particularly if you are to have contact with the public

* any registration or membership fees

FRANCE

GENERAL

NOTES

GERMANY

(DEMOCRATIC REPUBLIC)

Embassy of the German Democratic Republic
34 Belgrave Square, London SW1X 8QB
Tel 071-235 9941   Visa section: Tel 071-235 4465

British Embassy
Unter den Linden 32/34, Berlin 108

Tourist office
Berolina Travel Ltd, 22a Conduit Street,
London W1R 9TB Tel 071-629 1664

Youth & student information
Jugendtourist, Alexanderplatz 5, PSF 57, Berlin 1026

Studenten Reise Service (SRS), Alexanderplatz 25, PSF 57, Berlin 1026

INFORMATION

Entry regulations Workcamp organisations will inform volunteers how to obtain the necessary visa/permit, and hold orientation days for volunteers going to East Europe, giving information on all aspects of the work covered together with some political background and practical information.

Travel Campus Travel, 52 Grosvenor Gardens, London SW1W 0AG Tel 071-730 3402 offer

Eurotrain under 26 fares to destinations in the Democratic Republic.

Accommodation Jugendtourist, General-direktion, Alexanderplatz 5, Berlin 1026 operates a network of youth hostels and hotels all over the German Democratic Republic, including Berlin, Dresden, Potsdam, Rostock and Weimar.

WORKCAMPS

BRITISH COUNCIL OF CHURCHES Youth Unit, Inter-Church House, 35-41 Lower Marsh, London SE1 7RL Tel 071-620 4444
The Ecumenical Youth Council in Europe, the fellowship of national ecumenical youth councils or denominational bodies dealing with church youth work, offers young Christians from different countries and traditions the opportunity to meet and share their experiences and to discuss common issues and concerns. Promotes workcamps where international teams live and work together to serve the community on manual, society or study projects, offering an opportunity to share ideas on faith and life.
Recent projects have included renovating churches and church centres in Wasse, Rostock and Neschwitz, and a Russian Orthodox church in Leipzig; environmental protection work in Hirschluch; working at a centre for people with

handicaps in Altengesees; and maintenance work in the grounds of a castle in Liebstadt. All camps include a relevant theme for study and discussion. Basic knowledge of German usually necessary. Volunteers must be seriously motivated to contribute to the aims of the camp. Ages 18-30. 6 hour day, 2-3 weeks, July/August. Board and lodging usually provided. Volunteers pay their own travel and insurance costs. Registration fee approx £15. *Apply by 31 March.*

Organised by Oekumenischer Jugenddienst, Planckstrasse 20, Berlin 1080.

GDR SOCIETY The Secretary, 129 Seven Sisters Road, London N7 7QG
Can place a limited number of young people on workcamps in the German Democratic Republic. *Write for further details.*

GERMAN DEMOCRATIC REPUBLIC

INTERNATIONAL VOLUNTARY SERVICE
162 Upper New Walk, Leicester LE1 7QA
Tel Leicester 549430
IVS is the British branch of Service Civil
International which promotes international
reconciliation through work projects.
Volunteers are needed for manual work on
international workcamps. Recent projects have
included constructing a railway. Study
programmes are also arranged covering a wide
range of topics. A preparation seminar is
arranged in West Berlin one day before the
camp starts. Ages 18+. Applicants must have
previous workcamp experience, and should be
prepared to work hard and contribute to team
life. 35-40 hour week, 2-4 weeks, June-
September. Food, accommodation and
insurance provided, but not travel.
Membership fee £25 (students £15, unwaged
£10). Registration fee £40. **B D PH.**

Organised by Freie Deutsche Jugend (FDJ),
Unter den Linden 36-38, 1086 Berlin.

Applications from outside the UK: please see
workcamp information on page 27.

**When writing to any organisation it is
essential to mention Working Holidays 1991
and enclose a large stamped, self-addressed
envelope, or if overseas, a large addressed
envelope and at least two International Reply
Coupons.**

GERMANY

(FEDERAL REPUBLIC)

Embassy of the Federal Republic of Germany
23 Belgrave Square, London SW1X 8PZ
Tel 071-235 5033

British Embassy
Friedrich-Ebert Allee 77, 5300 Bonn

Tourist office
German National Tourist Office, Nightingale
House, 65 Curzon Street, London W1Y 7PE
Tel 071-495 3990

Youth hostels
Deutsches Jugendherbergswerk,
Bismarkstrasse 8, PO Box 220, 4930 Detmold

Youth & student information
Artu Berliner Gesellschaft für Studenten und
Jugendaustausch GmbH, Hardenbergstrasse 9,
1 Berlin 12 (Charlottenburg)

Youth Information Centre, Paul-Heyse-Strasse
22, 8000- Munich

INFORMATION

Entry regulations A UK citizen intending to work in the Federal Republic should have a full passport. EC nationals may stay in the Federal Republic for up to 3 months in order to seek employment; a person intending to stay longer than 3 months or who is taking up employment must obtain a residence permit from the local *Ausländerbehorde*, no later than 3 months after entry. Persons arriving seeking a job may call at the local employment office, *Arbeitsamt*. Non-EC nationals wishing to enter the Federal Republic require an entry visa which has to have the approval of the destination's *Ausländerbehorde*. This must be obtained prior to entering and applicants should be resident in an EC country for 12 months before their application can be considered. Application forms are obtainable from the Embassy of the Federal Republic in the country where they are staying. Clearance may take 6 weeks or more. If employment is intended, written confirmation of the job offer is required before an entry visa will be granted.

The German Embassy distributes an information booklet for non-resident workers and emigrants returning to the Federal Republic, containing background notes and details on all aspects of working and including entry requirements, employment regulations, social security and taxation. Also publishes *Residence and Work in Germany* a leaflet providing information likely to be needed upon taking up employment.

Job advertising The Axel Springer Publishing Group, Unit 2, Princeton Court, 53/55 Felsham Road, London SW15 1BY Tel 081-789 4929 is the UK office of a leading German publishing group which can place paid job advertisements in *Die Welt, Welt am Sonntag, Bild, Bild am Sonntag, Hamburger Abendblatt, Berliner Morgenpost, BZ* and approx 20 other national and local newspapers and magazines.

Publicitas Ltd, 525/527 Fulham Road, London SW6 1HF Tel 071-385 7723 are agents for *Rheinische Post, Stuttgarter Zeitung, Süddeutsche Zeitung, Der Tagesspiegel* and *Frankfurter Neue Presse.*

Travel DB Rail Pass offers unlimited travel for up to 21 days on the Federal Railways network, and on certain coach services. Cost from £80. Also available to those under 26; cost from £45. Tramper ticket offers unlimited rail travel for 1 month in the Federal Republic with free use of Intercity trains; for ages under 23, or students under 27. Cost £76.20. Details from DER Travel Service, 18 Conduit Street, London W1R 9TD Tel 071-408 0111.

Campus Travel, 52 Grosvenor Gardens, London SW1W 0AG Tel 071-730 3402 offer Eurotrain under 26 fares and youth and student airfares to destinations in the Federal Republic.

STA Travel, 86 Old Brompton Road, London SW7 3LQ Tel 071-937 9921 operate flexible,

FEDERAL REPUBLIC OF GERMANY

AU PAIR/CHILDCARE

low-cost flights between London and destinations throughout the Federal Republic.

Welcome to Germany, is a general folder with information on entry and visa regulations, advice on travel, accommodation, customs and other useful information for visitors. Available from the German National Tourist Office, see above.

Young People's Guide to Munich is an indispensable guide containing notes on where to stay, eating and drinking, walks in the Old City, public transport, maps, entertainment, places of interest, where to meet young people, special events and other useful information. Published by the Tourist Office of the City of Munich, Sendlinger Strasse 1, 8000 Munich 2.

International Youth Meetings in Germany 1991/92 lists services offered by German organisations to young visitors, and includes general information on youth work and details of international workcamps, environmental protection programmes, language courses and social services. Available from Studienkreis für Tourismus eV, Dampschiffstrasse 2, PO Box 1629, 8130 Starnberg.

Accommodation *Camping in Germany* lists over 400 campsites with a map indicating the locations. Available from the German National Tourist Office, see above.

Christlicher Verein Junger Menschen, Jugend-Gästehaus, Landwehrstrasse 13, 8000 Munich 2 offers YMCA accommodation in 1-3 bedded rooms for both sexes at Christian centre situated close to the station. Cost from DM34 per night includes breakfast and shower.

Haus International/Youth Hotel, Elisabethstrasse 87, 8000 Munich 40 offers cheap accommodation in 1-5 bedded rooms. Facilities include swimming pool, games room, bar and restaurant. Cost from DM28 includes breakfast. Reservations should be made in advance. PH

Large sleeping tent with space for 420, cooking area, canteen, showers, information bureau and recreation tent. Ages up to 23. Cost DM6 per night includes bedding and morning tea. Maximum stay 3 nights, end June-3 September.

Details from Jugendlager am Kapuzinerholzl, Kreisjugendring München, Franz-Schrank-Strasse, In den Kirchen, 8000 Munich 19.

AU PAIR/ CHILDCARE

Both males and females can be placed as au pairs with families in the Federal Republic provided they have experience of housework and childcare. Ages 18-28; 17 year old A level German students also accepted. Applicants must be single and without dependents, and should get their own room, board and lodging, DM200-DM300 per month pocket money, plus a travel ticket in order to attend language classes. EC nationals should register with the local immigration office, *Ausländermeldeamt* during the first 3 days of their stay. A 3 month residence permit will be granted which can later be extended to the whole length of the stay. Non-EC nationals must obtain a special au pair visa before entering the Federal Republic, obtainable from the German Consulate of their home country on production of their current passport and a letter of invitation from the host family. Applications for visas take 2-3 months to process, so early application is advisable. On arrival the au pair must register at the local *Ausländeramt* within 3 days and will be issued with a 4 week residence permit. During this time they are required to undergo a medical examination at the local health department *Gesundheitsamt*, the fee being paid by the host family. After a satisfactory medical the residence permit will be extended for one year, and a work permit will be issued by the labour exchange. Before returning to their own country, all au pairs must inform the local *Ausländeramt*. The host family insures the au pair against illness and accident, but this only covers 50% of dental fees and does not cover chronic illness. It is customary for au pairs to have a fortnight off after a stay of 6 months.

ANGLIA AGENCY 15 Eastern Avenue, Southend-on-Sea, Essex Tel Southend 613888 Au pair, mother's helps and nanny positions arranged throughout the year. Long and short-term placements available, including summer.

Hours and salaries vary; au pairs work 30 hours plus babysitting with 1 free day per week, and receive £25+ per week pocket money. Board and lodging provided. Ages 17+. Travel costs paid by the applicant. Service charge £40.

AVALON AGENCY Thursley House, 53 Station Road, Shalford, Guildford, Surrey GU4 8HA Tel Guildford 63640
Can place au pairs. Food, lodging and pocket money provided, with opportunity to attend language classes. 25-30 hour week, 6-12 months. Ages 18-30. Basic knowledge of German needed. Pocket money £25 per week. Positions also available for mother's helps and nannies. Ages 18+. Insurance provided. Service charge £40, if placement is accepted.

HELPING HANDS AU PAIR & DOMESTIC AGENCY 10 Hertford Road, Newbury Park, Ilford, Essex IG2 7HQ Tel 081-597 3138
Au pair and mother's help positions available all year. Au pairs work approx 30 hours plus 3 evenings babysitting per week, and earn approx £25 per week. Mother's helps work longer hours for a higher salary. Board and lodging provided. 6+ months. Ages 18-27. Applicants should be willing, helpful and adaptable. Insurance and travel costs paid by the applicant but assistance with arrangements provided. Introduction fee £40 on acceptance of a family. *UK nationals only.*

INTERLINGUA CENTRE Torquay Road, Foxrock, Dublin 18, Ireland Tel Dublin 893876
Can place au pairs in families throughout the Federal Republic. 30 hour week with one full day and some evenings off. Time to attend language classes 2-3 mornings or afternoons per week. 6+ months. Ages 18+. Experience desirable but not essential. £25-£40 pocket money per week, full board, lodging and insurance provided. Travel paid by applicants. Placement fee £55.

INTERNATIONAL CATHOLIC SOCIETY FOR GIRLS (ACISJF) St Patrick's International Youth Centre, 24 Great Chapel Street, London W1V 3AF Tel 071-734 2156
Au pair posts are arranged for 9+ months. Ages 18+. Assists girls/young women who are travelling and living away from home. Counselling and information service.

IN VIA Deutscher Verband Katholischer Mädchensozialarbeit eV, Karlstrasse 40, Lorenz-Werthmann-Haus, Postfach 420, 7800 Freiburg
Can place au pairs in towns throughout the Federal Republic. 5/6 hour day, 1 day free per week, including 1 Sunday per month. Knowledge of German and English essential. Ages 18-30. Applicants must supply a reference from their teacher or employer, a cv and medical certificate, and should have some experience of routine tasks and be prepared to adapt to a different lifestyle. 6+ months.

Board, lodging and basic medical insurance provided, plus DM300 pocket money per month. Travel paid by the applicant. Branch offices in 16 major towns in the Federal Republic. *Enclose 4 IRCs.*

JOLAINE AGENCY 18 Escot Way, Barnet, Hertfordshire EN5 3AN Tel 081-449 1334
Au pair and mother's help posts arranged throughout the year. Au pairs work a 5 hour day and 3/4 evenings babysitting per week. Afternoons plus 1 full day free per week. Mother's helps work an 8 hour day with 1½ days free per week, plus some evenings and other time by arrangement. Ages 18-30. June-October or 6+ months, all year. Must have reasonable German. Pocket money from £25 per week. Travel and insurance paid by the applicant. Introduction fee £40.

STUDENTS ABROAD AGENCY Elm House, 21b The Avenue, Hatch End, Middlesex HA5 4EN Tel 081-428 5823
Can place au pairs, usually for a minimum of 1 year; a few 3 month placements in summer. Au pairs are normally expected to work a 5/6 hour day. Usually 1 full day and 2/3 evenings free per week, but curriculum changes and applicants must be flexible during temporary summer season when no schooling available and families often go on holiday.

Board and lodging provided. Salary approx £25-£30 per week. Ages 18-27. Basic knowledge of German preferred. Applicants should like, and have the ability to cope with, children, babies, light housework and simple cooking. Applicants pay their own fare, but advice given on travel and insurance. Service charge £40.

FEDERAL REPUBLIC OF GERMANY

AU PAIR/CHILDCARE

UNIVERSAL CARE Chester House, 9
Windsor End, Beaconsfield, Buckinghamshire
HP9 2JJ Tel Beaconsfield 678811
Can place au pairs in most major cities in the
Federal Republic. Stays are usually for 6-12
months. Au pairs work a 5/6 hour day, may be
required to babysit 2-3 times per week and
have 1 full day off per week. Time off to attend
language classes should be negotiated. Ages
17-27. Knowledge of German necessary. Board
and lodging provided. Salary approx DM300
per month, with fares to language classes also
paid. Travel paid by the applicant, although
some families will sometimes help with the
return fare. Service charge £46. *Apply 2 months
before work period desired.*

VEREIN FÜR INTERNATIONALE
JUGENDARBEIT EV German YWCA/YMCA,
39 Craven Road, London W2 3BX
Tel 071-723 0216
Can place au pairs of both sexes in families all
over the Federal Republic. 5/6 hour day, plus
2/3 evenings of babysitting per week. At least
1 free day each weekend. Basic knowledge of
German essential. Ages 18-28, but exceptions
can be made for A level applicants. 6+ months.
Board, lodging and basic medical insurance
provided, plus DM250-DM350 pocket money
per month. Travel paid by the applicant. No
registration fee or service charge payable.
Arranges informal meetings for au pairs. Au
pairs attend language classes, travel for which
is paid for by family. Class fees paid by au
pair. Applicants must supply a cv, in German if
possible, a medical certificate (except EC
nationals), 2 referees and evidence of
experience of duties.

ZENTRALSTELLE FÜR ARBEITSVERMITT-
LUNG DER BUNDESANSTALT FÜR ARBEIT
Feuerbachstrasse 42-46, 6000 Frankfurt-am-
Main 1
A government agency offering a free placement
service for au pairs willing to work at least 9
months. Applicants must speak German. Ages
18+.

When writing to any organisation it is
essential to mention Working Holidays 1991
and enclose a large stamped, self-addressed
envelope, or if overseas, a large addressed
envelope and at least two International Reply
Coupons.

COMMUNITY WORK

BRITISH FORCES GERMANY Chief Youth
Service Officer, BFG Youth Service,
Education Branch, HQ, British Army of the
Rhine, BFPO 140 Tel 01049 2161-47-3176
Offers a voluntary service opportunity to those
seeking practical experience in working
informally with young people. Approx 30
student teachers/youth workers are recruited
for the Summer Student Volunteers Scheme, to
operate summer activity programmes in British
Forces youth clubs located in major garrison
towns and stations, and on RAF stations, in the
northern part of the Federal Republic. Clubs
have a mixed membership of 100-300 mainly in
the 10-16 age group. 6-8 weeks, summer.
The Scheme involves considerable
responsibility, and applicants should be
socially mature, persuasive, outgoing
individuals, capable of operating effectively on
their own initiative but also able to work with
other adults. Knowledge of German an
advantage, but not essential. Travel, full board
plus £30 per week pocket money provided.
Applicants are selected on the basis of relevant
training and experience. *Apply by 1 February;
interviews in April/May.*

Also recruits leaders for youth clubs on a
Trainee Youth Worker Scheme. Appointments
are normally for 12 months. Travel, full board,
plus £40 per week pocket money provided.
This Scheme is particularly suitable for mature
young adults wishing to gain full-time
professional training, and for newly-qualified
youth workers. *UK nationals only.*

CAMPHILL SCHOOLS Heimsonderschule
Brachenreuthe, 7770 Uberlingen - Bodensee
Tel 07551 80070
Aims to provide a new and constructive way of
life for mentally handicapped children,
assisting them to achieve individual
independence and social adjustment within
Camphill Trust communities. Volunteers are
needed to work alongside the residents in
every aspect of life and also as helpers in
school classes. As many of the children have
severe handicaps they are in need of care such

as bathing, dressing and other personal tasks. Volunteers must be willing to help wherever they are needed, and are encouraged not only to share in the responsibilities of living and working with the handicapped but also to participate in the cultural, recreational and social aspects of community life. Ages 19+. 60-70 hours per week, all year round. Full board, accommodation in single or double rooms and insurance provided, plus DM250 pocket money per month. Applicants pay their own travel expenses. Knowledge of German useful, but not essential. Participants staying for one year have an opportunity to take part in the first year of a training course in curative education. *Overseas applicants accepted.*

CHURCH ARMY Division of Evangelism, Independents Road, Blackheath, London SE3 9LG Tel 081-318 1226
Founded to train and equip men and women to share their living experience of Jesus Christ in a relevant and caring way. Works in residential and field social care; parish deanery and diocesan missions; youth and children's work; Forces' hospitals and prison chaplaincies; and an increasing number of urban and rural projects. Volunteers who are committed Christians are needed to work on children's holiday clubs for Forces' families, end July-end August. Work involves looking after 7-11 year olds, leading Bible quizzes, stories and choruses, organising outings, picnics, visits and tours. Ages 18+. Board, accommodation, insurance and return flight provided. *Apply by 31 January. British passport holders only.*

INTERNATIONALE JUGENDGEMEIN-SCHAFTSDIENSTE EV (IJGD) Kaiserstrasse 43, 5300 Bonn 1
A society for international and political education, organising approx 100 international workcamps each year, including 10-15 in West Berlin. Recent projects have included accompanying multiple sclerosis sufferers on evening visits, and caring for the elderly in Berlin; organising recreational activities for physically handicapped people in Schleswig-Holstein; building paths for wheelchairs at an old people's home in Munich; and running a summer holiday activity programme for children in Rheinland-Pfalz. On playschemes time for preparation and evaluation must be added to the normal 6 hour day. Ages 16-25.

Good knowledge of German needed. 30 hour, 5 day week. 3 weeks, June-September. Simple accommodation provided in schools, youth centres, boarding houses, tents or barns. All meals, often self-catering, and insurance provided. Excursions arranged to sites of interest. Registration fee DM93. Volunteers pay own travel costs. **B D PH**

Alternatively, UK applicants may apply to United Nations Association, International Youth Service, Welsh Centre for International Affairs, Temple of Peace, Cathays Park, Cardiff CF1 3AP Tel Cardiff 223088; or Concordia (Youth Service Volunteers) 8 Brunswick Place, Hove, East Sussex BN3 1ET Tel Brighton 772086.

TOC H National Projects Office, 38 Newark Street, London E1 Tel 071-247 5110
A voluntary movement which provides an opportunity to meet and work with a variety of different people on a range of challenging, high-energy projects. Volunteers are required to run a full programme of activities on playschemes in Berlin, Paderborn, Verden and Münster for children, aged 5-11, of British service families stationed in the Federal Republic. Ages 18+. 3 weeks, July/August. Applicants should preferably have experience of working with children, and are expected to comply at all times with Army protocol. Training and briefing weekend held in April. Food and accommodation provided but volunteers will be expected to pay £45 towards air travel costs. Registration fee £5.

CONSERVATION

CHRISTIAN MOVEMENT FOR PEACE Bethnal Green United Reformed Church, Pott Street, London E2 0EF Tel 071-729 1877
An international movement open to all who are concerned about violence, exploitation and injustice in society. Volunteers are needed to work in international teams on conservation projects. Recent projects have included helping to create protected areas for animals, plants and birds on sites near Gemersheim and Landau; and building a biological sewage plant and a greenhouse on an organic farm near Fulda. Volunteers share in discussions centring on the host community and world problems. Ages 18+. 6 hour day, 30-36 hour week. 2-3

FEDERAL REPUBLIC OF GERMANY

weeks, July-September. Food, accommodation and insurance provided, but participants pay their own travel. Registration fee £24. **PH**

Organised by Christlicher Friedensdienst, Deutscher Zweig eV, Rendelerstrasse 9-11, 6000 Frankfurt-Bornheim 60.

Applicants from outside the UK: please see workcamp information on page 27.

INTERNATIONAL VOLUNTARY SERVICE
162 Upper New Street, Leicester LE1 7QA
Tel Leicester 549430
IVS is the British branch of Service Civil International which promotes international reconciliation through work projects. Volunteers are needed to work in international teams on environmental protection and ecological workcamps. Recent projects have included planting vegetables, digging a clay pond and laying a footpath at an environmental education centre in Hamburg; preserving rare plants and animals living in dry meadows near Freiburg; tending orchards and harvesting hay on the edge of the Swabian forest; planning and constructing a water purification system in Prinzhofte bei Harpstedt at a former farmhouse and centre for ecological and holistic learning; clearing fields, cutting trees and generally studying the dangers of air pollution in the Alpine National Park in Burgberg/Allgau; and taking part in a cycle tour from Freiburg, examining ecological topics relevant to the region along the Upper Rhine including pollution of the Rhine River and changes in the landscape along the river. Opportunities to meet local members of the anti-nuclear and peace movements. All camps have a strong study element, linked to pollution, nature protection and ecological problems. Ecology cycle tours arranged. Knowledge of German needed on some camps. Ages 18+. Applicants should have previous workcamp experience and be prepared to work hard and contribute to team life. 35-40 hour week. 2-4 weeks, April-October. Board, lodging and insurance provided, but not travel. Membership fee £25 (students £15, unwaged £10). Registration fee £40. **B D PH**

Organised by Service Civil International, Deutscher Zweig eV, Blücherstrasse 14, 5300 Bonn 1.

CONSERVATION

Applications from outside the UK: please see workcamp information on page 27.

INTERNATIONALE BEGEGNUNG IN GEMEINSCHAFTSDIENSTEN EV (IBG)
Schlosserstrasse 28, 7000 Stuttgart 1
Founded by Scout leaders to organise work projects of benefit to the community and to promote better international understanding. Volunteers are needed on international workcamps; each camp is made up of 15-20 participants from 6-8 countries who work together on a common project. Recent projects have included forestry work, harvesting, woodcutting and gardening in Bavarian villages; plant and pond work in the Black Forest; and working on a footpath in the Taunus mountains. Ages 18-30. 30 hour week with weekends free. 3 weeks, July-September. Food, simple accommodation in schools, youth hostels, empty buildings, forest or mountain huts with self-catering facilities and insurance provided, but not travel. Participants should take a sleeping bag. Registration fee DM90.

Alternatively, UK applicants may apply to United Nations Association, International Youth Service, Welsh Centre for International Affairs, Temple of Peace, Cathays Park, Cardiff CF1 3AP Tel Cardiff 223088.

INTERNATIONALE JUGENDGEMEIN-SCHAFTSDIENSTE EV (IJGD)
Kaiserstrasse 43, 5300 Bonn 1
A society for international and political education, organising approx 100 international workcamps each year, including 10-15 in West Berlin. Recent projects have included restoring an old cloister wall in Niedersachsen; conservation work in the grounds of a bird sanctuary near Celle; planting trees in the Hausbrucher Forest; building dams, digging ponds and mowing fields on the Luneburger Heath; and coastal protection work on the East Frisian Islands. Ages 16-25. Basic knowledge of German needed, and previous workcamp experience preferable. 30 hour, 5 day week. 3 weeks, April and June-October. Simple accommodation provided in schools, youth centres, boarding houses, tents or barns. All meals, sometimes self-catering, and insurance provided. Volunteers pay their own travel costs. Excursions arranged to sites of interest. Registration fee DM93. Also arrange youth

workshops linked to workcamp tasks on ecology themes. **B D PH**

Alternatively, UK applicants may apply to United Nations Association, International Youth Service, Welsh Centre for International Affairs, Temple of Peace, Cathays Park, Cardiff CF1 3AP Tel Cardiff 223088; or Concordia (Youth Service Volunteers), 8 Brunswick Place, Hove, East Sussex BN3 1ET Tel Brighton 772086.

COURIERS/REPS

CANVAS HOLIDAYS LTD Bull Plain, Hertford SG14 1DY Tel Hertford 553535
Resident couriers are required to work on campsites for a holiday company providing accommodation for families in ready-erected fully equipped tents and mobile homes. The work involves a daily routine of tent cleaning as customers arrive and depart, providing information and advice on the local attractions and essential services, helping to sort out problems that might arise, and organising activities for the children and get-togethers for the families. 7 day week job with no fixed hours; the workload varies from day to day. At the beginning and end of the season there is a period of physical work when tents are put up and prepared for the customers or taken down and stored for the winter. Other tasks include administration, book keeping and stock control.
Working knowledge of German essential. Ages 18-25. Applicants are normally those with a year between school and further education, undergraduates or graduates. They need to be enthusiastic, practical, reliable, self-motivated, able to turn their hand to new and varied tasks, and with a sense of humour. 10-14 weeks, early April-mid July or July-late September. Return travel, dependent on successful completion of contract, accommodation in frame tents, and moped or bicycle for use on site provided. Salary approx £76 per week. *Applications accepted anytime; interviews commence early November for the following season.*

EUROCAMP Courier Department, Edmundson House, Tatton Street, Knutsford, Cheshire WA16 6BG Tel Knutsford 50444
Requires resident couriers to work on campsites throughout the Federal Republic.

Work involves cleaning tents and equipment prior to the arrival of new customers; checking, replacing and making repairs on equipment; replenishing gas supplies; keeping the store tent in order; keeping basic accounts and reporting on a weekly basis to England. Couriers are also expected to meet new arrivals and assist holidaymakers with any problems that may arise; organise activities and parties; provide information on local tourist attractions and maintain an information noticeboard. At the beginning and end of the season couriers are expected to help in erecting and dismantling tents. There are no set working hours or free days, as these depend on unpredictable factors.
Ages 18-28, although older applicants will be considered. Applicants should be familiar with working and travelling abroad, preferably with camping experience. They should also be adaptable, reliable, independent, efficient, hard working, sensible, sociable, tactful, patient and have a working knowledge of the language. Applications from couples welcome.
Applicants are expected to work one half of the season, early/mid April-mid July or mid July-late September/early October - exact dates depend on the campsite. Work is also available for the whole season. Accommodation in a frame tent with cooking facilities, insurance, return travel and moped for use on site provided. Salary approx £80 per week. Positions as senior couriers also available; salary approx £95 per week. Insurance and return fare provided. *Early application advisable interviews start in November.*

VENTURE ABROAD Warren House, High Street, Cranleigh, Surrey, GU6 8AJ Tel Cranleigh 273 027
Representatives are required by a tour operator specialising in holidays for youth groups. The work involves assisting and advising groups staying in Konigssee, Bavaria, meeting them on arrival, providing general local information, escorting on excursions and acting as a guide to the surrounding countryside. Ages 19+. University students with knowledge of German and experience of working with youth groups preferred. 50 hour week , end June-end August. Salary £65-£70 per week, self-catering accommodation , insurance, work permits and visas provided. Basic training given before departure. *Apply enclosing CV.*

FEDERAL REPUBLIC OF GERMANY

COURIERS/REPS

FEDERAL REPUBLIC OF GERMANY

DOMESTIC

ALPOTELS AGENCY PO Box 388, London SW1X 8LX

Alpotels carries out aptitude tests at the request of German hotels for work mainly as chambermaids or kitchen helpers. Ages 18+. Some knowledge of German useful but not essential. All jobs involve long hours and hard work in a professional team. 8 hours per day, with 2 days free per week. Jobs are available during 2 long seasons, December-May or May-November. Pay approx £80 per week. Board, lodging and insurance provided. Interview fee £1 plus subscription to JITA Club. *Closing dates for interviews, 30 September (winter) or 30 March/April (summer). EC nationals only.*

FARMWORK

Since farms in the Federal Republic tend to be small and highly mechanised, the opportunities for seasonal agricultural work are limited. The main crops are flour and feed grains, potatoes, sugar beet, vegetables, fruit and wine. The likelihood of employment is higher grape picking in the south west than in any other sector, although the grape harvests are late, from mid October to mid November.

INTERNATIONAL FARM EXPERIENCE PROGRAMME YFC Centre, National Agricultural Centre, Kenilworth, Warwickshire CV8 2LG Tel Coventry 696584

Provides assistance to young farmers and nurserymen by finding places in farms/nurseries abroad enabling them to broaden their knowledge of agricultural methods. Opportunities for practical horticultural/agricultural work, usually on mixed farms. Applicants live and work with a farmer and his family and the work is matched as far as possible with the applicant's requirements. The work is hard; 8-10 hour day, 6 day week, every other weekend free. 3-12 months throughout the year. Opportunities for farm and nursery work. Applicants pay own fares and insurance. Also opportunities to take part in practical training schemes, starting June. 4 month practical training scheme, preceded by a 6 week German language course in France,

starting February or June. Wages £30 on farm and pocket money on the course; board and lodging provided. Some travel costs paid. Ages 18-26. Applicants must have a minimum 2 years' practical experience, of which 1 year may be at agricultural college, and intend to make a career in agriculture/horticulture. Valid driving licence necessary. Registration fee £62. *Apply at least 3 months in advance. EC nationals only.*

German applicants should apply to Deutscher Bauernverband eV, Godesberger Allee 142-148, 5300 Bonn.

WILLING WORKERS ON ORGANIC FARMS (WWOOF) Hanna Blum, Rüdeshemerstrasse 33, 6222 Geisenheim

A non-profitmaking organisation which aims to help farmers and smallholders who need manpower to replace the use of herbicides, chemical fertilisers and heavy machinery. Provides unskilled voluntary workers with first hand experience of organic farming and gardening and a chance to spend some time in the country. Places exist on 29 farms throughout the Federal Republic. Work outside includes working in the fields, in the stable or on the market stall; indoor work includes spinning, weaving, cheesemaking, pottery and woodwork. Members receive a quarterly newsletter which details farms needing help. Ages 16+. 20-40 hour week. 1+ weeks. Full board and lodging provided in the farmhouse or in outbuildings; volunteers should take a sleeping bag. No wages paid, although long-term volunteers may receive small payment as arranged with host. Helpers pay own travel costs. Insurance and anti-tetanus vaccination recommended. Families welcome. Membership DM20.

MONITORS & TEACHERS

CENTRAL BUREAU Assistants Department, Seymour Mews House, Seymour Mews, London W1H 9PE Tel 071-486 5101

Opportunities for Helpers to work in state and private boarding schools, working under the supervision of the English teaching staff and assisting them in the classroom. Helpers may also take small groups of pupils to improve their command of spoken English and give them an insight into British life, customs and institutions, and are expected to participate fully in the life of the school. Schools are normally located in small towns or isolated country districts. Applicants must have A level German, and be aged 18-20. Board, lodging and approx DM250 monthly allowance provided. 2 or 3 terms, September-April/July. 12-14 hour week. It should be possible to attend classes in the school on subjects of particular interest. The number of posts is limited and competition strong. Travel paid by the applicant. Registration fee £5. *Apply by 31 March.*

PEACE CAMPS

CHRISTIAN MOVEMENT FOR PEACE
Bethnal Green United Reformed Church, Pott Street, London E2 0EF Tel 071-729 1877
An international movement open to all who share a common concern for lasting peace and justice in the world. Volunteers are needed to work in international teams on summer projects aimed at offering a service in an area of need and promoting self-help within the community, promoting international understanding and the discussion of social problems, and offering young people the chance to live as a group and take these experiences into the context of daily life. All workcamps are organised in cooperation with local groups to enable volunteers to gain an insight into the peace and anti-Fascist work being undertaken in the Federal Republic.

Recent peace projects have included repair work and gardening at a peace cottage in Herford; preparing an exhibition on the history of the international peace movement at a documentation centre and anti-war house at Sievershausen; decorating a training centre for non-violent action in Wustrow; and studying the current situation in Nicaragua and raising funds for a project there. Activities include discussions on peace problems, visits to events and contacts with local peace groups. Ages 18+. 30-36 hour week, 2-4 weeks, June-September. Food, accommodation and insurance provided, but participants pay their own travel costs. Registration fee £24. **PH**

Organised by Christlicher Friedensdienst, Deutscher Zweig eV, Rendelerstrasse 9-11, 6000 Frankfurt-Bornheim 60.

Applications from outside the UK: please see workcamp information on page 27.

INTERNATIONAL VOLUNTARY SERVICE
162 Upper New Walk, Leicester LE1 7QA
Tel Leicester 549430
IVS is the British branch of Service Civil International which promotes international reconciliation through work projects. Volunteers are needed to work in international teams on peace camps run to support peace information and activity centres, to promote international discussion of the nuclear threat, alternative security policies and non-violence, and to bring together peace movements in different countries. Camps are linked to peace study themes and opportunities to meet local peace groups. Also organise anti-Fascist camps, helping to maintain concentration camps as monuments, warning symbols and a means of raising awareness of history. Volunteers should be interested in and have some knowledge of the political background of this theme.
Recent projects have included repairing footpaths and working in the gardens at a holiday home for victims of Nazi persecution south of Hamburg; demolishing an abandoned barracks to build an arts workshop at a peace centre in Sievershausen; the construction of a meeting centre in Mutlangen sited near a military depot, with the objective of exercising non-violent conflict resolution as well as international understanding; involvement with the Idea Workshop in Wald, with the aim of breaking down political, social and cultural barriers; and manual work and gardening at the Jewish cemetery at Dachau. Study themes include history of the concentration camp and anti-Fascist resistance. Also international cycle and sailing tours for peace.
Ages 18+. Applicants should be committed to the camp theme, have previous workcamp, voluntary work or community service experience, and should be prepared to work hard and contribute to team life. Some camps require a knowledge of German. 35-40 hour week, 2-4 weeks, June-September, Christmas and Easter. Food and centre, tent or school accommodation plus insurance provided, but

FEDERAL REPUBLIC OF GERMANY

PEACE CAMPS

FEDERAL REPUBLIC OF GERMANY

WORKCAMPS

not travel. Volunteers prepare and cook their own meals. Membership fee £25 (students £15, unwaged £10). Registration fee £40. **B D PH**

Organised by Service Civil International, Deutscher Zweig eV, Blücherstrasse 14, 5300 Bonn 1.

Applications from outside the UK: please see workcamp information on page 27.

WORKCAMPS

ARBEITSGEMEINSCHAFT DER EVANGELISCHEN JUGEND IN DER BUNDESREPUBLIK DEUTSCHLAND UND BERLIN WEST EV Porschestrasse 3, 7000 Stuttgart 40
The umbrella organisation of Protestant youth organisations and youth work of the regional Protestant churches. Seeks to transmit insights into the way of thinking and into the lifestyle of young people in other nations and other church traditions, towards communication and peace education. Arrange international work/study camps. Ages 18+. Basic knowledge of German required. 30-35 hour week. 3 weeks, March, April and June-August.

UK applications to the British Council of Churches, Youth Unit, Inter-Church House, 35-41 Lower Marsh, London SE1 7RL Tel 071-620 4444.

AUFBAUWERK DER JUGEND IN DEUTSCHLAND EV Bahnhofstrasse 26, 3550 Marburg/Lahn
Founded after the Second World War and aims to promote cooperation and understanding between people from all over the world by providing opportunities for them to meet and work together. The accent is on learning new skills and gaining experience in a practical field. Recent projects have included restoring an old railway carriage for a museum; renovating and gardening at homes for the handicapped and at youth centres; renovating and clearing paths, playgrounds and parks; looking after and playing with children; and coastal protection work, stabilising the dunes and planting grass on the East Frisian Islands. Ages 16-26. Previous workcamp experience preferable; knowledge of German useful. 30-35 hour, 5 day week. 2-3 weeks, Easter, and June-

September. Board and accommodation provided in schools, old houses, youth hostels or tents. Volunteers help prepare meals and should take a sleeping bag. Travel extra. Registration fee DM50 includes insurance.

Alternatively UK applicants may apply to United Nations Association, International Youth Service, Welsh Centre for International Affairs, Temple of Peace, Cathays Park, Cardiff CF1 3AP Tel Cardiff 223088; or Concordia (Youth Service Projects) Ltd, 8 Brunswick Place, Hove, East Sussex BN3 1ET Tel Brighton 772086.

CHRISTIAN MOVEMENT FOR PEACE Bethnal Green United Reformed Church, Pott Street, London E2 0EF Tel 071-729 1877
An international movement open to all who share a common concern for lasting peace and justice in the world. Volunteers are required to work in international teams on summer projects aimed at offering a service in an area of need and promoting self-help within the community; promoting international understanding and the discussion of social problems; and offering young people the chance to live as a group and take these experiences into the context of daily life. All workcamps are organised in cooperation with local groups to enable volunteer teams to gain an insight into the peace, environmental and anti-Fascist work being undertaken in the Federal Republic.
Recent projects have included redecorating an educational and activities centre for immigrant workers' children and painting a Third World House, in Frankfurt; working in a cafe at a festival of Protestant churches in Frankfurt; assisting with the presentation of street theatre on the situation of political refugees, in Heppenheim; setting up an exhibition in Munich on living conditions of women and children in South Africa; and manual work at a communication centre based at an old mill in Willemrod. All camps have a strong study element. Ages 18+. Some camps require a basic knowledge of German. 30-36 hour week, 2-4 weeks, July-September. Food, accommodation and insurance provided, but participants pay their own travel. Registration fee £24. **PH**

Organised by Christlicher Friedensdienst, Deutscher Zweig eV, Rendelerstrasse 9-11, 6000 Frankfurt-Bornheim 60.

Applications from outside the UK: please see workcamp information on page 27.

INTERNATIONAL VOLUNTARY SERVICE
162 Upper New Walk, Leicester LE1 7QA Tel Leicester 549430

IVS is the British branch of Service Civil International which promotes international reconciliation through work projects. Volunteers are needed to work in international teams on social/manual projects in a variety of fields such as Third World solidarity and with self-help groups organised by young people facing long-term unemployment.

Recent projects have included building playground equipment at a youth farm near Stuttgart; constructing a camping place and renovating a half timbered building at Castle Waldeck in Dorweiler; converting an old button factory into a cultural centre in Reutlingen; painting a mural on a housing estate in Hamburg; renovating a 400 year-old farmhouse used by Scouts near Munich; and painting and carpentry work in Bohmte.

Solidarity camps are also organised, supporting Third World countries, helping organisations and projects involved in social, medical and educational work, by a combination of practical and educational assistance which includes providing materials for refugee camps and supporting self-reliant development and human rights. All camps include a strong study element, and support the struggles in Nicaragua, South Africa and Namibia. Also women's camps and East-West bicycle tour. Ages 18+. Applicants should have previous workcamp, voluntary work or community service experience and be highly motivated and prepared to work hard and contribute to team life. Good German needed for some camps. 40 hour week, 2-3 weeks, July-September, Christmas and Easter. Board, lodging and insurance provided, but not travel. Membership fee £25 (students £15, unwaged £10). Registration fee £40. **B D PH**

Organised by Service Civil International, Deutscher Zweig eV, Blücherstrasse 14, 5300 Bonn 1.

Applications from outside the UK: please see workcamp information on page 27.

INTERNATIONALE BEGEGNUNG IN GEMEINSCHAFTSDIENSTEN EV (IBG)
Schlosserstrasse 28, 7000 Stuttgart 1

Founded by Scout leaders to organise work projects of benefit to the community, and to promote better international understanding. Volunteers are needed on international workcamps; each camp is made up of 15-20 participants from 6-8 countries who work together on common projects which have recently included renovating buildings and working in parks in Bavaria; and renovating youth centres in Stuttgart and Mannheim. Ages 18-30. 30 hour week with free weekends. 3 weeks, July-September. Food, simple accommodation in schools, youth hostels, empty buildings, clubs or forest/mountain huts with self-catering facilities, and insurance provided, but not travel. Participants should take a sleeping bag. Registration fee DM90.

Alternatively, UK applicants may apply to United Nations Association, International Youth Service, Welsh Centre for International Affairs, Temple of Peace, Cathays Park, Cardiff CF1 3AP Tel Cardiff 223088.

INTERNATIONALE JUGENDGEMEIN-SCHAFTSDIENSTE EV (IJGD) Kaiserstrasse 43, 5300 Bonn 1

A society for international and political education, organising approx 100 international workcamps each year, including 10-15 in West Berlin. Recent projects have included constructing and renovating playground equipment in Berlin and Bielefeld; converting a 15th century farmhouse into an education centre in Schleswig-Holstein; collecting and repairing tools to send to Ghana, in Herford; building a wind-pump and bakery at an alternative meeting house in Niedersachsen; renovating a half-timbered building for use as a youth centre in Nordrhein-Westfalen; and constructing sand-dune protection fences on the East Frisian island of Wangeroog. Basic craftsmanship skills are taught for all projects. Parent/children and women only camps organised. Work/study camps also arranged on themes including Third World, peace and anti-Fascism. Ages 16-25. Basic knowledge of German needed. 30 hour, 5 day week. 3 weeks, June-September. Simple accommodation provided in schools, youth centres, flats, stations, boarding houses, tents or barns. All

FEDERAL REPUBLIC OF GERMANY

WORKCAMPS

GENERAL

meals, often self-catering, and insurance provided. Volunteers pay own travel. Registration fee DM93.

Alternatively UK applicants may apply to United Nations Association, International Youth Service, Welsh Centre for International Affairs, Temple of Peace, Cathays Park, Cardiff CF1 3AP Tel Cardiff 223088; or Concordia (Youth Service Volunteers) Ltd, 8 Brunswick Place, Hove, East Sussex BN3 1ET Tel Brighton 772086.

INTERNATIONALER BAUORDEN-DEUTSCHER ZWEIG EV Liebigstrasse 23, PO Box 1438, 6520 Worms-Horchheim
An international volunteers association with the aims of fighting misery and distress and making a contribution towards a better understanding between nations. Volunteers are needed to work in international teams for and together with the socially, mentally, economically and physically underprivileged. Recent projects have included painting and renovating an old people's home in Kirchheim; rebuilding a centre for young unemployed and socially deprived, at Kupferzell; preparing for a sports festival for the severely disabled in Krautheim; and converting an old railway station into a leisure centre in Hasel. Ages 18+ 40 hour, 5 day week, 3-4 weeks. Easter and June-September. Food prepared by the volunteers, tent, school or barrack accommodation and insurance provided, but volunteers should take a sleeping bag. Participants pay their own travel. *Apply 1 month in advance.*

NOTHELFERGEMEINSCHAFT DER FREUNDE EV Secretariat General, Auf der Kornerwiese 5, 6000 Frankfurt-am-Main 1
A fellowship founded on the conviction that peaceful coexistence is only possible if prejudices and differences between peoples are overcome. Aims to improve the situation of the needy and is working for a better understanding and reconciliation between peoples. Volunteers are needed on workcamps to help on projects which include manual and social work in homes for children, the elderly and the mentally handicapped, and in hospitals. Recent projects have included construction work, gardening and domestic work at centres for mentally handicapped people; path construction, farming and

gardening at Camphill village community farms for the handicapped; and repair work, painting and looking after elderly people at homes throughout the Federal Republic. Ages 18-30. Junior camps arranged for ages 16-18. Volunteers must be willing to work hard, show tolerance, initiative and enthusiasm, and be prepared to participate in discussions and seminars during their free time. Good knowledge of German needed on some camps. 30-35 hour week, 3/4 weeks, March, April, May-December. Self-catering accommodation, food and insurance provided. Registration fee DM50. *Apply by mid May.*

GENERAL

CANVAS HOLIDAYS LTD Bull Plain, Hertford SG14 1DY Tel Hertford 553535
Provides ready-erected fully equipped tents for holiday families. Requires applicants to form flying squads, teams of 2/3 people who help set up and equip 200-250 6 berth frame tents in an area containing approx 12 campsites. Similar work is also available taking down tents and cleaning and storing equipment. Ages 18-25. Knowledge of German not required but is an advantage as flying squad members sometimes have the opportunity to continue as couriers. Applicants must be sociable in order to work in a small community, fit and able to work for long hours under pressure, work without supervision and cope with living out of a rucksack. Early April-mid June, possibly longer, to set up the tents, and September to dismantle them. Valid driving licence an advantage. Salary approx £76 per week, tented accommodation, self-catering facilities and outward travel provided. Return travel dependent on the completion of contract dates.

EUROYOUTH LTD 301 Westborough Road, Westcliff-on-Sea, Essex SS0 9PT Tel Southend-on-Sea 341434
Holiday guest stays are arranged where guests are offered board and lodging in return for an agreed number of hours English conversation with hosts or their children. Time is also available for guests to practise German if desired. Mainly ages 15-25, but there are sometimes opportunities for older applicants. 2-3 weeks, June-August. Travel and insurance paid by the applicant. Registration fee approx

£80. *Apply at least 12 weeks prior to scheduled departure date; limited places. UK nationals only.*

GAP ACTIVITY PROJECTS LTD 44 Queen's Road, Reading, Berkshire RG1 4BB Tel Reading 594914

Recruits young people for a Live and Work in Germany scheme run by Deutsch-Britischer Jugendaustausch in cooperation with the Zentralstelle für Arbeitsvermittlung. Successful applicants spend some months working and gaining social and cultural experience, participating in the German way of life. The scheme runs from mid March or end April-end August , during which participants work in offices, banks, department stores, supermarkets, factories and help in social work in all parts of Germany including West Berlin. Each programme begins with a 1 week seminar in Berlin; a weekend evaluation seminar is held towards the end of the project. Applicants should be school leavers aged 18-19 who have up to a year before going on to further education. Participants must have a good command of spoken German, preferably A level, and must be confident of their ability to communicate easily and adapt quickly. Salary approx DM1400-DM2000 per month, less deductions for tax and national insurance. Participants pay for accommodation arranged either by employers or DBJ/ZAV in families. Cost £430 (6 month scheme) or £400 (4 month scheme) covers travel to Berlin, full board, lodging, travel for seminars and insurance. Interviews take place in November/December for 6 month scheme, and end of January for 4 month scheme, and are conducted in German. Applicants must enclose a letter of recommendation from their school, college or employer, a letter in German explaining their reasons for applying, and show a particular interest in German culture and political life. *Applications to be returned by 1 October.*

ZENTRALSTELLE FÜR ARBEITSVERMITT-LUNG DER BUNDESANSTALT FÜR ARBEIT Feuerbachstrasse 42-46, 6000 Frankfurt-am-Main 1

The central government office concerned with the recruitment of foreign workers, including the free placement of foreign students for temporary jobs of at least 2 months. Ages 18+. Applicants must speak good German.

APPLYING FOR A JOB

Read carefully all the information given before applying. Check in particular:

* the necessary skills/experience required

* the full period of employment expected

* any restrictions of age, sex or nationality

* application deadlines

* any other points, particularly details of insurance cover provided, and other costs such as travel and accommodation.

When applying be sure to include:

* name, address, date of birth, marital status, nationality, sex

* education, qualifications, relevant experience

* period of availability

* details of languages spoken

* a large stamped, self-addressed envelope plus, if overseas, 2 International Reply Coupons

* a passport-size photo, particularly if you are to have contact with the public

* any registration or membership fees

FEDERAL REPUBLIC OF GERMANY

GENERAL

NOTES

GREAT BRITAIN

Tourist offices
English Tourist Board, Thames Tower, Black's Road, Hammersmith, London W6 9EL Tel 081-846 9000

Scottish Tourist Board, 23 Ravelston Terrace, Edinburgh EH4 3EU Tel 031-332 2433

Wales Tourist Board, Brunel House, 2 Fitzalan Road, Cardiff CF2 1UY Tel Cardiff 499909

Youth hostels
YHA, Trevelyan House, 8 St Stephen's Hill, St Albans, Hertfordshire AL1 2DY

SYHA, 7 Glebe Crescent, Stirling FK8 2JA

Youth & student information
International Students House, 229 Great Portland Street, London W1N 5HD Tel 071-631 3223

National Union of Students, 461 Holloway Road, London N7 6LJ Tel 071-272 8900

UK Council for Overseas Students (UKCOSA), 60 Westbourne Grove, London W2 5SH Tel 071-229 9268

INFORMATION

Entry regulations Nationals of Belgium, Denmark, France, the Federal Republic of Germany, Gibraltar, Greece, the Republic of Ireland, Italy, Luxembourg and the Netherlands do not need a work permit to take up or seek employment in Great Britain. Nationals of Spain and Portugal still need to obtain work permits, where required, until 1993, when the provisions of the Treaty of Rome relating to employment will apply. Non-European Community nationals who are subject to immigration control need a work permit and will be refused entry if one cannot be produced at the port of entry. A work permit is not required for au pair posts or temporary employment at approved farmcamps, but a letter of invitation from the family or farmcamp must be produced. The letter does not provide entitlement to any other kind of paid work. Permits are not usually required for temporary employment on international workcamps or other voluntary opportunities, but it is advisable to obtain prior entry clearance from a British diplomatic post abroad.

Overseas students studying in Britain who wish to take paid work in their free time or during vacations do not require work permits but they must first obtain the consent of the Department of Employment through the local Jobcentre or employment office and provide evidence from their college that employment will not interfere with their studies. Further information on work permits may be obtained in leaflets OW5 and OW21, published by the Department of Employment, or from the Overseas Labour Section, Department of Employment, Caxton House, Tothill Street, London SW1H 9NF Tel 071-273 3000.

Commonwealth citizens with proof of a grandparent's birth in the UK do not need a work permit provided that they obtain prior entry clearance from a British Consular post overseas. Other Commonwealth citizens aged 17-27 inclusive may enter Britain for up to 2 years during which they can take work incidental to their holiday. They must have the means to pay for their return journey and not fall a charge on public funds. Further information on concessions for Commonwealth citizens of UK ancestry, the provisions for Commonwealth working holidaymakers and immigration requirements generally may be obtained from the Home Office, Lunar House, Wellesley Road, Croydon, Surrey CR9 2BY Tel 081-686 0688.

Job advertising Most newspapers in Britain carry classified advertising. There are several daily newspapers with national distribution

GREAT BRITAIN

and hundreds of local newspapers published on a daily or weekly basis. An evening daily newspaper circulating in London only is the *Evening Standard*, Classified Advertising, Northcliffe House, 2 Derry Street, London W8 5EE Tel 071-938 3838. As well as accepting paid advertisements this paper also advertises many short-term job opportunities, especially in the Tuesday edition. *Time Out* is a weekly magazine aimed at young people in London, giving details of events in the capital; to advertise contact Classified Advertising, Time Out, Tower House, Southampton Street, London WC2E 7HD Tel 071-836 5131.

Travel Anyone under 24 or a full-time student in the UK can buy a British Rail Young Person's Railcard, entitling the holder to 30% reduction on many tickets. Cost £15, valid 1 year. Further details and application forms are available from principal British Rail stations or most student travel offices. British Rail also offer a variety of discount tickets depending on age, time of day and distance to be travelled. Further information can be obtained from British Rail offices or agents outside Britain, and from any British Rail station. National Express operate extensive coach services to most major towns and cities throughout the UK. Full-time students can buy a Student Coach Card entitling them to 33% reduction on standard fares. Cost £5, valid 1 year. For further information contact National Express, Tel 081-770 7770.

Hitch-hikers' Manual Britain £4.70, is a comprehensive handbook including hints on techniques, route planning, legal matters, and how lifts can be found on boats, planes and hovercrafts. Contains descriptions of how to reach the best hitching points for 200 towns, plus a section on motorway hitching. Published by Vacation Work, 9 Park End Street, Oxford OX1 1HJ Tel Oxford 241978.

Information centres International Travellers' Aid, The Kiosk, Platform 8, Victoria Station, London SW1V 1JT is an interdenominational voluntary organisation helping and providing information to travellers, particularly if they have just arrived from overseas, are unfamiliar with English, need advice on accommodation, need to trace friends, relatives or lost possessions, or are in distress of any kind.

The National Youth Bureau, 17-23 Albion Street, Leicester LE1 6GD Tel Leicester 471200 can provide information on community involvement and young volunteer organisations in England and Wales.

The Scottish Community Education Council (SCEC), West Coates House, 90 Haymarket Terrace, Edinburgh EH12 5LQ Tel 031-313 2433 promotes community involvement and service by young people in Scotland. Although it does not recruit volunteers or find placements for them, it provides an information sheet giving details of volunteer projects in Scotland, including conservation work; workcamps; community projects; playschemes and some opportunities for long-term volunteers. It also operates the Young Scot Enterprise Project, which offers a wide range of discounts, benefits and information to European youth card holders.

The Volunteer Centre, 29 Lower King's Road, Berkhamsted, Hertfordshire HP4 2AB Tel Berkhamsted 73311 is the national advisory agency on volunteer and community involvement. It promotes voluntary action within statutory services, by voluntary organisations, self-help groups, or informally by individuals. Has a substantial library and information service.

Publications *Vac Work* details vacation work, sandwich placements, training and other types of employment available to undergraduates during the vacations. The main issues are published in February and November and supplements are available during the academic year. Published by Central Services Unit for Graduate Careers and Appointments Services. Available for consultation in university, polytechnic or college careers information rooms, or direct from CSU, Crawford House, Precinct Centre, Manchester M13 9EP, price £1.

Directory of Summer Jobs in Britain 1991 £6.95, lists opportunities all over Britain with details of wages and hours, conditions of work, and qualifications required. Published by Vacation Work, 9 Park End Street, Oxford OX1 1HJ Tel Oxford 241978.

Accommodation The International Friendship League, Peace Haven, 3 Creswick Road, Acton,

London W3 9HE works to promote a spirit of mutual respect and friendship among the peoples of the world. Offers accommodation at residential centres in London and Gloucester, all year. Cost from £9 per night, bed and breakfast. Advance booking usually necessary. Also offers a hospitality service throughout England, Scotland and Wales, of households prepared to provide accommodation at a reasonable charge and take visitors to places of interest. *Apply at least 8 weeks in advance enclosing 4 IRCs.*

Hackney Camping, Millfields Road, London E5 Tel 081-985 7656 a campsite for those taking their own tents/equipment. Mid June-end August. Cost £2 per night, including the use of hot showers, shop, snack bar and baggage store. From September-May contact Barnaby Martin, Tent City (address below) Tel 071-749 9074. B D PH

Tent City, Old Oak Common Lane, East Acton, London W3 7DP Tel 081-743 5708 offers camping accommodation for young travellers at a football pavilion and park, with 450 beds in 14 large mixed or single sex tents. Bedding available; also space for those taking their own tents. Early June-late September. Cost £4 per night including use of hot showers, snack bar and baggage store. B D PH

ARCHAEOLOGY

CANTERBURY ARCHAEOLOGICAL TRUST The Director, 92a Broad Street, Canterbury, Kent CT1 2LU Tel Canterbury 462062
Volunteers may be required to work on sites in and around the ancient Roman, Anglo-Saxon and medieval cities of Canterbury. Ages 17+. June-September. No experience necessary, training given on site. Accommodation available at local campsite; volunteers should take their own tents and equipment.

COUNCIL FOR BRITISH ARCHAEOLOGY 112 Kennington Road, London SE11 6RE Tel 071-582 0494
Ensures the safeguarding of all kinds of archaeological material, stimulates an informed interest in the past and provides information on how volunteers can assist in archaeological excavations. Opportunities on digs in all parts

of Britain; hours and payment vary, but where the work is organised by the Government some form of allowance is normally paid and hostel or camping accommodation provided. 2/3+ weeks. Applicants must be over 16 and fit. Details are published in *British Archaeological News*, bi-monthly; annual subscription £8.50. Lists sites in Britain where volunteer helpers are needed, giving brief details of accommodation, location and nature of the site.

DORSET NATURAL HISTORY & ARCHAEOLOGICAL SOCIETY Dorset County Museum, Dorchester, Dorset DT1 1XA Tel Dorchester 262735
Volunteers are required to help on rescue excavations all over Dorset; current excavations include prehistoric and Roman sites. Some training provided; experience preferable. Ages 16+. Volunteers must be fit, self-reliant and prepared for hard, disciplined work. 1+ weeks, April-September. Usually no wages paid. Volunteers should take tents and camping equipment if no other accommodation is provided. *Full details available in March.*

GROSVENOR MUSEUM EXCAVATIONS SECTION Field Officer, 27 Grosvenor Street, Chester CH1 2DD Tel Chester 316944
Volunteers are needed to assist the permanent excavations staff in recording the archaeology of Chester and the surrounding area. These have revealed the basic layout of the Roman fortress of Deva, buildings in nearby civil settlements, and parts of Saxon and medieval Chester. Further small excavations may be under way in the summer of 1991, carried out in advance of redevelopment and may be concerned with any historical period. Ages 16+. Volunteers should preferably have experience, and must be interested, intelligent and reasonably fit. 7½ hour day, 5-7 day week. 2-12 weeks, all year. Subsistence £3-£7 per day, depending on experience, plus return rail journey not exceeding £15.90. Accommodation list available.

When writing to any organisation it is essential to mention Working Holidays 1991 and enclose a large stamped, self-addressed envelope, or if overseas, a large addressed envelope and at least two International Reply Coupons.

GREAT BRITAIN

ARCHAEOLOGY

AU PAIR/ CHILDCARE

Au pair posts are intended only for unmarried girls aged 17-27 and without dependents, wishing to visit Britain to learn English while living as a member of an English-speaking family. Only nationals of western European countries, including Cyprus, Malta, Turkey and Yugoslavia, are eligible, and will be permitted to spend no more than a total of 2 years in Britain as an au pair. On arrival au pairs should provide the immigration officer with a letter of invitation from the host family, giving precise details of the au pair arrangements, including the amount of pocket money, accommodation, free time, details of the host family, house and household, and exact nature of assistance expected, and may also be required to produce a return ticket or evidence of sufficient funds to pay for return travel. As a general rule au pairs can expect to work up to 5 hours per day with 1 fixed day per week free. An au pair should have her own room, and receive approx £25+ per week pocket money. She may reasonably be asked to do light housework, cooking, childcare and occasional evening babysitting. EC nationals wishing to stay longer than 6 months must obtain a residence permit by filling in form EEC1, available from the Home Office, Department of Employment or police stations. Non-EC nationals staying longer than 6 months will normally have to register with the police, taking along their passport and two passport-sized photographs. Au pair posts should not be confused with regular domestic employment; *au pair plus* posts usually fall into this category. Information and advice on immigration matters can be obtained from British Embassies, Consulates and High Commissions or from the Home Office, Lunar House, Wellesley Road, Croydon, Surrey CR9 2BY Tel 081-686 0688.

ABOUT AU PAIRS 3 Garston Park, Godstone, Surrey RH9 8NE Tel Godstone 743735
Organises au pair placements throughout England. No experience necessary, but applicants must have a love of children and be willing to undertake domestic work. Single females only, ages 17-27. 30 hour week. 6+ months; some short-term summer positions. £30 per week pocket money, own room, board and lodging provided.

ANGLIA AGENCY 15 Eastern Avenue, Southend-on-Sea, Essex Tel Southend 613888
Au pair, mother's help and nanny positions arranged throughout the year. Long and short-term placements available including summer vacation period. Hours and salaries vary; au pairs work a 30 hour week plus babysitting, with 1 free day per week, and receive £25+ per week pocket money. Board and lodging provided. Ages 17+. Travel costs paid by applicant.

ANGLO PAIR AGENCY 40 Wavertree Road, Streatham Hill, London SW2 3SP Tel 081-674 3605
Arranges au pair and au pair plus posts in London. 30 hour week, plus 3 evenings babysitting and 1 full day off per week. Ages 17-27. 2-12 months. Applicants should have experience in childcare and light household duties. Pocket money per week £30+ au pairs, au pairs plus £40+. Board and lodging provided.

AVALON AGENCY Thursley House, 53 Station Road, Shalford, Guildford, Surrey GU4 8HA Tel Guildford 63640
Arrange au pair, *garçon familial* and *aide-de-famille* posts throughout the year. Au pairs work a maximum 5 hour day, with at least 1 day off per week. Pocket money £25-£35 per week. Ages 18-27. *Garçon familial* posts are for male EC nationals who act as mother's helps or general household helps. 5½ day week maximum. Pocket money £25-£45 per week depending on hours worked and length of stay. *Aide-de-famille* posts are for female EC nationals who work as mother's helps but are appointed without interview. 5½ day week. Wages £25-£50 per week. Board and lodging provided for all posts and sometimes travel costs.

EUROYOUTH LTD 301 Westborough Road, Westcliff-on-Sea, Essex SS0 9PT Tel Southend-on-Sea 341434
Au pair positions arranged throughout the year. Up to 5 hours work daily. One day and several evenings free per week. Language

courses available in all areas where au pairs are placed. Ages 18+. 3+ months. Knowledge of English desirable. Pocket money £24-£27 per week. Also opportunities for mother's helps, working 7-8 hours daily. Vacancies for holiday helps, working up to 3 hours per day, also available for up to 12 weeks during the summer. Full board and lodging provided, but applicants pay their own travel expenses and insurance. *Apply 9 weeks in advance.*

HELPING HANDS AU PAIR & DOMESTIC AGENCY 10 Hertford Road, Newbury Park, Ilford, Essex IG2 7HQ Tel 081-597 3138
Positions available all year, mainly in London suburbs, country areas and seaside towns, for demi pairs, au pairs, au pairs plus and mother's helps. 3-8 hours work per day and 2-4 evenings per week babysitting, in a 6 day week, depending on position. Salary approx £10-£40 per week depending on hours worked. Board and lodging provided. 6+ months. Ages 17-27. Insurance and travel costs paid by the applicant, but assistance provided with the arrangements.

HOME FROM HOME 10 Tackley Place, Oxford, Oxfordshire OX2 6RR Tel Oxford 512628
Placements found for au pairs to undertake childcare and light housework throughout Britain, all year. No experience necessary but at least basic English required. 30 hour, 5 day week. Ages 18+. Pocket money £28 per week. Applicants pay their own travel and insurance.

INTERNATIONAL CATHOLIC SOCIETY FOR GIRLS (ACISJF) St Patrick's International Youth Centre, 24 Great Chapel Street, London W1V 3AF Tel 071-734 2156
Au pair posts arranged for a few 3 month summer positions and also for 9+ months, usually from September. Ages 18+. Assists girls/young women who are travelling and living away from home. Counselling and information service.

JOLAINE AGENCY 18 Escot Way, Barnet, Hertfordshire EN5 3AN Tel 081-449 1334
Au pair, demi pair and mother's help posts arranged throughout the year with families in the London area, on the coast and in the country. Au pairs work 5 hours per day plus babysitting. Most afternoons free plus 1 full

day and some evenings. Pocket money from £25 per week, according to duties and responsibilities. Demi pairs do 3/4 hours light housework per day and 3 evenings babysitting per week. Pocket money £8-£15 per week. Ages 17+. Mother's helps work 8 hours per day with 1½ days free per week, plus some evenings and other times by arrangement; pocket money from £60 per week. Applicants must have experience in childcare and cleaning. 2 weeks, Easter/Christmas, and 3-24 months. Full board, accommodation and insurance provided.

JUST THE JOB EMPLOYMENT AGENCY 8 Musters Road, West Bridgford, Nottingham NG2 6JA Tel Nottingham 813224
Arrange au pair and au pair plus positions for females only in Blackpool, Cardiff, Derby, Leeds, Leicester, London, Manchester, Newcastle, Norwich, Nottingham, Sheffield, Aberdeen and Glasgow. Work includes helping to care for the children and with household duties such as hoovering, dusting, light washing, ironing and preparation of meals. Babysitting experience preferred. Au pairs work a 5/6 hour day, 6 day week, with 2/3 evenings babysitting; pocket money £24 per week. Au pairs plus work a 7/8 hour day, 6 day week; pocket money £32 per week. September-July, and a limited number of positions June-September. Ages 18+. Applicants pay their own travel and insurance.

MONDIAL AGENCY 32 Links Road, West Wickham, Kent, BR4 0QW Tel 081-777 0510
Can place au pairs with families in the south of London and the Home Counties. 6+ months. Au pairs work a 5 hour day with 2/3 afternoons free for language classes, and are expected to spend some evenings babysitting by arrangement with the family. Board and lodging provided. Pocket money £25-£30 per week. Ages 18-27. Applicants pay their own travel and insurance. Service charge £40.

THE NANNY SERVICE 9 Paddington Street, London W1M 3LA Tel 071-935 8247
Nannies and mother's helps are needed throughout Britain, mostly in London. Nannies are responsible for the complete care of the children and in some cases assist with light housework. Opportunities are available for temporary and permanent staff, daily or residential. Applicants should be qualified in

GREAT BRITAIN

AU PAIR/CHILDCARE

child care or have suitable experience with babies and young children. Written references essential. 6+ weeks, hours variable. Ages 20+. Board and lodging usually provided. Salary £100+ per week, according to age, experience and work involved. *UK nationals only.*

PROBLEMS UNLIMITED Au Pair Introduction Service, 86 Alexandra Road, Windsor, Berkshire SL4 1HU Tel Windsor 865776

Au pair posts arranged throughout the year, mainly in the south of England. 5 hours work daily with some evening babysitting. 3/4 evenings and 1 free day per week. Pocket money £25-£30 per week. Time for classes and study. Also opportunities for au pair plus, working approx 7 hours per day. Pocket money £30-£35 per week. Ages 17-27. Basic English and some experience of housework or childcare necessary. 6+ months. Full board and accommodation provided. Travel paid by applicants.

STUDENTS ABROAD AGENCY Elm House, 21b The Avenue, Hatch End, Middlesex HA5 4EN Tel 081-428 5823

Can place au pairs and mother's helps with families. 6+ months. Au pairs are normally expected to work a 5/6 hour day. Usually 1 full day and 2/3 evenings free per week, but curriculum changes and applicants must be flexible during temporary summer season when no schooling available. Pocket money £25+ per week. Mother's helps work longer hours for £40+ per week, depending on experience and qualifications. Ages 17+. Board and lodging provided. Basic requirements are adaptability and a liking for, and ability to cope with, children, babies and housework.

UNIVERSAL CARE Chester House, 9 Windsor End, Beaconsfield, Buckinghamshire HP9 2JJ Tel Beaconsfield 678811

Au pair positions available in London and throughout Britain. 6-12 months; 3 month stays also arranged. 5 hour day with 1 day free per week and occasional free weekend. Opportunities to attend language classes, sometimes paid for by the family. Pocket money £25-£30 per week with full board and accommodation. Ages 18-27. Also mother's help positions in London and south east

England. 6+ months . 8 hour day with 2 days off per week. Salary £50-£80 per week with full board and accommodation. Ages 18+. Travel costs paid by applicants but family will sometimes pay return travel. Medical insurance recommended.

CHILDREN'S PROJECTS

Involving Volunteers in Children's Play £3.50, is a useful booklet written for those who wish to advise volunteers on playschemes, or who wish to volunteer themselves. Provides advice on who does what in children's play, organising play, the scope and value of volunteer involvement, agency responsibilities towards volunteers, and the needs of volunteers. Published by the Volunteer Centre, 29 Lower King's Road, Berkhamsted, Hertfordshire HP4 2AB Tel Berkhamsted 73311.

ASSOCIATION FOR ALL SPEECH IMPAIRED CHILDREN 347 Central Markets, Smithfield, London EC1A 9NH Tel 071-236 6487

Works to improve educational provision for children and young people with speech and language impairments, and gives support and advice to parents and professionals. Arranges adventure holidays covering a wide range of outdoor pursuits and indoor activities. Age groups are 5-8, 9-14, 14-18 and 17+. The holidays are held in centres in the countryside or at the seaside for the younger children; recent venues have included Kincraig, Kendal, Whitby, Southport, Broadstairs, Basingstoke and Eyam. Committed volunteers are needed, with fluent English, and able to spend a week devoting time and energy. Work involves being a friend and constant companion on a 1:1 basis throughout the week, helping to stimulate and give supportive help. 1 week, mid July-end August. Ages 18+. No set hours. Full board and accommodation in hostel or youth centre provided, but help towards cost welcomed. No wages or travel paid, but insurance covered.

ATD FOURTH WORLD The General Secretary, 48 Addington Square, London SE5 7LB Tel 071-703 3231
Strives to protect and guarantee the fundamental rights of the most disadvantaged and excluded families to family life, education and representation. It is these families, denied the means of being fully active members of society, who constitute the Fourth World in every country. Volunteers are required to help on street libraries in order to help very disadvantaged children who are not reached by summer playschemes. They are run by permanent trained volunteers, and preparation and evaluation time is an important part of the programme. Applicants should have a love of books, music and painting that they wish to share with the children, and should be interested in better understanding the causes and effects of poverty and be willing to work hard with an outgoing, lively team. Ages 18+. Approx 40 hour, 5½ day week. 1-4 weeks, during school Easter, summer half-term and summer holidays. Accommodation provided. Volunteers asked to contribute to food costs.

BIRMINGHAM PHAB CAMPS Kate Price, 474 Kingsbury Road, Erdington, Birmingham B24 9NQ
Volunteers are needed to help on camps which aim to integrate physically handicapped and able-bodied children, aged 7-19, and break down isolation and prejudice. Work involves being responsible for the children 24 hours a day, supervising, caring and organising activities including riding, watersports, camping and excursions. Participants must be prepared for very demanding work, involving initiative and responsibility. Each camp has an experienced leader and qualified nurse; volunteers attend a training day when they are instructed by medical staff and have the opportunity to meet the rest of the volunteer team. Volunteers should have energy, imagination and the ability to get on with children; skills such as music and sports useful. Ages 17-30. Volunteers able to drive minibuses, ages 21+, particularly welcome, and qualified nurses and catering staff also required. 7-10 days, July and August. Board and lodging provided, but participants may be required to help with catering. Insurance and travel between Birmingham and the camp arranged.
B D PH

BIRMINGHAM YOUNG VOLUNTEERS ADVENTURE CAMPS 3rd floor, 24 Albert Street, Birmingham B4 7UD Tel 021-643 8297
Volunteers are needed to help on holidays at the seaside and near Malvern for disadvantaged children from the Birmingham area. 1 week, July-September. Volunteer helpers encourage close personal contact which allows development of personalities through new relationships and experiences. Experience of drama, art, games organisation, music or cooking useful. Ages 17+. Also opportunities for minibus drivers, ages 21+. Training given. Full board hostel or camping accommodation, insurance cover and travel costs from Birmingham to the holiday provided.

CHRISTIAN MOVEMENT FOR PEACE Bethnal Green United Reformed Church, Pott Street, London E2 0EF Tel 071-729 1877
An international movement open to all who share a common concern for lasting peace and justice in the world. Volunteers are required to work in international teams on summer projects aimed at offering service in an area of need and promoting self-help within the community; promoting international understanding and the discussion of social problems; and offering young people the chance to live as a group and take these experiences into the context of daily life. Recent projects have included running playschemes in County Durham, Liverpool, Leicester, Tiverton and Barnsley, involving fundraising, arts and craft activities, music and movement, sports, camping and bus trips. Participants are encouraged to become involved in the life of the host community.

Ages 17+. Ages 18+, overseas volunteers with fluent English. Volunteers must enjoy working with children, be able to contribute their own ideas to the schemes, show initiative in organising indoor and outdoor activities and be prepared to take a full part in all aspects of the project. 30-36 hour week. 2-3 weeks, July and August, and sometimes at Easter. Board, lodging and insurance provided, but participants pay their own travel costs. Registration fee £15.

Applications from outside the UK: please see workcamp information on page 27.

GREAT BRITAIN

CHILDREN'S PROJECTS

COMMUNITY ACTION PROJECTS
Camp Organiser, Goodricke College, University of York, Heslington, York, North Yorkshire YO1 5DD Tel York 433133
Volunteers are needed to help on an annual camp for disadvantaged children aged 6-13, who might not otherwise get a holiday. Many of the children are emotionally disturbed, hyperactive or come from unsettled backgrounds. The camp takes about 28 children per week and is usually held on the North Yorkshire Moors. Activities include drama, arts and crafts, canoeing, excursions, games, shows, community involvement and walks. Duties include supervising tents, playing with and looking after the children, dealing with emotional problems, taking responsibility for situations as they arise, driving the minibus, cooking and sharing camp duties/chores. The children are also encouraged to take part in the organisation of the camp and to help with daily chores. 3-4 weeks, during school summer holidays. The work is physically and emotionally tiring, so the maximum stay as a volunteer is 4 weeks, 2 weeks as a driver.

Ages 18+, 21+ for drivers, plus 1 year's clean driving licence. Volunteers should have initiative, enthusiasm, a sense of humour, lots of energy, the ability to take responsibility and participate fully in all camp activities, plus a liking for children, and be friendly and tolerant. Skills in games, arts/crafts, cookery, wildlife, sports or first aid are very useful, as well as the ability to drive a minibus. References required. Smaller camps, catering for up to 20, are also run at Easter, based in village schools or similar buildings. Food and accommodation provided. Venture weeks are run for 14-16 year olds in August, involving backpacking, setting up camp, orienteering and problem solving. Experience of camping and working with teenagers useful. A training day is arranged the day before each camp begins to give volunteers the opportunity to meet one another and discuss the running of the camp. *Overseas volunteers with a working knowledge of English accepted.*

EASTWOOD AREA COMMUNITY EDUCATION OFFICE 218 Ayr Road, Newton Mearns, Glasgow Tel 041-639 7160
Provides educational and recreational activities for all members of the community and needs volunteers to help on summer playschemes. Work involves supervising 5-16 year olds in sports, crafts, games, and taking them on outings or to special events. Ages 16+. No qualifications or experience required, but volunteers must be able to speak English. 25 hour week, July. Insurance provided, but not travel. Board and accommodation arranged with local families, cost approx £35 per week.

FLYSHEET CAMPS SCOTLAND
The Resident Organiser, Finniegill Children's Farm, Lockerbie, Dumfriesshire
A remote farmstead situated high in the hills of southwest Scotland, providing wilderness camps for children, mainly from families in need. The aim is to provide a setting where people of all ages and backgrounds can come together and experience living and working in ways that are different from their everyday life. All aspects of a simple lifestyle are explored, and the experience is as important as the end-product. There is no telephone, no electricity and no amenities for 15 miles.

A limited number of dedicated volunteers are needed, both for work on the 8 acres of woodland and on the children's camps. Ages 16+. 2-3+ weeks, Easter to late autumn. Primitive bothy or tent accommodation, pocket money £12 per week and insurance provided; volunteers pay their own travel costs. *Overseas applicants accepted; fluent English required for children's camp volunteers.*

GREAT GEORGES PROJECT Duty Officer, The Blackie, Great George Street, Liverpool L1 Tel 051-709 5109
The Great Georges Community Cultural Project, known locally as The Blackie, is a centre for experimental work in the arts, sports, games and education of today. Housed in a former church in an area typical of the modern inner-city: multi-racial, relatively poor, with a high crime rate and a high energy level; sometimes a lot of fun. Volunteers are needed to work with children/adults on playschemes, special projects and outdoor events. The general work of running the Project is shared as fairly as possible, with everyone doing some administration, repairs, building work, cleaning, talking to visitors and playing games with the children. Ages 18+. Applicants should have a good sense of humour, stamina,

a readiness to learn, and a willingness to work hard and to share any skills they may have. The children and young people who visit the Project are tough, intelligent, friendly and regard newcomers as a fair target for jokes, so the ability to exert discipline without being authoritarian is essential. 12 hour day, 5½ day week, 4+ weeks; volunteers particularly needed at Christmas, Easter and summer. Accommodation provided in shared rooms at staff house; volunteers should take a sleeping bag. Vegetarian breakfast and evening meal provided, cooking on a rota basis. Those who can afford to contribute approx £15 per week to cover food and housekeeping. *Overseas applicants welcome; good working knowledge of English required.*

INTERNATIONAL VOLUNTARY SERVICE 162 Upper New Walk, Leicester LE1 7QA Tel Leicester 549430

IVS is the British branch of Service Civil International which promotes international reconciliation through work projects. Volunteers are needed for children's projects on international workcamps. Recent projects have included helping to run summer playschemes in Cambridge, Edinburgh, Glastonbury, Liverpool and Stirling; involving local children in a water safety project on a canal in Glasgow; working among children with mental disabilities or emotional problems in Liverpool; and touring playschemes in Middlesbrough with an international arts and crafts workshop.

Ages 18+. 35-40 hour week, 2-4 weeks, June-September, Christmas and Easter. Preference given to those who are not students. Overseas volunteers must speak good English. Experience in working with children an advantage. Volunteers must be prepared to work hard and contribute actively to the work and team life, and be prepared for additional mental and emotional strain. Food, accommodation in village halls, houses, schools, homes, hospitals or community centres with self-catering facilities and insurance provided, but volunteers pay their own travel costs. Membership fee £25 (students £15, unwaged £10). Registration fee £20. B D PH

Applications from outside the UK: please see workcamp information on page 27.

LEICESTER BOYS' & GIRLS' SUMMER CAMP & INSTITUTE Shaftesbury Hall, Holy Bones, Leicester LE1 4LJ Tel Leicester 519863

Seasonal staff are required at a holiday home in Mablethorpe which provides the poorest and most deserving children aged 7-11 from Leicester and its neighbourhood with a fortnight's holiday. The home is situated on the sandhills and the children have their own path to the beach. Work includes looking after the children, playing with them, taking them to the beach, and perhaps making beds and a little housework. Ages 18+. 1+ months, May-August. Preference given to applicants able to work the whole season. Board and lodging provided plus a salary of £37.50 per week. *Apply to the Children's Holiday Home, The Matron, Quebec Road, Mablethorpe, Lincolnshire Tel Mablethorpe 472444. UK nationals only.*

LIVERPOOL CHILDREN'S HOLIDAY ORGANISATION Wellington Road School, Wellington Road, Liverpool L8 4TX Tel 051-727 7330

Volunteers are needed to help run holidays for Merseyside children, particularly those from low income families who would not otherwise be able to afford one, at centres throughout Britain. Volunteers are responsible for looking after the happiness and safety of groups of 4-6 children aged 7-14, providing them with a wide range of entertaining and stimulating activities. No experience necessary but volunteers must have plenty of energy and enthusiasm for being with children, and are on call 24 hours per day. All volunteers will be interviewed before attending a 1 week residential training course, usually at Easter. Ages 18+. Each holiday lasts 8 days. Full board and dormitory accommodation shared with the children. Accommodation and expenses covered during the holiday period. Pocket money approx £30 per week. Basic insurance and return travel from Liverpool to holiday centres provided. Participants pay nominal fee of £30 for training course. *UK nationals only.*

LONDON CHILDREN'S CAMP Recruitment Officer, 33 Farren Road, Forest Hill, London SE23 2DZ

Volunteers are required to provide a holiday for underprivileged children from London on a campsite in Kessingland, Suffolk. Leaders have pastoral care for a group of approx 6

children, aged 9-13, and are involved in inventing and organising different activities and in the day to day running of the camp. 11 days, July-end August.
Ages 18+. Applicants should be energetic, prepared to work 16-17 hours per day, have a sense of humour, be innovative, fairly thick-skinned, tolerant, able to listen, confident, willing to keep order and cope with the children who are sometimes difficult and hard to motivate. Camping accommodation provided plus washing facilities, leaders hut and a large dining room. Pocket money £20 per camp.

LOTHIAN PLAY FORUM Organising Secretary, c/o Dalry Primary School, Dalry Road, Edinburgh EH11 2BU
Organises over 130 playschemes for children in and around Edinburgh. Volunteers are needed to help with games, art, visits, camps and drama. Ages 18+. 4 weeks, July/August. Experience with children an advantage. Food and accommodation not provided but volunteers receive £20-£30 per week, depending on the playscheme. *Apply by end April.*

TADWORTH COURT CHILDREN'S SERVICES Tadworth Court Trust, The Chief Executive, Tadworth, Surrey KT20 5RU Tel Burgh Heath 357171
Requires volunteers for residential summer schemes for physically and mentally handicapped children, aged 4-16, who normally live at home. The services are provided in a children's hospital and at a residential school. Work involves acting as a friend to the children, carrying out basic personal care, organising games, encouraging them to take an active part in daily activities, escorting them on outings, and organising evening activities.

Previous experience with children or handicapped people preferable, but not essential. Creative skills, handicraft or musical ability welcomed. The work is very rewarding but can also be physically and emotionally tiring. Ages 18+. 9 hour day, worked in shifts, with 2 days off per week. 4+ weeks, mid July-mid September. Lodging provided, plus a meal allowance of £28 per week. Travel expenses within Britain can be reimbursed. *Apply by 31 May.* B D PH

TOC H National Projects Office, 38 Newark Street, London E1 Tel 071-247 5110
A voluntary movement which provides an opportunity to meet and work with a variety of different people on a range of challenging high-energy projects. Many of these involve running holiday playschemes or adventure camps for children who would otherwise be unable to have a holiday. Recent projects have included taking inner-city children on activity/adventure holidays in the Lake District and Norfolk Broads; walking, canoeing and dry-slope skiing in Snowdonia with children with special needs; running a playscheme in Mid-Glamorgan, involving swimming and riding; and running arts, crafts and drama workshops. Ages 16+. Weekends-3 weeks, all year. Volunteers need patience, energy, enthusiasm, understanding and a sense of humour. Accommodation provided but participants pay for travel to and from projects, although some financial assistance may be available. Registration fee £5. Projects may qualify under the Duke of Edinburgh's Award Scheme. *Overseas volunteers with good English accepted.*

UNITED NATIONS ASSOCIATION International Youth Service, Welsh Centre for International Affairs, Temple of Peace, Cathays Park, Cardiff CF1 3AP Tel Cardiff 223088
Aims to assist in community development by acting as a means to stimulate new ideas and projects, and encouraging the concept of voluntary work as a force in the common search for peace, equality, democracy and social justice. Volunteers are needed for community work on summer workcamps in various parts of Wales. Recent projects have included helping to run playschemes in the South Wales valleys, organising indoor and outdoor activities for children, some of whom are mentally and physically handicapped; and taking groups of deprived or socially handicapped children on holiday, including walks, swimming, sports and excursions. Ages 17+, 18+ for overseas volunteers. Volunteers are expected to join in the activities of the local community and to create a happy and effective project. 40 hour week, 2-4 weeks, April-May and July-September. Accommodation in church halls, youth hostels, schools or community centres, food and insurance provided.

Volunteers share the cooking, pay their own travel costs and should take a sleeping bag. Good command of English essential. Registration fee £25. **B D PH** on some projects.

Applications from outside the UK: please see workcamp information on page 27.

COMMUNITY
WORK

A Place for You in Britain? As a Volunteer is a free leaflet containing useful information on obtaining work as a volunteer and detailing opportunities available. *A Place for You in Britain? Working for World Development,* contains information on how to show concern for world development and the types of activities possible, plus organisations, development education centres and resource centres to contact. Both published by Christians Abroad, 1 Stockwell Green, London SW9 9HP Tel 071-737 7811.

Opportunities for Volunteers on Holiday Projects free on receipt of SAE/IRC and published annually, gives details of organisations needing volunteers to help physically disabled people on holiday. Published by RADAR (Royal Association for Disability and Rehabilitation), 25 Mortimer Street, London W1N 8AB Tel 071-637 5400, which works to remove the barriers which separate disabled people from society.

ASHRAM COMMUNITY SERVICE PROJECT 23/25 Grantham Road, Sparkbrook, Birmingham B11 1LU Tel 021-773 7061
A community project run jointly by Christians and Muslims in inner-city Birmingham, with the aims of working against racist patterns of employment, ensuring that women have access to resources, and putting local traditional skills to appropriate use by developing new employment initiatives. Volunteers are invited to help with general administration as well as horticulture, working with children, visiting women and helping with stalls at various events. Ages 21+. No experience necessary; training is usually given where required. Excursions sometimes arranged at weekends

with members of other projects. Hours negotiable; usually 09.00-17.00, all year. Insurance and accommodation in the Ashram community provided. Volunteers pay travel and board and lodging as far as possible. *Overseas applicants welcome.* **PH** but unsuitable for wheelchairs.

BEANNACHAR LTD Elisabeth Phethean, Banchory-Devenick, Aberdeen AB1 5YL Tel Aberdeen 861825/868605
A Camphill community for further education and training, with the aims of providing meaningful work and a home for young adults with varying degrees of handicap or disturbance. Students and staff live in 2 large family units in a pre-Victorian house in grounds on the outskirts of Aberdeen. Volunteers are required to help care for students and work with them on a communal basis. Work involves gardening, cooking, building, cleaning, looking after animals, laundry, weaving and woodwork. Volunteers are also expected to participate fully in other community activities such as folk dancing, drama, festivals, walking, swimming, games, lessons and outings. Ages 19+. Experience not necessary, but volunteers should be enthusiastic and willing to learn, preferably with fluent English. 6-12 months; longer-term commitment preferred, but also short-term opportunities over the summer. 6 days per week. Volunteers receive £18 per week pocket money, plus full board and lodging in the community. **D PH**

BREAK Mr GM Davison, 20 Hooks Hill Road, Sheringham, Norfolk NR26 8NL Tel Sheringham 823170
Provides holidays and respite for unaccompanied mentally, physically and emotionally handicapped children and adults from pre-school age upwards, and for socially deprived children. Holiday and special care opportunities also exist for mentally handicapped adults and families with special needs. Volunteers are needed as care assistants for residential work at two holiday homes at Sheringham and Hunstanton. Work involves helping with the personal welfare of the guests, their recreational programme and with essential domestic duties. Placements involving work discussions and assessments can be arranged for those seeking practical

experience prior to or as part of an educational course. Ages 17/18+. Applicants should be stable, conscientious, patient and understanding. The work is physically and emotionally demanding. 40 hour week. 1-9 months, all year. Board, lodging, £17 per week pocket money plus travel expenses within Britain provided. *Overseas volunteers accepted.*

CAMPHILL VILLAGE TRUST Loch Arthur Village Community, Beeswing, Dumfries DG2 8JQ Tel Kirkgunzeon 224

Aims to provide a new and constructive way of life for mentally handicapped adults, assisting them to achieve individual independence and social adjustment within Trust communities. Loch Arthur Village is one of the communities which provide a home, work, further education and general care for approx 30 handicapped adults, and consists of 5 houses, a farm and an estate of 500 acres. Volunteers are needed to work alongside the residents in every aspect of life and main areas of work are on the farm and in the garden, houses and workshops. As many of the adults have fairly severe handicaps they are also in need of care such as bathing, dressing and other personal tasks. Volunteers must be willing to help wherever they are needed, and are encouraged not only to share in the responsibilities of living and working with the handicapped but also to participate in the cultural, recreational and social aspects of Village life. Ages 18+. 3-48 weeks, throughout the year but especially during the summer. Food and accommodation provided, plus pocket money for long-term volunteers. *Overseas applicants accepted.*

CECIL HOUSES INC 2/4 Priory Road, Kew, Richmond, Surrey TW9 3DG Tel 081-940 9828

A housing association and charity providing hostels for homeless women, a sheltered hostel for active pensioners and residential care homes for the frail elderly. It aims to provide caring communities where individuals can mix with others in similar circumstances. Volunteers are needed to help the staff caring for the residents; work includes helping in social activities, domestic work and generally assisting in improving the residents' lifestyle. Ages 18+. No experience needed. 4+ months, all year. 39 hour week. Full board, lodging and £18.50 per week pocket money provided. *Overseas volunteers with good English accepted.*

CROYDON COMMUNITY & VOLUNTARY SERVICES Volunteer Organiser, Rehabilitation Services, Taberner House, Park Lane, Croydon, Surrey CR9 2BA Tel 081-760 5640

Volunteers are needed to help on holidays for adults with a physical or mental disabling condition, at holiday or activity centres. Venues have included Isle of Sheppey, West Country and the Lake District. Tasks include helping with personal care, meals, domestic chores, practical aid, socialising, outings and entertainments. 1 week, May-November. Ages 16+. Nursing experience useful but not essential. Volunteers should be cheerful, willing and sensible; those on activity holidays need outdoor sports experience or interest. References required. Board, accommodation and return travel from Croydon to holiday centre provided, plus pocket money and £10 towards fare to Croydon. *Overseas volunteers accepted.*

GLASGOW SIMON COMMUNITY 133 Hill Street, Garnethill, Glasgow G3 6UB Tel 041-332 3448

Aims to offer time, friendship, practical help and supportive accommodation to men and women who have been homeless for some time. There is an outreach team and 5 small group homes in which residents and volunteers live together, sharing in the running and day-to-day life. Contact is made with homeless people, especially rough sleepers, and friendship and practical help is offered. Volunteers will also maintain contact and good relations with relevant agencies. Ages 18+. No academic qualifications required but certain personal qualities essential - including a non-patronising attitude, the ability to accept people for what they are, the ability to cope with stress and emotional pressures. Recruitment takes place all year round. Informal, 1:1 training provided during the first month, with training visits to relevant agencies. Regular opportunities to participate in training events and attend conferences of the national servicing body in Birmingham. 5 day week, 24 hour day. 6+ months, preferably longer. Salary £15.70 per week; £18.63 per week compulsory savings, out of which Class III National Insurance contributions may be made, paid in lump sum at the end of placement. £40 shoe allowance and £53.75 for a holiday every 3 months. Full board and accommodation provided; separate accommodation for days off. Volunteers take their turn cooking along with the residents. Travel expenses are paid during the time in the community; for interview, arrival and departure £40 is paid. The work relies on commitment and involvement; the first 4 weeks are an introductory/trial period, at the end of which each member of the project votes on whether the person is suitable. *All nationalities welcome; applicants must have a good standard of spoken English.*

HELP THE HANDICAPPED HOLIDAY
FUND 147A Camden Road, Tunbridge Wells,
Kent TN1 2RA Tel Tunbridge Wells 547474
Aims to provide group holidays for physically handicapped people from the age of 11 upwards. Volunteers provide help and care during holiday visits in Cornwall, Dorset, Kent, Lancashire and Sussex. No experience necessary. Ages 18+. Hours depending on the guests' needs and level of care. Helpers must provide their own pocket money and new helpers are required to make a £30 refundable commitment fee. The cost of accommodation and transport within Britain for nominated holiday weeks, and medical and public liability insurance provided.

HOLIDAY HELPERS PO Box 20, Horley,
Surrey RH6 9UY Tel Horley 775137
Aims to recruit, train and match able-bodied volunteers to accompany elderly or disabled people on independent holidays, on a 1:1 basis. Volunteers provide personal care, help with wheelchairs, as well as companionship; they are matched with people who live near them, so that they can also be involved with holiday planning. Experience useful, though not essential. Ages 17+. 1-2 weeks, throughout the year. Travel and accommodation provided, but no pocket money. *UK residents preferred.* B D PH depending on ability.

INDEPENDENT LIVING ALTERNATIVES
Fulton House, Fulton Road, Empire Way,
Wembley, Middlesex HA9 OTF
Tel 081-902 8998
A non-profitmaking charity run by disabled people for disabled people, designed to promote independence. Volunteers are needed to provide physical support in the form of partnership, living with and giving full-time aid and companionship to a disabled person. Ages 17+. 3-5 day week depending on placement. Food, accommodation in own room in partner's home, £40 per week plus expenses provided. Training given prior to placement. B D PH depending on ability.

INDEPENDENT LIVING SCHEMES Room
306, Eros House, Brownhill Road, Catford,
London SE6 2EG Tel 081-695 6000
Aims to enable severely disabled people to live in the community with help from volunteers, who will assist in personal care, shopping, social and community activities. Ages 17+, no experience necessary. Two 24 hour shifts per week, sleeping in. Pocket money £20, food allowance £25, plus clothing and leisure allowance £3, per week. Self-contained flat, travel within the UK and insurance provided. Preferred placement period 6 months. B D PH depending on ability.

THE INTERNATIONAL FLAT Mrs B Gandhi,
20 Glasgow Street, Glasgow G12 8JP
Tel 041-339 6118
A voluntary organisation based in the Hillhead area of Glasgow, needing volunteers to help on a playscheme for children aged 6-12 from various ethnic backgrounds. Activities include puppet shows, films, indoor and outdoor games, arts and crafts and visits around Glasgow. Ages 18+. Experience preferred, but not essential. 30 hour week. 3 weeks, July. Self-catering accommodation provided. *Apply before mid May. Overseas volunteers accepted.*

INTERNATIONAL VOLUNTARY SERVICE
162 Upper New Walk, Leicester LE1 7QA
Tel Leicester 549430
IVS is the British branch of Service Civil International, which promotes international reconciliation through work projects. Volunteers are needed for community work on international workcamps. Recent projects have included building paths suitable for wheelchairs at a holiday centre for people with disabilities in Aviemore; living in a community of adults with social and mental disabilities in Loch Arthur, helping to restore old farm buildings and working on the organic farm; working on a 1:1 basis with the profoundly physically handicapped on holiday in Humberside; and organising crafts, drama and

outings for residents in a long-stay hospital in Birmingham. There are approx 80 international workcamps involving groups of 6-18 volunteers. Ages 18+. Preference given to those who are not students. Overseas volunteers must speak fluent English. Volunteers must be prepared to work hard and contribute actively to the work and team life, and be prepared for additional mental and emotional strain. 35-40 hour week, 2-4 weeks, June-September, and Christmas and Easter. Food, insurance and accommodation in village halls, houses, schools, homes, hospitals or community centres with self-catering facilities provided, but volunteers pay their own travel costs. Membership fee £25 (students £15, unwaged £10). Registration fee £20. B D PH

Applications from outside the UK: please see workcamp information on page 27.

THE LADYPOOL PROJECT The Honorary Secretary, 112 Whitecroft Road, Sheldon, Birmingham B26 3RG

A Christian organisation providing canal trips and sailing holidays for those who would not normally be able to participate in them, particularly the mentally and physically handicapped and the profoundly sick. Volunteers are needed to assist with day trips for schools, the handicapped and the elderly on the West Midlands canals, all year, and to accompany sailing holidays in Dartmouth for deaf and blind children, June. Duties include cleaning and moving the boats, and generally helping and entertaining the guests. Ages 17+. Experience useful but not essential; volunteers must be able to swim. Christian commitment preferred. Approx 40 hour week. Accommodation on boats, food and insurance provided. *Overseas applicants with a knowledge of English accepted.* B D PH

THE LEONARD CHESHIRE FOUNDATION Secretary to the Personnel Adviser, Leonard Cheshire House, 26/29 Maunsel Street, London SW1P 2QN Tel 071-828 1822

Runs over 80 homes throughout the UK, mostly in country areas, for the care of severely handicapped people, mainly physically disabled adults. Cheshire Homes offer the affection and freedom of family life, and the residents are encouraged to lead the most active lives that their disabilities permit.

Volunteers are needed in many Homes to assist with the general care of residents who require help in personal matters, including washing, dressing and feeding, as well as with hobbies, letter writing, driving, going on outings or holidays and other recreational activities. Ages 18-30. Preference generally given to those planning to take up medical or social work as a career. Volunteers must be adaptable, dedicated, hard working, punctual and willing to undertake a wide variety of tasks. Up to 39 hour, 5 day week. 1+ months, mostly 3-12 months. Board, lodging and at least £23 per week pocket money provided. Travel costs paid by the volunteer. *Overseas applicants must have a good working knowledge of English.*

LONDON CITY MISSION Youth Department, 175 Tower Bridge Road, London SE1 2AH Tel 071-407 7585

Volunteers are needed to help with outreach work in evangelical churches and mission centres around London, working alongside experienced Christian workers. Work includes open-air meetings, helping with vagrants, street witnessing, some visitation, practical and tourist work and children's evangelistic meetings. Experience in various evangelistic activities and knowledge of foreign languages helpful but not essential. Some in-service training given. Ages 18-30. 2-8 weeks, July-September. Other short-term opportunities available throughout the year. Hours worked depend on the individual placements, but volunteers should be prepared for hard work and long hours. Basic accommodation in church halls, with food provided. Expenses covered by the Mission, but participants are asked to donate towards the cost if possible. 1 year programme also available, beginning September. *Applicants must be practising evangelical Christians.*

MENCAP (Royal Society for Mentally Handicapped Children and Adults) National Centre, 123 Golden Lane, London EC1Y 0RT Tel 071-454 0454

Volunteer helpers are needed on adventure, guest house and special care holidays for unaccompanied mentally handicapped children and adults throughout England and Wales. Work involves being responsible for the personal care of each guest, including washing, feeding and other essential tasks as well as stimulating and interesting them in activities, communicating and being a friend. Duties are shared on a rota basis and can include cooking, cleaning, making beds and night duty. Much time is also spent playing, talking and planning activities. Ages 18+. No experience necessary, but volunteers need energy, enthusiasm and an interest in people with a mental handicap. Qualified nurses welcome. Maximum 14 hours' work per day. 1-2 weeks, Easter-September. Board and accommodation provided. Travelling expenses up to £15 will be reimbursed. *Applications from outside Britain welcome.* PH

All enquiries to MENCAP Holiday Services Office, 119 Drake Street, Rochdale, Lancashire OL16 1PZ Tel Rochdale 54111.

THE OCKENDEN VENTURE Personnel Officer, Ockenden, Guildford Road, Woking, Surrey GU22 7UU Tel Woking 772012
A voluntary organisation providing home, health, education and rehabilitation for displaced persons, refugees and young people, including intermediate treatment for young offenders, providing education, care and rehabilitation of children, particularly school refusers and those who are deprived, at risk or in trouble. There are Ockenden centres in North Wales, Yorkshire and Surrey. Volunteers are needed to assist in caring for refugee families, young unaccompanied refugees and a group of physically and mentally handicapped refugees, and to help with gardening, cooking, painting and maintenance. The communities are run on non-institutional lines in order to create homes, so volunteers are expected to accept a fair share of responsibility at all levels. The Venture aims to provide young volunteers with experience in community responsibility and awareness of social needs. Ages 18+. Approx 14 places per year for graduates or mature school leavers. Limited number of placements for summer volunteers; most positions for 1 year. 5½ day week. Full board and lodging plus £20 per week personal allowance.

OUTWARD BOUND CITY CHALLENGE Chestnut Field, Regent Place, Rugby, Warwickshire CV21 2PJ Tel Rugby 60423
Provides residential personal development courses for young people, based around the

social challenges of inner-city areas. Volunteers are needed to run group sessions and provide support and counselling for young people taking part in intensive voluntary service placements with disabled people, the homeless, elderly or mentally ill. Based mainly around Liverpool, Coventry and Humberside. Volunteers will need experience of working with 16+ age group, group work or counselling skills. Teaching or youth work qualifications preferred as well as a clean driving licence.

Ages 23+. 2-3 weeks, July/August and October/November. Tutors are residential and fully committed for the duration of the course, which includes working weekends and evenings. Canteen food organised by the students. All food, accommodation, insurance, travel expenses, honorarium of approx £80 and weekend staff training course provided. *Overseas applicants must have some knowledge of social conditions in UK cities. Near-native command of English essential.* B D PH

PETRUS COMMUNITY 82 Holt Road, Liverpool L7 2PR Tel 051-263 4543
A voluntary organisation providing a variety of accommodation and support for homeless single people in inner-city Liverpool. Currently run 3 projects including hostels providing long-stay accommodation and a dry house for recovering alcoholics. Many of the residents have been unemployed for long periods, are socially isolated and some have chronic medical or psychiatric problems. Main tasks include housekeeping, dealing with enquiries and day to day problems. Ages 18+. Volunteers are expected to be capable and responsible, able to cope with the demands of the job. Average 40 hour working week with 2 free days. Average length of stay 6 months, all year. £30 per week plus full board and accommodation provided. One week's holiday after 3 months service plus leaving bonus. *British applicants only.*

QUEEN ELIZABETH'S FOUNDATION FOR THE DISABLED Holiday Organiser, Lulworth Court, 25 Chalkwell Esplanade, Westcliff-on-Sea, Essex SS0 8JQ Tel Southend 431725
Volunteers are required to help give lively informal holidays to severely physically disabled people at a holiday home on the

GREAT BRITAIN

COMMUNITY WORK

seafront at Westcliff-on-Sea. Work involves assisting nursing staff to look after guests, many of whom are confined to wheelchairs and need complete help with all aspects of personal care as well as escorting on outings, shopping, theatre and pub trips. The work is hard but rewarding, requiring some heavy lifting. A sense of humour helps. Ages 18+. 2+ weeks, all year except Christmas. Full board and accommodation provided, and contribution made towards travel expenses. *Overseas volunteers with a good working knowledge of English accepted.*

THE RICHARD CAVE MULTIPLE SCLEROSIS HOLIDAY HOME The Administrator, Servite Convent, Leuchie House, North Berwick, East Lothian EH39 5NY Tel North Berwick 2864
Volunteers are needed at a holiday home for persons of all ages with multiple sclerosis. Applicants should be female, but no nursing qualifications necessary. Ages 18-30. Board and accommodation plus pocket money provided. Fares occasionally paid within Britain.

RIDING FOR THE DISABLED ASSOCIATION Avenue R, National Agricultural Centre, Kenilworth, Warwickshire CV8 2LY Tel Coventry 696510
Provides the opportunity of riding for disabled people who might benefit in their general health and well-being. Voluntary helpers are sometimes needed for riding holidays in the summer; a list is produced in March detailing the holidays available. Ages 17+. Experience with horses or disabled people useful. No set hours of work; volunteers will be expected to work a full week. Board and lodging plus travel expenses may be provided subject to the holiday organiser's discretion; helpers may be asked to contribute. No wages provided.

RITCHIE RUSSELL HOUSE The Churchill Hospital, Headington, Oxford, Oxfordshire OX3 7LJ Tel Oxford 741841
A purpose-built unit designed for disabled adults, the majority of whom suffer from chronic or progressive neurological diseases, such as multiple sclerosis, cerebro-vascular accidents, or the effects of head or spinal injury. Patients are intermittently resident, or attend daily, in a secure, lively and relaxed environment where patients and staff work

together to improve the quality of life. Each patient is given the opportunity of an annual holiday and volunteers are needed, responsible with the help of staff for the total care of patients on a 1:1 basis, including washing, dressing, toileting and feeding. Experience useful but not essential. Ages 18+, fluent English necessary. 12 hours per day, summer, except August. Half board usually in hotel or chalet, insurance and some travel provided. Volunteers are asked to contribute £35-£50.

SHAD Support and Housing Assistance for People with Disabilities, Deborah Livingstone, SHAD (Haringey), Selby Site, Selby Road, London N17 8JN Tel 081-885 5569
Aims to promote freedom for people with disabilities, offering housing and support in the community which leads to independence, integration and choice. Volunteers are required to assist disabled people with all aspects of daily living, including personal care, cooking, housework, and visits. No experience necessary; volunteers will receive instruction. Driving licence useful. Ages 18+. 4+ months, all year. Volunteers work full-time with one person, 3 volunteers to one disabled person on a rota basis. Salary £40 per week, fares, other expenses, separate accommodation and insurance provided. 4 days per fortnight and regular long weekends off.

THE SHAFTESBURY SOCIETY The Shaftesbury Society Holiday Centre, New Hall, Low Road, Dovercourt, Harwich, Essex CO12 3TS Tel Harwich 504219
Provides holidays for elderly and handicapped guests, and requires volunteers to assist guests in various ways, such as escorting them to the beach, the shops or on outings, and helping with personal needs such as getting up, washing, dressing, toilet, eating, going to bed, bed making. No experience necessary. Ages 16+. 1-2 weeks, April-October. Hours as required, and sometimes during the night. Single or double room accommodation, food, insurance and travel from London provided.

THE SIMON COMMUNITY St Joseph's House, PO Box 1187, London NW5 4HW Tel 071-485 6639
Works with homeless, rootless, socially isolated, inadequate and unemployable men and women, children and groups, providing a

long-term caring, supportive environment where the individual can regain self respect. A night shelter, reception and community houses and a farmhouse comprise a tier system enabling residents to move from house to house and find the appropriate level of support at a particular point in time.

Volunteers are needed to live at the same level as, and work with, the residents. Activities include helping to obtain medical care and social security, referral to other organisations, talking to the residents, cooking, fundraising, household work, administration, involvement in group meetings, night duty, going to rough sleeping sites in London with tea and sandwiches to make contact with homeless people and helping at a night shelter. The work is emotionally demanding, dealing with a wide range of problems and disorders from those who have been rejected by society and have slipped through the net of the welfare state.

Workers and residents share in the daily chores and decision making and volunteers must be caring, sensible, mature and stable enough to take the burden of other people's problems while retaining their own balance. They must also be capable of taking initiatives within the framework of a team, learning to cope with crises, so a sense of humour is an asset. Accommodation is very basic and conditions can be rough. The experience will be of particular interest to those seriously interested in social work. Ages 18+. Long working hours with 1 day free per week. 10 days leave after 3 months. Board, lodging and £12 per week pocket money provided. *EC nationals only; applicants must have a good grasp of English.*

ST EBBA'S HOSPITAL Hook Road, Epsom, Surrey KT19 8QJ Tel Epsom 22212

Cares for the mentally/physically handicapped, with about 400 adult residents, and aims to give the extra care and attention needed, and so help them lead a more contented life. Volunteers are needed to help in various departments: sports, physiotherapy, music and drama, gardening, training, and with general care. No experience necessary, just a sensible, caring nature. Work available for different periods, all year. 32 hour week. Ages 16+. Accommodation and food provided.

THE SUE RYDER FOUNDATION Administration Officer, Sue Ryder Home, Cavendish, Sudbury, Suffolk CO10 8AY Tel Glemsford 280252

Founded to help relieve physical and psychological suffering, the Foundation has over 80 homes, primarily for the disabled and incurables but also admits sick people who, on discharge from hospital, still need care and attention. Aims to give adults and children a family sense with something to contribute, as an individual, to the common good. Helpers are needed at headquarters and the Sue Ryder Home, Cavendish, and on occasions at other Foundation Homes. The work is largely domestic and nursing under supervision, including making beds, serving meals, feeding, working in the kitchen, laundry and gardens and possibly some office and maintenance work. Volunteers should be flexible and adaptable and are expected to help with whatever needs doing. Helpers are also required with training or experience in housekeeping, nursing, physio or occupational therapy, secretarial work, decorating, carpentry, plumbing, engineering, electrical work and bricklaying, as well as site supervisors, surveyors, draughtsmen, talks representatives and writers. Help is also needed in Sue Ryder gift and coffee shops, museum and retreat houses. Ages 18+. 35 hour week. 2+ months, all year. Preference given to students and graduates. Board and lodging provided, plus approx £10 pocket money per week. *Overseas volunteers with good command of spoken English accepted.*

TOC H National Projects Office, 38 Newark Street, London E1 Tel 071-247 5110

A voluntary movement which provides an opportunity to work with a variety of different people on projects aimed at meeting a need in the local community. Projects provide experience of working with the homeless; the unemployed; adults with learning difficulties or disabilities; and in other challenging areas. Recent projects have included running a holiday for homeless men in the Yorkshire Dales; taking people with special needs on trips and activity weeks; and doing conservation work with a groups of unemployed people in North Wales. Ages 16+. Weekends-3 weeks, all year. Volunteers need patience, energy and a sense of humour.

GREAT BRITAIN

COMMUNITY WORK

Accommodation and food provided, but participants pay for travel to and from the projects, although financial assistance may be available. Registration fee £5. Projects may qualify under the Duke of Edinburgh's Award Scheme. *Overseas volunteers with a good standard of English accepted.* PH

WINGED FELLOWSHIP TRUST Recruitment Officer, Angel House, 20-32 Pentonville Road, London N1 9XD Tel 071-833 2594
Aims to provide 2 week holidays for as many severely physically disabled people as possible, to give their families a break. Runs 5 holiday centres in Surrey, Essex, Hampshire, Merseyside and Nottinghamshire, each providing holidays for 32 disabled adults at a time. Volunteers are needed to provide the guests with help, companionship and entertainment. This includes washing, dressing and feeding the guests, helping them to bed, writing postcards, playing cards and accompanying them on outings, plus a certain amount of domestic work. Some volunteers may also be asked to help on night duty. Special fortnights include fishing, photography, music, drama and craft, so volunteers with these skills are particularly welcome. Opportunity to take part in country day trips. The atmosphere at the centres is informal and friendly. Hard physical work with long hours. Ages 16+. 1 or 2 weeks, almost all year round. Accommodation in 2-6 bunk bedded rooms, all meals, use of facilities and fares within Britain provided. *Overseas volunteers with good standard of spoken English welcome.*

WOODLARKS CAMP SITE TRUST Honorary Secretary, Kathleen Marshall House, Tilford Road, Lower Bourne, Farnham, Surrey GU10 3RN Tel Farnham 716279
Voluntary helpers are required on summer camps for severely physically handicapped adults and children at a 12 acre site of pinewoods and grassland on the Surrey/ Hampshire border. Emphasis is placed on the participants trying to do things they would not otherwise have the opportunity to do, and accomplishing things they had always thought impossible. Each week a different group goes to the camp from hospitals, special schools or private homes. Usually one volunteer for each disabled person, and they remain partners for

the duration of the camp. Facilities include heated swimming pool, sports equipment, dining/recreation room and open wood fires for cooking. 1+ weeks, mid May-mid September. Ages 12+. No experience needed, but commitment essential. A nominal fee is charged to help cover food costs. Camping equipment supplied. *Overseas volunteers accepted.* B D PH

YOUNG DISABLED ON HOLIDAY 33 Longfield Avenue, Heald Green, Cheadle, Cheshire SK8 3NH
Volunteers are needed to help on holidays for young physically disabled people. Activities include sightseeing, theatre visits, discos, shopping expeditions, and other adventure pastimes. Ages 18-30. Applicants should have a sense of fun and adventure. Each disabled person has at least 1 helper. 1 week, April-October. Volunteers are expected to contribute 25% of holiday costs.

CONSERVATION

BEACH HEAD NT c/o The National Trust, Cornwall Office, Lanhydrock, Bodmin, Cornwall PL30 4DE
Volunteers are needed to help clear litter from Cornish beaches. Each morning volunteers spend 2-3 hours collecting litter from among rocks and sand dunes; once the task is completed the rest of the day is free to discover and explore miles of fine coastal scenery. Ages 16-20. 12 days, July and August. Cost £99 covers all meals and accommodation at Beach Head NT basecamp, a converted barn on a remote and beautiful part of the coast. Facilities include hot showers, drying room, common room with log fire and fully equipped kitchen. Minibus available for outings and expeditions. Volunteers help with cleaning, preparing meals and washing up. Participants pay own travel expenses and should take a sleeping bag.

BRITISH TRUST FOR CONSERVATION VOLUNTEERS Room WH, 36 St Mary's Street, Wallingford, Oxfordshire OX10 0EU Tel Wallingford 39766
A charity promoting practical conservation work by volunteers; organises numerous conservation working holidays on sites

including nature reserves, country estates, National Trust properties and in National Parks. Volunteers are given a chance to contribute in a practical way to the conservation of rural and urban areas. Over 600 projects are organised each year. Recent projects have included conserving the sensitive coastal habitats of orchids, natterjack toads and sand lizards in Merseyside; clearing reeds from a medieval moat in Worcestershire; excavating a secret water garden in Wales; protecting the habitats of agile frogs in Jersey; and conserving floating acid bogs in Staffordshire. Instruction is given in the use of tools and equipment, traditional techniques and other conservation skills. Also provide slide shows, guided tours and talks on the conservation value of the work. Approx 12 volunteers work on each project with an experienced leader. Beginners welcome.

Ages 16-70. Overseas volunteers must be over 18, and speak reasonably good English. Some holidays are more arduous than others, and volunteers must be physically and mentally equipped to cope with working on remote and exposed sites. 8 hour day, 1 day off per week. 1 or 2 weeks, all year. Also weekends, when local groups will accept volunteers aged 12+. Food and accommodation in volunteer centres, tents, huts, youth hostels, estate cottages, village halls, farm buildings or basecamps provided. Volunteers should take a sleeping bag, waterproofs, boots and working clothes.

Cost from £25 includes food and accommodation and everyone takes it in turns to prepare food. Two friends can apply to work on the same project. Travel paid by the volunteer. Anti-tetanus vaccination essential. Projects qualify under the Duke of Edinburgh's Award Scheme. Full programme available by Easter. Weekend training courses in practical conservation skills and leadership arranged. Membership fee £10 (including overseas); £5.50 if unwaged, student or retired; £14 for families.

CATHEDRAL CAMPS Manor House, High Birstwith, Harrogate, North Yorkshire HG3 2LG Tel Harrogate 770385
Aims to preserve, conserve, restore and repair cathedrals and Christian buildings of the highest architectural significance. Volunteers can expect both spectacular and routine work,

maintenance work, cleaning roof voids, towers, spiral staircases, wall memorials, traceried woodwork and drain culverts, vacuum cleaning nave walls, washing floors, painting iron railings, plus gardening and renewing path areas, all under the guidance of craftsmen.

At some cathedrals volunteers are also able to work with professional conservators on projects concerning external stonework, internal marble pillars and memorials. 36 hour week, 08.30-17.00 each day with Saturday afternoon, Sunday and evenings free. Food and self-catering accommodation provided, sometimes in hostels, although usually in the cathedral hall; volunteers should usually take a sleeping bag. Ages 16-30. Volunteers should be willing to do a fairly hard day's work, contribute to the social life of the camp, and help with domestic duties on a rota system. Each camp is run by a leader and 2 assistants. A letter of recommendation is required from anyone attending a camp for the first time; two friends may apply to work in the same camp. Anti-tetanus vaccination advised. Camps are held at different cathedrals and churches for 1 week, mid July-early September. Travel and optional personal insurance paid by the volunteer. Projects qualify under the Duke of Edinburgh's Award Scheme. All volunteers receive an admission card valid for 1 year for all English cathedrals. Camp fee £25 per week; bursaries available for those who are unwaged, except on vacation, and for volunteers who can show they cannot afford to join a camp. B D PH

THE CENTAUR PROJECT 313/315 Caledonian Road, London N1 1DR Tel 071-609 3328
An organisation based in the Kings Cross area of London, which will suffer from a new development programme, particularly through environmental and social change. Concentrates on educational work to awaken greater interest in the environment, producing video films and holding an extensive reference collection on every kind of architectural and environmental site in the British Isles. Help is needed in manually cataloguing this and also entering details on the computer database. Knowledge and interest in the environment and old buildings is essential as is the ability to work diligently with minimum supervision. Ages 16/18+. Hours flexible within the centre's

opening hours, weekdays 09.00-17.00. No accommodation provided.

DERBYSHIRE INTERNATIONAL WORKCAMP Education Department, County Offices, Matlock, Derbyshire DE4 3AG Tel Matlock 580000 ext 6488

Organises international workcamps at Elvaston Castle Country Park and Shipley Park, aimed at improving the environment and developing understanding between young people from different countries. Recent projects have included constructing woodland walks, rebuilding a footbridge, erecting fencing, improving drainage, scrub clearance, plus work on a children's adventure play area. As well as undertaking manual work, participants are encouraged to help on community service projects, helping with general meal preparation and cleaning duties. Full training for manual work will be given, with trained supervisors available at all times. Extensive leisure programme arranged. Ages 16-21. 1/2 weeks, late July-mid August. Accommodation provided in a residential school with sports and recreational facilities. Cost approx £25 per week covers food and accommodation. 20 free places available for young Derbyshire people. Qualifies under the Duke of Edinburgh's Award Scheme. *Apply by 1 April.* B D PH

DYFED WILDLIFE TRUST Islands Booking Officer, 7 Market Street, Haverfordwest, Dyfed SA61 1NF Tel Haverfordwest 5462

Skomer Island is a 720 acre national nature reserve, renowned for the finest seabird colonies in the south west, with fulmars, guillemots, kittiwakes, oystercatchers, puffins, razorbills, large gulls and over 100,000 pairs of Manx shearwaters. In addition there are many land birds including buzzards, choughs, owls, skylarks, ravens and pheasants. Voluntary assistant wardens are required to help with a variety of tasks; the main work concerns the day visitors, helping to meet the boats, collect landing fees and give general information and advice. Also patrolling the island to ensure visitors keep to the footpaths, and possibly assisting with various management tasks such as repair and maintenance work, path clearance, driftwood collecting, and surveys and scientific work. Applicants should be fit and prepared for hard work and long hours. Experience useful but not essential. 1+ weeks,

mid April-September. Boat passage to Skomer and simple bunk bed accommodation with cooking facilities provided. Volunteers should take a sleeping bag and food.

FESTINIOG RAILWAY COMPANY Volunteer Officer, Harbour Station, Porthmadog, Gwynedd LL49 9NF Tel Porthmadog 512340

Volunteers are required to help in the maintenance and running of the 150 year old narrow gauge railway. A wide variety of work is available. Traffic and Commercial Department: working in booking offices, guard's vans, buffet cars, shops, cafes and small sales outlets; Locomotive Operating Department: cleaning locomotives, working on the footplate; Mechanical Department: turning, welding, machining, steam fitting, sheet metal work, joinery, upholstery and paintwork; Permanent Way/Civil Engineering Department: working on winter track relaying projects and summer siding work, helping to repair fences, bridges, culverts and heavy walling. The Active Parks and Gardens Department needs skilled and unskilled assistance with improving the appearance of the station surrounds and picnic areas. Qualified and experienced electricians and builders also needed. Training given where necessary. Qualifies under the Duke of Edinburgh's Award Scheme. Ages 16+, unless in a supervised party. All volunteers must be fit. All year. Limited self-catering hostel accommodation for regular volunteers, for which a small charge is made; food extra. Camping space and list of local accommodation also available. *Overseas volunteers with a good understanding of, and ability to speak clear English, accepted.*

FOREST SCHOOL CONSERVATION CAMPS The Workcamps Secretary, 110 Burbage Road, London SE24 9HD Tel 071-274 7566

Conservation workcamps are arranged throughout the year. Recent projects have included traditional coppicing techniques and working with timber in Essex; maintenance and reconstruction on buildings in Cambridgeshire; and restoring an old manorial farm complex and woodlands in Berkshire. 1/2 weeks, Easter and summer, and at weekends. Ages 17/18+. Volunteers pay their own fares; arrangements sometimes made regarding food, but volunteers may be asked to contribute up to £2.20 per day towards food and expenses. Lightweight camping accommodation only. *Overseas volunteers accepted.* **B D PH**

INTERNATIONAL VOLUNTARY SERVICE
162 Upper New Walk, Leicester LE1 7QA
Tel Leicester 5494230
IVS is the British branch of Service Civil International, which promotes international reconciliation through work projects. Volunteers are needed to work in international teams on various conservation projects. Recent projects have included building a greenhouse at an organic nursery near York, helping with the day-to-day tasks, digging, weeding, sowing, selling produce; constructing a cycle path along disused railway lines near Durham; helping school children in the Shetland Isles to restore a habitat for birds as part of their wildlife project; constructing a cycle path on a disused railway on the banks of Loch Venacher in Perthshire; and woodland conservation work, beach clearing and tree planting in the grounds of a castle on the Isle of Skye. Ages 18+. Applicants should be prepared to work hard and contribute actively to work and team life. 35-40 hour week. 2-4 weeks, June-September. Food, accommodation and insurance provided, but no travel. Membership fee £25 (students £15, unwaged £10). Registration fee £20. **PH**

Applications from outside the UK: please see workcamp information on page 27.

IRONBRIDGE GORGE MUSEUM TRUST
Volunteer Organiser, The Wharfage,
Ironbridge, Telford, Shropshire TF8 7AW
Tel Ironbridge 3522
Conserves, restores and interprets the rich industrial heritage of the Gorge, the birthplace of the Industrial Revolution. The Museum comprises six main sites and a number of smaller ones, and has been created around a unique series of industrial monuments concentrating on the iron and pottery industries, and spread over some 6 square miles. Volunteers are needed to work on various sites involving industrial archaeology, research, excavation, interpretation of exhibits and general site duties. At Blists Hill Open Air Museum demonstrators in Victorian costume

are needed to explain the site and its shops, works and houses to visitors. Training, costume, equipment and supervision provided as appropriate. Opportunities for talking to the public; those with good language skills particularly welcome. Ages 18+. 36 hour week, March-October. Low-cost self-catering hostel accommodation on site, £1.15 per night , or youth hostel nearby. Participants pay for their own food. Insurance provided. Own transport, bicycle or car, usually essential. Participants can enter sites free.

THE MONKEY SANCTUARY Looe,
Cornwall, PL13 1NZ Tel Looe 2532
Has received worldwide recognition as the first place where a natural colony of Woolly Monkeys has survived and bred outside the South American rainforests. It is a centre both for conservation and for the education of the public, who visit at Easter and during the summer months. Volunteers are required to help with various jobs including preparation of monkey foods; cleaning and maintenance of monkey enclosures and grounds; attending to visitors in the summer; and general maintenance work during the winter. They also spend time with monkeys in their territory. Informal discussions on subjects such as conservation, ecology, anthropology, ethology, philosophy, the arts, community living and alternative medicine. There is also a strong interest in music and volunteers are encouraged to take instruments. Ages 21+. No experience necessary, but applicants should have an interest in the field, and practical skills are always welcome. 2+ weeks, all year. Full board and accommodation provided, but volunteers pay their own travel. Food is usually vegetarian, and volunteers share accommodation with the sanctuary family team. Approx £5 per week pocket money provided for volunteers staying several weeks.

NATIONAL TRUST ACORN PROJECTS
Volunteer Unit, PO Box 12, Westbury,
Wiltshire BA13 4NA Tel Westbury 826826
The Trust was formed at the end of the 19th century for the preservation of places of historic interest and natural beauty. It owns and protects houses and gardens, parks and estates, mountains, moors, coastline, farms and nature reserves. Acorn Projects are organised at NT properties throughout England and

GREAT BRITAIN

CONSERVATION

Wales, providing young people with an opportunity to carry out conservation work and to encourage an active and practical interest in the Trust's work. Volunteers carry out essential tasks on the estates which could not otherwise be done.

Recent projects have included improving and widening coastal footpaths, scrub clearance on conservation sites, the repair of drystone walling; fenland conservation work, erosion control and scrub clearance to improve downland ecology; and archaeological digs. Majority of the work done outdoors, but there are occasionally wet weather tasks such as clearing out old buildings or cleaning, restoring or painting agricultural implements. Mainly ages 17-27, 18+ for overseas volunteers. Instruction given by experts. 8 hour day, 5½ day week, evenings free. 1+ weeks, March-October. Accommodation provided in NT hostels, village halls, stable blocks, farmhouses, cottages or converted barns. Volunteers should take sleeping bags and contribute approx £30 per week towards the cost of food and accommodation. Help with kitchen duties expected; travel costs paid by volunteers. The projects qualify under the Duke of Edinburgh's Award Scheme. Up to 2 friends may apply to work on the same project. Anyone completing a full week's work qualifies for 1 year's free admission to NT properties. *Application forms and annual programme available from January.*

NOAH'S ARK BTCV Senior Field Officer, Newtown, Newport, Isle of Wight PO30 4PA Tel Isle of Wight 78576

Volunteers are needed to help with conservation tasks in the area which includes a salt marsh, nature reserve, coppiced woodlands and meadows showing signs of medieval strip fields. Tasks vary according to the time of year but include coppicing, hedge laying, tree planting, hurdle making, drystone walling, stooking hay, clearing ponds, biological surveys and building farm trails. Ages 18+. 2+ weeks, all year. 4 day week with opportunities for sightseeing on days off. Self-catering accommodation available from £3.50 per week. Booking fee £5 covers supper on arrival and breakfast the following morning. Participants pay their own travel expenses up to arrival on the island.

NORTH NORFOLK RAILWAY PLC The General Manager, Sheringham Station, Sheringham, Norfolk NR26 8RA Tel Sheringham 822045

Runs a steam service along part of the former Great Northern and Midland line. Volunteers are needed throughout the year at Sheringham, Weybourne, Kelling and Holt to help with the restoration and preservation of steam locomotives and historical rolling stock, and with the operation of the regular service, museum and educational facilities. Work includes engineering, coachbuilding, trackwork, maintenance, catering, retail and administration. No experience necessary, but volunteers should be fit and in sound health, particularly for areas other than retail and administration. Training in all aspects of development of steam locomotives will be provided as required. Ages 16+. Insurance provided, but participants cover own travel and accommodation expenses. Bed and breakfast available locally.

OPERATION OSPREY The Royal Society for the Protection of Birds, c/o Stewart Taylor, Grianan, Nethy Bridge, Inverness-shire PH25 3EF Tel Boat of Garten 694

Volunteer wardens and cooks are needed at the Loch Garten Reserve in the ancient Caledonian Forest, Strathspey. Teams of volunteer wardens keep a 24 hour watch from the hide and are expected to maintain a log of the ospreys' activities and to spend time talking to visitors (72,000 in 1989) about the RSPBs work at Loch Garten, and acting as a guide. Volunteers work on a shift basis, with every third day free, and also help with camp chores. Bicycles available on day off, but own transport useful. Interest in ornithology preferable. Volunteer cooks are responsible for preparing meals for up to 18 people; after initial supervision they will be expected to cope on their own on a day on/day off basis. Ages 18+. 1+ weeks, 30 March-31 August. Full board and camping or caravan accommodation, washing facilities, kitchen/dining area and common room provided at Inchdryne Farm, for a nominal charge of £8 per week. Volunteers should take a sleeping bag, warm clothing and walking boots. Volunteer cooks who stay 1 week will have single fare paid; for 2+ weeks return travel paid. Overseas volunteer cooks have rail fare paid, London-Aviemore.

THE ROYAL SOCIETY FOR THE PROTECTION OF BIRDS Reserves Management Department, The Lodge, Sandy, Bedfordshire SG19 2DL Tel Sandy 680551
Protects wild birds and their threatened habitat by giving them a haven of 118 nature reserves all over Britain, publicising and enforcing bird protection laws, guarding rare breeding birds, studying environmental effects, protecting migratory birds and producing films, publications, lectures and displays. Volunteer wardens are needed on nature reserves, assisting the wardens by carrying out physical management work, helping to escort visitors around the reserve, helping in information centres and dealing with enquiries and keeping records of birds. Volunteers usually work in teams of 2-4. Ages 16+. An interest in, and knowledge of, birds an advantage. 1+ weeks, all year. Accommodation in chalets or cottages. Cooking facilities provided, but volunteers are responsible for their own food and transport, and should take a sleeping bag.

SCOTTISH CONSERVATION PROJECTS TRUST Director, Balallan House, 24 Allan Park, Stirling FK8 2QG Tel Stirling 79697
A charitable trust promoting practical conservation work by volunteers on Scottish projects including nature reserves, country estates, local authority sites and mountain footpaths. Volunteers are given a chance to contribute in a practical way to the conservation of rural and urban areas. Recent projects have included restoring an 18th century military bridge near Culloden Forest; stabilising sand dunes using marram grass in Gruinard Bay; footpath maintenance on Ben Nevis and along the West Highland Way; repairing drystane dykes on the Shetland seabird island of Ness; creating rabbit-fenced enclosures to protect a rare area of woodland on the Orkney island of Hoy; improving butterfly and dragonfly habitat in the native oakwoods of Sunart, Highland Region; and restoring an old flour mill and millpond in Grampian Region. Instruction is given in the use of tools and equipment, traditional techniques and other conservation skills. Also slide shows, guided tours and talks on the conservation value of the work. Approx 12 volunteers work on each project; beginners welcome. Ages 16-70. Some projects are more physically demanding than others and

volunteers must be prepared to cope with working on remote and exposed sites. 8 hour day, 1 day off per week. Normally 10 days, all year. Food, insurance and accommodation in centres, tents, huts, youth hostels, cottages, village halls, farm buildings or basecamps provided. Volunteers should take a sleeping bag, waterproof clothing, boots and midge repellent. Anti-tetanus vaccination advisable. Everyone helps to prepare food, and volunteers contribute £2.50 per day towards food and accommodation costs. Two friends can apply to work on the same project. Projects qualify under the Duke of Edinburgh's Award Scheme. Weekend training courses in practical conservation skills and leadership arranged. Membership fee £10; £6 if unwaged or student, £15 for family, £10 for overseas members.

THISTLE CAMPS National Trust for Scotland, 5 Charlotte Square, Edinburgh EH2 4DU Tel 031-226 5922 ext 257
Founded to promote the permanent preservation of countryside and buildings of historic interest or natural beauty. Thistle Camps are residential voluntary work projects organised by NTS to help in the conservation and management of properties in the care of the Trust. Recent projects have included sand dune stabilisation on the Isle of Iona; rhododendron clearance and upland footpath maintenance around the country park at Brodick Castle on the Isle of Arran; landscaping and scrub clearance on the Isle of Canna; improving wildlife habitats in the Old Wood of Drum; and upland footpath maintenance at Glencoe. Work parties on Fair Isle, Britain's most remote inhabited island, help the islanders repair buildings, maintain the airstrip and help with all kinds of croft work such as fencing, drystane dyking, painting, crop-cleaning, ditching and haymaking. Ages 16-70. Up to 3 friends can be placed together. Volunteers should be fit for hard, practical work. 8 hour day, 5 day week. 1-2 weeks, March-October. Similar weekend projects are carried out by local groups on NTS properties in their area. An experienced leader and/or a Trust Ranger Naturalist supervises all practical work, and gives instruction in the safe use of tools. One day free for recreation and exploration in the area. Insurance, hostel-type or basecamp accommodation and food provided, but volunteers help with

GREAT BRITAIN

CONSERVATION

GREAT BRITAIN

CONSERVATION

catering arrangements and other chores. Old clothes, waterproofs, a sleeping bag and boots or wellingtons should be taken to all camps. Qualifies under the Duke of Edinburgh's Award Scheme. Participants pay their own travel costs and contribute £16, £8 for unwaged, towards food and accommodation. *Overseas volunteers with good English welcome.*

TOC H National Projects Office, 38 Newark Street, London E1 Tel 071-247 5110
A voluntary movement which provides an opportunity to work with a variety of different people on a range of projects. Volunteers are needed on conservation projects involving other young people, including those with special needs. Recent projects have included clearing the grounds at Hanbury Hall in Worcestershire; working in the grounds of an 18th century mansion in the Scottish borders; building a walkway for students at Hinwich Hall in Northamptonshire; and pruning, brashing and building bonfires in the grounds of the National Centre for Epilepsy. Ages 16+. Weekends-3 weeks, all year. Accommodation and food provided, but participants pay for travel to and from projects; financial assistance may be available. Registration fee £5. Projects may qualify under the Duke of Edinburgh's Award Scheme. *Overseas volunteers with good standard of English accepted.* PH

UNITED NATIONS ASSOCIATION International Youth Service, Welsh Centre for International Affairs, Temple of Peace, Cathays Park, Cardiff CF1 3AP Tel Cardiff 223088
Volunteers are needed to work in international teams on conservation workcamps in various parts of Wales. Recent projects have included building footpaths and preserving sand dunes on Anglesey; laying stepping stones across a river in Pembrokeshire; clearing non-native plants and litter in the Great Orme country park; and clearing and restoring canals in West Glamorgan. Volunteers share in discussions centring on the host community and world problems, and are expected to take an active part in all aspects of the project. Ages 17+. 40 hour week. 2 weeks, June-August. Accommodation, food and insurance provided. Volunteers share the cooking, pay their own travel costs and should take a sleeping bag. Registration £25. B D PH

Applications from outside the UK: please see workcamp information on page 27.

THE WATERWAY RECOVERY GROUP Neil Edwards, Canal Camps, 24A Avenue Road, Witham, Essex CM8 2DT
The national coordinating body for voluntary labour on the inland waterways of Britain, it promotes and coordinates local trusts and societies involved in restoring abandoned and derelict waterways to a navigable state. Volunteers are needed on workcamps to help with this work. There are over 20 active restoration projects including excavating and laying foundations for a new canal bridge, building retaining walls, dredging and banking, clearing vegetation, pile driving, fitting lock gates, bricklaying and demolition work. Canals currently being restored include the Huddersfield, Montgomery, Wey and Arun, Droitwich, Hereford and Gloucester, Wiltshire and Berkshire, Basingstoke and Pocklington. Ages 16+. Parental consent required for those under 18. Work is unpaid and mostly unskilled; full training is given and work is directed by local experts. Volunteers should be fit and willing to work hard in all weathers, with enthusiasm and a sense of humour, and to live harmoniously in fairly close contact with approx 20 volunteers at each camp. Overseas volunteers must have a good command of English. 1+ weeks, March-October and at Christmas/New Year. 7½ hour day. Basic accommodation provided in village halls or similar, plus 3 good meals a day at charge of approx £18 per week. Volunteers should take a sleeping bag and old clothes and be prepared to help with domestic chores. Insurance provided. Qualifies under the Duke of Edinburgh's Award Scheme. Publish *Navvies* a quarterly journal which gives full details on camps arranged throughout the year.

COURIERS/REPS

BUTLIN'S LTD Head Office, Bognor Regis, West Sussex PO21 1JJ
Provides family holidays and leisure facilities, encompassing accommodation, retailing, catering, amusement parks, professional entertainment and conferences, all on the same site. Vacancies exist for Redcoats, hosts/hostesses responsible for entertainments and

organising children's programmes, at centres in Ayr, Bognor Regis, Minehead, Pwllheli and Skegness. Short and long term positions available virtually all year round, exact dates depending on each centre. Experience not normally necessary as training provided. 39-45 hour week. Ages 18+. Applicants should have enthusiasm, tact, attention to detail and the ability to integrate into a team. Salary, according to individual centres, accommodation in single or shared rooms, meals and uniform provided. Insurance and travel paid by applicants. Staff entertainment programmes, use of leisure facilities plus many of guest facilities, and holiday discounts available. *EC nationals only.*

Apply direct to the preferred centre: Wonderwest World, Heads of Ayr, KA7 4LB Scotland; Southcoast World, Bognor Regis, West Sussex PO21 1JJ; Somerwest World, Minehead, Somerset TA24 5SH; Starcoast World, Pwllheli, Gwynedd LL53 6HX, North Wales; or Funcoast World, Skegness, Lincolnshire PE25 1NJ.

FAIRTHORNE MANOR YMCA National Centre, Curdridge, Southampton, Hampshire SO3 2GH Tel Botley 5228
Offers a wide range of outdoor educational activities for young people aged 8-20 on residential or day camps, and provides visitors with a sense of community belonging in an outdoor environment. Volunteers are needed to act as couriers and course leaders. Duties involve being attached to a group of overseas/ UK visitors for their stay, and in cooperation with Centre staff, ensuring that they enjoy a full and interesting programme.

Ages 18+, preference given to older applicants. Couriers should have A level standard French or German, plus leadership ability, enthusiasm, loyalty and be in sympathy with the aims and purpose of the Young Men's Christian Association movement. Staff are carefully selected for their ability to relate to young people, and as activities are seen as a means to develop this relationship, applicants should have an interest/experience in the activities being taught. These include archery, campcraft, canoeing, sailing, windsurfing, climbing, riding, map reading, orienteering, life saving; sports and games, geology, hiking

and nature study; arts and crafts; and entertainment. No set hours, 5 day week. 6 weeks, April-September. Full board and tent/ other accommodation, £20 per week pocket money plus bonus, insurance, and assistance with travel from point of entry to UK provided that minimum work period of 6 weeks completed. 1 week obligatory leader training course at Easter. *Overseas applicants welcome.*

DOMESTIC

ADAIR INTERNATIONAL Hotel and Catering Personnel, 5 Sherwood Street, London W1V 7RA Tel 071-734 4000
Vacancies in the London area for temporary chambermaids, house and linen porters, housekeepers, cooks, chefs, kitchen porters, tea ladies, catering assistants, waiting staff and cloakroom attendants. Flexible hours. All year. Ages 18+. Meals whilst on duty, but no accommodation, travel or insurance provided. Experience not necessary, training given, though some jobs require appropriate qualifications. *Overseas applicants should speak good English and hold a work permit.*

ANGLIA AGENCY 15 Eastern Avenue, Southend-on-Sea, Essex Tel Southend 613888
Cook, housekeeper, daily help and hotel and catering positions arranged. Long and short term vacancies, all year. Board and lodging usually provided. Hours and wages vary according to type of work. Ages 17+. Travel costs paid by the applicant.

BEAUMONT CAMPS LTD Personnel Department, Corpus Christi House, 9 West Street, Godmanchester, Huntingdon, Cambridgeshire, PE18 8HG Tel Huntingdon 456123
Organises a wide range of holidays for children in American-style day and residential camps. Staff are recruited for 10 day and 8 residential camps throughout the country. Opportunities exist for caterers/head cooks, responsible for managing kitchen assistants, cooking meals for staff and campers, stock and portion control, and food ordering according to a strict budget. Back-up staff are also required as cleaners and kitchen assistants, which may also involve working as an assistant monitor looking after children at certain times of the day.

GREAT BRITAIN

Staff must be available for the whole season, March/April or July/September. 5-9 weeks, including compulsory day/weekend orientation course, setting up and clearing camps. Ages 18-35. Day camp staff work a 45 hour week; residential staff work a 24 hour day, with 1 free day per week plus alternate nights off; wages £40-£100 per week. Board and accommodation provided. PH

BRIGHSTONE HOLIDAY CENTRE The Personnel Manager, Brighstone, Isle of Wight PO30 4DB Tel Brighstone 740537
Staff are needed on a seasonal basis for a holiday centre catering for approx 300 guests. Work is available for waiting staff, snack bar, service room, washing up and other catering assistants. 39 hour per week. May-September. Full board and accommodation in single/twin bed chalet provided. Salary based on council rate. Ages 16+. No experience needed. Insurance and maximum of £12 towards return journey provided, if employment conditions are fulfilled. EC *nationals only*.

DOMESTIC

BUTLIN'S LTD Head Office, Bognor Regis, West Sussex PO21 1JJ
Provides family holidays and leisure facilities, encompassing accommodation, retailing, catering, amusement parks, professional entertainment and conferences, all on the same site. Catering and bar staff, waiters/waitresses, qualified chefs and cooks, cleaners and porters, are required at centres in Ayr, Bognor Regis, Minehead, Pwllheli and Skegness. Short and long term positions available virtually all year round, exact dates depending on each centre. Experience not normally necessary as training provided. 39-45 hour week. Ages 16+, local applicants, 18+ others. Applicants should have enthusiasm, tact, attention to detail and the ability to integrate into a team. Salary according to individual centres, accommodation, meals and uniform provided. Insurance and travel paid by applicants. Staff entertainment programmes, use of leisure facilities plus many of guest facilities, and holiday discounts available. EC *nationals only*.

Apply direct to the preferred centre: Wonderwest World, Heads of Ayr, KA7 4LB Scotland; Southcoast World, Bognor Regis, West Sussex PO21 1JJ; Somerwest World, Minehead, Somerset TA24 5SH; Starcoast

World, Pwllheli, Gwynedd LL53 6HX, North Wales; Funcoast World, Skegness, Lincolnshire PE25 1NJ.

THE COUNTRYWIDE HOLIDAYS ASSOCIATION Personnel Officer, Birch Heys, Cromwell Range, Manchester M14 6HU Tel 061-225 1000
Arranges holidays in centres throughout the UK, aiming to give people the opportunity of discovering the countryside through a range of outdoor activities. Centres provide inexpensive accommodation in a homely atmosphere, ranging from an Elizabethan manor house to a Scottish castle. Vacancies are available for general domestics and good all-round cooks with experience of cooking for 60-80, at 14 holiday centres. 40 hour, 6 day week. 8+ weeks, March-October, preferably working the whole season. Board and lodging provided. Salary from £50 for domestics and from £60-£90 for experienced cooks, per week.

FAIRTHORNE MANOR YMCA National Centre, Curdridge, Southampton, Hampshire SO3 2GH Tel Botley 785228
Offers a wide range of outdoor educational activities for young people aged 8-20 on residential and day camps, and provides visitors with a sense of community belonging in an outdoor environment. Domestic assistants are needed to carry out various duties and are responsible to the housekeeper; other work may involve sewing and assisting matron with sick bay duties. First aid certificate an advantage. Also tuck shop assistants needed, responsible for maintaining stock of sweets and drinks, opening tuck shop for evening sales and washing up; this is a part-time position so other duties are included. Ages 18+, but preference given to older applicants. Leadership ability, enthusiasm, loyalty and sympathy with the aims and purposes of the Young Men's Christian Association movement required. Staff are carefully selected for their ability to relate to young people and activities are seen as a means to developing this relationship. No set hours, 5 day week. 6 weeks, April-September. Full board and accommodation, £25 per week pocket money plus bonus, and assistance with travel from point of entry to UK provided that a minimum work period of 6 weeks completed. *Overseas applications welcome*.

FRIENDLY HOTELS PLC Premier House, 10 Greycoat Place, London SW1P 1SB Tel 071-222 8866
Hotel group requires waitresses, room attendants and porters in hotels in Birmingham, Burnley, Hull, London, Milton Keynes, Nottingham, Walsall and in Scotland. Experience useful but not essential. Work available all year round, minimum 4 months. 39 hour week. Ages 18+. Salary approx £80 per week. Accommodation in single or shared rooms, in or outside hotel, provided. B D PH limited opportunities.

HF HOLIDAYS LTD Redhills, Skirsgill Park, Penrith, Cumbria CA11 0DT Tel Penrith 67658
Seasonal staff are needed at 17 guest houses, each catering for 50-120 guests. General assistants are required for work in the house and dining room, to clean guests' rooms, serve tea and prepare packed lunches, and kitchen porters to assist in preparing food, cleaning work areas and equipment, and rubbish disposal. Cooks are also required. Staff are welcome to join in the programme of excursions and entertainments when off duty. 39 hour, 5 day week. Work available March-November. Board and lodging provided. Salary £46-£140 per week, according to position. Travel allowances given for satisfactory completion of appointment. *UK nationals only.*

HOTHORPE HALL Christian Conference Centre, Theddingworth, near Lutterworth, Leicestershire LE17 6QX Tel Market Harborough 880257
Provides conference facilities for groups of up to 120 people, mainly from church groups. Volunteers are required to undertake a variety of duties, including kitchen assistance, serving and washing up, and general domestic work. Gardening and maintenance also involved.

Ages 18+. Volunteers should have a Christian commitment and willingness to join in as a member of the community, showing a responsible attitude to their work. All year. 6 day week. 6-52 weeks. Pocket money £15 per week. Accommodation in shared rooms and all meals provided. No experience necessary. *Overseas applicants with good spoken English accepted.*

THE IONA COMMUNITY Voluntary Staff Coordinator, Isle of Iona, Argyll, Strathclyde PA76 6SN Tel Iona 404
An ecumenical Christian community seeking new and radical ways of living the Gospel in today's world. On Iona the Community runs two centres, each welcoming up to 50 guests to a common life of work, worship, meals and recreation.

Kitchen assistants and housekeeping assistants are required at both centres. Kitchen assistants help provide up to 90 meals, often vegetarian. Cooking skills not essential, but a willingness to learn is. Housekeeping assistants help with cleaning, washing and ironing, as well as supervising guests in household chores. Also requires assistants to work in the Coffee House, baking, preparing food, serving, clearing tables and keeping the place clean and tidy. On the nearby Island of Mull the Camas centre welcomes up to 16 guests each week, mainly unemployed or disadvantaged young people, to a common life of work, worship, arts, crafts and outdoor activities. Requires a competent cook to provide up to 25 meals over the summer months.

The work is demanding but rewarding, and the hours flexible. Most important is a willingness to join fully into the community life, which includes worship and social activities as well as work. Ages 18+. 6 day week, February-December. Full board, shared accommodation, pocket money of £14 per week and assistance with travel expenses within mainland Britain provided. *Applications received before 31 December given priority.*

KNOLL HOUSE HOTEL Staff Manager, Studland, Dorset BH19 3AH Tel Studland 251
A country house hotel with 80 rooms and a hundred acres of gardens and grounds adjoining the beach. Chefs (with previous experience), waiters, waitresses and kitchen staff are required from April-October. Willingness to learn is more important than experience. 39 hour week, 2 days free. Ages 17+. Pay approx £75.50 per week, full board, accommodation, insurance, and use of hotel amenities including swimming, boating, riding, tennis and golf, provided.

GREAT BRITAIN

DOMESTIC

LEICESTER BOYS' & GIRLS' SUMMER CAMP & INSTITUTE Shaftesbury Hall, Holy Bones, Leicester LE1 4LJ Tel Leicester 519863
Seasonal domestic staff are required at a holiday home in Mablethorpe which provides the poorest and most deserving children aged 7-12 from Leicester and its neighbourhood with a fortnight's holiday. The home is situated on the sandhills and the children have their own path to the beach. Positions include cooks and kitchen assistants, catering staff and dining room attendants to supervise children at mealtimes. Ages 18+. 1+ months, May-August. Preference given to applicants able to work the whole season. Board and lodging provided plus a salary of approx £36 per week. *Apply to the Children's Holiday Home, The Matron, Quebec Road, Mablethorpe, Lincolnshire Tel Mablethorpe 472444. UK nationals only.*

LONDON HOSTELS ASSOCIATION LTD Personnel Manager, 54 Eccleston Square, London SW1V 1PG Tel 071-834 1545
Part-time residential domestic work available in 10 London houses run mainly for young people in full-time employment or students. Female staff are employed as dining room assistants, serving meals, clearing tables and using washing up machines; also as junior housekeepers, involving normal housekeeping duties, cleaning public and residential rooms, changing linen and general evening duties once a week. Male staff are employed as kitchen or house porters, assisting in the preparation of food, cleaning the kitchen catering area and public utility rooms, washing up, and other manual duties. Ages 17+. 6+ months, possibly 3-4 months in summer, all year. 30-40 hour week. Working hours usually 07.00-11.00/17.00-19.30. 1½ days free per week. Board, accommodation and insurance provided. Salary approx £33-£44 net per week, according to hours worked. *EC nationals only.*

MAYDAY STAFF SERVICES 27 Noel Street, London W1V 3RD Tel 071-439 2056
An employment agency recruiting temporary and permanent catering staff of a high standard throughout central London and surrounding area. Can place experienced chefs, waiting and bar staff, as well as kitchen porters and general catering assistants with no experience. Catering assistants' work includes food preparation, serving food at counter, washing

up, clearing tables, and general kitchen duties. Kitchen porters' work includes washing up both manually and with a machine, cleaning and vegetable preparation. 25-40 hour week, all year. Ages 16+. Catering assistants and kitchen porters wages £2.95-£3.50 per hour. Meals usually available when on duty and public liability insurance provided. **B D PH** limited opportunities.

MECCA LEISURE HOLIDAYS 1 Port Way, Port Solent, Portsmouth, Hampshire PO6 4TY Tel Portsmouth 201201
Runs nearly 30 holiday centres in coastal locations, providing fun family holidays. Staff are required for a variety of positions, including housekeepers, chalet maids, chefs, kitchen, waiting and bar staff. Applicants should have a friendly, lively personality and fluent English. Full training given, although relevant qualifications are required for some positions, such as chefs. 39 hour week, plus overtime. 2+ months. Recruitment takes place all year; high season April-October. Ages 18+. Pay from £2.40 per hour, increasing after initial training; deduction made for live-in accommodation. Use of guest facilities when off-duty.

MONTPELIER EMPLOYMENT AGENCY 34 Montpelier Road, Brighton, Sussex BN1 2LQ Tel Brighton 778686
Introduces staff of all categories to hotels throughout Britain. Some previous experience preferred but not always essential. Applicants must be free of any work permit restrictions and already resident in Britain. Approx 39 hour week. Minimum 12 weeks during summer period. Ages 18+. Salary approx £80-£100 including accommodation; varies according to area, type of job, previous experience and whether accommodation is provided.

PGL YOUNG ADVENTURE LTD Personnel Department, Alton Court, Penyard Lane, Ross-on-Wye, Herefordshire HR9 5NR Tel Ross-on-Wye 764211
Organises outdoor adventure holidays for young people and families in England, Scotland and Wales. Catering and domestic assistants, cooks and assistant cooks required. Most centres run a self-service system with cooked breakfast, packed lunch and full evening meal. Ages 18+. Applicants should be

fond of children, responsible, flexible, patient, energetic and enthusiastic, reliable and mature, with a sense of humour and have the ability to cooperate with others as part of a team contributing fully to the life of the centre. 4+ weeks, February-September. Staff are also recruited for short periods at peak times such as Easter and the spring bank holiday. Catering staff generally work a split shift, with the middle hours of the day free. 1 day off per week. Full board accommodation provided. Pocket money from £25 per week depending on qualifications, responsibility and length of stay. Travel expenses paid by applicants. All staff can join in the activities during free periods and are encouraged to take part in evening activities with the guests. Staff may sometimes be asked to help out in areas other than their own. *Early application advisable; the majority of positions are filled by end June.*

PORTH TOCYN HOTEL Abersoch, Gwynedd LL53 7BU Tel Abersoch 2966
A country house hotel, requiring staff for all aspects of front of house hotel work. No experience necessary, but languages an advantage. Easter-November, hours variable. Ages 17+. Salary £6.50 per shift, accommodation in staff cottage, food, liability insurance, use of hotel facilities including tennis courts, swimming pool and windsurfers, provided. *EC nationals only.* B D PH limited opportunities.

SCATTERGOODS AGENCY Thursley House, 53 Station Road, Shalford, Guildford, Surrey GU4 8HA Tel Guildford 33732
Arranges posts in hotels, restaurants and public houses as chambermaids, plongeurs, barpersons, waiting staff, receptionists, cooks, kitchen assistants, porters and some general assistants. Experience sometimes required. Ages 18+. 40-50 hour week. Wages £45-£80 per week. Board, lodging and usually insurance provided. PH

SCOTTISH FIELD STUDIES ASSOCIATION LTD Kindrogan Field Centre, Enochdhu, Blairgowrie, Perthshire PH10 7PG Tel Strathardle 286
Aims to create a greater awareness and understanding of the Scottish countryside. The Centre is a large country house in the Highlands and provides accommodation,

laboratories and library for up to 80 people with opportunities for all aspects of field studies. Seasonal staff are needed for domestic duties such as cleaning, washing up, general maintenance and gardening. Ages 18+. No experience needed. 35 hour week, all year. Wages £40 per week. Accommodation and meals provided. Participants pay own travel and insurance costs. Staff may participate in field study courses when possible. *EC nationals only.* PH

TOPS HOLIDAYS (SUN LIVING LTD) Personnel Manager, Adventure House, 34-36 South Street, Lancing, West Sussex BN15 8AG Tel Lancing 751942
Organises a range of specialised activity and outdoor education programmes for groups of schoolchildren aged 7-17 at centres in Wales, Herefordshire and throughout south east England. Each centre has its own team of staff who ensure that high standards of safety, instruction and enjoyment are maintained. Staff are required for catering and domestic teams: chefs/assistant chefs required to manage a small kitchen team, working to a strict budget managing stock control and food ordering, as well as catering for up to 200 guests; kitchen assistants helping chefs with food preparation and general work in the kitchen; domestic staff, responsible for maintaining a high standard of hygiene and cleanliness, and also assisting in the centre's activities. Staff often assist in other areas of the centre's operation and will need to be flexible. Ages 18+, preference given to ages 20+. Experience required varies according to post: chefs and assistant chefs should come from a home cooking or small restaurant background. The jobs demand a high level of commitment both physically and mentally; applicants should enjoy being with children all day and have a genuine interest in their welfare. Fitness, stamina, enthusiasm and the ability to live and work as part of a team are also essential. 40+ hour week, 1 day free per week. 1+ months, March-October. Most staff work the full season; extra staff are also taken on for shorter periods during peak times at Easter and during July and August. There are opportunities for staff to move from centre to centre. Pay from £25 per week or negotiable for chefs, depending on experience and responsibilities. Training is provided to ensure

staff are confident and able to carry out their responsibilities. Social and recreational activities such as parties, barbecues and outings arranged for staff. *British nationals only.* B D PH limited opportunities.

UNIVERSAL AUNTS PO Box 304, London SW4 0NN Tel 071-371 9766

Vacancies are available for resident and non-resident housekeepers, nannies and mother's helps. Also opportunities for cooks, waitresses, washers up, cleaners and drivers. Ages 18+. Permanent and temporary positions, all year. Salary according to qualifications.

FARMWORK

Most fruit picking jobs are paid at piece-work rates so it is important to remember that inclement weather can affect the ripening and amount of crops to be picked. On most farmcamps emphasis is on living and working in an international community with sports and social activities, rather than on earning money. The wages paid may be sufficient only to cover food and accommodation costs and provide pocket money. While every effort is made to provide full-time employment, on occasions work may be temporarily limited; it is therefore essential that workers have enough money to cover basic living expenses throughout their stay.

ASHRAM COMMUNITY SERVICE PROJECT 23/25 Grantham Road, Sparkbrook, Birmingham B11 1LU Tel 021-773 7061

A community project jointly run by Christians and Muslims in inner-city Birmingham, with the aims of working against racist patterns of employment, ensuring that women have access to resources, and putting local traditional skills to appropriate use by developing new employment initiatives. Volunteers are invited to help with a land use project set up in order to deal pragmatically with unsightly and unused parts of the neighbourhood such as neglected gardens and land awaiting development. Work involves organic gardening, working in a dairy, caring for animals, woodwork, building and maintenance work. Ages 21+. No experience necessary, training is usually given where required. Excursions sometimes arranged at weekends

with members of other projects. Hours negotiable; usually 09.00-17.00, all year. Insurance and accommodation in the Ashram community provided. Volunteers pay own travel, and are expected to pay as far as possible for board and lodging. PH but unsuitable for wheelchairs.

SC & JH BERRY LTD Gushmere Court Farm, Selling, Faversham, Kent ME13 9RF Tel Faversham 795205

Assistance needed with the harvest of hop, apple and pear crops. Work includes loading and unloading kilns and pressing hops in the oast house, cutting and loading bines in the hop garden, work on the hop picking machines, loading, sorting, clearing up, and picking apples and pears in the orchards. A few tractor-driving posts are available for which instruction is given; UK or international driving licence required. End August-end September. Basic 40 hour week plus 15 hours overtime, Saturday afternoon/Sunday off. Ages 18+. On the job training given. Wages approx £120 per week. Caravan accommodation with all facilities available; workers will need to buy and cook their own food. Insurance not provided. Workers should provide their own clothing, including waterproofs and rubber boots, and sleeping bag and towels. *All nationalities welcome; non-EC nationals should apply through Concordia, see below.*

JM BUBB & SON Pave Lane Farm, Newport, Shropshire TF10 9AX Tel Newport 811 497

A family partnership producing quality potatoes, vegetables and fruit. Workers are needed to assist in the picking and packing of the produce; experience not essential, but working conditions can be tough. Ages 16+. 50 hour week, beginning July-end September. Piece-work rates paid weekly in accordance with the Agricultural Wages Board. Public liability insurance provided. No food or accommodation provided; land available for camping.

When writing to any organisation it is essential to mention Working Holidays 1991 and enclose a large stamped, self-addressed envelope, or if overseas, a large addressed envelope and at least two International Reply Coupons.

TJ & BJ CASE (FRUITGROWERS) Coombe Farm, West Monkton, Taunton, Somerset TA2 8RB

Jobs at Giffords Farm, Langford Lane, Norton Fitzwarren, Taunton, Somerset Tel West Monkton 413228/337416

A commercial fruitgrowers offering strawberry picking and packing work. No experience necessary. June-August. 7 hour day, 6 day week, not including Saturday. Piece-work rates paid. Ages 17+. Campsite facilities available at £2 per week; workers should take their own tents and camping equipment. *All nationalities welcome; non-EC applicants should apply through Concordia, see below.*

CAWLEY FARMS Ashton Fruit Farm, Castle Grounds, Ashton, Leominster, Herefordshire Tel Brimfield 401
Fruit pickers needed. Ages 16+. Hours variable, end June-early August. Piece-work rates paid. Campsite provided, but workers should take their own food and camping equipment. *EC nationals only.*

CONCORDIA (Youth Service Volunteers) Ltd, Recruitment Secretary, 8 Brunswick Place, Hove, Sussex BN3 1ET Tel Brighton 772086
Aims to bring together the youth of all nations throughout the world, to promote a better understanding between them of their ideas, beliefs and ways of living. Can place applicants on international farmcamps in the UK: hop picking in Kent; soft fruit picking in Scotland, Kent, Lincolnshire, Oxfordshire, Herefordshire, Sussex and Devon; apple picking in Hampshire and Kent; and vegetable picking in Cambridgeshire, Devon, Kent and Somerset. Volunteers must be prepared to work hard when and where required.
Although every effort will be made to find alternative work in the event of bad weather or crop failure, it should be stressed that work cannot be guaranteed. Mainly ages 18-25. June-October; soft fruit June-August, hops and apples late August-October. Piece-work rates paid for soft fruit picking; hop/apple pickers receive wages as laid down by the Agricultural Wages Board. All workers are subject to tax on their weekly earnings. Conditions and costs of board and lodging vary according to location.

The majority of accommodation is provided in huts, caravans or farm cottages but workers are expected to take their own food and sleeping bags. In some camps workers provide their own tents and cooking equipment. Registration fee £23. Travel paid by the volunteer. *Overseas applicants accepted.*

DOUGLAS COURTS Teafrish Farm, Beauly, Inverness-shire Tel Inverness 782102
A farm 7 miles from Inverness on the route north to John O' Groats, close to Loch Ness. Raspberry picking work is available, 6-7 weeks, July-August. 48 hour, 6 day week, weather permitting, with optional evening work. No experience necessary. Ages 17+. Piece-work rates paid. Campsite facilities and some caravans available; applicants should take their own tents, cooking equipment and suitable warm and waterproof clothing. After 2½ weeks work, travel costs to a maximum of £8 refunded. Occasional excursions organised. *Non-EC applicants should apply through Concordia, see above.*

FRIDAY BRIDGE INTERNATIONAL FARMCAMP LTD The Manager, March Road, Friday Bridge, Wisbech, Cambridgeshire PE14 0LR Tel Wisbech 860255
A cooperative set in the heart of the Fen Country with 140 local growers and farmers needs seasonal workers to harvest its crops. Work involves weeding and strawing, and also picking gooseberries, strawberries, plums, apples, blackberries, pears, potatoes, courgettes and beans. Campers are collected from and returned to the camp daily by the farmer for whom they are working. Ages 17-30. 1+ weeks, approx 30 May-23 October. Hourly and piece-work rates normally paid. Indoor processing work also available. Many social and sports facilities available including swimming pool, tennis courts, games field, games/TV room, bar, discos and dances. Other facilities include hot showers, drying rooms and camp shop. Cost £30 per week covers full board accommodation in huts and facilities. Registration fee £30. *EC nationals only.*

GREAT HOLLANDEN FARM Mr BR Brooks, Mill Lane, Hildenborough, near Sevenoaks, Kent TN15 0SG Tel Hildenborough 832276
Fruit pickers and agricultural workers are needed to pick all types of soft fruit to a very

GREAT BRITAIN

FARMWORK

high standard. Work is also available harvesting and pruning raspberries at the end of the season. Pickers are trained and should be hard working and conscientious. Ages 18+. 2+ weeks, end June-end September. Hours 06.00-15.00 with opportunities for evening work. Piece-work rates paid. Campsite and showers provided; workers should take their own tents and cooking equipment. Nominal charge of £3 per week for use of facilities. Farm shop offering food on site. *Early booking advised; notification of acceptance early May.*

GREENS OF DEREHAM Norwich Road, Dereham, Norfolk Tel Dereham 692014
Fruit pickers are required throughout July to pick strawberries. Ages 17+. Work may take place until 16.00. Workers paid in cash daily. Camping area provided. Applicants pay own insurance and travel costs. *UK nationals only.*

HUDSON FARMS Badliss Hall, Ardleigh, Colchester, Essex Tel Colchester 230306
A soft fruit production and plant raising farm. Work includes the picking, planting and pruning of strawberries, raspberries and vegetables. June-October. 30 hour week, Monday-Friday with occasional weekend work. Ages 18+. Piece-work rates paid. No work in bad weather and no wet weather equipment provided. Campsite facilities with cooking areas available at £5 per week; workers should take their own sleeping bags and tents.

INTERNATIONAL FARM CAMP The Organiser, Hall Road, Tiptree, Colchester, Essex CO5 0QS Tel Tiptree 815496
Fruit picking and general farm labouring work available. Ages 18-25. 35 hour, 5 day week. 2+ weeks, end May-September; few places available mid July-end August. Facilities include hot showers, drying and ironing rooms, shop, table tennis and TV. Piece-work rates paid. Cost approx £35 per week includes full board accommodation in huts or tents. Workers must help with kitchen duties 1 day during their stay. £25 deposit, £15 of which is refundable. *Students only.*

KENT SALADS LTD Valerie Dodrill, Northbourne, Deal, Kent CT14 0LW Tel Deal 366947
Growers of salad and vegetable crops; require harvesters and packers. No experience

necessary, but knowledge of English required. 35-40 hour week, April-September. Ages 19+. Wages £2.80 per hour, overtime (after 8 hour day) £4.20 per hour, and production bonus. Accommodation provided in self-catering caravans at a cost of £15 per week.

MARE HILL FRUIT FARM Mare Hill, Pulborough, West Sussex RH20 2EA
Fruit pickers are needed to pick strawberries, raspberries, blackcurrants and gooseberries on a farm 15 miles from the sea. Early June-early August. Ages 18-24, mainly students. Piece-work rates paid. Campsite provided; participants must take their own tent and cooking equipment. Facilities include community hut with TV and radio; no showers. *Early booking necessary; EC nationals only.*

NAIRN VALLEY FRUIT GROWERS DWM Fraser, Cantraybruich, Culloden Moor, Inverness IV1 2EG Tel Inverness 790260
Fruit pickers required to pick raspberries. Ages 18-30. 40+ hour week over 7 day period including evenings when required. Usually 4+ weeks, mid July-end August. Piece-work rates paid. Campsite with showers and self-catering facilities. Workers should take their own tents and camping equipment. Transport to shops twice a week and insurance cover provided.

NEWTON FRUIT FARMS Mudcroft Farm, Newton, Wisbech, Cambridgeshire PE13 5HF Tel Wisbech 870254
Apple pickers are needed on a family-run farm in the Fens. Ages 20+. 40-50 hour week. 4/5 weeks, September/October. Piece-work or hourly rates with bonuses paid. Campsite and accommodation available in self-catering 4/5 berth modern caravans in orchard. Workers should take their own cooking equipment and bedding. Food can be bought from local tradesmen. Deposit payable. *EC nationals only.*

OAK TREE FARM RES Stephenson, Hasketon, Woodbridge, Suffolk Tel Grundisburgh 218
Strawberry pickers needed. Piece-work rates paid. Ages 18+, girls and couples only. 8 hour day, 6 day week excluding Saturday. 3+ weeks, approx 25 June-25 July. Self-catering hostel or camping accommodation approx £3 per week. Campers should take their own tents and equipment. *Apply by mid March.*

R & JM PLACE LTD International Farm Camp, Church Farm, Tunstead, Norwich, Norfolk NR12 8RQ Tel Smallburgh 225
Strawberry, raspberry and blackberry pickers and agricultural workers needed. Other work, such as crop irrigation, fruit inspection or packing, may also be available. Ages 17-30. 8 hour day, 5/6 day week. 21 June-13 September. Piece-work rates paid. Bed and breakfast provided from £22 per week in converted farm buildings; the remaining meals are self-catering. Workers should take a sleeping bag, and help with essential camp duties. Facilities include kitchen, dining hall, bar, showers, shop, laundry room, pool tables, table tennis, darts, volleyball, football and canoeing instruction. Registration fee £20 includes membership of social club. *Overseas applicants accepted.*

JAMES A ROBERTSON & SONS Barnyards, Beauly, Inverness-shire IV4 7AT Tel Beauly 782533
Raspberry pickers required. 40 hour week minimum with extra work available during evenings and weekends. Only students willing to work hard should apply. Approx 20 July-20 August. Piece-work rates paid. Basic facilities provided including camping site and showers. Shops available in nearby village. Participants should take their own camping/cooking equipment.

SPELMONDEN ESTATE CO LTD
The Director, Spelmonden Farm, Goudhurst, Kent TN17 1HE Tel Goudhurst 211400
Hop pickers are required, and also a very limited number of apple pickers. Ages 18+. 5 weeks, from 1 September. Hop pickers receive £2.11 per hour for up to 40 hour week, and £3.16 per hour overtime. Apple pickers paid at piece-work rates. Self-catering accommodation and facilities free of charge. *British nationals only.*

TINKLETOP AND LEROCH FARM CAMPS
Mr P Barron, Tinkletop Farm, Blairgowrie, Perthshire PH10 6TB
Strawberry and raspberry pickers required at 2 farm camps. Ages 17-30. Applicants should be prepared to live simply and work hard in all weathers. Hours 08.00-17.00, 6 day week. 1+ weeks, July and August. Piece-work rates paid. Self-catering campsite or dormitory

accommodation in converted barn provided, but workers should take a sleeping bag, waterproof clothing and boots, and tent and cooking equipment if camping. Communal duties worked on a rota basis. Work accident insurance provided. *Written applications only. Overseas applicants accepted.*

WORKING WEEKENDS ON ORGANIC FARMS (WWOOF) 19 Bradford Road, Lewes, Sussex BN7 1RB
A non-profitmaking organisation which aims to help farmers and smallholders who need manpower to replace the use of herbicides, chemical fertilisers and heavy machinery. Provides unskilled voluntary workers with first hand experience of organic farming and gardening, and a chance to spend an energetic weekend in the country.
Working weekends are organised on 200 organic farms, smallholdings and gardens throughout Britain and Ireland. The work can include hedging, ditching, pond and scrub clearance, haymaking, fruit and vegetable cropping, dairy work, beekeeping, stone walling, sheep shearing, rearing kids and ducklings, building renovation, peat cutting, hooking and scything, seaweed spraying and compost making.
Members receive a bi-monthly newsletter which details places needing help on specific weekends, and also lists job opportunities in the organic movement. After completing 2 scheduled weekends members may apply for their own copy of the complete list of WWOOF places, including some overseas, so that independent arrangements for longer periods can be made. Ages 16+. Families welcome on some farms; vegetarians on many farms. Opportunities to learn crafts. 8 hour day, weekends all year. Full board and lodging provided in the farmhouse or outbuildings; volunteers should take a sleeping bag. No wages paid, and helpers must pay their own travel costs. Insurance and anti-tetanus vaccination recommended. Membership fee £6. Training scheme available.

When writing to any organisation it is essential to mention Working Holidays 1991 and enclose a large stamped, self-addressed envelope, or if overseas, a large addressed envelope and at least two International Reply Coupons.

LEADERS & GUIDES

FAIRTHORNE MANOR YMCA National Centre, Curdridge, Southampton, Hampshire SO3 2GH Tel Botley 5228

Offers a wide range of outdoor educational activities for young people aged 8-20 on residential or day camps, and provides visitors with a sense of community belonging in an outdoor environment.

Volunteers are needed as leaders and assistant leaders. Section leaders are responsible to the camp chief for groups of 40 campers, programme arrangements, camp tidiness plus general supervision including equipment. Group leaders are in charge of approx 8 campers, and must supervise, lead and relate to the group in many different activities, deal with personal problems and be responsible for their physical well being. Centre staff ensure that the visitors enjoy a full and interesting programme. Arts and handicrafts assistants are responsible to the programme director for running the arts and crafts department, purchasing equipment and planning and running sessions. Initiative, enthusiasm, loyalty and sympathy with the aims and purposes of the Young Men's Christian Association movement needed. Ages 18+, preference given to older applicants.

Leadership ability plus qualifications to lead/teach in one sphere of activity, and interest in other activities needed; staff are carefully selected for their ability to relate to young people, and activities are seen as a means to developing this relationship. Language qualifications an advantage. Activities include archery, campcraft, canoeing, sailing, windsurfing, climbing, orienteering. No set hours, 5 day week. 6 weeks, April-September. Full board and tent or other accommodation, £20 per week pocket money plus bonus, insurance and assistance with travel from point of entry provided that a minimum work period of 6 weeks completed. *Overseas applicants welcome.*

THE IONA COMMUNITY Voluntary Staff Coordinator, Isle of Iona, Argyll, Strathclyde PA76 6SN Tel Iona 404

An ecumenical Christian community seeking new and radical ways of living the Gospel in today's world. On Iona the Community runs two centres, each welcoming up to 50 guests to a common life of work, worship, meals and recreation. Volunteers are required to help run the children's programme for those staying at the centres. Some experience of working with children, flexibility and organisation essential, as is the willingness to work as part of a team. Also require guides to offer guided tours of the Abbey, a rebuilt Benedictine monastery, for guests and visitors, often many hundreds each day in the summer months. Duties include keeping the Abbey clean, preparation for worship and welcoming people to services. An interest in history, meeting people and worship is essential.

On the nearby Island of Mull the Camas Centre welcomes up to 16 guests each week, mainly unemployed or disadvantaged young people, to a common life of work, worship, arts, crafts and outdoor activities. Requires programme workers and general assistants with experience and, if possible, qualifications in one or more of the following: outdoor skills (canoeing, walking, camping, abseiling), arts and crafts, working with groups of sometimes very demanding teenagers, games, driving and maintenance. All the work is demanding but rewarding, but most important is a willingness to join fully in the community life, which includes worship and social activities as well as work. Ages 18+. 6 day week, February-December. Full board, shared accommodation, pocket money of £14 per week and assistance with travel expenses within mainland Britain provided. *Applications received before 31 December given priority.*

JOLLY ROGER DAY CAMPS Broome House, 152 Palatine Road, Didsbury, Manchester M20 8QH Tel 061-434 8454

Staff are required for children's summer day camps based in Altrincham, Cheshire and Greater Manchester. Positions include group leaders, with responsibility for supervising a group of children and their activities, making sure they arrive at activities on time, checking on safety procedures and ensuring that children are enjoying their holiday. Group leaders also instruct/supervise non-specialist activities such as sports, games, discos and barbecues. Monitors are also needed to accompany children on the coach from pickup points to the camps and assist group leaders with activities and supervision. Ages 18+, preferably 20+ for group leaders. Applicants should have boundless energy and enthusiasm, preferably with interests or skills in a number of activities, and experience of working with children. Native English speakers preferred. 5 day week, July-August. Wages £55 per week. Lunch and insurance provided. No accommodation or travel, except £5 per week for monitors doing bus courier duty.

LONDON SIGHTSEEING TOURS
3A Victoria House, South Lambeth Road, London SW8 Tel 071-582 2838
Require guides for panoramic tours of London by double-decker bus. Applicants should be good communicators, have a flexible attitude, good English and a clear voice; foreign languages useful but not vital. No experience necessary; full training provided. Work available throughout the summer, 3+ months. 48 hour week. Ages 18+. Salary £3.50 per hour and uniform provided; generous tips can usually be expected. No accommodation or meals provided.

NORD-ANGLIA INTERNATIONAL LTD
Broome House, 152 Palatine Road, Didsbury, Manchester M20 8QH Tel 061-434 7475
Organises holidays, based on English language courses, for overseas students at centres throughout England, Scotland and Wales. Social activity monitors are needed for supervision and courier duties, to liaise with the course director and help with the organisation, animation and supervision of sports. Mostly 5 afternoons per week. Ages 18+. No formal teaching qualifications required, but applicants must be native speakers of English. 2-10 weeks, Easter and July/August. Most courses last 3 weeks, July. Insurance provided, but not board, accommodation or travel. Wages £50-£105 per week depending on duties. Successful applicants are expected to attend a 1 day training and information session before commencing employment. B D PH in certain cases.

PGL YOUNG ADVENTURE LTD Personnel Department, Alton Court, Penyard Lane, Ross-on-Wye, Herefordshire HR9 5NR Tel Ross-on-Wye 764211
Organises outdoor adventure holidays for young people and families in England, Wales and Scotland. Activities include pony trekking, sailing, canoeing, computing, archery, judo, fencing, rifle shooting, hill walking, orienteering, swimming and many others. Group leaders are required to take charge of a group of young people, joining in the activities and developing group identity, as well as planning and organising the evening programme of activities. They are responsible for looking after the welfare of the group, and must expect to be fully involved with them throughout their stay, with the prime task of ensuring that the guests enjoy their holiday and get the most out of the experience. Ages 20+. Applicants should have a strong sense of responsibility and total commitment, be well organised, calm, patient, flexible and caring, have a wide range of skills, experience of working with children in informal or formal settings, an ability to cope with demands on their time, initiative, imagination, stamina, energy, enthusiasm, a good sense of humour and a strong personality. It is not necessary to be an extrovert - different types of personality will tackle the post in different ways, and all can be equally successful. Previous experience of working with young people useful. 4+ weeks, February-September. Staff are also recruited for short periods, such as Easter and the spring bank holiday. 1 day off per week. Full board and accommodation provided. Pocket money from £25 per week, depending on qualifications and length of stay. Applicants pay their own travel expenses. All staff are encouraged to take part in evening activities with the guests, and may sometimes be asked to help out in areas other than their own. *Early application advisable; majority of positions filled by end June.*

TOPS HOLIDAYS (SUN LIVING LTD)
Personnel Manager, Adventure House, 34-36 South Street, Lancing, West Sussex BN15 8AG Tel Lancing 751942
Organises a range of specialised activity and outdoor education programmes for groups of schoolchildren aged 7-17 at centres in Herefordshire, Wales and throughout south

east England. Each centre has its own team of staff to ensure that high standards of safety, instruction and enjoyment are maintained. Group leaders are required, looking after the general welfare of a group of 12-15 children and making sure they get the most from their holiday. Leaders are also responsible for ensuring their group arrives at activities, meals and events on time, sorting out problems and organising entertainments.

Ages 18+, preference is given to ages 20+. Experience of working with children, and of at least one of the activities organised an advantage. The jobs demand a high level of commitment both physically and mentally; applicants should enjoy being with children all day, have a genuine interest in their welfare, be patient, sympathetic and diplomatic. Fitness, stamina, energy, enthusiasm and the ability to live and work as part of a team also essential. 40+ hour week, 1 day free per week. 1+ months, March-October. Most staff work the full season; extra staff are also taken on for shorter periods during peak times at Easter and during July and August. Opportunities for staff to move from centre to centre. Full board and shared accommodation provided. Pay £25 per week, rising to £35 after 4 weeks. Training provided to ensure staff are confident and able to carry out their responsibilities. Social and recreational activities such as parties, barbecues and outings arranged for staff. Senior positions also available. *British nationals only.* B D PH limited opportunities.

YHA ACTIVITY HOLIDAYS Trevelyan House, 8 St Stephen's Hill, St Albans, Hertfordshire AL1 2DY Tel St Albans 55215
Leaders and assistant leaders are required for walking tours and holidays in many parts of England and Wales. Leaders and assistants are responsible for groups of participants, many of whom have no experience of hostelling or of the countryside. It is the responsibility of the leaders to guide participants safely from point to point and to ensure that they get the most from their walking holiday. Ages 18+. 1+ weeks, April-October. Applicants must have experience of dealing with people, and be prepared to be on the go all day. Experience of walking long distance routes such as the Pennine Way, useful. Nominal wages plus board and lodging provided.

MONITORS & INSTRUCTORS

**ACADEMIC TRAVEL (LOWESTOFT) LTD
The Briar School of English, 8 Gunton Cliff, Lowestoft, Suffolk NR32 4PE
Tel Lowestoft 573781**
Aims to provide an educational and cultural experience for young people from overseas, providing sports, visits and social activities in addition to English lessons. Requires experienced teachers and instructors to teach English and sports. Appropriate qualifications necessary; TEFL English, LTA tennis, RYA sailing and BCU kayak/canoe. Knowledge of French, German, Italian and Spanish useful. End June-end August, average 25 hours per week. Ages 18+. Salaries according to position and insurance provided. Accommodation and catering not provided but help given.

**ACTION HOLIDAYS LTD Windrush, Bexton Lane, Knutsford, Cheshire WA16 9BP
Tel Knutsford 54775**
Runs children's multi-activity holidays at two centres in Cheshire and Surrey. Requires supervisors and instructors with some experience of working with children, although full training is given before the work starts. Enthusiasm for the job and enjoyment of sports activities essential. Specialist activities include archery, go-karting and performing arts. 50+ hour week with 1 day off. Salary £40-£90 per week, depending on responsibility, all meals, and shared accommodation provided. Participants pay their own travel expenses and insurance. *Overseas applicants will need to arrange their own work permit.*

ADVENTURE INTERNATIONAL Belle Vue, Bude, Cornwall EX23 8JP Tel Bude 355551
Aims to develop participants' respect for themselves, others, and the environment through a range of experience-based courses to be pursued within a framework of safety. Requires outdoor pursuits and development training instructors to take part in teaching a range of activities including surfing, canoeing, sailing, climbing, plus a pastoral role looking after young people's welfare.
March-November. Up to 36 hour week.

Nationally recognised qualifications in outdoor pursuits preferred. Ages 18+. Salaries from £25-£125 per week, depending on experience, qualifications and post; board, accommodation and insurance provided. B D PH

ANGLO-CONTINENTAL Director of Studies, 33 Wimborne Road, Bournemouth, Dorset BH2 6NA Tel Bournemouth 557414
An English language school which as part of a wide range of programmes organises junior holiday courses for those aged 8-18, combining English language and creative leisure. Staff are required for sports coaching and residential supervision, with additional responsibility for recreational and social activities. The posts involve careful supervision of junior students in and out of school hours. There are opportunities to teach and organise sports, lead educational visits and excursions and to conduct other activities such as computer programming, arts and crafts, cookery and give talks on British life, literature and institutions. A number of administrative posts also available in the areas of travel and social activities. Applicants should have organising ability, drive and enthusiasm plus wide sporting and cultural interests. Irregular working hours including evening activities. 6 day week, June-August. Staff may be required to attend brief training seminars in the week prior to the arrival of students. Residential accommodation provided at most centres in return for extra duties. Weekly salaries, paid according to qualifications and experience. All applicants must attend for interview; successful candidates will have travelling expenses refunded.

ARDMORE ADVENTURE 11-15 High Street, Marlow, Buckinghamshire SL7 1AU Tel Marlow 890060
Organises activity holidays for young people at residential and day centres in the Thames Valley, Dorset and Wales. Specialist instructors with relevant experience and qualifications are required to teach abseiling, aerobics, archery, arts and crafts, BMX bikes, canoeing, computing, fencing, go-karting, gymnastics, horse riding, judo, karate, mini motorbikes, performing arts, pottery, rifle shooting, sailing, tennis, trampolining and windsurfing. Ages 18+. Applicants should preferably have experience of working with children.

2/3+ weeks, Easter and mid June-early September. Day centres 40 hours per week, residential centres 60 hours per week. Wages from £45 per week, depending on position. Full board, single or shared accommodation and insurance provided, but no travel. UK nationals only.

BEAUMONT CAMPS Personnel Department, Corpus Christi House, 9 West Street, Godmanchester, Huntingdon, Cambridgeshire PE18 8HG Tel Huntingdon 456123
Organises a wide range of holidays for children in American-style day and residential camps. Staff are recruited for 10 day and 8 residential camps throughout the country. Opportunities exist for general monitors, specialist instructors and group leaders. General monitors are chosen for their experience with children and their sports or activity skills. Activities include pioneering, waterfront, ball games, music, dance, arts and crafts. Each monitor is assigned to a group of 8-10 children, taking them to the activities and ensuring their safety throughout the day, and is responsible to a group leader. Day camp monitors accompany children daily by coach from pick-up points, and must live in the Greater London area.
Specialist instructors are needed to teach a limited number of activities where special caution is required; these include canoeing, sailing, archery, judo, fencing, trampolining, caving, subaqua, rifle-shooting, horseriding, soccer, tennis, swimming, mini motorbikes and computing. Specialists assume total responsibility for the safety of both children and staff during the activity under instruction, and should have relevant qualifications or experience. Group leaders liaise with the camp director, coordinate groups and organise monitor duties, timetables and catering arrangements. Also opportunities for waterfront, TEFL and computing staff. Residential staff are responsible for groups of children aged 8-17, during the day, in the evening and at night when they sleep in the same tent or dormitory. All staff must genuinely enjoy working with children, possess leadership ability, and be willing to work a long, hard exhausting day enthusiastically in a structured setting where regulations apply to all. Staff must be available

for the whole season, March/April or July/September. 5-9 weeks, including compulsory day/weekend orientation course, setting up and clearing camps. Ages 18-35. Day camp staff work a 45 hour week. Residential staff work a 24 hour day, with 1 free day per week plus alternate nights off. Wages £40-£50 per week. Board, accommodation and travel provided PH

CAMP WINDERMERE Low Wray Farm, Ambleside, Cumbria LA22 0JJ
Tel Ambleside 32163
A full-time training centre for school parties and youth groups with the emphasis on training, safety and enjoyment. Recognised as an approved establishment by the Mountain Leadership Training Board, the British Canoe Union and the Royal Yachting Association. Volunteer assistant outdoor pursuits instructors are needed to teach walking, canoeing, sailing, camping and other activities in the Lake District. Experience useful but not essential. 24 hour day, 7 day week, March-October. Ages 18+. Full training to national standards in canoeing, sailing and walking, tent accommodation and catering provided.

DOLPHIN ADVENTURE HOLIDAYS (SUN LIVING LTD) Personnel Manager, Adventure House, 34-36 South Street, Lancing, West Sussex BN15 8AG Tel Lancing 751942
Opportunities exist for general counsellors and specialist instructors to help with the organisation and supervision of children's American-style activity camps throughout the country. Camps are set in schools, universities and colleges, all of which have extensive grounds and facilities. Applicants should have a sense of humour, enthusiasm, qualifications, energy, commitment, stamina and initiative, and be able to demonstrate the ability to communicate well, particularly with children. Experience in teaching and working with children helpful, and ability to take initiative useful. Knowledge of French, Italian or Spanish helpful.
Instructors are needed in sailing, windsurfing, canoeing, swimming, tennis, football, squash, cricket, badminton, table tennis, volleyball, fencing, golf, American football, baseball, archery, trampolining, rifle, judo, horse riding, dance and drama, video, BMX bikes, motorbikes, arts and crafts, computing and TEFL. They must be able to teach the activity

combined with an understanding of how to create a safe environment, plus the ability to make it fun for all age groups.
General counsellors provide continual supervision of a group of children throughout their stay and create group interaction, maximum excitement and ensure the best possible time for the children. Staff with a particular aptitude for dealing with children aged 3-6 are also needed to work on day camps as teenies staff. Opportunities also exist for camp directors with proven ability and experience, qualified nurses, SRN or SEN, to provide medical care, and to help with general organisation and supervision. Wages depend on experience and amount of on-camp responsibility. Ages 18+. 40 hour week. 3-9 weeks, Easter and summer. Day camp staff receive £45 per week with lunches and, where possible, transport to and from camp; residential staff receive £30 per week plus full board and at least 1 day and 1 evening off per week. All staff attend an initial training course and pay for uniform and travel. Liability insurance provided. *British nationals only.*

ERA ADVENTURE HOLIDAYS LTD Director of Personnel, 2 Mays Road, Teddington, Middlesex TW11 0SQ
Aims to provide a memorable and stimulating holiday for ages 6-15. Children are given the opportunity to follow many activities including craftwork, sports instruction, discos, competitions, trips and camping. Staff are required for various duties at a centre based at a school in the New Forest. Sports instructors in gymnastics, archery, judo, canoeing, tennis, motor sports, windsurfing, squash and badminton are required who must be prepared to take groups of youngsters of varying abilities and standards. Supervisors, teachers of English, nurses and drivers are also required. Applicants must have a mature attitude, enjoy being with children and be willing to take the initiative by participating and involving the youngsters in all activities. The work can be at times very demanding and tiring but is enjoyable and rewarding. Ages 21+. Experience preferred. End July-end August. Hours of work variable; 1 day off per week plus set off-duty periods. Some residential duties are expected. Full board, accommodation and insurance provided. Wages £25-£100 per week.

FAIRTHORNE MANOR YMCA National Centre, Curdridge, Southampton, Hampshire SO3 2GH Tel Botley 785228
Offers a wide range of outdoor educational activities for young people aged 8-20 on residential or day camps and provides visitors with a sense of community belonging in and outdoor environment. Sports instructors are needed. Canoeing (kayak) instructors conduct groups under the supervision of the waterfront director, sharing in the camp duty rota and occasionally in other activities. Fluency in French and German plus BCU certificate desirable. Sports and games organisers arrange sport tournaments and large group games; sound knowledge of a wide variety of sports and games essential. Archery instructors' work involves responsibility to the programme director for the smooth running of the theoretical and practical sessions on the archery range and for the upkeep of equipment; GNAS certificate desirable. Applicants will also be expected to participate in other activities. Qualified sailing and climbing instructors also needed. Ages 18+, preference given to older applicants. Leadership ability, enthusiasm, loyalty, and sympathy with the aims and purposes of the Young Men's Christian Association movement plus qualifications to lead/teach in one sphere of activity and interest in other activities needed; staff are carefully selected for their ability to relate to young people, and activities are seen as a means to develop this relationship. Language qualification an advantage. 5 day week. 6 weeks, April-September. Full board, tent or other accommodation, £20 per week pocket money plus bonus, insurance and assistance with travel provided that minimum work period of 6 weeks completed. 1 week obligatory leader training course arranged at Easter. *Overseas applicants welcome.*

HYDE HOUSE ACTIVITY HOLIDAY CENTRE c/o 6 Kew Green, Richmond, Surrey Tel 081-940 7782
Situated on a 50 acre estate 9 miles from Poole, organising outdoor multi-activity holidays and courses for schools and groups. Sports include windsurfing, water skiing, dinghy and longboat sailing, snorkelling, canoeing, climbing, abseiling, parascending, grass skiing, orienteering, riding and archery. Full and part-time instructors are required; qualifications preferred. 6 day week. 8+ weeks, March-October. Salary £40 per week and full board accommodation provided.

JOLLY ROGER DAY CAMPS Broome House, 152 Palatine Road, Didsbury, Manchester M20 8QH Tel 061-434 7475/8454
Specialist instructors are required for a children's summer day camp based in Altrincham, Cheshire and Greater Manchester, to teach archery, rifle shooting, judo, fencing, motorsports and mechanics. As well as organising the activities, instructors may also be required to assist in other aspects of the camp, such as sports, games, discos and barbecues. Ages 18+. Applicants must have a good basic level of skill, plus the ability to impart that skill to children. Boundless energy and enthusiasm, experience of working with children and ability to evaluate their capabilities also required. Native English speakers preferred. 5 day week, July-August. Wages £50 per week. Lunch and insurance provided, but no accommodation or travel. Also require centre managers with organisational ability to help run the camps, wages £125-£150 per week; also qualified nurses who can undertake general administration. Wages £120 per week.

KIDS KLUB The Hall, Great Finborough, near Stowmarket, Suffolk IP14 3EF Tel Stowmarket 675 907
Provides activity holidays for 6-15 year olds at a country house. Staff are needed to organise and play with the children, creating a happy family atmosphere and holiday of a lifetime. Activities include watersports, horse riding, dry skiing, tennis, arts and crafts. Staff are chosen for their enthusiasm and love of children. Knowledge of European languages an asset but not essential. Ages 18+. 48 hour week during Easter, and beginning July-end August. Wages negotiable; full board and accommodation provided. Participants pay own travel and insurance costs.

MILLFIELD SCHOOL Village of Education, Street, Somerset BA16 0YD Tel Somerset 45823
An independent school organising a range of special interest holidays for children and adults, with over 100 different activities and

350 courses to choose from. Instructors are needed to teach a wide variety of outdoor pursuits, sports, arts, crafts and cookery courses, plus EFL. Facilities include sports halls, games fields, swimming pool, dance/ health studios and technology centre. Ages 20+. Degree or teaching qualifications and/or relevant sports coaching qualifications essential. 25 hour week. 4 weeks, July and August. Wages £85 per week. Small group accommodation and catering provided in exchange for evening or weekend supervisory duties. Staff pay own travel and insurance costs. PH

OUTDOORS UNLIMITED National Westminster Bank Chambers, 52/54 Lichfield Street, Wolverhampton WV1 1DG Tel Wolverhampton 310020
Provides a centralised employment opportunities information service to the outdoor pursuits industry, placing instructors throughout Britain. Experience not essential, but more positions open to experienced instructors. Work available all year round. Ages 18+.

PGL YOUNG ADVENTURE LTD Personnel Department, Alton Court, Penyard Lane, Ross-on-Wye, Herefordshire HR9 5NR Tel Ross-on-Wye 764211
Organises outdoor adventure holidays in England, Wales and Scotland. Instructors are needed for sailing, windsurfing, pony trekking, canoeing, hill walking, orienteering and archery. Staff are also needed with particular interest and skills in swimming, campcraft, caving, basketball, football, aerobics, tennis, squash, badminton, volleyball, judo, fencing, cycling, drama, gymnastics, golf, computing, trampolining, rollerskating, climbing, abseiling, assault courses, nature trails, and arts and crafts. At some centres, instructors are needed who are proficient in a number of activities.

Ages 18+, preference given to ages 21+. Instructors should ideally have a qualification or previous experience of teaching with a good basic level of skill, but consideration will be given to candidates who are competent in the given activity. Training can be arranged. Enthusiasm and stamina essential, plus the ability to adhere to strict safety standards and the foresight to deal with emergency situations, and recognise the limitations of each child.

Applicants should have a strong sense of responsibility and total commitment, enjoy the company of young people, be self-motivated, tolerant, flexible, positive, mature, with vitality and a good sense of humour. 4+ weeks, February-September. Staff are also recruited for short periods such as Easter and the spring bank holiday. 1 day off per week. Full board and accommodation provided. Pocket money from £25 per week, depending on qualifications and length of stay. Senior activity instructors receive from £50 per week; senior watersports instructors and canoeists receive £45-£80 per week. Applicants pay own travel expenses. All staff are encouraged to take part in evening activities with the guests, and may sometimes be asked to help out in areas other than their own. *Early application advisable; majority of positions are filled by end June.*

PIONEER ACTIVITY HOLIDAYS Buckingham House, 12 Buckingham Road, Brighton, East Sussex BN1 3RA Tel Brighton 821968
Aims to provide exciting, educational and safe holiday programmes for children. Specialises in sports camps for children from Britain and mainland Europe. Instructors are required at residential camps in southern England to teach aerobics, American football, archery, badminton, baseball, basketball, canoeing, computing, dryslope skiing, first aid, fitness training, golf, indoor hockey, orienteering, riding, rifle shooting, sailing, soccer, squash, swimming, table tennis, tennis, trampolining, volleyball, windsurfing and water polo. Camp counsellors also required to supervise and take care of children.

Ages 20+. Applicants must have recognised teaching/proficiency qualifications in the sport/subject they wish to teach, plus a genuine liking for children. Previous summer camp experience preferred. Knowledge of French, Italian or Spanish an advantage. Work is physically hard, but very rewarding. 60+ hours per week; work available from 24 June-31 August. Pay from £40 per week, plus full board accommodation and insurance. Travel can be arranged from certain points in the UK. *EC nationals only.*

**RANK EDUCATIONAL SERVICES LTD
Castle Mill, Lower Kings Road, Berkhamsted,
Hertfordshire HP4 2AP
Tel Berkhamsted 876641**
Designed to help organisations concerned with
the character development of young people,
arranging a variety of residential activity
holidays. Instructors are required for school
venture and language weeks which cater for
groups of children aged 8-14 in Cornwall, Kent,
Somerset, Sussex, the Isle of Wight, Scotland
and Wales. A wide range of crafts and outdoor
activities are taught including judo,
badminton, boating, fencing, swimming, ball
games, abseiling, orienteering, gymnastics,
aerobics, archery, art, crafts, drama, and
video-making. Qualifications or experience
preferable but not always essential. For
language weeks fluent French or German and
English are required. Applicants must be
friendly and enthusiastic, and have a genuine
interest in working with children. October,
November, January, February and March-May.
Instructors also required for pre-vocational
education programmes which cater for older
children and trainees aged 15-18. Involves a
balanced range of team-building activities,
both mental and physical, designed to motivate
and create self-confidence and other skills
necessary in vocational and life-skills
curricula. October-December, February and
March. Wages approx £70-£85 per week. Board
and lodging provided.

**ROCKLEY POINT SAILING SCHOOL
Hamworthy, Poole, Dorset BH15 4LZ
Tel Poole 677272**
Teaches sailing to individuals and groups in
dinghies and yachts, and requires instructors
with RYA qualifications. Those with the ability
to achieve RYA qualifications within a short
time may also apply. Some posts for house
mothers, to look after the children when not
sailing. Ages 18+, 40 hour week, March-
October. Wages dependent on experience.
Accommodation provided in caravans near the
school.

**STUDENTOURS 3 Harcourt Street, London
W1H 1DS Tel 071-402 5131**
Monitors are required to organise sports
programmes and supervise children's activities
at summer camps in Kent and Sussex. Ages
17+. 5+ hour day, 5 day week with evenings

free. 2-6 months, all year. Board, lodging and
insurance provided. Pocket money from £35
per week.

**TIGHNABRUAICH SAILING SCHOOL
Tighnabruaich, Argyll PA21 2BD**
Instructors are needed to teach sailing and
windsurfing to high standards in a relaxed
holiday atmosphere. Appropriate sailing or
windsurfing qualifications required. Approx
36 hour week, June-September. Ages 18+.
Salary £40 per week and self-catering youth
hostel accommodation provided.

**TOPS HOLIDAYS (SUN LIVING LTD)
Personnel Manager, Adventure House, 34-36
South Street, Lancing, West Sussex BN15 8AG
Tel Lancing 751942**
Organises a range of specialised activity and
outdoor education programmes for groups of
school children aged 7-17 at centres in
Herefordshire, Wales and throughout south
east England. Each centre has its own team
staff who ensure that high standards of safety,
instruction and enjoyment are maintained.
Activity instructors are required to teach horse
riding, trail riding, sailing, windsurfing,
canoeing, climbing, abseiling, archery, rifle
shooting and motorsports. Instructors spend
most of the time teaching their specialist
activity, so must have the ability to teach it to a
good basic level and impart the knowledge to a
variety of ages in an imaginative, interesting
way. The emphasis is on safety, fun and
participation rather than achievement.

Ages 18+, preference given to ages 20+.
Qualifications from the relevant sporting body
are a definite advantage, but applicants with
just teaching experience will be considered.
Instructors with experience in or an aptitude
for BMX bikes, orienteering, assault course,
photography, hill walking, camping, raft
building, caving, swimming and trials bikes
are also needed. In these activities prior
technical skills are less significant than
personality and teaching ability; a full
residential training course is available for the
inexperienced during the spring. In addition
there are a number of senior instructor
positions, such as river leader and head
activity instructor, for which applicants with
extensive experience and maturity will be
considered. All jobs demand a high level of

commitment both physically and mentally; applicants should enjoy being with children all day and have a genuine interest in their welfare. Fitness, stamina, energy, enthusiasm and the ability to live and work as part of a team are also essential. 40+ hour week, 1 day free per week. 1+ months, March-October.

Most staff work the full season; extra staff are also taken on for shorter periods during peak times at Easter and during July and August. There are opportunities for staff to move from centre to centre. Full board and shared accommodation provided. Pay from £25 per week rising to £35 after 4 weeks and for returning staff, according to experience and responsibilities. Training is provided to ensure staff are confident and able to carry out their responsibilities. Social and recreational activities such as parties, barbecues and outings arranged for staff. *British nationals only.* B D PH limited opportunities.

THE WOODSIDE ADVENTURE CENTRE c/o 6 Kew Green, Richmond, Surrey Tel 081-940 7782
The Centre is situated in Bideford and organises outdoor activity holidays and courses for all ages and levels. Sports include water skiing, canoeing, sailing, surfing, riding, abseiling, sand yachting, climbing, snorkelling, coastal/hill walking, orienteering, skate sailing, grass slope skiing and archery. Full or part-time instructors required. Qualifications preferred. 36 hour, 6 day week. 8+ weeks, March-October. Full board centre accommodation provided. Salary £40 per week.

YHA ADVENTURE HOLIDAYS Trevelyan House, 8 St Stephen's Hill, St Albans, Hertfordshire AL1 2DY Tel St Albans 55215
Instructors are required for multi-activity holidays including sailing, canoeing, hillwalking, archery, rifle shooting, mountain biking, orienteering and climbing, organised at YHA activity centres in England and Wales. 1+ months, during summer season. Ages 18+.

Applicants should be proficient and qualified in at least one of the activities, articulate, cheerful, enjoy working with children and capable of imparting their knowledge to beginners. They must also be well aware of

safety considerations, be able to act sensibly on their own initiative, and be prepared to supervise evening activities. Opportunities for improving qualifications available to longer-term staff. Full board and lodging plus weekly payment offered.

TEACHERS

ANGLO-CONTINENTAL Director of Studies, 33 Wimborne Road, Bournemouth, Dorset BH2 6NA Tel Bournemouth 557414
A group of schools providing English language courses for overseas students. Qualified teachers and university graduates, preferably with EFL experience, are required at international vacation centres (ages 14+) and at an international school for juniors (ages 8-18). English is taught at 6 levels, with emphasis on oral English; maximum class size 15. Junior school staff will also be expected to take part in out-of-class activities, including excursions, sports and social activities, and general student welfare. 30-40 hour week, June-August. Staff may be required to attend brief training seminars in the week prior to the arrival of the students. Residential accommodation provided in return for extra duties at junior school, but at some centres staff have to arrange their own accommodation. Weekly salary according to qualifications and experience. Vacation course teachers are carefully chosen for their skill and enthusiasm, and for a lively, interesting and entertaining approach. Applicants must attend for interview and successful candidates will have travelling expenses refunded.

ANGLO EUROPEAN STUDY TOURS LTD 8 Celbridge Mews, London W2 6EU Tel 071-229 4435
Runs English language courses for foreign students during the summer at centres in Bristol, Edinburgh, London, Norwich, Swansea and Tunbridge Wells. Teachers with TEFL qualifications and at least 1 year's teaching experience are required. Applicants should be of English mother tongue and preferably have an additional language. Ages 24+. 15-25 hour week, mid June-end August. Salary £140+ per week. Applicants arrange their own accommodation and travel.

ELIZABETH JOHNSON ORGANISATION
Education Department, West House, 19/21
West Street, Haslemere, Surrey GU27 2AE
Tel Haslemere 52751
Arranges short-term holiday courses in English
for young students, particularly from Europe,
the Middle East and Japan. Teachers are needed
at more than 35 centres in the areas around
Eastbourne, Portsmouth, Bristol, Southampton,
Bournemouth, Reading, Guildford, Cambridge,
Farnham and Weybridge. Work normally
involves 4 mornings teaching per week,
accompanying students on excursions and
supervising activities in the afternoons and
sometimes in the evenings; occasionally
escorting between course centre and arrival/
departure point. Weekends are normally free,
although some programmes involve weekend
activities.

Applicants should be qualified and/or
experienced teachers, in particular those with
TEFL experience, or graduates/final year
students at colleges, especially those studying
languages. On some courses there are
vacancies for those with qualifications to teach
art, drama, riding, tennis and indoor sports.
Flexibility and enthusiasm essential. All
applicants should be capable of carrying out
programmes in a lively and responsible way as
a full-time commitment. 2-3 weeks, Easter and
2-8 weeks, June-September. Salary according to
programme. Accommodation can be arranged,
although preference is given to local
applicants. All new teachers attend a 1 day
briefing workshop.

ENGLISH HOME HOLIDAYS 4 Albert
Terrace, High Street, Bognor Regis, West
Sussex PO21 1SS Tel Bognor Regis 865793
EFL teachers are needed to teach groups of
French students at centres along the south
coast, Cornwall, Inverness, Galway and North
Wales. Ages 21+. 5 mornings per week plus 1
full day excursion to London. March/April,
July and August. Salary £75 per week. No
board or accommodation provided. *British
nationals only.*

THE ENGLISH LANGUAGE CENTRE 163/169
Old Christchurch Road, Bournemouth, Dorset
BH1 1JU Tel Bournemouth 291919
Requires teachers to teach English to overseas
students and accompany them on Saturday
excursions. Applicants should be English
speakers with a minimum of 2 A levels;
preference given to graduates or those with a
TEFL qualification. Some experience of
teaching or youth or social work an advantage.
4-8 weeks, from 2 July. 22½ hour week,
teaching 30 x 45 minute lessons. Ages 21+.
Salary £6 per lesson plus £25 per day for
Saturday excursions. Workplace insurance
provided. Accommodation with families £55
per week. B D PH

EUROYOUTH LTD 301 Westborough Road,
Westcliff-on-Sea, Essex SS0 9PT
Tel Southend-on-Sea 341434
Organises stays for overseas students which
can be combined with language and activity
courses. Part-time EFL teachers required for
English language courses for students aged
14-17. 12 hour week, 3 weeks, Easter and July-
August. Ages 20+. TEFL training or experience
desirable, and knowledge of foreign languages
useful. Salary approx £7 per hour depending
on qualifications or experience. Apply giving
personal particulars, experience, qualifications
and availability dates. No accommodation
provided. *British nationals only.*

GABBITAS, TRUMAN AND THRING
6-8 Sackville Street, London W1X 2BR
Tel 071-734 0161
Recruits teaching and non-teaching staff for
independent schools and colleges. For
unqualified staff work includes domestic and
supervisory duties, and possibly some teaching
if appropriate. No experience or qualifications
necessary but school leavers should generally
have A levels and be going on to university.
Overseas applicants must have appropriate
visa/work permit and be available for
interview. Work available all academic year,
3-9 months. Salary according to placement.
Accommodation usually within the school,
plus institutional meals.

INTERLINK SCHOOL OF ENGLISH
126 Richmond Park Road, Bournemouth,
Dorset BH8 8TH Tel Bournemouth 290983
Requires experienced teachers with degree and
preferably TEFL qualification, to teach English
to overseas students. 20 hour week, July-
August. Ages 21+. Salary £134-£200 per week.
Applicants must arrange their own board and
lodging.

INTERNATIONAL STUDY PROGRAMMES
The Manor, Hazleton, Cheltenham, Gloucestershire GL54 4EB Tel Cotswold 60379
Organises educational visits and arranges holiday language courses, international holiday camps, study tours and homestay programmes. EFL tutors required to teach on a wide variety of language programmes at approx 20 centres and camps throughout Britain. Work includes planning and carrying out tuition programmes (14 hours per week), supervising group activities, including sports sessions, excursions and evening activities, liaising with group leaders and local organisers and escorting groups to and from port, airport or station. Ages 21+. Tutors must have TEFL experience and/or degree and PGCE or other teaching qualifications in English or modern languages. 2-3 weeks, Easter and June-August. Salary approx £160-£210 per week including camp, family or residential board and accommodation or £190-£240 per week if own accommodation provided. Tutors also receive £20 travel allowance per course. *Native English speakers only.* B D PH on request.

KING'S SCHOOL OF ENGLISH (LONDON)
25 Beckenham Road, Beckenham, Kent BR3 4PR Tel 081-650 5891
Staff are needed to teach EFL and to organise activities and excursions for groups of 10-14 foreign students aged 16+. Applicants should preferably have a TEFL qualification and relevant experience of teaching and of organising tours and social activities. 16-32 hour week, July and August. Ages 22-40. Salary approx £8 per lesson; help given in finding accommodation. *Native English speakers only.*

LTC INTERNATIONAL COLLEGE OF ENGLISH Compton Park, Compton Place Road, Eastbourne, East Sussex, BN21 1EH Tel Eastbourne 27755
Runs a residential college for overseas students. Experienced teachers, preferably with TEFL qualifications, are required to teach English, supervise students and organise extra-curricular activities. Ages 21+.
Applicants must be native English speakers and candidates with qualifications such as a degree plus RSA Preparatory certificate in TEFL are preferred. 20 hour week plus 15-20 hours of supervision and extra-curricular

activities. Mid June-end August. Salary £550+ per month. Residential accommodation in shared bedrooms, full board and National Insurance provided; applicants arrange their own travel. One-day induction programme. Also vacancies for residential or non-residential social organisers and welfare assistants. *Apply after 1 January.*

NORD-ANGLIA INTERNATIONAL LTD
Broome House, 152 Palatine Road, West Didsbury, Manchester M20 8QH Tel 061-434 7475
Organises holidays, based on English language courses, for overseas students at 85 centres throughout England, Scotland and Wales. Staff are required to teach English and supervise social and cultural activity sessions. Ages 21+. Applicants must be graduates, preferably with TEFL experience, and must be native speakers of English. 15+ hours teaching, plus up to 5 afternoon or evening activity sessions per week. Full day excursions count as 2 activity sessions. 2-10 weeks, Easter and July/August, most courses being 3 weeks, July. Insurance provided, but not board or travel. Accommodation provided in some residential centres, where teachers have responsibility for supervising students in the evenings. Salary from £125 per week, depending on hours worked and accommodation. Successful applicants are expected to attend a 1 day training and information session before commencing employment. B D PH in certain cases.

OXFORD INTENSIVE SCHOOL OF ENGLISH Unit 1, Kings Meadow, Ferry Hinksey Road, Oxford, Oxfordshire OX2 0DP Tel Oxford 792799
Requires teachers for schools in the Midlands, East Anglia and the South West, to provide intensive EFL tuition for teenagers in their vacations, teaching English in small classes and supervising during leisure activities. Applicants should be graduates with English as their mother tongue, preferably with a modern language background; teaching experience advantageous, but not essential. 3/4 hours per weekday plus supervision during afternoons and at weekends, Easter and July/August. Wages £135+ per week and public liability insurance provided. Applicants will have to arrange their own board and lodging.

RICHARD LANGUAGE COLLEGE 43-45 Wimborne Road, Bournemouth, Dorset BH3 7AB Tel Bournemouth 25932
Graduates are required to teach EFL to groups of 12-14 adults. Duties include teaching, correction of homework, and some participation in extra-curricular activities on the extensive sports and social programme. Applicants should have a degree in English, French or German, and preferably RSA Cambridge Certificate in TEFL. Ages 22+. Maximum 30 x 45 minute lessons per week. Late June-mid September. Part board family accommodation can be arranged at cost of £50-£55 per week, full board at weekends. Salary according to qualifications and experience. Public liability insurance and interview travel expenses provided.

STUDIO SCHOOL OF ENGLISH 6 Salisbury Villas, Station Road, Cambridge CB1 2JF Tel Cambridge 69701
A recognised language school with vacancies for high calibre EFL teachers. Applicants should have a degree/PGCE, and ideally a TEFL qualification. Native English speakers only. 15-30 hour week. June/July-August/September. Wages according to qualifications and experience. Board and accommodation not provided. PH

WORKCAMPS

ATD FOURTH WORLD The General Secretary, 48 Addington Square, London SE5 7LB Tel 071-703 3231
Strives to protect and guarantee the fundamental rights of the most disadvantaged and excluded families to family life, education and representation. It is these families, denied the means of being fully active members of society, who constitute the Fourth World in every country. Volunteers are required for a workcamp at the family centre in Surrey. Work is mainly manual, such as building, painting and landscaping, with some secretarial and translation work. The camp is run by permanent volunteers. Applicants should be interested in better understanding the causes and effects of persistent poverty and be willing to work hard with others as a team. Ages 18+. Approx 40 hour, 5½ day week. 2 weeks, July. Also weekends, June and September and 3

month volunteer scheme April-July or September-December. Simple camping or prefab self-catering accommodation provided. Volunteers are asked to contribute approx £40 towards living expenses, and should take a sleeping bag and all-weather working clothes. PH

CHRISTIAN MOVEMENT FOR PEACE Bethnal Green United Reformed Church, Pott Street, London E2 0EF Tel 071-729 1877
An international movement open to all who share a common concern for lasting peace and justice in the world. Volunteers are required to work in international teams on summer projects aimed at offering a service in an area of need and promoting self-help within the community; promoting international understanding and the discussion of social problems; and offering young people the chance to live as a group and take these experiences into the context of daily life. Recent projects have included running a city farm in a multi-cultural area of Birmingham; participating in music workshops; renovating buildings on the isle of Iona; decorating, gardening and general maintenance work at a Christian retreat centre in Essex; raising awareness of the Namibian situation by working alongside Namibians to prepare a float for the Notting Hill Carnival; and converting an army truck into an ambulance for use in health and education settlements for Namibian refugees in Angola. Ages 17+. Volunteers must be prepared to take a full part in all aspects of the camp. Overseas volunteers must have fluent English and be over 18. 30-36 hour week. 2 weeks, May-September. Board, lodging and insurance provided but volunteers pay their own travel costs and sometimes contribute towards living expenses. Registration fee £15. B D PH

Applications from outside the UK: please see workcamp information on page 27.

INTERNATIONAL VOLUNTARY SERVICE 162 Upper New Walk, Leicester LE1 7QA Tel Leicester 549430
IVS is the British branch of Service Civil International, which promotes international reconciliation through workcamps. Recent projects have included constructing log cabins at the Centre for Alternative Technology in

Machynlleth to be fitted with woodburning stoves, hydro-electric power sources, wind turbines and solar panels; working with the Dandelion Trust in Devon to restore land and buildings to be used for artistic events and social projects; living in a community of crofters on the Shetland Islands and helping them with everyday tasks as well as constructing a track to enable access to the other side of the island; gardening and working in the print shop at a community based in railway cottages in the Pennines; painting, decorating and building work at an 18th century mansion run by a cooperative in Leeds; renovating an old church for use as a peace centre in Berwick-upon-Tweed; and helping with general farmwork and restoring farm buildings at a Camphill village near Dumfries. Projects combining manual and social work also arranged; these normally involve painting, decorating, converting, renovating, maintenance and conservation work, building and gardening at schools, homes and residential centres for the elderly and handicapped or emotionally disturbed children or adults, often working alongside the residents and joining in with the life of the community. Work/study camps are also organised on specific themes such as anti-racism, Third World solidarity, East-West cooperation, and tools for self-reliance for the Third World. There are approx 80 international workcamps all over Britain involving groups of 6-18 volunteers.

Ages 18+. Overseas volunteers must speak fluent English. Volunteers must be prepared to work hard, contributing actively to the work and team life. 35-40 hour week, 2-4 weeks, June-September. Food, accommodation and insurance provided, but not travel. Membership fee £25 (students £15, unwaged £10). Registration fee £20. B D PH

Applications from outside the UK: please see workcamp information on page 27.

UNITED NATIONS ASSOCIATION

International Youth Service, Welsh Centre for International Affairs, Temple of Peace, Cathays Park, Cardiff CF1 3AP Tel Cardiff 223088

Aims to assist in community development by acting as a means to stimulate new ideas and projects, encouraging the concept of voluntary work as a force in the common search for peace, equality, democracy and social justice. Volunteers are needed on workcamps. Recent projects have included the construction of the Welsh National Garden of Peace in Cardiff; excavating a medieval castle in Powys; helping at the Llangollen International Eisteddfod; and looking after handicapped children on holiday in Mid Glamorgan. Ages 17+, 18+ for overseas volunteers. Volunteers are expected to join in the activities of the local community, and to create a happy and effective project. 40 hour week. 2-4 weeks, July-September. Accommodation in church halls, hospitals, homes or community centres, food and insurance provided. Some camps are self-catering. Volunteers pay their own travel costs and pocket money and should take a sleeping bag. Registration fee £25. B D PH

Applications from outside the UK: please see workcamp information on page 27.

GENERAL

ARDMORE ADVENTURE LTD 11-15 High Street, Marlow, Buckinghamshire SL7 1AV Tel Marlow 890060

Organises activity holidays for young people at residential and day centres in the Thames Valley, Dorset and Wales. Administrative and managerial positions exist as centre directors and senior group leaders. Ages 18+. Applicants should be English speakers, preferably with experience of working with children. 2/8+ weeks, Easter and mid June-early September. Day centres 40 hours per week, residential centres 60 hours per week. Wages £45+ per week, depending on position. Full board, single or shared accommodation and insurance provided, but not travel. *UK nationals only.*

BEAUMONT CAMPS LTD Personnel Department, Corpus Christi House, 9 West Street, Godmanchester, Huntingdon, Cambridgeshire, PE18 8HG Tel Huntingdon 456123

Organises a wide range of holidays for children in American-style day and residential camps. Staff are recruited for 10 day and 8 residential camps throughout the country. Opportunities exist for NNEB qualified nursery leaders responsible for looking after and organising a programme for 3-5 year olds, SRN qualified camp nurses, administrative and book keeping staff, programme organisers, transport coordinators and PSV/HGV drivers. Staff at residential camps are responsible for groups of children aged 8-17, during the day, in the evening and at night when they sleep in the same tent or dormitory. Fluent French required for administrative posts at some residential centres. All staff must genuinely enjoy working with children, possess leadership ability, and be willing to work a long, hard, exhausting day enthusiastically in a structured setting where regulations apply to all. They must be available for the whole season, March/April or July/September. 5-9 weeks, including compulsory day/weekend orientation course, setting up and clearing camps. Ages 18-35. Day camp staff work a 45 hour week; residential staff work a 24 hour day, with 1 free day per week plus alternate nights off. Salary £40-£75 per week. Board and accommodation provided. PH

BUTLIN'S LIMITED Head Office, Bognor Regis, West Sussex PO21 1JJ
Provides family holidays and leisure facilities, encompassing accommodation, retailing, catering, amusement parks, professional entertainment and conferences, all on the same site. Vacancies exist in the retail and leisure areas, and for lifeguards, nurses, nursery nurses, entertainers, security staff, electricians and technicians, at centres in Ayr, Bognor Regis, Minehead, Pwllheli and Skegness. Relevant qualifications such as RGN, NNEB useful. Short and long term positions almost all year, exact dates varying according to centre. 39-45 hour week. Ages 16+, local applicants, 18+ others. Salary dependent on individual centres, accommodation, meals, uniform and staff entertainment programme provided. Use of the leisure and guest facilities and holiday discounts available. Applicants pay own insurance and travel costs. *EC nationals only.*

Apply direct to the preferred centre to: Wonderwest World, Heads of Ayr, KA7 4LB, Scotland; Southcoast World, Bognor Regis, West Sussex PO21 1JJ; Somerwest World, Minehead, Somerset TA24 5SH; Starcoast World, Pwllheli, Gwynedd, North Wales LL53 6HX; Funcoast World, Skegness, Lincolnshire PE25 1NJ.

CAREERS RESEARCH AND ADVISORY CENTRE (CRAC) Britain Australasia Vocational Exchange Scheme, 2nd floor, Sheraton House, Castle Park, Cambridge CB3 0AX Tel Cambridge 460277
Opportunities are available for Australian and New Zealand students to work and travel in Britain during their summer vacation. Gives students an opportunity to combine the adventure of travel with the challenge of meaningful work experience. 12 weeks, December-March. Students work for a minimum period of 8 weeks relating, wherever possible, to university studies. The remainder of the time is spent touring. Jobs have included work in commerce, government departments, industry and laboratories, with particular demand for those studying business studies, commerce, computing, engineering, electronics and laboratory work. Preference given to students in the penultimate or final year of a first degree course. Salary not less than £120 per week. Participants are responsible for own travel arrangements, accommodation and living costs. Registration fee £14. Placement fee £60. *Apply by 30 September.*

CHESSINGTON WORLD OF ADVENTURES Leatherhead Road, Chessington, Surrey KT9 2NE Tel Epsom 29560
A zoo and theme park, requiring seasonal staff to work as catering assistants, cashiers, ride operators, site cleaners, gardeners and shop assistants. No experience necessary as training is given, but staff must be enthusiastic and enjoy working as part of a team. 40 hour week, March-October. Ages 16+. Salary £2-£3 per hour, employers' liability insurance and subsidised staff canteen, but no accommodation provided. *Overseas applicants with work permits and good English welcome.*

COUNCIL ON INTERNATIONAL EDUCATIONAL EXCHANGE (CIEE) Work Abroad Department, 205 East 42nd Street, New York NY 10017, United States
Work in Britain/Student Exchange Employment Programme (SEEP) enables American students to have an educational and cultural experience through a period of work in Britain of up to 6 months. Programme participants may enter Britain at any time of year, and work in any type of employment; most students work in the service industries,

GREAT BRITAIN

GENERAL

GREAT BRITAIN

although many undertake career-oriented jobs. Ages 18+. Students must be residing and studying in the US at the time of application and enrolled as a matriculating student at an accredited college or university, or taking at least 8 credit hours. Applicants may either find a job before leaving the US or look for one on arrival. Advice on accommodation, travel, administrative procedures and finding a job provided at orientation session on arrival. The *SEEP Handbook* includes information contacts for employment and a regional employment guide. Administration fee $96.

UK partner organisation: British Universities North America Club (BUNAC), 16 Bowling Green Lane, London EC1R 0BD Tel 071-251 3472.

GENERAL

EUROP ASSISTANCE LTD 252 High Street, Croydon, Surrey CR0 1NF Tel 081-680 1234
Provides a 24 hour, year round worldwide medical, motoring and personal travel insurance service. Staff are required to work as coordinators/clerks and telex operators at the Croydon office. Experience not necessary, but a good telephone manner and English mother tongue preferred; fluency in other European languages a distinct advantage. Work involves liaising with agents in more than 200 countries to provide on the spot help, working with contacts in garages, transport companies, airlines, hospitals, doctors and local authorities. Ages 18+. 35 hour week in shifts. Approx 10 weeks, June-September. Salary by arrangement.

FAIRTHORNE MANOR YMCA National Centre, Curdridge, Southampton, Hampshire SO3 2GH Tel Botley 785228
Offers a wide range of outdoor educational activities for young people aged 8-20 on residential and day camps and provides visitors with a sense of community belonging in an outdoor environment. Volunteers are needed as groundstaff. Work involves being responsible to the estate manager for duties including grass cutting, tent erection and maintenance, preparation of estate for sports events and generally helping to maintain a high standard of cleanliness and tidiness. Ages 18+, preference given to older applicants. Leadership ability, enthusiasm, loyalty, sympathy with the aims of the Young Men's Christian Association movement needed. Staff

are carefully selected for their ability to relate to young people, and activities are seen as a means to develop this relationship. No set hours, 5 day week. 6 weeks, April-September. Full board, tent or other accommodation, £20 per week pocket money plus bonus, insurance and assistance with travel from point of entry provided that minimum work period of 6 weeks completed. *Overseas applicants welcome.*

HARRODS LTD Prospects, Brompton Road, Knightsbridge, London SW1X 7XL Tel 071-730 1234
London's famous department store requires seasonal staff for sales, administration, portering, driving and warehouse work. 41 hour week, July and January sales and pre-Christmas, September-December. Experience useful but not essential. Ages 16+. Salary £130 per week, sales/administration, £137 per week, warehouse work. Insurance and subsidised staff restaurant provided. *Overseas applicants must obtain their own work permits.* B D PH limited opportunities.

HUNTSHAM COURT Huntsham Village, Near Tiverton, Devon EX16 7NA Tel Clayhanger 210
Staff are required all through the year at a country house hotel in the heart of Devon. Offers the opportunity to learn different aspects of catering and hotel management in a warm, friendly atmosphere. Work is varied and interesting, and includes acting as waiter/waitress, catering and gardening. Classical musicians are also welcome, to assist with evening entertainment. Ages 18+. Willingness to learn is more important than experience, although cooks do require qualifications. Knowledge of English necessary. 15-40 hours per week. Pay from £45 per week, plus full board accommodation and insurance. *EC nationals only.*

THE IONA COMMUNITY Voluntary Staff Coordinator, Isle of Iona, Argyll, Strathclyde PA76 6SN Tel Iona 404
An ecumenical Christian community seeking new and radical ways of living the Gospel in today's world. On Iona the Community runs two centres, each welcoming up to 50 guests to a common life of work, worship, meals and recreation. Volunteers are needed to work in the Abbey shop. The work involves contact

with a large number of people and includes till work, serving, stocking shelves and cleaning. The ability and willingness to serve and work quickly under pressure for prolonged periods is essential. Also require a driver/general assistant to take luggage and provisions between the centres and the jetty. A full driver's licence is required, as is a willingness to work responsibly, often alone. An interest in meeting people is useful: the driver comes into contact with many staff, guests, day villagers and islanders. The work is demanding but rewarding, and the hours flexible. Most important is a willingness to join fully into the community life, which includes worship and social activities as well as work. Ages 18+. 6 day week, February-December. Full board, shared accommodation, pocket money of £14 per week and assistance with travel expenses within mainland Britain provided. *Applications received before 31 December given priority.*

MECCA LEISURE HOLIDAYS Personnel Department, 1 Portway, Port Solent, Portsmouth PO6 4TY Tel Portsmouth 201201
Runs nearly 30 holiday centres in coastal locations, providing fun family holidays. Staff are required for a variety of positions, including retail shop assistants, clerical/ reception workers, entertainments staff, nurses, nursery and playgroup staff. Applicants should have fluent English and a friendly, lively personality. Relevant qualifications required for some positions such as nurses, though full training is given. 39 hour week, plus overtime. 1+ months. Recruitment takes place all year; high season April-October. Ages 18+. Pay from £2.20 per hour, increasing after initial training; deduction made for live-in accommodation. Use of guest facilities when off duty.

PAX CHRISTI 9 Henry Road, London N4 2LH Tel 081-800 4612
Promotes international exchanges, forming an international community spirit to spread the church's teaching on peace, and encourages Christian participation in social and political life. Volunteers are needed to work in international summer youth hostels in London and possibly other cities, usually set up in school buildings, and providing bed and breakfast and light refreshment in the evenings. Each hostel is run by a team of 10-18

volunteers; approx two-thirds are from overseas. The aim is for the volunteers to form a lively international community to provide a welcoming and friendly atmosphere. Work involves reception duties, cleaning, cooking, shopping, laundry, publicity, accounts and the setting up and dismantling of beds, and is hard but often rewarding. Duties and free time are allocated on a rota basis so that everyone shares the menial as well as the more enjoyable aspects. Free time activities include picnics, sightseeing, sports, games, parties, theatre and cinema trips. Ages 19+. Approx 40 hour week. 4/5 weeks, July/August. Food, dormitory accommodation with self-catering facilities and insurance provided. Volunteers pay their own travel costs.

PGL YOUNG ADVENTURE LTD Personnel Department, Alton Court, Penyard Lane, Ross-on-Wye, Herefordshire HR9 5NR Tel Ross-on-Wye 764211
Organises outdoor adventure holidays in England, Wales and Scotland. Activities include pony trekking, sailing, canoeing, archery, hill walking, tennis, squash, arts and crafts, fencing, judo, rifle shooting, cycling, grass skiing, gymnastics, golf, badminton and many others. Staff are required for the following service and supplies positions:

Administrative assistants, generally acting as assistants to the manager and responsible for petty cash, staff wage sheets, lost property, programme schedules, reception, telephone enquiries and correspondence. Stores and site maintenance staff, responsible for the general appearance and cleanliness of the centre, with duties including litter control, maintaining tents and equipment, cutting grass, cleaning, painting, looking after stores, and maintenance and repair work; carpentry, plumbing, electrical experience welcome. Nurses, preferably RGN/SEN qualified, with a driving licence and experience in child nursing. Drivers, including PSV and HGV, responsible for looking after passengers and maintenance of vehicles. Gardeners, with horticultural interest and ability. Coffee bar/tuck shop staff, responsible for cleaning and organising the shop, displaying and selling the goods, stocktaking and taking charge of the money. Ages 18+, 21+ for drivers. Applicants should be fond of children, responsible, flexible, energetic and enthusiastic, patient, reliable and mature with a sense of humour, capable of working on their own initiative, and have the ability to cooperate with others as part of a team, contributing fully to the life of the centre. 4+ weeks, February-September. Staff are also recruited for short periods at Easter and the spring bank holiday. 1 day off per week. Full board and accommodation provided. Pocket money from £25-£40 per week for general positions, from £50 for nurses, from £75 for HGV/PSV drivers. Travel expenses paid by applicants. All staff can join in the activities during free periods and are encouraged to take part in evening activities with the guests. Staff may sometimes be asked to help out in areas other than their own. *Early application advisable; majority of positions filled by end June.*

STUDENTOURS 3 Harcourt Street, London W1H 1DS Tel 071-402 5131
Volunteers are required for various duties at youth centres in Kent and Sussex. Staff are needed to help on children's farms, looking after the animals plus maintenance of the nature study trails and assault course. Other duties involve gardening, maintenance of fences, restoring Victorian architecture and the Italian gardens. Workers are also required for general maintenance work in the grounds of the centres, for painting, cementing, building, construction and driving work. Volunteers can participate in the sports and activities organised at the centres. Ages 17+. 5+ hour day, 5 day week with evenings free. 2-6 months, all year. Accommodation, insurance and meals whilst on duty provided. At other times workers are provided with food but must do their own cooking. Pocket money from £35 per week. All tools and equipment supplied.

TOPS HOLIDAYS (SUN LIVING LTD) Personnel Manager, Adventure House, 34-36 South Street, Lancing, West Sussex BN15 8AG Tel Lancing 751942
Organises a range of specialised activity and outdoor education programmes for groups of school children aged 7-17 at centres in Herefordshire, Wales and throughout south east England. Each centre has its own team of staff who ensure that high standards of safety, instruction and enjoyment are maintained. Requires centre managers, responsible for running the centres and directing a large team

of young, inexperienced staff. Applicants should have wide ranging experience, proven ability, total commitment, good administrative and organisational skills and a willingness to work hard for the whole operational period. Staff often assist in all areas of the centre's operation and will need to be flexible.

Ages 18+; preference given to ages 20+. Applicants should enjoy being with children all day and have a genuine interest in their welfare. Fitness, stamina, enthusiasm and the ability to live and work as part of a team also essential. 40+ hour week, 1 day free per week. 1+ months, March-November. Most staff work the full season. Opportunities for staff to move from centre to centre. Full board provided, pay negotiable. Training provided to ensure staff are confident and able to carry out their responsibilities. Social and recreational activities such as parties, barbecues and outings arranged. *British nationals only.* B D PH limited opportunities.

WINDSOR SAFARI PARK Personnel Department, Winkfield Road, Windsor, Berkshire SL4 4AY Tel Windsor 830886
Famous for its reserves where animals live as in the wild and can be viewed by visitors from their cars. Requires seasonal workers to act as food and beverage assistants, rides and amusements operators, house and grounds maintenance staff and guest relations personnel in a leisure park with an African theme.No experience necessary. Also occasional possibility of specialised work in the animal sections; applicants must have relevant experience/qualifications. 40-48 hour week, February-October. Ages 16+. Salary dependent on age. Uniform and local travel provided; staff canteen available. No accommodation provided. B D PH

YOUTH HOSTELS ASSOCIATION England and Wales, National Office, Trevelyan House, 8 St Stephen's Hill, St Albans, Hertfordshire AL1 2DY Tel St Albans 55215
Aims to help all, especially young people of limited means, to a greater knowledge, love and care of the countryside particularly by providing hostels or other simple accommodation. Assistant wardens are required at youth hostels throughout England and Wales. Work involves domestic and

catering duties, helping to manage the hostel, reception work and other general duties, including shopping, cleaning, serving in the shop, bookwork and maintenance. Applicants should have a cheerful, outgoing personality; experience not necessary. Preference given to applicants prepared to work for most of the season. 2-6 months, all year; peak periods March-September. 5 day week, 2 days off per week or payment/time in lieu. Ages 18+. Salary £55-£60 per week, depending on location, full board accommodation and insurance provided. Travel expenses paid by applicants.

For further details contact the regional office of the area in which you wish to work: Cardiff 396766 (Wales); 091-284 7414 (Northern); Matlock 57751 (Central); or Salisbury 337515 (Southern).

APPLYING FOR A JOB

Read carefully all the information given before applying. Check in particular:

* the necessary skills/experience required

* the full period of employment expected

* any restrictions of age, sex or nationality

* application deadlines

* any other points, particularly details of insurance cover provided, and other costs such as travel and accommodation.

When applying be sure to include:

* name, address, date of birth, marital status, nationality, sex

* education, qualifications, relevant experience

* period of availability

* details of languages spoken

* a large stamped, self-addressed envelope plus, if overseas, 2 International Reply Coupons

* a passport-size photo, particularly if you are to have contact with the public

* any registration or membership fees

When applying to any organisation it is essential to mention Working Holidays 1991 and enclose a large stamped, self-addressed envelope, or if overseas, a large addressed envelope and at least two International Reply Coupons.

NOTES

GREECE

Greek Embassy
1a Holland Park, London W11 3TP
Tel 071-727 8040

British Embassy
1 Ploutarchou Street, Athens

Tourist office
National Tourist Organisation of Greece,
4 Conduit Street, London W1R 0DJ
Tel 071-734 5997

Youth hostels
Greek YHA, 4 Dragatsaniou Street, Athens

Youth & student information
British Travel and Student Service, 10 Stadiou
Street, Athens

International Student & Youth Travel, 11 Nikis
Street, Syntagma Square, 105 57 Athens

STS, 1 Felellindy Street, Syntagma Square,
Athens

INFORMATION

Entry regulations A UK citizen intending to work in Greece should have a full passport. EC nationals may stay for up to 3 months in order to look for or take up employment, after which a residence permit will be required. To obtain a residence permit, applicants should go to the Aliens' Department of the Ministry of Public Order in Athens, or outside Athens, to the local police station. Citizens of non-EC countries require a work permit and a temporary residence permit, which should be applied for by the prospective employer from the local prefecture. Applicants will be notified once permission has been granted, and should take their passport to the Greek Consulate in their home country to be stamped. This entitles the applicant to obtain a residence permit from the Aliens' Department and a work permit from the local prefecture, on arrival in Greece. During the time of this procedure the applicant should not be resident in Greece. Job opportunities are extremely limited and permits are only issued in cases where the work necessitates the employment of a foreigner, and in some professions of special interest. It is against the immigration regulations to enter Greece as a tourist to seek and/or take up employment, and any persons so doing risk refusal of leave to enter Greece and/or deportation. An information sheet, *Residence and Employment*, is available from the Labour Counsellor Office, the Greek Embassy.

Job advertising Publicitas Ltd, 525/527 Fulham Road, London SW6 1HF Tel 071-385 7723 are agents for various Greek morning and evening journals, weeklies, monthlies and magazines.

Travel STA Travel, 86 Old Brompton Road, London SW7 3LQ Tel 071-937 9921 operates flexible low cost flights between London and destinations throughout Greece.

Campus Travel, 52 Grosvenor Gardens, London SW1W 0AG Tel 071-730 3402 offers student/youth fares and summer charter flights to Athens, plus Eurotrain under 26 fares.

The Greek Tourist Card allows unlimited travel on rail and bus services of the Greek State Railways. Reduced rates available where 2-5 travel together. Cost from £23.70 (10 days). Available from YHA Travel, 14 Southampton Street, London WC2E 7HY Tel 071-240 5236.

The Rough Guide to Greece £6.95 and *The Rough Guide to Crete* £4.95 are practical handbooks with full details on historic sites, including some of the less well-known ones, plus a wealth of practical information on getting around the country and on cheap places to stay. Published by Harrap Columbus, Chelsea House, 26 Market Square, Bromley, Kent BR1 1NA.

GREECE

Information centres International Student & Youth Travel Service, 11 Nikis Street, 2nd Floor, Syntagma Square, 105 57 Athens is the official student and youth travel service specialising in tickets for domestic and international air, sea and land travel, plus information on cheap hotel accommodation, excursions, tours, cruises and festivals. Also issues student cards and provides free welcome and poste restante service.

Accommodation National Tourist Organisation of Greece, see above, issues *Camping*, a booklet listing sites run by them, situated by the sea and equipped with modern facilities.

Young Women's Christian Association of Greece, 11 Amerikis Street, 106 72 Athens offers accommodation at Heliopolis YWCA centre near Athens airport for all young people. Can also provide bed and breakfast hostel accommodation in single and double bedded rooms for females only travelling through Athens or Salonika.

AU PAIR/ CHILDCARE

AU PAIR/CHILDCARE

HELPING HANDS AU PAIR & DOMESTIC AGENCY 10 Hertford Road, Newbury Park, Ilford, Essex IG2 7HQ Tel 081-597 3138
Au pair and mother's help positions available all year. Au pairs work approx 30 hours per week plus 3 evenings babysitting and earn approx £25 per week. Mother's helps work longer hours for a higher salary. Board and lodging provided. 6+ months. Ages 18-27. Applicants should be willing, helpful and adaptable. Insurance and travel costs paid by the applicant, but assistance with the arrangements provided. Introduction fee £40 on acceptance of a family. *UK nationals only.*

CONSERVATION

JOLAINE AGENCY 18 Escot Way, Barnet, Hertfordshire EN5 3AN Tel 081-449 1334
Au pair and mother's help posts arranged throughout the year. Au pairs work a 5 hour day with 3/4 evenings babysitting per week. Afternoons plus 1 full day free per week. Mother's helps work an 8 hour day with 1½

days free per week, plus some evenings and other time by arrangement. Ages 17-27. 6+ months, all year. Summer holiday posts also available, looking after children and doing light household duties. 3+ months, June-October. Pocket money from £25+ per week. Travel and insurance paid by applicants. Introduction fee £40.

STUDENTS ABROAD AGENCY Elm House, 21b The Avenue, Hatch End, Middlesex HA5 4EN Tel 081-428 5823
Can place au pairs and mother's helps. Long-term positions available all year as well as a number of 3+ month placements during the summer. At least 1 full day free per week. Salary from £25 per week. Board and lodging provided. Ages 18+. Knowledge of Greek not necessary. Applicants should like, and have the ability to cope with, children, babies and housework. Advice given on travel and insurance. Service charge £40. *Apply early for temporary summer positions.*

YOUNG WOMEN'S CHRISTIAN ASSOCIATION OF GREECE 11 Amerikis Street, 106 72 Athens
Offer a counselling service which can provide information on au pair work with Greek families.

CONSERVATION

BRITISH TRUST FOR CONSERVATION VOLUNTEERS Room IWH, 36 St Mary's Street, Wallingford, Oxfordshire OX10 0EU
The largest charitable organisation in Britain to involve people in practical conservation work. Following the success of the Natural Break Programme in the UK, BTCV is now developing a series of international working holidays with the aim of introducing the volunteering ethic to communities abroad. It is hoped that British volunteers will adapt to and learn from local lifestyles as well as participate in the community. Recent projects have included footpath construction in the Evros Forest. 2-3 weeks. Ages 18-70. Cost from £100 includes food and camping/dormitory accommodation. Everyone shares in the cooking. Membership fee £10.

WORKCAMPS

INTERNATIONAL VOLUNTARY SERVICE 162 Upper New Walk, Leicester LE1 7QA Tel Leicester 549430

IVS is the British branch of Service Civil International, which promotes international reconciliation through work projects. Volunteers are needed to work in international teams on various workcamps. Recent projects have included preparing a holiday camp for autistic children on Aegina and planning entertainment evenings, games and sports; gathering water samples from springs on the island of Andros for analysis; building low stone walls on the island of Naxos to prevent further soil erosion; organising a campaign promoting cycling in Thessalia; creating a forest park in Ferres in Thrace; and renovating houses and bridges in Zagoria. Volunteers should preferably have previous workcamp experience.

Ages 18+. Applicants should be prepared to work hard and contribute to team life. 35-40 hour week. 2-4 weeks, June-September. Food and basic accommodation provided but not travel. Volunteers prepare and cook their own meals. Membership fee £25 (students £15, unwaged £10). Registration fee £40. B D PH

Organised by Service Civil International, Erika Kalamatzi, 59 Kefallimias Street, 11 251 Athens.

Applications from outside the UK: please see workcamp information on page 27.

GENERAL

EUROYOUTH LTD 301 Westborough Road, Westcliff-on-Sea, Essex SS0 9PT Tel Southend-on-Sea 341434

Offers holiday guest stays where guests are offered board and lodging in return for an agreed number of hours English conversation with hosts or their children. Time is also available for guests to practise Greek if desired. Mainly ages 15-25, but there are sometimes opportunities for ages 13-16 and for older applicants. 2-3 weeks, June-August. Travel and insurance paid by the applicant. Registration fee £60. *Apply at least 12 weeks prior to scheduled departure date. UK nationals only.*

INTERTOM HELLAS International Trust Office Mediators, 24-26 Halkokondili Street, Athens 104 32 Tel 52 39 470

Can place hotel, bar, disco and office staff throughout Greece including Athens and a number of the islands. Salaries from 40,000-65,000 drachmas per month, plus board and lodging provided. Can also place house keepers, mother's helps, nannies and au pairs. Airport reception service.

NATIONAL TOURIST ORGANISATION OF GREECE 4 Conduit Street, London W1R 0DJ Tel 071-734 5997

Publishes an annual guide of UK tour companies operating in Greece, including student travel and educational organisations. Lists a range of holidays, including camping, cruising, yachting, flotilla, island-hopping, coach tours and special interest, in Athens, the Apollo, East and South Western coasts of Attica, Central, Western and Northern Greece, Peloponnese, the North Eastern Aegean, Sporades, Dodecanese, Cyclades, Saronic and Ionian Islands, and Crete. Many tour operators need staff during the high season, such as couriers, representatives, domestics, chalet maids, yacht skippers, crews and maintenance staff, and the guide gives a comprehensive list of organisations to contact.

PIONEER TOURS Working Holiday, 11 Nikis Street, Syntagma Square, Athens 105 57

Organises a variety of working holidays all over Greece, including hotel work, au pair work and fruit picking. Ages 18+. Relevant experience sometimes required, also knowledge of English. 8 hour day, 6 day week. Work available mainly in summer. Pay Drs1000 per day, plus food and accommodation. Travel paid from Athens to place of work by employer; return fare back to Athens paid after 1+ month's work. Registration fee £20. *EC nationals only.*

SUNSAIL The Port House, Port Solent, Portsmouth PO6 4TH Tel Portsmouth 219847

Crew members required to work aboard cruising yachts sailing in flotillas around the Greek islands. Vacancies for experienced skippers to be responsible for the wellbeing of up to 13 cruising yachts and 60 holiday makers, to give daily briefings on navigation, and provide sailing assistance where necessary.

GREECE

Applicants must have considerable sailing experience, be cheerful, hardworking and able to deal with people of varying backgrounds and ages. Ages 23-30.

Also bosuns/mechanics needed, responsible to the skipper for maintaining the marine diesel engines and repairing any other items aboard. Must have excellent knowledge of marine diesels and practical ability to cope with all sorts of breakdowns and repairs. Ages 22-30.

Hostesses are required to look after laundry, accounting, and cleaning of boats, to advise holiday makers on shops and restaurants, and to organise social events and barbecues. Sailing experience useful, but bright personality, patience and adaptability essential. Ages 22-30.

GENERAL

All staff should be prepared for very hard work and long hours. 12+ hour day, 1 free day per week. Knowledge of German advantageous but not essential. Mid March-November. Wages approx £85 per week, paid monthly. Accommodation on board, return travel and medical insurance provided.

When writing to any organisation it is essential to mention Working Holidays 1991 and enclose a large stamped, self-addressed envelope, or if overseas, a large addressed envelope and at least two International Reply Coupons.

HUNGARY

Hungarian Embassy
35 Eaton Place, London SW1X 8BV
Tel 071-235 4048   Visa section: Tel 071-235 2664

British Embassy
Budapest V, Harmincad Utca 6

Tourist office
Danube Travel Ltd, 6 Conduit Street, London
W1R 9TG Tel 071-493 0263

Youth hostels
Hungarian YHA, 1395 Budapest V,
Semmelweis utca 4

Youth & student information
International Bureau for Youth Tourism &
Exchange (BITEJ), Budapest VI, Kaldygy 6

Express Youth & Student Travel Bureau, 1395
Budapest V, Semmelweis utca 4

INFORMATION

Entry regulations Workcamp organisations will inform volunteers how to obtain the necessary visa/permit and hold orientation days for volunters going to East Europe, giving information on all aspects of the work covered together with some political background and practical information.

Travel Campus Travel, 52 Grosvenor Gardens, London SW1W 0AG Tel 071-730 3402 offer Eurotrain under 26 fares and student/youth flights to Budapest.

Hungary Tourist Information is a free annual booklet giving information on travel, entry formalities, customs, insurance, transport, accommodation, entertainment, sports and other useful information and addresses. Available from Danube Travel Ltd, see above.

The Rough Guide to Eastern Europe £7.95 is a practical handbook covering Hungary, Bulgaria and Romania, and packed with useful and unusual information. Published by Harrap Columbus, Chelsea House, 26 Market Square, Bromley, Kent BR1 1NA.

FARMWORK

INTERNATIONAL FARM EXPERIENCE PROGRAMME YFC Centre National Agricultural Centre, Kenilworth, Warwickshire CV8 2LG Tel Coventry 696584
Provides assistance to young farmers and nurserymen by finding places on farms and nurseries, with opportunities to live and work with the Hungarian people. Placements provide a varied programme offering experience of private farms as well as state cooperatives. Ages 18-26. 3-12 months. Board, lodging, pocket money and some travel expenses provided. Applicants must have at least 2 years practical experience, 1 year of which may have been at agricultural college, and intend to make a career in agriculture or horticulture. Registration fee £62. *British nationals only.*

MONITORS & TEACHERS

CENTRAL BUREAU Schools Unit, Seymour Mews House, Seymour Mews, London W1H 9PE Tel 071-486 5101 ext 277
Teachers, students and sixth formers are required at English language camps, the main objective of which is to provide Hungarian pupils, aged 16-19, with the opportunity of practising English learnt in school, and by spending 3 weeks in the company of a group of British teachers and young people to acquire a deeper awareness of the British way of life. Duties include assisting with the teaching of English as a foreign language, running conversation classes and organising sporting, musical and social activities including drama,

HUNGARY

embroidery, folk dancing and singing workshops. Ages up to 45. Applicants should be native English speakers, sixth formers or those aged 16-19 and willing to assist the staff; or teachers qualified in the teaching of any discipline: EFL or ESL qualifications an advantage. Applicants should have a sense of responsibility, organisational skill, adaptability to new surroundings, a sociable nature and an ability and interest in sports and/or drama and music, plus experience in working with or teaching children. Participants must fully commit themselves to the teaching of English and the organisation of various educational, outdoor and social activities. 3 weeks, July/August. Board and accommodation at school, sharing with the pupils, provided. Excursions and visits to places of interest arranged by the host school and 3 day trip to visit places of interest on the return to Budapest. Group travel cost approx £150, including insurance and visa, paid by applicants. 1 day briefing session in June/July. Organised by the Hungarian Ministry of Education under the auspices of UNESCO. *Apply by mid April.*

MONITORS & TEACHERS

WORKCAMPS

INTERNATIONAL VOLUNTARY SERVICE
162 Upper New Walk, Leicester LE1 7QA
Tel Leicester 549430

UNITED NATIONS ASSOCIATION
International Youth Service, Welsh Centre for International Affairs, Temple of Peace, Cathays Park, Cardiff CF1 3AP Tel Cardiff 223088

Apply to either of the above to join a work/study camp. Camps are organised for 40-80 participants and dedicated to themes of common concern and interest; volunteers share information about their experiences relating to the themes. Work begins very early in the morning, with afternoons and evenings free for discussions, lectures, excursions, visits plus cultural and leisure activities. Recent projects have included laying paths through a forest; excavation work at an old mine; working in the canning factory of an agricultural cooperative; gardening, painting and environmental work; and park cleaning in the city of Szeged. Study

WORKCAMPS

themes include important issues of our planet, South Africa and present day Hungary. The official languages of the camps are English and Russian. Ages 18-30. Previous workcamp experience essential. 6-8 hour day, 5 day week. 2-3 weeks, July and August. Board and lodging provided in student hostels, huts or tents. Travel costs to camp not included. Participants applying through IVS should attend an orientation meeting.

Organised by KISZ, PO Box 72, 1138 Budapest.

Applications from outside the UK: please see workcamp information on page 27.

When writing to any organisation it is essential to mention Working Holidays 1991 and enclose a large stamped, self-addressed envelope, or if overseas, a large addressed envelope and at least two International Reply Coupons.

ICELAND

Icelandic Embassy
1 Eaton Terrace, London SW1W 8EY
Tel 071-730 5131

British Embassy
Laufasvegur 49, 101 Reykjavik

Tourist office
Icelandair, 172 Tottenham Court Road, London
W1P 9LG Tel 071-388 5599

Youth hostels
Icelandic YHA, Bandalag Islenskra Farfugla,
Laufasvegur 41, 101 Reykjavik

Youth & student information
Iceland Tourist Board, Laufasvegur 3, 101
Reykjavik

INFORMATION

Entry regulations Foreign nationals may not seek or accept employment in Iceland after their arrival in the country unless they have a prior working permit. This must be applied for from the Ministry of Social Affairs by the prospective employer on behalf of the foreign national, and the employer must show sufficient proof that the foreign national will fill a position for which no skilled Icelander is presently available. British nationals do not need a visa to visit Iceland, but must be in possession of a return travel ticket, have a re-entry permit into their country of origin, and show sufficient funds for their support during their intended stay. Provided these requirements are met, they may stay in Iceland for a period of up to 3 months; extensions may be granted by the nearest police authority.

Information centres Dick Phillips, Specialist Icelandic Travel Service, Whitehall House,

Nenthead, Alston, Cumbria CA9 3PS Tel Alston 381440 can give details on the physical environment and general advice, and stocks maps and most of the relevant English language publications including guides and books on Icelandic life, environment and history. Hostelling, walking, riding and motorised tours of Iceland organised. Can also book travel by ferry from Lerwick or Scrabster, from £124 single, May-September.
25% reduction to holders of international student cards. Sea passage from Aberdeen to Lerwick can be arranged. *Personal callers welcome October-June.*

The Rough Guide to Scandinavia £7.95 is a practical handbook which includes concise, up-to-date information on getting around Iceland. Published by Harrap Columbus, Chelsea House, 26 Market Square, Bromley, Kent, BR1 1NA.

CONSERVATION

BRITISH TRUST FOR CONSERVATION VOLUNTEERS Room IWH, 36 St Mary's Street, Wallingford, Oxfordshire OX10 0EU
The largest charitable organisation in Britain to involve people in practical conservation work. Since 1983 Trust members have been assisting the Icelandic Nature Conservancy Council with footpath maintenance work in the Skaftafell National Park. Volunteers work alongside

locals, and should be prepared for hard physical work. The constant daylight means that there are plenty of opportunities for walking, climbing and exploring the spectacular land and ice scape. Ages 18+.
10-14 days, June-July. Cost £300+ includes food and flight. Camping accommodation, cooking facilities and insurance provided.

NOTES

IRELAND

Irish Embassy
17 Grosvenor Place, London SW1X 7HR
Tel 071-235 2171

British Embassy
33 Merrion Road, Dublin 4 Tel Dublin 695211

Tourist office
Irish Tourist Office, Ireland House, 150 New
Bond Street, London W1Y 0AQ
Tel 071-493 3201

Youth hostels
An Oige Irish YHA, 39 Mountjoy Square,
Dublin 1 Tel Dublin 363111

Youth & student information
Union of Students in Ireland, 16 North Great
George's Street, Dublin 1 Tel Dublin 786020

Union of Students in Ireland Travel Service
(USIT), Aston Quay, O'Connell Bridge, Dublin
2 Tel Dublin 778117

National Youth Council of Ireland, 3 Montague
Street, Dublin 2 Tel Dublin 784122

INFORMATION

Entry regulations UK citizens intending to
work in Ireland do not need a passport, but
should produce evidence of their place of birth;
those born in Northern Ireland may claim Irish
nationality. Citizens of other member states of
the EC do not require work permits. Those
interested in working in Ireland can consult the
training and employment authority, FAS, 27-33
Upper Baggot Street, Dublin 4 Tel Dublin
685777, or consider advertising in a newspaper.
UK applicants for work may complete form
ES13 at their local Jobcentre, which is then
forwarded to the FAS.

Information centres Community and Youth
Information Centre, Sackville House, Sackville
Place, Dublin 1 Tel Dublin 786844 offers
information on a wide range of subjects
including education, employment agencies,
rights, sports, travel and accommodation.

Travel CIE Tours International, 185 London
Road, Croydon, Surrey CR0 2RJ Tel 081-667
0011 issues the Rambler ticket entitling the
holder to unlimited rail and bus travel; cost
£75/£110 (8/15 days).

Campus Travel, 52 Grosvenor Gardens, London
SW1W 0AG Tel 071-730 3402 offers student/
youth airfares, student coach fares and

Eurotrain under 26 fares. Student/youth ferry
fares for car travel also available. Issues
Travelsave stamps for ISIC cards, entitling
holders up to 50% discount on Irish rail and
coach travel.

Publications *Irish Youth Handbook* £1.95 plus
£1.50 postage, is a useful reference and
resource aid which provides detailed
information on voluntary youth organisations
together with a comprehensive list of useful
addresses, youth travel and accommodation.
Published by and available from the National
Youth Council of Ireland, 3 Montague Street,
Dublin 2 Tel Dublin 784122.

Accommodation Kinlay House
Accommodation Centre, 2-12 Lord Edward
Street, Dublin, owned and run by USIT, see
above, provides low cost hostel
accommodation in the centre of Dublin.

**When writing to any organisation it is
essential to mention Working Holidays 1991
and enclose a large stamped, self-addressed
envelope, or if overseas, a large addressed
envelope and at least two International Reply
Coupons.**

AU PAIR/ CHILDCARE

INTERLINGUA CENTRE Torquay Road, Foxrock, Dublin 18 Tel Dublin 893876
Can place au pairs in Irish families. 30 hour week with one full day and some evenings off. Time off to attend language classes 2-3 mornings or afternoons per week. Experience desirable but not essential. 6+ months. Ages 18+. £25-£40 per week pocket money, full board, lodging and insurance provided. Travel paid by applicant. Placement fee £55.

COMMUNITY WORK

INTERNATIONAL VOLUNTARY SERVICE 162 Upper New Walk, Leicester LE1 7QA Tel Leicester 549430
IVS is the British branch of Service Civil International which promotes international reconciliation through work projects. Volunteers are needed to work in international teams on various community workcamps. Recent projects have included helping to run the Navan Travellers Summer Project with the aim of improving facilities for Travellers, organising sports, arts/crafts, games, discos and outings for Travellers' children and youth with talks on their life and culture, in Co Meath; organising playschemes of creative, recreational and educational activities in an inner city area of Dublin and in Kilkenny; and helping to clean, paint and repair a drop-in centre/restaurant for unemployed teenagers in Waterford. Ages 18+. Previous workcamp or other voluntary experience preferred. Volunteers must be prepared to work hard and contribute to team life. 35-40 hour week, 2-4 weeks, June-September. Food, accommodation and insurance provided, but not travel. Membership fee £25 (students £15, unwaged £10). Registration fee £40. **B D PH**

Organised by Voluntary Service International, 37 North Great George's Street, Dublin 1 Tel Dublin 788679.

Applications from outside the UK: please see workcamp information on page 27.

CONSERVATION

GROUNDWORK (IRELAND) 43 Bayview Drive, Killeney, Co Dublin
A branch of the Irish Wildlife Federation which carries out vital conservation tasks that would otherwise not be possible. Volunteers of all nationalities are required to assist with this work by taking part in workcamps. Recent projects have included blocking drainage channels in Mongans and Clara Bogs to prevent them drying out; and clearing rhododendron which is threatening the ecosystems of oak and birch woodlands in the Killarney and Glenveagh National Parks. Terrain is difficult and the weather and insects sometimes make conditions unpleasant. Access to woods is by Landrover or boat. Ages 16+. No experience necessary. Basic English required. Volunteers should be prepared for demanding, messy work. 35 hour week. 1+ weeks, end June-end August. Opportunities to visit local places of interest and take boat trips. Self-catering hostel or camping accommodation and insurance provided. IR£10 booking fee for first week, IR£5 for successive weeks.

IRISH GEORGIAN SOCIETY Leixlip Castle, Leixlip, County Kildare Tel Dublin 244211
Works for the preservation of Ireland's architectural heritage, with particular reference to the Georgian period. It carries out rescue and repair work and has helped to save many buildings. Under the supervision of craftsmen, volunteers carry out a wide variety of work including painting, cleaning, stripping and reglazing windows, removing rubble, stripping wallpaper, eradicating rotten timbers and oil treating doors. Recent projects have included removing ivy and replacing missing slates at a mausoleum in Shanrahan, Co Tipperary; assisting in the renovation of Doneraile Court, a large country house in Co Cork; and working on the restoration of paintings at Woodbrook, Portarlington. Excursions arranged to local buildings of interest. No experience needed.

Ages 17+. 8 hour day. 2 weeks, May-August. Basic accommodation and public liability insurance provided. Participants pay own travel costs, contribute IR£20 towards food and should take plenty of old clothes and a sleeping bag. *Applications should be made early in the year as places are limited.*

UNITED NATIONS ASSOCIATION
International Youth Service, Welsh Centre for International Affairs, Temple of Peace, Cathays Park, Cardiff CF1 3AP Tel Cardiff 223088
Volunteers are needed on conservation, renovation and other manual projects, organised by Comhchairdeas, an organisation providing practical assistance to Irish communities with the aim of supporting and stimulating local voluntary efforts while giving young people an insight into existing problems and living conditions and enabling them to contribute to their solution. Recent projects have included restoring the Royal gunpowder mills at Ballincollig, County Cork; working on an organic farm in County Dublin; renovating a Georgian mansion in County Roscommon; and conservation work in County Wicklow and the Killarney National Park. Ages 17/18+. 40 hour week. Approx 3 weeks, June-August. Food and accommodation provided in school halls, youth clubs or community centres. Communal cooking on rota basis. Registration fee from £35 includes insurance. Travel paid by applicants. **B D PH**

Organised by Comhchairdeas, The Irish Workcamps Movement, 7 Lower Ormond Quay, Dublin 1 Tel Dublin 729681.

Applications from outside the UK: please see workcamp information on page 27.

FARMWORK

WILLING WORKERS ON ORGANIC FARMS (WWOOF) c/o Annie Sampson, Crowhill, Newgrove, Tulla, Clare
A non-profitmaking organisation which aims to help farmers and smallholders who need manpower to replace the use of herbicides, chemical fertilisers and heavy machinery. Provides unskilled voluntary workers with first hand experience of organic farming and gardening, and a chance to spend some time on thirty eight holdings throughout Ireland. The work can include working with horses, cows,

goats, sheep, pigs and various fowl; all aspects of organic gardening, cutting turf, preserving fruit and vegetables; making various cheeses and yoghurt, stonewalling, hedging and renovating. Members receive a current list of holdings together with a short description of each one. Length of stay can be weekend, week, month or longer by arrangement. Ages 16+. Opportunities to learn crafts. Full board and lodging provided in the farmhouse and outbuildings; volunteers should take sleeping bags. No wages paid, and helpers must pay their own travel costs. Insurance and anti-tetanus vaccination recommended. Membership fee £3.

WORKCAMPS

INTERNATIONAL VOLUNTARY SERVICE 162 Upper New Walk, Leicester LE1 7QA Tel Leicester 549430
IVS is the British branch of Service Civil International, which promotes international reconciliation through work projects. Volunteers are needed to work in international teams on various workcamps, which have recently included cleaning, renovating and painting in the James Joyce Cultural Centre in Dublin; clearing and terracing a section of the Royal Canal near Ballinaacarrigy; helping to create a nature garden in a school in Cork; cutting, stacking and transporting peat, and preparing for a summer festival at a centre for reconciliation in Wicklow; reclaiming an overgrown field to convert into a tree nursery in Leitrim; and outdoor manual work at a Camphill Community for handicapped adults in Wexford.
Ages 18+. Previous workcamp or other voluntary experience preferred. Volunteers must be prepared to work hard and contribute to team life. 35-40 hour week, 2-4 weeks, June-September. Food, accommodation and insurance provided, but not travel. Membership fee £25 (students £15, unwaged £10). Registration fee £40. **PH**

Organised by Voluntary Service International, 37 North Great George's Street, Dublin 1 Tel Dublin 788679.

Applications from outside the UK: please see workcamp information on page 27.

NOTES

ISRAEL

Israeli Embassy
2 Palace Green, London W8 4QB Tel 071-937 8050

British Embassy
192 Rehov Hayarkon, Tel Aviv 63405

Tourist office
Israel Government Tourist Office, 18 Great Marlborough Street, London W1V 1AF Tel 071-434 3651

Youth hostels
Israel Youth Hostels Association, Youth Travel Bureau, PO Box 1075, 3 Dorot Rishonim Street, Jerusalem

Youth & student information
Israel Students' Tourist Association (ISSTA), 109 Ben Yehuda Street, Tel Aviv 63401

Kibbutz Representatives, 1a Accommodation Road, London NW11 8ED Tel 081-458 9235

The Public Council for Exchange of Youth and Young Adults, 67 Pinsker Street, Tel Aviv

INFORMATION

Entry regulations A work permit is required for employment in Israel, and this should be obtained by the prospective employer on application to the Ministry of the Interior, who will then authorise the issue of a visa. It is important that a permit is arranged before leaving for Israel; volunteers on kibbutzim, moshavim or archaeological digs will receive their visas on arrival.

Applicants should be aware that it is now more difficult to find a place on a kibbutz, and are strongly advised not to travel to Israel if they have not arranged a place prior to departure. Immigration officials are making it very difficult for one-way ticket holders to enter Israel; kibbutz and moshav volunteers should be able to produce a return or open ticket plus proof of sufficient means of support whilst in the country, at the port of entry. The cost of living is high and no volunteer should leave for Israel with less than £100 spending and emergency money. General employment opportunities are limited and a work permit will only be granted if a vacancy cannot be filled by local manpower. British Visitors Passports are not accepted for entry into Israel; all passports must be valid for 6+ months from the date of departure from Israel.

Travel North-South Travel Ltd, Moulsham Mill, Parkway, Chelmsford CM2 7PX Tel Chelmsford 492882 arranges competitively priced, reliably planned flights to Israel. Profits are paid into a trust fund for the assignment of aid to projects in the poorest areas of the South.

STA Travel, 86 Old Brompton Road, London SW7 3LQ Tel 071-937 9921 operates flexible low-cost flights between London and Tel Aviv.

Israel: A Youth and Student Adventure is a comprehensive booklet with information on cheap accommodation, free tours, museums, home hospitality, sports facilities, events, study courses and volunteer work, plus medical aid, hitching and useful addresses. A *Visitor's Companion* is a free 48 page booklet containing a wealth of useful information covering entry regulations, currency, climate, accommodation, travel, shopping, eating out, cultural activities and entertainment and sport. Both available from the Israel Government Tourist Office, see above.

Accommodation *Israel Chalets & Camping* gives details of facilities, local places of interest and dates of opening of 16 sites run by the Israel Camping Union.
Kibbutz Inns Guest Houses lists 25 inns offering board and accommodation; facilities include private beaches, swimming pools and tennis courts. *Christian Hospices in Israel* lists approx 40 hospices offering board and accommodation. All available from the Israel Government Tourist Office, see above.

ISRAEL

ARCHAEOLOGY

ARCHAEOLOGY

DOR/NAHSHOLIM CENTER OF NAUTICAL AND REGIONAL ARCHAEOLOGY Mr Kurt Raveh, Department of Antiquities and Museums Maritime Center, PO Box 114, Kibbutz Nahsholim, Doar-Na Hof Carmel 30815

Located in a 19th century glass factory, the Dor Center is the home base for the Department's maritime inspection team, underwater archaeology and Tel Dor area excavations. Volunteers are needed throughout the year to help with rescue excavations, underwater survey and excavation, field work including diving, technical and restoration work, and in the museum for clerical and tour guide work. Reduced rate accommodation in kibbutz beach guest houses. Applicants arrange own insurance and pay travel costs.

DEPARTMENT OF CLASSICAL STUDIES Professor M Gichon, Division of Archaeology, Yad Avner, Ramat Aviv, Tel Aviv 69978

Volunteers are required for excavations of town fortifications and public buildings at two sites at Horvat Eqed and Emmaus, dating from the Hellenistic to the Roman and Byzantine period, located in the Judaean foothills. 1+ weeks, July-August. 6½ hour day with 1 hour rest. Accommodation provided at a cost of $13 per day. No charge for senior students, postgraduates in archaeology or experienced diggers, provided arrangements are made in advance. No fares, insurance or wages paid. Ages 16+. Lectures in history, archaeology and geography provided as well as trips and recreational activities. Also opportunities for volunteers to work on processing of archaeological finds, under supervision, November-June.

THE HEBREW UNIVERSITY OF JERUSALEM The Director, Institute of Archaeology, Mount Scopus, Jerusalem 91905

Conducts excavations all over Israel, concerned with the prehistoric, Biblical and classical periods. Recent excavations have included a dig at Yoqne'am which include Islamic, Crusader and Bronze Age remains near Haifa; a large Iron Age site at Miqne/Ekron, one of 5 Philistine capital cities; and Persian, Iron Age,

Hellenistic and Roman period remains at Tel Dor. 2-6 weeks, June-August. Lectures on Biblical archaeology and visits to other sites. 7-9 hour day, starting early in the morning. Accommodation provided for small fee. Volunteers pay own travel and insurance. Applicants should write, indicating the period and vicinity they are interested in, and the dates when they will be available.

ISRAEL ANTIQUITIES AUTHORITY Ministry of Education and Culture, PO Box 586, Rockefeller Museum, Jerusalem 91004

Volunteers are needed to help on excavations dating from the prehistoric era through to Crusader times. Recent excavations have been carried out at over 30 sites and have included a major port on the Mediterranean coast dating back to the Herodian, Roman, Early Byzantine and Islamite periods; an ancient city with early Bronze, Hellenistic and Roman remains in the Golan Heights; a castle and village with Crusader, Mamluk and Ottoman remains; Bronze Age remains of a fortified city near Naharriya; a Chalcolithic village in the Negev desert; an Iron Age site in the Inner Coastal Plain; and a prehistoric site in Galilee. Work includes digging, shovelling, and hauling baskets, with cleaning and sorting pottery in the afternoons. Excavations are conducted throughout the year, but the main season is May-September. 2+ weeks. The Authority also conducts rescue excavations and emergency surveys throughout the year on short notice. Ages 18+. Experience not needed, but volunteers should be highly motivated, fit and able to work long hours in very hot weather. Lectures and field trips organised. On some sites volunteers may have to pay a fee or provide a medical certificate. Insurance obligatory. Travel to Israel paid by volunteers. *Archaeological Excavations* published annually in March, gives details of digs arranged all over Israel. When applying it is helpful to indicate any previous studies or experience in archaeology, anthropology, geography, excavation work or related fields such as architecture, surveying, graphic arts, photography or pottery restoration.

JEWISH NATIONAL FUND Eli Shenhav, 11 Zvi Shapira Street, Tel Aviv 64538

Volunteers required to help excavate a Shuni Roman theatre at Binyamina. Ages 17+. 1+

weeks, July-August. Cost $20 per day includes medical and accident insurance, meals and accommodation in tents at the youth summer camp. Lectures arranged. 5 day week. Hours of work 06.00-13.00; other work 17.00-19.00. Volunteers pay own travel costs and should take a sleeping bag.

PROJECT 67 LTD 10 Hatton Garden, London EC1N 8AH Tel 071-831 7626

Organises digs at various sites in cooperation with the Antiquities Authority. The work consists of clearing away debris, shovelling, hauling baskets, cleaning fragments of pottery and other artefacts. Hours of work 05.00-12.30. Afternoons usually free. Evening lectures and trips arranged to nearby sites and museums. 2 weeks, May-October. Ages 18+; no maximum limit. Previous experience not necessary, but volunteers should be fit, enthusiastic and prepared for hard work in a hot climate. Cost from £289 covers return flight, full board and insurance.

TEL AVIV UNIVERSITY Institute of Archaeology, Ramat Aviv, PO Box 39040, Tel Aviv 69978

Volunteers are required to excavate the remains of Bronze Age Tel Kabri near Nahariya. Excavations have revealed fortification systems and urban remains of a Canaanite city and a Phoenician town. 3 weeks, July-August. Lectures and classes arranged. Ages 18+. Campsite accommodation $12 per day. Registration fee $25. Hours of work 05.30-13.00 and 17.00-19.00. Volunteers pay their own travel costs.

AU PAIR/ CHILDCARE

ANGLIA AGENCY 15 Eastern Avenue, Southend-on-Sea, Essex Tel Southend 613888

Au pair, mother's help and nanny positions arranged throughout the year. 6+ months; return fare for 12 month stays. Hours and salaries vary; au pairs work 30 hours per week plus babysitting, with 1 free day and £25+ pocket money per week. Board and lodging provided. Ages 18+. Travel costs paid by applicants. Service charge £40.

AVALON AGENCY Thursley House, 53 Station Road, Shalford, Guildford, Surrey GU4 8HA Tel Guildford 63640

Can place au pairs. Food, lodging and pocket money provided, with opportunity to attend language classes. 30-36 hour week. Positions are for 6-12 months. Ages 18-30. Pocket money £18 per week. Insurance provided. Service charge £34.50.

STAR AU PAIRS INTERNATIONAL 16 Michal Street, Tel Aviv 63903

Can place mother's helps, nannies and au pairs, especially in Tel Aviv, Haifa and Jerusalem. Previous childcare experience preferred but not essential. Knowledge of English and driving licence an advantage. 4+ months. Also summer stays, 1+ months, July/August. Ages 18+. Wages $400+ per month, board and lodging provided. Travel costs paid by applicants. Applicants receive return fare after completing 1 year's contract.

STUDENTS ABROAD AGENCY Elm House, 21b The Avenue, Hatch End, Middlesex HA5 4EN Tel 081-428 5823

Can place au pairs plus, mother's helps and housekeepers with families. Positions available all year for 6+ months. Some experience preferred. Au pairs plus normally work a 6/7 hour day. Usually 1 full day and 2/3 evenings free per week. Salary approx £30+ per week. Mother's helps work longer hours for a higher salary, and salary is double for experienced housekeepers. Board and lodging provided. Ages 19-30. Applicants should like, and have the ability to cope with, children, babies, and housework. Applicants pay their own fare, but advice given on travel and insurance. Service charge £40.

COMMUNITY WORK

GAP ACTIVITY PROJECTS LTD 44 Queen's Road, Reading, Berkshire RG1 4BB Tel Reading 594914

Recruits volunteers for a modern children's orthopaedic hospital outside Jerusalem. Male volunteers help with heavy lifting and may help the ambulance teams; both male and

ISRAEL

female volunteers share the nursing with professional staff. Also recruit volunteers for work at an ambulance centre in Jerusalem, equivalent to the Red Cross. Volunteers go out with the ambulances, accompanied by a doctor, to help in cases of accident, illness or transfer to and from hospital. Applicants should be school leavers aged 18-19 who have up to a year before going on to further education. Six months, beginning August or February. Accommodation, communal meals and a small amount of pocket money provided. Cost £200 plus airfare and insurance costs. *Apply early September of last school year; applications close March. UK nationals only.*

KIBBUTZIM

KIBBUTZIM

A kibbutz is a communal society in which all the means of production are owned by the community as a whole. Members do not receive wages or salaries but give their labour in return for the provision of their basic needs. Kibbutzim welcome volunteers who are prepared to live and work within the community and abide by the kibbutz way of life. Volunteers share all communal facilities with kibbutz members and should be capable of adapting to a totally new society. Some of the work during the summer months is citrus, melon and soft fruit harvesting, and volunteers may also be involved in haymaking, gardening or working in the fish ponds, cow sheds or chicken houses. Work is also available in the kibbutz factory, helping in non-specialist, light industrial work. For those who find the heat uncomfortable, indoor work is usually available in the kitchens, dining rooms, laundries or factories. Volunteers work approx 8 hour day, 6 day week, with Saturdays free. Work often starts at 05.00 so that afternoons are free. Volunteers live together in wood cabins or stone houses with food provided in the communal dining room. Laundry, toilet requisites, entertainment, medical care and other basic needs, such as stamps and cigarettes, usually available as required, and some kibbutzim have bars and discos. A small amount of pocket money, approx £20 per month, may also be provided. Kibbutzim should not be regarded as holiday bases; volunteers can make arrangements for sightseeing at the end of their work period.

Kibbutz - The Way We Live 90p, is an illustrated booklet describing the kibbutzim movement. Published by Kibbutz Representatives, 1a Accommodation Road, London NW11 8ED Tel 081-458 9235.

Kibbutz Volunteer £5, describes kibbutzim and how they function, conveying the atmosphere of the communities and explaining what to expect when working in one. There are details of 200 kibbutzim plus a map showing locations and how to apply. Also includes other vacation and short-term work opportunities in Israel, including the moshav movement, au pair work, archaeological digs, fruit picking and social work. Published by Vacation-Work, 9 Park End Street, Oxford, Oxfordshire OX1 1HJ Tel Oxford 241978.

GAP ACTIVITY PROJECTS LTD 44 Queen's Road, Reading, Berkshire RG1 4BB Tel Reading 594914
Places volunteer on selected kibbutzim throughout Israel. 5+ months, starting October or February. The work is hard, but volunteers are given ample opportunity to travel. Applicants should be school leavers aged 18-19 who have up to a year before going on to further education. Cost £150 plus airfare and insurance. *Apply early September of last school year; applications close March. UK nationals only.*

KIBBUTZ REPRESENTATIVES Volunteer Coordinator, 1a Accommodation Road, London NW11 8ED Tel 081-458 9235
Operates a working visitor scheme throughout the year whereby volunteers spend 5-12 weeks on a kibbutz. Volunteers pay their own travel costs and must be in possession of a return ticket or adequate funds for the return journey. All applicants must supply a medical certificate and two letters of reference, and attend an orientation interview. Ages 18-32. Registration fee £29. *Limited places during July and August; apply before Easter.*

PROJECT 67 LTD 10 Hatton Garden, London EC1N 8AH Tel 071-831 7626
Arranges working holidays on kibbutzim for 5+ weeks, all year. Cost from £235 covers return flight, transfer to kibbutz and registration fee. Tel Aviv office assists with queries and onward travel. Ages 18-32. *All nationalities welcome.*

WST CHARTERS Priory House, 6 Wrights Lane, London W8 6TA Tel 071-938 4362
Arranges working holidays on kibbutzim for 6+ weeks. Ages 18-32. Volunteers usually work 6 mornings per week and receive approx £10 per month pocket money. Volunteers pay their own travel costs. Registration fee £50 covers transfer to kibbutz and medical insurance. All applicants must supply a medical certificate and two letters of reference. Ages 18-32.

MOSHAVIM

A moshav is a collective of individual smallholders, based on the family unit. Each family works and develops its own plot of land/farm while sharing the capital costs of equipment and marketing. Moshavim are different from kibbutzim in that each family lives in its own house and makes its own living; there are some communal buildings and facilities such as a club house or swimming pool. Volunteers on moshavim live and work as a member of an Israeli family and are expected to share in the social and cultural activities of the family and village. In some cases a small group of volunteers may live in their own bungalow, but they will each be 'adopted' by the family for whom they are working. Most of the work is on the land, with emphasis on flower growing, market gardening and specialist fruit farming. It should be stressed that work on a moshav is tougher and more demanding than on a kibbutz, and working hours may be long. Volunteers are expected to develop close relationships with the family, which demands a far greater personal effort than in the communal life of a kibbutz. In return for their work volunteers receive board and lodging plus wages of approx £100 per month, more than the pocket money given on a kibbutz. Lectures, cultural activities and excursions arranged.

GIL TRAVEL LTD 65 Gloucester Place, London W1 3PF Tel 071-935 1701
Arranges moshav volunteer places throughout the year for 8+ weeks, maximum 1 year. 8 hour day, 6 day week, 1 day free per month. Ages 18-35. Wages US$320 per month. Self-catering accommodation, food cost approx US$50 per month. Registration fee £25-£30. Open return flights available from £199. Health insurance

must be taken out at the moshav volunteer office in Tel Aviv.

PROJECT 67 LTD 10 Hatton Garden, London EC1N 8AH Tel 071-831 7626
Arranges working holidays in moshav families for 2+ months, all year. Ages 21-35. Wages approx US$320 per month. Cost to participants from £220 covers return flight and registration fee. *All nationalities welcome.*

WST CHARTERS Priory House, Wrights Lane, London W8 6TA Tel 071-838 4362
Arranges working holidays for 2+ months. 6 day week. Ages 18-35. Wages £50-£80 per month. Volunteers pay their own travel costs. Registration fee £45 covers medical insurance. Applicants must supply a medical certificate and two letters of reference.

WORKCAMPS

CHRISTIAN MOVEMENT FOR PEACE Bethnal Green United Reformed Church, Pott Street, London E2 0EF Tel 071-729 1877
An international movement open to all who share a common concern for lasting peace and justice in the world. Volunteers are needed to work in international teams on summer projects aimed at offering a service in an area of need and promoting self-help within the community; promoting international understanding and the discussion of social problems; and offering young people the chance to live as a group and take these experiences into the context of daily life.

Recent projects have included cleaning streets and public areas, creating a public garden and reconstruction work in Jaffa for the Palestinian community; paving roads, repairing schools and cultural institutions and building retaining walls in Nazareth; and living and working with Palestinians in the villages and refugee camps of the West Bank. Ages 18+. Volunteers should have some interest in the Palestinian cause. 6 hour day, 30-36 hour week. 1+ weeks, August. Food, school, centre or tent accommodation and insurance provided. Participants pay their own travel costs.

Applications from outside the UK: please see workcamp information on page 27.

ISRAEL

MOSHAVIM

WORKCAMPS

ISRAEL

WORKCAMPS

THE ELCHANAN ELKES ASSOCIATION FOR INTER-COMMUNITY UNDERSTANDING Sara Elkes, Director, 8 Amaziah Street, Greek Colony, Jerusalem
Aims to further inter-community understanding between Jews and non-Jews. Volunteers are needed to work in both Arab and Jewish institutions and communities. Recent projects have included helping at a peace village for Arabs and Jews at Neveh Shalom; working in the fields, building a herb garden and looking after sheep; spring cleaning and preparing for Passover at a home for the handicapped in Akim Jerusalem; office work and gardening at a school for the study of the Holocaust, near Natanyah; and working with children at an Arab kindergarten in Jaffa. Ages 21+. 1-3 weeks, November-April. Also opportunities for experienced volunteers to work with handicapped or elderly people, 6-8 weeks. Applicants should have previous workcamp, voluntary work or community service experience, and should be fit, prepared to work hard and contribute to team life. Skills in music, crafts or dance helpful. All applicants must produce a medical certificate and attend an interview. Food and accommodation provided but not insurance or travel. *British volunteers only; apply with cv and 3 references to Joan Margaret Burn, 2 Linden Farm Drive, Countesthorpe, Leicestershire LE8 3SX Tel Leicester 775369.*

When writing to any organisation it is essential to mention Working Holidays 1991 and enclose a large stamped, self-addressed envelope, or if overseas, a large addressed envelope and at least two International Reply Coupons.

ITALY

Italian Consulate General
38 Eaton Place, London SW1X 8AN
Tel 071-235 9371

British Embassy
Via XX Settembre 80A, 00100 Rome

Tourist office
Italian State Tourist Office (ENIT), 1 Princes
Street, London W1R 8AY Tel 071-408 1254

Youth hostels
Associazione Italiana Alberghi per la Gioventu,
Via Cavour 44, 3rd floor, 00184 Rome

Youth & student information
Centro Turistico Studentesco et Giovanile CTS
(Student Travel), Via Nazionale 66, 00184 Rome
and Via Genova 16, 00184 Rome

Student Travel Service Florence, Via Zanetti 18,
50123 Florence

ESTC, Largo Brancaccio 55, 00184 Rome

Intercultura, Piazza San Pantaleo 3, 00186
Rome

INFORMATION

Entry regulations UK citizens intending to
work in Italy should have full passports. Police
registration is required within 3 days of
entering Italy. EC nationals may stay for up to
3 months, and those wishing to stay longer
must obtain an extension from the police. When
status changes from visitor to employee the
individual must immediately apply for a work
permit.

Job advertising Publicitas Ltd, 525/527
Fulham Road, London SW6 1HF Tel 071-385
7723 are agents for a number of Italian
newspapers and magazines including *Corriere
della Sera* (largest national morning daily);
Il Gazzettino (Venice daily); *Il Messagero*
(leading Rome newspaper); *La Sicilia* (leading
Sicilian newspaper), plus a great number of
trade, technical and general interest magazines.

Travel Centro Turistico Studentesco UK Ltd, 33
Windmill Street, London W1P 1HH Tel 071-
580 4554 offers low cost rail travel and charter
flights, and reductions on Mediterranean
shipping lines, for students and young people.

CIT (England) Ltd, 3-5 Landsdowne Road,
Croydon, Surrey Tel 081-686 0677 issues a
Kilometric ticket valid for 3000 km (maximum
20 journeys) which can be used by up to 5
people at the same time, the 3000 km being

divided by the number of passengers. Valid 2
months; cost £60. A Travel at Will ticket
entitles the holder to unlimited travel on the
Italian rail network. Valid for up to 60 days;
cost from £65 (8 consecutive days).

STA Travel, 86 Old Brompton Road, London
SW7 3LQ Tel 071-937 9921 operates flexible,
low cost flights between London and
destinations throughout Italy.

Campus Travel, 52 Grosvenor Gardens, London
SW1W 0AG Tel 071-730 3402 offers Eurotrain
under 26 fares to destinations all over Italy,
and flexible youth/student weekly charter
flights to Milan and Rome.

Italy, Travellers Handbook is a free booklet
containing useful information for visitors with
notes on accommodation, culture and leisure,
sports, and travel. Also includes general
information, and the addresses of provincial
and local tourist boards. Available from the
Italian State Tourist Office, see above.

Information centres Servizio Turistico Sociale,
Youth and Student Travel Service, Via Zanetti
18, 50123 Florence provides a reception and
information service and can arrange
accommodation and travel. Information on
Italian courses and events. B D PH

ITALY

Publications *Young Rome* is an invaluable source of information, containing advice on where to sleep and eat, health and public services, details on museums, galleries and monuments, universities and cultural institutions, transport, excursions, maps and a host of other useful information and addresses. Available free from Regional Tourist Organisation, Region of Latium, Tourist Assessor's Office, Via Rosa Raimondi Garibaldi 7, Rome.

Welcome to Italy is a guide for young people, covering what to do before you leave, travel, money, accommodation, food, postal services, tourism and leisure; and also provides information on study and work in Italy and useful addresses. Published by Intercultura and available from the Central Bureau, Seymour Mews, London W1H 9PE, price £3.20 including UK postage.

Accommodation Europa Youth & Student Travel Centre, Via Mezzocannone 87-119, 80134 Naples offers cheap accommodation at international student halls of residence in Naples, June-September. Also at international holiday centres in Sorrento, March-October. Cost from £10 per day includes bed and breakfast.

Federazione Italiana del Campeggio e del Caravanning, Via V Emanuele 11, PO Box 23, 50041 Calenzano, Florence operates an international campsite booking centre and publishes a list of member campsites which can accept bookings, with details of costs, opening dates and facilities. *Apply by 15 May.*

ARCHAEOLOGY

ARCHAEOLOGY

ARCHEOCLUB D'ITALIA Arco de' Banchi 8, 00186 Rome
Volunteers are required to assist on archaeological excavations arranged throughout Italy. Sites include Bronze Age remains, medieval monasteries and castles. Work involves research, excavating, gathering and cataloguing finds and drawing up plans of sites. Ages 16+; those under 18 will need parental consent. No experience necessary, but volunteers should have some knowledge of

Italian. 2-3 weeks, August. Approx 24 hours per week, mornings only. Cultural/educational activities organised in afternoons, including one guided visit per week in nearby town. No wages or travel paid. Cost L250000 per week covers insurance and full board accommodation in youth hostel, school or inn.

DIPARTIMENTO SCIENZE DELL'ANTICHITA Prof Francesco d'Andria, Universita, 73100 Lecce
Volunteers are required for the excavation of a site at Otranto-Veste on the Adriatic coast of Apilia, a long-term project to investigate the Messapian culture and its relations with Greece and Magna Graecia in the Archaic period. Experienced volunteers with knowledge of the period preferred. 4 weeks, July. Food and accommodation provided; no fares or wages provided. *Apply by 30 May.*

GRUPPI ARCHEOLOGICI D'ITALIA Via Tacito 41, 00193 Rome
Volunteers are required for the excavation and restoration of various sites. Recent projects have included excavation of a 6th century BC Etruscan necropolis near Viterbo in Tuscania; excavation of a Roman villa and documentation and excavation of a 10th-15th century medieval town, near Tolfa; excavation of the Diana Nemorense Sanctuary, 1st century BC, in Nemi; and excavation of the Appia Antica near Rome. Ages 16+. 2+ weeks, July-September. 6 hour day. Experience in excavation techniques preferable but not essential. Cost L350000-L450000, 2 weeks, includes full board hostel or centre accommodation and insurance. Lectures and excursions. No fares or wages paid. *Apply by 15 June.*

AU PAIR/ CHILDCARE

ANGLIA AGENCY 15 Eastern Avenue, Southend-on-Sea, Essex Tel Southend 613888
Au pair, mother's help and nanny positions arranged throughout the year. Long and short-term placements available, including summer. Hours and salaries vary; au pairs work 30 hours per week plus babysitting, with 1 free day and £25+ pocket money per week. Board

and lodging provided. Ages 17+. Travel costs paid by applicants. Service charge £40.

AU PAIRS-ITALY 46 The Rise, Sevenoaks, Kent TN13 1RJ

Can place au pairs, mother's helps and nannies in families throughout Italy, including Sicily and Sardinia. Families include members of the nobility and some of Italy's most distinguished households. Stays are usually for 6-12+ months, with vacancies for 1-3 months, June-September. Many families have holiday accommodation by the sea, in the country or mountains where they spend long summer holidays and weekends. Girls live as members of the family, looking after the children, their rooms, laundry and meals, speaking English with them and helping with light housework. Au pairs work a 5 hour day plus some babysitting. Mother's helps work a full day. All girls have 1 free day per week plus at least 1 free evening. Board and lodging provided, plus salary approx £120+ au pairs, £175+ mother's helps, per month. Positions for qualified nannies, junior nannies and nanny governesses; salary approx £250-£600 per month, depending on experience. Ages 18+. Older applicants often requested. Applicants must have a love of children, be patient with them, have a cheerful, outgoing personality and be willing, reliable and adaptable. Applicants must supply 3 references and a medical certificate. Knowledge of Italian not essential. Advice can be given on travel and insurance. Applicants pay for own fares, but many families pay the return fare after a year's service. *EC nationals only.*

AVALON AGENCY Thursley House, 53 Station Road, Shalford, Guildford, Surrey GU4 8HA Tel Guildford 63640

Can place au pairs in all areas excluding Rome. Food, lodging and pocket money provided, with opportunity to attend language classes. 25-30 hour week, 6-12 months. Ages 18-30. Basic knowledge of Italian needed. Pocket money £25 per week and insurance provided. Service charge £40, if job is accepted.

HELPING HANDS AU PAIR & DOMESTIC AGENCY 10 Hertford Road, Newbury Park, Ilford, Essex IG2 7HQ Tel 081-597 3138

Au pair and mother's help positions available all year. Au pairs work approx 30 hours plus 3 evenings babysitting each week and earn approx £25 per week. Mother's helps work longer hours for a higher salary. Board and lodging provided. 6+ months. Ages 17-27. Applicants should be willing, helpful and adaptable. Insurance and travel costs paid by applicants, but assistance with arrangements provided. Introduction fee £40 on acceptance of a family. *UK nationals only.*

HOME FROM HOME 10 Tackley Place, Oxford, Oxfordshire OX2 6RR Tel Oxford 512628

Placements found for au pairs to undertake childcare and light housework in northern Italy. No experience necessary but basic knowledge of Italian an advantage. All year. 5 hour day, 30 hour week. Ages 18+. Pocket money £25 per week; travel and insurance not provided. Service charge £40.

INTERLINGUA CENTRE Torquay Road, Foxrock, Dublin, Ireland 18 Tel Dublin 893876

Can place au pairs with Italian families. 30 hour week with one full day and some evenings off. Time to attend classes 2-3 mornings or afternoons per week. Experience desirable but not essential. 6+ months. Ages 18+. £25 per week pocket money, full board, lodging and insurance provided. Travel paid by applicants. Placement fee £55.

JOLAINE AGENCY 18 Escot Way, Barnet, Hertfordshire EN5 3AN Tel 081-449 1334

Au pair and mother's help posts arranged throughout the year. Au pairs work a 5 hour day with 3/4 evenings babysitting per week. Afternoons plus 1 full day free per week. Mother's helps work an 8 hour day with 1½ days free per week, plus some evenings and other time by arrangement. Ages 17-27. 6+ months, all year. Summer holiday posts also available, looking after children and doing light household duties. 3+ months, June-October. Pocket money from £25+ per week. Travel and insurance paid by applicants. Introduction fee £40.

STUDENTS ABROAD AGENCY Elm House, 21b The Avenue, Hatch End, Middlesex HA5 4EN Tel 081-428 5823

Can place au pairs and mother's helps. Long-term positions available all year, but a number of holiday stays, usually in coastal, lakeside

ITALY

AU PAIR/CHILDCARE

and/or mountain areas are available for 2+ months, July and August. Au pairs normally work a 5/6 hour day with usually 1 full day and 2/3 evenings free per week. 3-4 hours allowed per day for language classes, but curriculum changes and applicants must be flexible during temporary summer season when no schooling available and families often go on holiday. Salary approx £25 per week. Mother's helps work longer hours for a higher salary. Board and lodging provided. Ages 17-27. Basic knowledge of Italian useful, but not essential. Applicants should like, and have the ability to cope with, children, babies, light housework and simple cooking. Applicants pay own fare, but advice given on travel and insurance. Service charge £40. *Apply early for summer positions.*

UNIVERSAL CARE Chester House, 9 Windsor End, Beaconsfield, Buckinghamshire HP9 2JJ Tel Beaconsfield 678811
Can place au pairs and mother's helps in families. 6+ months; 3 month summer positions also available. Some Italian families go to the coast in summer and to the mountains in September, taking their au pair or mother's help with them. Au pairs work a 5/6 hour day, with occasional babysitting; regular time off for language classes. Mother's helps work an 8 hour day, without free time for classes. Ages 17-27. Knowledge of Italian not essential, but applicants must love children and be willing to help. Experience with children desirable, and O level English preferred. All girls generally have 1 day plus 2 evenings free per week. Board and lodging provided. Salary approx L300000 per month. Travel paid by applicant. Service charge £46. *Apply 2 months before work period desired.*

COMMUNITY
WORK

INTERNATIONAL VOLUNTARY SERVICE 162 Upper New Walk, Leicester LE1 7QA Tel Leicester 549430
IVS is the British branch of Service Civil International, which promotes international reconciliation through work projects. Volunteers are needed to work in international teams on various community workcamps. Recent projects have included working with residents on manual projects and organising activities at social centres for ex-prisoners and people with disabilities in Torino and Milan; working with residents on manual projects and organising activities at training centres for people with mental disabilities in Piemonte and Torino; and riding tandem cycles with blind people on tours of the Italian countryside. Ages 18+. Knowledge of Italian necessary for some camps. Applicants should have previous workcamp experience, be highly motivated and prepared to work hard and contribute to team life. 35-40 hour week. 1-3 weeks, June-September. Food, accommodation and insurance provided, but not travel. Membership fee £25 (students £15, unwaged £10). Registration fee £40. **B D PH**

Organised by Service Civil International, Via dei Laterani 28, 00184 Rome.

Applications from outside the UK: please see workcamp information on page 27.

CONSERVATION

ALTERNATIVE TRAVEL GROUP LTD Restoration Project, 1-3 George Street, Oxford, Oxfordshire OX1 2AZ Tel Oxford 251195
Volunteers are required to help with the restoration of an 11th century convent in the Tuscany countryside, and with its conversion into a staging post for those on walking holidays. Ages 16+. Applicants must be hard-working and reliable. 5+ weeks, January-November. 35 hour week. Knowledge of Italian not essential. £1.50 pocket money per day worked, full board accommodation in convent and return travel provided. Swimming pool nearby; bicycles available, and at least one excursion organised each week. Applicants must attend for interview in Oxford.

When writing to any organisation it is essential to mention Working Holidays 1991 and enclose a large stamped, self-addressed envelope, or if overseas, a large addressed envelope and at least two International Reply Coupons.

CHRISTIAN MOVEMENT FOR PEACE
Bethnal Green United Reformed Church, Pott
Street, London E2 0EF Tel 071-729 1877

UNITED NATIONS ASSOCIATION
International Youth Service, Welsh Centre for
International Affairs, Temple of Peace,
Cathays Park, Cardiff CF1 3AP Tel Cardiff
223088

Apply to either of the above to work in
international teams on summer projects aimed
at offering a service in an area of need and
promoting self-help within the community;
promoting international understanding and the
discussion of social problems; and offering
young people the chance to live as a group and
take these experiences into the context of daily
life. Recent projects have included working
with a local groups to prevent fires in an area
south of Rome; organic farming in R Emilia;
and gardening and restoration work at an old
church in Novara. Ages 18+. A knowledge of
Italian may be required. 6 hour day, 30-36 hour
week. 2-4 weeks, July-August. Food,
accommodation and insurance provided, but
participants pay own travel costs.

Organised by Movimento Cristiano per la Pace,
Via Rattazi 24, 00185 Rome.

*Applications from outside the UK: please see
workcamp information on page 27.*

INTERNATIONAL VOLUNTARY SERVICE
162 Upper New Walk, Leicester LE1 7QA
Tel Leicester 549430
IVS is the British branch of Service Civil
International which promotes international
reconciliation through work projects.
Volunteers are needed to work in international
teams on various conservation workcamps,
which have recently included organic farming
at a small village in the Appennines; clearing
and repairing footpaths at a nature reserve
near Rome; restoring old houses in an Alpine
village in Sondrio; and building mountain
footpaths and clearing forests in Como. Ages
18+. Applicants must have previous SCI
experience and should be prepared to work
hard and contribute to team life. 40 hour week.
2-4 weeks, June-September. Food,
accommodation and insurance provided, but
not travel. Membership fee £25 (students £15,

unwaged £10). Registration fee £40. **B D PH**

Organised by Service Civil International, Via
dei Laterani 28, 00184 Rome.

*Applications from outside the UK: please see
workcamp information on page 27.*

**LA SABRANENQUE CENTRE
INTERNATIONAL 30290 Saint Victor la
Coste, France**
A small, non-profitmaking organisation that
has been working since 1969 to preserve,
restore and reconstruct abandoned rural sites,
and bring them back to life. Aims to give
volunteers the chance to discover the interest
and pleasure of working directly on genuine
rural restoration projects while being part of a
cooperative team. In collaboration with Italian
preservation organisations, supervises several
conservation projects. Volunteers are needed to
work in small teams in Gnallo, a hamlet in
northern Italy, learning traditional
construction techniques on-the-job from
experienced leaders. Work can include
masonry, stone-cutting, floor or roof tiling,
interior restoration, drystone walling, path
paving and planting trees. Ages 18+. No
experience necessary. 3 weeks, August. Cost
FF55 per day includes full board
accommodation. Registration fee FF120.

COURIERS/REPS

BLADON LINES Personnel Department,
56-58 Putney High Street, London SW15 1SF
Tel 081-785 2200
Opportunities for representatives to work in
the Italian ski resorts of Courmayeur and San
Viglio. Relevant experience an advantage, and
good spoken Italian essential. Hours are very
variable; applicants must be prepared to work
hard but will get time to ski. December-May.
Ages 24+. Salary approx £50-£70 per week,
board, lodging, return travel, insurance, ski
pass, ski hire and company ski jacket provided.
Training week held in London before
departure.

Also a few places for ski guides who act as
assistant representatives and whose work
involves showing guests around the slopes,
helping with coach transfers and organising

ITALY

COURIERS/REPS

après ski. Ages 22+ with fluent Italian. Applicants should have good leadership qualities and be proficient skiers. Salary approx £50 per week. A week's training is held in Val d'Isère before the season starts. *EC nationals only.* PH depending on ability.

CANVAS HOLIDAYS LTD Bull Plain, Hertford SG14 1DY Tel Hertford 553535

Resident couriers are required to work on campsites for a holiday company providing accommodation for families in ready-erected fully equipped tents and mobile homes. The work involves a daily routine of tent cleaning as customers arrive and depart, providing information and advice on the local attractions and essential services, helping to sort out problems that might arise, and organising activities for the children and get-togethers for the families. 7 day week with no fixed hours; the workload varies from day to day. At the beginning and end of the season there is a period of physical work when tents are put up and prepared for the customers or taken down and stored for the winter. Other tasks include administration, book keeping and stock control.

Ages 18-25. Working knowledge of Italian essential. Applicants are normally those with a year between school and further education, undergraduates or graduates. They need to be reliable, self-motivated, able to turn their hand to new and varied tasks, and with a sense of humour. 10-14 weeks, early April-July or July-late September. Return travel, dependent on successful completion of contract, and accommodation in frame tents provided. Salary approx £76 per week. *UK nationals only. Applications accepted anytime; interviews commence early November.*

CLUB CANTABRICA HOLIDAYS LTD Personnel Department, Holiday House, 146-148 London Road, St Albans, Hertfordshire AL1 1PQ Tel St Albans 33141

Organises holidays providing fully equipped tents and caravans. Requires couriers and maintenance staff to work from mid May-early October. Some experience an advantage. 6 day week. Ages 21+. Salary from £40 per week, bonus at end of the season, self-catering accommodation in tents or caravans, travel costs from Watford and insurance provided.

COACH EUROPE Personnel Manager, 47 Gratten Road, Bradford, West Yorkshire BD1 2QF

Operates holiday tours to destinations in Italy including Lido di Jesolo. Coach/train couriers are needed to organise and assist clients at their pick-up point and during the Channel crossing, provide information whilst travelling and ensure all-round first class service. 6+ months. April-mid October and occasionally in winter. Ages 19+. Fluent English essential; knowledge of Italian an advantage. Salary approx £90 per week. 3-4 days off in the resort with free accommodation until the return journey. *Early application advisable; recruitment starts October.*

EUROCAMP Courier Department, Edmundson House, Tatton Street, Knutsford, Cheshire WA16 6BG Tel Knutsford 50052

Requires resident couriers to work on campsites by the Italian Lakes, near Venice, in Tuscany and near Grosetto. Work involves cleaning tents and equipment prior to the arrival of new customers; checking, replacing and making repairs on equipment; replenishing gas supplies; keeping the store tent in order; keeping basic accounts and reporting on a weekly basis to England. Couriers are also expected to meet new arrivals and assist holidaymakers with any problems that may arise; organise activities and parties; provide information on local tourist attractions and maintain an information noticeboard. At the beginning and end of the season couriers are expected to help in erecting and dismantling tents. There are no set working hours or free days, as these depend on unpredictable factors. Ages 18-28; older applicants will be considered. Applications from couples welcome. Applicants should be familiar with working and travelling abroad, preferably with camping experience. They should also be adaptable, reliable, independent, efficient, hard working, sensible, sociable, tactful, patient and have a working knowledge of the language. Applicants are expected to work one half of the season, early/mid April-mid July or mid July-late September/early October; exact dates depend on the campsite. Work is also available for the whole season. Accommodation in frame tent with cooking facilities, moped for use on site, insurance and return fare provided. Salary approx £80 per week. Positions as senior couriers also available; salary £95 per week. *Early application advisable; interviews start November.*

ILG COACH & CAMPING DIVISION (incorporating NAT Holidays and Intasun Camping), Overseas Personnel Manager, Devonshire House, Elmfield Road, Bromley, Kent Tel 081-466 6660
Vacancies exist for campsite representatives. Work involves welcoming and visiting clients, accompanying excursions, organising and taking part in evening entertainments, and generally looking after clients. Ages 19+. Applicants must have the desire and ability to get on with people and to handle pressure. April-October, with some positions available for students only in June/July. Applicants should be reliable, hardworking, prepared to work as part of a team, and have enough staying power to last the season. Knowledge of Italian an advantage. Staff are required to take an active part in their resort entertainment programme, helping to organise events such as parties, barbecues, and games evenings. Salary approx £70 per week. Accommodation and return travel provided. All staff are required to take part in a 2 week training programme in April. *Early application advisable; recruitment starts October and applicants should write then for details. Interviews commence December.*

QUEST TRAVEL Olivier House, 18 Marine Parade, Brighton, East Sussex BN2 1TL Tel Brighton 677777
Provides ski and summer tours for groups, mainly school parties, individuals and youth and adult organisations. Requires resort representatives for the summer and winter seasons, December-April and May-July/ August, in Pinzolo, Andalo, Aprica and other resorts. Duties include meeting groups at airports or hotels, room allocation, liaising with group leaders, organising entertainments, arranging ski passes and lessons, and promoting good local relations. Fluent Italian necessary. Applicants should be enthusiastic, have a flair for organising and enjoy hard stimulating work. On call 24 hours per day. Ages 21+. Salary £75-£110 per week, full board, lodging in shared accommodation, medical insurance and return travel provided. Training course at beginning of season. B D PH limited opportunities.

SEASUN/TENTREK HOLIDAYS 71/72 East Hill, Colchester, Essex CO1 2QW Tel Colchester 861886
Provides self-catering family holidays in apartments, mobile homes and tents plus activity holidays for schools and groups. Requires representatives for the summer season, beginning April-mid November, in Venice. 50/60 hour week. Ages 19+. Applicants should be independent, resourceful, with good communication skills and commitment. Knowledge of Italian an advantage, but not essential. Training provided. Salary and subsistence £260 per month; £40 per month extra paid on successful completion of contract. Accommodation and travel provided; personal insurance cost £55, uniform cost £60. B D PH depending on ability.

DOMESTIC

BLADON LINES Personnel Department, 56-58 Putney High Street, London SW15 1SF Tel 081-785 2200
Opportunities for chalet girls to work in the Italian ski resorts of Courmayeur and San Viglio. The work involves cleaning chalets, making beds, caring for guests, shopping and preparing meals. Ages 20+. Experience and/or qualifications in catering or domestic work essential, and must be able to cook well. Hours are very variable; applicants must be prepared to work hard but will get time to ski. Season lasts December-May. Salary approx £40 per week, board, lodging, return travel, insurance, ski pass, ski hire and company ski jacket provided. One day briefing held in London before departure. *EC nationals only.* PH depending on ability.

SNOW WORLD (SUN LIVING LTD) 34-36 South Street, Lancing, West Sussex BN15 8AG Tel Lancing 750310
Opportunities for chalet maids to work in ski resorts. Work involves keeping chalets tidy, looking after guests, and in certain cases preparing meals. Ages 18-30. Relevant experience in domestic and/or catering essential. Usually 8-10 hour day, 6 day week, but hours vary depending on the needs of clients. Applicants should be prepared to work for the whole season December-April. Extra staff may also be required at peak times such

as Christmas. Board, lodging and travel provided. Salary from £45 per week. Training given at the resort during the week before clients arrive.

FARMWORK

Seasonal farmwork is available through local agricultural cooperatives, at *Ufficio di Collocamento* (job centres) or by applying direct to the farms. Information on cooperatives, job centres and farms is available at *Centri Informazione Giovani*, youth information centres, regional addresses of which are given below.

The harvesting seasons are:

May-August
Strawberries, cherries, peaches and plums in Emilia Romagna

September-October
Apples and pears in Emilia Romagna, Piemonte and Trentino. Grapes in Emilia Romagna, Lazio, Piemonte, Puglia, Trentino, Veneto and Toscana

November-December
Olives in Puglia, Toscana, Liguria, Calabria and Sicilia. Flowers in Liguria, Toscana, Lazio and Puglia. Tobacco in Umbria, Puglia and Campania

CENTRI INFORMAZIONE GIOVANI IN THE AGRICULTURAL REGIONS

Campania
Centro Informagiovani, piazza Dante 4, 81100 Caserta

Informagiovani, piazza Vittorio Emanuele 10, 80046 S Giorgio A Cremano

Emilia Romagna
Centro Informazione Giovani, Via Scudari 8, 41100 Modena

Centro Informazione e Orientamento Professionale, Via Zamboni 8, 40126 Bologna

Centro Informagiovani, Via Mazzini 8, 48100 Ravenna

Lazio
Informagiovani, Villa Delfico, 65016 Montesilvano

Piemonte
Informagiovani, Via Caviglietti 1, 10017 Montanaro

Informagiovani, Via Assarotti 2, 10122 Torino

Informalavaro, Piazza della Libertà 4, 10036 Settimo Torinese

Toscana
Centro Oz, Via Corsica 3, 57025 Piombino

Informagiovani, Via Goldoni 83, 57125 Livorno

Centro Informagiovani, Provincia di Lucca, 55100 Lucca

Veneto
Informagiovani, contra S Tommaso 7, 36100 Vicenza

Informagiovani, vicolo Ponte Molino 7, 35137 Padova

MONITORS & INSTRUCTORS

BRITISH SCHOOL (Summer Camps), Via Matteotti 34, 18038 Sanremo
Organises English language courses combined with multi-activity holidays for Italian children under 16 at summer camps in the pine forests and mountain areas of Northern Italy. Staff are needed to teach the children English, develop creative thinking and stimulate their appreciation of the natural environment. As well as teaching and supervising children, work involves organising evening entertainment, a gala day and participating in all aspects of camp duties. Activities include hill walking, sports, excursions, handicrafts and drama. Ages 18+. TEFL qualifications and knowledge of Italian useful, but more importantly, applicants must have a genuine interest in children, be fun-loving, energetic, innovative and enthusiastic. Experience of working with children necessary. Also

opportunities for actors and sports/survival instructors. 65-75 hours per week, mid June-end August. Salary £250 per month, plus full board accommodation. Return travel paid for 2 months' work.

CLUB CANTABRICA HOLIDAYS LTD Overseas Department, Holiday House, 146-148 London Road, St Albans, Hertfordshire AL1 1PQ Tel St Albans 33141
Organises camping holidays, providing fully equipped tents, caravans and mobile homes. Kiddies and club staff are required for the summer season, mid May-early October. 25-35 hour week. Ages 21+. Nursery or NNEB qualifications required; experience an advantage. Salary from £40 per week, plus bonus at end of season. Self-catering accommodation in tents and caravans, travel costs from Watford and insurance provided.

SKI EUROPE Northumberland House, 2 King Street, Twickenham, Middlesex TW1 3RZ Tel 01-891 4400
A company with its own ski school operating holidays for groups and school parties. Part-time ski instructors are required for winter sports in Piemonte. Work involves 4 hours teaching per day. BASI or full ASSI qualifications essential, together with a high level of teaching skill. Knowledge of foreign languages useful but not essential; fluent English a prerequisite. 1-2 week periods over Christmas and the New Year, February and April. Instructors receive full board accommodation and ski pass plus travel expenses London/resort, and have access to the same facilities as the clients. Wages approx £75 per week, depending on qualifications. *Interviews take place May-November.*

SNOW WORLD (SUN LIVING LTD) Personnel Manager, Adventure House, 34-36 South Street, Lancing, West Sussex BN15 8AG Tel Lancing 750310
Opportunities exist for ski instructors. Applicants with BASI grade 3 or equivalent qualifications. Ages 18-30. 8-10 hour day, 6 day week, although hours vary depending on needs of clients. Also opportunities for ski technicians. Applicants should be prepared to work for the whole season, December-April. Extra staff may also be required at peak times such as Christmas. Board, lodging and travel provided. Salary from £80 per week. Training is given at the resort in the week before clients arrive.

WORKCAMPS

ASSOCIAZIONE ITALIANA SOCI COSTRUTTORI via Cesare Battisti 3, 20071 Casalpusterlengo, Milan
An international volunteers association with the aims of fighting misery and distress, and making a contribution towards a better understanding between nations. Volunteers are needed on workcamps; projects involve living and working in small communities, often rural, which are socially or economically underprivileged. Recent projects have included building, cleaning or renovating community centres, houses, kindergartens, playgrounds, centres for youth at risk and the handicapped, village schools, churches, rehabilitation centres or farm buildings such as granaries, sheep folds and cowsheds; harvesting grain and fruit, collecting firewood, fencing pastures and planting vines; or helping the disadvantaged and physically handicapped. Importance is given to volunteers understanding the significance and purpose of each project and realising the importance of their personal contribution. Ages 18+. 40-48 hour, 5 day week. 3 weeks, July/August. Food, prepared by the volunteers, and tent, family, school or centre accommodation provided, but volunteers should take sleeping bags. Volunteers pay own travel, 40% of which may be refunded. Registration fee L13000 includes insurance. *Apply 2 months in advance.*

CHRISTIAN MOVEMENT FOR PEACE Bethnal Green United Reformed Church, Pott Street, London E2 0EF Tel 071-729 1877

UNITED NATIONS ASSOCIATION International Youth Service, Welsh Centre for International Affairs, Temple of Peace, Cathays Park, Cardiff CF1 3AP Tel Cardiff 223088

Apply to either of the above to work in international teams on summer projects aimed at offering a service in an area of need and promoting self-help within the community; promoting international understanding and the discussion of social problems; and offering young people the chance to live as a group and take these experiences into the context of daily life. Recent projects have included bricklaying in Rome; working with the disabled in a special centre; and restoring a 17th century building for use as a community arts centre. Ages 18+. Knowledge of Italian may be required. 6 hour day, 5/6 day week. 2-4 weeks, July-August. Food, accommodation and insurance provided, but participants pay own travel costs.

Organised by Movimento Cristiano per la Pace, via Rattazi 24, 00185 Rome.

Applications from outside the UK: please see workcamp information on page 27.

COMUNITA EMMAUS Segretariato Campi di Lavoro, Via la Luna 1, 52020 Pergine Valdarno, Arezzo
Volunteers are needed to join international workcamps in various towns throughout Italy, organised by individual Emmaus communities which are self-supporting through recycling raw materials and old items. This involves collecting, sorting and selling paper, books, clothes, furniture, household apparatus, ironware and metals. Proceeds from the sale of items is often directed to development projects in the Third World. The camps aim to create a community in each location. Volunteers should be committed to community living and solidarity. Ages 18+. 8 hour day, 6 day week. 3+ weeks, July and August. Board, accommodation and accident insurance provided. Volunteers pay own travel costs and should take a sleeping bag and work clothes.

INTERNATIONAL VOLUNTARY SERVICE 162 Upper New Walk, Leicester LE1 7QA Tel Leicester 549430
IVS is the British branch of Service Civil International, which promotes international reconciliation through work projects. Volunteers are needed to work in international teams. Recent projects have included setting up stands and preparing a park for a young people's festival in Monza; living with and understanding the problems of immigrants near Milan; and collecting and repairing old bicycles in Turin to send to a Namibian refugee camp. Most camps include a study element on ecology, peace and disarmament. Some camps

include local volunteers who are recovering from drug-abuse problems, in an effort to help them readapt to social life, and volunteers should be sensitive to their need for a drug-free environment. Ages 18+. Applicants must have previous SCI experience, and should be prepared to work hard and contribute to team life. Knowledge of Italian useful. 40 hour week. 2-4 weeks, June-September. Food, accommodation and insurance provided, but not travel. Membership fee £25 (students £15, unwaged £10). Registration fee £40. *Limited places.*

Organised by Service Civil International, via dei Laterani 28, 00184 Rome.

Applications from outside the UK: please see workcamp information on page 27.

GENERAL

CANVAS HOLIDAYS LTD Bull Plain, Hertford SG14 1DY Tel Hertford 553535
A company providing ready-erected fully-equipped tents for family holidays, requires a number of applicants to form flying squads, teams of 2/3 people who help set up and equip 200-250 6 berth frame tents in an area containing approx 12 campsites. Similar work is also available dismantling tents and cleaning and storing equipment. Ages 18-25. Knowledge of Italian not required, but is an advantage as flying squad members sometimes have the opportunity to continue as couriers.

Applicants must be sociable in order to work in a small community, fit and able to work hard for long hours under pressure, work without supervision and cope with living out of a rucksack. Driving licence an advantage. Early April-mid June, possibly longer to set up the tents, and September to dismantle them. Salary £76 per week. Tented accommodation, self-catering facilities and outward travel provided; return travel dependent on the completion of contract dates. *UK nationals only.*

COMUNITA' DI AGAPE Centro Ecumenico, Segreteria, 10060 Prali, Torino
An international ecumenical community centre in a remote part of the Italian Alps, constructed by workcamp volunteers in response to the

need for reconciliation after the Second World War. Now used for national and international conferences, study camps, courses and other meetings on ecological, peace, Third World, political, cultural, theological and women's issues. A service group made up of volunteers from many countries works alongside the resident community during the summer months. The work is varied and can include kitchen duties, housework, cleaning, working in the coffee bar or laundry, babysitting, maintenance, construction or repair work. There are opportunities for volunteers to take part in the conferences. Knowledge of at least basic Italian useful. Applicants should be willing to make a contribution to the collective life of the community.

Ages 18+. 36 hour, 6 day week. 1+ months, June-September. Volunteers are sometimes taken on outside the summer period. Full board accommodation and insurance provided. Volunteers pay own travel costs. Anti-tetanus vaccination advised. *Apply at least 2 months in advance; limited number of places.*

EUROYOUTH LTD 301 Westborough Road, Westcliff-on-Sea, Essex SS0 9PT Tel Southend-on-Sea 341434
Holiday guest stays arranged where guests are offered board and lodging in return for an agreed number of hours English conversation with hosts or their children. Time is also available for guests to practise Italian if desired. Mainly ages 15-25, but there are sometimes opportunities for older applicants. 2-3 weeks, mainly July/August. Travel and insurance paid by the applicant. Registration fee approx £60. *Apply at least 12 weeks prior to scheduled departure date. UK nationals only.*

SUNSAIL The Port House, Port Solent, Portsmouth, Hampshire PO6 4TH Tel Portsmouth 370566
Crew members are required to work aboard cruising yachts flotilla sailing off Sardinia and Corsica. Vacancies for experienced skippers, responsible for the well-being of up to 13 cruising yachts and 60 holiday-makers, giving daily briefings on navigation and providing sailing assistance where necessary. Applicants must have considerable sailing experience, be cheerful, hardworking and able to deal with people of varying backgrounds and ages. Ages 23-30. Also bosuns/mechanics needed, responsible to the skipper for maintaining the marine diesel engines and repairing any other items aboard. Must have excellent knowledge of marine diesels and practical ability to cope with all sorts of breakdowns and repairs. Ages 22-30. Hostesses are required to look after laundry, accounting and cleaning of boats, advising holidaymakers on shops and restaurants, and organising social events and barbecues. Sailing experience useful, but bright personality, patience and adaptability essential. Ages 22-30.

All staff should be prepared for very hard work and long hours. 12 hour day, 1 free day per week. Knowledge of German advantageous, but not essential. Mid March-November. Salary approx £85 per week, paid monthly. Accommodation on board, return travel and medical insurance provided.

ITALY

GENERAL

When writing to any organisation it is essential to mention Working Holidays 1991 and enclose a largestamped, self-addressed envelope, or if overseas, a large addressed envelope and at least two International Reply Coupons.

NOTES

JAPAN

Japanese Embassy
9 Grosvenor Square, London W1X 9LB

Consulate General
101/104 Piccadilly, London W1V 8FN
Tel 071-465 6500

British Embassy
1 Ichiban-cho, Chiyoda-ku, Tokyo 102

Tourist office
Japan National Tourist Organisation,
167 Regent Street, London W1R 7FD
Tel 071-734 9638

Youth hostels
International Youth Hostel Association, Hoken
Kai Kan, 1-2 Sado Hara-Cho, Ichigaya,
Shinjuku-ku, Tokyo 162

Youth & student information
International Student Association of Japan,
Tokyo Chapter, c/o Kokusai Kyoiku,
Shinko-kai, 1-21 Yotsu Ya, Shinjuku-ku,
Tokyo 160

Japan Information Centre, Japanese Embassy,
9 Grosvenor Square, London W1X 9LB

INFORMATION

Entry regulations A visa is required for all types of employment. This can only be obtained once a job has been secured and application must be made from outside Japan. Before granting a visa the Japanese Embassy will require various documents, including copies of the contract or agreement made between the applicant and the employer in Japan, details of the applicant's personal history and proof of qualifications, plus details of the company/firm by whom the applicant will be employed; a complete list of the documents required can be obtained from the Embassy. If entering Japan by the Polar Route via Moscow no vaccinations are necessary; however, if any countries on the Southern Hemisphere Route have been visited, vaccination against cholera is strongly recommended. For further details, contact the Consular Section of the Embassy.

Job advertising Publicitas Ltd, 525/527 Fulham Road, London SW6 1HF Tel 071-385 7723 are agents for *Nihon Keizai Shimbun*, the leading financial business daily.

Travel The Japan National Tourist Organisation, 167 Regent Street, London W1R 7FD Tel 071-734 9638 can provide information on the Home Visit System, where under a

goodwill programme organised in 12 cities, families have volunteered to open their homes to foreign visitors.

North-South Travel Ltd, Moulsham Mill, Parkway, Chelmsford CM2 7PX Tel Chelmsford 492882 arranges competitively priced, reliably planned flights to Japan. Profits are paid into a trust fund for the assignment of aid to projects in the poorest areas of the South.

Your Guide to Japan is a 35 page booklet containing notes on history, frontier formalities, climate, currency and travel to and within Japan, accommodation, places of interest, what to do, including festivals, arts and traditional sports plus general information. Available from the Japan National Tourist Organisation, see above.

Japan - A Travel Survival Kit £7.95, is a handbook for travellers to Japan, with comprehensive information on where to stay, what to eat, the best places to visit and how to travel around. Available from Trailfinders, 194 Kensington High Street, London W8 7RG Tel 071-938 3939.

Publications *Jobs in Japan* has information and advice for English-speakers wishing to work in

JAPAN

Japan. Most opportunities are in the teaching field, but details of other possibilities are also given. Appendix includes list of employment sources, private English language schools, international schools and survival Japanese. Knowledge of Japanese and teaching credentials not essential. Published by Global Press, 1510 York Street, Suite 204, Denver, CO 80206, United States. Available in the UK from Vacation Work, 9 Park End Street, Oxford OX1 1HJ Tel Oxford 241978, price £9.95.

TEACHERS

TEACHERS

Teaching Tactics for Japan's English Classrooms US$6.95 + $3 airmail, a supplement to *Jobs in Japan*, see above, is a useful guide for anyone teaching EFL in Japan. Includes section on teaching methods, common student errors, ideas for games and classroom activities, together with addresses of private English language schools throughout Japan.

JAPAN EXCHANGE AND TEACHING (JET) PROGRAMME, JET Programme Officer, Japan Information Centre, Embassy of Japan, 101/104 Piccadilly, London W1V 9FN Tel 071-465 6500
The Programme seeks to promote mutual understanding between Japan and other countries, and fosters international perspectives by promoting international exchange at local levels, as well as intensifying foreign language education in Japan. Conducted under the co-sponsorship of local government authorities in Japan, and the Ministries of Foreign Affairs, Education, and Home Affairs. Vacancies for English teaching assistants, carrying out coaching in English language and pronunciation, preparation of teaching materials and participation in extra-curricular activities, under the guidance of Japanese academic staff. Placements are mostly in lower and upper secondary schools. Teaching experience or training an advantage. Knowledge of Japanese not essential, but candidates are expected to devote some effort to learning the language before they leave for Japan and whilst they are there. Before departure successful candidates will receive written materials on the programme and on basic Japanese, and further orientation is provided on arrival in Tokyo.

Contracts are for 1 year, commencing 1 August, and may be renewed in certain circumstances by mutual consent. Salary Yen 3,600,000+ per year, tax free; paid holiday on similar terms to Japanese colleagues. Participants are expected to work an average of 40 hours a week. Assistance given with return air ticket and health insurance. Advice given on finding accommodation. *British nationals only, under 35 years of age, and graduates of a British college or university holding at least a Bachelor's degree. Closing date for applications end December; interviews take place February/March.*

Nationals of Ireland, Canada, France, the Federal Republic of Germany, the United States, Australia and New Zealand should apply to the Japanese Embassy in their home country.

YOUNG ABROAD CLUB Kowa Building, 4th floor, 2-3-12 Shinjuku, Shinjuku-ku, Tokyo 160
Cultivates international understanding by promoting youth abroad. Qualified English teachers are needed to work in local cities, for at least 1 year, starting at various times throughout the year. Contracts depend on qualifications and place of work. 5-7 hour day, 6 day week. Salary Yen 200,000 per month. Lodging provided in company dormitory. Travel paid by applicants.

LUXEMBOURG

Luxembourg Embassy
27 Wilton Crescent, London SW1X 8SD
Tel 071-235 6961

British Embassy
14 boulevard Roosevelt, 2018 Luxembourg

Tourist office
Luxembourg National Tourist and Trade
Office, 36/37 Piccadilly, London W1V 9PA
Tel 071-434 2800

Youth hostels
Centrale des Auberges de Jeunesse
Luxembourgeoises, 18 place d'Armes, 2013
Luxembourg

Youth & student information
Service National de la Jeunesse, 1 rue de la
Poste, BP707, 2017 Luxembourg

Union Nationale des Etudiants
Luxembourgeois, 20 avenue Marie-Therese,
2132 Luxembourg

INFORMATION

Entry regulations UK citizens intending to work in Luxembourg should have full passports. EC nationals may stay in Luxembourg for up to 3 months; those wishing to stay longer must apply to the local police for a residence permit. Non-EC nationals must have a job and a work permit (*Déclaration Patronale*), and have *Permis de Séjour* stamped in their passport before entering Luxembourg. French and German, in addition to the Luxembourg language, are commonly used in business and industry, and anyone seeking employment should have a good knowledge of at least one of these languages.

Job advertising *Letzeburger Journal*, rue A Fischer 123, PO Box 2101, 1251 Luxembourg is a leading daily newspaper which will accept advertisements for jobs.

Luxemburger Wort, rue Christophe-Plantin 2, PO Box 1908, 2988 Gasperich-Luxembourg is the largest and most important daily newspaper in Luxembourg accepting job advertisements.

Travel Campus Travel, 52 Grosvenor Gardens, London SW1W 0AG Tel 071-730 3402 offers Eurotrain under 26 fares and youth/student airfares to Luxembourg.

Grand Duchy of Luxembourg contains practical information for visitors covering entry requirements, climate, transport, accommodation, outdoor activities, museums, special events and places of interest. Available from the Luxembourg National Tourist and Trade Office, see above.

Accommodation Gites d'Etape Luxembourgeois, Caritas, 29 rue Michel Weiter, 2730 Luxembourg have rest houses and vacation homes available throughout Luxembourg. All year; cost approx FB120-FB180 per night, self-catering.

The Luxembourg National Tourist & Trade Office, see above, can provide a booklet listing accommodation in Luxembourg City. Also a leaflet *Camping* which lists all the authorised camping sites in the Grand Duchy, together with facilities available.

When writing to any organisation it is essential to mention Working Holidays 1991 and enclose a large stamped, self-addressed envelope, or if overseas, a large addressed envelope and at least two International Reply Coupons.

LUXEMBOURG

AU PAIR/ CHILDCARE

ADMINISTRATION DE L'EMPLOI 38a rue Philippe II, 2340 Luxembourg
There is no special legislation or agency for the employment of au pairs, but prospective au pairs may contact the Administration, the government office dealing with all employment enquiries.

DOMESTIC

LUXEMBOURG EMBASSY 27 Wilton Crescent, London SW1X 8SD Tel 071-235 6961
Can supply a booklet *Hotels, Auberges, Restaurants, Pensions,* published annually, which includes detailed listings of establishments all over Luxembourg which often need seasonal domestic staff.

TEACHERS

LUXEMBOURG EMBASSY 27 Wilton Crescent, London SW1X 8SD Tel 071-235 6961
Publishes an information sheet on education in Luxembourg, listing English-speaking schools, language and secretarial schools, *lycées,* and *collèges d'enseignement* which may have vacancies for teachers. Opportunities exist in private schools; only Luxembourg nationals can teach in state schools.

GENERAL

ADMINISTRATION DE L'EMPLOI 38a rue Philippe II, 2340 Luxembourg
The government employment office dealing with all employment enquiries, can provide information on the availability of work in Luxembourg.

BUREAU-SERVICE 2 allée Leopold Goebel, Luxembourg
Can provide information on temporary office jobs.

CERCLE DE COOPERATION ET D'AIDE AU DEVELOPPEMENT DU TIERS MONDE 5 avenue Marie-Thérèse, 2132 Luxembourg
Can provide information on voluntary work opportunities.

LUXEMBOURG EMBASSY 27 Wilton Crescent, London SW1X 8SD Tel 071-235 6961
Can provide lists for those interested in working in Luxembourg; one gives the addresses of British and American firms, the other lists Luxembourg's major companies, classified according to their branch of activity.

MANPOWER-AIDE TEMPORAIRE 19 rue Glesener, Luxembourg
Can provide information on temporary jobs in all professions.

OFFICENTER 25 boulevard Royal, Luxembourg
Can provide information on temporary office jobs for students.

MALTA

Malta High Commission
16 Kensington Square, London W8 5HH
Tel 071-938 1712

British High Commission
17 St Anne Street, Floriana

Tourist office
Malta National Tourist Organisation, Suite 300,
Mappin House, 4 Winsley Street, London W1N
7AR Tel 071-323 0506

Youth hostels
Malta Youth Hostels Association, 17 Tal-Borg
Street, Pawla

Youth & student information
Youth Service Organisation, c/o Director of
Education, 33-34 Marsamett Road, Valletta

NSTS, Student and Youth Travel, 220 St Paul
Street, Valletta

INFORMATION

Entry regulations Foreign nationals may not
seek or accept employment in Malta after their
arrival in the country unless they have a prior
work permit. Work permits must be applied
for by the prospective employer on behalf of
the foreign national; the employer must show
sufficient proof that the foreign national will
fill a position for which no skilled Maltese
national is presently available. British
nationals do not need a visa to visit Malta and
may stay for up to 3 months.

Travel *Malta and its islands* is an information
sheet giving brief details of history, climate,
health, currency regulations, accommodation,
food, shopping, places of interest, sport,
festivals and other events. Available free from
the Malta National Tourist Organisation, see
above.

Campus Travel, 52 Grosvenor Gardens, London
SW1W 0AG Tel 071-730 3402 offers youth/
student airfares to Malta.

GENERAL

**MALTA YOUTH HOSTELS ASSOCIATION,
17 Triq Tal-Borg, Pawla**
Volunteers motivated to help and work hard to
develop Malta's tourist industry are needed to
work as directed by the Malta Youth Hostels
Association. This will mainly involve support
work in Malta and Gozo's youth hostels,
including office work and administration,
renovation and construction work such as
painting, plastering, building walls and
repairing roofs. Ages 16-50; those under 18
must provide a letter giving parental consent.
21 hours per week, or 3½ days per 2 weeks.
2-12 weeks, all year, commencing the 1st and
15th of each month. Transport from port of
entry and hostel accommodation with breakfast

provided; volunteers prepare other meals.
Participants pay insurance and travel costs.
£21 deposit.

**When writing to any organisation it is
essential to mention Working Holidays 1991
and enclose a large stamped, self-addressed
envelope, or if overseas, a large addressed
envelope and at least two International Reply
Coupons.**

NOTES

MEXICO

Mexican Embassy
8 Halkin Street, London SW1X 7DW
Tel 071-235 6393

British Embassy
Rio Lerma 71, Col Cuauhtémoc, 06500 Mexico, DF

Tourist office
Mexican Ministry for Tourism, 60-61 Trafalgar Square, London WC2 5DS Tel 071-734 1058

Youth hostels
CREA Red Nacional De Albergues Turisticos,

Oxtopulco No 40, Col Oxtopulco Universidad, 04310 Mexico, DF

Youth & student information
Secretaria de Turismo, Mariano Escobedo 726, 11590 Mexico, DF

SETEJ, Servicio Educativo de Turismo de los Estudiantes y de la Juventud de Mexico AC, Hamburgo 301, Col Juàrez, 06600 Mexico, DF

Consejo Nacional de Atencion de Recursos para la Juventud, Serapio Rendon 76, Colonia San Rafael, 06470 Mexico, DF

INFORMATION

Entry regulations It is very difficult to obtain a work permit; if, however, a company requires your services, they will apply for the permit.

Travel *Mexico - A Travel Survival Kit* £4.95 has comprehensive information on where to stay, what to eat, the best places to visit and how to travel around. Available from Trailfinders, 194 Kensington High Street, London W8 7RG Tel 071-938 3939.

Campus Travel, 52 Grosvenor Gardens, London SW1W 0AG Tel 071-730 3402 offer competitive airfares to destinations in Mexico.

The Rough Guide to Mexico £6.95, is a practical handbook with details on historical sites and a wealth of information on getting around. Published by Harrap Columbus, Chelsea House, Market Square, Bromley, Kent BR1 1NA.

Accommodation SETEJ, Servicio Educativo de Turismo de los Estudiantes y de la Juventud de Mexico AC, Hamburgo 301, Col Juàrez, 06600 Mexico, DF can provide information on campsites around Mexico City and in the states of Morelos, Hidalgo, Michoacàn and Chiapas. Also hostel accommodation in Mexico City, Acapulco and San Pedro Amuzgos; cost approx $5 per night, bed and breakfast.

COMMUNITY WORK

AMERICAN FRIENDS SERVICE COMMITTEE INC Personnel Department, 1501 Cherry Street, Philadelphia, Pennsylvania 19102, United States
A Quaker organisation undertaking programmes of relief, service and education. Volunteers are needed for manual and educational work on community service projects in villages in Mexico and occasionally other Latin American countries, living and

working with the community. Projects involve constructing and repairing schools, irrigation systems, clinics, roads and houses destroyed by natural disasters. Other work includes reafforestation, gardening, nutrition and health. Project life follows the patterns of village life, and volunteers must fit into and respect local customs. Groups consist of about 15 volunteers; half of the project leaders and volunteers are Mexican. Participants live as a

MEXICO

COMMUNITY WORK

group, sharing in work and maintenance tasks such as cooking, cleaning, carrying water and weekly market trips. Work can be physically and psychologically strenuous; each unit responds to its situation with creativity and flexibility, and each project develops from the initiatives and skills of the participants.

Ages 18-26. Applicants should be healthy, willing to adapt to group living, prepared to respond positively to the unexpected, be fluent in Spanish and have had some workcamp or community experience. Construction, gardening, arts, crafts, childcare or recreation experience useful. 7 weeks, July-August. Cost approx US$700 includes orientation conferences, food, accommodation in schools or unused buildings and insurance. Travel and pocket money not provided. Registration fee US$50. *Limited scholarships available. Apply by 1 March.*

GAP ACTIVITY PROJECTS LTD 44 Queen's Road, Reading, Berkshire RG1 4BB Tel Reading 594914
Several attachments are available for volunteers wishing to undertake community work. Some of the placements are made under the auspices of the Salvation Army, where the work is particularly demanding, varying from teaching to general assistance in orphanages. Applicants should ideally have a working knowledge of Spanish, or be prepared to learn before they go, and have an interest in music. Those wishing to teach are required to undertake a one week TEFL course before departure. Applicants should be school leavers aged 18-19 who have up to a year before going on to further education. Six months, starting September or February. Basic accommodation, food and a small amount of pocket money provided. Cost £350, plus airfare, insurance, and TEFL course, if applicable. *Apply early September of last school year; applications close March. UK nationals only.*

WORKCAMPS

INSTITUTO FENIX RURAL PROGRAM Guadelupe 108, Apdo Postal 1, Chalchihuites, Zacatecas
Organises rural programmes in the village of Chalchihuites in the foothills of the Sierra Madre Occidental, offering a unique opportunity to study the language and life of rural Mexico. Students live with local families,

study Spanish language and culture in the mornings and participate in a voluntary work programme in the village or on a farm in the afternoons, which is integrated into the daily life. Work may include sandal making, leather curing, bee keeping, weaving, working in fruit orchards, the market or general stores, or teaching English in local schools. No wages are paid, but in some cases there are opportunities for students to learn a new skill as well as contribute to the well-being of the village. The programme aims to develop and monitor small family industries, such as rabbit breeding or ceramics, and to create groups which could work to provide a service to the town, such as reafforestation and repair. It includes weekend excursions to the Chalchihuites ruins, the mines of Sierra, local haciendas, and nearby cities, and a series of seminars exploring the history and culture of Chalchihuites and Mexico. Students with little or no knowledge of Spanish may apply. 3+ weeks, all year. Cost $585, 3 weeks, covers full board and lodging, job placement, excursions, language instruction and seminars. Registration fee $75. *Apply 2 months in advance for summer period.*

Alternatively apply to Instituto Fenix, Cathy Fagan, 721 S Bruce Street, PO Box 5095, Anaheim, California, CA 92804, United States.

WORKCAMPS

SETEJ Servicio Educativo de Turismo de los Estudiantes y de la Juventud de Mexico AC, Hamburgo 301, Col Juàrez, 06600 Mexico, DF
Volunteers are needed on workcamps in small communities in the states of Morelos, Michoacàn, Guerrero and Oaxaca. Projects involve construction work, health programmes and social work. Ages 18+. Basic knowledge of Spanish essential. 30 hour week. 3+ weeks, June-September. Food and accommodation provided by local families. Volunteers should be prepared for a very low standard of living; few of the homes have bedrooms or toilets and food is scarce. Volunteers pay own travel and insurance costs. Administration fee $50. *Apply 3 months in advance.*

MOROCCO

Moroccan Embassy
49 Queen's Gate Gardens, London SW7 5NE
Tel 071-581 5001

Consular Section: Diamond House, 97/99
Praed Street, London W2 Tel 071-724 0719

British Embassy
17 boulevard de la Tour Hassan, Rabat

Tourist office
Moroccan Tourist Office, 205 Regent Street,
London W1R 7DE Tel 071-437 0073

Youth hostels
Union Marocaine des Auberges de Jeunesse, 6
Place Amiral Philibert, Casablanca

Fédération Royale Marocaine des Auberges de
Jeunesse, avenue Oqba Ibn Nafii, Meknes

INFORMATION

Entry regulations British nationals require a
full passport and a work permit before taking
up employment in Morocco and this will be
applied for by the prospective employer, and
issued by the Ministry of Labour. British
passport holders are free to travel without a
visa, but their passport must be valid for
6+ months on their day of entry into Morocco.
Those wishing to stay for over 3 months must
register with the police, justifying their stay
with a valid work permit. It should be noted
that it is difficult for foreigners to obtain
employment in Morocco. An information sheet,
Employment in Morocco, is available from the
Moroccan Consulate.

Travel Campus Travel, 52 Grosvenor Gardens,
London SW1W 0AG Tel 071-730 3402 offers
Eurotrain under 26 fares to destinations in
Morocco.

The Rough Guide to Morocco £6.95 is a practical
handbook covering all aspects of Moroccan life,
travel, places to stay and things to see.
Published by Harrap Columbus, Chelsea
House, 26 Market Square, Bromley, Kent BR1
1NA.

WORKCAMPS

**LES AMIS DES CHANTIERS
INTERNATIONAUX DE MEKNES (ACIM)
PO Box 8, Meknes**
Volunteers are needed to work on international
camps. Projects usually include agricultural
and construction work. Excursions, cultural
and social evenings arranged. Ages 18+.
Applicants should have previous workcamp or
voluntary work experience. 30-35 hour week,
afternoons and weekends free. 3 weeks, July/
August. Board, lodging and insurance
provided, but no pocket money. Travel costs
paid by volunteers.

**CHANTIERS JEUNESSE MAROC CCP Rabat
No 1234, PO Box 566, Rabat Chellah**
Volunteers are needed on international
workcamps concerning the economic, social
and cultural development of the people. Recent
projects have included creating green spaces at
Asilah; making a garden for children at
Chefchaouen; and constructing lanes and
alleyways in shanty towns near Mohammedia.
Ages 18+. 35 hour week. 3 weeks, July and
August. Food, school accommodation and some
insurance cover provided, but not travel. Basic
accommodation provided, sometimes with no
running water. Applicants should have
previous workcamp or voluntary work
experience.

MOROCCO

CHRISTIAN MOVEMENT FOR PEACE
Bethnal Green United Reformed Church, Pott
Street, London E2 0EF Tel 071-729 1877

UNITED NATIONS ASSOCIATION
International Youth Service, Welsh Centre for
International Affairs, Temple of Peace,
Cathays Park, Cardiff CF1 3AP Tel Cardiff
223088

Apply to either of the above to work in
international teams on manual and community
projects. Recent projects have included
construction work at children's centres in
Benmim and Harhoura; renovation work at
youth centres in Kenitra and Marakesh; and
conservation and clearance work at Al
Houcima, Sidi Kacem and other towns and
villages. Volunteers share in discussions
centring on the host community and world
problems and are expected to take a full part in
all aspects of the camp. Walks and excursions
arranged. Ages 18+. 35 hour week. 2-3 weeks,
July and August. Food, accommodation in
colleges, schools, centres or rural communes
and insurance provided. Participants cook on a
rota basis and should take a sleeping bag.
Applicants pay their own travel.

Organised by Chantiers Sociaux Marocains,
PO Box 456, Rabat RP.

*Applications from outside the UK: please see
workcamp information on page 27.*

WORKCAMPS

**PENSEE & CHANTIERS 26 rue de Pakistan,
BP 1423, Rabat RP**
Arranges various cultural and social activities,
training schemes and workcamps. Volunteers
are needed for a variety of workcamps aimed at
helping community schemes. Projects include
work on schools, youth clubs, social centres
and green spaces, involving construction,
restoration, painting and gardening tasks. No
experience necessary. Ages 17+. All
nationalities accepted. 5 hour day, 6 day week.
3 weeks, July and August. Food,
accommodation and insurance provided, but
participants should take a sleeping bag and
work clothes. Social and cultural activities
organised, including excursions and
discussions. PH

NETHERLANDS

Netherlands Embassy
38 Hyde Park Gate, London SW7 5DP
Tel 071-584 5040

British Embassy
Lange Voorhout 10, 2514 ED The Hague

Tourist office
Netherlands Board of Tourism, 25-28
Buckingham Gate, London SW1E 6LD
Tel 071-630 0451

Youth hostels
Stichting Nederlandse Jeugdherberg Centrale
(NJHC), Prof Tulpplein 4, 1018 GX Amsterdam

Youth & student information
EXIS, Centre for International Youth Activities,
Prof Tulpstraat 2, 1018 HA Amsterdam/PO
Box 15344, 1001 MH Amsterdam

Foreign Student Service, Oranje Nassaulaan 5,
1075 AH Amsterdam

INFORMATION

Entry regulations UK citizens intending to work in the Netherlands should have a full passport. EC nationals may stay for up to 3 months; those wishing to stay longer should contact the local police within 8 days of arrival in order to apply for a residence permit. Citizens of non-EC countries must possess a work permit, which can be applied for by the employer. Visitors may be asked to prove that they have adequate means of self-support for the duration of their proposed stay and that the cost of the return journey can be covered.

Further details of the regulations governing temporary employment in the Netherlands, plus useful information for those seeking a job, are contained in an information sheet, *Information about working and residence in the Netherlands*, available from the Economic Department of the Netherlands Embassy.

Job advertising Frank L Crane (London) Ltd, International Press Representation, 5/15 Cromer Street, Grays Inn Road, London WC1H 8LS Tel 071-837 3330 are agents for *Het Parool*, *De Volkskrant* and *Trouw*, all leading Dutch newspapers, for which they can accept job advertisements.

Publicitas Ltd, 525/527 Fulham Road, London SW6 1HF Tel 071-385 7723 are agents for *De Telegraaf* (largest morning daily) and numerous magazines.

Travel NBBS Travel, Informatiecentrum, Schipholweg 101, PO Box 360, 2300 AJ Leiden is the national office for youth and student travel, and administers 33 travel offices including 5 in Amsterdam, and can arrange cheap travel and hotel accommodation.

Rail Rovers entitle the holder to unlimited travel for 3/7 days on the Netherlands Railways network; cost approx £24.50/£35.50. A Public Transport Link Rover, for use in conjunction with Rail Rovers, entitles the holder to unlimited travel on Amsterdam and Rotterdam metro systems and on buses and trams throughout the Netherlands. Costs approx £6.50 for 3/7 days. The Teenage Rover Ticket is available for 4 days within a period of 10 days, June-August, to those aged up to 19; cost approx £15. The Benelux Tourrail Card is available for 5 days within a period of 17 days, allowing unlimited travel on the national railway networks of the Netherlands, Luxembourg and Belgium. March-October; cost from £43.50. Bicycle hire is available at reduced rates for rail ticket holders at many stations. Details from Netherlands Railways, 25/28 Buckingham Gate, London SW1E 6LD Tel 071-630 1735.

Campus Travel, 52 Grosvenor Gardens, London SW1W 0AG Tel 071-730 3402 offers Eurotrain under 26 fares and youth/student flights to destinations in the Netherlands.

NETHERLANDS

Holland, a young and lively country, is a free booklet for young visitors including details of transport, accommodation, eating, sightseeing, events, shopping, entertainment and useful addresses; plus details of organisations providing advice and information on looking for work, legal assistance, medical problems, courses and details of hostels, student hotels, campsites and sleep-ins. *Useful hints for your stay in the Netherlands* is a brochure providing useful information on where to eat and sleep, travel, customs formalities, health care, places of interest, currency, climate, events and museums, plus other general information. Also a booklet listing holiday and recreational opportunities for the disabled, covering travel, accommodation, restaurants and tourist attractions. All available from the Netherlands Board of Tourism, see above. **PH**

Publications *The Rough Guide to Amsterdam* £5.95 is a practical handbook, full of essential information. Published by Harrap Columbus, Chelsea House, 26 Market Square, Bromley, Kent BR1 1NA.

Information centres EXIS, Centre for International Youth Activities, PO Box 15344, 1001 MH Amsterdam/Prof Tulpstraat 2, 1018 Amsterdam is the national centre fostering international contacts between young people. Provides information and advice on holidays, paid and voluntary work, au pair placements plus other opportunities for Dutch people, cheap travel and accommodation, courses and exchanges. Publishes *Young Visitors to the Netherlands*, a guide for young EC nationals with information on working, studying and practical training, language courses, transport, money, accommodation and a list of useful addresses. Available from the Central Bureau, Seymour Mews House, Seymour Mews, London W1H 9PE price £3.10 including UK postage.

Accommodation Cok Hotels Amsterdam, Koninginneweg 34-36, 1075 CZ Amsterdam offers low-cost accommodation in 3 modern hotels situated in the green heart of Amsterdam. Facilities include self-service restaurant, bars and function rooms. Cost from Dfl 35 per night includes accommodation in 5/6 bedded rooms and breakfast.

Ernst Sillem Hoeve, Soestdykerweg 10b, 3734 MH Den Dolder is an international YMCA conference and holiday centre with 100 beds. Open all year; all ages. Also YMCA camps with 25-60 beds in tents and dormitories, May-September; ages up to 24.

Hans Brinker Hotel, Kerkstraat 136-138, 1017 GR Amsterdam has budget accommodation in a variety of rooms from singles to dormitories of up to 12 beds. Facilities include restaurants, cafe, bar and tourist information. Open all year. Cost from Dfl 23 bed and breakfast..

Netherlands Board of Tourism, see above, can provide information on virtually every type of accommodation available in the Netherlands.

AU PAIR/ CHILDCARE

AVALON AGENCY Thursley House, 53 Station Road, Shalford, Guildford, Surrey GU4 8HA Tel Guildford 63640
Can place au pairs. Opportunity to attend language classes. 25-30 hour week. Ages 18-30. 6+ months. Basic knowledge of Dutch needed. Food, lodging, £18 pocket money per week and insurance provided. Service charge £40, if placement is accepted.

EXIS Centre for International Youth Activities, PO Box 15344, 1001 MH Amsterdam/ Prof Tulpstraat 2, 1018 HA Amsterdam
Arranges au pair positions throughout the year. Experience not essential, but a basic knowledge of Dutch helpful. Au pairs work a 30 hour week plus babysitting, with 1 free day per week. 6+ months. Ages 18-30. £27 per week pocket money, board, lodging and insurance provided. Travel costs paid by applicants.

HOME FROM HOME 10 Tackley Place, Oxford, Oxfordshire OX2 6RR Tel Oxford 512628
Can place au pairs to undertake childcare and light housework in the Netherlands, all year round. 5 hour day, 30 hour week. No experience necessary. Ages 18+. Pocket money £25 per week. Applicants pay own travel and insurance costs. Placement fee £40.

AU PAIR/CHILDCARE

INFORMATION

INTERLINGUA CENTRE Torquay Road, Foxrock, Dublin, Ireland 18 Tel Dublin 893876
Can place au pairs families throughout the Netherlands. 30 hour week with one full day and some evenings off. Time to attend language classes 2-3 mornings or afternoons per week. Experience desirable but not essential. 6+ months. Ages 18+. £25-£40 per week pocket money, full board, lodging and insurance provided. Travel paid by applicants. Placement fee £55.

CONSERVATION

INTERNATIONAL VOLUNTARY SERVICE 162 Upper New Walk, Leicester LE1 7QA Tel Leicester 549430

UNITED NATIONS ASSOCIATION International Youth Service, Welsh Centre for International Affairs, Temple of Peace, Cathays Park, Cardiff CF1 3AP Tel Cardiff 223088

Apply to either of the above to work in international teams on conservation projects. Recent projects have included mowing grass and reeds, and cleaning ditches in the fen area of Guisveld; reconstruction of a Stone Age burial place in Stadskanaal, near Groningen; measuring water samples to expose cases of commercial pollution, on a ship harboured in Amsterdam; and repairing old barns at an educational farm for children in Soest. Study elements included environmental education and nature protection. Ages 18-30. Volunteers with previous workcamp experience preferred. 30-35 hour, 5 day week, with weekends free. 2/3 weeks, July-August. Food, accommodation in schools, community centres, farms or tents and insurance provided, but not travel. Some camps accept children. B D PH

Organised by Stichting Internationale Vrijwilligersprojekten, Willemstraat 7, 3511 RJ Utrecht.

Applications from outside the UK: please see workcamp information on page 27.

COURIERS

PGL YOUNG ADVENTURE LTD Personnel Department, Alton Court, Penyard Lane, Ross-on-Wye, Herefordshire HR9 5NR Tel Ross-on-Wye 764211
Couriers are required to escort groups of young people on Dutch barge holidays, starting and finishing in London. Couriers are totally responsible for the welfare of their group, and for giving them an enjoyable holiday. The barge provides accommodation for up to 34 guests, and each group has 2 couriers. Holidays run for 10 days and the itinerary allows for frequent stops at centres of interest within easy access of the moorings. Ages 21+. Applicants should have skill and experience of working with children, and in controlling groups of teenagers aged 12-15 and 16-18. They should be committed, tolerant, flexible, enthusiastic and have stamina, energy and a sense of humour. Fairly demanding job; preference will be given to those with maturity, resourcefulness, strong personality and a previous knowledge of the area. Couriers are employed for 1 or 2 trips, July-September. Pocket money £4 per day plus expenses.

VENTURE ABROAD Warren House, High Street, Cranleigh, Surrey GU6 8AJ Tel Cranleigh 273027
Representatives are required by a tour operator specialising in holidays for youth groups. The work involves assisting and advising groups staying in Eemhof, helping them to get the most out of their stay. Representatives meet groups on arrival, provide general local information, escort on excursions and act as a guide to the surrounding countryside. Ages 19+. University students with knowledge of Dutch or German and experience of working with youth groups preferred. 50 hour week, end June-end August. Salary £65-£70 per week, insurance, self-catering accommodation, work permits and visas provided. Basic training given before departure. *Apply enclosing cv.*

When writing to any organisation it is essential to mention Working Holidays 1991 and enclose a large stamped, self-addressed envelope, or if overseas, a large addressed envelope and at least two International Reply Coupons.

FARMWORK

INTERNATIONAL FARM EXPERIENCE PROGRAMME YFC Centre, National Agricultural Centre, Kenilworth, Warwickshire CV8 2LG Tel Coventry 696584
Provides assistance to young farmers and nurserymen by finding places in farms and nurseries abroad to enable them to broaden their knowledge of agricultural methods. Opportunities to take part in practical training schemes which involve living and working on a farm, where the work is matched as far as possible with the applicant's requirements. 3-12 months, all year. Wages £30; board and lodging provided. Applicants pay own travel. Also 4 month practical training scheme preceded by a 6 week French/German language course in France, starting February or June. The work is hard; 8-10 hour day, 6 day week, every other weekend free. Wages £30 on farm and pocket money on the course; board and lodging provided. Ages 18-26. Applicants must have at least 2 years practical experience, 1 year of which may be at an agricultural college, and intend to make a career in agriculture or horticulture. Valid driving licence necessary. Registration fee £62. *British nationals only; apply at least 4 months in advance.*

Dutch applicants should apply to Stichting Uitwisseling, Postbus 97, 1860 Bergen NH.

MINISTERIE VAN SOCIALE ZAKEN EN WERKGELEGENHEID Directoraat-Generaal voor de Arbeidsvoorziening, Bureau Internationale Arbeidsbemiddeling & Stagiaires, Visseringlaan 26, Postbus 5814, 2280 HV Rijswijk
Can assist young people interested in holiday or seasonal farmwork by putting them in touch with potential employers. Most vacancies occur in the floriculture/flower bulb sector, in the provinces of Noord-Holland and Zuid-Holland. Work involves digging, peeling, sorting, counting and packing bulbs, and getting bulbs and flowers ready for transport. Also some vacancies in fruit/vegetable greenhouses of the Westland in Zuid-Holland, helping with the harvest, sorting and packing produce. Ages 16+. Applicants should be fit and prepared for hard, dirty work outdoors in all weathers, and/or indoors in hot greenhouses. 8+ weeks, peak period mid June-mid August. Hours variable. Salary dependent on the employee's age, circumstances, hours worked and form of payment. Transport and accommodation usually arranged by applicants. *EC nationals only.*

WORKCAMPS

CHRISTIAN MOVEMENT FOR PEACE Bethnal Green United Reformed Church, Pott Street, London E2 0EF Tel 071-729 1877
An international movement open to all who share a common concern for lasting peace and justice in the world. Volunteers are needed to work in international teams on summer projects aimed at offering a service in an area of need and generating self-help within the community; promoting international understanding and the discussion of social problems; and offering young people the chance to live as a group and take these experiences into the context of daily life. Recent projects have included repairing tools to be sent to Nicaragua and Zimbabwe for the Dutch branch of Tools for Self-Reliance; fruit picking and construction work in a former monastery at De Weyst; manual work at an organic mixed farm at Beemster; and converting a farmhouse into a centre for people who have had traumatic experiences, in Giethoorn. Ages 18+. 6 hour day, 30-36 hour week. 2-3 weeks, June-August. Food, accommodation and insurance provided, but participants pay their own travel. Registration fee £24.

Organised by ICVD, Pesthuislaan 25, 1054 RH Amsterdam.

Applications from outside the UK: please see workcamp information on page 27.

INTERNATIONAL VOLUNTARY SERVICE 162 Upper New Walk, Leicester LE1 7QA Tel Leicester 549430
IVS is the British branch of Service Civil International which promotes international reconciliation through work projects. Recent projects have included repairing old tools to send to schools in Zimbabwe; working to conserve peaty areas in Kortenhoef; repairing secondhand tools to be sent to a small

technological centre in Zambia; helping to organise and publicise a Third World Festival in Tilburg to draw attention to developments there; renovating and painting an Emmaus centre in Haarzuilens; and gardening with disabled people at an activity centre in Scheveningen. Study themes include Third World problems, human rights, peace, apartheid systems, women and violence. Ages 18+. Applicants should have previous workcamp, voluntary work or community service experience, and should be prepared to work hard and contribute to team life. 35-40 hour week. 2-4 weeks, June-September. Food, accommodation and insurance provided, but not travel. Membership fee £25 (students £15, unwaged £10). Registration fee £40. B D PH

Organised by Vrijwillige Internationale Aktie, Pesthuislaan 25, 1054 RH Amsterdam.

Applications from outside the UK: please see workcamp information on page 27.

INTERNATIONAL VOLUNTARY SERVICE 162 Upper New Walk, Leicester LE1 7QA Tel Leicester 549430

UNITED NATIONS ASSOCIATION International Youth Service, Welsh Centre for International Affairs, Temple of Peace, Cathays Park, Cariff CF1 3AP Tel Cardiff 223088

Apply to either of the above to work on international social service workcamps. Recent projects have included repairing bicycles for refugees at a centre in Goes; organising holiday activities for ethnic minority children in Amersfoort; repairing and painting a women's centre in Amsterdam; and construction and decoration work for a Third World solidarity group in Groningen. All camps include related study theme. Excursions and films. Ages 18-30. Volunteers with previous workcamp experience preferred. 30-35 hour, 5 day week, weekends free. 2/3 weeks, July and August. Food, accommodation in schools, centres, farms or tents and insurance provided, but not travel. Some camps accept children. B D PH

Organised by Stichting Internationale Vrijwilligersprojekten, Willemstraat 7, 3511 RJ Utrecht.

Applications from outside the UK: please see workcamp information on page 27.

GENERAL

MINISTERIE VAN SOCIALE ZAKEN EN WERKGELEGENHEID Afdeling Internationale Arbeidsbemiddeling, Visseringlaan 26, 2288 ER Rijswijk
The Ministry of Social Affairs and Labour may be able to assist young people in finding temporary employment for at least 8 weeks during the summer, or from mid October-end December.

ROYAL NETHERLANDS EMBASSY Economic Department, 38 Hyde Park Gate, London SW7 5DP Tel 071-584 5040
Can provide a list of labour exchanges in some major towns in the Netherlands, as well as information sheets on social security and income tax.

NETHERLANDS

GENERAL

NOTES

NEW ZEALAND

New Zealand High Commission
New Zealand House, 80 Haymarket, London
SW1Y 4TE Tel 071-930 8422

British High Commission
Reserve Bank Building, 2 The Terrace, PO Box
1812, Wellington 1

Tourist office
New Zealand Tourist Office, 5th floor, New
Zealand House, 80 Haymarket, London SW1Y
4TE Tel 071-973 0360

Youth hostels
YHA of New Zealand Inc, PO Box 436,
Christchurch 1

Youth & student information
New Zealand University Students Association,
Student Travel Bureau, PO Box 6368, Te Aro,
Wellington

INFORMATION

Entry regulations A work permit is required
for all types of employment. Those entering
New Zealand temporarily for full-time and
pre-arranged employment, as distinct from a
working holiday, should apply to the
Immigration Service, at New Zealand House,
see above, at least 4 weeks before the intended
date of departure, earlier in the case of
teachers, doctors, nurses or other hospital staff.
A request for a permit will only be considered
if the applicant has a firm guarantee of
employment in an occupation in which they are
qualified and experienced, and which is
currently in demand in New Zealand, and for
which overseas recruitment is being approved.

Young people on a bona fide holiday,
especially where employment is being offered
by relatives or sponsors, may lodge an
application after arrival with the nearest office
of the Immigration Service, and should enclose
a written offer of employment from the
employer concerned. The employer may
consult the Immigration Service in advance,
but there is no guarantee that a permit will be
issued. Applicants must have a passport valid
for at least 3 months beyond the last day of
their proposed stay, a fully paid return or
onward ticket, plus proof that they will have a
minimum of NZ$1000 per month of stay on

arrival or have made prior arrangements for
their support while in the country. Permits are
granted for an initial period of 3 months, 6
months for UK passport holders, although
extensions for up to a total of 12 months may
be considered. Fees are payable for all services.

Travel Compass, 9 Grosvenor Gardens, London
SW1W 0BH Tel 071-828 4111 are agents for
New Zealand Railways. Travelpass provides
unlimited travel on trains, buses and ferry.
Cost from £138 (8 days).

Publications *Travellers Survival Kit Australia &
New Zealand* £6.95, is a handbook for those
going down under, giving information on
travelling as cheaply as possible, local culture,
restaurants, beaches and reef, flora and fauna.
Published by Vacation Work, 9 Park End
Street, Oxford OX1 1HJ Tel Oxford 241978.

**When writing to any organisation it is
essential to mention Working Holidays 1991
and enclose a large stamped, self-addressed
envelope, or if overseas, a large addressed
envelope and at least two International Reply
Coupons.**

NEW ZEALAND

GENERAL

FARMWORK

FARMWORK

INTERNATIONAL AGRICULTURAL EXCHANGE ASSOCIATION YFC Centre, National Agricultural Centre, Kenilworth, Warwickshire CV8 2LG Tel Coventry 696578
Operates opportunities for agricultural students and young people to acquire practical work experience in the rural sector, and to strengthen and improve their knowledge and understanding of the way of life in other countries. Participants are given an opportunity to study practical methods on approved training farms, and work as trainees, gaining further experience in their chosen field. Types of farm include cattle and sheep; mixed (cattle, sheep and field crops); dairy; horticultural enterprises; plus a very limited number of bee farms.
Participants undertake paid work on the farm, approx 45 hours per week, and live as members of the host family. Full board and lodging, insurance cover and a net weekly wage of £50-£60 provided. All programmes include 3/4 weeks unpaid holiday. 3/5 day orientation courses held at agricultural colleges and universities throughout New Zealand. Educational sightseeing trips (4 days-3 weeks) within New Zealand and in Australia, Thailand, Singapore, Fiji, Hawaii and the US arranged for participants en route for all programmes. Ages 19-28. Applicants should be single, and have good practical experience in the chosen training category, plus a valid driving licence. 6 months (departing October), 8 months (departing July), 13 months - 6½ in New Zealand plus 6½ in Canada/US departing October) or 15 months - 8 months in New Zealand plus 7 months in Australia (departing July). Cost from £1250 (6/8 months). £200 deposit payable. Costs cover airfare, work permit, administration fee, orientation courses and insurance, plus travel and half board accommodation on sightseeing trips. *Apply at least 4 months in advance. British nationals only.*

New Zealand applicants requiring an exchange should apply to IAEA, PO Box 328, Whakatane, North Island.

TEACHERS

GAP ACTIVITY PROJECTS LTD 44 Queen's Road, Reading, Berkshire RG1 4BB Tel Reading 594914
Work is available in independent boarding schools acting as house tutors, helping with activities, games, music, drama, expeditions, private tuition, supervisory duties and laboratory work. Most placements are in the North Island, but volunteers will have ample opportunity to travel to the South. Applicants should be school leavers aged 18-19 who have up to a year before going on to further education. September or January/February-mid August. Board, lodging and pocket money provided. Cost £325 plus airfare and insurance. *Apply early September of final school year; applications close March. British nationals only.*

GENERAL

CAREERS RESEARCH & ADVISORY CENTRE (CRAC) Sheraton House, Castle Park, Cambridge CB3 0AX Tel Cambridge 460277
Opportunities are available to work, travel and live in New Zealand for up to 3 months. The Britain Australasia Vocational Exchange scheme aims to widen the experience and understanding of industrial, commercial and business life, providing work experience to help British undergraduates relate and apply their studies to career opportunities. 12 weeks, July-September. Students work for a period of 8 weeks in jobs relating wherever possible to university studies, then have approx 4 weeks holiday time. Jobs have included work in retail distribution, mining and metallurgy, farming, engineering, geology, planning, marketing, personnel, accountancy, astronomy, banking, computing, nursing and research. Those studying engineering, economics, commerce, computing or applied science stand a higher chance of being placed. Preference given to students in the penultimate year of a first degree course. Average weekly wage NZ$340. Flight, visa, work permit and insurance organised. Participants pay their airfare, but should earn sufficient to cover board, lodging and living expenses. Insurance £60; registration fee £8. *Application forms available November.*

NORTHERN IRELAND

Tourist office
Northern Ireland Tourist Board, 11 Berkeley Street, London W1X 6BU Tel 071-493 0601

Northern Ireland Tourist Board, River House, 48 High Street, Belfast BT1 2DS
Tel 0232-2315906

Youth hostels
Youth Hostels Association of Northern Ireland, 56 Bradbury Place, Belfast BT7 1RU
Tel 0232-324733

Entry regulations governing the employment of overseas workers are given under **Great Britain**

CHILDREN'S PROJECTS

FELLOWSHIP OF RECONCILIATION Workcamps, c/o 24 Pinehill Road, Ballycairn, Lisburn, Co Antrim BT27 5TU Tel Lisburn 826341
Volunteers are needed for a workcamp in Lurgan, helping to run constructive Catholic and Protestant playschemes for the children of the Shankhill, Avenue Road and Wakehurst estates. Concurrently organises a playschemes workcamp in Belfast between Tiger Bay and New Lodge estates, a deprived and deeply segregated area. Ages 18+. 3 weeks, July/ August. Volunteers receive maintenance but pay their own travel costs. A few days are set aside before the camp for briefing and consultation. *Apply by 1 April.*

PAX CHRISTI 9 Henry Road, London N4 2LH Tel 081-800 4612
An international Catholic movement for peace, founded at the end of the Second World War. Volunteers are needed to work on summer playschemes for Catholic and Protestant children and young people from housing estates, based at schools, community centres and youth clubs in Belfast, Dungannon and Antrim. The schemes aim to ease tension and promote integration by providing happy and creative play opportunities for those for whom there is otherwise very little provision. Each

scheme has 6-20 volunteers and daily attracts up to 500 young people aged 5-21. Volunteers work in international teams and in close collaboration with the local community. Work involves helping to plan, organise and supervise indoor and outdoor activities including sports and team games, hiking, nature studies, drama, arts and crafts, discos, day trips, weekend camping trips, talent shows and fancy dress parades.
Ages 18+. Experience with children desirable and volunteers must be self-disciplined, energetic, committed to community living, sensitive to the local situation, prepared to work together as an international team and to take considerable personal responsibility and initiative in planning, assessing and maintaining the schemes. Approx 30 hour, 5 day week, with some weekend work. 3-5 weeks, July/August. Self-catering accommodation in schools, empty houses, youth clubs, church halls or with families provided, plus food. Help may be given with travel costs if necessary. Volunteers arrange their own insurance. Orientation weekend arranged, which volunteers are strongly urged to attend. It is essential that time is taken to study the history and current situation in Northern Ireland before arrival. *British nationals only.*

NORTHERN IRELAND

COMMUNITY WORK

CONSERVATION

COMMUNITY WORK

CHRISTIAN MOVEMENT FOR PEACE
Bethnal Green United Reformed Church, Pott Street, London E2 0EF Tel 071-729 1877
An international movement open to all who share a common concern for lasting peace and justice in the world. Volunteers are needed to work in international teams on summer projects aimed at offering a service in an area of need and promoting self-help within the community; promoting international understanding and the discussion of social problems; and offering young people the chance to live as a group and take these experiences into the context of daily life. Recent projects have included working in a deprived, high unemployment area of Belfast and running a playscheme for children from both Loyalist and Nationalist areas. Ages 18+. 6 hour day, 30-36 hour week. 2-3 weeks, July-September. Food, accommodation and insurance provided, but participants pay their own travel. Registration fee £24. **PH**

Applications from outside the UK: please see workcamp information on page 27.

THE CORRYMEELA COMMUNITY
Volunteer Coordinator, Corrymeela Centre, 5 Drumaroan Road, Ballycastle BT54 6QU Tel Ballycastle 62626
An interdenominational Christian community working for reconciliation in Northern Ireland, and promoting a concern for issues of peace and justice in the wider world. Volunteers are needed at the Community's ecumenical centre on the north Antrim coast, helping to run youth camps/projects and family weeks for children and families under stress and from troubled areas. Volunteers must be prepared to spend 6 days living, working and playing with a group as one community in a residential setting. Involves looking after and planning activities for children, building up relationships with parents and organising outings. Ages 18+. 1-3 weeks, July and August. Cost £27, £18 unwaged, per week includes board and accommodation. Applicants are expected to attend preparation weekend. *Apply by mid May. Overseas volunteers accepted.* **PH**

INTERNATIONAL VOLUNTARY SERVICE
162 Upper New Walk, Leicester LE1 7QA Tel Leicester 549430
IVS is the British branch of Service Civil International which promotes international reconciliation through work projects. Volunteers are needed for community work on international workcamps. Recent projects have included running playschemes for children in Derry and Newry; organising recreational activities for the patients of a psychiatric hospital in Holywell; constructing an adventure playground for a community centre in Banbridge; and running a holiday in the west of the Province for underprivileged children. Ages 18+. Experience in working with children an advantage. Overseas volunteers must speak at least basic English. Applicants should be prepared to work hard and contribute to team life. 35-40 hour week. 2-3 weeks, July and August, and Christmas and Easter. Food, accommodation in schools, hospitals or community centres with self-catering facilities, and insurance provided, but not travel. Membership fee £25 (students £15, unwaged £10). Registration fee £20. **B D PH**

Organised by IVS Northern Ireland, 122 Great Victoria Street, Belfast BT2 7BG Tel 0232-238147.

Applications from outside the UK: please see workcamp information on page 27.

CONSERVATION

CONSERVATION VOLUNTEERS
(NORTHERN IRELAND) The Pavilion, Cherryvale Park, Ravenhill Road, Belfast BT6 0BZ Tel 0232-645169
The Northern Ireland branch of the British Trust for Conservation Volunteers, a charity promoting practical conservation work by volunteers. Organises numerous projects on nature reserves, country estates, NT properties and country parks. Recent projects have included restoring the famous Brandy Pad in the Mourne Mountains; fencing and woodland management on Strangford Lough; drystone walling in the Fermanagh countryside; and clearing gorse and habitat management in the Murlough national nature reserve. Also family holidays with a variety of work for adults and

alternative entertainment for the children. Instruction is given in the techniques of drystone walling, fencing, coppicing, woodland and wetland management, footpath repair and many other conservation skills. Approx 12 volunteers work on each task with an experienced leader; beginners welcome. Ages 16+. 7/8 hour day with 1 day off per week. 1 week, March-September. Food, insurance, accommodation in training centre, tents, youth hostels or cottages provided. Everyone helps to prepare the food and volunteers are asked to contribute approx £2 per day towards camp costs. Tasks qualify under the Duke of Edinburgh's Award scheme.

INTERNATIONAL VOLUNTARY SERVICE 162 Upper New Walk, Leicester LE1 7QA Tel Leicester 549430
IVS is the British branch of Service Civil International, which promotes international reconciliation through work projects. Volunteers are needed for conservation work on international projects. Recent projects have included clearing a nature walk, cutting back undergrowth and making paths alongside Carlingford Lough; carrying out a land use survey on the shores of Strangford Lough, an area rich in wildlife; and helping to re-lay the old railway line between Downpatrick and Ardglass to establish a permanent tourist attraction. Ages 18+. Applicants should be prepared to work hard and contribute to team life. 35-40 hour week. 2-4 weeks, June-September. Food, accommodation in schools or community centres with self-catering facilities and insurance provided, but not travel. Membership fee £25 (students £15, unwaged £10). Registration fee £20. **B D PH**

Organised by IVS Northern Ireland, 122 Great Victoria Street, Belfast BT2 7BG Tel 0232-238147.

Applications from outside the UK: please see workcamp information on page 27.

NATIONAL TRUST COMMITTEE FOR NORTHERN IRELAND Irene Murphy, Regional Volunteer Organiser, Rowallane House, Saintfield, Ballynahinch, Co Down BT24 7LH Tel Saintfield 510721
A major conservation society, organising several workcamps each year at its estate at

Castle Ward on the shores of Strangford Lough. Typical projects include scrub clearance, fencing, conservation work and helping with the wildfowl collection. Ages 16+. July/August. Basecamp accommodation provided in stone houses. Participants should take sleeping bags.

DOMESTIC

THE CORRYMEELA COMMUNITY Volunteer Coordinator, Corrymeela Centre, 5 Drumaroan Road, Ballycastle BT54 6QU Tel Ballycastle 62626
An interdenominational Christian community working for reconciliation in Northern Ireland, and promoting a concern for issues of peace and justice in the wider world. Youth camps/projects and family weeks are organised for children and families under stress and from troubled areas, at the Community's ecumenical centre at Ballycastle on the north Antrim coast. Opportunities for volunteers to supplement the resident domestic staff, including assisting in the laundry, general housework and the kitchen, where experience of cooking for large groups is an asset; and to work in reception, receiving groups and visitors and performing routine administrative tasks. Ages 18+. Applicants must be able to cope with very hard and demanding work. 1-3 weeks, July and August. Full board and accommodation provided. Applicants are expected to attend a preparation weekend. *Apply by mid May. Overseas volunteers accepted.* **PH**

MONITORS & INSTRUCTORS

THE CORRYMEELA COMMUNITY Volunteer Coordinator, Corrymeela Centre, 5 Drumaroan Road, Ballycastle BT54 6QU Tel Ballycastle 62626
An interdenominational Christian community working for reconciliation in Northern Ireland, and promoting a concern for issues of peace and justice in the wider world. Youth camps/projects and family weeks are organised for children and families under stress and from troubled areas, at the Community's ecumenical

NORTHERN IRELAND

MONITORS & INSTRUCTORS

WORKCAMPS

centre on the north Antrim coast.
Opportunities for volunteers to supplement the resident staff include a music resource person to accompany singing at worship, barbecues and general sing-songs; assisting in drama and arts and crafts such as weaving, printing, macrame and candle making; and organising and supervising recreational activities. Ages 18+. Applicants must have relevant experience or skills and be able to cope with very hard and demanding work. 1-3 weeks, July and August. Full board and accommodation provided. Applicants are expected to attend a preparation weekend. *Apply by mid May. Overseas volunteers accepted.* PH

GLEN RIVER YMCA National Centre, Rathmourne House, 143 Central Promenade, Newcastle, County Down BT33 0AU Tel Newcastle 24488/23172
Offers a wide range of outdoor activities aiming to introduce young people to nature and improve their quality of life in a Christian atmosphere. Volunteers are needed to work as counsellors, instructors, domestic assistants and day camp leaders. Training is given in basic activities such as ropes course, archery, orienteering, adventure and nature walks. Opportunity to take part in canoeing, walking, climbing and abseiling as well as opportunities to participate in programmes and excursions with the clients. All staff will be expected to participate in domestic and other duties related to the running of the centre. Applicants should agree with the aims and purposes of the YMCA, be articulate, enjoy working with children and fit easily into the staff team. Good knowledge of English required. Ages 18+. June-August. 6 day week. All meals, accommodation, public liability insurance and £18 per week pocket money provided. Participants pay own travel and insurance.

WORKCAMPS

INTERNATIONAL VOLUNTARY SERVICE 162 Upper New Walk, Leicester LE1 7QA Tel Leicester 549430
IVS is the British branch of Service Civil International, which promotes international reconciliation through work projects. Volunteers are needed for manual work on international workcamps. Recent projects have included harvesting fruit and vegetables, making jam, constructing and repairing a cowshed, painting and cleaning at Glebe House, a children's holiday centre at Strangford in Co Down; building an adventure playground at a community centre in Bainbridge; helping with organic farming and repainting buildings at a peace people farm in Coleraine; and helping a community theatre group stage a play in Belfast's Botanic Gardens. Ages 18+. Applicants should be prepared to work hard and contribute to team life. 40 hour week. 2-3 weeks, June-September. There are also a few camps at Christmas and Easter. Food, accommodation in schools or community centres with self-catering facilities, and insurance provided, but not travel. Membership fee £25 (students £15, unwaged £10). Registration fee £20. **B D PH**

Organised by IVS Northern Ireland, 122 Great Victoria Street, Belfast BT2 7BG Tel 0232-238147.

Applications from outside the UK: please see workcamp information on page 27.

NORWAY

Royal Norwegian Embassy
25 Belgrave Square, London SW1X 8QD
Tel 071-235 7151

British Embassy
Thomas Heftyesgate 8, 0264 Oslo 2

Tourist office
Norwegian National Tourist Office, 20 Pall
Mall, London SW1Y 5NE Tel 071-839 6255

Youth hostels
Landslaget for Norske Ungdoms-herberger,
Dronningensgate 26, Oslo 1

Youth & student information
Universitetenes Reisebyra (Norwegian Student
Travel Office), Universitets-sentret, Blindern,
Boks 55, Oslo 3

Norwegian Foundation for Youth Exchange,
Rolf Hofmosgate 18, 0655 Oslo 6

INFORMATION

Entry regulations A work permit is required
for all types of employment. This can only be
obtained before arrival in Norway, when a job
has been secured with an employer who has
been approved by the Norwegian labour
authorities to employ foreign personnel. An
Offer of Employment form must be completed
and signed by the employer before a work
permit can be applied for. A work permit is
very difficult to obtain and only people with
special skills are accepted, if a Norwegian
national cannot fill the job. The application will
be sent to the competent authorities in Norway,
who normally require 3-6 months for
investigations; in special cases and at peak
times the time required may be longer. A
current full passport is required; identity cards
or visitors' passports are not valid for
employment purposes. Applications for work
in Norway can be made under the International
Clearing of Vacancies (ICV) scheme; for more
details contact the Training Agency. Because of
the labour situation, work permits will not
usually be given to foreign nationals seeking
seasonal employment. If a person has had an
offer for seasonal employment, they should
apply for a work permit through the Consular
Section of the Norwegian Embassy, see above,
or to the Royal Norwegian Consulate General,
86 George Street, Edinburgh EH2 3BU Tel 031-
226 5701; Royal Norwegian Consulate, 470
India Building, Water Street, Liverpool L2 0QT
Tel 051-236 2787; or Royal Norwegian
Consulate General, Tyne Commission Quay,

Albert Edward Dock, North Shields NE29 EA
Tel 091-259 5490. Only in special cases, when
the labour exchange has agreed to the job in
question, is it advisable to go to Norway.
Under the Norwegian Aliens Regulations
applicants should not, in their own interest,
enter the country during the period in which
the application for a work permit is under
consideration.

Job advertising Frank L Crane (London) Ltd
International Press Representation, 5/15
Cromer Street, Grays Inn Road, London WC1H
8LS Tel 071-837 3330 are agents for the daily
newspaper *Dagbladet*, for which they can accept
job advertisements.

Publicitas Ltd, 525/527 Fulham Road, London
SW6 1HF Tel 071-385 7723 are agents for a
number of magazines.

Travel The Nordic Tourist Ticket entitles the
holder to unlimited travel on trains in Norway,
Denmark, Finland and Sweden, and is also
valid on some inter-Scandinavian ferries.
Valid for 21 days; cost £113, ages under 26,
£151 ages over 26. Details from Norwegian
State Railways, 21-24 Cockspur Street, London
SW1Y 5DA Tel 071-930 6666.

Campus Travel, 52 Grosvenor Gardens, London
SW1W 0AG Tel 071-730 3402 offers Eurotrain
under 26 fares and youth/student flights to
destinations in Norway.

NORWAY

The Rough Guide to Scandinavia £7.95 is a practical handbook which includes concise, up-to-date information on getting around Norway. Published by Harrap Columbus, Chelsea House, 26 Market Square, Bromley, Kent BR1 1NA.

AU PAIR/ CHILDCARE

NORWEGIAN FOUNDATION FOR YOUTH EXCHANGE Rolf Hofmosgate 18, 0655 Oslo 6
Can place English-speaking au pairs in Norwegian families, to provide an experience of Norwegian culture. 6+ months. Ages 18-28. Board, lodging, health insurance and NKr2000 per month provided. Travel and language course fees paid by applicants. *Apply 4 months in advance of work period desired.*

COMMUNITY WORK

NANSEN INTERNASJONALE CENTER Barnegarden Breivold, Nesset, 1400 Ski
Aims to help teenagers with social problems at a relief and activity centre in a renovated farm 25 km south of Oslo, based on total participation and involvement from the voluntary staff as well as the permanent staff and residents. Volunteers are needed, from cleaning and preparation tasks to creative work, hobbies, sports and the care of animals. The projects take approx 20 children, aged 5-17, per week, and there are many opportunities to develop and use creative skills. The work is physically and mentally demanding, but rewarding. Ages 22+. Applicants should be mature, practical and have experience or strong motivation and commitment to work with children who are in need of care, and willing to take part in all activities. The staff is international and the working languages are English and Norwegian. Beginning June-mid August, and all year round. Long working hours on a rota basis, with approx 3 days free per fortnight. Board and lodging in barracks or houses, plus NKr300 per week pocket money and opportunities to travel in Norway.

FARMWORK

INTERNATIONAL FARM EXPERIENCE PROGRAMME YFC Centre, National Agricultural Centre, Kenilworth, Warwickshire CV8 2LG Tel Coventry 696584
Provides assistance to young farmers and nurserymen by finding places in farms and nurseries abroad to enable them to broaden their knowledge of agricultural methods. Opportunities for practical horticultural or agricultural work, usually on mixed farms. Applicants live and work with a farmer and his family and the work is matched as far as possible with the applicant's requirements. The work can be strenuous. Girls should be prepared to work inside the home as well as outside. 2-3 months, May-September. Salary £30 per week; board and lodging provided. Ages 18-26. Applicants must have at least 2 years practical experience, 1 year of which may be at an agricultural college, and intend to make a career in agriculture or horticulture. Valid driving licence necessary. Applicants pay own fare. Registration fee £62. *British nationals only.*

Norwegian applications to the Norwegian Foundation for Youth Exchange, Rolf Hofmosgate 18, 0655 Oslo 6.

NORWEGIAN FOUNDATION FOR YOUTH EXCHANGE Working Guest Programme, Rolf Hofmosgate 18, 0655 Oslo 6
Opportunities to stay on a farm as a working guest. The work involves haymaking, weeding, milking, picking fruit, berries and vegetables, tractor driving, feeding cattle, painting, housework and/or taking care of the children, combined with outdoor work. Most farmers and/or their children speak some English or German. Ages 18-30. Farming experience desirable but not essential; applicants must be willing to work hard. Up to 35 hour week, 1½+ consecutive free days. 4-12 weeks, all year. Board and lodging, health insurance and NKr500+ per week pocket money provided; work permits arranged. Participants pay their own travel costs. Registration fee NKr830; NKr700 refundable if not placed. Some farms accept 2 people who apply together. Applicants should receive job offers 4-6 weeks before their proposed date of arrival. *Apply by February.*

WORKCAMPS

INTERNATIONAL VOLUNTARY SERVICE
162 Upper New Walk, Leicester LE1 7QA
Tel Leicester 549430
IVS is the British branch of Service Civil
International, which promotes international
reconciliation through work projects.
Volunteers are needed to work on international
workcamps. Recent projects have included
painting, haymaking and gardening at a Rudolf
Steiner community for the handicapped at
Jossasen; gardening and wood chopping at a
farm for young people with social problems in
Numedal; painting a museum and organising
an anti-racism project in Oslo; manual work
and traditional farming at a mountain school in
the Rondane mountains; and clearing a forest
to prevent toxic spraying in South Trondelag.
Ages 18+. Applicants should have previous
workcamp, voluntary work or community
service experience, and should be prepared to
work hard and contribute to team life. 35-40
hour week. 2-4 weeks, June-September. Food,
accommodation and insurance provided, but
not travel. Membership fee £25 (students £15,
unwaged £10). Registration fee £40. **B D PH**

Organised by Internasjonal Dugnad,
Rozenkrantzgate 18, 0160 Oslo 1.

Applications from outside the UK: please see
workcamp information on page 27.

APPLYING FOR A JOB

Read carefully all the information given before
applying. Check in particular:

* the necessary skills/experience required

* the full period of employment expected

* any restrictions of age, sex or nationality

* application deadlines

* any other points, particularly details of
insurance cover provided, and other costs
such as travel and accommodation.

When applying be sure to include:

* name, address, date of birth, marital status,
nationality, sex

* education, qualifications, relevant
experience

* period of availability

* details of languages spoken

* a large stamped, self-addressed envelope
plus, if overseas, 2 International Reply
Coupons

* a passport-size photo, particularly if you are
to have contact with the public

* any registration or membership fees

NOTES

POLAND

Polish Embassy
47 Portland Place, London W1N 3AG
Tel 071-580 4324
Visa section: Consulate General, 19 Weymouth
Street, London W1N 3AG Tel 071-580 0476

British Embassy
Aleje Roz 1, 00-556 Warsaw

Tourist office
Polorbis Travel Ltd, 82 Mortimer Street,
London W1N 7DE Tel 071-637 4971

Youth hostels
Polskie Towarzystwo Schronisk
Mlodziezowych, Chocimska 28, 00-791 Warsaw

Youth & student information
Almatur, Travel Bureau of the Polish Students'
Association, ul Kopernika 23, 00-359 Warsaw

Juventur Youth Travel Bureau, Union of
Socialist Polish Youth, Malczewsksiego 54,
02-622 Warsaw

INFORMATION

Entry regulations Details of entry
requirements can be obtained from the Visa
Section of the Polish Embassy. Workcamp
organisations will inform volunteers how to
obtain the necessary visa/permit and hold
orientation days for volunteers going to East
Europe, giving information on all aspects of the
work covered together with some political
background and practical information.

Travel Fregata Travel Ltd, 100 Dean Street,
London W1V 6AQ Tel 071-734 5101 offers
express rail travel London-Poznan/Warsaw
from £155 return including couchettes, and a
coach service Manchester/Nottingham/
Birmingham-Poznan/Warsaw, from £139
return.

The Polrailpass entitles the holder to unlimited
travel on local and express trains. Valid for 8/

15/21/30 days, cost from £35. Available from
Polorbis Travel Ltd, 82 Mortimer Street,
London W1N 7DE Tel 071-636 2217.

Campus Travel, 52 Grosvenor Gardens, London
SW1W 0AG Tel 071-730 3402 offers Eurotrain
under 26 fares and youth/student flights to
destinations in Poland.

Accommodation Polorbis Travel Ltd, see
above, can provide student and youth tourist
vouchers which guarantee bed and breakfast in
2-4 bedded rooms in international student
hotels in 20 major university cities. Vouchers
can be used without advance reservation,
provided check in is before 16.00. July-August.
Cost approx £10 per night. Vouchers can also
be used in payment for Almatur services,
equipment hire and tickets for cultural events.

COMMUNITY WORK

**ZWIAZEK SOCJALISTYCZNEJ MLODZIEZY
POLSKIEJ Union of Socialist Polish Youth,
International Department, ul Smolna 40,
00-920 Warsaw**
A social, political and cultural organisation
arranging special forms of activity for disabled
young people. Places are offered to foreign

physically handicapped young people to take
part in a 24 day programme which combines
voluntary work with medical therapy at a
health resort. Ages 18+. 24 hour week, June-
August. Board and accommodation, plus
Zl 3600 pocket money provided, but not travel
or insurance. **PH**

CONSERVATION

CHRISTIAN MOVEMENT FOR PEACE
Bethnal Green United Reformed Church, Pott
Street, London E2 0EF Tel 071-729 1877

INTERNATIONAL VOLUNTARY SERVICE
162 Upper New Walk, Leicester LE1 7QA
Tel Leicester 549430

UNITED NATIONS ASSOCIATION
International Youth Service, Welsh Centre for
International Affairs, Temple of Peace,
Cathays Park, Cardiff CF1 3AP Tel Cardiff
223088

Apply to one of the above to work on
international workcamps aiming to give young
people from foreign countries an insight into
the real social, economic, political and cultural
conditions in present day Poland. Recent
projects have included land reclamation and
lake construction in a former mining region at
Walbrzych; conservation work at Kakonosze
National Park, under threat from acid rain; and
restoring a cemetery and clearing parkland in
Warsaw. Educational, cultural and recreational
activities, including visits to national parks,
factories, museums, sports and meeting local
people. Ages 18-30. Previous workcamp
experience essential. Applicants should be
prepared to work hard and contribute to team
life. 30-35 hour week. 2-4 weeks, July and
August. Food and accommodation in schools,
hostels, houses or under canvas provided.
Compulsory orientation meeting for those
applying through IVS.

Organised by Ochotnize Hufce Pracy, ul
Kosynierow 22, 04-641 Warsaw.

*Applications from outside the UK: please see
workcamp information on page 27.*

**When writing to any organisation it is
essential to mention Working Holidays 1991
and enclose a large stamped, self-addressed
envelope, or if overseas, a large addressed
envelope and at least two International Reply
Coupons.**

FARMWORK

**INTERNATIONAL FARM EXPERIENCE
PROGRAMME** YFC Centre, National
Agricultural Centre, Kenilworth,
Warwickshire CV8 2LG Tel Coventry 696584
Provides assistance to young farmers and
nurserymen by finding places on farms and
nurseries, giving opportunities to live and
work with local people. Placements provide a
varied programme offering experience of
private farms as well as state cooperatives. 3-12
months. Ages 18-26. Pocket money, some travel
expenses, board and lodging provided.
Applicants must have at least two years
practical experience, one year of which may be
at an agricultural college and intend to make a
career in agriculture or horticulture.
Registration fee £62. *British nationals only.*

MONITORS & TEACHERS

**CENTRAL BUREAU Schools Unit, Seymour
Mews House, Seymour Mews, London W1H
9PE Tel 071-486 5101 ext 243**
Teachers and sixth formers are required at
English language camps held concurrently at
boarding schools at 3 venues, each
accommodating approx 100 pupils from
UNESCO associated schools which have
specialised courses in foreign languages.
The main objective is to provide Polish pupils
aged 15-18 with the opportunity of practising
English learnt in school, and by spending 4
weeks in the company of a group of British
teachers and young people to acquire a deeper
awareness of the British way of life. Duties
include assisting with the teaching of English
as a foreign language, running conversation
classes and organising sporting, musical and
social activities. Ages up to 45. Applicants
should be native English speakers, sixth
formers willing to assist the staff; or teachers
qualified in the teaching of any discipline: EFL
or ESL qualifications an advantage. Applicants
should have a sense of responsibility,
organisational skill, adaptability to new
surroundings, a sociable nature and an interest
in sports and/or drama and music, plus

experience of working with or teaching children. Participants must fully commit themselves to the teaching of English and the organisation of various educational, outdoor and social activities. 4 weeks, July-August, including a 4 day trip to places of interest at the end. Board and accommodation provided, plus honorarium in Polish currency towards pocket money. Travel cost approx £190 including insurance and visa, paid by applicants. Organised by the Polish Ministry of Education and UNESCO. *Apply by mid April.*

GAP ACTIVITY PROJECTS LTD 44 Queen's Road, Reading, Berkshire RG1 4BB Tel Reading 594914
A limited number of placements are available for girls to work at a school outside Warsaw, assisting the nuns to look after blind children, aged 4-12, and also to help teach English to 12-19 year old residents and staff. 8 hour day, 5½ day week. Applicants must have total confidence in their resilience to undertake a very demanding, but worthwhile job with few luxuries, and will be expected to undertake a one week TEFL course before departure. 6 months, from September or March. Board, lodging and a small monthly stipend provided. Cost £250 plus airfare, insurance and TEFL course fee. *Apply early September of last school year; applications close March. British nationals only.*

PEACE CAMPS

CHRISTIAN MOVEMENT FOR PEACE Bethnal Green United Reformed Church, Pott Street, London E2 0EF Tel 071-729 1877

INTERNATIONAL VOLUNTARY SERVICE 162 Upper New Walk, Leicester LE1 7QA Tel Leicester 549430

UNITED NATIONS ASSOCIATION International Youth Service, Welsh Centre for International Affairs, Temple of Peace, Cathays Park, Cardiff CF1 3AP Tel Cardiff 223088

Apply to one of the above to work on international peace camps, aiming to give young people from foreign countries an insight into the real social, economic, political and cultural conditions in present day Poland. Recent projects have included renovation work and preparation of the museum at Stutthof concentration camp in Elblag; and preservation work and constructing monuments at the Majdanek concentration camp in Lublin. In the context of Polish history one of the most important ways of working for peace is to recognise the horrors of war; it is important to keep alive an understanding of what happened in order to prevent history repeating itself. Volunteers should be aware that they will be confronted with very disturbing situations and they should give a lot of thought to the subject before participating, but should also be aware that they will be making an important contribution to promoting tolerance and justice. Educational, cultural and recreational activities, including visits to national parks, factories, museums, sports and meeting local people. Ages 18-30. Previous workcamp experience essential. Applicants should be prepared to work hard and contribute to team life. 30-35 hour week. 2-3 weeks, July-September. Food and accommodation in schools, hostels, houses or under canvas provided. Participants applying through IVS must attend an orientation meeting.

Organised by Ochotnize Hufco Pracy, ul Kosynierow 22, 04-641 Warsaw.

Applications from outside the UK: please see workcamp information on page 27.

WORKCAMPS

CHRISTIAN MOVEMENT FOR PEACE Bethnal Green United Reformed Church, Pott Street, London E2 0EF Tel 01-729 1877
An international movement open to all who share a common concern for lasting peace and justice in the world. Volunteers are needed to work on international workcamps aiming to promote mutual understanding among young people from different countries, and to present the achievements, traditions and culture of Poland. Recent projects have included carpentry, construction and cleaning at student riding centres at Zbroslawice and Trachy, with opportunities to ride and groom horses; and construction and maintenance work with Polish students at hikers' cottages in the

POLAND

PEACE CAMPS

WORKCAMPS

POLAND

Beskidy Mountains. Working language is
English; knowledge of French or German
useful. Recreational activities include
excursions to salt mines, towns and cities,
tennis, riding, swimming and cycling.
Ages 18-30. 40 hour week. 2 weeks, July and
August. Food and self-catering accommodation
provided, but participants pay their own travel
costs and insurance.

Organised by Almatur Travel Bureau, Polish
Students' Association, ul Kopernika 23, 00-359
Warsaw. Registration fee $25.

*Applications from outside the UK: please see
workcamp information on page 27.*

GENERAL

GENERAL

**POLISH JAZZ SOCIETY ul Mazowiecka 11,
00-052 Warsaw**
Set up in 1959 to teach jazz and to organise
festivals and charity concerts. Volunteers are
needed to participate in a jazz workshop at
Chodziez near Pila, receiving training in a
variety of instruments in small groups and big
bands, with joint sessions on music theory and
the history of jazz. Participants must be able to
read music fluently, should have a knowledge
of basic jazz standards and must submit a brief
summary of their musical knowledge. 2 weeks,
15 July-3 August, 10.00-19.00 with an evening
jam session. Ages 16/17+. No wages paid but
each participant receives assistance, approx
20% of total cost, to cover the organisation of
the workshop. Accommodation in hotels or
camping, with meals; cost from US$298.
Participants pay own travel costs. Open to
those with a secondary school knowledge of
music, professional musicians or amateurs
with a recommendation from a qualified
musician, music school or club. *All nationalities
welcome; working languages English, German and
Russian.* B D PH

PORTUGAL

Portuguese Embassy
11 Belgrave Square, London SW1X 8PP
Tel 071-235 5331
Visa section: Consulate General, Silver City
House, 62 Brompton Road, London SW3 1BJ
Tel 071-581 8722

British Embassy
35/37 Rua S Domingos a Lapa, Lisbon 3

Tourist office
Portuguese National Tourist Office, New Bond
Street House, 1/5 New Bond Street, London
W1Y 0NP Tel 071-493 3873

Youth hostels
Associacâo Portuguesa de Pousadas de
Juventude, Rua Andrade Corvo 46, 1000 Lisbon

Youth & student information
Associacâo de Turismo Estudantil e Juvenil, PO
Box 586, 4009 Porto Cedex

Instituto da Juventude, Avenida Duque d'Avila
137, 1097 Lisbon

Turicoop, Turismo Social e Juvenil, Rua Pascoal
de Melo, 15-1, Dto, Lisbon 1

INFORMATION

Entry regulations Although Portugal is now a member state of the European Community, the reciprocal arrangements governing the employment of EC nationals will not come into effect until 1993. A work permit and a residence visa are required for all types of employment. A work permit will be applied for by the prospective employer from the local authorities, and applications for a residence visa should be made to the Consulate General at least 6 months in advance. Volunteers on workcamps do not require work permits.

Notes on Employment, Travel and Opportunities in Portugal for Foreigners and Students includes details on office employment, summer jobs, teaching opportunities, grants and scholarships, workcamps, house exchanges, travel and contacts for further information. Available from the Hispanic and Luso Brazilian Council, Canning House, 2 Belgrave Square, London SW1X 8PJ Tel 071-235 2303; price £2 (free to members).

Job advertising Publicitas Ltd, 525/527 Fulham Road, London SW6 1HF Tel 071-385 7723 are agents for *Diario de Noticias* (Lisbon daily), *Journal de Noticias* (Oporto daily) and *Expresso* leading business weekly.

Anglo-Portuguese News Apartado 113, 2765 Estoril, Lisbon, can accept job advertisements, especially for work in families as au pairs or domestics.

Travel STA Travel, 86 Old Brompton Road, London SW7 3LQ Tel 071-937 9921 operates flexible low-cost flights between London and destinations throughout Portugal.

Campus Travel, 52 Grosvenor Gardens, London SW1W 0AG Tel 071-730 3402 offers Eurotrain under 26 fares and youth/student flights to destinations in Portugal.

Portugal Enjoy It is a brochure providing descriptions of regions, information on food, wines, folklore, handicrafts, fairs, festivals, travel, accommodation and other general information. Available from the Portuguese National Tourist Office, see above.

The Rough Guide to Portugal £5.95 is a practical handbook to Portugal, with full details on historic sites, cities and towns, including some of the less well-known ones, plus a wealth of practical information on how to get around and on cheap places to stay. Published by Harrap Columbus, Chelsea House, 26 Market Square, Bromley, Kent BR1 1NA.

Accommodation The Portuguese National Tourist Office, see above, can provide a brochure listing *pousadas* (state tourist inns) in historic houses, castles, palaces, convents and monasteries, and situated in areas of natural beauty. Also publish a leaflet with a map showing the location of campsites with information on dates and facilities. Information sheet on accommodation for the disabled available. PH

Residência Universitária, Estrada da Costa, 1495 Cruz Quebrada, Lisbon has accommodation available for students during August. 170 beds in double/triple rooms; cost Esc1500 per night. Meals available in restaurant; cost Esc400 each. Also runs a service offering discounts on train, boat and air travel. Further information from Servicos Socaiais da Universidade Técnica de Lisboa, Servico de Cultura e Turismo, Rua Goncalves Crespo 20, 1100 Lisbon.

Turicoop, Turismo Social e Juvenil, Rua Pascoal de Melo, 15-1, Dto, Lisbon 1 can arrange cheap accommodation for young people in youth hostels, pensions and hotels. Also runs youth holiday centres and provides information on campsites.

ARCHAEOLOGY

CONCORDIA (Youth Service Volunteers) Ltd, Recruitment Secretary, 8 Brunswick Place, Hove, East Sussex BN3 1ET Tel Brighton 772086

INTERNATIONAL VOLUNTARY SERVICE 162 Upper New Walk, Leicester LE1 7QA Tel Leicester 549430

UNITED NATIONS ASSOCIATION International Youth Service, Welsh Centre for International Affairs, Temple of Peace, Cathays Park, Cardiff CF1 3AP Tel Cardiff 22308

Apply to one of the above to work on international workcamps assisting with archaeological digs and aimed at discovering and preserving Portugal's heritage. Recent projects have included excavating, drawing, recording and cataloguing finds at prehistoric sites, Roman thermal baths, castles and other historic monuments in Beja, Braga, Braganca, Castelo Branco, Coimbra, Faro, Guarda, Leiria,

Portalegre, Porto, Santarém, Setùbal and Viseu. Visits to local places of interest and sports activities arranged. Ages 18-25. 40 hour, 5 day week. 2 weeks, July-September. Food, accommodation in houses, schools or tents and insurance provided. Participants cook on a rota basis and must take a sleeping bag. Applicants pay their own travel.

Organised by Instituto da Juventude, Avenida Duque D'Avila 137, Lisbon.

Applications from outside the UK: please see workcamp information on page 27.

AU PAIR/ CHILDCARE

CENTRO DE INTERCAMBIO E TURISMO UNIVERSITARIO avenida Defensores de Chaves, 67-6, Dto, Lisbon
Can provide information on au pair work.

TURICOOP rua Pascoal de Melo, 15-1, Dto, 1100 Lisbon
Can arrange au pair placements with families during the summer, for girls aged 18+.

CONSERVATION

BRITISH TRUST FOR CONSERVATION VOLUNTEERS Room IWH, 36 St Marys Street, Wallingford, Oxfordshire OX10 0EU
The largest charitable organisation in Britain to involve people in practical conservation work. Following the success of the Natural Break Programme in the UK, BTCV is now developing a series of international working holidays with the aim of introducing the volunteering ethic to communities abroad. It is hoped that British volunteers will adapt to and learn from local lifestyles as well as participate in the community. Projects last for 2-3 weeks, and are organised in partnership with a Portuguese nature conservation society.

Recent projects have included river revetment, footpath construction and woodland management. Ages 18-70. Cost from £50 per week includes food and camping/dormitory accommodation; everyone shares in the cooking. Membership fee £10.

CONCORDIA (Youth Service Volunteers) Ltd, Recruitment Secretary, 8 Brunswick Place, Hove, East Sussex BN3 1ET Tel Brighton 772086

INTERNATIONAL VOLUNTARY SERVICE 162 Upper New Walk, Leicester LE1 7QA Tel Leicester 549430

UNITED NATIONS ASSOCIATION International Youth Service, Welsh Centre for International Affairs, Temple of Peace, Cathays Park, Cardiff CF1 3AP Tel Cardiff 223088

Apply to one of the above to work on international workcamps assisting with conservation projects. Recent projects have included restoring 16th-18th century ceramic tiles in Beja; renovating an old watermill in Braga; cleaning up the Esmoriz lagoon; biological and geological studies in natural caves in Portalegre; coastal protection work in Setúbal; and renovating a Benedictine convent in Serra da Arrabida. Visits to local places of interest and sports activities arranged. Ages 18-25. 40 hour, 5 day week. 2 weeks, July-September. Food, accommodation in houses, schools or tents and insurance provided; participants cook on a rota basis and must take a sleeping bag. Applicants pay their own travel.

Organised by Instituto da Juventude, Avenida Duque D'Avila 137, Lisbon.

Applications from outside the UK: please see workcamp information on page 27.

COURIERS/REPS

ILG COACH & CAMPING DIVISION (incorporating NAT Holidays and Intasun Camping), Overseas Personnel Manager, Devonshire House, Elmfield Road, Bromley, Kent Tel 081-466 6660
Vacancies exist for campsite representatives. Work involves visiting clients, providing information on the local area, restaurants,

shops and sports facilities available, and generally looking after clients. Ages 19+.

Applicants must be fluent in Portuguese and hold a full UK driving licence. They must be of a very independent nature, have the desire and ability to get on with people and be capable of working on their own initiative. Staff are on call 24 hours a day, 6 days a week. April-October, with some positions available for students only in June/July. Applicants should be reliable, hardworking, prepared to work as part of a team, and have enough staying power to last the season. All staff are required to take an active part in their resort entertainment programme, helping to organise events such as parties, barbecues, and games evenings. Salary approx £70 per week. Accommodation and return travel provided. All staff are required to take part in a 2 week training programme in April. *Early application advisable; recruitment starts October and applicants should write then for details. Interviews commence December.*

SEASUN/TENTREK HOLIDAYS 71/72 East Hill, Colchester, Essex CO1 2QW Tel Colchester 861886
Provides self-catering family holidays in apartments, mobile homes and tents plus activity holidays for schools and groups. Requires representatives for the summer season, beginning April-mid November, in Albuseira. 50/60 hour week. Ages 19+.

Applicants should be independent, resourceful with good communication skills and commitment. Knowledge of Portuguese an advantage, but not essential. Training provided. Salary and subsistence £260 per month; £40 per month extra paid on successful completion of contract. Accommodation and travel provided; personal insurance cost £55, uniform cost £60. B D PH depending on ability.

TEACHERS

PORTUGUESE CONSULATE GENERAL Silver City House, 62 Brompton Road, London SW3 1BJ Tel 071-581 8722
Can provide a list of English-speaking schools indicating the addresses to which applications for teaching posts may be sent.

WORKCAMPS

ATEJ (Associacâo de Turismo Estudantil e Juvenil), Portuguese Youth and Student Travel Association, rua Joaquim Antonio de Aguiar 255, 4300 Porto

A non-profit association which organises a variety of workcamps; volunteers are needed to work in international teams. Recent projects have included cleaning beaches, nature protection, reconstructing monuments, and constructing children's playgrounds. Previous experience not necessary, but volunteers should have a commitment to understanding and learning about other cultures and nationalities. Ages 16-30. Applicants should have a knowledge of French, English, Spanish or Portuguese. 5/6 hour day. June-September. Accommodation and self-catering facilities in youth hostels or camp sites and insurance provided. Travel paid by volunteers. Excursions arranged. Registration fee payable. PH

CHRISTIAN MOVEMENT FOR PEACE Bethnal Green United Reformed Church, Pott Street, London E2 0EF Tel 071-729 1877

An international movement open to all who share a common concern for lasting peace and justice in the world. Volunteers are needed to work in international teams on summer projects aimed at offering a service in an area of need and promoting self-help within the community; promoting international understanding and the discussion of social problems; and offering young people the chance to live as a group and take these experiences into the context of daily life.

Recent projects have included building and improving houses near St Cruz; rebuilding houses damaged by the weather, for poor families; and helping to build and set up a children's home with a library and a garden. Ages 18+. Knowledge of Portuguese or French desirable. 6 hour day, 30-36 hour week. 2 weeks, August. Food, accommodation and insurance provided, but participants pay their own travel costs. Registration fee £24 plus FF150 at the camp towards food costs.

Applications from outside the UK: please see workcamp information on page 27.

COMPANHEIROS CONSTRUTORES Rua Pedro Monteiro 3-1, 3000 Coimbra

An international volunteers' association with the aims of fighting misery and distress and making a contribution towards a better understanding between nations. Volunteers are needed to work in international teams on behalf of the socially, mentally, economically and physically underprivileged.

Recent projects have included building and renovation work on homes for the handicapped, the elderly, and socially deprived families; in kindergartens, children's villages and creches; on agricultural cooperatives, roads and drainage systems; and in social and cultural community centres. Ages 18+. 40 hour week. 3-4 weeks, July September. Cost US$200 covers accident insurance, food prepared by the volunteers, and tent, family or centre accommodation; volunteers should take a sleeping bag. Volunteers pay their own travel, 40% of which may be refunded.

Also opportunities for long-term volunteers on development projects in rural areas, 1-12 months. *Apply 2 months in advance.*

CONCORDIA (Youth Service Volunteers) Ltd, Recruitment Secretary, 8 Brunswick Place, Hove, East Sussex BN3 1ET Tel Brighton 772086

INTERNATIONAL VOLUNTARY SERVICE 162 Upper New Walk, Leicester LE1 7QA Tel Leicester 549430

UNITED NATIONS ASSOCIATION International Youth Service, Welsh Centre for International Affairs, Temple of Peace, Cathays Park, Cardiff CF1 3AP Tel Cardiff 223088

Apply to one of the above to work on international workcamps. Recent projects have included renovating a youth hostel in Beja; restoring an old castle in Portalegre; constructing kayaks in Porto; preserving an abandoned village in Viano do Castelo; studying and documenting caves in Serra de Montejunio; and building a children's playground and an open-air theatre in Vila Real. Ages 18-25. 40 hour, 5 day week. 2 weeks, July-September. Food, accommodation in houses, schools or tents and insurance provided. Participants cook on a rota basis and must take a sleeping bag. Applicants pay their own travel.

Organised by Instituto da Juventude, Avenida Duque D'Avila 137, Lisbon.

Applications from outside the UK: please see workcamp information on page 27.

GENERAL

EUROYOUTH LTD 301 Westborough Road, Westcliff-on-Sea, Essex SS0 9PT
Tel Southend-on-Sea 341434
Arranges stays where guests are offered board and lodging in return for an agreed number of hours English conversation with hosts or their children. Time is also available for guests to practise Portuguese. Mainly ages 15-25, but there are sometimes opportunities for ages 13-16 and for older applicants. The scheme is open to British students interested in visiting Portugal and living with a local family for a short time. Compulsory language course. 2-3 weeks, June-August. Travel and insurance paid by the applicant. Registration fee approx £50. *Apply at least 12 weeks prior to scheduled departure date.*

APPLYING FOR A JOB

Read carefully all the information given before applying. Check in particular:

* the necessary skills/experience required

* the full period of employment expected

* any restrictions of age, sex or nationality

* application deadlines

* any other points, particularly details of insurance cover provided, and other costs such as travel and accommodation.

When applying be sure to include:

* name, address, date of birth, marital status, nationality, sex

* education, qualifications, relevant experience

* period of availability

* details of languages spoken

* a large stamped, self-addressed envelope plus, if overseas, 2 International Reply Coupons

* a passport-size photo, particularly if you are to have contact with the public

* any registration or membership fees

NOTES

SOUTH & CENTRAL AMERICA

See also Mexico

Bolivian Embassy
106 Eaton Square, London SW1W 9AD
Tel 071-235 4248

Brazilian Embassy
32 Green Street, London W1Y 4AT
Tel 071-499 0877

Chilean Embassy
12 Devonshire Street, London W1N 2FS
Tel 071-580 6392

Costa Rica Embassy
Flat 1, 14 Lancaster Gate, London W2 3LH
Tel 071-723 9630

Cuban Embassy
167 High Holborn, London WC1V 6PA
Tel 071-240 2488

Ecuador Embassy
Flat 3b, 3 Hans Crescent, London SW1X 0LS
Tel 071-584 1367

Honduras Embassy
115 Gloucester Place, London W1H 3PJ
Tel 071-486 4880

Panama Embassy
119 Crawford Street, London W1H 1AF
Tel 071-487 5633

Paraguay Embassy
Braemar Lodge, Cornwall Gardens, London
SW7 4AQ Tel 071-937 1253

Peruvian Embassy
52 Sloane Street, London SW1X 9SP
Tel 071-235 1917

INFORMATION

Entry regulations Details of work permits and entry requirements can be obtained in Britain from the embassies listed above.

Latin America: Notes on Employment and Opportunities, includes information on teaching and assistantship opportunities, volunteer work, exchange schemes, grants, fundraising and travel. Available from the Hispanic & Luso Brazilian Council, Canning House, 2 Belgrave Square, London SW1X 8PJ Tel 071-235 2303; price £2 (free to members).

Travel North-South Travel Ltd, Moulsham Mill, Parkway, Chelmsford CM2 7PX Tel Chelmsford 492882 arranges competitively priced, reliably planned flights to all parts of South America. Its profits are paid into a trust fund for the assignment of aid to projects in the poorest areas of the South.

STA Travel, 74 Old Brompton Road, London SW7 3LQ Tel 071-937 9962 operates flexible, low-cost flights with open-jaw facility - enter one country, leave by another - between London and destinations throughout South America. Internal flights, accommodation and tours also available.

Campus Travel, 52 Grosvenor Gardens, London SW1W 0AG Tel 071-730 3402 offers competitive flexible flights with open jaw facility to destinations throughout Central and South America.

The Rough Guide to Peru £6.95, is a practical handbook with full details on how to get around, places to stay and eat and things to see. Published by Harrap Columbus, Chelsea House, 26 Market Square, Bromley, Kent BR1 1NA.

The Travellers Survival Kit Central America £8.95, is a detailed handbook on the region and covers Guatemala, Belize, Honduras, El Salvador, Nicaragua, Costa Rica and Panama. Contains information on where it's safe to go, travel bargains, budget accommodation and eating and drinking. *The Travellers Survival Kit Cuba* £6.95, gives full information for visitors to Cuba on how to get there, eating out, where to stay, how to get around, what to see and what to do, and includes a set of 20 maps. Both published by Vacation Work, 9 Park End Street, Oxford OX1 1HJ Tel Oxford 241978.

South America on a Shoestring £7.95, is a useful handbook for anyone who wants to get from Tijuana to Tierra del Fuego and anywhere vaguely in between. Information given includes cheap travel and accommodation, details on climate and geography plus practical information on where to stay and what to visit, with sections on each country. *South American Handbook*, £19.95 has detailed information on countries throughout South America, Mexico and the Caribbean. Revised annually and includes the current political situation in each country, border formalities, public transport, health, plus town and regional plans and maps. Both available from Trailfinders, 194 Kensington High Street, London W8 7RG Tel 071-938 3939.

ARCHAEOLOGY

EARTHWATCH EUROPE Belsyre Court, 57 Woodstock Road, Oxford, Oxfordshire Tel Oxford 311600
Aims to support field research in a wide range of disciplines including archaeology, ornithology, animal behaviour, nature conservation and ecology. Support is given to researchers as a grant and in the form of volunteer assistance.

Recent projects have included conducting the first formal study of royal Inca architecture in Peru; sorting and matching frieze fragments which could reveal the reason for the Mayan collapse, in Honduras; and mapping and excavating artefacts to aid the study of the rise and fall of civilisation on Easter Island. 2-3 weeks, October-April. Ages 16-80. No special skills are required although each expedition

may, because of its nature, demand some talent or quality of fitness. Volunteers should be generally fit, able to cope with new situations, able to mix and work with people of different ages and backgrounds, and a sense of humour will help. Members share the costs of the expedition, from £500, which includes meals, transport and all necessary field equipment, but does not include the cost of travel, although assistance may be given in arranging it. Membership fee £22 includes magazines and newsletters providing information on joining an expedition.

COMMUNITY WORK

AMIGOS DE LAS AMERICAS 5618 Star Lane, Houston, Texas 77057, United States
An international non-profitmaking, private voluntary organisation that provides leadership development opportunities for young people, improved community health for the people of Latin America and better cross-cultural understanding on both American continents.

Volunteers are needed to work in teams in schools, health clinics and house-to-house in Latin American countries including Brazil, Mexico, Costa Rica, the Dominican Republic, Paraguay and Ecuador. In addition to providing technical knowledge and supplies, volunteers assume leadership roles as health educators. Projects include animal health and rabies inoculation; human immunisation; oral rehydration therapy; community sanitation; latrine construction and dental hygiene.

Ages 16+, no upper limit. Volunteers must complete a training programme. One year of secondary school Spanish required. 4-8 weeks, mid June-mid August. Volunteers live with families or in schools or clinics; food provided by the community. Cost US$2100-US$2500, depending on the region visited, includes international travel, board, lodging, in-country transportation, supplies and training materials. Volunteers arrange and pay for domestic travel to point of departure, and are advised to take out health insurance.

VOLUNTARIOS EN ACCION (VEA) PO Box 3556, La Paz, Bolivia Tel 36 23 46
A voluntary service organisation aiming to aid rural education. Volunteers are required to help build furniture for schools in rural areas, at the carpentry shop at Huarina on the Bolivian high plateau. 40 hour week, all year round. Ages 19+. Applicants must be fluent in Spanish; carpentry skills an asset. Food, accommodation and local travel provided, but no pocket money or insurance. Visits to neighbouring communities, local festivals and fairs arranged whenever possible. B D PH

CONSERVATION

EARTHWATCH EUROPE Belsyre Court, 57 Woodstock Road, Oxford, Oxfordshire Tel Oxford 311600
Aims to support field research in a wide range of disciplines including archaeology, ornithology, animal behaviour, nature conservation and ecology. Support is given to researchers as a grant and in the form of volunteer assistance. Recent expeditions have included recording the behaviour of katydids in the Amazon rainforests of Peru; monitoring tropical plants in Brazil; and analysing plant data on the slope of a live volcano in Costa Rica. Ages 16-75. No special skills are required although each expedition may, because of its nature, demand some talent or quality of fitness. Volunteers should be generally fit, able to cope with new situations, able to mix and work with people of different ages and backgrounds, and a sense of humour will help. 2-3 weeks, July and August. Members share the costs of the expedition, from £500, which includes meals, transport and all necessary field equipment, but does not include the cost of travel, although assistance may be given in arranging it. Membership fee £22 includes magazines and newsletters providing information on joining an expedition.

GENESIS II - TALAMANCA CLOUD FOREST Apdo 655, 7.050 Cartago, Costa Rica
Volunteers are needed to help with new trail routing, construction, maintenance and upgrade work on existing trails, in a rare tropical white oak cloud forest in the mountains of Costa Rica. The forest is situated at a height of 2360m and is being preserved for academic research and recreational activities such as bird watching. Ages 17+. Experience preferred, but not essential as training can be given. All nationalities welcome; some knowledge of Spanish helpful. 25 hour week, weekends free. 6+ weeks, all year. Volunteers contribute $50 per week to cover dormitory style accommodation, all meals and laundry service, but make own travel and insurance arrangements. *Only fully fit and dedicated people need apply; competition for places is strong.*

UNIVERSITY RESEARCH EXPEDITIONS PROGRAM University of California, Desk L-10, Berkeley CA 94720, United States
Volunteers are needed to provide field assistance for research in the natural and social sciences. Projects include studying and documenting the survival strategies and farming techniques of share-croppers in the drought-stricken regions of northeastern Brazil; and exploring the benefits of the relationship between plants and insects in the tropical rainforest of the Atlantic lowlands of Costa Rica. Ages 16+. Applicants should be in good health, have a desire to learn, enthusiasm, a willingness to undertake rigourous but rewarding work, flexibility and sensitivity to other cultures. Skills such as sketching and photography, plus wilderness or camping experience, some knowledge of animal behaviour, general ecology and botany useful. 2/3 weeks, December-February and June-October. Contribution to costs from US$985 covers research equipment and supplies, meals, accommodation, ground transportation and preparation materials. Travel to site not provided but route guidance given. *Partial scholarships available. Apply at least 2 months before session.*

LEADERS & GUIDES

EXODUS EXPEDITIONS 9 Weir Road, London SW12 0LT Tel 081-675 7996
Operates a large range of expeditions including those by truck to South America plus foot treks and shorter adventure holidays to Peru, Ecuador, Bolivia and Brazil. Expedition leaders are needed to lead and drive expeditions; each

SOUTH & CENTRAL AMERICA

LEADERS & GUIDES

expedition lasts 4-6 months, but leaders can expect to be out of the country for up to 24 months at a time. The work involves driving, servicing and when necessary repairing the vehicle; controlling and accounting for expedition expenditure; dealing with border formalities and other official procedures; helping clients with any problems that may arise and informing them on points of interest in the countries visited. Ages 25-30. Applicants must be single and unattached, able to commit themselves for 2 years, with no personal or financial commitments. Driving experience of large vehicles plus HGV/PSV licence and a good basic knowledge of mechanics required. Applicants must have leadership qualities and be resourceful, adaptable and have a good sense of humour. Previous travel experience and a knowledge of foreign languages an advantage. It is not expected that applicants will have all the necessary qualifications and basic training will be given to suitable candidates. Trainees spend 2 months in the company's Wiltshire workshop and then go on an expedition with an experienced leader before leading on their own. Salary £50 per week with food and accommodation provided on site when training and £20 per week plus food and accommodation with £28 per week expenses on the first expedition. Salary £80-£115 per week for a full expedition leader plus food and accommodation.

GENERAL

BRITAIN-CUBA RESOURCE CENTRE José Marti International Work Brigade, Latin America House, Priory House, Kingsgate Place, London NW6 Tel 071-388 1429
Offers western Europeans a unique way of seeing life in Cuba and of learning in detail how the people have organised their society since the beginning of the revolution in 1959. Volunteers are needed for agricultural and construction work in the Caimito area of Havana province. As well as tending and picking fruit, the Brigade has contributed to the construction of a polytechnic, a college for building workers and housing for textile workers. Ages 17+. Volunteers must be fit. 4½ day, 35 hour week. September-October. Participants work for 3 weeks and spend the final week travelling around. 2 days per week

are spent visiting factories, schools, hospitals, industry, agriculture and seeing Havana and its surroundings. A full programme of activities is organised including lectures, concerts and films. Applications are encouraged from those who have undertaken active political work within ethnic groups, the women's movement, industry, the Labour movement and solidarity organisations. Cost to participants approx £650 covers airfare, food, hostel accommodation, insurance and travel within Cuba, allowing approx £100 for pocket money. Compulsory orientation weekends organised. *Apply by end March.*

Irish applications to Ireland-Cuba Friendship Society, c/o Margaret O'Leary, 93 Jamestown Road, Finglas East, Dublin 11, Ireland.

BRITISH UNIVERSITIES NORTH AMERICA CLUB (BUNAC) 16 Bowling Green Lane, London EC1R OBD Tel 071-251 3472
A non-profit, non-political educational student club venture which aims to encourage interest and understanding between students in Britain and the Americas. Operates a small programme in Jamaica for adventurous people for whom the unique experience gained is more important than the money earned.
The programme is open to full time degree/HND students aged 18+. Work is available for the summer months, from end June onwards. Orientation programmes held throughout Britain give advice on finding and choosing a job, obtaining a visa, income tax, accommodation, travel food and budgeting. Cost £582-£637, depending on departure date, includes administration fees and round trip flight to Montego Bay. Insurance fee £72. Applicants will need to show proof of purchase of £150 travellers' cheques. EC *nationals only. Application forms available January; apply by 30 April.*

When applying to any organisation it is essential to mention Working Holidays 1991 and enclose a large stamped, self-addressed envelope, or if overseas, a large addressed envelope and at least two International Reply Coupons.

GENERAL

SPAIN

Spanish Embassy
24 Belgrave Square, London SW1X 8QA
Tel 071-235 1484

Visa section: Spanish Consulate General, 20
Draycott Place, London SW3 2RZ
Tel 071-581 5921

British Embassy
Calle de Fernando El Santo 16, 28010 Madrid

Tourist office
Spanish National Tourist Office, 57/58 St
James's Street, London SW1A 1LB
Tel 071-499 0901

Youth hostels
Red Espanola de Albergues Juveniles, Jose
Ortega y Gasset 71, 28006 Madrid

Youth & student information
TIVE, Oficina Nacional de Intercambio y
Turismo de Jovenes y Estudiantes, Jose Ortega
y Gasset 71, 28006 Madrid

INFORMATION

Entry regulations Although Spain is now a member state of the European Community, the reciprocal arrangements governing the employment of EC nationals will not come into effect until 1993. Those offered a job by a firm in Spain must apply personally for the appropriate visa at the Spanish Consulate. To do this they must present proof of the offer of employment and complete four application forms, one of which will be sent to the future employer who will take the necessary steps with the Spanish employment authorities. The Consulate will then notify the applicant of the decision taken. The consular fee is £36. It should be noted that in the present circumstances, where there is a high level of unemployment in Spain, it is very difficult to obtain a work permit. Bilingual secretarial posts for those with a knowledge of shorthand/typing can sometimes be found in the larger cities. Casual employment such as fruit picking and harvesting is not easy to obtain as the number of applicants greatly exceeds the amount of work available. Those taking a car or motorbike temporarily into Spain may not undertake paid employment during the 6 month period of temporary importation. Full details of the regulations governing residence and employment in Spain are given in information sheets available from the Consular Section of the Spanish Embassy see above.

Notes on Employment and Opportunities in Spain for Foreigners and Students includes information on teaching opportunities, office employment, summer jobs, voluntary work, au pair work, exchanges, travel and contacts for further information. Available from the Hispanic & Luso Brazilian Council, Canning House, 2 Belgrave Square, London SW1X 8PJ Tel 071-235 2303; price £2 (free to members).

Job advertising Publicitas Ltd, 525/527 Fulham Road, London SW6 1HF Tel 071-385 7723 are agents for *El Pais* (leading national daily), *La Vanguardia* (leading Barcelona daily) and regional newspapers throughout Spain.

Travel STA Travel, 86 Old Brompton Road, London SW7 3LQ Tel 071-937 9921 operates flexible, low-cost flights between London and destinations throughout Spain.

Campus Travel, 52 Grosvenor Gardens, London SW1W 0AG Tel 071-730 3402 offers Eurotrain under 26 fares, the Eurotrain Costa Brava Explorer valid for 2 months travel through France and Spain and youth/student charter flights and airfares to destinations throughout Spain.

The Rough Guide to Spain £6.95 is a comprehensive handbook for travellers, giving detailed information on cheap places to stay and eat, things to see, local buses and trains, and Spanish life and culture. Published by Harrap Columbus, Chelsea House, 26 Market Square, Bromley, Kent BR1 1NA.

ARCHAEOLOGY

CHRISTIAN MOVEMENT FOR PEACE Bethnal Green United Reformed Church, Pott Street, London E2 0EF Tel 071-729 1877

UNITED NATIONS ASSOCIATION International Youth Service, Welsh Centre for International Affairs, Temple of Peace, Cathays Park, Cardiff CF1 3AP Tel Cardiff 223088

Volunteers with a genuine interest in archaeology can apply to either of the above to work on sites throughout Spain. Recent projects have included excavating Roman villages near Madrid; recovering remains from the sea and excavating a Bronze Age settlement in Murcia; restoring a 17th century tannery in Palencia; excavating a Tartesian settlement and burial ground in Cadiz; discovering Roman and Greek ruins in Ciudad Real; and excavating and cleaning mosaics in Sovia.

Some of the projects include topographic studies, research, finds classification, lectures and discussions as well as excavation work. Cultural and sports activities and excursions arranged. Ages 18-26. 40 hour week. 2/3 weeks, July and August. Food and accommodation in schools, youth hostels, centres or tents, and accident insurance provided. Participants pay own travel costs.

Organised by Instituto de la Juventud, Servicio Voluntario Internacional de España, Jose Ortega y Gasset 71, Madrid 28006.

Applications from outside the UK: please see workcamp information on page 27.

DEYA ARCHAEOLOGICAL MUSEUM AND RESEARCH CENTRE Dr W H Waldren, Deya, Mallorca, Baleares
Participants are needed for excavation of a Chalcolithic settlement complex at Ferrandell-Oleza, Valldemosa on Majorca. A Copper Age site with evidence of Beaker culture, it is the

most important open-air settlement in this area. Excavations have so far revealed fortified compound walls, water channels, habitations and other structures. The work involves excavation, site surveys, lectures, courses, study of the material, classifying artefacts and laboratory work. 2 weeks, May-September. Volunteers of all ages, backgrounds, skills and interests welcome, but people with specialised skills especially welcome. Cost £250 covers food, lodging at research centre and on-site transportation for 14 days. No fares or wages paid. *Apply by May, with detailed cv, references and £25 deposit.*

AU PAIR/ CHILDCARE

ANGLIA AGENCY 15 Eastern Avenue, Southend-on-Sea, Essex Tel Southend 613888
Positions for au pairs, mother's helps and nannies arranged throughout the year. Long and short-term placements available, including summer. Hours and salaries vary; au pairs work a 30 hour week plus babysitting, with 1 free day per week, and receive £25+ per week pocket money. Board and lodging provided. Ages 17+. Travel costs paid by the applicant. Service charge £40.

AVALON AGENCY Thursley House, 53 Station Road, Shalford, Guildford, Surrey GU4 8HA Tel Guildford 63640
Can place au pairs throughout Spain. Opportunity to attend language classes. 25-30 hour week. 6+ months. Ages 18-30. Basic knowledge of Spanish needed. Pocket money approx £20+ per week. Food, lodging and insurance provided. Service charge £40, if placement accepted.

CENTROS EUROPEOS English for Executives, C/Principe 12, 6A, 28012 Madrid
Arranges au pair stays in Madrid, Alicante and Valencia for girls aged 18+. 2+ months, summer or 6+ months during the year. 30 hour week helping with children and housework plus 2 evenings babysitting; 1 day off per week. Pocket money Pts4000-Pts4500, board and lodging provided. Language classes can be arranged in local schools.

CLUB DE RELACIONES CULTURALES INTERNACIONALES Calle de Ferraz 82, 28008 Madrid
Can place au pairs in families all over Spain. Ages 18-28. Applicants must like working with children. Knowledge of Spanish not necessary. Up to 6 hour day. 1 free day per week, plus time for language classes. 6+ months, September-April; stays of 4-12 weeks possible in summer. Board, lodging, Pts4000 pocket money per week and insurance with medical and repatriation cover, provided. Travel paid by applicant. Provides a social service for all applicants, plus language programmes, weekend excursions and a social club. Registration fee £25.

HELPING HANDS AU PAIR & DOMESTIC AGENCY 10 Hertford Road, Newbury Park, Ilford, Essex IG2 7HQ Tel 081-597 3138
Au pair and mother's help positions available throughout the year. Au pairs work approx 30 hours plus 3 evenings babysitting each week and earn approx £25 per week. Mother's helps work longer hours for a higher salary. Board and lodging provided. Minimum stay 6 months. Ages 18-27. Applicants should be willing, helpful and adaptable. Insurance and travel costs paid by the applicant but assistance with arrangements provided. Introduction fee £40 on acceptance of a family. *UK nationals only.*

HOME FROM HOME 10 Tackley Place, Oxford, Oxfordshire OX2 6RR Tel Oxford 512628
Can place au pairs to undertake childcare and light housework in all areas of Spain, all year round. No experience necessary but basic knowledge of Spanish preferable. 5 hour day, 30 hour week. Ages 18+. Pocket money £28 per week; travel and insurance not provided. Placement fee £40.

INTERLINGUA CENTRE Torquay Road, Foxrock, Dublin, Ireland 18 Tel Dublin 893876
Can place au pairs in Spanish families. 30 hour week with one full day and some evenings off. Time to attend language classes 2-3 mornings or afternoons per week. Experience desirable but not essential. 6+ months. Ages 18+. Pocket money £25 per week, full board, lodging and insurance provided. Travel paid by applicants. Placement fee £55.

JOLAINE AGENCY 18 Escot Way, Barnet, Hertfordshire EN5 3AN Tel 081-449 1334
Au pair and mother's help posts arranged throughout the year. Au pairs work a 5 hour day and 3/4 evenings babysitting per week. Afternoons plus 1 full day free per week. Mother's helps work an 8 hour day with 1½ days free per week, plus some evenings and other time by arrangement. Ages 17-27. 6+ months. Summer posts also available to look after children and do light household duties; hours of work arranged with the employer. 3+ months, June-October. Pocket money £25+ per week, au pairs; £40+ per week, mother's helps. Full board and accommodation provided. Travel and insurance paid by applicants. Introduction fee £40.

STUDENTS ABROAD AGENCY Elm House, 21b The Avenue, Hatch End, Middlesex HA5 4EN Tel 081-428 5823
Can place au pairs with families. Long-term positions available all year as well as a number of 2+ months summer placements. Occasional temporary posts available throughout the year. Au pairs normally work a 5/6 hour day with 3-4 hours per day for language classes. Usually 1 full day and 2/3 evenings free per week, but curriculum changes and applicants must be flexible during temporary summer season when schooling rarely available and families often go on holiday. Salary approx Pts12000-Pts16000 per month. Board and lodging provided. Ages 17-27. Basic knowledge of Spanish useful, but not essential. Applicants should like, and have the ability to cope with, children, babies, light housework and simple cooking. Applicants pay their own fare, but advice given on travel and insurance. Service charge £40. *Apply early for summer positions.*

UNIVERSAL CARE Chester House, 9 Windsor End, Beaconsfield, Buckinghamshire HP9 2JJ Tel Beaconsfield 678811
Can place au pairs in families in many areas of Spain. Some families visit the coast and the country during the summer holidays. Stays are usually 6+ months; some summer stays, 2+ months. Hours are slightly longer than in other European countries and help is mainly needed with children and some light housework, as many families employ maids for domestic work. 1 day and 2 evenings off per week. During the winter girls have 5-6 hours per day

SPAIN

for studying. Ages 17-27. Girls must love children, and should be prepared to become involved in family life. Knowledge of Spanish desirable. Board and lodging provided. Salary approx Pts15000 per month. Travel paid by the applicant although families will sometimes help with return fare. Service charge £46. *Apply 2 months before work period desired.*

COMMUNITY WORK

INTERNATIONAL VOLUNTARY SERVICE 162 Upper New Walk, Leicester LE1 7QA Tel Leicester 549430

Volunteers are needed to work in international teams on community service in workcamps organised by SCCT, the Catalan branch of Service Civil International. Recent projects have included helping at a drug rehabilitation centre in Alicante; organising summer playschemes for children from low-income families and helping at institutes and homes which integrate people with disabilities, in Barcelona; looking after physically disabled children on holiday in the countryside, organising activities and outings to the Pyrenees; constructing play amenities, arranging a sports field and assisting with workshops for young people in La Mina, one of Barcelona's largest slum areas; and working with African immigrant families in El Maresme helping them to repair their homes and putting together a report on their living conditions in order to raise awareness in the local community. Ages 18+. Applicants should have previous workcamp experience and be highly motivated and prepared to work hard and contribute to team life. Good knowledge of Spanish essential for some camps. 35-40 hour week. 2-4 weeks, June-September. Food, accommodation and insurance provided, but no travel. Membership fee £25 (students £15, unwaged £10). Registration fee £40. PH

Organised by SCI-SCCT (Servei Catala de Camps de Treball) Rambla Catalunya 5, pral 2a, 08007 Barcelona, Catalonia.

Applications from outside the UK: please see workcamp information on page 27.

CONSERVATION

AULA VERDE EL CAMPILLO 46165 Bugarra (Valencia)

An environmental education centre consisting of an organic farm and ecological park. Volunteers are required to assist with all aspects of the centre's work, which can involve general maintenance, cleaning, painting, gardening, farming and helping to run children's activities. Ages 18+. No experience necessary, but knowledge of English or Spanish required. 20-25 hours per week, all year, especially summer. Full board and accommodation provided for 4 weeks, plus pocket money depending on volunteer's individual circumstances. Contributions to board requested for stays of 4+ weeks. Volunteers may also take part in educational programmes offered, including excursions, arts and crafts, paper recycling and environmental education. Volunteers pay their own travel. *All nationalities welcome.*

CHRISTIAN MOVEMENT FOR PEACE Bethnal Green United Reformed Church, Pott Street, London E2 0EF Tel 071-729 1877

UNITED NATIONS ASSOCIATION International Youth Service, The Welsh Centre for International Affairs, Temple of Peace, Cathays Park, Cardiff CF1 3AP Tel Cardiff 223088

Apply to either of the above to work on voluntary conservation projects. Recent projects have included coastal protection work on Gran Canaria; cleaning the facade of a Renaissance church in Guipuzcoa; repairing forest pathways in Alicante; cleaning a river and creating a bathing pool in Asturias; painting and renovating churches and hermitages on Tenerife; planting trees in Castellon; restoring abandoned mountain villages using traditional techniques in Huesca; and conservation work in a seabird sanctuary on a river delta in Tarragona. Some of the projects include ecological studies and population surveys as well as conservation work. Cultural and sports activities and excursions arranged. Ages 18-26. 40 hour week. 2/3 weeks, July and August. Food, accommodation in schools, youth hostels, centres or tents and accident insurance provided. Participants pay own travel costs.

Organised by Instituto de la Juventud, Servicio Voluntario Internacional de Espana, Jose Ortega y Gasset 71, Madrid 28006.

Applications from outside the UK: please see workcamp information on page 27.

INTERNATIONAL VOLUNTARY SERVICE 162 Upper New Walk, Leicester LE1 7QA Tel Leicester 549430

Volunteers are needed to work in international teams on conservation projects in workcamps organised by SCCT, the Catalan branch of Service Civil International.

Recent projects have included clearing forest, building observation hides and planting trees at an Eastern philosophy centre near Barcelona; repairing damage caused by heavy rain and clearing paths alongside a group concerned with rural depopulation in the mountain villages of Gerona; renovating a traditional Catalan house to be used as a shelter for travellers in the Parc Natural de la Serra del Montsec; replanting trees, painting and setting up solar cells at a centre used to host groups interested in discussing alternative ways of living; and pruning olive trees, farming and converting an old house into a hikers' shelter in western Catalonia. Volunteers participate in local festivals. Ages 18+. Applicants should have previous workcamp experience and be highly motivated, and prepared to work hard and contribute to team life. Good knowledge of Spanish essential on some camps. 35-40 hour week. 2-4 weeks, June-September. Food, accommodation and insurance provided, but not travel. Membership fee £25 (students £15, unwaged £10). Registration fee £40. **PH**

Organised by SCI-SCCT (Servei Catala de Camps de Treball), Rambla Catalunya 5, pral 2a, 08007 Barcelona, Catalonia.

Applications from outside the UK: please see workcamp information on page 27.

LA SABRANENQUE CENTRE INTERNATIONAL 30290 Victor la Coste, France

A small, non-profitmaking organisation that has been working since 1969 to preserve, restore and reconstruct abandoned rural sites, and bring them back to life. Aims to give volunteers the chance to discover the interest and pleasure of working directly on genuine rural restoration projects while being part of a cooperative international team. Helps to supervise a project in Ibort, Spain, a small village near the Pyrenees which was abandoned until several years ago. Volunteers work in small teams, learning the traditional construction techniques on-the-job from experienced leaders. Work can include masonry, stone cutting, floor or roof tiling, interior restoration, drystone walling and path paving. Visits are made to the Pyrenees and nearby towns. No experience necessary. 2+ weeks, 1 June-30 September. Ages 18+. Cost FF65 per day includes full board and dormitory accommodation in restored houses. Registration fee FF120.

COURIERS/REPS

CANVAS HOLIDAYS LTD Bull Plain, Hertford, Hertfordshire SG14 1DY Tel Hertford 553535

Resident couriers are required to work on campsites for a holiday company providing accommodation for families in ready-erected fully equipped tents and cabins. The work involves a daily routine of tent cleaning as customers arrive and depart, providing information and advice on the local attractions and essential services, helping to sort out problems that might arise, and organising activities for the children and get-togethers for the families. 7 day week with no fixed hours; the workload varies from day to day. At the beginning and end of the season there is a period of physical work when tents are put up and prepared for the customers or taken down and stored for the winter. Other tasks include administration, book keeping and stock control. Working knowledge of Spanish essential. Ages 18-25. Applicants are normally those with a year between school and further education, undergraduates or graduates. They need to be reliable, self-motivated, able to turn their hand to new and varied tasks, and with a sense of humour. 10-14 weeks, early April-late July or July-late September. Return travel, dependent on successful completion of contract, and accommodation in frame tents

SPAIN

provided. Salary approx £76 per week. *UK nationals only; applications accepted anytime, interviews commence early November.*

CLUB CANTABRICA HOLIDAYS LTD
Overseas Department, Holiday House, 146-148 London Road, St Albans, Hertfordshire AL1 1PQ Tel St Albans 33141
Organises holidays providing fully equipped tents, caravans and mobile homes. Requires couriers and maintenance staff to work the whole summer season, mid May-early October. 6-day week. Some experience an advantage. Ages 21+. Wages from £40 per week, plus bonus at end of season. Self-catering accommodation in tents or caravans, travel costs from Watford and insurance provided.

EUROCAMP Courier Department,
Edmundson House, Tatton Street, Knutsford, Cheshire WA16 6BG Tel Knutsford 50052
Requires resident couriers to work on campsites on the Costa Brava and the Costa Dorada. Work involves cleaning tents and equipment prior to the arrival of new customers; checking, replacing and making repairs on equipment; replenishing gas supplies; keeping the store tent in order; keeping basic accounts and reporting on a weekly basis to England. Couriers also meet new arrivals and assist holidaymakers with any problems that may arise, organise activities and parties, provide information on local tourist attractions and maintain an information noticeboard. At the beginning and end of the season couriers are expected to help in erecting and dismantling tents. There are no set working hours or free days, as these depend on unpredictable factors. Ages 18-28, although older applicants will be considered. Applications from couples welcome.

COURIERS/REPS

Applicants should be familiar with working and travelling abroad, preferably with camping experience. They should also be adaptable, reliable, independent, efficient, hard working, sensible, sociable, tactful, patient and have a working knowledge of Spanish. Applicants are expected to work one half of the season, early/mid April-mid July or mid July-late September/early October - exact dates depend on the campsite; work is also available for the whole season. Accommodation in frame tents with cooking facilities, moped for use on

site, insurance and return fare provided. Salary approx £80 per week. Also senior couriers, salary £95 per week. *Early application advisable; interviews start November.*

ILG COACH & CAMPING DIVISION
(incorporating NAT Holidays and Intasun Camping), Overseas Personnel Manager, Devonshire House, Elmfield Road, Bromley, Kent Tel 081-466 6660
Vacancies exist for campsite representatives. Work involves welcoming and visiting clients, accompanying excursions, organising and taking part in evening entertainments, and generally looking after clients. Applicants must have the desire and ability to get on with people and to handle pressure. Ages 19+. Applicants must hold a full UK driving licence and be capable of working on their own initiative. April-October, with some positions available for students only in June/July.

Applicants should be reliable, hard working, prepared to work as part of a team, and have enough staying power to last the season. Staff are required to take an active part in their resort entertainment programme, helping to organise events such as parties, barbecues, and games evenings. Salary approx £70 per week. Accommodation and return travel provided. All staff are required to take part in a 2 week training programme in April. *Recruitment starts October; applicants should write then for details. Interviews commence December.*

SEASUN/TENTREK HOLIDAYS
71/72 East Hill, Colchester, Essex CO1 2QW
Tel Colchester 861886
Provides self-catering family holidays in apartments, mobile homes and tents plus activity holidays for schools and groups. Requires representatives for the summer season, beginning April-mid November, in Castelli Montgri, Estarti and Lafosca. 50/60 hour week. Ages 19+. Applicants should be independent, resourceful with good communication skills and commitment. Knowledge of Spanish an advantage, but not essential. Training provided. Salary and subsistence £260 per month; £40 per month extra paid on successful completion of contract. Accommodation and travel provided; personal insurance cost £55, uniform cost £60. B D PH depending on ability.

SOLAIRE INTERNATIONAL HOLIDAYS
1158 Stratford Road, Hall Green, Birmingham
B28 8AF Tel 021-778 5061
Organises camping and mobile home holidays in Spain, from the Costa Brava to Costa Dorada, including Llafranc and Salou. Staff are required to prepare tents and mobile homes when the season begins in May and then close down at the end of the season in October. During the season staff act as couriers, ensuring the smooth running of the camps, and undertake some maintenance work. No fixed hours. No previous experience necessary; foreign languages preferable but not essential. Ages 18+. Wages £40-£60 per week, accommodation in tents or mobile homes, insurance and travel provided.

DOMESTIC

SNOW WORLD (SUN LIVING LTD)
Personnel Manager, Adventure House, 34-36 South Street, Lancing, West Sussex BN15 8AG Tel Lancing 750310
Opportunities for chalet maids to work in ski resorts, keeping chalets tidy, looking after guests, and in certain cases preparing meals. Ages 18-30. Relevant experience in domestic and/or catering essential. Usually 8-10 hour day, 6 day week, but hours vary depending on the needs of clients. Applicants should be prepared to work for the whole season, December-April. Extra staff may also be required at peak times such as Christmas. Board, lodging and travel provided. Salary from £45 per week. Training given at the resort during the week before clients arrive.

LEADERS & GUIDES

CLUB DE RELACIONES CULTURALES INTERNACIONALES Calle de Ferraz 82, 28008 Madrid
Young people are required to work at hotels in coastal resorts, looking after children and arranging entertainments for them such as contests and parties. Full use of hotel facilities in spare time. Ages 18-28. Applicants must have patience, imagination and experience of working with children. Knowledge of Spanish and other languages welcome. 4-6 hours per day. 1-3 months, April-September. Board, lodging, insurance and £40+ per week pocket money provided. Registration fee £25. Apply January-March.

TOPS HOLIDAYS (SUN LIVING LTD)
Personnel Manager, Adventure House, 34-36 South Street, Lancing, West Sussex BN15 8AG Tel Lancing 750310
Organises a range of specialised activity and outdoor education programmes for groups of school children aged 12-17 at a centre in L'Escala. The centre has its own team of staff to ensure that high standards of safety, instruction and enjoyment are maintained. Group leaders are required, looking after the general welfare of a group of up to 50 children and making sure they get the most from their holiday. Leaders are also responsible for ensuring their group arrives at activities, meals and events on time, sorting out problems and organising entertainments. Ages 20+. Experience of working with children, and of at least one of the activities organised an advantage. The work demands a high level of commitment both physically and mentally; applicants should enjoy being with children all day, have a genuine interest in their welfare, be patient, sympathetic and diplomatic. Fitness, stamina, energy, enthusiasm and the ability to live and work as part of a team also essential. 40+ hour week, 1 day free per week. 1+ months, May-September. Most staff work the full season; extra staff are also taken on during peak times at Easter and during July and August. Opportunities for staff to move to other centres in Europe. Travel costs from Dover, full board, apartment accommodation and insurance provided. Pay from £25 per week paid in local currency. Training provided to ensure staff are confident and able to carry out their responsibilities. Social activities such as parties, barbecues and outings arranged for staff. Senior positions also available. *British nationals only.* B D PH limited opportunities.

When writing to any organisation it is essential to mention Working Holidays 1991 and enclose a large stamped, self-addressed envelope, or if overseas, a large addressed envelope and at least two International Reply Coupons.

SPAIN

DOMESTIC

LEADERS & GUIDES

SPAIN

MONITORS & INSTRUCTORS

CLUB CANTABRICA HOLIDAYS LTD
Overseas Department, Holiday House,
146-148 London Road, St Albans,
Hertfordshire AL1 1PQ Tel St Albans 33141
Organises camping holidays, providing fully equipped tents caravans and mobile homes. Kiddies and club staff are required to work the whole summer season, mid May-early October. Nursery or NNEB qualifications necessary. Ages 21+. Salary from £40 per week, plus bonus at end of season. Self-catering accommodation in tents and caravans, travel from Watford and insurance provided.

CLUB DE RELACIONES CULTURALES
INTERNACIONALES Calle de Ferraz 82,
28008 Madrid
Young people are required to work as monitors on summer camps in Santander, Malaga, Segovia and Madrid. Work involves teaching English to the children and helping with sports, recreational and social activities. Some jobs involve working with mentally or physically handicapped children. Ages 18+. Applicants with experience of working with children particularly welcome. July and August. Board and lodging, pocket money and a 4 day tour of Spain provided. Short and long-term teaching posts available throughout the year for young people with EFL experience. Language helpers also needed to live with families and help with spoken English and children's homework. No housework or other duties involved. Ages 18-25. 5 hour day, 1-12 months, all year. Pocket money Pts2500 per week. Provide social service for all applicants, plus language programmes, weekend excursions and a social club. Registration fee £25.

SNOW WORLD (SUN LIVING LTD)
Personnel Manager, Adventure House, 34-36
South Street, Lancing, West Sussex BN15 8AG
Tel Lancing 750310
Opportunities for ski instructors. Ages 18-30. Applicants must have BASI grade 3 or equivalent qualifications. 8-10 hour day, 6 day week, although hours vary depending on needs

of clients. Also opportunities for ski technicians. Applicants should be prepared to work for the whole season, December-April. Extra staff may also be required at peak times such as Christmas. Board, lodging and travel provided. Salary from £80 per week. Training is given at the resort in the week before clients arrive.

TOPS HOLIDAYS (SUN LIVING LTD)
Personnel Manager, Adventure House, 34-36
South Street, Lancing, West Sussex BN15 8AG
Tel Lancing 750310
Organises a range of specialised activity and outdoor education programmes for groups of school children aged 12-17 at a centre in L'Escala. The centre has its own team of staff who ensure that high standards of safety, instruction and enjoyment are maintained. Activity instructors are required to teach sailing, windsurfing and canoeing. Instructors spend most of the time teaching their specialist activity, so must have the ability to teach it to a good basic level and impart the knowledge to a variety of ages in an imaginative, interesting way. The emphasis is on safety, fun and participation rather than achievement. Ages 18+, preference given to ages 20+.

Qualifications from the relevant sporting body are a definite advantage, but applicants with just teaching experience will be considered. All jobs demand a high level of commitment both physically and mentally; applicants should enjoy being with children all day and have a genuine interest in their welfare. Fitness, stamina, energy, enthusiasm and the ability to live and work as part of a team are also essential. 40+ hour week, 1 day free per week. 1+ months, May-September. Most staff work the full season; extra staff are also taken on for shorter periods during peak times at Easter and during July and August. Opportunities for staff to move to other centres in Europe. Travel costs from Dover, full board apartment accommodation and insurance provided. Pay from £35 per week paid in local currency, and varying according to experience and responsibilities. Training provided to ensure staff are confident and able to carry out their responsibilities. Social and recreational activities such as parties, barbecues and outings arranged for staff. *British nationals only.* B D PH limited opportunities.

TEACHERS

BRITISH COUNCIL Director of Studies, Almagro 5, 28010 Madrid 4
Teachers with TEFL qualifications and experience required for British Institute schools in Madrid, Valencia, Barcelona, Mallorca and Granada. Can also provide lists of English language establishments all over Spain where teachers can apply.

CENTRAL BUREAU Assistants Department, Seymour Mews House, Seymour Mews, London W1H 9PE Tel 071-486 5101
Opportunities exist for Junior Assistants in Spanish independent secondary boarding schools, working under the supervision of the English teaching staff and assisting them in the classroom. Junior Assistants also take small groups of pupils to improve their command of spoken English and give them insight into British life, customs and institutions, and are expected to participate fully in the life of the school. Ages 18-20. Board and lodging, usually within the school, and weekly allowance of approx Pts4000-Pts5000 provided. 12-15 hours teaching per week, 2 terms, January-June. Short briefing session usually arranged at the Central Bureau in mid December. Assistance given with travel arrangements and advice on insurance also available. The schools are very often situated in relatively small localities, mostly in the province of Malaga, often some distance from the nearest large town. Applicants must have A level Spanish. Number of posts limited and competition very strong. Registration fee £5. *Apply by mid September.*

CENTROS EUROPEOS English for Executives, C/ Principe 12, 6 A, 28012 Madrid
Teachers with enthusiasm, imagination, and good communication skills are required to teach English, French, and occasionally German or Italian to small groups of mainly adult students. Classes take place within companies or privately. Ages 20+. Applicants should have a university background and be reliable, conscientious and vivacious. Some experience preferred. Those without experience, but who have the necessary qualities and who attend an introductory course, may be accepted. Some knowledge of Spanish helpful but not essential. 15-25 hour week, October-June. Pts1750 per

hour. Accommodation can be arranged with families. Travel and insurance paid by the applicant. *Native speakers only.* PH

ESCUELAS DE IDIOMAS BERLITZ DE ESPANA Ms Susan Taylor, Gran Via 80, 4°, 28013 Madrid Tel 542 35 86
Opportunities for graduates of any discipline to teach English as a foreign/second language. Applicants will teach adult professionals in beginner through to advanced levels, at centres in Madrid, Barcelona, Bilbao, Sevila, Valencia and Palma de Mallorca. Also possibility of teaching English for Special Purposes in the areas of commerce, finance, science and engineering. The work may involve frequent travel within and around the city of allocation. Irregular timetable hours, 08.00-21.30, and Saturday mornings. Ages 21+. Applicants should be mature, responsible, flexible regarding timetabling, and have an outgoing personality. TEFL training/experience not necessary; full in-house training provided. 9 month contracts, salary by negotiation. *Apply by mid April, sending cv and recent photograph. Interviews held April/May in London, Manchester, Edinburgh and Dublin.*

LANGUAGE EXPORT Dr JL Kettle-Williams, PO Box 1574, London NW1 4NJ
Applications are invited for a number of vacancies, teaching English in a variety of institutions, mainly in Madrid. Ages 21-42. Applicants should be highly motivated and suitably qualified, with RSA and/or degree in any discipline. Preference will be given to those with TEFL experience. 20-35 hour week, October-June. Wages approx Pts80000 per month. Schools will usually advise on accommodation. Growing number of opportunities available for short-term posts and in other countries. *Apply in writing with cv.*

THE MANGOLD INSTITUTE Avda Marques de Sotelo 5, Pasaje Rex, Valencia 46002
Offers day and evening courses at all levels in languages, secretarial skills and computing. Languages taught include English, French, German, Italian, Russian, Arabic, and intensive summer courses in Spanish. EFL teachers and secretarial staff are needed in Valencia and surrounding areas; native English speakers with knowledge of Spanish preferred. Teachers should have 1+ year's experience.

SPAIN

Ages 25+. 34 hour week. 9+ months, October onwards for teachers; April-June/October-December, secretarial staff. Wages according to qualifications, approx Pts90000 per month. Accommodation approx Pts2000-Pts2500 per day, full board. Staff should allow Pts1750 per month, medical insurance.

WORKCAMPS

WORKCAMPS

CHRISTIAN MOVEMENT FOR PEACE
Bethnal Green United Reformed Church, Pott Street, London E2 0EF Tel 071-729 1877

UNITED NATIONS ASSOCIATION
International Youth Service, Welsh Centre for International Affairs, Temple of Peace, Cathays Park, Cardiff CF1 3AP
Tel Cardiff 223088

Apply to either of the above to work in international workcamps on a variety of projects. Recent projects have included renovating an old youth hostel in Asturias; reconstructing a bridge and the city walls in Vallodolid; gardening in the grounds of a monastery in Madrid; renovating a Red Cross centre on Tenerife; and reconstructing old houses in a village in Soria. Cultural and sports activities and excursions arranged. Ages 18-26. 2/3 weeks, July and August. Food, accommodation in schools, youth hostels, centres or tents, and accident insurance provided. Participants pay own travel costs.

Organised by Instituto de la Juventud, Servicio Voluntario Internacional de Espana, Jose Ortega y Gasset 71, Madrid 28006.

Applications from outside the UK: please see workcamp information on page 27.

CLUB DE RELACIONES CULTURALES INTERNACIONALES Calle de Ferraz 82, 28008 Madrid
Volunteers are required to work on social and community projects organised throughout Spain in conjunction with local governments or national schemes. Work involves care of the elderly or of children, as well as some construction work on rural sites. Ages 18-28. 4-6 hours per day, 5 days a week during the summer. £20-£25 per week pocket money,

GENERAL

board and lodging provided. Spanish language courses also offered on some projects. Registration fee £25. *Apply January-March.*

INTERNATIONAL VOLUNTARY SERVICE
162 Upper New Walk, Leicester LE1 7QA
Tel Leicester 549430
Volunteers are needed to work in international teams on workcamps organised by SCCT, the Catalan branch of Service Civil International. Recent projects have included carpentry, plumbing and renovation work at an alternative economy study centre; renovating an educational centre in the Pyrenees; painting, decorating and repairing the roof of a community centre near Barcelona; and repairing tools to be sent to a Namibian refugee camp and organising a solidarity campaign in Gerona. Ages 18+. Applicants should have previous workcamp experience and be highly motivated and prepared to work hard and contribute to team life. Good knowledge of Spanish essential on some camps. 40 hour week. 2 weeks, July and August. Food, accommodation and insurance provided, but no travel. Membership fee £25 (students £15, unwaged £10). Registration fee £40. PH

Organised by SCI-SCCT (Servei Catala de Camps de Treball), Rambla Catalunya 5, pral 2a, 08007 Barcelona, Catalonia.

Applications from outside the UK: please see workcamp information on page 27.

GENERAL

CANVAS HOLIDAYS LTD Bull Plain, Hertford SG14 1DY Tel Hertford 553535
Provides ready-erected fully-equipped tents for family holidays, and requires a number of applicants to form flying squads, teams of 2/3 people who help set up and equip 200-250 6 berth frame tents in an area containing approx 12 campsites. Similar work is also available dismantling tents and cleaning and storing equipment. Ages 18-25. Knowledge of Spanish not required, but is an advantage as flying squad members sometimes have the opportunity to continue as couriers. Applicants must be sociable in order to work in a small community, fit and able to work hard for long hours under pressure, work without

supervision and cope with living out of a rucksack. Driving licence an advantage. Early April-mid June, possibly longer to set up the tents, and September to dismantle them. Salary £76 per week, tented accommodation, self-catering facilities and outward travel provided. Return travel dependent on the completion of contract dates. *UK nationals only.*

CLUB DE RELACIONES CULTURALES INTERNACIONALES Calle de Ferraz 82, 28008 Madrid

In cooperation with the Spanish Red Cross, arranges positions for 2nd year medical students wishing to gain professional experience by working in hospitals and emergency departments. Applicants should have good spoken Spanish. 1-3 months, April-September. Board, accommodation, insurance and Pts15000-Pts20000 pocket money per month provided. *Apply January-March.*
Also arranges positions throughout Spain for 2nd year vocational, secretarial or university students wishing to obtain work experience. Typing and other skills an advantage. Knowledge of Spanish or other languages welcome but not essential. Ages 18-25. 1-3 months, all year. Insurance and Pts35000-Pts40000 per month provided. Help given in finding accommodation. *Apply all year.* Registration fee £25.

EUROYOUTH LTD 301 Westborough Road, Westcliff-on-Sea, Essex SS0 9PT
Tel Southend-on-Sea 341434

Arranges holiday guest stays where guests are offered board and lodging in return for an agreed number of hours English conversation with hosts or their children. Time is also available for guests to practise Spanish if desired. Mainly ages 15-25, but there are sometimes opportunities for older applicants. 2-3 weeks, and occasionally 1-2 months, mainly July and August. Travel and insurance arranged by applicants, but tickets at reduced rates can be obtained on request. Registration fee approx £60. *Apply at least 12 weeks prior to scheduled departure date. UK nationals only.*

SINDICATO ESPANOL UNIVERSITARIO (Spanish Union of Students), Reina 33, Madrid 4

Can provide information on voluntary work throughout Spain.

APPLYING FOR A JOB

Read carefully all the information given before applying. Check in particular:

* the necessary skills/experience required

* the full period of employment expected

* any restrictions of age, sex or nationality

* application deadlines

* any other points, particularly details of insurance cover provided, and other costs such as travel and accommodation.

When applying be sure to include:

* name, address, date of birth, marital status, nationality, sex

* education, qualifications, relevant experience

* period of availability

* details of languages spoken

* a large stamped, self-addressed envelope plus, if overseas, 2 International Reply Coupons

* a passport-size photo, particularly if you are to have contact with the public

* any registration or membership fees

NOTES

SWEDEN

Swedish Embassy
11 Montagu Place, London W1H 2AL Tel 07
1-724 2101

British Embassy
Skarpogatan 6-8, 115 27 Stockholm

Tourist office
Swedish National Tourist Office, 29/31 Oxford
Street, London W1R 1RE Tel 01-437 5816

Youth hostels
STS, Vasagatan 48, 101 20 Stockholm

Youth & student information
SFS Resor, Kungsgatan 4, 103 87 Stockholm

Östermahus Fritidsgard, Valhallavagen 142,
115 24 Stockholm

INFORMATION

Entry regulations A work permit is required
for all types of employment, including au pair
positions. Applications should be made to the
Swedish Embassy or a Swedish Consulate once
an offer of employment has been secured.
Work permits are issued for a specific job and
period by the National Immigration Board and
applicants will be notified of the decision by
the Embassy. It must be noted that an offer of
employment is no guarantee that a work
permit will be granted. Students should
indicate their status when applying; vacation
employment may cover a period of 3 months,
15 May-15 October. Opportunities are
extremely limited and students without a
specific skill or knowledge of Swedish may
have difficulty in obtaining a permit.

Applications for work permits are not accepted
by the Immigration Board from visitors already
in Sweden; if an applicant enters Sweden
before the work permit is granted, the permit
will be refused. It usually takes 6-8 weeks to
process an application. Applications for work
in Sweden can be made under the International
Clearing of Vacancies (ICV) scheme; for more
details contact the Training Agency. Those
intending to remain in Sweden for more than 3
months will require a residence permit which
must be issued before entering Sweden, and if
the period of work exceeds 3 months it will
usually be necessary to attend an interview at
the Embassy.

Job advertising Frank L Crane (London) Ltd,
International Press Representation, 5/15
Cromer Street, Grays Inn Road, London WC1H
8LS Tel 071-837 3330 are agents for *Dagens
Nyheter* (largest morning daily in Stockholm),
Expressen (largest afternoon daily), *Goteborgs-
Posten* (largest morning daily) and many other
newspapers for which they can accept job
advertisements.

Travel Norwegian State Railways, 21/24
Cockspur Street, London SW1Y 5DA Tel 071-
930 6666 issues the Nordic Tourist Ticket which
entitles the holder to unlimited travel on trains
in Sweden, Norway, Denmark and Finland, and
is also valid on some inter-Scandinavian ferry
services. Valid 21 days; cost £113 for ages
under 26, and £151 for ages over 26.

Campus Travel, 52 Grosvenor Gardens, London
SW1W 0AG Tel 071-730 3402 offers Eurotrain
under 26 fares and competitive airfares to
destinations in Sweden.

Sweden Holiday Guide is a free magazine
providing general information on travel to and
around the country, places of interest, public
services, medical treatment, eating,
accommodation and outdoor activities, plus
maps and colour photographs. Also *Holiday
Guide for the Disabled*. Available from the
Swedish National Tourist Office, see above. PH

The Rough Guide to Scandinavia £7.95 is a
practical handbook which includes concise

SWEDEN

up-to-date information on getting around Sweden. Published by Harrap Columbus, Chelsea House, 26 Market Square, Bromley, Kent, BR1 1NA.

Accommodation Ostermahus Fritidsgard, Valhallavagen 142, 115 24 Stockholm has accommodation available for young people. Facilities include information centre, washing machines, lockers, bike hire, kitchen and coffee shop. 5 consecutive nights only, mid June-end July. Cost Skr35 per night, bed and shower; membership Skr10.

FARMWORK

FARMWORK

INTERNATIONAL FARM EXPERIENCE PROGRAMME YFC Centre, National Agricultural Centre, Kenilworth, Warwickshire CV8 2LG Tel Coventry 696584 Provides assistance to young farmers and nurserymen by finding places in farms and nurseries abroad to enable them to broaden their knowledge of agricultural methods. Opportunities for practical horticultural or agricultural work, usually on mixed farms. Applicants live and work with a farmer and his family and the work is matched as far as possible with the applicant's requirements. 3-12 months, mostly spring and summer. Some au pair positions for girls. Wages approx £30; board and lodging provided. Ages 18-26. Applicants must have at least 2 years practical experience, 1 year of which may be at an agricultural college, and intend to make a career in agriculture or horticulture. Valid driving licence necessary. Applicants pay own fares. Registration fee £62. *British applicants only; apply at least 3 months in advance.*

Swedish applicants requiring an exchange should contact Arbetsmarknadsstyrelsen, 17199 Solna.

TEACHERS

TEACHERS

FOLK UNIVERSITY OF SWEDEN The British Centre, c/o International Language Services (Scandinavia), 36 Fowlers Road, Salisbury, Wiltshire SP1 1ED Tel Salisbury 331011 The British Centre is part of the Folk University, the only organisation concerned with promoting adult education in Sweden with no political, religious or sociological affiliations. The majority of English teachers are placed in Type B posts, in smaller towns, where they teach mainly general English at all levels for adults in study circles, plus some teaching in schools, with a limited number in Kursverksamheten (KVs), extra-mural departments of local universities. The largest KVs, in Gothenburg, Stockholm, Lund and Uppsala, employ teachers in Type A posts where work is of a more demanding nature.

Ages 22-40. Applicants must be British citizens and hold a university degree and/or qualified teacher status in the UK or recognised TEFL qualifications granted in the UK. For Type A posts 2+ years EFL experience and the RSA TEFL Diploma or equivalent also required. Applicants must be in excellent health and should be sociable, adaptable and well informed. Candidates with children will not be considered. Approx 26 academic hours per week, September-May. Limited number of vacancies available in January. Teachers must be prepared to work every weekday evening; some weekend work possible. Accommodation provided during initial training course. Salary approx Kr8000 per month, plus supplement of Kr1500-Kr2000 per month for Type A posts. Travel provided; teachers working 4+ terms receive contribution to return journey. Most teachers stay for at least 2 years. *Apply at any time; interviews held spring, early summer and November.*

WORKCAMPS

INTERNATIONAL VOLUNTARY SERVICE 162 Upper New Walk, Leicester LE1 7QA Tel Leicester 549430 IVS is the British branch of Service Civil International, which promotes international reconciliation through work projects. International teams of 8-10 volunteers live and work together on workcamps where the work may vary from manual labour to social activities or study. Recent projects have included planting trees for an ecology cooperative near Storuman; sorting and packing secondhand clothes and equipment to send to refugees at Emmaus centres in Skane and Smaland; helping with the harvest and caring for animals at an organic farm on a nature reserve near Karlstad; painting and working in the grounds of a Rudolf Steiner school near Stockholm; renovating an alternative community centre for creative and social activities in Uppsala; and renovating a building in Verkstaden to be used as an arts/activity centre with workshops for ceramics, fine art and photography. Study themes are linked to the camps.

Ages 18+. Applicants should preferably have previous workcamp, voluntary work or community service experience, a real interest in living and working together with people from other countries to better understand other cultures, and should be prepared to work hard and contribute to team life. 35-40 hour week. 2 weeks, June-September. Food, accommodation and insurance provided, but not travel. Membership fee £25 (students £15, unwaged £10). Registration fee £40. **PH**

Organised by Internationella Arbetslag (IAL), Barnangsgatan 23, 11641 Stockholm.

Applications from outside the UK: please see workcamp information on page 27.

When writing to any organisation it is essential to mention Working Holidays 1991 and enclose a large stamped, self-addressed envelope, or if overseas, a large addressed envelope and at least two International Reply Coupons.

APPLYING FOR A JOB

Read carefully all the information given before applying. Check in particular:

* the necessary skills/experience required

* the full period of employment expected

* any restrictions of age, sex or nationality

* application deadlines

* any other points, particularly details of insurance cover provided, and other costs such as travel and accommodation.

When applying be sure to include:

* name, address, date of birth, marital status, nationality, sex

* education, qualifications, relevant experience

* period of availability

* details of languages spoken

* a large stamped, self-addressed envelope plus, if overseas, 2 International Reply Coupons

* a passport-size photo, particularly if you are to have contact with the public

* any registration or membership fees

SWEDEN

WORKCAMPS

NOTES

SWITZERLAND

Swiss Embassy
16-18 Montagu Place, London W1H 2BQ
Tel 071-723 0701

Swiss Consulate General
Sunley Building, 24th floor, Piccadilly Plaza,
Manchester M1 4BT Tel 061-236 2933

British Embassy
Thunstrasse 50, 3005 Bern

Tourist office
Swiss National Tourist Office, Swiss Centre,

1 New Coventry Street, London W1V 8EE
Tel 071-734 1921

Youth hostels
Schweizerischer Bund für Jugendherbergen
(SJH), Postfach 265, Engelstrasse 9, 3000
Bern 26

Youth & student information
Swiss Student Travel Office, SSR-Reisen,
Bäckerstrasse 40, Postfach, 8026 Zürich

INFORMATION

Entry regulations An *assurance of a residence permit* is required for all types of employment; this is a combination of both a residence and work permit, entitling the holder to live in a particular canton and work for a specified employer. It should be obtained by the prospective employer by applying to the Cantonal Aliens Police before the applicant's arrival in Switzerland. This procedure also applies to au pairs and trainees. The economic situation and quota restrictions imposed by the Federal Government on the granting of seasonal permits has resulted in a considerable decrease in employment opportunities for foreign nationals. The number of permits granted is extremely limited and only applicants offering specific skills or qualifications are likely to succeed. As a rule, only those who have been offered a job which cannot be filled by a Swiss national have a chance of receiving a permit. The few jobs for which permits may be granted are mainly in the hotel and catering trades, and in shops and on farms. Seasonal permits are granted to holders of assurance of a residence permits after arrival in Switzerland for seasonal employment in the building, hotel and holiday industry for a period of 4/5-9 months; entry and exit dates must be strictly adhered to. Those married to Swiss women, and foreign children of a Swiss mother are not subject to the quota restrictions. The Federal Office for

Industry, Crafts and Labour in Bern publishes a booklet covering information on entry and residence, job availability, living and working conditions, wages, taxes and insurance schemes; available from the Swiss Embassy.

Job advertising Publicitas Ltd, 525/527 Fulham Road, London SW6 1HF Tel 071-385 7723 are agents for *Basler Zeitung* (Basle daily), *Der Bund* (Bern daily), *Journal de Genève* (high class daily), *Neue Zürcher Zeitung* (leading high class daily), *La Suisse* (Geneva daily), *Tandem* (leading Lucerne daily), *24 Heures* (Lausanne daily) and other newspapers.

Travel STA Travel Ltd, 86 Old Brompton Road, London SW7 3LQ Tel 071-937 9921 operates flexible, low-cost flights between London, Geneva and Zürich.

Campus Travel, 52 Grosvenor Gardens, London SW1W 0AG Tel 071-730 3402 offers Eurotrain under 26 fares and charter flights to destinations in Switzerland.

Swiss National Tourist Office, Swiss Centre, New Coventry Street, London W1V 8EE Tel 071-734 1921 issues the Swiss Pass which gives unlimited travel on rail, boat and postbus routes, plus trams and buses in 24 towns, and reductions on mountain railways and cable cars. Cost SF160-SF325, 4-31 days.

Swiss Student Travel Office, SSR-Reisen, Bäckerstrasse 52, Postfach, 8026 Zürich offers reduced air and rail fares including daily departures from London Gatwick to Geneva and Zürich from £70 return.

Travel Tips for Switzerland is a booklet containing information on travel formalities and facilities including sports, culture and general information and advice. Available from the Swiss National Tourist Office, see above.

Accommodation *Student Lodgings at University Cities in Switzerland* is a booklet giving the addresses of student accommodation. Available from the Swiss National Tourist Office, see above.

Swiss Student Travel Office, see above, offers accommodation at hotels in the Swiss alps. Holders of ISIC cards are entitled to 10% discount, plus various other reductions.

Information centres Swiss Student Travel Office, see above, provides general tourist information, details of cheap places to stay, where to go and what to see.

AU PAIR/ CHILDCARE

INTERLINGUA CENTRE Torquay Road, Foxrock, Dublin, Ireland 18 Tel Dublin 893876
Can place au pairs with Swiss families. 30 hour week with one full day and some evenings off. Time to attend classes 2-3 mornings or afternoons per week. Experience desirable but not essential. 6+ months. Ages 18+. £25-£40 per week pocket money, full board, lodging and insurance provided. Travel paid by applicants. Placement fee £55.

JOLAINE AGENCY 18 Escot Way, Barnet, Hertfordshire EN5 3AN Tel 081-449 1334
Au pairs and mother's help posts arranged. Ages 17-27. 6+ months, all year. Summer posts also available, looking after children and doing light household duties. 3+ months, June-October. Pocket money from £25+ per week. Travel and insurance paid by applicants. Introduction fee £40.

UNIVERSAL CARE Chester House, 9 Windsor End, Beaconsfield, Buckinghamshire HP9 2JJ Tel Beaconsfield 678811
Can place au pairs and mother's helps in most parts of Switzerland. Stays are usually a minimum of 6 months. Ages 17-27. Board and lodging provided. Salaries vary but are usually £25 per week; higher for mother's helps. Travel paid by applicant, but sometimes families help with return fare. Service charge £46. *Apply 2 months before work period desired.*

COMMUNITY WORK

INTERNATIONAL VOLUNTARY SERVICE 162 Upper New Walk, Leicester LE1 7QA Tel Leicester 549430
IVS is the British branch of Service Civil International, which promotes international reconciliation through work projects. Volunteers are needed to work in international teams on community projects. Recent projects have included helping disabled children at a holiday camp near Olten, with the aim of fighting isolation and creating opportunities for new friendships; working on a holiday camp for handicapped and able-bodied children in Berguen; carrying out renovation and agricultural work in a Pestalozzi children's village which cares for refugee orphans; and collecting information on museums, cinemas, restaurants and other public buildings in Basle, in order to update a guide for handicapped people.

Ages 18+. Applicants should have previous workcamp, voluntary work or community service experience, and should be prepared to work hard and contribute to team life. Good knowledge of German needed on some camps. 35-40 hour week. 2-4 weeks, June-September. Food, accommodation and insurance provided, but not travel. Membership fee £25 (students £15, unwaged £10) Registration fee £40. B D PH

Organised by Service Civil International, Postfach 246, Waldhoheweg 33a, 3000 Bern 25.

Applications from outside the UK: please see workcamp information on page 27.

CONSERVATION

INTERNATIONAL VOLUNTARY SERVICE
162 Upper New Walk, Leicester LE1 7QA
Tel Leicester 549430
IVS is the British branch of Service Civil
International which promotes international
reconciliation through work projects.
Volunteers are needed to work in international
teams on conservation projects which have
recently included building a barrier to protect
reed zones from erosion, fixing stakes and
planting osiers in marshland along the shore of
Lake Neuchâtel; trying out ecological
construction techniques at an environmental
centre in Lucerne; restoring buildings in an
abandoned village in Ticino; and clearing
overgrown mountain pastures near Grimentz,
a village in the Valaisan Alps. Ages 18+.
Knowledge of French or German useful.
Applicants should have previous workcamp,
voluntary work or community service
experience, and should be prepared to work
hard and contribute to team life. 35-40 hour
week. 2-4 weeks, June-September. Food,
accommodation and insurance provided, but
not travel. Membership fee £25 (students £15,
unwaged £10). Registration fee £40. **B D PH**

Organised by Service Civil International,
Postfach 246, Waldhoheweg 33a, 3000 Bern 25.

Applications from outside the UK: please see
workcamp information on page 27.

INTERNATIONALE ARBEITSGEMEIN-
SCHAFT fur Wander, Ski-, Rad- and
Rettungswesen (AWSR), Rosengartenstrasse
17, 9000 St Gallen
Volunteers are needed for conservation work at
international camps in Zermatt, Saas Fee,
Sustenpass/Steingletscher and possibly
Schwägalp. Small teams of volunteers go out
from the basecamp to work on a variety of
projects, which may include environmental
protection on alpine roads and the shores of
rivers and lakes; building footpaths and small
bridges, clearing litter; or repairing damage
caused by avalanches. Ages 18-26. Knowledge
of German required. 5-7 hour day, excluding
travel to and from work place. 5 day week. 8-22
days; mid June-end August. Full board and
accommodation provided, plus SF6 per day

pocket money. Volunteers must take mountain
boots, warm clothes, rainwear, sleeping bag,
first aid kit, pocket knife, torch, sunglasses and
signal whistle; anyone arriving insufficiently
equipped will not be accepted. Volunteers pay
their own travel costs. Registration fee SF50.
Families welcome. *Apply at least 4 weeks before*
intended date of arrival; applications confirmed 2+
weeks before start date.

INTERNATIONALE BEGEGNUNG IN
GEMEINSCHAFTSDIENSTEN EV (IBG)
Schlosserstrasse 28, 7000 Stuttgart 1, Federal
Republic of Germany
Founded by Scout leaders to organise work
projects of benefit to the community and to
promote better international understanding.
Volunteers are needed on international
workcamps; each camp is made up of 15-20
participants from 6-8 countries who work
together on a common project. Recent projects
have included forestry work at Olten; and
preparing footpaths near Brig, Altdorf and
Munster. Ages 18-30. 30 hour week with
weekends free. 3 weeks, end June-September.
Food, accommodation in youth hostels or
schools with self catering facilities and
insurance provided, but not travel. Volunteers
should take a sleeping bag. Registration fee
DM90.

UK applicants may apply to United Nations
Association, International Youth Service, Welsh
Centre for International Affairs, Temple of Peace,
Cathays Park, Cardiff CF1 3AP Tel Cardiff
223088.

COURIERS/REPS

BLADON LINES Personnel Department, 56-58
Putney High Street, London SW15 1SF
Tel 081-785 2200
Opportunities for representatives to work in
the ski resorts of Verbier, Crans Montana, Les
Diablerets, Haute Nendaz, Saas Fee and
Zermatt. Work involves welcoming and
looking after guests, providing information,
organising coach transfers and ensuring
everything is running smoothly. Ages 24+.
Relevant experience an advantage, and good
spoken French or German essential. Hours are
very variable; applicants must be prepared to
work hard but will get time to ski. December-

SWITZERLAND

May. Salary £50-£100, depending on the size of the resort. Board, lodging, return travel, insurance, ski pass, ski hire and company ski jacket provided. Training week held in London before departure. There are also a couple of places in each resort for ski guides who act as assistant representatives and whose work involves showing guests around the slopes, helping with coach transfers and organising *après ski*. Age 22+ with good spoken French or German. Applicants should have good leadership qualities and be proficient skiers. Salary approx £50 per week. A week's training held in Val d'Isère before the season starts. *EC nationals only*. PH depending on ability.

CANVAS HOLIDAYS LTD Bull Plain, Hertford SG14 1DY Tel Hertford 553535
Resident couriers are required to work on campsites for a holiday company providing accommodation for families in ready-erected fully equipped tents and cabins. The work involves a daily routine of tent cleaning as customers arrive and depart, providing information and advice on the local attractions and essential services, helping to sort out problems that might arise and organising activities for the children and get-togethers for the families. 7 day week job with no fixed hours; the workload varies from day to day. At the beginning and end of the season there is a period of physical work when tents are put up and prepared for the customers or dismantled and stored for the winter. Other tasks include administration, book keeping and stock control. Working knowledge of French or German essential. Ages 18-25. Applicants are normally those with a year between school and further education, undergraduates or graduates. They need to be reliable, self-motivated, able to turn their hand to new and varied tasks, and with a sense of humour. 10-14 weeks, early April-July or July-late September. Return travel, dependent on successful completion of contract, and accommodation in frame tents provided. Salary approx £76 per week. *UK nationals only. Applications accepted anytime; interviews commence early November.*

EUROCAMP Courier Department, Edmundson House, Tatton Street, Knutsford, Cheshire WA16 6BG Tel Knutsford 50052
Requires resident couriers to work on various campsites. Work involves cleaning tents and equipment prior to the arrival of new customers, checking, replacing and making repairs on equipment, replenishing gas supplies, keeping the store tent in order, keeping basic accounts and reporting on a weekly basis to England. Couriers are also expected to meet new arrivals and assist holidaymakers with any problems that may arise; organise activities and parties; provide information on local tourist attractions and maintain an information noticeboard. At the beginning and end of the season couriers are expected to help in erecting and dismantling tents. There are no set working hours or free days, as these depend on unpredictable factors. Ages 18-28; older applicants considered. Applications from couples welcome. Applicants should be familiar with working and travelling abroad, preferably with camping experience. They should also be adaptable, reliable, independent, efficient, hard working, sensible, sociable, tactful, patient and have a working knowledge of the language. Applicants are expected to work one half of the season, early/mid April-mid July or mid July-late September/early October; exact dates depend on the campsite. Work also available for the whole season. Accommodation in frame tent with cooking facilities, moped for use on site, insurance and return fare provided. Salary approx £80 per week. *Early application advisable; interviews start November.*

QUEST TRAVEL Olivier House, 18 Marine Parade, Brighton, East Sussex BN2 1TL Tel Brighton 677777
Provides ski and summer tours for groups, mainly school parties, individuals and youth and adult organisations. Requires resort representatives for the summer and winter seasons, December-April and May-July/August, in Crans Montana. Duties include meeting groups at airports or hotels, room allocation, liaison with group leaders, organising entertainments, arranging ski passes and lessons, and promoting good local relations. On call 24 hours per day. Applicants should have fluent French, be enthusiastic, have a flair for organising and enjoy hard stimulating work. Ages 21+. Wages £75-£110 per week, full board, lodging in shared accommodation, medical insurance and return travel provided. Training course at beginning of season. B D PH limited opportunities.

COURIERS/REFS

SUPERTRAVEL Alpine Operations Department, 22 Hans Place, London SW1X 0EP Tel 071-589 5161

Arranges skiing holidays in the Swiss alpine resorts of Murren, Wengen, Zermatt and Verbier. Opportunities for resort representatives, responsible for looking after guests and supervising staff. Ages 24-30. Work involves travelling to the airport each weekend to welcome guests; organising their ski passes, ski hire and ski school; informing them of local events; overseeing the work of chalet girls and ensuring that chalets are kept in perfect running order. There are also opportunities for managers in jumbo chalets (24-60 beds) who are responsible for the smooth running of their chalets and should be experienced in managing others if not experienced in hotel work. Applicants should be used to working on their own initiative, often under pressure. Stamina, a sense of humour and fluent French or German essential. Applicants must be available for the whole season, early December-end April. Approx 40+ hours per week. Board, lodging, ski pass, ski and boot hire and return travel provided; also insurance in return for approx £35 contribution. Salary £55-£85 per week, paid in local currency. Two day briefing held in London before departure, plus individual session to learn about the resort. *British nationals only.*

VENTURE ABROAD Warren House, High Street, Cranleigh, Surrey GU6 8AJ Tel Cranleigh 273027

Representatives are required by a tour operator specialising in European holidays for youth groups. The work involves assisting and advising groups staying in Adelboden, Grindelwald, Gstaad, Meiringen, Interlaken and the Bernese Oberland, helping them to get the most out of their stay. Representatives meet groups on arrival, provide general local information, hire coaches, escort on excursions and act as a guide to the surrounding countryside. Ages 19+. University students with knowledge of French or German and experience of working with youth groups preferred. 50 hour week, end June-end August. Salary £65-£70 per week, self-catering accommodation, insurance, work permits and visas provided. Basic training given before departure. *Apply enclosing cv.*

DOMESTIC

BLADON LINES Personnel Department, 56-58 Putney High Street, London SW15 1SF Tel 081-785 2200

Opportunities for cooks and cleaners to work in the ski resorts of Verbier, Crans Montana, Les Diablerets, Haute Nendaz, Saas Fee and Zermatt. Also opportunities for chalet girls, whose work involves cleaning chalets, making beds, caring for guests, shopping and preparing meals. Ages 20+. Experience and/or qualifications in catering or domestic work essential. However, there are also positions for hostesses to work in the larger chalets where no cooking experience is required.

Hours are very variable; applicants must be prepared to work hard but will get time to ski. December-May. Salary approx £40 per week, ski pass, ski hire, company ski jacket, board, lodging, return travel and insurance provided. One day briefing in London before departure. *EC nationals only.* PH depending on ability.

JOBS IN THE ALPS AGENCY PO Box 388, London SW1X 8LX

Work is available for hall and night porters, waiters, waitresses, and occasionally receptionists or barmaids, in hotels with international clientele. Good knowledge of French or German required. Limited number of other jobs such as chambermaids and kitchen helpers, and in mountain cafes, may be available for those with limited languages. Some jobs available for girls with a good knowledge of French in village cafes, not in tourist resorts; isolated jobs with a local clientele. Ages 18+.

Applicants must be prepared to work hard and to a high standard, alongside an international workforce. 9 hour day with afternoons usually free. 2 days free per week, of which one may be paid in lieu during the high season. Jobs are for the whole season, December-April or June-September. Pay from approx £100 per week, board, lodging and insurance provided. Interview fee £1, plus £25 service charge and £10 per month depending on length of contract. *Closing dates for interviews 30 September (winter) or 30 April (summer). EC nationals only.*

SWITZERLAND

DOMESTIC

FARMWORK/GRAPE PICKING

SNOW WORLD (SUN LIVING LTD)
Personnel Manager, Adventure House, 34-36 South Street, Lancing, West Sussex BN15 8AG Tel Lancing 750310
Opportunities for chalet maids to work in ski resorts, keeping chalets tidy, looking after guests, and in certain cases preparing meals. Ages 18-30. Relevant experience in domestic and/or catering essential. Usually 8-10 hour day, 6 day week, but hours vary depending on the needs of clients. Applicants should be prepared to work the whole season, December-April. Extra staff may also be required at peak times such as Christmas. Board, lodging and travel provided. Salary from £45 per week. Training given at the resort during the week before clients arrive.

SUPERTRAVEL Alpine Operations
Department, 22 Hans Place, London SW1X 0EP Tel 071-589 5161
Arranges skiing holidays in the Swiss alpine resorts of Murren, Wengen, Zermatt and Verbier. Opportunities for chalet girls, responsible for looking after guests and keeping chalet clean and tidy. Ages 21-30. Work involves cooking, cleaning, acting as hostess, sitting down to dinner with guests, advising them on skiing areas and keeping them up to date with events in the resort. Chalet girls must work to a budget and account for expenditure. Applicants must have cooking experience and preferably qualifications, be capable of running a chalet of approx 8 guests and have an outgoing and helpful personality. In the jumbo chalets (24-60 beds) there are opportunities for chalet girl helpers, whose duties are similar to the chalet girls but do not involve cooking, and also for chalet boy helpers, who look after the heavier duties such as cleaning of general areas, washing up, snow clearing, maintenance and sometimes bar work. Ages 20+. Applicants must be available for the whole season, early December-end April. Approx 40+ hours per week. Board, lodging, ski pass, ski and boot hire and return travel provided; also insurance in return for approx £35 contribution. Salary £45 per week, paid in local currency. Briefings held in London before departure. *British nationals only.*

VILLAGE CAMPS Chalet Seneca, 1854 Leysin
Organises a range of holidays in American-style camps for children aged 8-16 from the international business and diplomatic communities. Opportunities for chalet girls to work on winter programmes at camps in Saas Fee, Anzere, Leysin, Saas Grund and Champery. Chalet girls are responsible for the overall operations of a single chalet, including general cleaning, meal planning and preparation, ordering and/or shopping for food, and preparing the chalet for the weekly arrival of guests, which may involve clearing snow from the chalet path. Ages 21+. Applicants should have specialised training and experience in cooking, household or hotel management, and nutrition. They should be independent, proficient in budgeting, well-organised, friendly and capable of dealing with small groups of people of different ages and nationalities. English is the first language but priority consideration is given to applicants with additional French and German language skills. 45 hour week, 2+ weeks, December-Easter. 2 evenings free per week. Accommodation, ski pass and accident and liability insurance provided. Wages SF150 per week. Applicants pay their own travel costs. Compulsory pre-camp training course arranged.

FARMWORK/ GRAPE PICKING

VACATION WORK INTERNATIONAL 9
Park End Street, Oxford, Oxfordshire OX1 1HJ Tel Oxford 241978
Grape pickers are needed in the French-speaking canton of Vaud, an area of small villages and vineyards. Applicants should expect to work a hard 10 hour day, 6 day week. Approx 8 10 days, 30 September-20 October. Wages approx SF55+ per day. Travel allowance of SF30 paid on completion of work period. During bad weather only the actual hours worked will be paid for. Board and lodging provided, but participants must take sleeping bags. Ages 17-35. Work is strenuous and applicants should be fit. Cost £109 includes outward rail travel; insurance extra. *Applicants must hold a full UK, Australian or New Zealand passport; apply by 1 September.*
Vacancies also exist on small Swiss farms, mainly in German-speaking Baselland. The

farms are usually scattered and remote, and work consists of a mixture of farm and domestic jobs including work with animals, in the fields and housework. Long hours, 6 day week. 3-8 weeks, mid August. Wages SF120 per week. Participants who work 3+ weeks will receive a travel voucher for the return journey to Basle. Board and lodging provided on the farm. Ages 17-30. Applicants must be fit for manual work. Knowledge of French, German or Italian to GCSE standard essential. Cost £109 includes outward rail travel. Insurance extra. *British applicants only; apply by 12 April for work in May or 22 June for work in August.*

ZENTRALSTELLE FUR FREIWILLIGEN LANDDIENST Bahnhofplatz 1, PO Box 6331, 8023 Zürich
Workers are required for strenuous agricultural and domestic work on small farms in French and German-speaking cantons. Work involves cleaning out cowstalls, haymaking, grass cutting, poultry feeding, transporting milk, manure spreading and spraying, vegetable and fruit picking, wood cutting, gardening and housework. Ages 17+. Basic knowledge of French or German essential. Working hours 07.00-19.00; Sundays free. 3-8 weeks, March-October. Full board and lodging with the farmer's family, insurance and SF19+ per day pocket money provided. It is not possible to place 2 people with the same farmer. Applicants from western Europe can enter Switzerland under a global residence guarantee. Applications should be made 4 weeks before intended date of arrival, and successful applicants will be sent details of arrangements before they are due to start work.

MONITORS & INSTRUCTORS

ARENA Hameau de la Pinéde, Traverse Valette, 13009 Marseille, France
Volunteers are needed to work as monitors on a holiday camp for North African children from the shanty towns of Marseille. Each volunteer is responsible for looking after a group of 6-8 children and organising activities. Ages 18+. Experience with children and a knowledge of French essential. 4 weeks, 5 July-5 August.

Board and lodging provided and help may be given with travel expenses. *Alternatively apply to Christoph McHale, Berchtoldstrasse 19, 3012 Bern.*

SKI EUROPE Northumberland House, 2 King Street, Twickenham, Middlesex TW1 3RZ Tel 01-891 4400
A company with its own ski school, operating holidays for groups and school parties. Part-time ski instructors are required for winter sports in the Bernese Oberland, Grisons, Valais and Graubunden regions. Work involves 4 hours teaching per day. BASI or full ASSI qualifications essential, together with a high level of teaching skill. Knowledge of foreign languages useful; fluent English a prerequisite. 1-4 week periods over Christmas, the New Year, February and April. Instructors receive full board accommodation and ski pass, plus travel expenses London/resort, and have access to the same facilities as the clients. Wages approx £75 per week, depending on qualifications. *Interviews held May-November.*

SNOW WORLD (SUN LIVING LTD) Personnel Manager, Adventure House, 34-36 South Street, Lancing, West Sussex BN15 8AG Tel Lancing 750310
Opportunities for ski instructors with BASI grade 3 or equivalent qualifications. Ages 18-30. 8-10 hour day, 6 day week, although hours vary depending on needs of clients. Also opportunities for ski technicians. Applicants should be prepared to work the whole season, December-April. Extra staff may also be required at peak times such as Christmas. Board, lodging and travel provided. Salary from £80 per week. Training given at the resort in the week before clients arrive.

VILLAGE CAMPS Chalet Seneca, 1854 Leysin
Organises a range of holidays in American-style camps for children aged 8-16 from the international business and diplomatic communities. Opportunities for counsellors, special activity counsellors, programme leaders, special instructors, ski counsellors and nurses. Staff live, work and play with the children and are responsible for their safety, health and happiness. Counsellors plan, organise and direct daytime and evening programmes, accompany campers on excursions and may be called upon to

TEACHERS

WORKCAMPS

supervise other counsellors and take charge of a camper group. Evening activities include sports and games, films, competitions, fondues and discos. Special activity counsellors having a high degree of proficiency organise, execute and instruct specific programmes such as sports, arts and crafts, nature study and basic computer science. Counsellors with a substantial amount of leadership experience in recreational programmes can be appointed programme leaders, which includes running a camp programme and direction and supervision of adult counsellors. Assistant and junior counsellors are responsible for supporting counsellors in all activities and assisting with special activities at day camps as required. Specialist instructors should have 2 years training and experience and be able to instruct children of all ability levels; they are responsible for the concentrated teaching of their subject at a speciality camp such as football, golf, tennis, computer science or French and English language. Ski counsellors must be good parallel skiers, with a thorough understanding of mountain safety. Nurses are responsible for the general health and welfare of campers and counsellors, attending to accidents and maintaining an infirmary. Compulsory pre-camp training course arranged for all staff. Summer camps are organised in Leysin; winter camps at Saas Fee, Anzere, Leysin, Saas Grund and Champery. Ages 21+, 26+ for programme leaders. Applicants must have training and/or experience of working with children and have an interest in children from many ethnic and religious backgrounds. English is the first language, but priority consideration given to applicants with additional French, Italian or German language skills. For day camps preference is given to applicants living within commuting distance of the camp. 45 hour week. Summer camps 1+ months, June-August; 1½ days, plus 3 evenings free per 2 week session. Winter camps 1-4 weeks, December-Easter; 2 evenings free per week. Full board and accommodation, accident and liability insurance provided, but not travel costs. Summer wages SF325 per two week session; winter wages SF100 per week plus ski pass for area worked. Wages for day camps are paid per 10 day session: counsellors, special activity counsellors and nurses SF275; assistant counsellors SF225; junior counsellors SF150.

TEACHERS

SWISS FEDERATION OF PRIVATE SCHOOLS Service Scolaire, Tour de l'Ile 1, PB 43, 1211 Geneva 11
Publishes *Private Schools in Switzerland*, a booklet giving full details of schools to which teachers may apply, many international, from elementary to adult formation and including finishing schools. Many of them have English-speaking sections which prepare for GCSE and A level examinations, and include commercial, technical, secretarial, language and domestic branches with sports facilities. *Does not arrange individual placements; apply directly to the schools.*

SWISS NATIONAL TOURIST OFFICE Swiss Centre, New Coventry Street, London W1V 8EE Tel 071-734 1921
Can provide a booklet, *Switzerland - Country for Children*, published by the Association Suisse des Homes d'Enfants, which contains a large selection of schools and homes for children in the lowlands, mountains and towns to which teachers may apply. Some offer tutoring in English of American/English curricula.

WORKCAMPS

ATD QUART MONDE 1733 Treyvaux
Strives to protect and guarantee the fundamental rights of the most disadvantaged and excluded families to family life, education and representation. It is these families, being denied the means of being fully active members of society, who constitute the Fourth World in every country.

Volunteers are required to help in the construction of an international centre for the movement in Treyvaux, undertaking such jobs as masonry, painting, gardening, secretarial work, cooking, carpentry, and electrical work. Applicants should be interested in better understanding the causes and effects of poverty and be willing to work hard with others as a team. Evening meetings and lectures focus on the concerns of the movement and are given by people working in the field. Occasional visits to deprived areas arranged. Ages 18+. No experience necessary. 30 hour week. Cost FF400, 2 weeks. Accommodation provided in bungalows or tents, with rooms for older volunteers. Some insurance provided, but applicants pay their own travel. **B D PH**

BRITISH COUNCIL OF CHURCHES Youth Unit, Inter-Church House, 35-41 Lower Marsh, London SE1 7RL
The Ecumenical Youth Council in Europe is the fellowship of national ecumenical youth councils or denominational bodies dealing with church youth work, and through this offers young Christians from different countries and traditions the opportunity to meet and share their experiences and to discuss common issues and concerns. Promotes workcamps where international teams live and work together to serve the community on manual, social or study projects, offering an opportunity to share ideas on faith and life.

Recent projects have included renovating a cabin used as a youth centre in the Alps; and assisting on a Swiss holiday camp from children from the poorer areas of Marseille. All camps include a relevant theme for study and discussion. Volunteers must be highly motivated to contribute to the aims of the camp. Ages 18-30. 1-3 weeks, July-October. Board and lodging usually provided. Volunteers pay their own travel and insurance. *Apply by mid May.*

GRUPPO VOLUNTARI DELLA SVIZZERA ITALIANA CP 12, 6517 Arbedo
Based in Ticino in Italian-speaking Switzerland, exists to promote communal activity for the good of society and recruits volunteers to assist in reconstruction, maintenance and other essential work after natural disasters. Projects have included helping the inhabitants of Fusio which was struck by a flood; building river bridges in the Mogno region; operating schemes for young and handicapped people; excavating an aqueduct in Borgnone; and restoring a small church in Cess. Sports, social and cultural activities and excursions arranged. Ages 18+. Applicants should enjoy living and working together and want to help the community in which they are based. No previous experience or special skills required. 4/6 hour day, 30 hour week. 1-3 weeks, July and August. Self-catering accommodation provided. Fee SF100. **B D PH**

INTERNATIONAL VOLUNTARY SERVICE 162 Upper New Walk, Leicester LE1 7QA Tel Leicester 549430
IVS is the British branch of Service Civil International which promotes international reconciliation through work projects. Volunteers are needed to work in international teams on manual/social projects. Recent projects have included setting up a street bicycle repair shop, organising bicycle tours and courses, carrying out research on the provisions made for cyclists in Basle; renovating a holiday centre for women in the Jura; repairing tracks and haymaking at a farming community for ex drug-abusers in the mountains near Locarno; and participating in the cleaning of the alpine tourist resort of Salecina at the end of the summer season.

Ages 18+. Applicants should have previous workcamp, voluntary work or community service experience and be highly motivated and prepared to work hard and contribute to team life. Some camps require a knowledge of French or German. 25-40 hour week. 2-4 weeks, June-September. Food, accommodation and insurance provided, but not travel. Membership fee £25 (students £15, unwaged £10). Registration fee £40. **B D PH**

Applications from outside the UK: please see workcamp information on page 27.

GENERAL

CANVAS HOLIDAYS LTD Bull Plain, Hertford SG14 1DY Tel Hertford 553535
Provides ready-erected fully equipped tents for family holidays, and requires a number of applicants to form flying squads, teams of 2/3 people who help set up and equip 200-250 6 berth frame tents in an area containing approx 12 campsites. Similar work also available dismantling tents and cleaning and storing equipment. Ages 18-25. Knowledge of the native languages not required, but is an advantage as flying squad members sometimes have the opportunity to continue as couriers.

Applicants must be sociable in order to work in a small community, fit and able to work hard for long hours under pressure, work without supervision and cope with living out of a

SWITZERLAND

rucksack. Driving licence an advantage. Early
April-mid June, possibly longer to set up the
tents, and September to dismantle them. Salary
£75 per week. Tented accommodation, self-
catering facilities and outward travel provided;
return travel dependent on the completion of
contract dates. *UK nationals only.*

**When writing to any organisation it is
essential to mention Working Holidays 1991
and enclose a large stamped, self-addressed
envelope, or if overseas, a large addressed
envelope and at least two International Reply
Coupons.**

TUNISIA

Tunisian Embassy
29 Prince's Gate, London SW7 1QG
Tel 071-584 8117

British Embassy
5 Place de la Victoire, Tunis

Tourist office
Tunisian Tourist Office, 77a Wigmore Street,
London W1H 9LS Tel 071-224 5561

Youth & student information
Association Tunisienne Tourisme et Jeunesse,
1 avenue de Carthage, Tunis

INFORMATION

Entry regulations Details of the regulations governing temporary work can be obtained from the Consular Section of the Embassy. Applications for a work permit should be made to the Ministry of Social Affairs.

Travel STA Travel, 86 Old Brompton Road, London SW7 3LQ Tel 071-937 9921 operates flexible low-cost flights between London and destinations throughout Tunisia.

The Rough Guide to Tunisia £5.95 is a practical handbook covering all aspects of Tunisian life and travel, with practical information on how to get around the country and on cheap places to stay. Published by Harrap Columbus, Chelsea House, 26 Market Square, Bromley, Kent BR1 1NA.

WORKCAMPS

CONCORDIA (Youth Service Volunteers) Ltd, Recruitment Secretary, 8 Brunswick Place, Hove, Sussex BN3 1ET Tel Brighton 772086

UNITED NATIONS ASSOCIATION International Youth Service, Welsh Centre for International Affairs, Temple of Peace, Cathays Park, Cardiff CF1 3AP Tel Cardiff 223088

Apply to either of the above to work on international camps in towns and villages throughout Tunisia, carrying out community development work. Recent projects have included preventing sand movement and dune erosion in Tozeur and El Faouar; building an archaeological museum in Kalaa Kebira; and helping to construct or renovate youth centres in various towns throughout Tunisia. Study themes include youth participation in national development, peace and solidarity. Sports, cultural activities and excursions arranged. Ages 18-35. Applicants must be in good health

and with a good knowledge of French/Arabic and a background knowledge of Africa. Previous workcamp experience essential. 30 hour, 6 day week. Hours of work usually 05.00/06.00-12.00. 2/3 weeks, June-September. Food, accommodation with basic facilities and insurance provided, but volunteers pay own travel costs.

Organised by Association Tunisienne d'Action Volontaire, Maison du RCD, boulevard du 9 Avril 1938, La Kasbah, 1002 Tunis.

Applications from outside the UK: please see workcamp information on page 27.

When writing to any organisation it is essential to mention Working Holidays 1991 and enclose a large stamped, self-addressed envelope, or if overseas, a large addressed envelope and at least two International Reply Coupons.

NOTES

TURKEY

Turkish Consulate General
Rutland Lodge, Rutland Gardens, London SW7
1BW Tel 071-589 0360

British Embassy
Sehit Ersan Caddesi 46/A Cankaya, Ankara

Tourist office
Turkish Tourist Office, 1st Floor, 170-173
Piccadilly, London W1V 9DD Tel 071-734 8681

Youth & student information
Genctur, Tourism and Travel Agency,
Yerebatan Caddesi 15/3, Sultanahmet, Istanbul
Postal address: PO Box 1263, Sirkeci-Istanbul

INFORMATION

Entry regulations A working visa is required for all types of employment. This may be applied for from the Consulate General once an offer of work has been secured. Alternatively, the prospective employer may make the necessary application to the Turkish authorities. In either case the applicant will be informed of the decision by the Consulate. Those who enter Turkey as a tourist are not permitted to take up employment.

Travel North-South Travel Ltd, Moulsham Mill, Parkway, Chelmsford CM2 7PX Tel Chelmsford 492882 arranges competitively priced, reliably planned flights to all parts of Turkey. Profits are paid into a trust fund for the assignment of aid to projects in the poorest parts of the South.

STA Travel, 86 Old Brompton Road, London SW7 3LQ Tel 071-937 9921 operates flexible low cost flights between London and destinations throughout Turkey, and also offers accommodation and tours.

Campus Travel, 52 Grosvenor Gardens, London SW1W 0AG Tel 071-730 3402 offers Eurotrain under 26 fares to destinations in Turkey, and flexible low-cost youth/student charter flights to Istanbul several days weekly from £69 single and £129 return.

Turkey Holiday Guide is a booklet containing information, useful tips, addresses, accommodation and maps. Available from the Turkish Tourist Office, see above.

Turkey - A Travel Survival Kit £5.95, is a handbook for travellers, with comprehensive information on where to stay, what to eat, the best places to visit and how to travel around. Available from Trailfinders, 194 Kensington High Street, London W8 7RG Tel 071-938 3939.

AU PAIR/CHILDCARE

ANGLO PAIR AGENCY 40 Wavertree Road, Streatham Hill, London SW2 3SP Tel 081-674 3605
Arranges au pair and au pair plus posts in Turkey. Some positions also available for English nannies and mother's helps. Au pairs work 5-6 hours per day plus babysitting, with 1 full day free and study time. Au pairs plus work 8 hours per day, with 2 days free and 2/3 evenings study time. Ages 17-27. 2-12 months. Applicants must have experience in childcare and light household duties. Pocket money £25+ per week au pairs, £30+ per week au pairs plus. Board and lodging provided. Agency fee £40. Advice given on travel and insurance.

When writing to any organisation it is essential to mention Working Holidays 1991 and enclose a large stamped, self-addressed envelope, or if overseas, a large addressed envelope and at least two International Reply Coupons.

WORKCAMPS

CHRISTIAN MOVEMENT FOR PEACE
Bethnal Green United Reformed Church, Pott
Street, London E2 0EF Tel 071-729 1877

INTERNATIONAL VOLUNTARY SERVICE
162 Upper New Walk, Leicester LE1 7QA
Tel Leicester 549430

UNITED NATIONS ASSOCIATION
International Youth Service, Welsh Centre for
International Affairs, Temple of Peace,
Cathays Park, Cardiff CF1 3AP Tel Cardiff
223088

Apply to one of the above to participate in
international camps working in groups of 12-20
volunteers from at least 4 countries. Recent
projects have included digging freshwater
canals, building schools and village centres,
planting trees, clearing forests, cleaning up
beaches and assisting at archaeological digs in
different regions of the country. The camps are
organised in small villages with a peasant
population, where living conditions are
primitive, and village customs must be
respected. The aim of the camps is to do a job
which benefits all the villagers and fulfils a
basic need. Volunteers will share in the life of
villagers in all aspects, living under the same
conditions, eating the same food and joining in
social activities. Ages 18-35. Applicants must
be prepared for hard, manual work which is
often slow and repetitious, with a lack of tools
and equipment. 6-8 hour day, with 1 free day
per week. 2 weeks, June-September.
Accommodation provided in schools or village
centres, sleeping on the floor, or sometimes
under canvas, with food cooked by the
villagers or self-catering. Volunteers pay for
travel to Turkey. Those applying through IVS
must attend orientation meeting; further
orientation provided by Genctur in Istanbul
before each camp. D

Organised by Genctur, Tourism and Travel
Agency, PO Box 1263, Sirkeci-Istanbul.

*Applications from outside the UK: please see
workcamp information on page 27.*

GSM YOUTH ACTIVITIES SERVICE
Bayindir sok, 45/7 Kizilay, Ankara
Requires volunteers for workcamps throughout
Turkey. Projects include living in small village
communities, helping with farmwork and
learning rural traditions; working on a
Development Foundation non-profitmaking
farm, including rug and carpet-weaving, milk
and cheese production and poultry farming;
and working in the underdeveloped seaside
towns of Anatolia. International workcamps
will be in Avanos and Marmaris. 5 hour day,
weekends free. 3/4+ weeks, July/August. Ages
16+. Excursions organised at weekends. Board
and lodging provided in small hotels in towns,
or in farmhouses in the rural communities.
Volunteers pay their own travel costs.
Registration fee £50-£80.

GENERAL

**EUROYOUTH LTD 301 Westborough Road,
Westcliff-on-Sea, Essex SS0 9PT
Tel Southend-on-Sea 341434**
Holiday guest stays arranged where guests are
offered board and lodging in return for an
agreed number of hours English conversation
with hosts or their children. Time is also
available for guests to practise the language if
desired. Mainly ages 17-25, but there are
sometimes opportunities for older applicants.
The scheme is open to anyone whose mother
tongue is English, interested in visiting Turkey
and living with a local family for a short time.
2-3 weeks, and occasionally 1-2 months, mainly
during July and August, but on occasions also
during the year. Travel and insurance arranged
by the applicant, but tickets at reduced rates
can be obtained on request. Registration fee
approx £80. *Apply at least 12 weeks prior to
scheduled departure date.*

**SUNSAIL The Port House, Port Solent,
Portsmouth, Hampshire PO6 4TH
Tel Portsmouth 219847**
Crew members are required to work aboard
cruising yachts sailing in flotillas off the
Lycian coast of Turkey. Vacancies for
experienced skippers, responsible for the
wellbeing of up to 13 cruising yachts and 60
holidaymakers, giving daily briefings on
navigation and providing sailing assistance
where necessary. Applicants must have

considerable sailing experience, be cheerful, hard working and able to deal with people of varying backgrounds and ages. Ages 23-30. Also bosuns/mechanics needed, responsible to the skipper for maintaining the marine diesel engines and repairing any other onboard items. Must have excellent knowledge of marine diesels and practical ability to cope with all sorts of breakdowns and repairs. Ages 22-30. Hostesses are required to look after laundry, accounting, and cleaning of boats, to advise holidaymakers on shops and restaurants, and to organise social events and barbecues. Sailing experience useful, but bright personality, patience and adaptability essential. Ages 22-30.

All staff should be prepared for very hard work and long hours. 12+ hour day. 1 day free per week. Knowledge of German useful but not essential. Mid March-November. Wages approx £85 per week, paid monthly. Half board accommodation for shore-based staff, on board accommodation for crew members, return travel and medical insurance provided.

APPLYING FOR A JOB

Read carefully all the information given before applying. Check in particular:

* the necessary skills/experience required

* the full period of employment expected

* any restrictions of age, sex or nationality

* application deadlines

* any other points, particularly details of insurance cover provided, and other costs such as travel and accommodation.

When applying be sure to include:

* name, address, date of birth, marital status, nationality, sex

* education, qualifications, relevant experience

* period of availability

* details of languages spoken

* a large stamped, self-addressed envelope plus, if overseas, 2 International Reply Coupons

* a passport-size photo, particularly if you are to have contact with the public

* any registration or membership fees

NOTES

NITED STATES

, London W1A 2JB

Visa branch: 5 Upper Grosvenor Street, London
W1A 2JB Tel 071-493 5322

British Embassy
3100 Massachusetts Avenue NW, Washington
DC 20008

Tourist office
United States Travel & Tourism Administration,
22 Sackville Street, London W1X 2EA

Youth hostels
American Youth Hostels Inc, 1332 1 Street NW,
Suite 800, Washington DC 20005

Youth & student information
Council on International Educational Exchange
(CIEE), 205 East 42nd Street, New York,
NY 10017

ISSTA, Suite 1204, 211 East 43rd Street, New
York NY 10017

Student Travel Network, Suite 307, Geary
Street, San Francisco, CA 94108

Student Travel Network, Suite 728, 6151 West
Century Boulevard, Los Angeles 90034

US-UK Educational Commission, 6 Porter
Street, London W1 Tel 071-486 1098

INFORMATION

Entry regulations A visa is required for all types of temporary employment. The applicant must generally either be the beneficiary of a petition approved by the US Immigration and Naturalization Service or qualify as an exchange visitor. Exchange Visitor Programmes are operated by a number of organisations; anyone wanting to work in the United States should check whether they qualify under one of the programmes offered and if so should apply as early as possible.

Once an application has been accepted, the participant will receive form IAP-66 for a non-immigrant Exchange Visitor Visa, which should be posted to the visa branch of the US Embassy, address above; or for residents of Northern Ireland to the American Consulate General, Queens House, 14 Queen Street, Belfast BT1 6EQ. Generally, physically handicapped people are not ineligible to receive visas; those having, or having had mental disabilities may, however, be ineligible and would have to submit a letter outlining the disability. Holders of non-immigrant Exchange Visitor Visas may work in the US only under the terms of the programme and are not eligible to seek other employment while in

the country. They are automatically exempt from paying social security and income tax. Participants should not plan to stay in the US longer than the duration of the programme, though the visa is valid for a period of travel, normally of 2/3 weeks, at the end of the programme. If the holder visits Canada or Mexico during the programme, a Multiple Entry Visa is needed for re-entry into the US. If only a Single Entry Visa has been granted, the participant should not plan to leave the US during the programme. Changing to another visa is a difficult and complicated procedure, and there is no guarantee that it will be granted; full details available from the visa branch at the US Embassy.

Travel Compass, 9 Grosvenor Gardens, London SW1W 0BH Tel 071-828 4111 are agents for Amtrak. National USA Rail Pass offers unlimited travel on trains in the US. Cost from $299 (45 days). Regional USA Rail Pass offers unlimited travel on trains over key routes in 3 major regions. Cost from $179 (45 days). Bicycle boxes available.

Ameripass offers unlimited bus travel in the US, also valid in eastern and western Canada;

UNITED STATES

cost from £80 (7 days). Helping Hand service, enables a companion to travel free to assist a handicapped person who needs help in travelling on a bus. Certificate of eligibility required from a doctor; wheelchairs and other aids carried free. All tickets must be purchased in Britain. Details from Greyhound International Travel Inc, 14-16 Cockspur Street, London SW1Y 5BL Tel 071-839 5591.

North-South Travel Ltd, Moulsham Mill, Parkway, Chelmsford CM2 7PX Tel Chelmsford 492882 arranges competitively priced, reliably planned flights to all parts of America. Profits are paid into a trust fund for the assignment of aid to projects in the poorest areas of the South.

STA Travel, 74 Old Brompton Road, London SW7 3LQ Tel 071-937 9971 operates flexible low cost flights with open-jaw facility - enter one country, leave by another - between London and destinations throughout the US. Internal flights, accommodation, tours and air passes available from STA offices throughout the US.

The Moneywise Guide to North America £8.85 including UK postage, provides information for anyone travelling on a budget in the US or Canada, with useful details on getting around, where to stay, what to eat and places to visit. Published by BUNAC, 16 Bowling Green Lane, London EC1R OBD Tel 071-251 3472.

INFORMATION

The Rough Guide to New York £5.95 is a comprehensive handbook which balances informed detail on sights and sounds with practical money-saving hints on where to stay and how to get around. Published by Harrap Columbus, Chelsea House, 26 Market Square, Bromley, Kent BR1 1NA.

Travellers Survival Kit USA & Canada £6.95, is a down-to-earth, entertaining guide for travellers to North America. Describes how to cope with the inhabitants, officialdom and way of life in the US and Canada. Published by Vacation Work, see below.

Publications *The Summer Employment Directory of the United States 1991* £8.95, gives details of thousands of summer jobs for students in the US and Canada, including work in ranches, summer camps, national parks, theatres,

resorts, restaurants and many more. Includes a special section giving advice on requirements and visa procedures for non-US citizens. Also *Internships USA 1991* £14.95, which lists career-oriented positions enabling students and graduates to train through a period of work with an established employer. Both published by Writer's Digest Books and available in Britain from Vacation Work, 9 Park End Street, Oxford OX1 1HJ Tel Oxford 241978.

The Students Guide to the Best Summer Jobs in Alaska £6.95, gives a complete picture of the summer job opportunities on the fishing boats and in the salmon processing plants of Alaska. Explains where the jobs are and how to get them. Published by Mustang Publishing, New Haven, Connecticut and available in Britain from Vacation Work, see above.

Accommodation *Handbook of USA Youth Hostels* £4.95, lists addresses and telephone numbers of youth hostels throughout the US with details of location and costs. Also includes practical information and maps. Available from YHA Services Ltd, 14 Southampton Street, London WC2E 7HY Tel 071-836 8541.

The Council on International Educational Exchange (CIEE), 205 East 42nd Street, New York, NY 10017 publishes *Where to Stay USA 1991/92* $12.95 plus postage, a paperback listing over 1700 places to spend the night from $5, including hostels, motels, campsites and university halls of residence. Also information on hotlines and switchboards, plus a special section for foreign visitors.

The Ys Way International, 356 West 34th Street, New York, NY 10001 operates the Ys Way to Visit North America, offering inexpensive accommodation at YMCAs in major cities from coast to coast in the US and Canada, with single or double rooms. Cost from $24 per night including use of sports facilities. Details in Britain from STA Travel, 74 Old Brompton Road, London SW7 3LQ Tel 071-937 9971.

When writing to any organisation it is essential to mention Working Holidays 1991 and enclose a large stamped, self-addressed envelope, or if overseas, a large addressed envelope and at least two International Reply Coupons.

ARCHAEOLOGY

Archaeological Fieldwork Opportunities Bulletin
$8 plus $2.50 postage, lists archaeological sites
throughout the US at which excavation and
research work is being carried out. Details are
given of staff needed at each site, with ages,
experience required, board and lodging, wages,
training and equipment provision, any costs
involved and other conditions. Also lists
archaeological field schools which provide
practical training for students. Published
annually in January by the Archaeological
Institute of America, 675 Commonwealth
Avenue, Department GG, Boston,
Massachusetts 02215.

**BUFFALO STATE COLLEGE Dr Bill
Engelbrecht, Anthropology, Buffalo State
College, 1300 Elmwood Avenue, Buffalo, NY
14222**
Offers opportunities for volunteers to work on
open archaeological excavations in West
Seneca, south east of Buffalo. No experience
necessary. 25 June-3 August. 40 hour week,
Monday-Friday. Ages 18+. Insurance and
travel within Buffalo state provided.
Volunteers pay their own food and
accommodation costs; cheap lodgings available
in Buffalo State College dormitories. One field
trip per week generally organised.

**EARTHWATCH EUROPE Belsyre Court, 57
Woodstock Road, Oxford, Oxfordshire
Tel Oxford 311600**
Aims to support field research in a wide range
of disciplines including archaeology,
ornithology, animal behaviour, nature
conservation and ecology. Support is given to
researchers as a grant and in the form of
volunteer assistance.

Recent projects have included mapping and
photographing by hot air balloon the complex
geometrical patterns of stone alignments traced
by early hunter gatherers on the floor of the
Panamint Valley, California; excavating a
workshop and quarry complex with tools made
10,000 years ago, in Montana; and recording
artefacts in an underwater excavation of the
first cod fisheries of the early settlers to
America, in the Isles of Shoals, New
Hampshire. Ages 16-80. No special skills are

required, but each expedition may, because of
its nature, demand some talent or quality of
fitness. Volunteers should be generally fit, able
to cope with new situations, able to mix and
work with people of different ages and
backgrounds, and a sense of humour will help.
2-3 weeks, June-October. Members share the
costs of the project, from £500, which includes
meals, transport and all necessary field
equipment, but does not include the cost of
travel although assistance may be given in
arranging it. Membership fee £22 includes
magazines and newsletters providing the
information needed on joining a project.

**FOUNDATION FOR FIELD RESEARCH
PO Box 2010, Alpine, California 92001**
A non-profitmaking organisation sponsoring
research expeditions by finding volunteers to
assist scientists in the field. Volunteers are
required to help on archaeological projects,
which have recently included assisting with the
excavation of a 19th century frontier trading
post, and surveying for archaeological sites in
California; scuba diving at Hudson's Bay
Company dock sites in Oregon and
Washington; recording rock art in Arizona; and
excavating at a site in Connecticut. Ages 14+.
No special experience or skills required, but
always welcome. 20-25 hour week; 3 days-4
weeks; spring, summer, autumn and winter.
Participants are given responsibilities to fulfil,
so applicants should be willing to do their part
to become active members of the research team.
Members share the costs of the project, from
$120-$495 which includes transportation
during the expedition, insurance, a preparatory
booklet, most field gear, tent or dormitory
accommodation and 3 meals per day. Travel to
assembly point not provided. Scholarships
available. PH on certain expeditions.

**LUBBOCK LAKE LANDMARK The Director,
The Museum, PO Box 4499, Lubbock TX 79409**
Volunteers are needed for research on
Paleo-Indian, Archaic, Ceramic, Protohistoric
and historic remains. Ages 18+. Applicants
should be willing to work hard. 6+ weeks,
June-August. Board and lodging, major
equipment, instruction and training provided.
Volunteers pay own fares, personal expenses
and $35 for small equipment needs. Academic
credit available. Sponsored by Texas Tech
University. *Apply by 1 May.*

UNITED STATES

ARCHAEOLOGY

AU PAIR/CHILDCARE

MISSION SAN ANTONIO ARCHAEOLOGICAL SCHOOL Dr Robert Hoover, Social Sciences Department, California Polytechnic State University, San Luis Obispo, California 93407

Volunteers are needed to assist in research into Spanish colonial archaeology at the Mission, one of the Franciscan establishments of Spanish California founded to convert the Indian population. Since 1976 the school has been excavating the 18th century site, including the Indian dormitories, the first brick and tile kiln excavated in Spanish California and the nearby barracks, and examining historical and cultural materials from the vineyardist's house to interpret the role of agriculture in educating the converts to the culture of 18th century Spain. Work involves excavating, recording and laboratory processing. Evening lectures and activities arranged; opportunities for weekend sightseeing. Ages 18+. Applicants must be in good health. Interest and dedication essential; no experience necessary. Knowledge of English required. 35 hour, 5 day week. 3+ weeks, mid June-end August. Cost approx $75 per week includes board and accommodation as guests of the Mission's Franciscan friars. Housekeeping chores are cooperative. No wages. Volunteers pay for insurance and travel.

MOUNT CLARE RESTORATION OFFICE Kristen L Stevens, Carroll Park, 1500 Washington Boulevard, Baltimore MD 21230

Volunteers are needed to participate in a full range of archaeological activities involved in unearthing Baltimore's history and restoring the city's heritage. The excavation, entering its sixth year, seeks clues about this 18th century plantation's original appearance so that the entire landscape and numerous outbuildings may be reconstructed with as much care and accuracy as the main house. Areas scheduled for research are the parterre garden, kitchen garden, ice house, wash house, milk house and sheds. The work includes excavation and laboratory processing of artefacts, reconstruction of pots, historical research, surveying, analysis, report writing and acting as a tour guide for visitors. Ages 13+; those under 13 must be accompanied by an adult who will also dig. Applicants should have a desire to learn about and participate in archaeological activities. Previous experience

not essential, but useful for certain tasks. Volunteers individually assigned to trained archaeologists. Up to 20 hour week, 10.00-16.00. Wednesday-Sunday, seasonal. Insurance provided, but volunteers must pay their own travel, board and accommodation costs. No wages paid.

UNIVERSITY RESEARCH EXPEDITIONS PROGRAM University of California, Desk L-10, Berkeley CA 94720

Volunteers are needed to assist on archaeological excavations. Recent projects have included excavating a Chinese gold rush town in north California; researching the survival strategies of Anasazi Indians in New Mexico; and locating, mapping, drawing and photographing ancient Polynesian rock carvings on Hawaii. 2 weeks, June-September. Ages 16+. Applicants should be in good health, have a desire to learn, enthusiasm, a willingness to undertake rigourous but rewarding work, flexibility and sensitivity to other cultures. Skills such as surveying and photography, plus wilderness experience, some knowledge of archaeology, history, anthropology or geology useful. Contribution to costs from US$865 covers research equipment and supplies, meals, accommodation, ground transportation and preparation materials. Travel to site not provided but route guidance given. *Partial scholarships available.*

AU PAIR/ CHILDCARE

AMERICAN INSTITUTE FOR FOREIGN STUDY Au Pair in America Programme, 37 Queens Gate, London SW7 5HR Tel 071-581 2730

The Programme is open to western Europeans; non-British nationals should have a fair degree of fluency in English. Work involves 45 hours per week childcare and related duties. All au pairs will be expected to take advantage of the educational and cultural opportunities in their community; up to $300 tuition costs paid by host family. Applicants must have some childcare experience, hold a full driving licence and be a non-smoker. Ages 18-25. Character references and medical certificate required. Applicants are interviewed and, if accepted, matched according to interests and experience with a selected host family, and issued with a J-1 Exchange Visitor Visa authorised by the US Government. All participants attend a 5 day training and orientation session in New York before joining their host families. Local counsellors in each area provide a constant source of support for both au pairs and families, and organise activities. 1 weekend free each month. 1 year, applications/ departures all year. Return flight London-New York, single travel New York-host family, $100+ per week pocket money, 2 weeks holiday with pocket money, and medical insurance provided. Participants pay good faith deposit of £300, refundable upon successful completion of the placement and return to Europe.

AVALON AGENCY Thursley House, 53 Station Road, Shalford, Guildford, Surrey GU4 8HA Tel Guildford 63640
Can place nannies; duties include childcare and assisting with domestic chores. Food, lodging, medical insurance and approx $100 per week pocket money provided by host family. 40-45 hour week including babysitting. Arranged on the basis of a 1 year working study visit. Ages 18-25. Applicants must either be taking a year out before attending higher education, or preferably be qualified in a childcare course (such as NNEB or BTEC) and seeking to gain experience for a career in childcare. They must be non-smokers, have a full driving licence and 6+ months childcare experience. Visas arranged and return travel paid if contract completed. Good faith deposit of £350 repaid on completion of contract.

CAMP AMERICA Dept WH, 37A Queens Gate, London SW7 5HR
An Exchange Visitor Programme offering a limited number of places for females as companions in selected American families. Participants live as a member of the family, responsible for care and supervision of the children from 0-10 years of age, and undertake light household duties. 1½ days free per week. Ages 18 (by 1 June)-24. Applicants must have a genuine love of children, enthusiasm to work and play with them in an imaginative manner, and the ability to adapt readily to different lifestyles. Driving licence preferred. 10 weeks,

June-September. Pocket money $400. The programme includes return flight from London, orientation, sightseeing and accommodation in New York, and transfer. Applicants must have a willingness to work hard, be fit with a doctor's certification of good health, and speak good English. 1-8 weeks at the end of the programme for travel, the cost of which is not included. Deposit £50. Medical insurance fee £50. *Apply September-May. Interviews throughout Europe, Scandinavia, Australia and India.*

CBR AU PAIR 34a Foregate Street, Worcester WR1 1EE Tel Worcester 26671
Operates a government authorised programme to place au pairs with families throughout the US. Work involves entertaining children, helping with homework, supervising games and visits, bathing, feeding and dressing children, putting them to bed and waking them in the morning; plus light housework such as preparing children's meals, tidying their room, doing their laundry, making beds and dusting. Ages 18-25. Applicants should be non-smokers and have a full driving licence. 45 hour, 5½ day week for 12 months, with 2 weeks vacation in first 10 months, and one full weekend off per month. $100+ per week pocket money plus $300 assistance towards a study course. 3-4 day induction programme held on arrival. Monthly meeting with local community coordinator to discuss any problems. Assistance in finding a study course; seminars and special events also offered. Good faith bond of £350 repaid when programme successfully completed. Return air fare and medical/accident insurance provided

EXPERIMENT IN INTERNATIONAL LIVING Au Pair Homestay USA, Otesaga, Upper Wyche, Malvern, Worcestershire WR14 4EN Tel Malvern 562577
A non-profitmaking organisation which aims to promote international understanding as a means of achieving world peace. Operates a government authorised programme to place au pairs with families throughout the US. Maximum 45 hour week. Ages 18-24. Applicants should be non-smokers, hold a current driving licence, have good childcare/ babysitting experience, a genuine love of children and fluent English. 12 months; placements available monthly except December. Two day orientation session soon

UNITED STATES

after arrival, with detailed training and advice on adaptation and getting the most out of the stay. Local coordinators arrange monthly meetings, providing support and guidance. $100 per week pocket money, accommodation, travel, insurance, work permits, visas and $300 for course of study at local school or college provided. Two week paid holiday and discount travel opportunities. £350 good faith bond, returnable at end of year; administration and orientation fee £150. *British nationals only; other EC nationals should apply to the EIL office in their own country.* B D PH

COMMUNITY WORK

COMMUNITY WORK

BENEDICTINE LAY VOLUNTEERS Summer Experience Program, Mother of God Monastery, Box 254, Watertown, South Dakota 57201
The Program is designed for people interested in experiencing life in a monastic community, and is offered in the expectation that the volunteer might serve and at the same time grow spiritually. Volunteers serve primarily in South Dakota, in rural parishes, on summer day camp programmes with native American children, as well as in the monastery and the Harmony Hill Centre. Orientation to the monastery life and ministries. Sharing in the life of the religious community, such as reflection and days of prayer, is an important aspect of the programme. Ages 18+. 2-10 weeks, June-August. Board and lodging provided. Volunteers pay their own travel and insurance costs. *Apply by 1 May.*

BETTERWAY INC 612 Middle Avenue, Elyria, Ohio 44035
A non-profitmaking private social organisation providing homes for adults and children aged 12+ who are homeless, in trouble, or have AIDS or HIV. Also operates a gift shop, a 150-acre wooded farm and a ropes course. Volunteers are required to assist with looking after the people in the homes, helping with the cooking and other domestic chores. Ages 19+. No experience necessary. 40-50 hour week, all year. Full board and accommodation provided. Applicants pay their own travel costs.

CHRISTIAN MOVEMENT FOR PEACE Bethnal Green United Reformed Church, Pott Street, London E2 2EF Tel 071-729 7985

INTERNATIONAL VOLUNTARY SERVICE 162 Upper New Walk, Leicester LE1 7QA Tel Leicester 549430

UNITED NATIONS ASSOCIATION International Youth Service, Welsh Centre of International Affairs, Temple of Peace, Cathays Park, Cardiff 223088

Apply to one of the above to work on community projects organised by an independent, non-aligned, non-profit American organisation working for peace through youth exchanges and voluntary service. Recent projects have included building housing for low-income families and providing services for the homeless in New Hampshire; clearing and landscaping an old mail route for wheelchair access in Alaska; building a cabin as a mountainside farm for inner city children in Virginia; food salvaging and clothing distribution in Washington; and assisting with a children's summer school programme in Newport. Ages 18-35. Applicants should have previous workcamp, voluntary work or community service experience, preferably already involved in the peace movement, and be highly motivated and prepared to work hard and contribute to team life. 2/3 weeks, June-August. Food, accommodation and insurance provided, but volunteers pay their own travel costs.

Organised by Volunteers for Peace Inc, Tiffany Road, Belmont, Vermont 05730.

Applications from outside the UK: please see workcamp information on page 27.

INTERNATIONAL VOLUNTARY SERVICE 162 Upper New Walk, Leicester LE1 7QA Tel Leicester 549430
IVS is the British branch of Service Civil International, which promotes international reconciliation through work projects. Volunteers are needed to work on community projects. Recent projects have included working with children and the elderly at a centre for transients, homeless people and families of prison inmates in Iowa; assisting in

children's day camp activities at a youth centre in the Bronx; assisting in the running of a children's camp in Alaska; helping to provide housing for low-income families in Philadelphia; working in a prevention programme for youth at risk, building a base lodge, storage shed and outhouse in Canterbury, New Hampshire; and doing painting and decorating and other small jobs alongside disabled adults at a working community for the handicapped in the Blue Ridge Mountains, Virginia. Ages 18+. Applicants should have previous workcamp experience and should be prepared to work hard and contribute to team life. 3-8 weeks, June-August. Food, accommodation and insurance provided, but not travel. Membership fee £25 (students £15, unwaged £10). Registration fee £40. B D PH

Organised by Service Civil International, c/o Innisfree Village, Route 2, Box 506, Crozet, Virginia 22932.

Applications from outside the UK: please see workcamp information on page 27.

THE SIOUX INDIAN YMCA PO Box 218, Dupree, South Dakota 57623

The Sioux YMCAs were first founded in Dakota Territory in 1879 and today serve in 28 communities on 5 reservations in South Dakota, the only YMCAs operated by and serving primarily Indian people. Volunteers are required to live and work individually on small, remote reservation communities under the supervision of the YMCA. Projects may include developing recreational and children's activities; work in elementary and pre-schools; assisting with the nutrition programme for the elderly; alcohol and drug abuse counselling; and developing libraries and health services. Time not spent in formally organised activity may be spent in a variety of counselling, recreation and community development activities, visiting homes, arts, crafts and sports, talking with children and getting to know the families and the communities. What is done largely depends on the volunteer's own abilities and the needs and supervision of the community and local YMCA. The personal relationships formed are at least as important as the specific activities carried out. Ages 18+. Volunteers should speak good English, and

preferably be skilled in recreation, leadership development, childcare and working with people. A love of children and people in general, and an ability to adapt to a different socio-economic and cultural setting are also necessary. Because of the poverty/alcohol syndrome on the reservation, volunteers are expected not to drink alcohol for the project period. Those from all religious faiths and commitments are accepted, but are expected to respect and participate in the Christian life of the community. 4 weeks, January or 10 weeks, March-end of summer. Time commitment should be to a 24 hour day, 7 day week. Full board and accommodation provided with families or in small community buildings, but volunteers must arrange own insurance and travel. Orientation and evaluation sessions arranged. Help given in obtaining a visa. PH depending on ability.

WINANT-CLAYTON VOLUNTEERS ASSOCIATION The Chairman, 38 Newark Street, London E1 2AA

A community service exchange scheme which aims to provide assistance to city community projects in the eastern states and to give volunteers an insight into a different culture. Volunteers are assigned to social work agencies, selected for their interest in the cultural exchange of young people. Projects include assisting at psychiatric rehabilitation centres and homes for emotionally disturbed children, working with the elderly and housebound, and helping organise day camps and centres for teenage groups and deprived children in the inner city.

Ages 19+. Applicants should have some experience of working with children, youth and community work or other voluntary social work. They should be flexible, with a sense of humour and a real interest in people. Hours worked are comparable to full-time staff on the project. 3 months, June-September, including time for own travel. 2 days free per week. Board, accommodation, insurance and pocket money provided. Volunteers pay travel costs; small grants may be available. Participants should take enough money to support themselves during free time at the end of the project. Weekend orientation course organised. Registration fee £10. *UK residents only; apply by 30 November.* PH depending on ability.

CONSERVATION

CHRISTIAN MOVEMENT FOR PEACE
Bethnal Green United Reformed Church, Pott Street, London E2 0EF Tel 071-729 1877

INTERNATIONAL VOLUNTARY SERVICE
162 Upper New Walk, Leicester LE1 7QA Tel Leicester 549430

UNITED NATIONS ASSOCIATION
International Youth Service, Welsh Centre for International Affairs, Temple of Peace, Cathays Park, Cardiff CF1 3AP Tel Cardiff 223088

Apply to one of the above to work in international teams on summer conservation projects aimed at offering a service in an area of need and promoting self-help within the community. Recent projects have included rebuilding log cabins in Baxter State Park; cheesemaking, gardening, wood gathering, looking after animals and organising an art exhibition on an educational farm in Pennsylvania; and conservation work in woods bordering Lake Michigan. Ages 18+.
6 hour day, 30-36 hour week. 2-3 weeks July-August. Food, accommodation and insurance provided, but volunteers pay their own travel.

Organised by Volunteers for Peace Inc, Tiffany Road, Belmont, Vermont 05730

Applications from outside the UK: please see workcamp information on page 27.

EARTHWATCH EUROPE Belsyre Court, 57 Woodstock Road, Oxford, Oxfordshire Tel Oxford 311600
Aims to support field research in a wide range of disciplines including archaeology, ornithology, animal behaviour, nature conservation and ecology. Support is given to researchers as a grant and in the form of volunteer assistance. Recent projects have included tracking and studying timber wolfs by night in Minnesota; tracking killer whales and recording their behaviour in Puget Sound, Washington; monitoring chuckwalla lizards in lava fields of the Mojave Desert; helping on a long-term study of threatened sub-alpine meadows, counting flowers, butterflies and pollinators in the Rocky Mountains, Colorado; studying individual behaviour patterns of the dolphin community in Sarasota Bay, Florida; and recording wading birds, American crocodile, bald eagle, shrimp and spiny lobsters to protect the area from suburban growth, at Everglades National Park. Ages 16-80. No special skills are required, but each expedition may, because of its nature, demand some talent or quality of fitness. Volunteers should be generally fit, able to cope with new situations, able to mix and work with people of different ages and backgrounds, and a sense of humour will help. 2-3 weeks, March-December. Members share the costs of the project, from £500 which includes meals, transport and all necessary field equipment, but does not include the cost of travel although assistance may be given in arranging it. Membership fee £22 includes magazines and newsletters providing information on joining a project.

NEW YORK STATE DEPARTMENT OF ENVIRONMENTAL CONSERVATION
Five Rivers Environmental Education Center, Game Farm Road, Delmar, New York 12054-9776
Has a statewide responsibility to manage natural resources and to protect the environment. Education centres contribute to this effort by offering stimulating and enjoyable education programmes which help develop the public's understanding of complex environmental concerns. Offer naturalist internships to persons seeking professional experience in environmental communications and education. Each intern will receive training in a wide variety of education centre programmes, the operations and activities of a centre, and in principles of environmental interpretation. A basic core of work will be required of each intern. Additional opportunities for training and development of skills will be available depending on each intern's interests and the centre's needs. Each centre provides living space, with kitchen, living room and private bedroom, plus a workspace. Approx 12 weeks, all year round. Preference given to those with backgrounds in natural history and environmental science. Ages 18+ with a demonstrated interest in environmental education. US$50 per week and some insurance provided. Participants must supply own means of transportation.

STUDENT CONSERVATION ASSOCIATION INC, PO Box 550, Charlestown NH 03603
Aims to provide resource management agencies with qualified and motivated volunteers, and to give volunteers educational opportunities and professional work experience in conservation and resource management in over 200 national parks, forests, wildlife refuges and similar areas throughout the US, including Hawaii, Alaska and the Virgin Islands. Specific duties vary with location, but may include trail patrol, wildlife management, visitor contact, natural science interpretation, forestry, archaeological surveys or recreation management. Recent opportunities have included rehabilitating Yellowstone National Park after wildfires; monitoring fledgeling Peregrine falcons in Glen Canyon, Arizona; assisting with the relocation of black bears in the Great Smokey Mountains; protecting nesting bird colonies at a wildlife refuge in New York; identifying and sampling marine fish, invertebrates and vegetation in the Everglades, Florida; conducting tours of a life saving station museum on Cape Cod; developing and presenting short programs and nature walks interpreting Indian legends in Mt Hood National Forest, Oregon; and patrolling the remote wilderness areas of the Grand Canyon. Ages 18+. Volunteers should have an interest in conservation or resource management. Some positions may require specific experience in public speaking, hiking or other outdoor activities, or in a particular academic field. Fluency in English essential; knowledge of other languages also helpful. 12+ weeks, all year. 40 hour week. Accommodation in apartment, trailer or ranger station, information and assistance with visas and partial travel reimbursement provided. Volunteers also receive $45-$90 per week to cover food expenses, and a uniform allowance if required. Training, guidance and supervision provided by professional staff. Application fee $15. *Apply 2 months in advance.*

UNIVERSITY RESEARCH EXPEDITIONS PROGRAM University of California, Desk L-10, Berkeley CA 94720
Volunteers are needed to provide field assistance for research in the natural and social sciences. Projects include studying Strangler Fig trees on St John Island, part of the US

Virgin Islands group, investigating the leaf structure and metabolism of the plants in an attempt to better understand their unique anatomy and physiology; gathering information on the distribution and feeding patterns of seabirds in the Pribilof Islands of Alaska; and tracking elk and mule deer in the High Sierra of California, to determine if competition occurs in their activity and feeding patterns. Ages 16+. Applicants should be in good health, have a desire to learn, enthusiasm, a willingness to undertake rigourous but rewarding work, flexibility and sensitivity to other cultures. Skills such as surveying and photography, plus wilderness experience, some knowledge of botany, taxonomy and ecology useful. 2 weeks, June-August. Contribution to costs from $685 covers equipment, supplies, meals, accommodation, ground transportation and preparation materials. Travel to site not provided but route guidance given. *Partial scholarships available. Apply at least 2 months before session.*

DOMESTIC

BRITISH UNIVERSITIES NORTH AMERICA CLUB (BUNAC) 16 Bowling Green Lane, London EC1R 0BD Tel 071-251 3472
Operates KAMP (Kitchen and Maintenance Programme), an Exchange Visitor Programme offering opportunities to work on children's summer camps in the US as domestic or maintenance staff. The camps are permanent sites catering for 40-600 children at one time. Camps can be organised privately, by the YMCA, Girl Scouts or Salvation Army, or they can be institutional camps for the physically, mentally or socially handicapped. Vacancies for kitchen assistants, dining room staff, chambermaids, cleaners, laundry workers, dishwashers, assistant cooks and bakers, porters, janitors and nightwatchmen. Ground staff and general maintenance workers are also required for mowing, weeding, plumbing, carpentry, electrical work, building, moving rubbish, painting, cleaning and repairing. Vacancies for drivers (ages 21+ with full UK and international drivers licences) transporting children, staff and equipment. Relevant skills required for some jobs. Ages 18+. Applicants must be full-time students studying at HND or degree level in Britain, who like children and

UNITED STATES

CONSERVATION

DOMESTIC

sports, and must be cooperative, energetic, sociable, conscientious, outgoing and cheerful. June-August. Hours vary from camp to camp, but can be long; the work is hard and often tedious and staff have to organise their own free time. Most camps allow staff to use recreational facilities. 8-10 hour day, 5½-6 day week. Contracts are for the full camp period, normally 9 weeks, but occasionally longer. Cost £58 towards flight to New York, transfer to camp, full board and basic accommodation in wooden cabins at camp, and visa charges. Insurance cost approx £72. Participants receive a salary of approx $490, at the end of the camp. Approx 6 weeks are free at the end of the programme for independent travel. Advice can be provided on onward travel. Friends can sometimes be placed on the same camp. Applicants will receive a list of jobs available, with details of camps, types of work available and any special facilities. Two references required. Compulsory orientation programmes held at Easter throughout Britain. Membership fee £3. *Apply from October-November; directory available January/February.*

Irish applicants should apply to USIT, Aston Quay, O'Connell Bridge, Dublin 2, Ireland Tel Dublin 778117.

CAMP AMERICA Dept WH, 37A Queens Gate, London SW7 5HR
An Exchange Visitor Programme enabling young people to spend the summer in the US. Openings at summer camps in the US on the Campower programme, working in utility areas. Assignments include working with automatic washing and drying machines in the laundry; helping with food preparation, serving, dish and pot washing in the kitchen; dining room service; indoor and outdoor work, grass cutting, painting, moving and clearing rubbish, cleaning and general repair work; driving camp vehicles; and general secretarial work. Experienced cooks and bakers also required. On some camps workers are needed before camp opens, preparing the activity and living areas. 10+ hour day. Students aged 18+. Pocket money $300. The programmes include return flight from London, orientation, sightseeing and accommodation in New York, transfer to camp, plus full board and lodging. Applicants must have a willingness to work hard, be fit, with a doctor's certification of

good health, and speak good English. 1-6 weeks are left free at the end of the camp for travel, the cost of which is not included in the programme. Deposit £50. Medical insurance fee £50. *Apply September-May.*

FARMWORK

INTERNATIONAL AGRICULTURAL EXCHANGE ASSOCIATION YFC Centre, National Agricultural Centre, Kenilworth, Warwickshire CV8 2LG Tel Coventry 696578
Operates opportunities for agricultural students and young people to acquire practical work experience, and to strengthen and improve their knowledge and understanding of the way of life in other countries. Opportunities to study practical methods on approved training farms; categories include agriculture (all general farm operations); horticulture (working with pot plants, trees, landscape gardening, vegetables, fruit and cut flowers); home management (household duties, child care and gardening); or agri-mix (farming and household management). Farms include mixed (grain production and livestock); grain; plus a limited number of bee farms and horticultural enterprises. Participants undertake approx 45 hours work per week, and live as members of the host family. Long hours during peak periods. Full board and lodging, insurance cover and a net weekly wage of £50-£60 provided. All programmes include 3-6 weeks unpaid holiday. 5 day orientation courses held at the beginning of each programme. Educational sightseeing trips (4 days-3 weeks) within the US and in Australia, Thailand, Singapore, Fiji and Hawaii arranged for participants en route for the 13 month programme. Ages 19-28. Applicants should be single, and have good practical experience in the chosen training category, plus a valid driving licence. 7 months, departing April; cost £1530. Also 13/14 months - 6½ in the US plus 6½ in Australia, departing September; cost £3550. £200 deposit payable. Costs cover airfare, work permit, administration fee, orientation courses and insurance. *UK nationals only; apply at least 4 months in advance.*

American applicants requiring an exchange should apply to IAEA, 1000 1st Avenue South, Great Falls, Montana 59401 Tel 406 727 1999

INTERNATIONAL FARM EXPERIENCE PROGRAMME YFC Centre, National Agricultural Centre, Kenilworth, Warwickshire CV8 2LG Tel Coventry 696584
Provides assistance to young farmers and nurserymen by finding places in farms/nurseries abroad to enable them to broaden their knowledge of agricultural methods. Several schemes exist providing applicants with the opportunity to experience North American farm life. The University of Minnesota scheme involves 5-8 months on a farm/nursery followed by 3 months in the University. There are a variety of farms and the work is matched as far as possible with the applicants' requirements. Salary $300 per month including board and lodging. The Ohio State University scheme involves 12 months practical work in orchards, farms or nurseries. Salary $3.35+ per hour. Also operates a combining scheme whereby trainees work on some of the large contract-combining crews. Crews generally leave Texas or Oklahoma in April or May, reach Canada in September, then head towards the Rockies and continue into Montana in October. Work involves combine and truck driving, and machinery maintenance. 12 months, starting March-May. Accommodation usually in mobile homes. Salary $3.35+ per hour, from which tax, board and lodging may be deducted. Future Farmers of America also offer agricultural and some horticultural placements. 3, 6 or 12 months, beginning late March or late June. Salary from $3.35 per hour, from which tax, board and lodging are deducted. Programme fee $50 per month. 2 day orientation seminar arranged in Alexandria, Virginia before placements begin. Ages 20-30. Applicants must have at least 2 years' practical experience, or at least 1 year at agricultural college and 1 year's practical experience, and intend to make a career in agriculture or horticulture. Valid driving licence necessary. Applicants pay own travel and insurance. Registration fee £160. *Apply early; EC nationals only.*

American applicants requiring an exchange should apply to one of the following: MAST/PART Program, Office of Special Programs, 405 Coffey Hall, 1420 Eckles Avenue, St Paul, Minnesota 55108; Ohio Agricultural Intern Program, Ohio State University, 113 Agricultural Admin Building, 2120 Fyffe Road, Columbus, Ohio 43210; Future Farmers of America, National FFA Center, PO Box 15160, Alexandria, Virginia 22309.

MONITORS & TEACHERS

AMERICAN CAMPING ASSOCIATION Publications, Bradford Woods, Martinsville, IN 46151-7902
Publishes *Guide to Accredited Camps* $15.95 including airmail postage, listing over 2,000 residential and day camps throughout the US. Written primarily for parents choosing a camp for their children, it also includes a section on the camp job market which is estimated to provide more than 330,000 full-time posts. The majority of opportunities are for counsellors and skills are needed in over 50 activities, including outdoor living, sports, climbing, horse riding, ocean biology projects, drama and music. The guide also gives details of practical job finding services operated by the American Camping Association. **B D PH**

BRITISH UNIVERSITIES NORTH AMERICA CLUB (BUNAC) 16 Bowling Green Lane, London EC1R 0BD Tel 071-251 3472
A non-profit, non-political educational student club which aims to encourage interest and understanding between students in Britain and North America. Operates opportunities for some 4000 young people to work as counsellors on summer camps across the US, but mostly in the north east, upper mid west, south east and west coast. The camps are permanent sites and cater for 40-600 children at a time. Camps can be organised privately, by the YMCA, Girl Scouts, Salvation Army or they can be institutional camps for the physically, mentally or socially handicapped. Camp counselling involves living, working and playing with groups of 3-8 children aged 6-16. General counsellors are responsible for the full-time supervision of their group and ensure that the children follow the set routine, and should be able to provide counsel and friendship and must therefore have fairly general experience and aptitude in the handling of children. Specialist counsellors must have a sporting or craft interest, qualifications or skills plus

ability and enthusiasm to organise or teach specific activities. These include sports, watersports, music, arts and crafts, science, pioneering, entertainments and dance. Counsellors with secretarial skills are needed for office work, and counsellors are also needed in institutional camps. Ages 19½ (by 1 July)-35. Applicants must be resident in UK, single, hard working as hours are long, with a genuine love of children and relevant experience. They should be able to show firm, fair leadership and be flexible, cooperative, energetic, conscientious, cheerful, patient, positive and able to adapt to new situations, and to function enthusiastically in a structured setting. 8/9+ weeks, with 1 day off most weeks, mid June-end August, followed by 1-6 weeks free for travel after the camp. Return flight, overnight hostel accommodation, transfer to camp, orientation and training, guide to North America, plus board and lodging at the camp provided. Counsellors live with the children in log cabins or tents. Registration fee £48. Insurance fee approx £72. Salary approx £360; £420 for those aged 21+. Suitable for students, teachers, social workers and those with other relevant qualifications. Interviews held throughout the UK, mid November-early May. Compulsory orientation programme held at Easter. Membership fee £3. *Apply early.*

Irish applicants should apply to USIT, Aston Quay, O'Connell Bridge, Dublin 2, Ireland Tel Dublin 778117.

CAMP AMERICA Dept WH, 37A Queens Gate, London SW7 5HR

An Exchange Visitor Programme which recruits young people to work as general or activities counsellors on summer camps in the US, mainly in New England, the middle Atlantic and mid-west states. Camps can be organised privately, by agencies such as the Boy Scouts, Jewish Youth Centres and YMCA, or they can be institutional, organised specially for the handicapped and the learning disabled. General counsellors will be responsible for the care and supervision of a group of 8-10 American children aged 6-16. The work involves working, playing and living with children 24 hours a day, and duties include supervising the camp and personal cleanliness, helping to maintain a high level of camp morale, ensuring that campers receive proper

medical care, supervising rest hours, conducting activities and being on duty several nights a week. Specialist counsellors are responsible for instructing the children in specific activities such as sports, waterfront, sciences, arts and crafts, pioneering and performing arts. Other counsellors may be responsible for both activities and general work. Nurses and student nurses are also required as camp aides. Ages 18 (by 1 June)-35. Applicants must be flexible, cooperative and adaptable, like and get on with children, prepared to work intensively in an outdoor educational environment, and be willing to adjust to camp life. They must be fit, with a doctor's certification of good health, and speak good English. Applicants must be available June-September. The programme includes return flight, orientation in the US, transfer to camp, full board and lodging for 9 weeks at camp plus pocket money of $150-$450, according to age and experience. Up to 8 weeks are free at the end of the camp for travel, the cost of which is not included in the programme. Refundable deposit £50. Medical insurance fee £50. *Apply September-May.*

THE SIOUX INDIAN YMCA PO Box 218, Dupree, South Dakota 57623

The Sioux YMCAs were founded in 1879 and today serve in 28 communities on five reservations in South Dakota, and are the only YMCAs operated by and serving primarily Indian people. Volunteers are needed to plan for and work at a residential summer camp on the Oahe Reservoir of the Missouri River. Volunteers will provide partial leadership for a workcamp as it prepares the campground, and will assume staff responsibilities for five 8 day camp sessions, plus shorter special camps for families, teenagers and canoeing. A camp director, head cook, nurse, waterfront director, maintenance person, crafts director and general counsellors are required. Staff live in tents with campers, without electricity and running water; applicants should have skills suitable for primitive camping. Volunteers are also required to plan, organise and conduct 2-3 week day camps in small reservation communities at the request of, in cooperation with and under the direct supervision of the indigenous community YMCA. Camp activities may include basketball, volleyball, arts and crafts, storytelling, hiking, swimming, canoeing, baseball and group games. Time not spent in leadership of camps may be spent in a variety of counselling, recreation and community development activities and in just getting to know the families and the communities. Self-catering accommodation provided in one-room community buildings. Ages 18+. Volunteers should be mature and committed, with definite camp skills, prepared to accept the disciplines of camp routine. They should be creative, responsible and flexible, speak good English, and be skilled in recreation, leadership development, childcare and working with people. A love of children and people in general, the ability to adapt to a different socio-economic setting and to relate meaningfully to other cultures are also necessary. Because of the poverty/alcohol syndrome on the reservation, volunteers are expected not to drink alcohol for the project period. Those from all religious faiths and commitments accepted, but are expected to respect and participate in the Christian life of the community. 10 weeks, summer. 24 hour day, 7 day week. Volunteers pay own insurance and travel costs. Orientation and evaluation sessions; help given in obtaining visa. PH depending on ability.

PEACE CAMPS

CHRISTIAN MOVEMENT FOR PEACE
Bethnal Green United Reformed Church, Pott Street, London E2 0EF Tel 071-729 1877

INTERNATIONAL VOLUNTARY SERVICE
162 Upper New Walk, Leicester LE1 7QA
Tel Leicester 549430

UNITED NATIONS ASSOCIATION
International Youth Service, Welsh Centre for International Affairs, Temple of Peace, Cathays Park, Cardiff CF1 3AP Tel Cardiff 223088

Apply to one of the above to work on peace projects organised by an independent organisation working for peace through youth exchanges and voluntary service. Recent projects have included working alongside volunteers from Eastern bloc countries to renovate low income housing; painting, gardening and studying peace and justice

issues in New York; and running a Peace Day camp for children at a Quaker Conference Centre in Massachusetts. Opportunities for discussions, study groups, social and cultural activities, all linked to camp themes. Ages 18-35. Applicants should have previous workcamp, voluntary work or community service experience, preferably already involved in the peace movement, and be highly motivated and prepared to work hard and contribute to team life. 2/3 weeks, June-August. Food, accommodation and insurance provided, but volunteers pay their own travel.

Organised by Volunteers for Peace Inc, Tiffany Road, Belmont, Vermont 05730.

Applications from outside the UK: please see workcamp information on page 27.

WORKCAMPS

INTERNATIONAL VOLUNTARY SERVICE
162 Upper New Walk, Leicester LE1 7QA
Tel Leicester 549430
IVS is the British branch of Service Civil International which promotes international reconciliation through work projects. Volunteers are needed to work in international teams on workcamps. Recent projects have included renovating a residence for teenage parents in Lebanan, New Hampshire; path building, gardening and landscaping at an alternative medicine centre in Hillsboro, Virginia; helping to make programmes for a community-based radio station, Illinois; indoor renovation work at Fort Apache youth centre, in the Bronx; and converting an abandoned building into a youth centre with cafeteria, gym and classroom space at a Navaho Reservation in Shiprock, New Mexico. Ages 18+. Applicants should have previous workcamp, voluntary work or community service experience, and should be prepared to work hard and contribute to team life. 35-40 hour week. 2-4 weeks, July-September. Food, accommodation and insurance provided, but not travel. Membership fee £25 (students £15, unwaged £10). Registration fee £40. B D PH

Organised by Service Civil International, c/o Innisfree Village, Route 2, Box 506, Crozet, Virginia 22932.

UNITED STATES

Applications from outside the UK: please see workcamp information on page 27.

UNITED NATIONS ASSOCIATION
International Youth Service, Welsh Centre for International Affairs, Temple of Peace, Cathays Park, Cardiff CF1 3AP Tel Cardiff 223088
Volunteers are needed on international workcamps in the states of California, Florida, Idaho, Iowa, Kentucky, Maine, Montana, New York and Rhode Island, organised by a non-governmental organisation seeking to promote international understanding and friendship. Recent projects have included helping at an archaeological excavation on a prehistoric site; working on historical preservation projects at the Lyndhurst American Gothic Mansion; cataloguing and arranging museum exhibits at the Statue of Liberty; and general conservation work on various sites. Ages 18+. Applicants should have previous workcamp experience. 3 weeks, July-September. Food and self-catering accommodation provided. Participants should take work clothes and a sleeping bag, and pay their own travel costs. Registration fee £22.

Organised by the Council on International Educational Exchange (CIEE), 205 East 42nd Street, New York, NY10017.

Applications from outside the UK: please see workcamp information on page 27

GENERAL

GENERAL

BRITISH UNIVERSITIES NORTH AMERICA CLUB (BUNAC) 16 Bowling Green Lane, London EC1R 0BD Tel 071-251 3472
A non-profit, non-political educational student club which aims to encourage interest and understanding between students in Britain and North America. Operates the Work America Programme, a general work and travel Exchange Visitor Programme for full-time British college and university students aged 18+ who wish to work and travel in the US. Participants can visit the US between 15 June-3 October, working for up to 15 weeks; most work about 8 weeks and travel for 4. Members receive a handbook on how to get to the US, and a job directory which lists hundreds of jobs

including hotel, restaurant and shop work, making and selling fudge, ice cream, sandwiches, soft drinks and fast food, laundry work, and helping in amusement parks. Alternatively members can go to the US on sponsorship and find a job once they are there. Compulsory orientation programmes held throughout Britain and upon arrival give advice on finding and choosing a job, obtaining a visa, income tax, accommodation, travel, food and budgeting. Flights arranged and include overnight accommodation in New York, cost £349 (1990); information also provided on onward travel, together with a guide to budget travel in North America and Mexico. Assistance provided by the summer office in New York. Cost £59 (1990) covers visa and administration costs. Insurance £72. Participants can earn enough to cover the cost of the return flight, plus travel and all living expenses. Wages average $200+ per week. Operates a loan scheme to help with flight costs. To qualify participants must be able to provide evidence that they can support themselves during their stay, such as $300 in dollar travellers cheques, plus proof of round-trip transportation, and a definite job offer or individual sponsorship. Membership fee £3. *Apply for information in November.*

GAP ACTIVITY PROJECTS LTD 44 Queen's Road, Reading, Berkshire RG1 4BB Tel Reading 594914
A number of placements are available for volunteers to undertake committed but rewarding work throughout the US. Volunteers can be placed in a hostel for the homeless, run by the volunteers, who live as a community. Also placements at an outdoor activity centre, helping to run programmes introducing people, from schoolchildren to pensioners, to outdoor activities, camping and ecology. A small number of attachments are available on a large ranch which raises cattle for the Third World. No wages at the hostel, but food, toiletries and other essentials provided. Board, lodging and pocket money provided at the activity centre and on the ranch. Applicants must be school leavers aged 18-19 who have up to a year before going on to further education. 5+ months, beginning September or January. Cost £300 plus airfare and cover insurance. *Apply early September of last school year; applications close March. UK nationals only.*

USSR

Embassy of the USSR
13 Kensington Palace Gardens, London W8 4QX Tel 071-229 3628
Consular section: 5 Kensington Palace Gardens, London W8 4QS Tel 071-229 8027

British Embassy
Naberezhnaya Morisa Toreza 14, Moscow 72

Tourist office
Intourist Moscow, Intourist House, 219 Marsh

Wall, Isle of Dogs, London E14 9JF
Tel 071-538 8600

Youth & student information
Sputnik, Youth & Student Tourist Bureau of the USSR, 15 Kosygin Street, Moscow 117946

Society for Cultural Relations with the USSR, 320 Brixton Road, London SW9 6AB
Tel 071-274 2282

INFORMATION

Entry regulations Workcamp organisations will inform volunteers how to obtain the necessary visa/work permit and hold orientation days for volunteers going to East Europe, giving information on all aspects of the work covered together with some political background and practical information.

Travel *The Travellers Survival Kit Soviet Union & Eastern Europe* £8.95, is an invaluable guide for travellers, containing advice on where to go, travel bargains, budget accommodation and dealing with bureaucracy. Published by Vacation Work, 9 Park End Street, Oxford, Oxfordshire OX1 1HJ Tel Oxford 241978.

WORKCAMPS

GAP ACTIVITY PROJECTS 44 Queen's Road, Reading, Berkshire RG1 4BB
Tel Reading 594 914
A small number of placements are available for volunteers to help teach sport, drama and English to primary school children. Applicants must be school leavers aged 18-19 who have up to a year before going on to further education. Fluent A level Russian essential; interview conducted mainly in Russian. Placements will normally last 6 months, and volunteers will be expected to take a one week TEFL course before departure. Board, lodging and pocket money provided. Cost £250 plus airfare, insurance and TEFL course fee. *Apply early September of last school year; applications close March. British nationals only.*

INTERNATIONAL VOLUNTARY SERVICE 162 Upper New Walk, Leicester LE1 7QA
Tel Leicester 549430
IVS is the British branch of Service Civil International, which promotes international reconciliation through work projects.

Volunteers are needed for manual work on international workcamps which have recently included preserving rare plants and renovating paths at a nature reserve south of Moscow; constructing and renovating buildings in Voronezh; excavating archaeological remains in Latvia; and agricultural work at Kalinin. 4 hour day, with study programmes in the afternoons covering a wide range of topics, as well as study visits to Moscow, Vilnius and Kiev. Ages 18+. Applicants must have previous SCI experience, preferably in East Europe, and should be prepared to work hard and contribute to team life. 35-40 hour week. 1-2 weeks, June-August. Food, accommodation and

USSR

insurance provided, but not travel.
Membership fee £25 (students £15, unwaged
£10). Registration fee £40. Study programme
cost approx US$150. **B D PH**

Organised by the Committee of Youth
Organisations (KMO).

Applications from outside the UK: please see
workcamp information on page 27.

YUGOSLAVIA

Yugoslav Embassy
5-7 Lexham Gardens, London W8 5JU
Tel 071-370 6105

British Embassy
46 Ulice General Zdanova, 11000 Belgrade

Tourist office
Yugoslav National Tourist Office, 143 Regent
Street, London W1R 8AE Tel 071-734 5243

Youth hostels
Ferijalni Savez Jugoslavije, 11000 Belgrade,
Mose Pijade 12/1

Youth & student information
Karavan-Naromtravel, Organisation for
International and Domestic Youth Travel,
11000 Belgrade, Knez-Mihailova 50

Omladinski Turisticki Centar, Youth Tourist
Agency, Petrinjska 73, Zagreb

INFORMATION

Entry regulations British nationals do not need
a visa to enter Yugoslavia. Visitors may stay in
Yugoslavia for up to 90 days, and permission
for an extension may be obtained from the local
authorities within 7 days of arrival. It is very
difficult to find employment in Yugoslavia, a
situation which is not made easier if the
applicant has no knowledge of the native
languages. Local employment bureaux or
tourist associations may be able to help find a
temporary or seasonal job, but applications and
arrangements must be made in person.

Travel STA Travel, 86 Old Brompton Road,
London SW7 3LQ Tel 071-937 9921 operates
flexible low cost flights between London and
destinations throughout Yugoslavia.

Campus Travel, 52 Grosvenor Gardens, London
SW1W 0AG Tel 071-730 3402 offers Eurotrain
under 26 fares and competitive airfares to
destinations in Yugoslavia.

The Rough Guide to Yugoslavia £5.95 is a
practical handbook full of information on
travel, accommodation and cheap places to eat.
Published by Harrap Columbus, Chelsea
House, 26 Market Square, Bromley, Kent BR1
1NA.

Yugoslavia - Travel Information is a booklet
containing brief information on travel,
accommodation, formalities, events and
entertainment, sports, customs, medical care
plus useful addresses, including tourist
information centres all over Yugoslavia.
Available from the Yugoslav National Tourist
Office, see above.

Accommodation *Private Accommodation Rates*
gives details of accommodation available
throughout the year in private homes,
including rented apartments, family houses
and bungalows. Also *Camping Yugoslavia,*
providing a listing of all official campsites with
details of facilities and a map. Available from
the Yugoslav National Tourist Office, see
above.

Youth Hostel, Petrinjska 77, Zagreb, has 215
beds in 55 double, triple and multi-bedded
rooms. Also shower and toilet facilities and
maid service. Guests can also use facilities of
nearby youth travel agency who run the hostel
and provide information for young visitors to
Yugoslavia.

**When writing to any organisation it is
essential to mention Working Holidays 1991
and enclose a large stamped, self-addressed
envelope, or if overseas, a large addressed
envelope and at least two International Reply
Coupons.**

COMMUNITY WORK

INTERNATIONAL VOLUNTARY SERVICE
162 Upper New Walk, Leicester LE1 7QA
Tel Leicester 549430

UNITED NATIONS ASSOCIATION
International Youth Service, Welsh Centre for International Affairs, Temple of Peace, Cathays Park, Cardiff CF1 3AP Tel Cardiff 223088

Apply to either of the above to work in international teams on various projects in Slovenia, Vojvodina and Macedonia. Recent projects have included working alongside residents of a castle for people suffering mental and nervous disorders in Hrastovec; running workshops and excursions for physically disabled people in Dva Topola; and running a playscheme for disadvantaged children in Llubljana. Ages 18+. Applicants must have previous workcamp experience and be highly motivated and prepared to work hard and contribute to team life. 40 hour week, 3-4 weeks, July-September. Food, accommodation and medical insurance provided, but volunteers pay their own travel costs. **PH**

Organised by Zveza Socialisticne Mladine Slovenije (RK-ZSMS), Dalmatinova ul 4, Dom Sindikatov, 61000 Llubljana.

Applications from outside UK: please see workcamp information on page 27.

CONSERVATION

INTERNATIONAL VOLUNTARY SERVICE
162 Upper New Walk, Leicester LE1 7QA
Tel Leicester 549430

UNITED NATIONS ASSOCIATION
International Youth Service, Welsh Centre for International Affairs, Temple of Peace, Cathays Park, Cardiff CF1 3AP Tel Cardiff 223088

Apply to either of the above to work in international teams on various projects in Slovenia and Vojvodina. Recent projects have

included collecting herbs in the mountains of Serbia for research into medical properties; rehabilitating the shores and surroundings of Lake Dojran, after a serious drought; taking photographs and preparing an exhibition on the ecological decline of parts of the city of Llubljana; preparing feeding places for wildlife in the forests of Zlatna Dolina; clearing lakes and monitoring bird migration in Ludos; and preservation work on an abandoned castle in Krumperk. Ages 18+. Applicants must have previous workcamp experience and be highly motivated and prepared to work hard and contribute to team life. 6 hour day, 5-6 day week, 3-4 weeks, June-August. Food, basic accommodation and medical insurance provided, but volunteers pay their own travel costs. **PH**

Organised by Zveza Socialisticne Mladine Slovenije (RK-ZSMS), Dalmatinova ul 4, Dom Sindikatov, 61000 Llubljana.

Applications from outside UK: please see workcamp information on page 27.

COURIERS/REPS

EUROCAMP Courier Department,
Edmundson House, Tatton Street, Knutsford,
Cheshire WA16 6BG Tel Knutsford 50052
Requires resident couriers to work on various campsites. Work involves cleaning tents and equipment prior to the arrival of new customers; checking, replacing and making repairs on equipment; replenishing gas supplies; keeping the store tent in order; keeping basic accounts; and reporting on a weekly basis to England. Couriers are also expected to meet new arrivals and assist holidaymakers with any problems that may arise; organise activities and parties; provide information on local tourist attractions and maintain an information noticeboard. At the beginning and end of the season couriers are expected to help in erecting and dismantling tents. There are no set working hours or free days, as these depend on unpredictable factors. Ages 18-28; older applicants considered. Applications from couples welcome. Applicants should be familiar with working and travelling abroad, preferably with camping experience. They should also be

adaptable, reliable, independent, efficient, hard working, sensible, sociable, tactful, patient and have a working knowledge of the language. Applicants are expected to work one half of the season, early/mid April-mid July or mid July-late September/early October; exact dates depend on the campsite. Work also available for the whole season. Accommodation in frame tent with cooking facilities, moped for use on site, insurance and return fare provided. Salary approx £80 per week. *Early application advisable; interviews start November.*

ILG COACH & CAMPING DIVISION (incorporating NAT Holidays and Intasun Camping), Overseas Personnel Manager, Devonshire House, Elmfield Road, Bromley, Kent Tel 081-466 6660
Vacancies exist for campsite representatives. Work involves welcoming and visiting clients, accompanying excursions, organising and taking part in evening entertainments, and generally looking after clients. Ages 19+. Applicants must have the desire and ability to get on with people and to handle pressure. April-October, with some positions available for students only in June/July. Applicants should be reliable, hard working, prepared to work as part of a team, and have enough staying power to last the season. Knowledge of German or Serbo-Croat an advantage. Staff are required to take an active part in their resort entertainment programme, helping to organise events such as parties, barbecues, and games evenings. Salary approx £70 per week. Accommodation and return travel provided. All staff are required to take part in a 2 week training programme in April. *Early application advisable; recruitment starts October and applicants should write then for details. Interviews commence December.*

SEASUN/TENTREK HOLIDAYS 71/72 East Hill, Colchester, Essex CO1 2QW Tel Colchester 861886
Provides self-catering family holidays in apartments, mobile homes and tents plus activity holidays for schools and groups. Requires representatives for the summer season, beginning April-mid November, in Rovinj. 50/60 hour week. Ages 19+. Applicants should be independent, resourceful with good communication skills and commitment. Knowledge of German or Serbo-Croat an

advantage, but not essential. Training provided. Salary and subsistence £260 per month; £40 per month extra paid on successful completion of contract. Accommodation and travel provided; personal insurance cost £55, uniform cost £60. B D PH depending on ability.

GENERAL

PREDSEDNISTVO KONFERENCIJE SAVEZA SOCIJALISTICKE OMLADINE JUGOSLAVIJE Medjunarodno Odeljenje, Bul Lenjina 6, Belgrade
The Division for International Relations of the Students Union, who may be able to help foreign students find temporary employment during the summer.

SUNSAIL The Port House, Port Solent, Portsmouth, Hampshire PO6 4TH Tel Portsmouth 219847
Crew members required to work aboard cruising yachts sailing in flotillas around the Kornati and Dalmatian islands. Vacancies for experienced skippers, responsible for the wellbeing of up to 13 cruising yachts and 60 holidaymakers, giving daily briefings on navigation and sailing assistance where necessary. Applicants must have considerable sailing experience, be cheerful, hard working and able to deal with people of varying backgrounds and ages. Ages 23-30. Also bosuns/mechanics needed, responsible to the skipper for maintaining the marine diesel engines and repairing any other onboard items. Must have excellent knowledge of marine diesels and practical ability to cope with all sorts of breakdowns and repairs. Ages 22-30. Hostesses are required to look after laundry, accounting, and cleaning of boats, to advise holidaymakers on shops and restaurants, and to organise social events and barbecues. Sailing experience useful, but bright personality, patience and adaptability essential. Ages 22-30.

All staff should be prepared for very hard work and long hours. Knowledge of German advantageous but not essential. Mid March-November. Wages approx £85 per week, paid on a monthly basis. Accommodation on board, return travel and medical insurance provided.

NOTES

WORLDWIDE
INFORMATION

Travel Eurolines, 23 Crawley Road, Luton LU1 1HX Tel Luton 404511 offers a range of coach services to over 190 destinations on mainland Europe, including daily services to Paris and Amsterdam.

Odyssey International, 21 Cambridge Road, Waterbeach, Cambridge CB4 9NJ Tel Cambridge 861079 is a travel club which aims to match like-minded travelling partners. An advice line is run by members who have just returned from abroad giving details of visa problems, vaccination requirements and employment prospects. Publishes a biannual newsletter detailing travel offers. Annual membership fee £20.

Touring Guide to Europe £7.25 including UK postage, gives information on 22 countries, what to see, and background details about the people and way of life. Some chapters are available separately in handy pocket form: Benelux and Denmark/Iceland, each 45p; Switzerland 50p; Federal Republic of Germany, Norway and Spain/Portugal, each 60p. Available from YHA Services Ltd, 14 Southampton Street, London WC2E 7HY Tel 071-836 8541 or YHA (England & Wales), National Office, Trevelyan House, St Stephen's Hill, St Albans, Hertfordshire AL1 2DY Tel St Albans 55215.

Europe by Train £6.70 including UK postage, is a paperback guide for young European train travellers, giving advice on where to stay. Published annually in January. Also *Thomas Cook Rail Map of Europe* £3.15 including UK postage, shows passenger lines throughout Europe and in countries bordering the Mediterranean, including enlargements of 36 city plans. Both available from Thomas Cook Publications, PO Box 36, Peterborough PE3 6SB

Europe - A Manual for Hitch-hikers £3.95, gives country by country information on hitching techniques, route planning, entry procedures

and attitudes towards hitch-hikers. Also includes an essential vocabulary in 9 languages, advice on how to cross the channel cheaply and for free, how to read foreign number plates, addresses of hitch-hiking agencies, sources of free maps and how to get help with legal problems. *Travellers Survival Kit Europe* £6.95, is a practical guide covering over 36 European countries, including details on the cost of food and accommodation, rules of the road, how the telephone systems work, car hire, health tips, public transport, shopping hours, customs regulations, the law, where to get help and information and many useful addresses. Both published by Vacation Work, 9 Park End Street, Oxford , Oxfordshire OX1 1HJ Tel Oxford 241978.

The Traveller's Handbook £9.95 (£6.95 to members), is an 864 page reference and source book for the independent traveller, with chapters on travel, camping and backpacking, hitch-hiking, health, clothing, luggage and survival kits, where to stay, dealing with people when things go wrong, photography, choosing maps, passports, visas, permits, insurance, currency and customs. Also includes special chapters for students, single women and the handicapped. Published by WEXAS International, 45 Brompton Road, London SW3 1DE Tel 071-589 0500.

Accommodation The YMCA Inter-Point Programme offers low-cost accommodation for young travellers in various centres throughout Europe. All offer a warm welcome, advice and information. Available July-August/September. Cost from approx £4, bed and breakfast. Inter-Point card £2. Brochure giving full information available from YMCA Inter-Point Programme, Training Services, Crown House, 550 Mauldeth Road West, Manchester M21 2SJ Tel 061-881 5321.

YMCA World Directory £4 including UK postage, lists over 2,400 YMCA addresses in

WORLD WIDE

90+ countries offering accommodation for men and women. *Pack for Europe* £2, post free, is a handbook containing addresses of hostels and restaurants of the YMCA, YWCA and other recognised youth organisations, offering accommodation within a reasonable price range in Europe and the Middle East. Available from National Council of YMCAs, 640 Forest Road, London E17 3DZ Tel 081-520 5599.

International Youth Hostel Handbook Vol I gives addresses and brief details of all the permanent hostels in Europe, North Africa and the Near East with the principal hostel regulations. Large folding map showing locations. Published annually in March. *International Youth Hostel Handbook Vol II* details hostels in Australasia, America and Asia. Price £6.55 each including UK postage. Available from YHA Services Ltd, 14 Southampton Street, London WC2E 7HY Tel 071-836 8541 or YHA (England & Wales), National Office, Trevelyan House, St Stephen's Hill, St Albans, Hertfordshire AL1 2DY Tel St Albans 55215.

INFORMATION

Publications *Work Your Way Around the World* £8.95, is an informative book including firsthand accounts and details on preparation, working a free passage, opportunities in tourism, fruit picking, farming, teaching, domestic work, business and industry. Also contains details of areas of work and seasonal and temporary employment available. *Directory of Summer Jobs Abroad 1991* £6.95, details vacancies in over 40 countries, including information on jobs offered, wages given and addresses of employers. *Working in Ski Resorts - Europe* £5.95, has information on finding work as a ski instructor, courier, chalet girl, teacher, au pair, ski technician, shop assistant, disc jockey, snow clearer, office worker or representative in a ski resort. All published by Vacation Work Publications, 9 Park End Street, Oxford OX1 1HJ Tel Oxford 241978.

A Place for You Overseas? In the Summer is a free leaflet containing addresses of organisations who can be contacted for details of workcamp, community and voluntary work opportunities for 1-3 months. Published by Christians Abroad, 1 Stockwell Green, London SW9 9HP Tel 071-737 7811.

ARCHAEOLOGY

ARCHAEOLOGY

Archaeological Fieldwork Opportunities Bulletin $8 + $2.50 postage, lists archaeological sites at which excavation and research work is being carried out. Details are given of staff and volunteers needed at each site, age/experience required, board and lodging, wages, training and equipment provision, any costs involved and other conditions. Also lists archaeological field schools which provide practical training. Published annually in January by the Archaeological Institute of America, 675 Commonwealth Avenue, Department GG, Boston, Massachusetts 02215, United States.

ARCHAEOLOGY ABROAD The Secretary, 31-34 Gordon Square, London WC1H 0PY Provides information on opportunities for archaeological fieldwork and excavations outside Britain. Three bulletins are published annually which provide details of digs, dates, the number of places offered, conditions of participation, details of board and lodging, and addresses of where to apply. Also publishes two news sheets, spring and autumn.

FOUNDATION FOR FIELD RESEARCH PO Box 2010, Alpine, California 92001, United States
A non-profitmaking organisation sponsoring research expeditions by finding volunteers to assist scientists in the field. Volunteers are required to help on archaeological projects which have recently included studies of textiles from pre-Columbian mummies in Peru; excavations at a 2,000 year old Amerindian site on the island of Grenada; and studying prehistoric lakeside rock art carved by the Ojobway in central Canada. Ages 14+. Special experience or skills are always welcome, but not necessary. Participants are given responsibilities to fulfil, so applicants should be willing to do their part and become active members of the research team. Members share the costs of the project, from US$550-$1500 for 1-4 weeks, which covers transportation during the expedition, a preparatory booklet, most field gear, tent or dormitory accommodation and three meals a day. Travel to assembly point not provided. Scholarships available. PH on certain expeditions.

COMMUNITY WORK

ACTION D'URGENCE INTERNATIONALE Secretariat International, rue Felix Ziem 10, 75018 Paris, France
A grouping of associations and volunteers who, conscious of the problems faced in time of natural disaster, wish to bring into being a supranational structure for practical assistance, wholly unconcerned with political or territorial rivalries. Mobilises trained volunteers to go anywhere at any time in the event of a natural disaster requiring sound organisation. During the past few years volunteers have been called for relief, reconstruction and medical work after earthquakes in Italy, Algeria, Yugoslavia, Mexico and Chile; a volcanic eruption in Colombia; flooding in India and the north of England; a typhoon in the Dominican Republic; a tornado in France and a cyclone in the West Indies. Tasks may include setting up rescue services, procurement and distribution of vital supplies, erection of temporary accommodation, provision of medical assistance, restoration of transport and communication facilities, repair of damaged property, and helping survivors re-establish their lives and independence. International training courses are held during the summer in the UK, France, Morocco, Guadeloupe, Colombia, Chile and India, to introduce volunteers to the problems that go with natural disasters and to give them the basic skills needed for emergency action, in particular life saving, rescue and the clearing out of debris. Membership fee FF120.

UK applicants may apply through Mike Fraser, 22 Raphael Drive, Shoeburyness, Southend-on-Sea, Essex SS3 9UW.

ACTION HEALTH 2000 International Voluntary Health Association, The Director, The Bath House, Gwydir Street, Cambridge CB1 2LW Tel Cambridge 460853
A voluntary charitable society concerned with health care issues in developing countries. Applications for a medical electives scheme are invited from medical school, nursing and physiotherapy students in Britain; students from other European medical schools may also apply but must be prepared to travel to England to attend orientation course. Placements available in India, Bangladesh, China and East and Southern Africa. 6-8 weeks. Locations and type of work vary considerably, but personal interests are matched as far as possible. Participants are attached to the existing health team, often following a special programme. Returned elective students are encouraged to maintain links with the organisation and with the projects. The scheme is operated on a non-profit basis. The fee of £62 covers selection, placement, orientation courses, practical help and advice with travel and insurance, and a support service during and after the placement. Participants also pay annual membership fee of £10, and approx £120 to cover hospital board and lodging. Applications considered throughout the year, but students are strongly advised to apply at least 6, and preferably 12 months before the elective date. Also operates short-term visitor and volunteer schemes for health professionals including doctors, dentists, physiotherapists, nurses, midwifes and health visitors in India and Tanzania. Placements are in rural, semi-rural or deprived urban areas, often isolated, and may involve work in any area of primary health care. Positions may also be available in district general or specialist hospitals, teaching local health staff and passing on specific skills. 3+ months; may vary in special circumstances. Short-term visitors pay £125 fee to cover selection, placement, orientation courses and administrative costs, plus approx £250 towards board and lodging, and pay their own travel and insurance costs. **PH**

THE DISAWAY TRUST 2 Charles Road, Merton Park, London SW19 3BD Tel 081-543 3431
Formed to enable physically disabled people to take holidays in the UK and abroad, the Trust needs able-bodied volunteers to look after disabled holidaymakers aged 16-80 on a 1:1 basis, helping with all their personal needs and ensuring that they gain the greatest possible enjoyment from their holiday. In 1990 holidays were arranged in Corfu, England and Israel. Ages 18+. Experience not necessary; volunteers who have never assisted disabled people before are particularly welcome. 8-10 days, May-late September. Volunteers are asked to pay 50% of

WORLD WIDE

total cost of the holiday; minimum contributions £150-£265 cover transport, half board accommodation, excursions and insurance.

HELP THE HANDICAPPED HOLIDAY FUND (3Hs Fund) Holiday Organiser, 147A Camden Road, Tunbridge Wells, Kent TN1 2RA Tel Tunbridge Wells 47474

Provides large group holidays for physically handicapped people from the age of 11 upwards. Able-bodied volunteers are required to care for the guests and help them enjoy their stay. Holiday venues have included Spain, Swanage, Isle of Sheppey, Cliftonville and an adventure holiday in Cornwall. Ages 18+. No experience necessary. Tasks include washing, dressing, feeding and taking the guests on outings. Most holidays take place in the summer and last 1 week; volunteers have 1 afternoon off during the week. Full board and accommodation in hotels/holiday camps, insurance and travel provided for UK venues. For continental holidays a nominal contribution is required to offset medical insurance and travel. *British applicants preferred.*

CONSERVATION

PROJECT PHOENIX TRUST, The Secretary, 68 Rochfords, Coffee Hall, Milton Keynes MK6 5DJ Tel Milton Keynes 678038

Runs overseas study tours and interest holidays for adults who would not be able to travel without physical assistance, or who are prepared to give such help as is needed in order that others may travel. Able-bodied helpers are needed to provide care for disabled adults. Holidays last 7-14 days, spring and September, and include Tunisia, Rome, Pompeii, Venice, Vienna, Florence, Andalucia, Bruges, Athens, Israel, Sweden and Leningrad. Ages 20+. Long hours and hard but rewarding work. Helpers should be strong and fit as tasks include pushing and lifting wheelchairs, and night attendance for turning patients in bed. Experience of caring for disabled people welcome, but not essential, providing there is genuine motivation to help. Accommodation in twin-bedded rooms shared by one handicapped and one able-bodied person. Volunteers are required to contribute 25% of the full costs, and organise their own insurance, pocket money and travel to and from London. *Apply well in advance; most places are allocated in January/ February.*

UNIVERSITIES' EDUCATIONAL FUND FOR PALESTINIAN REFUGEES (UNIPAL) Volunteer Programme Organiser, 12 Helen Road, Oxford OX2 0DE Tel Oxford 241537

Volunteers are needed to help on projects run by Palestinians on the occupied West Bank and in the Gaza Strip, Jordan, and in Arab villages in Israel. The work is mainly teaching English as a foreign language to older children or students, but there are some opportunities for working with the handicapped, helping with children's activities, and also for manual work. Usually ages 20-40. Applicants should have sensitivity, tolerance, a readiness to learn, political awareness, adaptability and a sense of responsibility. Relevant experience desirable. 3-8 weeks depending on the project, June-August. Food and simple accommodation provided, but volunteers pay own travel costs and insurance. Selection process involves references and interview in Oxford. Registration fee £5. *Apply by April.*

CONSERVATION

EARTHQUEST 54 Sunderland Terrace, Ulverston, Cumbria LA12 Tel Ulverston 57885

Organises worldwide adventure, research and development expeditions. Recent expeditions have included rainforest and ornithological research on New Zealand's South Island; coral reef research and scuba diving off the archipelagos of Samoa and Tonga in the South Pacific; and investigating Viking settlement sites and studying glaciers, geology, weather and botany in Greenland. Volunteer leaders, support staff members and adventure task leaders are required to motivate young people in their appreciation of the natural world and the power and enjoyment of purposeful, meaningful teamwork. Experience is preferred for the scientific research aspects of the programme and mountaineering, canoeing and rafting are useful skills where outdoor activities are involved. Applicants should be enthusiastic and willing, conscious of the importance of the natural environment. Work available year round, 6 weeks-6 months. Ages 18+. Accommodation in three-person tents. Catering provided by expedition teams. Subsistence and accommodation charges vary according to the operation; insurance, visas and subsidised travel organised.

EARTHWATCH EUROPE Belsyre Court, 57 Woodstock Road, Oxford, Oxfordshire Tel Oxford 311600

Aims to support field research in a wide range of disciplines including archaeology, ornithology, animal behaviour, nature conservation and ecology. The support is given as a grant and in the form of volunteer assistance. Recent expeditions have included recording the behaviour of orang-utans in Borneo; monitoring giant clams in Tonga; tagging sharks for a population survey in the Bahamas; saving baby leatherback turtles in the Virgin Islands; and examining coral communities in Fiji. Ages 16-80. No special skills are required although each expedition may, because of its nature, demand some talent or quality of fitness. Volunteers should be generally fit, able to cope with new situations, able to mix and work with people of different ages and backgrounds, and a sense of humour will help. 2-3 weeks, all year. Members share the costs of the expedition, from £500, which includes meals, transport and all necessary field equipment, but does not include the cost of travel, although assistance may be given in arranging it. Membership fee £22 includes magazines and newsletters providing information on joining an expedition.

FOUNDATION FOR FIELD RESEARCH PO Box 2010, Alpine, California 92001, United States

A non-profitmaking organisation sponsoring research expeditions by finding volunteers to assist scientists in the field. Volunteers are required to help on conservation study projects, which have recently included studying the habitats of chimpanzees, colobus monkeys and other primates in a national park, and meeting medicine men to research into native medical uses of plants, in Liberia; patrolling a beach where turtles lay their eggs in Mexico; and helping to track and study the mona monkey in the rainforests of Grenada. Ages 14+. Special experience or skills always welcome, but not necessary. Participants are given responsibilities to fulfil, so applicants should be willing to become active members of the research team. Members share the costs of the project, from US$515-US$1285 for 1-4 weeks, depending on destination. This covers transportation during the expedition, a preparatory booklet, most field gear, tent or

dormitory accommodation and food. Travel to assembly point not provided. Scholarships available. PH on certain expeditions.

UNIVERSITY RESEARCH EXPEDITIONS PROGRAM University of California, Desk L-10, Berkeley CA 94720, United States

Volunteers are needed to provide field assistance for research in the natural and social sciences. Recent projects have included collecting, photographing and sorting sponges and other marine animals from the reef environments of the Fiji Islands; studying the mother-pup interactions of sea-lions in Australia; and recording data on sheep flock numbers in Morocco. Ages 16+. Applicants should be in good health, have a desire to learn, enthusiasm, a willingness to undertake rigourous but rewarding work, flexibility and sensitivity to other cultures. Divers need SCUBA certification. Sailing and photographic skills desirable; background in marine biology, chemistry, ecology or natural history useful. 3 weeks, February-May, July-August or October. Contribution to costs US$1025-$1325 covers research equipment and supplies, meals, accommodation, ground transportation and preparation materials. Travel to site not provided but route guidance given. Partial scholarships available. *Apply at least 2 months before session.*

COURIERS/REPS

AMERICAN EDUCATIONAL TRAVEL INC 650 Cambridge Street, Cambridge, Massachusetts 02141, United States

Promotes educational travel for American high school students, and requires tour escorts for groups of students visiting countries all over Europe, including Britain, Austria, Belgium, France, Federal Republic of Germany, Italy, the Netherlands, Spain and Switzerland. Ages 19+. No experience required, but applicants must have fluent English and a good command of French, German, Italian or Spanish. Tours take place during the Easter vacation and in June/July. Escorts are on call 24 hours a day, 7 days a week. Full board hotel accommodation, travel, insurance and expenses provided. Wages US$25 per day, plus up to $10 per day performance bonus and tips.

WORLD WIDE

COURIERS/REPS

DOMESTIC

CLUB 18-30 HOLIDAYS Overseas Personnel Department, Academic House, 24/28 Oval Road, London NW1 7DE Tel 071-267 7044
Operates holidays in several countries, and employs overseas representatives for seasonal work, May-October, in hotels and apartments. There are also vacancies in the high season, July-September, suitable for students. Ages 20-26. Applicants must have a friendly personality and be bright and outgoing preferably with experience in organising special events, entertainment, administration, the travel business or sales ability. *Apply early; interviews held December-January.*

THOMSON HOLIDAYS Overseas Personnel Department, Greater London House, Hampstead Road, London NW1 7SD Tel 071-387 3685
Britain's largest holiday company, operating throughout the world. Overseas representatives are required, meeting clients at the airport and transferring them by coach to their hotel, organising social occasions and generally giving assistance and advice on hotel and resort facilities. Representatives should be flexible and may be moved to different resorts during the season. Ages 21-30. Applicants should be fluent in English and at least one of the following: Spanish, Italian, French, German, Greek, Portuguese, Serbo-Croat or Russian. The work involves close contact with clients and experience with the general public is desirable. No set working hours as representatives are expected to be on call to deal with any problems. Salary paid monthly in local currency with commission on excursion sales.
Also work as youth representatives, which entails close contact with the younger clients, organising excursions, beach parties, outdoor sports and games to ensure they enjoy the holiday of a lifetime. Ages 21-35. Applicants should have a good working knowledge of Spanish or Greek, an extrovert but balanced personality and stamina as the job is very demanding. Children's representatives are also required, which involves organising activities, supervising meals, reading bedtime stories, evening patrolling services and ensuring the safety of the children is maintained at all times. Variable hours of work. Ages 18-28. Applicants must have childcare or nursing experience, should be friendly, and like children. Salary

paid monthly in local currency.
Accommodation, meals and uniform provided. For all these jobs, applicants must have a high degree of patience, tact, a strong sense of responsibility, a friendly, outgoing nature, and the ability to use their own initiative. April-October, with the possibility of winter employment.

TRACKS EUROPE LTD The Flots, Brookland, Romney Marsh, Kent TN29 9TG Tel Brookland 343/454
Couriers required by a coach/camping tour operator arranging tours of Europe, including Russia and Scandinavia, for groups of 35-45 people, mostly in the 18-35 age range. Ages 25+. Applicants must be English speakers, prepared to work extremely hard for long hours to ensure the safety and comfort of passengers and deal with any contingencies that may arise. In return, they will have the opportunity to see many European and Scandinavian countries. Successful applicants attend a 6½ week training trip around Europe and Scandinavia, departing in March. Participants pay £130 contribution to food kitty on the training trip, plus refundable bond of £250. Tours operate May-October. Trainee couriers receive £65 per week whilst on tour. Food and tent accommodation provided. *Applications accepted December-February only.*

DOMESTIC

CLUB MEDITERRANEE 106-110 Brompton Road, London SW3 1JJ Tel 071-225 1066
Housekeepers, kitchen, laundry and bar staff, food buyers and chefs are required to work in holiday villages in the Bahamas, Brazil, Bulgaria, Dominican Republic, Egypt, France, Greece, Guadeloupe, Indonesia, Israel, Italy, Ivory Coast, Malaysia, Martinique, Mauritius, Mexico, Morocco, New Caledonia, Romania, Senegal, Spain, Switzerland, Tahiti, Thailand, Tunisia, Turkey, United States and Yugoslavia. Applicants should be single, possess relevant qualifications and experience, must have minimum A level French, and, if possible, one other language. Ages 21-30. 6 months, April-October. It should be noted that applications cannot be made to work in a specific country; preference to work in a particular country can be indicated once applicants have worked for a

few seasons. *Apply with cv from November-January. UK nationals only.*

TRACKS EUROPE LTD The Flots, Brookland, Romney Marsh, Kent TN29 9TG Tel Brookland 343/454
Cooks required by a coach/camping tour operator arranging tours of Europe, including Russia and Scandinavia, for groups of 35-45 people, mostly in the 18-35 age range. Ages 25+. Applicants must be English speakers, with previous experience, prepared to work extremely hard for long hours. In return they will have the opportunity to see many European and Scandinavian countries. Successful applicants attend a 6½ week training trip around Europe and Scandinavia, departing in March. Participants pay £130 contribution to food kitty on the training trip, plus refundable bond of £250. Tours operate May-October. Trainee cooks receive £60 per week whilst on tour, and bonus on completion. Food and tent accommodation provided. *Applications accepted December-February only.*

FARMWORK

INTERNATIONAL FARM EXPERIENCE PROGRAMME YFC Centre, National Agricultural Centre, Kenilworth, Warwickshire CV8 2LG Tel Coventry 696584
Provides assistance to young farmers and nurserymen by finding places in farms/nurseries abroad to enable them to broaden their knowledge of agricultural methods. Exchange schemes are operated with Austria, Canada, Denmark, Finland, France, Federal Republic of Germany, Hungary, Israel, Netherlands, Norway, Poland, Sweden, Switzerland and the US, whereby agricultural and horticultural trainees can be placed in work positions. The work is matched as far as possible with the applicant's requirements and is physically hard. 3-12 months. Positions are mostly available spring and summer, based on mutual convenience for farmer and applicant. Ages 18-30. Applicants must have at least 2 years practical experience, 1 year of which may be at an agricultural college, and intend to make a career in agriculture/horticulture. Valid driving licence necessary. Applicants pay own fare. Registration fee £62 or £160, depending on destination. *EC nationals only.*

MONITORS & INSTRUCTORS

CLUB MEDITERRANEE 106-110 Brompton Road, London SW3 1JJ Tel 071-225 1066
Qualified tennis, riding, golf, judo, cycling, skiing, windsurfing, kayaking, swimming, archery, yoga, scuba diving, water skiing and sailing instructors, playgroup leaders and arts and crafts, dance, aerobics, theatrics, games and children's activities monitors, are required to work in holiday villages in the Bahamas, Brazil, Bulgaria, Dominican Republic, Egypt, France, Greece, Guadeloupe, Indonesia, Israel, Italy, Ivory Coast, Malaysia, Martinique, Mauritius, Mexico, Morocco, New Caledonia, Romania, Senegal, Spain, Switzerland, Tahiti, Thailand, Tunisia, Turkey, United States and Yugoslavia. Applicants should be single, possess relevant qualifications and experience, must speak have minimum A level French, and, if possible, one other language. Ages 20 (19 for playgroup leaders)-30. 5 months, May-October. It should be noted that applications cannot be made to work in a specific country; preference to work in a particular country can be indicated once applicants have worked for a few seasons. *Apply with cv from November-January. UK nationals only.*

WORKCAMPS

BRITISH COUNCIL OF CHURCHES Youth Unit, Inter-Church House, 38-41 Lower Marsh, London SE1 7RL Tel 071-620 4444
The Ecumenical Youth Council in Europe is the fellowship of national ecumenical youth councils or denominational bodies dealing with church youth work, and through this offers young Christians from different countries and traditions the opportunity to meet and share their experiences and to discuss common issues and concerns. Promotes international exchanges and seminars for young people; also workcamps where international teams live and work together to serve the community on manual, society or study projects, offering an opportunity to share ideas on faith and life. Recent projects have included cleaning up a centre for children with behavioural difficulties

WORLD WIDE

in Belgium; conservation work and maintenance work at a former concentration camp in the Federal Republic of Germany; working in the garden, fields and kitchen of a monastery in Finland; renovating a Russian Orthodox church in the German Democratic Republic; painting and carpentry in Cyprus; and renovation work in the Lebanon. All camps include a relevant theme for study and discussion. Volunteers must be highly motivated to contribute to the aims of the camp. Ages 18-30. 2-3 weeks, July-October. Board and lodging usually provided. Volunteers pay their own travel and insurance costs. *Apply by mid May. Applicants from outside Europe should enclose a letter of support from a church or ecumenical youth body in their region.*

WORKCAMPS

WORLD COUNCIL OF CHURCHES Ecumenical Youth Action, 150 route de Ferney, PO Box 2100, 1211 Geneva 2, Switzerland Tel 791 61 11
Within the programme of the Ecumenical Youth Action of the World Council of Churches there are opportunities for young people to participate in international workcamps, contributing to local and national development schemes. Recent workcamps have been held in Africa, Asia and the Middle East. Volunteers assist local groups in manual work such as agriculture, construction and renovation of buildings. The camps have theological reflections and discussions on vital issues affecting the local situation. Ages 18-30. 1-2 weeks, July and August. Volunteers pay travel and insurance costs and contribute approx $3 per day towards camp expenses.

GENERAL

GENERAL

CHRISTIAN SERVICE CENTRE Unit 2, Holloway Street West, Lower Gornal, West Midlands DY3 2DZ
Matches the personnel needs of missions and Christian organisations in Britain and abroad with the availability of those offering themselves for service, and also provides a counselling and advisory service for prospective workers. Both short and long-term paid and voluntary positions are available throughout the year in a wide variety of areas, ranging from pioneer missionary work, agriculture, community development and

engineering, to jobs in the fields of radio, literacy, publicity, translation, accountancy and administration, and short-term work on summer camps and building projects. Vacancies in Britain also cover maintenance staff, cooks, housekeepers, social workers, secretaries and book-keepers in residential, rehabilitation or conference centres, and secretarial posts in mission offices. Experience/ qualifications needed vary from post to post, as do hours, wages/pocket money, and provision of board, lodging and insurance cover. Ages 17+. No charge is made for the service, but enquirers are encouraged to make a donation as approx £30 is involved in handling each application.

CLUB MEDITERRANEE 106-110 Brompton Road, London SW3 1JJ Tel 071-225 1066
Receptionists, secretaries, couriers, computer operators, book-keepers, hostesses, cashiers, entertainments organisers and presenters, seamstresses, musicians, photography lab workers, sound and lighting technicians, disc jockeys, administrative staff, boutique staff, hairdressers, electricians, plumbers, painters, mechanics, carpenters, dressmakers, gardeners, laundry workers, doctors, dieticians, lifesavers, and nurses are required to work in holiday villages in the Bahamas, Brazil, Bulgaria, Dominican Republic, Egypt, France, Greece, Guadeloupe, Indonesia, Israel, Italy, Ivory Coast, Malaysia, Martinique, Mauritius, Mexico, Morocco, New Caledonia, Romania, Senegal, Spain, Switzerland, Tahiti, Thailand, Tunisia, Turkey, United States and Yugoslavia. Applicants should be single, possess relevant qualifications and experience, must have minimum A level French, and, if possible, one other language. Ages 20-30. 6 months, April-October. It should be noted that applications cannot be made to work in a specific country; preference to work in a particular country can be indicated once applicants have worked for a few seasons. *Apply with cv from November-January. UK nationals only.*

COMMUNITY ACTION PROGRAMME FOR EDUCATION AND TRAINING FOR TECHNOLOGY (COMETT) Task Force Human Resources, Education, Training & Youth, 200 rue de la Loi, 1049 Brussels, Belgium
Set up by the EC Commission with the aim of developing trans-national training to help

ensure the industrial and technological development of a unified Europe. The programme includes opportunities for 3-24 month student placements in enterprises located in another member state. The placement should familiarise the student with career prospects in the field concerned, bring a European perspective to the training and stimulate the student's entrepreneurial abilities. Applicants must be registered students, or undertaking the placement immediately after graduation. An agreement between the university and enterprise concerned must have been made prior to submitting the application.

UK applicants can obtain further details from Mrs Elizabeth Moss, Department of Education and Science, Elizabeth House, York Road, London SE1 7PH Tel 071-934 9654.

EUROPEAN COMMUNITY YOUNG WORKER EXCHANGE PROGRAMME
Commission of the European Communities, rue de la loi 200, 1049 Brussels, Belgium
Aims to give young EC nationals, aged 18-28, who are employed or actively seeking employment and who have completed vocational training, an opportunity to widen their vocational skills and experience and gain an insight into life in another EC member country. The projects are short-term (3-12 weeks) or long-term (up to 16 months). The EC can contribute to the cost of accommodation, meals, and in some cases, language training courses. Up to 75% of travel expenses can be reimbursed.

UK nationals can apply to the Central Bureau for Educational Visits & Exchanges, Vocational and Technical Education Department, Seymour Mews House, Seymour Mews, London W1H 9PE Tel 071-486 5101.

INTERNATIONAL ASSOCIATION FOR THE EXCHANGE OF STUDENTS FOR TECHNICAL EXPERIENCE (IAESTE-UK)
Seymour Mews House, Seymour Mews, London W1H 9PE Tel 071-486 5101
The UK office of an international exchange scheme operating in 51 countries worldwide, and providing undergraduate students with course-related industrial, technical or commercial experience in another country. IAESTE covers a wide range of subject fields and operates in North and South America,

Europe, the Middle East, Asia and Australia. Minimum 8-12 weeks during summer vacation, maximum 1 year. Students pay own travel expenses; a salary is paid by the firm. Accommodation arranged. Apply to own university or college, which normally must be affiliated to the national IAESTE office. Students should check application procedures with the IAESTE office in their own country. In the UK applications should be supported by the student's sponsoring company or by his/ her university or college which should be affiliated to IAESTE-UK.

TRACKS EUROPE LTD **The Flots, Brookland, Romney Marsh, Kent TN29 9TG Tel Brookland 343/454**
Drivers required by a coach/camping tour operator arranging tours of Europe, including Russia and Scandinavia for groups of 35-45 people, mostly in the 18-35 age range. Ages 25+. Experience of driving large vehicles preferred, and British PSV licence essential. Applicants must be English speakers, prepared to work extremely hard. In return, they will have the opportunity to see many European and Scandinavian countries. Successful applicants attend a 6½ week training trip around Europe and Scandinavia, departing in March. Participants pay £120 contribution to food kitty on the training trip, plus refundable bond of £200. Tours operate May-October. Trainee drivers receive £55 per week whilst on tour, and bonus on completion of each tour. Food and tent accommodation provided.
Applications only accepted December-February.

VACATION WORK INTERNATIONAL CLUB **9 Park End Street, Oxford, Oxfordshire OX1 1HJ Tel Oxford 241978**
Offers a number of services, including discounts on summer job directories, work/ travel publications, spring and summer job bulletins and an information service to answer enquiries. Provides information sheets on a range of countries, giving information on organisations which arrange work, plus a list of useful addresses and suggestions for finding work. Initial membership fee £10; renewal £6 per year.

WORLD WIDE

GENERAL

INDEX

INDEX

INDEX

INDEX

Y

Z

REPORT FORM

Up-to-date reports on working holidays enable us to improve the accuracy and standard of information in this guide. Your completion and return of this form to the Print, Marketing and IT Unit, Central Bureau for Educational Visits & Exchanges, Seymour Mews House, Seymour Mews, London W1H 9PE, would therefore be much appreciated. **All reports will be treated in strict confidence.**

Name and address of employing organisation(s)

Where work was undertaken

Period of work

Type of work

Ratio of work : free time

Salary/terms of employment

Food and accommodation provided?   Yes ☐   No ☐

Were you offered visits/excursions?   Yes ☐   No ☐

Age group of other participants

PLEASE TURN OVER

REPORT FORM

Nationality of the other participants

Any other comments

Age

Occupation

Knowledge of foreign languages

Have you travelled overseas before?   Yes ☐   No ☐

If yes, which countries?

Have you been on a working holiday before?   Yes ☐   No ☐

Name

Address

Signed   Date